'Up until this volume, no scholarly study has been dedicated to exploring the intersection of memory and religion. To this end, *Memory and Religion from a Postsecular Perspective* offers new vistas on how political and social change comes into being by reinterpreting well known theories.'

Catherine Wanner, *Pennsylvania State University, USA*

'The book asks fundamental questions about the relations and boundaries between the sacred and profane, the religious and secular, the political uses of religious narratives and media, and the features and contexts of memory processes within the sphere of religion in both its institutional and vernacular, lived forms. Elaborating such important issues needs the kind of intellectual courage and sensitivity that enables the in-depth and refreshing analyses that we can find in this book.'

Małgorzata Zawiła, *Jagiellonian University, Poland*

Memory and Religion from a Postsecular Perspective

The book argues that religion is a system of significant meanings that have an impact on other systems and spheres of social life, including cultural memory.

The editors call for a postsecular turn in memory studies, which would provide a more reflective and meaningful approach to the constant interplay between the religious and the secular. This opens up new perspectives on the intersection of memory and religion and helps memory scholars become more aware of the religious roots of the language they are using in their studies of memory. By drawing on examples from different parts of the world, the contributors to this volume explain how the interactions between the religious and the secular produce new memory forms and content in the heterogenous societies of the present-day world. These analyzed cases demonstrate that religion has a significant impact on cultural memory, family memory and the contemporary politics of history in secularized societies. At the same time, politics, grassroots movements and different secular agents and processes have so much influence on the formation of memory by religious actors that even religious, ecclesiastic and confessional memories are affected by the secular.

This volume is ideal for students and scholars of memory studies, religious studies and history.

Zuzanna Bogumił, PhD, works at the Institute of Archaeology and Ethnology at the Polish Academy of Sciences. Her published works include *Gulag Memories: The Rediscovery and Commemoration of Russia's Repressive Past* (2018) and a co-authored study titled *Milieux de mémoire in Late Modernity: Local Communities, Religion, and Historical Politics* (2019).

Yuliya Yurchuk, PhD, teaches history at Umeå University, Sweden. She specializes in memory, the history of religion and Eastern Europe. She is the author of the book *Reordering of Meaningful Worlds: Memory of the Organization of Ukrainian Nationalists and the Ukrainian Insurgent Army in Post-Soviet Ukraine* (2014).

European Remembrance and Solidarity Series

The recent crisis of the European project (the Euro, migration, Brexit, the rise in national populism) has brought about new questions about the direction of EU integration. The debate on a common European memory and identity has been equally dramatic, and in particular since the expansion of the EU towards the east, as pleas for proper recognition of the 'new' Europe within a common European historical awareness have emerged. With a number of volumes studying social memories in connection to art, religion, politics and other domains of social life, the series editors wish to contribute to the debate on European memory and identity and shed fresh light on the region of Central and Eastern Europe and Europe more broadly, a region stretched between the past and the future in the negotiation of identities – both national and transnational. The editors encourage comparative studies of two or more European countries, as well as those that highlight Central and Eastern Europe in reference to other regions in Europe and beyond.

The book series is developed in cooperation with the European Network Remembrance and Solidarity (www.enrs.eu).

Editorial Board of the book series: Marek Cichocki, Peter Haslinger, Catherine Horel, Csaba Gy. Kiss, Dušan Kováč, Elena Mannová, Andrzej Nowak, Attila Pók, Marcela Sălăgean, Arnold Suppan, Stefan Troebst, and Jay Winter.

Coordination: Małgorzata Pakier, Ewelina Szpak

Image, History and Memory
Central and Eastern Europe in a Comparative Perspective
Edited by Michał Haake and Piotr Juszkiewicz

Memory and Religion from a Postsecular Perspective
Edited by Zuzanna Bogumił and Yuliya Yurchuk

A New Europe, 1918–1923
Instability, Innovation, Recovery
Edited by Bartosz Dziewanowski-Stefańczyk and Jay Winter

For more information about this series, please visit: https://www.routledge.com/European-Remembrance-and-Solidarity/book-series/REMEMBER

The European Network Remembrance and Solidarity

The European Network Remembrance and Solidarity is an international initiative the aim of which is to research, document and enhance public knowledge of the 20th-century history of Europe and European cultures of remembrance, with particular emphasis on periods of dictatorships, wars and resistance to political violence. The members of the Network are Germany, Hungary, Poland, Romania, and Slovakia, with representatives from Albania, Austria, the Czech Republic, Estonia, Georgia, Latvia and Lithuania present in its advisory bodies.

More information: www.enrs.eu

ENRS is funded by: the German Federal Government Commissioner for Culture and the Media, the Ministry of Human Capacities of Hungary, the Ministry of Culture and National Heritage of the Republic of Poland, the Ministry of Culture of Romania and the Ministry of Culture of the Slovak Republic.

Memory and Religion from a Postsecular Perspective

Edited by Zuzanna Bogumił and
Yuliya Yurchuk

LONDON AND NEW YORK

First published 2022
by Routledge
2 Park Square, Milton Park, Abingdon, Oxon OX14 4RN

and by Routledge
605 Third Avenue, New York, NY 10158

Routledge is an imprint of the Taylor & Francis Group, an informa business

© 2022 selection and editorial matter, Zuzanna Bogumił and Yuliya Yurchuk; individual chapters, the contributors

The right of Zuzanna Bogumił and Yuliya Yurchuk to be identified as the authors of the editorial material, and of the authors for their individual chapters, has been asserted in accordance with sections 77 and 78 of the Copyright, Designs and Patents Act 1988.

All rights reserved. No part of this book may be reprinted or reproduced or utilised in any form or by any electronic, mechanical, or other means, now known or hereafter invented, including photocopying and recording, or in any information storage or retrieval system, without permission in writing from the publishers.

Trademark notice: Product or corporate names may be trademarks or registered trademarks, and are used only for identification and explanation without intent to infringe.

British Library Cataloguing-in-Publication Data
A catalogue record for this book is available from the British Library

Library of Congress Cataloging-in-Publication Data
A catalog record for this book has been requested

ISBN: 978-1-032-20698-1 (hbk)
ISBN: 978-1-032-20699-8 (pbk)
ISBN: 978-1-003-26475-0 (ebk)

DOI: 10.4324/9781003264750

Typeset in Bembo
by Apex CoVantage, LLC

This publication was financed by the European Network Remembrance and Solidarity. ENRS is funded by: the German Federal Government Commissioner for Culture and the Media, the Ministry of Human Capacities of Hungary, the Ministry of Culture and National Heritage of the Republic of Poland, the Ministry of Culture of Romania and the Ministry of Culture of the Slovak Republic.

 Federal Government Commissioner for Culture and the Media

 Ministry of **Culture** and National Heritage of the Republic of Poland

This volume has been written in partnership with
the European Network Remembrance and Solidarity.

Contents

List of figures	xiv
Notes on contributors	xvi
Acknowledgements	xxi
Foreword	xxiv

1 Introduction: memory and religion from a postsecular perspective   1

ZUZANNA BOGUMIŁ AND YULIYA YURCHUK

PART I
Memory and religion: theoretical considerations   27

2 Religion and collective memory of the last century: general reflections and Russian vicissitudes   29

ALEXANDER AGADJANIAN

3 Sacred religio-secular symbols, national myths and collective memory   49

GENEVIÈVE ZUBRZYCKI

PART II
Postsecularity and politics of memory   67

4 The Armenian genocide: extermination, memory, sacralization   69

ADAM POMIECIŃSKI

5 Building a patrimonial Church: how the Orthodox Churches in Ukraine use the past   89

YULIYA YURCHUK

xii *Contents*

6 'God is in truth, not in power!' the re-militarization
of the cult of St Alexander Nevsky in contemporary
Russian cultural memory   111

LILIYA BEREZHNAYA

7 The martyrdom of Jozef Tiso: the entanglements of
the sacred and secular in post-war Catholic memories   133

AGÁTA ŠÚSTOVÁ DRELOVÁ

8 Remembering and enforced forgetting: the dynamics
of remembering Cardinal József Mindszenty in the
Cold War decades   156

RÉKA FÖLDVÁRYNÉ KISS

PART III
Post-conflict memories   179

9 Evocation and the June Fourth Tiananmen candlelight
vigil: a ritual-theological hermeneutics   181

LAP YAN KUNG

10 Religious echoes of the Donbas conflict: the
discourses of the Christian, Muslim and Jewish
communities in Ukraine   200

NADIA ZASANSKA

11 Official quests, vernacular answers: the Macedonian
Orthodox Church – Ohrid Archbishopric (MOC-OA)
as a memory actor in the post-conflict Republic of
North Macedonia (2001–19)   222

NAUM TRAJANOVSKI

12 Negotiating the sacred at non-sites of memory. The
religious imaginary of post-genocidal society   243

KARINA JARZYŃSKA

PART IV
Media and postsecular memory   265

13 The Crimean Tatars' memory of deportation and Islam   267

ELMIRA MURATOVA

Contents   xiii

14 **The Soviet past in contemporary Orthodox hymnography and iconography**   284
PER-ARNE BODIN

15 **Whose Church is it? the nonreligious use of religious architecture in Eastern Germany**   308
AGNIESZKA HALEMBA

PART V
Transnational and vernacular memories   327

16 **The political use of the cult of St Tryphon of Pechenga and its potential as a bridge-builder in the Arctic**   329
ELINA KAHLA

17 **'Vernacular' and 'official' memories: looking beyond the annual Hasidic pilgrimages to Uman**   348
ALLA MARCHENKO

18 **Memory as a religious mission? religion and nation in local commemoration practices in contemporary Poland**   369
MAŁGORZATA GŁOWACKA-GRAJPER

19 **Critical juxtaposition in the post-war Japanese mnemoscape: Saint Maksymilian Kolbe of Auschwitz and the atomic bomb victims of Nagasaki**   388
JIE-HYUN LIM

Afterword: from *Religion as a Chain of Memory* to memory from a postsecular perspective   407
KATHY ROUSSELET

Index   413

Figures

3.1	Popular postcard published circa 1891	51
3.2	Postcard circulated in 1980	53
3.3	The papal cross surrounded by smaller crosses in the summer of 1998	55
3.4	Makeshift altars to the memory of President Kaczyński	59
3.5	As of 2018, a small group of self-proclaimed Defenders of the Cross continued to meet in front of the Presidential Palace every evening	61
3.6	Studded *Cross*, metal, by Polish street artist Peter Fuss	62
6.1	St. Alexander Nevsky Southern Russia, Trubchevsk. End of 18th century	116
12.1	Stanisław Zybała, *Menorka* ('Little Menorah')	249
12.2	Stanisław Zybała's sculptures (untitled)	250
12.3	Stanisław Zybała's sculpture (view from above)	251
12.4	Stanisław Zybała, *Cemetery Symbol* (recto)	252
12.5	Stanisław Zybała, *Cemetery Symbol* (verso)	253
12.6	'Temporary' *matzevot* for burials of victims of the Holocaust erected by the Zapomniane ('Forgotten') Foundation in Chodówki forest, Poland	258
14.1	The *Assembly (or Synaxis) of New Martyrs* icon	292
14.2	Ilia Glazunov, *The Eternal Russia* 1988	293
14.3	The murder of the tsar and his family	295
14.4	Patriarch Tikhon in confinement	296
14.5	The murder of Andronik and Ermogen	297
14.6	Caricature of Patriarch Tikhon from the journal *Bezbozhnik*	299
14.7	The Red Army attacks a religious procession	300
14.8	The *Novorussian Mother of God* icon	301
14.9	The Tower of Babel	303
14.10	The consecration of the Cathedral of Christ the Saviour	304
15.1	The church in Rosow with its openwork steel tower	313
15.2	Obelisk in front of the church in Rosow	315

17.1	Hasidim praying in the yard of a private house near the grave of Rebbe Nachman	359
17.2	A wall commemorating Chief Sephardi Rabbi of Israel Ovadia Yosef	360
Diagram 17.1	Important personalities in the history of Uman	363

Notes on contributors

Alexander Agadjanian is Professor at the Center for the Study of Religion at the Russian State University of the Humanities, and the Russian Academy of National Economy and Public Administration, Moscow. His fields of interest include religion in the modern world, in particular in Russia and post-Soviet Eurasia, where he focuses on religion's cultural and socio-political dimensions. His most recent publications include *World Christianities: Russia* (Fortress 2021; co-author); *Turns of Faith, Search of Meaning: Orthodox Christianity and Post-Soviet Experience* (Peter Lang 2014; author); *Armenian Christianity Today: Identity Politics and Social Practices* (Routledge 2014; editor and author); *Religion, Nation and Democracy in the South Caucasus* (Routledge 2015; co-editor and author); *Prikhod i Obshchina v russkom pravoslavii (Parish and Community in Russian Orthodoxy)* (Ves' mir, 2011; co-editor and author); and *Eastern Orthodoxy in a Global Age* (Altamira Press 2005; co-editor and author).

Liliya Berezhnaya was an associate professor at the University of Münster's Religion and Politics Cluster of Excellence in Germany and is currently a research associate at the University of Amsterdam. Her research interests are focused on comparative borderland studies, imperial and national discourses in Eastern European history, symbolic geography and the construction of 'the other', Ukrainian religious and cultural history and eschatological notions in Christian traditions. Her recent publications include *Die Militarisierung der Heiligen in Vormoderne und Moderne* (Duncker & Humblot 2020); *Iconic Turns: Nation and Religion in Eastern European Cinema since 1989* (Brill 2013; co-edited with Christian Schmitt); *Rampart Nations: Bulwark Myths of East European Multiconfessional Societies in the Age of Nationalism* (Berghahn 2019; co-edited with Heidi Hein-Kircher); and *The World to Come: Ukrainian Images of the Last Judgment* (Harvard University Press 2015; co-authored with John-Paul Himka).

Per-Arne Bodin is Professor Emeritus of Slavic Literatures at Stockholm University. His main research interests are Russian poetry, Russian cultural history (with a particular focus on the importance of the Russian Orthodox tradition) and Polish literature after the Second World War. His most recent books are *Language, Canonization and Holy Foolishness: Studies in Postsoviet Russian Culture and the Orthodox Tradition* (Acta Universitatis Stockholmiensis

2009) and *Från Bysans till Putin: Historier om Ryssland* (From Byzantium to Putin: Histories about Russia) (Norma 2016).

Zuzanna Bogumił is Assistant Professor at the Institute of Archaeology and Ethnology at the Polish Academy of Sciences (Warsaw, Poland). Her research interests include Gulag memories, museum studies and postsecular memory. At present she is the coordinator of a project on postsecular memory of Soviet repressions in Russia titled 'From the Enemy to a New Martyr', which is supported by the National Science Centre in Poland (2017–21). Her publications include *Gulag Memories: The Rediscovery and Commemoration of Russia's Repressive Past* (Berghahn 2018) and the following co-authored studies: *Milieux de mémoire in Late Modernity: Local Communities, Religion, and Historical Politics* (Peter Lang 2019) and *The Enemy on Display: The Second World War in Eastern European Museums* (Berghahn 2015).

Grace Davie is a professor emeritus in the Sociology of Religion at the University of Exeter UK. In 2000–2001 she was the Kerstin-Hesselgren Professor at Uppsala, where she returned for extended visits in 2006–07, 2010 and 2012, receiving an honorary degree in 2008. She has also held visiting appointments at the École pratique des hautes études (1996) and at the École des hautes études en sciences sociales (1998 and 2003) in Paris. Her latest publications include *Religion in Britain: A Persistent Paradox* (Wiley-Blackwell 2015) and *Religion in Public Life: Levelling the Ground* (Theos 2017).

Małgorzata Głowacka-Grajper is Assistant Professor at the Faculty of Sociology at the University of Warsaw. Her research interests include social memory, ethnic tradition, contemporary developments in ethnic identity and minority group activism. Her current research projects concern the relation between memory and religion and the class dimension of social memory. She is the author of the book *The Transmission of Memory. Memory Activists and Narratives of Former Eastern Borderlands in Contemporary Poland* (*Transmisja pamięci. Działacze sfery pamięci i przekaz o Kresach Wschodnich we współczesnej Polsce*) (Wydawnictwa Uniwersytetu Warszawskiego 2016) and co-author of *Milieux de mémoire in Late Modernity: Local Communities, Religion, and Historical Politics* (Peter Lang 2019).

Agnieszka Halemba has been a Professor of Social Anthropology at the Institute of Archeology and Ethnology at the Polish Academy of Science since 2019. Her main field is the anthropology of religion, but she has a special interest in relations between religious organizations and the practices of lived religion. She is the author of two books: *The Telengits of Southern Siberia: Landscape, Religion and Knowledge in Motion* (Routledge 2006) and *Negotiating Marian Apparitions: The Politics of Religion in Transcarpathian Ukraine* (Central European University Press 2015). At present, she is the Principal Investigator on a project titled 'Churches in Secular Space. Relational Approach to the Reconstruction and Use of Church Buildings in North-Eastern Germany' (National Science Centre 2020–23).

xviii *Notes on contributors*

Karina Jarzyńska is Assistant Professor at the Faculty of Polish Studies at the Jagiellonian University in Kraków and a member of the Research Center for Memory Cultures, which functions within this institution. Her research interests include the history of Polish literature of the twentieth century, relations between religion and literature in modernity, and heritology. She has authored the following books: *Literature as Spiritual Exercise: The Work of Czeslaw Milosz from a Post-secular Perspective (Literatura jako ćwiczenie duchowe. Dzieło Czesława Miłosza w perspektywie postsekularnej)* (Universitas 2018) and *Epics of the World. At the Sources of Cultures (Eposy świata. U źródeł kultur)* (Wydawnictwo Szkolne PWN 2011).

Elina Kahla is Adjunct Professor and Principal Investigator at the Aleksanteri Institute at Helsinki University, which is one of the world's largest and best-known research centres in the field of Russian and Eastern European studies. She has published widely on Russian cultural history, hagiography and the Russian Orthodox Church in postsecular society. Her research interests also include modernization studies and the cultural practices of Eastern Orthodox Christianity.

Réka Földváryné Kiss is a historian and the Chair of the Hungarian Committee of National Remembrance. Since 2018 she has been the Chair of the Department of Church History at the Faculty of Theology at Károli Gáspár University of the Reformed Church in Hungary. Her main research areas are the relations between the Church and the Hungarian State during the communist period, the retaliations and political trials after the Hungarian Revolution of 1956 and social history post 1945. She is author, co-author and editor of ten books and some eighty scientific articles. Földváryné Kiss is a member of the European Network Remembrance and Solidarity (ENRS) Steering Committee and coordinates the Hungarian branch in the ENRS.

Lap Yan Kung received his education in Hong Kong, Denmark and Scotland. He has taught at the Divinity School of Chung Chi College at the Chinese University of Hong Kong since 1996. His current research is on memory and religion, yoga and spiritual fervour in China, and justice and peace in world Christianity. His recent publications are found in *The Oxford Handbook of Mission Studies* (Oxford University Press 2021); *Hong Kong Protests and Political Theology* (Rowman and Littlefield 2021); and *Human Dignity, Human Rights and Social Justice* (Springer 2020). He is the honorary general secretary of the Hong Kong Christian Institute (a non-governmental organization committed to human rights and democracy).

Jie-Hyun Lim is Professor of Transnational History and Founding Director of the Critical Global Studies Institute at Sogang University in Seoul, and the Principal Investigator of an international research project titled 'Mnemonic Solidarity: Colonialism, War, and Genocide in the Global Memory Space' (from 2017 to 2024). He is also the co-editor of the Palgrave series titled *Entangled Memories in the Global South*. Most recently, he published a book titled 희생자의식민족주의 (*Victimhood Nationalism - A Global History*; Humanist, 2021).

Notes on contributors xix

His most recent books are *Mnemonic Solidarity-Global Interventions* (co-edited with Eve Rosenhaft; Palgrave Macmillan 2021) and *Global Easts: Remembering-Imagining-Mobilizing* (Columbia University Press, under publication).

Alla Marchenko is a sociologist. She is currently writing her second doctoral thesis as a doctoral candidate at the Institute of Philosophy and Sociology at the Polish Academy of Sciences (Warsaw, Poland). The topic is 'A Comparative Analysis of the Hasidic Pilgrimage's Effects upon Local Frames of Memory in Poland and Ukraine'. Alla has worked as a researcher on an EU project titled *ReHerit: Common Responsibility for Shared Heritage*, which was implemented by the Center for Urban History of East Central Europe (Lviv, Ukraine) in 2018–20. She previously studied and worked at Taras Shevchenko National University of Kyiv. Alla is an alumna of the Carnegie Research Fellowship Program and Carnegie Scholar Publication Program at New York University.

Elmira Muratova is a senior lecturer in Political Science at Taurida National University (Crimean Federal University) in Simferopol. She holds a PhD in political science from Taurida National University (2005). Her major research topics include the Crimean Tatars, ethnic and religious relations and conflicts in Crimea, and the history and contemporary development of Islam in Crimea. Her most recent publications have been devoted to various issues relating to ethnic and religious developments among the Crimean Tatars following the 2014 annexation of Crimea.

Adam Pomieciński is Professor at the Institute of Anthropology and Ethnology at the Adam Mickiewicz University in Poznań (Poland). His main research interests are Armenian studies, the culture of ethnic and religious minorities in the Caucasus and the problematics of social movements. His publications include *Alter-globalists. Anthropology of the Global Justice Movement* (*Alterglobaliści. Antropologia ruchu na rzecz globalnej sprawiedliwości*) (Adam Mickiewicz University Press 2013), and *National Minorities in Poland. An Anthropological Outline* ("Chelovek.ru" 2019; co-author).

Kathy Rousselet is a political scientist. She is a Research Professor at the Center for International Studies at Sciences Po (Paris) and an Associate Fellow of the Centre d'études des mondes russe, caucasien et centre-européen at the École des hautes études en sciences sociales. She authored many articles, edited or co-edited several books and special journal issues on Russia and on religious issues, mainly in post-Soviet Russia. Her recent publications include studies on the New Martyrs, memory of Soviet repression in the Russian Orthodox Church and the worship of the imperial family.

Agáta Šústová Drelová is a researcher at the Institute of History at the Slovak Academy of Sciences, Slovakia. She obtained her PhD from the University of Exeter, England; her doctoral thesis explored the cultural history of Catholic nationalism in late socialist and early post-socialist Slovakia. She has been the beneficiary of various scholarships, including most recently a

xx *Notes on contributors*

junior fellowship at the Imre Kertész Kolleg in Jena, Germany. Her recent publications include studies of post-war Catholicism and nationalism in Central Eastern Europe.

Naum Trajanovski is a PhD candidate in sociology at the Graduate School for Social Research at the Institute of Philosophy and Sociology of the Polish Academy of Sciences. He was a project coordinator at the European Network Remembrance and Solidarity (2017) and a researcher at the Faculty of Philosophy, Ss. Cyril and Methodius University–Skopje (2018–20). His major academic interests include memory politics in North Macedonia and sociological knowledge transfer in 1960s Eastern Europe. He is the author of a book in Macedonian titled *Operacijata Muzej: Muzejot na makedonskata borba i makedonskata politika na sekjavanje* (*Operation Museum: The Museum of the Macedonian Struggle and the Macedonian Memory Politics*) (Templum, 2020).

Yuliya Yurchuk is a senior lecturer of history at Umeå University, Sweden. She worked on the present book when she was a postdoctoral researcher at the Department of History and Contemporary Studies at Södertörn University, Sweden. This research was funded by the Foundation for Baltic and East European Studies. She specializes in memory studies, history of religion, and the study of nationalism in East European countries. She is the author of a book titled *Reordering of Meaningful Worlds: Memory of the Organization of Ukrainian Nationalists and the Ukrainian Insurgent Army in Post-Soviet Ukraine* (Acta 2014). Her articles have appeared in *Memory Studies, Nationalities Papers, Europe-Asia Studies, Nordisk Østforum, Baltic Worlds* and *Ukraina Moderna.*

Nadia Zasanska is a postdoctoral researcher at the Department of Media and Center for Studying Foreign Languages at the Ukrainian Catholic University in Lviv. Her research interests include applied linguistics and lexical semantics with a specific focus on political and religious discourses, media and memory studies.

Geneviève Zubrzycki is Professor of Sociology and Director of the Weiser Center for Europe and Eurasia at the University of Michigan. She studies national identity and religion, collective memory and national mythology, and the contested place of religious symbols in the public sphere. She is the author of the award-winning books *The Crosses of Auschwitz: Nationalism and Religion in Post-Communist Poland* (University of Chicago Press 2006; Polish trans. 2014) and *Beheading the Saint: Nationalism, Religion and Secularism in Quebec* (University of Chicago Press 2016; French and Polish trans. 2020) and the editor of *National Matters: Materiality, Culture, and Nationalism* (Stanford University Press 2017).

Acknowledgements

In this volume, we propose a postsecular turn in memory studies. The path we took to conceptualizing the exact nature of this 'turn' (in all senses of the word) was winding, but the road ahead became visible as we made progress. Before we stepped onto this path together, we had both been working on the questions of memory and religion, although we did not know each other at the time: Yuliya was dealing with the memory politics of the Churches in Ukraine and Zuzanna, the postsecular memory of Soviet repressions in Russia. It was Małgorzata Pakier, the head of the Academic Section of the European Network of Remembrance and Solidarity (ENRS), who introduced us to each other in 2017 and offered us the opportunity to jointly organize a conference on memory and religion within the framework of the Genealogies of Memory series. That was the moment when our paths crossed and our long journey together began. We are very grateful to Małgorzata Pakier and to Rafał Rogulski, director of the European Network of Remembrance and Solidarity, for the exceptional opportunity they granted us and their assistance with organizing the conference. Their support and patience during the conference preparations and later during the writing of the book were generous indeed and most invaluable. Moreover, Małgorzata Pakier was always ready to respond to our requests and actively encouraged us in our work by offering help and expressing her firm confidence in our endeavours.

The *Memory and Religion: Central and Eastern Europe in a Global Perspective* conference took place in Warsaw in October 2018. At this event, we discussed the impact of religion on memory. It was probably the first memory studies conference fully dedicated to questions relating to the connection between memory and religion. We would like to thank the participants of the conference for sharing with us their research and reflections, which helped us to see links between memory and religion in a broader interdisciplinary perspective.

After the conference, we started to work on the publication, and Małgorzata Pakier and Rafał Rogulski offered us the opportunity to publish it in a new ENRS Routledge book series. We invited both the conference participants and some new authors to join the project. We would like to express our words of gratitude to the contributing authors for their strong engagement in the project, patience, hard work on the chapters and deep interest in the subject.

xxii *Acknowledgements*

The conference and our ongoing online discussions clearly showed us that reflection on memory and religion within memory studies is very limited, and if we want to reintroduce such issues into the sphere of interests of memory researchers, we need to propose a new theoretical framework. Drawing from the rich literature on postsecularism, we started to develop the idea of a postsecular turn in memory studies. We would like to acknowledge Alexander Agadjanian, Małgorzata Głowacka-Grajper, Agnieszka Halemba and Karina Jarzyńska for their careful reading of our introduction and their critical comments, which helped us to improve and sharpen our arguments. Zuzanna Bogumił is particularly thankful to Małgorzata Głowacka-Grajper, with whom she published a book titled *Milieux de mémoire in Late Modernity: Local Communities, Religion and Historical Politics* (2019), in which they investigated the impact of local religiosity on the memory of traumatic events of the Second World War. The collaborative work on that book and the discussions this provoked were an important step in Zuzanna's thinking about memory–religion relations.

We would like to express our great debt to other people who made this book possible, especially Karolina Dziełak, who was the conference coordinator and generously supported our ideas and made the whole organization of the conference smooth and effective. We would also like to acknowledge Laura Galian, Victoria Tkachenko, Kim Groop and Chanan Yitzchaki, who participated in the *Religious Memory Devices* panel that was held at the Memory Studies Association conference in Madrid in 2018, for their interesting papers on memory and religion, which enriched our understanding of the phenomenon. We are also grateful to Catherine Wanner and Małgorzata Zawiła for their reviews of the manuscript, which were invaluable for improving the text. Moreover, Irina Paert took the time to read and comment on several chapters, which was very stimulating for us, and we are very appreciative. Finally, we would like to express our deep gratitude towards Philip Palmer, the proofreader and editor of the book, for his engagement in the project, invaluable comments and hard work making the chapters understandable to an anglophone reader while maintaining the stylistic particularity of each of the authors.

Yuliya Yurchuk would also like to express her gratitude to Catherine Wanner, Iuliia Buyskykh and Tetiana Kalenychenko for granting her a valuable opportunity to participate at the series of conferences titled Working Group on Religion in the Black Sea Region, where she could discuss her ideas about postsecular memory in an intellectually stimulating environment. Yuliya is also grateful to the Foundation of Baltic and East European Studies, which generously financed her postdoctoral project, part of which was the work on this book. Zuzanna Bogumił, in turn, acknowledges Tatiana Voronina for discussions within the framework of the *From the Enemy to a New Martyr* project, supported by The National Science Centre in Poland, which is dedicated to postsecular memory of the Soviet repressions in Russia.

Finally, we would like to direct our words of gratitude towards our families, who provided their support and understanding throughout the course of our work on this volume. The fact that most of the editing work and the writing of the introduction were carried out during the Covid-19 lockdown made our common journey unforgettable indeed.

Zuzanna Bogumił and Yuliya Yurchuk

Foreword

I was delighted to take part in a conference in Warsaw on memory and religion, which set a series of case studies from Central and Eastern Europe in a global perspective. I say this for several reasons: the connections between memory and religion have long intrigued me; both the venue and the work presented were located in a part of Europe that I wanted to know more about; the cross-disciplinarity of the meeting appealed to me; and I had personal as well as professional reasons for visiting Warsaw. In my laptop was a transcript of a diary written by my mother during a trip to Central Europe (including several days in Warsaw) in the spring of 1933. I was anxious to explore further.

Both the visit to Warsaw and the meeting itself met every expectation; I very much enjoyed my time in the city and its environs and I learnt a huge amount from the conference papers and subsequent discussion. This is equally the case with respect to the chapters brought together in this volume, many of which had their first hearing in Warsaw. The first section sets out the theoretical underpinning of the conference; the following, thematically arranged chapters illustrate the subtle, complex and constantly evolving connections between religion and memory in a wide variety of contexts, most but not quite all of which are located in Central and East Europe.

I found – and continue to find – resonances with my own work at every turn, not least with the monograph that I published in 2000 titled *Religion in Modern Europe: A Memory Mutates* (Davie 2000). This in turn drew on Danièle Hervieu-Léger's *Religion as a Chain of Memory* (Hervieu-Léger 2000), a book that I got to know well in the course of its translation into English. Both Hervieu-Léger and I consider religion as a form of memory, asking how this is, or is not, sustained as the societies of which this memory is part evolve. What might happen, moreover, if that memory no longer exists? Put differently, both volumes explore the complex relationship between religion and modernity in the West, specifically in an increasingly secular West Europe. Neither volume, however, anticipated the shift that underpins this volume, that is, the notion of the postsecular per se and its deployment in the field of memory studies more generally.

Debates surrounding the postsecular have been heated. This is unsurprising in my view, given the unresolved ambiguity at the heart of this discussion that is best articulated as a question: is the 'turn to the postsecular' a shift in the state of religion per se, or is it a shift in our perceptions of this? Is it the case, in other words, that religion has once again asserted itself in modern or late modern societies, or is it simply that scholars have – for whatever reason – reconnected with something that was always there but was ignored for most of the time? The answer lies in a complex combination of both: the realities that surround us have most certainly evolved but so too have our capacities to understand them. And either way, a new and very significant agenda opens up as the relationships between religion, politics, conflict and the media are examined in new ways, paying attention to the place of memory in these, both within and across national contexts. It is this rich and innovative agenda that underpins the chapters that follow.

As I read though these, I reflected further on the connections with my own thinking. I recalled, for example, an invitation to review a fascinating research project dealing with the place of religion in the lives of elderly people in three European countries: Romania, Bulgaria and England (Coleman, Koleva, and Bornat 2013). I was captivated – as I am once again – by the richness of the data deriving from primarily qualitative methods and by the differences between East and West Europe. I warmed in particular to the experiential dimensions that stood out in the former. Despite – or perhaps because of – my familiarity with the rather more cerebral West, I found the first-hand accounts of three generations in an Orthodox family tending the icon lamp as they rose in the morning extraordinarily vivid, a reaction that came back to me again and again as I heard, and then read, the accounts gathered here.

A second example draws on a rather different enterprise: this was my involvement in an extended chapter on religion within an initiative titled the International Panel on Social Progress (IPSP).[1] The details of the IPSP lie beyond the limits of a short foreword, but a key question emerged from our deliberations regarding the place of religion in both conflict and peacemaking. It became increasingly clear that it is unhelpful to ask whether or not religion causes conflict, expecting a yes or no answer. It is (much) more constructive to formulate the question as follows: under what circumstances is religion likely to become involved in conflict – or indeed peacemaking – and with what consequences in any particular situation? I am wondering if there might be parallels in the case of memory studies. Might it be possible, in other words, to consider the circumstances in which religion is, or is not, likely to become involved in memory work or memory making and the consequences that follow for both the memories that ensue and for the religious narratives deployed in this way? And once again, I find considerable potential for this way of working in the material assembled in these pages.

xxvi *Foreword*

For all these reasons, I conclude by commending these chapters to the widest possible audience. Readers may arrive by different disciplinary routes; all of them, however, will be richly rewarded for the time they invest in this volume.

Grace Davie

Note

1 For more information about the International Panel on Social Progress, see https://blogs.lse. ac.uk/religionglobalsociety/2019/01/a-lived-situated-and-constantly-changing-reality-why-religion-is-relevant-to-the-pursuit-of-social-progress/.

References

Coleman, Peter, Daniela Koleva, and Joanna Bornat. 2013. *Ageing, Ritual and Social Change: Comparing the Secular and Religious in Eastern and Western Europe.* Farnham: Ashgate.

Davie, Grace. 2000. *Religion in Modern Europe.* Oxford: Oxford University Press.

Hervieu-Léger, Danièle. 2000. *Religion as a Chain of Memory.* Translated by Simon Lee. Cambridge: Polity Press (translation of *La Religion pour mémoire*, Paris: Cerf, 1993).

1 Introduction

Memory and religion from a postsecular perspective

Zuzanna Bogumił and Yuliya Yurchuk

Sociologists and anthropologists of religion have made an impressive contribution to the body of literature that draws attention to the close affinity between memory and religion. Some of these scholars regard religion as an integral part of cultural memory (Paert 2016a) or a 'chain of memory' (Hervieu-Léger 2000), while others identify it with the paradigmatic forms of cultural mnemotechnics (Assmann 2006). However, even a cursory analysis of the theoretical literature produced by memory studies scholars will swiftly reveal that the relationship between memory and religion is yet to receive the close attention its importance warrants. However, this was not always the case. Religion did in fact hold a prominent position in memory studies during the field's inception but lost this status once the field had begun its rapid development (Brown et al. 2009). This period of growth led, from the 1980s onwards, to the formation of various centres and organizations devoted to memory research. The most important of these is the Memory Studies Association, which was established in 2017 as a global interdisciplinary forum connecting 'scholars and practitioners interested in the ways we draw on, shape, and are shaped by the past' (Memory Studies Association 2017). The association collaborates with the *Memory Studies* journal, which promotes interdisciplinary approaches. A number of other journals devoted to memory-related issues have also appeared in recent years. Furthermore, many prestigious publishing houses have their own memory studies series, not to mention their own handbooks (Tota and Hagen 2016; Nardi et al. 2019; Kim 2015; Erll 2010; Olick, Vinitzky-Seroussi, and Levy 2011; Rossington and Whitehead 2007). These publications are further supplemented by the thousands of independent monographs and edited volumes being published all around the world. Nevertheless, religion is largely absent as an object of study from this constantly growing memory studies field (Urbaniak 2015; Sakaranaho 2011; Váně et al. 2018).

In fact, since the memory boom of the 1980s, not a single handbook, special issue or edited volume has appeared on the relationship between memory and religion. Furthermore, the theoretical literature on memory contains no systematic scholarly studies devoted to the complex memory–religion relationship that take into account the role played by religious traditions in the production of narratives about the past as well as independent cases. In those few cases where

DOI: 10.4324/9781003264750-1

2 Zuzanna Bogumił and Yuliya Yurchuk

religion is mentioned, it is generally presented as a marginal phenomenon. This lack of interest in religion among memory studies scholars is somewhat surprising because throughout history, it is religious traditions that have been the main producers and global distributors of narratives about the past (Casanova 1994). Believers live in secular societies, so the ways religious people remember the past will inevitably influence the ways other groups – secular included – deal with the past and commemorate it. Similarly, the religious texture of memory does not function in a vacuum. Conversely, it is in a constant relationship with other, secular commemorative languages and practices. Moreover, as we will show, it is often not possible to draw a clear distinction between the religious and the secular, which makes it even more important to highlight the interplay between different elements in a concrete memory work.

In this introduction, we reflect on the relationship between religion and memory, a subfield that should, as we argue, become more visible within memory studies. First, we show how religion was originally conceptualized by the founders of memory studies and how it is being discussed today by contemporary memory scholars. We demonstrate that religion is present, though often unnamed, in contemporary memory studies. Despite its presence being unacknowledged, religion functions as a hidden discourse that merely hints at the potential role religion can play in memory work and seldom positions it at the centre of researchers' scrutiny. We argue for a more focused and explicit approach that acknowledges the true impact of religion and religious influences. Finally, we call for a postsecular turn in memory studies, which we believe will help researchers to better understand how much religion and religious imagination shape memory. We claim that such a critical turn could help memory scholars be more reflective and become more aware of the religious roots of the language they are using when they approach memory. The perspective we present may also open up new theoretical possibilities for a more nuanced understanding of how memory works. Our aim is to demonstrate the widely neglected memory-forming potential of religion. We approach religion as a system of significant meanings that have an impact on other systems and spheres of social life. While we do not deny the existence of secular actors and fields, we also recognize their origins can often be traced back to a religious past. Moreover, we underline the constant interplay between the religious and the secular, an interaction that has the potential to produce new forms and contents in the heterogenous societies of the present-day world. As the authors who have contributed to this volume show, religion has a significant impact on cultural memory, family memory and the contemporary politics of history in secularized societies. At the same time, politics, grassroots movements and other secular agents and processes have so much influence on the formation of memory by religious actors that even religious, ecclesiastic and confessional memories are affected.

Religion and the origins of memory studies

It should be remembered that one of the 'fathers' of memory studies, Maurice Halbwachs, devoted special attention to the issue of religion in his groundbreaking work that laid the foundation for further interest in memory among sociologists, historians and scholars of other disciplines (Halbwachs 1992). Halbwachs first referred to religion in his book *Les cadres sociaux de la mémoire* (1925), in which he illustrates the work of social frameworks of memory by analyzing the way that memory functions within religious groups. Halbwachs drew a clear distinction between religious memory and the memory of other social groups. He then drew a further distinction between two key dimensions of religious memory: normative dogma and experiential mysticism. However, when many contemporary memory researchers formally reference his writings, they tend to focus on whether they should adopt or dispute his notion of 'collective memory' rather than using his writings to further their empirical research (Gensburger 2016). This explains why the most elaborated and widely used concept attributed to Halbwachs is that of 'frameworks of memory', which is often applied by researchers interested in the way social memory functions, tradition is invented and sites of memory are constructed. By contrast, the interrelations between religion and memory continue to be a marginal area of investigation (Hervieu-Léger 2017), and any scholars who do choose to tackle them largely go along with the clear distinction that has been drawn between religious memory and other forms of memory.

This was the case for another 'father' of memory studies, the German Egyptologist Jan Assmann, who drew inspiration from Halbwachs's reflections on religion and memory. What Halbwachs called memory and tradition, Assmann named communicative and cultural memory, although he did, at the same time, propose a much more complex theoretical concept when explaining the processes lying behind memory transformations (Assmann 2011). In his analysis, he refers to religion extensively and explains the significance for world history of the appearance of monotheism (Assmann 1997, 2006, 2009). According to Assmann, the world we live in was affected to a great extent by 'the shift from "polytheistic" to "monotheistic" religions, from cult religions to religions of the book, from culturally specific religions to world religions' (Assmann 2009, 1). Assmann generally confines his reflections on religion to the Judaeo-Christian tradition and concentrates on the cultural dimension of religion. Memory scholars influenced by Assmann's writings primarily focus on his concept of cultural memory, disregarding the fact that this prominent scholar also stressed that cultural memory owed its modus operandi to the mechanisms of the monotheistic Judaeo-Christian tradition.

As memory studies developed, religion was increasingly marginalized. In the 1980s Pierre Nora proclaimed that *milieux de memoire*, by which he meant real environments of memory typical of peasant culture and supported by religion and the Churches, no longer exist. He asserted that they have now been completely replaced by *lieux de memoire*, that is, sites of memory where a sense of historical continuity persists through organized and, most often, state-sanctioned efforts (Nora 1989). Essentially, Nora was contending that the loss of religious power and secularization of society are part and parcel of the process whereby *milieux de memoire* vanish and *lieux de memoire* appear in their place. Clearly, Nora's understanding of *milieux de memoire* is somewhat idealistic, as he conceives of them being completely authentic and untouched by politics and present-day needs. However, German historian Thomas Wünsch has argued that 'untouched memory', as such, has never really existed. Even memory supported by religion and religious actors has always been formed under the influence of external needs, as religious actors have not only had to address believers but also the strangers to whom they have conveyed ideas that could potentially influence them to join the Church (Wünsch 2013). Nevertheless, most scholars accept the distinction that Nora drew between *milieux de memoire* and *lieux de memoire*.

Consequently, many contemporary memory researchers followed Nora's lead and started to describe sites of memory as a new phenomenon in the post-traditional world. Nevertheless, they quickly discovered that these sites of memory are sacred, though in a secularized rather than religious sense. Geneviève Zubrzycki presents religion as a reservoir of symbols secularized by nation states and then sacralized as national, even within Poland and in other such apparently 'religious' societies (Zubrzycki 2006, 2016). However, even this promising approach, which shows that religion forms the basis of national and political secular memories, requires further elaboration. Even so, within memory studies, everything that was previously regarded as religious is often now being reduced to the secular sacred, and religion itself is increasingly beginning to be perceived as a reservoir of symbols used by political and national stakeholders rather than the type of cultural memory that Halbwachs and Assmann described. The main focus of reflections on religion is often limited to the role played by institutional Churches as agents of politics of memory (Klimenko 2020; Smolkin 2018; Yamashiro, Van Engen, and Roediger 2019; Turoma, Aitamurto, and Vladiv-Glover 2019; Haskins 2009).

Another problem is that religion is perceived as a static and atavistic phenomenon belonging to a pre-secular world. This tendency was perfectly expressed by Aleida Assmann in a discussion of what she considers cultural memory to be. She claimed that there are three core areas of 'active cultural memory': religion, art and history. She argues that in secular modernity the religious canon was translated into the arts and became a canon of classics. For her, this canon of classics 'is not as fixed and closed as the religious canon but open to changes and exchanges' (Assmann 2008, 101). The chapters in this volume show that examining memory and religion more closely can reveal that the 'religious canon' is not as closed and unchangeable as Assmann presumed. In fact, her contention about the immutability of the religious canon largely reflects assumptions inherent in the main approach that memory scholars (from Halbwachs onwards) have taken towards religion in relation to memory, namely, that a clear distinction should be drawn between secular and religious memory and the secular should be regarded as a developmental stage in the formation of modernity that followed on from a religious stage. This volume is, in many ways, a response to such long-held assumptions about the relationship between memory and religion.

Memory and religion beyond memory studies

Besides exploring common ground between religion and memory, Halbwachs, Assmann and Nora all discussed the relationship between memory and history. It was the latter relationship that drew the attention of most scholars engaged in memory studies, while links between memory and religion were left relatively unexplored. However, sociologists of religion have continued to expand their reflections on the memory–religion relationship, frequently building on Durkheimian thought. For example, the French sociologist of religion, Daniele Hervieu-Léger, highlighted the role religion has played in modern societies (2000). She discusses how religion is transformed when the continuity of religious memory has been broken by secularization and goes on to reflect on how institutional Churches adapt to this new situation. She does, however, limit her reflections to the Christian tradition, with a particular focus on Catholicism – a rather narrow viewpoint when the growing diversity of religions in the contemporary world is taken into account (Vance 2005).

Grace Davie, another sociologist of religion, introduced memory theory as an explanatory framework for the sociological analysis of religion and modernity. Inspired by Hervieu-Léger, Davie explains religion through its relationship to history (Davie 2000). Davie draws attention to the fact that when religion is being spoken of as a form of memory, two sides of the issue must be considered, 'one concerning the continuation of the dominant Christian memory and the other concerning the diversification of religion in Europe' (Davie 2000, 176–77).

Yet, despite the richness of Hervieu-Léger and Davie's conceptualizations of religion, their ideas largely failed to draw the attention of memory scholars. In fact, further analysis reveals that scholars of religions are just as reluctant as memory scholars to enter into meaningful dialogue on this issue. It is also important to stress that some of the critics encountered by both Hervieu-Léger and Davie were researchers from their own field who accused them of reducing religion to memory (Vance 2005).

Our discussion above could give the impression that religion is completely absent from memory studies, but this is not the case. Recently, memory scholars have published several studies on the memory of religious groups that discuss the religious dimension of memory and try to demonstrate its particularity. These works deal with different societies and are written within different research fields. However, they are united by a common conviction that the religious cannot be reduced in its totality to the secular sacred. They show the limitations of existing concepts and theories in memory studies and call for a new approach to the relationship between memory and religion (Urbaniak 2015; Sakaranaho 2011; Váně et al. 2018; Stroumsa 2016).

Of particular importance are works written by researchers of post-conflict studies who have examined the role played by religion in societies that have experienced trauma. They argue that religion offers distinct strategies for the 'representation of trauma' that enable it to manage change both in the personal lives of individual believers and within societies going through the process of coping with trauma (van der Merwe 2012). As Rios Oyola and Sandra Milena show in their analysis of a grassroots initiative to memorialize the Massacre of Bojayá in Colombia, which was perpetrated in 2002, religion offers a mechanism that can regulate emotions, thereby helping to transform the way the past is interpreted in a way that can be of assistance to survivors needing to deal with painful memories (Oyola and Milena 2015).

The role of religion in dealing with traumatic experiences is also stressed by postcolonial researchers (van der Merwe 2012). They also show how the texture and forms of memory carriers are a complex phenomenon. Although monuments and museums are the forms typically used by Western societies to commemorate the past, it should not be taken for granted that they constitute the best forms of remembering for all societies. As the South African sociologist Sabine Marschall claims, postcolonial communities use different markers and material objects to remember the past. Their memories are strongly linked to grassroots traditions and should therefore be analyzed as such rather than through reference to external Western patterns and commemorative systems (Marschall 2013).

Researchers investigating vernacular communities have independently come to similar conclusions. They show that vernacular communities have their own locally shaped strategies, which are rooted in their local religiosity, for dealing with the past (Lubańska 2018; Oyola and Milena 2015). Even if they perceive themselves as members of a national community, their local identity remains strong. This is most evident when there is a conflict between national and local memory. In such a case, local factors turn out to be more important for local actors. In other words, religion may sometimes prevail over the national in local understandings of the past (Bogumił and Głowacka-Grajper 2019; see also Głowacka-Grajper in this volume).

It is also worth mentioning a number of authors who have tried to expand on Halbwachs's and Assmann's reflections. Some of them have proposed new theoretical insights into the understanding of religious memory. Guy G. Stroumsa, whose main research focus is early Christianity, has argued that a distinction should be made between two kinds of religious memory: implicit and explicit. He shows how these two systems of religious memory once functioned together, complementing one another. Even if his analysis is rich, it is ultimately historical. The primary focus of Stroumsa's enquiry is how societies based on oral traditions progress to ones based on a written tradition (Stroumsa 2016). By contrast, the Czech sociologists Jan Váně and Dušan Lužný attempt to operationalize the concept of religious memory in such a manner that it can be used in an empirical survey. Inspired by the conceptualization of memory proposed by Jan Assmann, they distinguish two levels of religious memory. One is cultural and the other is communicative (Váně et al. 2018). When designing their research, they paid attention to the place held by religion in the Czech national myth and the way in which religious memory is transmitted to the next generation when the structures through which it traditionally passed have been disrupted. However, as they acknowledge, their theory of religious memory requires more development (Váně et al. 2018, 9). Finally, Francisca Metzger perceives religion as a system of communication and tries to systematize forms and modes of religious memory by taking a poststructuralist approach to memory studies and a cultural historical perspective on religion (Metzger 2019).

Some important insights have appeared in the literature that address different dimensions of the production of the sacred. In 2011, one of the field journals devoted to memory studies, *History and Memory*, published a special issue titled *Landscapes of Violence: Memory and Sacred Space* (Schramm 2011), in which the authors look at the sacralization of landscapes of violence and analyze remembrance practices by taking into consideration the relationship between violence, memory, the body and landscape. In the introduction, Katharina Schramm claims that the sacred is less an unchanging quality than the potentiality of objects and sites, which may take different forms for different actors. Consequently, the actualization of a violent past in the present at sites of memory can happen in religious or secular settings.[1] However, the authors do not develop how these settings work, preferring instead to concentrate on the authentication and imaginative potential of landscapes of violence.

It is also important to recall the works of researchers dealing with societies where religion was either banned or forced to play a limited role under communism but is now undergoing a revival. These works mostly concern memory work undertaken by institutional Churches in particular post-socialist European countries that have become actively engaged in the analysis of religion's cultural, political and social significance (Christensen 2018; Bodin 2007, 2009; Kahla 2010; Kormina 2013; Fedor 2014). What such Churches are effectively attempting to achieve is the 're-religionization' of sacred symbols that were secularized by communist or nation states. The novelty of these studies lies in the fact that they show that religious working through the past is not so much an internal matter for the Churches as a process strongly entangled with contemporary political, historical and memory discourses. Interestingly, the Churches not only use traditional religious means of commemoration but are increasingly referring to the secular language of commemoration to talk about their experience of the past (Bogumił and Łukaszewicz 2018; Fedor 2014). However, researchers investigating how Churches use secular language for their own needs do not propose any new theoretical frame for approaching the subject of their analysis. Instead, they mostly refer to Assmann's concept of communicative and cultural memory (Christensen 2018; Váně et al. 2018).

Finally, the problems presented by the need to deal with a difficult past and the role performed by religion in the process of working through the resultant trauma have been intensively discussed by theologians. Works written by theologians from Eastern Europe that describe the faith of their own religious communities are deserving of special attention because they try to explain the nature of the region's memory in all its complexity. They do this by analyzing the ambivalent role played by institutional Churches under communism and consider the impact of the social, cultural and political circumstances within which the life of these Churches was reshaped after 1989 (Noble 2008). The works of

8   *Zuzanna Bogumił and Yuliya Yurchuk*

theologians specializing in this region clearly show that even if religious memory is no longer the dominant form of memory there, it still constitutes an important part of its cultural memory. Moreover, the theological approach has provided some new insights that can be fruitfully applied to memory research, in particular that relating to traumatic twentieth-century experiences of mass repressions (Tolstaya 2013), understandings of the victim and perpetrator (Noble 2008; Paert 2016a) and the impact of a religious understanding of repentance and forgiveness on memory work in the region. Theologists have also contributed new insights on generational memory in post-communist societies by presenting how the manner in which religious socialization varies between generations can affect believers' memory activism (Paert 2016b).

Even though the abovementioned works are clearly throwing new light on memory and religion, they lie on the periphery of memory studies discussions and are making little impact on the field's development. As we have already noted, the fact that the fathers of memory studies perceived religion as a formative element of cultural memory did little to prevent it from disappearing from theoretical reflection once the field started to develop, or from the religious being reduced to the 'national secularized sacred'. When memory researchers exclude relations between religion and memory from their interpretations or present them in a rather narrow way, they are effectively limiting their focus to some groups while excluding others, and proposing a very West-centric perspective on memory processes. Such limiting theories and concepts are incapable of fully describing the complexities inherent in the memory of contemporary multi-ethnic and multireligious societies. When the investigation of the memory–religion relationship is restricted to discussions on the politics of memory of institutionalized Churches, the significance of the lived religion of believers is effectively being ignored. Moreover, believers quite often play the role of 'exotic others' in memory studies works that fail to take into account that believers are very diverse and often enter into alliances with both secular actors and representatives of other religious denominations. As a result, the consequences of such alliances for memory are also neglected in studies of memory. Finally, the fact that religion itself is effectively being perceived through the prism of Western Christianity excludes from scholarly analysis any other religion and religious behaviours unfamiliar to that tradition.

Postsecularism incorporates a wide and diverse spectrum of discipline-specific approaches (McLennan 2010), and our call for a postsecular turn within memory studies follows corresponding developments in other fields including literature, sociology, anthropology, philosophy and religious studies. In the next section, we explain what a postsecular turn within memory studies would potentially entail and what kind of benefits this could bring to scholarly memory analysis.

Rethinking memory studies through the prism of postsecularism

The term 'postsecularism' is used to refer to various theories and approaches that not only help scholars to determine where exactly religion has re-emerged in the contemporary secular world but also support their reflections on religion's place in the current public domain (Ratti 2019). Vivid discussions on postsecularism were first held across various disciplines following the terrorist attack on the World Trade Center in 2001 (Habermas 2008). However, even though the 'postsecular' continues to be widely discussed, the manner in which it is primarily understood and the methodologies used to investigate it vary from discipline to discipline. In philosophy, for instance, scholars tend to discuss the rejection of Weber's thesis that growing rationality leads to complete secularization. Philosophers of postsecularity postulate that we do not have to be rational purists and concur that religion has not disappeared from social life and the public sphere. Consequently, the relationship between religion, politics and society needs to be rethought (Blond 1998; Habermas 2008). Moreover, many philosophers and sociologists acknowledge the possibility that religious theories and language can be used to describe contemporary political and social disputes. Some look for inspiration in theology or even call for a closer cooperation between the disciplines. In the historical field, some scholars also draw attention to the fact that religion influences historiography and ways of thinking about the past to a much greater extent than we used to think. Historians have been attempting to disentangle the complex relationship between history and religion and approach religious traditions both as producers of historical narratives and distinct topics for historiographical research (Otto, Rau, and Rüpke 2015).

This interest in religion visible across different disciplines does not, however, mean that religion has regained the status it held in premodern society as the primary regime of truth-making. The postsecular approach also does not call for the religious to be focused on to the exclusion of all other aspects of social life. In fact, its primary focus is on interrelations between the diverse religious, humanist and secularist positions present in contemporary societies. It perceives the public presence of various religions as a manifestation of the kind of societal plurality that primarily draws attention to the limitations of the secular. This explains why scholars engaged in contemporary philosophy (McLennan 2010), the political sciences (Mavelli and Petito 2012), sociology (Rosati 2016) and literature studies (Ratti 2013) are currently showing such a keen interest in religion. Even if some scholars have shown the limitations to, and problems raised by, postsecular approaches (Fessenden 2014; Obirek 2019), we believe that an appropriately critical postsecular rethinking within memory studies may enrich the field by encouraging greater self-reflexivity and, ultimately, by urging scholars to pursue new theoretical options. However, it first needs to be asked how this rethinking should proceed. In short, what form would a postsecular turn within memory studies take?

As we mentioned earlier, there is no single understanding of what postsecularism entails. Each discipline has its own approach and multiple theories. Moreover, memory studies is an interdisciplinary field rather than a single discipline. Consequently, a postsecular turn within memory studies would be an even more complex and multivocal process that would draw on understandings of postsecularism adopted by the disciplines particular scholars originally came from or work in. On the one hand, memory scholars working on different aspects of memory may look for inspiration in their primary fields and then present their findings to the public. On the other, memory scholars would also surely need to discuss among themselves what postsecularism may mean for the field of memory studies. We would like to open the discussion by concentrating on the most pivotal aspects of our understanding of what a postsecular turn within a memory studies context would entail and what its advantages could be for the field.

The first task for memory scholars seeking to introduce a postsecular turn into memory studies would be to rethink how religion itself is understood within the field. As we have already mentioned, religion is generally perceived in the field as a given, something that is static, a reservoir of symbols or something belonging to the premodern, presecular world and a tool used by nation states to sacralize their regimes (Winter 2017). We propose to change perceptions of religion in the field by adopting the postsecular concept proposed by the American anthropologist Talal Asad, who argued that religion is more of a historical category and so needs to be regarded as being in a close relationship with secularization (Asad 1993). According to Asad, there was no linear shift from religion to secularization. Instead, religion and secularization mutually constituted one another. As religion is strongly dependent on secular understanding, it must be defined within a given historical context (Asad 1993). Consequently, the main challenge scholars should set themselves is to properly define and describe the relationships between religion and the secular in a given society (Asad 2003). Therefore, Asad calls for religion to be perceived more as 'practice, language and sensibility set in social relationships' (Martin and Asad 2014, 12) than as a separate, independent and unchangeable system of meanings. Asad explained his theoretical elaborations on the postsecular as follows: 'I was looking for ways of formulating the most fruitful questions about how people enact, declare, commit to – or repudiate – things when they talk about "religion"' (Martin and Asad 2014, 13).

Scholars of religion who have expanded on Asad's reflections on religion and the secular have demonstrated that secularizing and sacralizing processes often go hand in hand at the same time and within the same context. It is therefore possible, by focusing in on concrete practices and discourses, to perceive the intricate dynamics at play between secularization and sacralization, which need not be viewed as polarities (Baraniecka-Olszewska and Lubańska 2018). Even in societies with state-led secularization policies, as was the case in the USSR, religion did not disappear: instead, forced secularization led to the kind of 'religious change' that was reflected in the transformation of religious practices and discourses (Wanner 2012, 2018; Steinberg and Wanner 2008). It should be stressed here that although the studies discussed in this paragraph were produced by scholars of religion, they all discussed different aspects of memory that shed light on the intricate dynamics between secularization and sacralization.

Implementing Asad's understanding of religion and secularism within memory studies would open up a new interpretative perspective within which the religious and secular could be investigated within a dynamically changing relationship rather than being viewed as a static dichotomy. This would make the whole analysis of memory processes much more complex and also require scholars in the field to adopt a more reflective attitude that takes into account that religious languages – like all languages – are interwoven with life itself and produced by different actors. Moreover, adopting such an approach would show that religious elements are intertwined within different networks of the individual, collective, cultural and public memories of today's secularized societies, and it is this nexus that is deserving of further analysis and understanding. As Geneviève Zubrzycki shows in this volume, the way the cross is perceived in Polish culture is the result of over two centuries of mutual negotiations between the religious and secular. Even if she states that the national secular eventually prevailed over the religious, there are still some people for whom the cross has more of a religious meaning, and this has an impact on their agency (Golonka-Czajkowska 2018). Clearly, any postsecular rethinking of religion would necessarily entail accepting the fact that there has never been any lineal development from the time of religion to the time of postsecularism. The reality is, and was in the past, non-lineal and asynchronous. The religious exists in parallel with the secular, and the secular and religious sometimes merge and sometimes clash with or reinforce each other, directly or indirectly. Therefore, the role of the memory scholar is to understand, describe and interpret these interrelations within the sphere of memory.

The perspective we are proposing does not, however, mean that religion should now be placed at the centre of memory studies research and we should be looking for traces of religion in every dimension of memory representation and practice. We fully acknowledge that there are spheres that exclusively belong to the secular or religious and should be analyzed as such. What we are arguing for is for researchers to be more aware that secular forms of life and religious traditions coexist, so the memory researcher should take a reflective approach to any memory issue and look for a dialectical, rather than an oppositional, relationship between the religious and secular. As Massimo Rosati has stressed: 'awareness is a key term in . . . understanding of the postsecular' (Rosati 2016, 33).

We argue that a postsecular turn within memory studies would enable memory scholars to rethink the origins of their field and reassess their multifaceted personal connections with religion, which are quite often unconscious. Despite the fact that memory studies closely reflected on religion in the early days of its development, it later became a field that regarded memory as a purely secular phenomenon. But secularity has its own history, which it understands in its own way. Asad has showed that secularization is inextricably linked to the internal transformation of European Christianity (Asad 2003). Thus, the way we understand secularism and postsecularism should be based on how we understand the development of European Christian societies. Halbwachs's and Assmann's concepts of memory were also restricted to the monotheistic Judaeo-Christian tradition. Many scholars in memory studies have followed

12 *Zuzanna Bogumił and Yuliya Yurchuk*

this research path without always realizing that the epistemological tradition of memory studies rooted in this tradition is not always relevant to other contexts, especially when it is non-European memories and remembering processes that are being investigated.

Let us consider, for instance, such concepts as global (or 'cosmopolitan') memory, which clearly conceals a similar universalistic dream to the one that once stood behind strivings for a global Christianity. According to Levy and Sznaider, who sought to valorize cosmopolitan memory, most Europeans agreed that the memory of the European Jews murdered in the Holocaust was 'European common memory' and, as such, this memory should become a foundational moment for the idea of European identity in the third millennium (Levy and Sznaider 2002, 102). However, as memory scholars in East European countries have shown, such an assertion needs to be qualified, as the ways of remembering the Holocaust prescribed by the old democracies and then presented to the new members of the European Union have often revealed hegemonic tendencies and insensibilities to local histories and historical legacies (Pakier and Wawrzyniak 2015; Törnquist-Plewa and Yurchuk 2019; Yurchuk 2017; Mälksoo 2009, 2015). Moreover, the concept of cosmopolitan memory uses moral categories like 'good' and 'evil', whose understanding is rooted in the Judaeo-Christian tradition. Thus, promoting the commemoration of all other crimes and genocides in the twentieth century as a universal model has become problematic, because this form of commemoration sacralizes memory (Misztal 2004). In fact, close analysis of this model reveals similarities of approach between the proponents of cosmopolitan memory's attempts to construct a universal language of remembrance and religious actors for whom religion is such a universal language that it does indeed transcend nations and cultures.

By sanctioning a postsecular turn in memory studies, scholars would effectively be shifting towards a position that would enable them to better realize the epistemic and emic assumptions that laid the foundations for the field. Notwithstanding all the historical developments that have taken place since religion maintained a powerful hold on Western society, it should be acknowledged that deep-rooted religious traditions are continuing to influence the ways we deal with the past. Even though such influence is often indirect and unconscious, the task of scholars of memory is to increase their awareness of how it might be affecting their approach to their area of research. Below, we will mention some of the areas where this influence of religion on memory is most visible. We hope, through our reflections here and the chapters published in this volume, to establish a dialogue with other memory scholars. We therefore propose that our introduction be seen as the beginning of a fruitful discussion and an invitation to start thinking in terms of a postsecular memory studies.

Postsecularity and memory

One of the realms in which the traces of religion in memory are most visible is the language of memory and consequently the language and terms used by memory scholars. This is hardly surprising, as the topics we deal with most often in memory studies, namely trauma and death, have been dealt with by religion through the millennia (see Agadjanian in this volume). Jacques Derrida eloquently argued that we ought to keep in mind that the terms we use when speaking about religion already bear their history within themselves (Derrida and Vattimo 1996, 4). Moreover, Derrida, like Asad, shows the limitations of our understanding of religion itself. He argues we perceive religion from our Judaeo-Christian position (Derrida and Vattimo 1996). Thus, the postsecular turn would mean more critical use of terms and a deeper awareness of the genealogy of memory language. This also suggests a change of mindset and acknowledgement of the presence of religion in memory processes as well as the awareness that secular memory may also be a site of 'isolation, domination, violence and exclusion' (Mavelli and Petito 2014, 1).

Furthermore, the language we are highlighting here is not only present in discourses but in practices as well. If we take, for instance, historical justice, we can say that religious terms such as 'redemption', 'atonement', 'reconciliation', 'truth' and 'justice' are not only used in discussions on redressing past wrongs but also in practices that are produced to the same end (Berg and Schaefer 2009; Szablewska and Bachmann 2015; Tuttle 2015; Gabowitsch 2017). Thus, certain historic acts that shape our contemporary understanding and imagination of what reconciliation is and should be were actually completed under the direct influence of religious actors. Suffice it to mention that South Africa's Truth and Reconciliation Commission (which began its hearings in 1996) was led by Archbishop Desmond Tutu (Graybill 1998). Furthermore, the symbolic act of reconciliation between Poles and Germans that took place after the Second World War was initiated by bishops of the Catholic Churches in both countries, who signed a mutual 'letter of forgiveness' (in 1965) containing the symbolic formula, 'we forgive and ask for forgiveness' (Wigura 2011). The globally recognizable act of reconciliation between Germans and Jews symbolized by Willy Brandt kneeling in front of the monument to the Ghetto Heroes in Warsaw (in 1970) can be seen, in turn, as a postsecular gesture. What did the German Chancellor have in mind when he explained his unexpected behaviour in the following words: 'Under the weight of recent history, I did what people do when the words fail. That's how I thought of millions of murdered people'? (Brandt 1970). All these symbolic acts of reconciliation, which set examples to follow and are generally perceived as secular acts (Gabowitsch 2017), can in fact be more constructively perceived from a postsecular perspective. Similar examples may be found in other spheres of life, and the role of memory researchers is to decode and describe them.

A postsecular turn would also result in more complex analysis of the agency of believers. Rather than simply reducing ordinary believers to official representatives of the traditional Churches, genuine attempts could also be made to analyze their personal commemorative activity. To paraphrase Tariq Modood, who has claimed that secularism may even pose a threat to democracy because it ignores the implications of religious identity for active citizenship (Modood 2007), one may say that it is not possible to attain a full picture of memory processes in the contemporary global, multicultural world while remaining ignorant of the commemorative activities of various religious groups and churches. The postsecular approach would not only show how both religious people and non-believers engage in the process of memory work, how their works affect each other's memory activity and how they learn from each other, but also how their memory work comes to incorporate new configurations and practices.

It is important to stress that some works have already been published that attempt to describe commemorative activity from a postsecular perspective. The most prominent of these is a book written by Massimo Rosati, in which he analyzes the formation of a postsecular society in Turkey (Rosati 2016). Rosati describes the process of the formation of a postsecular collective macro-imaginary and draws on Halbwachs's reflections to show the importance of memory and space in this process. He analyzes postsecular sanctuaries, which he perceives as spaces of performative memory where the process of 'constantly redrawing the borders and engraving the content of a central value system' takes place (Rosati 2016). One such postsecular site of memory is the figure of Hrant Dink, editor-in-chief of the *Agos* newspaper, who worked to build bridges between the Turkish and Armenian communities until his assassination in January 2007. Rosati shows how various groups, some of which were religious, work together on understanding the meaning of Hrant Dink for Turkish society. In a similar vein, Magdalena Lubańska shows (in her study of the commemoration of the victims of killings that local gang members perpetrated in the Dębrzyna forest in south-eastern Poland after the Second World War) how a religious community unable to perpetuate traumatic memory in a traditional religious manner may feel a need to do this by drawing from secular commemorative practices (Lubańska 2018). All the chapters in this volume show the multilevel and highly complex engagements of believers in the formation of memory of events of importance to both believers and non-believers. They clearly demonstrate Wünsch's argument, mentioned above, that no memory, even if it is religious, exists in a vacuum, cut off from other developments in society (Wünsch 2013).

Another important issue is the relationship between religion and politics. Not only does religion become enmeshed with political power, but religious actors also have their own agenda in society. There is a huge literature describing the relationship between religion and nation, most of which shows how religion looms in representations of the nation and inspires nationalism (Smith 1986; Zubrzycki 2016; Berezhnaya and Schmitt 2013). It was often religious actors who shaped, strengthened and disseminated the historical myths that have served until now as sites of memory (Berezhnaya and Hein-Kircher 2019).[2] Other case studies in this volume show how churches have become the guardians of national identity and have been mobilizing memory of past events to support the state in the process of nation formation. But this is only one side of the coin. As Chris Hann stressed: 'the role of religion in the formation and persistence of modern nation-states is extremely variable' (Hann 1997,

27). The postsecular turn in the political sciences and international relations therefore calls for a more complex approach to politics and religion (Mavelli and Petito 2012, 2014). One aspect of these discussions that could be appropriated by memory scholars is a more nuanced perception of religion and the Churches in the politics of memory. This would help memory scholars to avoid reducing religion to a tool for sacralizing the nation and perceiving religious institutions as servants of nation state fatherlands. It would also help them to acknowledge the capacity of religion to promote more inclusive narratives and representations of the past, thus contributing to a more complex analysis of the religious arguments being used in memory politics that would distinguish the various voices existing within the Churches (Bogumił and Voronina 2020). This approach would assist the tracing of links between secular and religious imaginaries in the politics of memory in a more attentive way.

The postsecular turn would also mean more attention being paid to the presence of religion and religious language in the media and communication, which are approached in memory studies as both bearers and shapers of cultural memory (Erll and Nunning 2008; Erll and Rigney 2009). As Jan Assmann has claimed: 'on the *social level*, memory is a matter of communication and social interaction' (Assmann 2008, 109). This explains why the role of memory from a media cultures perspective is widely investigated by memory researchers. There are already studies that show that religious symbols are widely used in contemporary art and media, architecture, landscaping and monuments with different purposes. Often, these symbols function as transmitters for nationalist and patriotic ideologies (Berezhnaya and Schmitt 2013; Klimenko 2020; Norris 2013). For instance, the iconography of martyrs that die for their faith is well recognized in films produced in both Hollywood and Europe (Berezhnaya and Schmitt 2013). The chapters of this volume written by Berezhnaya and Yurchuk show that religion and the Church have become an important ingredient in national (or transnational, as in the case of the 'Orthodox world') identity formations. On the other hand, there are also works showing the power of religion for working through grief after the losses of war. Such masterpieces as Paweł Pawlikowski's Oscar-winning movie *Ida* (Vredenburgh 2016) or the poem *A Poor Christian Looks at the Ghetto* (1943), written by the Nobel Prize winner Czesław Miłosz (Jarzyńska 2018), make religion a means to discuss the memory of Poland's lost Jewish community.

The postsecular approach has also attracted a great deal of interest from art and literature studies scholars because it can offer new insight into classical and modern literature (Coviello and Hickman 2014; Kaufmann 2007; McClure 2007). The role of memory researchers would be to follow the existing literature in these fields and link it to their own research on memory. There is also a close relationship between postsecularism, on the one hand, and postcolonialism, which encourages people to think beyond categories and concepts produced in the Global North. As Ratti claims: 'whereas a western postsecularism can entail the rethinking of Christianity, an Indian postsecularism can entail the rethinking of a political formulation, of secularism as a state policy where the state assumes a principled distance from religion' (Ratti 2015). Adopting a postsecular approach in memory studies would therefore lead to deeper analysis of differing constellations and contexts of power relations.

Religion and churches also influence digital memory. Existing research shows that religion is very present, for instance, in the everyday online practices of migrants. Moreover, Churches themselves use the Internet for virtual re-evangelization in the Western megapolis. Similarly, as those participating in digital practices and religious social networking sites construct affective alternative networks that form 'counter-publics' – that is, spaces where it is possible to discuss and contest the images imposed on migrant groups and beliefs by secular society – the Internet offers possibilities for the manifestation of religious counter-memories. The investigation of these may throw new light on postsecular and transnational engagements in memory formation, not only in virtual reality but also in city space (Oosterbaan 2010; Leurs and Ponzanesi 2014; Bordyugov 2010; Molendijk, Beaumont, and Jedan 2010; Beaumont and Baker 2011).

This brings us to one more domain where a close relationship between memory and religion can be observed: space. Maurice Halbwachs, who was one of the first scholars to investigate the relationship between space and memory, claimed that 'a society first of all needs landmarks' (Halbwachs 1992, 122). In his book On Collective Memory, Halbwachs discussed the role of space and objects in collective memory work, and in his book The Legendary Topography of the Gospels in the Holy Land (*La topographie légendaire des Évangiles en Terre Sainte: étude de mémoire collective* 1941), the formation of sacred space in Jerusalem. Memory researchers have mostly focused on the secular dimension of cities, investigating national shrines and other material carriers of memory. However, recent postsecular researchers have stressed the need to be 'more sensitive to the religious dimensions of the "postmetropolis"' (Rosati 2016). The implication here is that religions are an integral part of city life. They are not only a source of conflicts and contestations but also spaces of dialogue integrated into global cities (Becci, Burchardt, and Casanova 2013). According to Baker and Beaumont, contemporary postsecular cities are spaces where religious, secular and postsecular representations coexist (Beaumont and Baker 2011) and should therefore be investigated as such. Such cities contain postsecular temples (Rosati 2016), postreligious spaces (see Halemba in this volume) and purely secular post-Christian heritage, but also new sacred spaces of generalized religiosity and post-Lutheran civil religion where people may contemplate 'heritage, spirituality and aesthetics' (Harding 2019).

Another important process that takes place at the intersection of religion and memory, where space, art politics and the abovementioned secular and religious actors converge, is the patrimonialization of religion. Hervieu-Léger has argued that it is through patrimonialization that 'religion is constituted as a collective patrimony, theologically neutralized and capable of being claimed by one and all: it has become a set of markers rooted in a distant past' (2015, 19). The authors in our volume show how the patrimonialization process works in contexts different from Western Europe, Hervieu-Léger's main area of focus.

Introduction 17

In Eastern Europe, for instance, religion, conceived as a collective patrimony, is far from being theologically neutralized. In fact, it is often less of a marker of unity than a marker of differentiation and a trigger for mobilization (see Berezhnaya, Kahla and Yurchuk in this volume). The patrimonialization of religion is also realized by protecting the religious objects and buildings perceived as national heritage. This trend is well observed in contexts where religion was once suppressed and liberalization has started to gather considerable momentum (Darieva, Mühlfried, and Tuite 2018).

By applying a postsecular understanding of memory, we can better grasp the complexities of the texture of remembrance. If we agree that religion coexists in our reality alongside rationality as an alternative source of knowledge, we are then in a position to scrutinize the religious currents crossing the memory studies discipline to better understand the contexts we study and belong to as well as the actors they contain. In the chapters collected in the volume, we can clearly see how, by focusing on the intersection of memory and religion, we can take a practice-based approach to transnational, transconfessional, transcultural and translocal subjectivities that are very often hard to embrace beyond the theory. For example, Elina Kahla in her chapter on the cult of St Tryphon of Pechenga shows how the figure of a seemingly very local Orthodox saint crosses the borders of three countries, revealing complex relations not only between countries but between humans and nature. Thus, we even can speak, albeit tentatively, of an ecological memory that transcends purely interhuman relations. Alla Marchenko and Jie-Hyun Lim very interestingly analyze the use of religion in memory work drawn from global contexts in specific local circumstances and show the transformations of different memories and their mutual influence on each other in practice. Marchenko's revelations about the intricate memory work undertaken by the Hasidic pilgrims who come from all over the world to a small locality in Ukraine enable us to clearly perceive how pilgrims can become transnational players in a global 'memory game' and a local Ukrainian town can become the space for these negotiations. Jie-Hyun Lim traces how the cult of St Maksymilian Kolbe is being used to negotiate and merge memory of the Holocaust with memory of the atomic bombing. He shows that these memories, rather than competing with each other, work '*productively* through negotiation, cross-referencing, and borrowing' in the manner elaborated by Michael Rothberg in his concept of 'multidirectional memory' (Rothberg 2014, 176). All the above examples show how examining memory from a postsecular perspective can be realized in practice and the kind of findings that such an approach can enable. Below we present a summary of all the chapters according to the structure of our book.

The book's structure

The fact that most of the case studies in this book come from post-socialist Europe or post-communist countries is by no means a coincidence. In general, post-conflict societies demonstrate a special interest in reworking the past

18 *Zuzanna Bogumił and Yuliya Yurchuk*

and look for various explanatory narratives, some of which are religious. The countries of Central and Eastern Europe are often described as post-totalitarian, post-catastrophic and post-genocidal, which makes them 'a fascinating laboratory in which to study cultural memory in action' (Blacker and Etkind 2013, 10). The authors of this volume enrich our understanding of this laboratory by proposing studies of religion, conceived as a kind of cultural memory. There is one additional factor that makes Central and Eastern Europe so special in religious terms. Communist regimes officially forced atheism through all state channels (Smolkin 2018). Religion was simply erased from public life and was forced to function through transformed practices and discourses (Wanner 2012, 2018; Steinberg and Wanner 2008). With the collapse of the socialist regimes in 1989 and dismantling of the Soviet Union in 1991, religion returned with renewed force to the forefront of public life. Many chapters in this book discuss various aspects of this return of religion to public life. All the chapters in this volume refer to Cold War or post–Cold War contexts and focus on a postsecular understanding of the interplay between religion and memory.

The book starts with a foreword by Grace Davie, whose works on religion, postsecularity and memory both inspired us and encouraged us to reflect on these topics and develop them further. This is followed by a theoretical part, in which Alexander Agadjanian and Geneviève Zubrzycki show how the relationship between memory and religion can be conceptualized theoretically. Agadjanian argues that religion is involved in a network of entangled memory agendas and narratives. He shows how religion provides tools and media for memory production. Taking the Russian Orthodox Church and the way it is dealing with the traumatic Soviet past as an example, Agadjanian demonstrates that religion has a rich range of resources for coping with a traumatic past that can vitalize the language and practice allied to the transcendental justification of history. This author also discusses the role of quasi-religious languages and techniques borrowed by nonreligious agents that can lead to the rejection of a confessional memory discourse in favour of one that is more universalistic. Zubrzycki draws on Durkheim's conceptualization of the sacred and profane, arguing for the destabilization of false 'sacred = religious' and 'profane = secular' associations. Zubrzycki focuses on the cross in Poland, arguing that it serves as a sacred religio-secular symbol. She encourages scholars to distinguish when and why certain symbols may be sacred or profane and when the religious is political (and vice versa). The scholar also draws attention to the role played by historical narrative in the creation of such sacred religio-secular symbols.

Part II of the book presents a discussion on postsecularity and the politics of memory. Here, it is made very clear how the postsecular is not only influencing secular politics but also the ecclesiastical politics of memory. This is the exact situation described by Asad, one in which it becomes impossible to distinguish where the contours of the secular and religious lie. Adam Pomieciński clearly shows that the mass canonization of all the victims of the Armenian genocide is being realized in a politically polarized environment in which a

Introduction 19

lack of international recognition of that genocide is being compensated for by the sacralization of human tragedy. Yuliya Yurchuk shows another context where politics and religion intersect on the cross-currents of discussions about the past. In the Ukrainian context, the plurality of Orthodox Churches in the 1990s and early 2000s created fertile ground for the creation of multiple narratives on these Churches' histories, each of which contributed to the formation and mobilization of multiple national identities. Liliya Berezhnaya shows in her chapter how the politics of memory in Russia and within the Russian Orthodox Church (ROC) have led to the militarization of St Alexander Nevsky, who was one of the first saints in the ROC and whose image has been an object of negotiation between the religious and secular, or in this case the military, through the centuries. It is noteworthy that the trends favouring this saint's militarization have ebbed and flowed along with the needs and desires of political elites. In her chapter, Agáta Šústová Drelová deals with Slovak memory of Jozef Tiso, a Catholic priest who served as president of Slovakia during the Second World War, collaborating with Nazis and later being murdered by the socialist regime. Šústová Drelová shows how the shaping of Slovak Catholic memory was strongly influenced by the secular memory of the socialist regime developed by the Slovak diaspora and later promoted as a symbol of the country's victimhood under both the Nazi and communist regimes. In the final chapter of Part II, Réka Földváryné Kiss shows the multiplicity of layered meanings attributed to the symbolic figure of the head of the Hungarian Catholic Church, Cardinal József Mindszenty, as well as his political trial, which took place in 1949. She demonstrates how memory of the cardinal developed through decades of communist rule and following the collapse of the dictatorial regime. In her chapter, she underlines the role played by transnational actors in forming memory of this prominent religious figure within the context of a political and ideological struggle.

Part III opens a discussion on the role religion plays in the formation of memory in post-conflict societies. Lap Yan Kung comprehensively demonstrates the power religions can wield when victims need to be remembered in a society where other, nonreligious forms of remembrance are suppressed and therefore not possible. Nadia Zasanska deals with the most recent military conflict in Europe, showing how different Churches have framed narratives about the war in Donbas, Eastern Ukraine, and how their narratives are affecting public interpretation of the past in Ukraine. She demonstrates that the position of different religious organizations in Ukraine depends on how they view their own position in national contexts and how they see the nation and its future in general. Naum Trajanovski analyzes commemorations of the state holiday known as Republic Day or Ilinden and the annual vernacular commemorations dedicated to a Macedonian-born Bulgarian revolutionary Mara Buneva to show how the Macedonian Orthodox Church – Ohrid Archbishopric has become the main memory actor in the politics and cultures of remembrance in the post-conflict Republic of North Macedonia. Karina Jarzyńska discusses the role performed by religion in remembering the Holocaust in

Polish villages, where people try to mark the genocide in their own way by combining Christian and Jewish religious imaginaries. As the author shows, the religious and secular are negotiated in such a way as to allow such interreligious combinations.

In Part IV, we move on to discussions on how religion and memory emerge in the media and spaces of memory. Elmira Muratova discusses the Crimean Tatars' memory of Stalin's deportations and shows the intricate interplay between politics, religion and memory in films and other artistic projects depicting this traumatic experience. Moreover, she shows the generational impact on the formation of memory and how this is interwound with religion. Per-Arne Bodin focuses on other media – in particular, icons and hymnography – to show how Russian modernist art is influencing the creation of contemporary Orthodox sacred images and texts. It soon becomes very clear that the line between the religious and secular art is obscure. Indeed, it is even open to question whether such a line even exists. Agnieszka Halemba approaches architecture as a space and medium of memory. She vividly demonstrates how religious architecture is used for nonreligious needs. Nevertheless, her case study also shows that the mere fact of a religious building's existence invites rather than excludes its religious use.

Part V examines transnational and vernacular memories. This part highlights the fluidity and imbalance inherent within such categories as nation or the confession, and even religions. Elina Kahla's case study on the cult of St Tryphon of Pechenga shows that, for each of the groups she examines in Russia, Norway and Finland, the cult means different things and stands for different ideals, especially when this issue is examined from national perspectives. However, if we zoom in to examine the context locally, the national 'grand narratives' dissolve, enabling us to see the potential of a form of translocal memory that establishes a dialogue between local inhabitants and nature. Taking such an approach enables us to reach a new, ecological understanding of memory. Alla Marchenko presents a case study that also shows how 'cosmopolitan' memory can work in peripheral contexts. Hasidic pilgrims serve as transnational actors bringing their memories to a provincial town in Ukraine, pushing local actors into formulating their own responses to this memory. Małgorzata Głowacka-Grajper analyzes how local communities in Poland draw from the Roman Catholic religion to transmit values they consider to be important. She shows how national memory is being contextualized and redefined within a local context. Jie-Hyun Lim focuses on a complex entanglement of memory of the Holocaust with memory of the bombing of Nagasaki. He demonstrates that the cult of Maksymilian Kolbe, Saint of Auschwitz, has become a mnemonic nexus for Japanese Catholic victims in Nagasaki. Through this process, religion has become, for the Catholics in Japan, the main tool for translating global memory of the Holocaust into memory of the bombing.

The book ends with an afterword by Kathy Rousselet, whose works, much like Grace Davie's, awakened our interest in memory and religion.

Notes

1 In religious settings, sacralization of 'past violence may reverberate in the articulations and demands of ancestral and other spirits, which need to be constantly addressed by the living; or, it may be incorporated into religious liturgy, in prayers, votive shrines and the like'. Sacralization in more secular settings takes place, for instance, when 'the victim, the martyr and the hero are narrative figures' (Schramm 2011).

2 For the 'symbiosis of the religious and national', see Krumeich and Lehman, 'Nation, Religion und Gewalt: zur Einführung', in *"Got mit uns": Nation, Religion und Gewalt im 19. und frühen 20. Jahrhundert* (Göttingen: Vandenhoeck & Ruprecht, 2000, 1). See also M. Schulze Wessel, 'Einleitung: Die Nationalisierung der Religion und die Sakralisierung der Nation im Östlichen Europa', in *Nationalisierung der Religion und die Sakralisierung der Nation im Östlichen Europa* (Stuttgart: Franz Steiner Verlag, 2006, 7–14); Anthony Smith, 'Ethnic Election and National Destiny: Some Religious Origins of National Ideals', *Nations and Nationalism* 5, no. 3, 1999; Anthony Smith, *Myths and Memories of the Nation* (Oxford: Oxford University Press, 1999); and Adrian Hastings, *The Construction of Nationhood. Ethnicity, Religion, and Nationalism* (Cambridge: Cambridge University Press, 1997).

References

Asad, Talal. 1993. *Genealogies of Religion: Discipline and Reasons of Power in Christianity and Islam.* Baltimore: Johns Hopkins University Press. https://doi.org/10.2307/3712068.

———. 2003. *Formations of the Secular: Christianity, Islam, Modernity.* Stanford, CA: Stanford University Press.

Assmann, Aleida. 2008. "Cultural Working Memory: The Canon." In *Cultural Memory Studies: An International and Interdisciplinary Handbook*, edited by Astrid Erll and Ansgar Nünning, 100–7. Berlin: De Gruyter.

Assmann, Jan. 1997. *Moses the Egyptian: The Memory of Egypt in Western Monotheism.* Cambridge, MA: Harvard University Press.

———. 2006. *Religion and Cultural Memory: Ten Studies.* Stanford, CA: Stanford University Press.

———. 2008. "Communicative and Cultural Memory." In *Cultural Memory Studies: An International and Interdisciplinary Handbook*, edited by Astrid Erll and Ansgar Nünning, 109–18. Berlin: De Gruyter.

———. 2009. *The Price of Monotheism.* Translated by Robert Savage. Stanford, CA: Stanford University Press.

———. 2011. *Cultural Memory and Early Civilization: Writing, Remembrance, and Political Imagination. Cultural Memory and Early Civilization: Writing, Remembrance, and Political Imagination.* Cambridge: Cambridge University Press. https://doi.org/10.1017/CBO9780511996306.

Baraniecka-Olszewska, Kamila, and Magdalena Lubańska. 2018. "Material, Political and Postsecular Dimensions of Polish Catholicism. An Anthropological Perspective." *Ethnologia Polona* 38: 5–14.

Beaumont, Justin, and Christopher Baker. 2011. "Introduction: The Rise of the Postsecular City." In *Postsecular Cities: Space, Theory and Practice*, edited by Justin Beaumont and Christopher Baker, 1–14. New York: Continuum.

Becci, Irene, Miran Burchardt, and Jose Casanova. 2013. *Topographies of Faith: Religion in Urban Spaces.* Leiden: Brill.

Berezhnaya, Liliya, and Heidi Hein-Kircher. 2019. "Introduction. Constructing a Rampart Nation. Conceptual Framework." In *Rampart Nations. Bulwark Myths of East European Multiconfessional Societies in the Age of Nationalism*, edited by Liliya Berezhnaya and Heidi Hein-Kircher, 3–30. New York: Berghahn Books.

Berezhnaya, Liliya, and Christian Schmitt, eds. 2013. *Iconic Turns: Nation and Religion in Eastern European Cinema Since 1989*. Leiden: Brill.

Berg, Manfred, and Bernd Schaefer. 2009. *Historical Justice in International Perspective: How Societies Are Trying to Right the Wrongs of the Past*. Washington, DC: Cambridge University Press.

Blacker, Uilleam, and Alexander Etkind. 2013. "Introduction." In *Memory and Theory in Eastern Europe. Palgrave Studies in Cultural and Intellectual History*, edited by Uilleam Blacker, Alexander Etkind and Julie Fedor, 1–24. New York: Palgrave Macmillan.

Blond, Phillip, ed. 1998. *Post-Secular Philosophy. Between Philosophy and Theology*. London: Routledge. https://doi.org/10.4324/9780203423516.

Bodin, Per-Arne. 2007. *Eternity and Time: Studies in Russian Literature and the Orthodox Tradition*. Södertälje: Amqvist & Wiksell International.

———. 2009. *Language, Canonization and Holy Foolishness: Studies in Postsoviet Russian Culture and the Orthodox Tradition*. Stockholm: Acta Universitatis Stockholmiensis.

Bogumił, Zuzanna, and Małgorzata Głowacka-Grajper. 2019. *Milieux de Mémoire in Late Modernity*. Bern, Switzerland: Peter Lang. https://doi.org/10.3726/b15596.

Bogumił, Zuzanna, and Marta Łukaszewicz. 2018. "Between History and Religion: The New Russian Martyrdom as an Invented Tradition." *East European Politics and Societies* 32 (4): 936–63.

Bogumił, Zuzanna, and Tatiana Voronina. 2020. "A Time of Persecution or a Time of Glory? The Russian Orthodox Church's Centenary Commemorations of the 1917 Revolution." *Religion, State & Society* 48 (2–3): 161–79. https://doi.org/10.1080/09637494.2020.1761756.

Bordyugov, Gennadiy. 2010. *Oktyabr'. Stalin. Pobeda Kul't Yubileyev v Prostranstve Pamyati*. Moscow: Akademie Verlag.

Brandt, Willy. 1970. "Warschauer Kniefall, Willy Brandt Falls to His Knees, 1970." *Deutsche Geschichten*. www.deutschegeschichten.de/popup/objekt.asp?OzIID=6264&Seite=6.

Brown, Adam D., Yifat Gutman, Lindsey Freeman, Amy Sodaro, and Alin Coman. 2009. "Introduction: Is an Interdisciplinary Field of Memory Studies Possible?" *International Journal of Politics, Culture, and Society* 22 (2): 117–24.

Casanova, José. 1994. *Public Religions in the Modern World*. Chicago: University of Chicago Press.

Christensen, Karin Hyldal. 2018. *The Making of the New Martyrs of Russia: Soviet Repression in Orthodox Memory*. Avignon: Routledge.

Coviello, Peter, and Jared Hickman. 2014. "Introduction: After the Postsecular." *American Literature* 86 (4): 645–54.

Darieva, Tsypylma, Florian Mühlfried, and Kevin Tuite, eds. 2018. *Sacred Places, Emerging Spaces: Religious Pluralism in the Post-Soviet Caucasus*. New York: Berghahn Books.

Davie, Grace. 2000. *Religion in Modern Europe: A Memory Mutates*. Oxford: Oxford University Press.

Derrida, Jacque, and Gianni Vattimo. 1996. *Religion*. Stanford, CA: Stanford University Press.

Erll, Astrid, ed. 2010. *A Companion to Cultural Memory Studies*. Berlin: De Gruyter.

Erll, Astrid, and Ann Rigney. 2009. *Mediation, Remediation, and the Dynamics of Cultural Memory*. New York: De Gruyter.

Erll, Astrid, and Ansgar Nunning. 2008. *Media and Cultural Memory: An International and Interdisciplinary Handbook*. Berlin: De Gruyter.

Fedor, Julie. 2014. "Setting the Soviet Past in Stone: The Iconography of the New Martyrs of the Russian Orthodox Church." *Australian Slavonic and East European Studies* 28 (1–2): 121–54.

Fessenden, Tracy. 2014. "The Problem of the Postsecular." *American Literary History* 26 (1): 154–67.

Gabowitsch, Mischa, ed. 2017. *Replicating Atonement Foreign Models in the Commemoration of Atrocities*. Cham: Palgrave Macmillan.

Gensburger, Sarah. 2016. "Halbwachs' Studies in Collective Memory: A Founding Text for Contemporary 'Memory Studies'?" *Journal of Classical Sociology* 16 (4): 396–413.

Golonka-Czajkowska, Monika. 2018. "In the Shadow of the Sacred Bodies: The Monthly Smolensk Commemorations in Krakow." *Ethnologia Polona* 38: 107–23.

Graybill, Lyn S. 1998. "South Africa's Truth and Reconciliation Commission: Ethical and Theological Perspectives." *Ethics & International Affairs* 12: 43–62.

Habermas, Jürgen. 2008. "Notes on a Postsecular Society." *New Perspectives Quarterly* 25 (4): 17–29.

Halbwachs, Maurice. 1925. *Les cadres sociaux de la mémoire*. Paris: Librairie Félix Alcan.

———. 1941. *La topographie légendaire des Évangiles en Terre Sainte: étude de mémoire collective*. Paris: Presses Univ. de France.

———. 1992. *On Collective Memory*. Chicago: University of Chicago Press.

Hann, Chris. 1997. "The Nation-State, Religion, and Uncivil Society: Two Perspectives from the Periphery." *Daedalus* 126 (2): 27–45.

Harding, Tobias. 2019. "Heritage Churches as Post-Christian Sacred Spaces: Reflections on the Significance of Government Protection of Ecclesiastical Heritage in Swedish National and Secular Self-Identity." *Culture Unbound* 11 (2): 209–30.

Haskins, Ekaterina V. 2009. "Russia's Postcommunist Past: The Cathedral of Christ the Savior and the Reimagining of National Identity." *History and Memory*. https://doi.org/10.1353/ham.0.0015.

Hervieu-Léger, Danièle. 2000. *Religion as a Chain of Memory*. New Brunswick, NJ: Rutgers University Press.

———. 2015. "Religion as Grammar of Memory: Reflections on the Comparison between Britain and France." In *Modernity, Memory, and Mutations: Grace Davie and the Study of Religion*, edited by Abby Day and Mia Lövheim. London, New York: Routledge.

———. 2017. "La Religion Comme Chaîne de Mémoire." In *Maurice Halbwachs. La Topographie Légendaire Des Évangiles En Terre Sainte*, edited by Marie Jaisson, 31–41. Paris: Presses Universitaires de France.

Jarzyńska, Karina. 2018. *Literatura Jako Ćwiczenie Duchowe. Dzieło Czesława Miłosza w Perspektywie Postsekularnej*. Kraków: Universitas.

Kahla, Elina. 2010. "The New Martyrs of Russia – Regeneration of Archaic Forms or Revival?" *Ortodoksia* 51: 193–208.

Kaufmann, Michael W. 2007. "The Religious, the Secular, and Literary Studies: Rethinking the Secularization Narrative in Histories of the Profession." *New Literary History* 38 (4): 607–28.

Kim, Mikyoung, ed. 2015. *Routledge Handbook of Memory and Reconciliation in East Asia*. London: Routledge.

Klimenko, Ekaterina V. 2020. "Building the Nation, Legitimizing the State: Russia – My History and Memory of the Russian Revolutions in Contemporary Russia." *Nationalities Papers* (February): 1–17. https://doi.org/10.1017/nps.2019.105.

Kormina, Jeanne. 2013. "Canonizing Soviet Pasts in Contemporary Russia: The Case of Saint Matrona of Moscow." In *Companion to Anthropology of Religion*, edited by Janice Boddy and Michael Lambek, 409–24. London: Wiley-Blackwell.

Leurs, Koen, and Sandra Ponzanesi. 2014. "Remediating Religion as Everyday Practice: Postsecularism, Postcolonialism, and Digital Culture." In *Transformations of Religion and the Public Sphere Postsecular Publics*, edited by Rosi Braidotti, Bolette Blaagaard, and Tobijn de Graauw, 152–74. New York: Palgrave Macmillan.

Levy, D., and N. Sznaider. 2002. "Memory Unbound: The Holocaust and the Formation of Cosmopolitan Memory." *European Journal of Social Theory* 5 (1): 87–106. https://doi.org/10.1177/13684310222225315.

Lubańska, Magdalena. 2018. "Postmemory of Killings in the Woods at Dębrzyna (1945–46): A Post-Secular Anthropological Perspective." *Ethnologia Polona* 38: 15–45.

Mälksoo, Maria. 2009. *The Politics of Becoming European: A Study of Polish and Baltic Post-Cold War Security Imaginaries. The Politics of Becoming European: A Study of Polish and Baltic Post-Cold War Security Imaginaries*. London: Routledge. https://doi.org/10.4324/9780203871898.

———. 2015. "'Memory Must Be Defended': Beyond the Politics of Mnemonical Security." *Security Dialogue*, 221–37. https://doi.org/10.1177/0967010614552549.

Marschall, Sabine. 2013. "Collective Memory and Cultural Difference: Official vs. Vernacular Forms of Commemorating the Past." *Journal of South African and American Studies* 14 (1): 77–92.

Martin, Craig, and Talal Asad. 2014. "Genealogies of Religion, Twenty Years On: An Interview with Talal Asad." *Bulletin for the Study of Religion* 43 (1): 12–17. https://doi.org/10.1558/bsor.v43i1.12.

Mavelli, Luca, and Fabio Petito. 2012. "The Postsecular in International Relations: An Overview." *Review of International Studies* 38 (5): 931–42. https://doi.org/10.1017/s026021051200040x.

———. 2014. "Towards a Postsecular International Politics." In *Towards a Postsecular International Politics: New Forms of Community, Identity, and Power*, 1–26. Palgrave Macmillan.

McClure, John A. 2007. *Partial Faiths: Postsecular Fiction in the Age of Pynchon and Morrison*. Athens: University of Georgia Press.

McLennan, Gregor. 2010. "The Postsecular Turn." *Theory, Culture & Society* 27 (4): 3–20. https://doi.org/10.1177/0263276410372239.

Memory Studies Association. 2017. www.memorystudiesassociation.org/about_the_msa/.

Metzger, Franziska. 2019. "Devotion and Memory – Discourses and Practices." *Kirchliche Zeitgeschichte* 31 (2): 329–47. https://doi.org/doi.org/10.13109/kize.2018.31.2.329.

Misztal, Barbara. 2004. "The Sacralization of Memory." *European Journal of Social Theory* 7 (1): 67–84.

Modood, Tariq. 2007. *Multiculturalism. A Civic Idea*. Cambridge: Polity Press.

Molendijk, Arie L., Justin Beaumont, and Christoph Jedan. 2010. *Exploring the Postsecular: The Religious, the Political and the Urban*. International Studies in Religion and Society. Leiden: Brill.

Nardi, Sarah De, Hilary Orange, Steven High, and Eerika Koskinen-Koivisto, eds. 2019. *The Routledge Handbook of Memory and Place*. London: Routledge.

Noble, Ivana. 2008. "Memory and Remembering in the Post-Communist Context." *Political Theology* 9 (4): 455–75. https://doi.org/10.1558/poth.v9i4.455.

Nora, Pierre. 1989. "Between Memory and History: Les Lieux de Mémoire." *Representations*. https://doi.org/10.2307/2928520.

Norris, Stephen M. 2013. "Blessed Films: The Russian Orthodox Church and Patriotic Culture in the 2000s." In *Iconic Turns: Nation and Religion in Eastern European Cinema Since 1989*, edited by Liliya Berezhnaya and Christian Schmitt, 65–80. Leiden: Brill.

Obirek, Stanisław. 2019. "The Challenge of Postsecularism." *Journal of Nationalism, Memory & Language Politics* 13 (2): 239–50. https://doi.org/10.2478/jnmlp-2019-0009.

Olick, Jeffrey K., Vered Vinitzky-Seroussi, and Daniel Levy, eds. 2011. *The Collective Memory Reader*. Oxford: Oxford University Press.

Oosterbaan, Martijn. 2010. "Virtual Re-Evangelization: Brazilian Churches, Media and The Postsecular City." In *Exploring the Postsecular the Religious, the Political and the Urban*, edited by Arie Molendijk, Justin Beaumont, and Christoph Jedan, 281–308. Cham: Brill. https://doi.org/doi.org/10.1163/ej.9789004185449.i-406.111.

Otto, Bernd-Christian, Susanne Rau, and Jörg Rüpke, eds. 2015. *History and Religion*. Berlin: De Gruyter.

Paert, Irina. 2016a. "Memory of Socialism and the Russian Orthodox Believers in Estonia." *Journal of Baltic Studies* 47 (4): 497–512. https://doi.org/10.1080/01629778.2016.1248681.

———. 2016b. "Religion and Generation: Exploring Conversion and Religious Tradition Through Autobiographical Interviews with Russian Orthodox Believers in Estonia." In *Generations in Estonia: Contemporary Perspectives on Turbulent Times*, edited by Raili Nugin, Anu Kannike, and Maaris Raudsepp, 188–211. Tartu: University of Tartu Press. https://doi.org/10.26530/OAPEN_606515.

Pakier, Małgorzata, and Joanna Wawrzyniak, eds. 2015. *Memory and Change in Europe: Eastern Perspectives*. New York: Berghahn Books.

Ratti, Manav. 2013. *The Postsecular Imagination: Postcolonialism, Religion, and Literature. The Postsecular Imagination: Postcolonialism, Religion, and Literature*. London: Routledge. https://doi.org/10.4324/9780203071786.

———. 2015. "Rethinking Postsecularism through Postcolonialism." *Interdisciplinary Journal for Religion and Transformation in Contemporary Society – J-RaT*. https://doi.org/10.14220/jrat.2015.1.1.57.

———. 2019. "Theoretical Framings of the Postsecular." In *The Routledge Handbook of Postsecularity*. London: Routledge. https://doi.org/10.4324/9781315307831-9.

Rios Oyola, Sandra, and Sandra Milena. 2015. *Religion, Social Memory and Conflict. The Massacre of Bojayá in Colombia*. New York: Palgrave Macmillan UK.

Rosati, Massimo. 2016. *The Making of a Postsecular Society. A Durkheimian Approach to Memory, Pluralism and Religion in Turkey*. Burlington: Ashgate. https://doi.org/10.4324/9781315555867.

Rossington, Michael, and Anne Whitehead, eds. 2007. *Theories of Memory: A Reader*. Edinburgh: Edinburgh University Press.

Rothberg, Michael. 2014. "Multidirectional Memory." *Témoigner. Entre Histoire et Mémoire* 119. https://doi.org/https://doi.org/10.4000/temoigner.1494.

Sakaranaho, Tuula. 2011. "Religion and the Study of Social Memory." *The Finnish Society for the Study of Religion* 47 (2): 135–58.

Schramm, Katharina. 2011. "Introduction: Landscapes of Violence: Memory and Sacred Space." *History and Memory*. https://doi.org/10.1353/ham.2011.0001.

Smith, Anthony D. 1986. *The Ethnic Origins of Nations*. Oxford: Blackwell.

Smolkin, Victoria. 2018. *A Sacred Space Is Never Empty: A History of Soviet Atheism*. Princeton, NJ: Princeton University Press.

Steinberg, Mark D., and Catherine Wanner. 2008. *Religion, Morality, and Community in Post-Soviet Societies*. Bloomington: Indiana University Press. https://catalog.loc.gov/vwebv/citeRecord?searchId=21895&recPointer=0&recCount=25&searchType=0&biblId=15348615.

Stroumsa, Guy G. 2016. "Religious Memory, Between Orality and Writing." *Memory Studies*. https://doi.org/10.1177/1750698016645271.

Szablewska, Natalia, and Sascha-Dominik Bachmann, eds. 2015. *Current Issues in Transitional Justice Towards a More Holistic Approach*. Cham: Springer International.

Tolstaya, Katya. 2013. "Theology and Theosis after Gulag. Varlam Shalamov's Challenge to Theological Reflection in Postcommunist Russia." In *Just Peace: Ecumenical, Intercultural, and Interdisciplinary Perspectives*, edited by F. Enns and A. Mosher, 50–69. Eugene: Wipf and Stock Publishers.

Törnquist-Plewa, Barbara, and Yuliya Yurchuk. 2019. "Memory Politics in Contemporary Ukraine: Reflections from the Postcolonial Perspective." *Memory Studies* 12 (6): 699–720. https://doi.org/10.1177/1750698017727806.

Tota, Anna Lisa, and Trever Hagen, eds. 2016. *The Routledge International Handbook of Memory Studies*. London: Routledge.

Turoma, Sanna, Kaarina Aitamurto, and Slobodanka Vladiv-Glover, eds. 2019. *Religion, Expression, and Patriotism in Russia*. Stuttgart: Ibidem Press.

Tuttle, K. 2015. "Truth and Reconciliation Commission." In *Africana: The Encyclopedia of the African and African American Experience*, edited by Henry Louis Gates and Anthony Appiah. Oxford: Oxford University Press.

Urbaniak, Jakub. 2015. "Religion as Memory: How Has the Continuity of Tradition Produced Collective Meanings? – Part One." *HTS Teologiese Studies / Theological Studies* 71 (3): 1–8. https://doi.org/10.4102/hts.v71i3.2815.

van der Merwe, Chris. 2012. "Rethinking Religion in a Time of Trauma." In *Trauma, Memory, and Narrative in the Contemporary South African Novel: Essays*, edited by Ewald Mengel and Michela Borzaga, 195–215. Amsterdam: Rodopi.

Vance, Laura. 2005. "Review: Danièle Hervieu-Léger, Religion as a Chain of Memory." *Nova Religio: The Journal of Alternative and Emergent Religions* 8 (3): 128–29.

Váně, J., D. Lužný, F. Kalvas, M. Štípková, and V. Hásová. 2018. *Continuity and Discontinuities of Religious Memory in the Czech Republic*. Barrister & Principal. https://books.google.pl/books?id=wbnwxwEACAAJ.

Vredenburgh, Steven. 2016. "Finding God in Pawlikowski's Ida." *Religions* 7 (6). https://doi.org/doi.org/10.3390/rel7060072.

Wanner, Catherine, ed. 2012. *State Secularism and Lived Religion in Soviet Russia and Ukraine*. New York: Oxford University Press.

———. 2018. "Public Religions after Socialism: Redefining Norms of Difference." *Religion, State and Society* 46 (2): 88–95. https://doi.org/10.1080/09637494.2018.1465245.

Wigura, Karolina. 2011. *Wina Narodów. Przebaczenie Jako Strategia Prowadzenia Polityki*. Warsaw, Gdańsk: Wydawnictwo Scholar.

Winter, Jay. 2017. "Commemorating Catastrophe: 100 Years On." *War and Society* 36 (4): 239–55. https://doi.org/10.1080/07292473.2017.1384137.

Wünsch, Thomas. 2013. "Einleitung: Religiöse Erinnerungsorte in Ostmitteleuropa." In *Religiöse Erinnerungsorte in Ostmitteleuropa. Konstitution Und Konkurrenz Im Nationen- Und Epochenübergreifenden Zugriff*, edited by Joachim Bahlcke, Stefan Rohdewald, and Thomas Wünsch, xv–xxxiii. Berlin: De Gruyter.

Yamashiro, Jeremy K., Abram Van Engen, and Henry L. Roediger. 2019. "American Origins: Political and Religious Divides in US Collective Memory." *Memory Studies*. https://doi.org/10.1177/1750698019856065.

Yurchuk, Yuliya. 2017. "Reclaiming the Past, Confronting the Past: OUN-UPA Memory Politics and Nation-Building in Ukraine (1991–2016)." In *War and Memory in Russia, Ukraine, and Belarus,* edited by Julie Fedor, Markku Kangaspuro, Jussi Lassila, and Tatiana Zhurzhenko. London: Palgrave Macmillan.

Zubrzycki, Geneviève. 2006. *The Crosses of Auschwitz: Nationalism and Religion in Post-Communist Poland*. Chicago: University of Chicago Press.

———. 2016. *Beheading the Saint: Nationalism, Religion, and Secularism in Quebec*. Chicago: University of Chicago Press.

Part I

Memory and religion

Theoretical considerations

2 Religion and collective memory of the last century

General reflections and Russian vicissitudes

Alexander Agadjanian

Framing religion within collective (post)memory of a secular age

The expansion of memory studies has led to the field dramatically growing in complexity, and 'religion' is but a small segment of a picture that not only includes all manner of memories experienced by a variety of subjects, from individuals and families, through local communities and business corporations, to ethnic groups and nations, but also incorporates what is now tentatively perceived as global memory (Assmann and Conrad 2010). My assumption in this chapter is that religion has a certain special affinity to what we assume to be the collective memory process, and it is this affinity that makes religion highly relevant to the field. The reason for this affinity is threefold. First, as we shall see, religion, by definition, tends to be organized as a memory-oriented institutional, normative and behavioural social phenomenon. Second, patterns of religious memory-oriented communication have been largely borrowed by secular institutions and milieux, so religious patterns are latently present in forms or memory techniques that would otherwise appear to be purely secular. Third, in sociological terms, the re-activation of public religion in the twenty-first century (as can be seen, for example, in the former socialist nations) appears to have boosted the public visibility of explicitly religious forms of memory work.

When speaking of these three aspects of 'religion', I am certainly mainly referring to the monotheistic Abrahamic traditions that possess certain 'theologized' rituals, symbols, norms and metaphors. The material I will be drawing upon in the rest of this text has obvious associations with Christianity and its respective language and style. (Yet I would hazard a guess that all other religions, as a matter of fact, possess in various forms those same mnemonic qualities that I have just described.) From the perspective of Mircea Eliade's account of the 'eternal return' paradigm, even archaic preliterate religions were memory centred and elaborated continuity-protecting imagery, mythology and rituals (Eliade 1987, chap. 2).

According to a well-known definition by Danièle Hervieu-Léger, religion is a 'chain of memory' that derives its temporal narrative from the myth of creation, presenting this narrative as 'tradition' and the respective community as 'lineage', thereby making religion a quintessential agent of memory

DOI: 10.4324/9781003264750-3

30 *Alexander Agadjanian*

(Hervieu-Léger 1993). Religion's very function is to re-enact the past, or keep it functioning in the present, by maintaining and continuously reproducing a sense of continuity going back to the 'Great Beginning'. Religion's obsession with continuity leads it to 'resist' time and position itself, as Jan Assmann points out, as a 'counterpresent' (Assmann 2004, 89). Even though religious people would assume that their religion is deeply embedded in the present and relevant to our days, such embeddedness is based upon the presumption of the immutability of 'eternal truth'. This metaphysical presumption makes religion, even when it is conceived sociologically (as a set of institutions and identities), predominantly a force for continuity and tradition. To be sure, there have been instances in human history when religious agency has detonated the present (like the European Reformation), but again, the goal in that case was to bring the present back to an ideal, sacral *past*, to re-enact the *past*, and the anticipated eschatological *future* was only part of a past prediction.

All this means that religion, *ex definitio*, possesses, so to speak, the requisite professional skills, means and media (and most importantly, as we shall see, the language) to either make sense of the past, re-present the past or make the past present. Religions have accumulated the means and mechanisms to fix and transfer memory of the past through the creation of a sacred map of the past that is supposed to be deeply meaningful to the present because it is energized by primal sacred meanings. Assmann called this the 'semiotization of history under the sign of salvation' (Assmann 2004, 263). He specified that history was *theologized* at some point in ancient history when 'religion' started to provide not only a magical-mechanical (ritual-based) resistance to the forces of chaos but also an overall divine legitimation of world events as hyper-meaningful (my wording; Assmann 2004, 263–66).

There are at least three ways in which religion can produce and maintain this sacred map of the past. One way is, indeed, ritual. Rituals have outlived the 'theologization' mentioned by Assmann, who rightly believes that rituals have survived as the primal form of organizing cultural memory, or as 'the oldest and the most fundamental medium for bonding memory' (Assmann 2006, 11). Ritual has persisted, in textual religions as well, as a symbolic, emotional and bodily performative technique for re-enacting the past. The most powerful and meaning-generating of all rituals is the cult of the dead. In fact, it is the most archaic and fundamental form of religion, as can be seen from all its various ideas of coping with death and, most importantly, its complex material and sensual system of commemorative techniques.

The second way of producing and maintaining the sacred map of the past is 'writing space' using the symbolic visual language highly elaborated by religious traditions to create various kinds of mnemotopes (religious buildings and other material objects) or produce symbolic imagery that creates an emotional impact.[1]

The third way religion creates a sacred map of the past is the normative structure that it claims to authoritatively maintain and support. This normative structure is translated into the language of moral discourse, rhetoric and judgments about both the past and present. The 'text-based religions' provide an elaborated system of normative references, which are not only used in other written or audible texts but also in rituals and visual symbolism. The 'language' of memory – the ultimate medium possessed by religions working with memory – is infused with metaphors and carries meanings assuming the form of myths. We know that metaphors and myths are the most suitable material for memory, as they contain a combination of the two major forms of remembering: narrative and image (Leontieva 2011, 16–17).

Therefore, religion is indeed well equipped for the process of memorialization. The very fact that it claims to deal with an allegedly unchanged matrix of ultimate knowledge makes it, along with art, one of the 'antidotes' (*Gegenmittel*) to the 'stifling' of life by history, or the 'historical sickness', as this process is termed in the Ricoeurian interpretation of Nietzsche (Ricoeur 2006, 292). A more specific example of this approach, in this case relating to religious language, is Ricoeur's acknowledgement of Jacques Derrida's intuition that an 'Abrahamic heritage', or 'Abrahamic language', is widely felt in the contemporary discourse of memory (see Derrida 1999; Ricoeur 2006, 468–69). We will see more examples of this semantic influence below.

The assumption that religion is prominent in today's memory processes does, however, require at least two important elaborations. Our first task is to specify what we actually mean here by *religion*, or *the religious*, and identify the religious agents of the memory work. The most crucial distinction here should be drawn between official religious institutions, on the one hand, and what can be called vernacular discourses and practices on the other. The official dogmatic position tends to be unitary and presented as an authoritative, canonical univocality, be it a liturgical text, an official judgment (of the past) or a pattern of ritual performance (even though the challenges posed by social turmoil, such as that caused by the dissolution of empires or collapsing regimes, can produce varying responses within these institutions). However, vernacular religious memories are, by definition, multivocal, and more often in contradiction than in harmony with 'official religion'. In a sense, the distinction between institutional and vernacular religious memory can be meaningfully compared to the opposition of cultural and communicative (social) memory developed by Assmann (2008).

The second fundamental elaboration is that today religion, in whatever form, can by no means claim a monopoly over the work of collective memory or pretend to hold any exclusivity over commemorative practices and moral judgments, or indeed claim any form of linguistic/discursive domination. The very fact of secularization might lead us to reflect on whether secularized societies have, as a matter of fact, *ceased* to be societies of memory (Hervieu-Léger 1993; Davie 2000). This diagnosis, however, would appear to be overstating the case, and it does, in fact, contradict some more recent trends. In the secularized world, there are other agents that need memory and work to shape it. The main competitors to religious memory in the work of creating a meaningful map of the past have probably been nation states and ethnic groups; or, more precisely, the subjects of national and ethnic collective memories that are either state-sponsored or represented by spontaneous groups/actors who claim the right to do so. There are also a variety of collective memory actors who appear in the form of vernacular civil and professional groups of various social provenance and

32 *Alexander Agadjanian*

ideological tenor. Today's landscape of collective memory includes a complex intermixture of new rituals, textbooks, family legends, literature, state propaganda, monuments and professional histories. All these secular actors are producing their own new dialects of memory, new myths, new media and methods of remembrance and new forms of performative embodiment of the past.

What is of most interest here is the undeniable fact that religious elements are present and intertwined within this entire network of collective memories belonging to today's secularized society – partly because of the old special skills developed by religions and partly because in many societies, as mentioned before, religious actors are simply maintaining, or even enhancing, their stakes. Both the religious and secular fields of memory work are multiple and plural; the memory landscape is full of controversies, contestations, rivalries and competition. We have known since Maurice Halbwachs published his seminal works that collective memory cannot be anything other than plural, because collective memories are linked to 'affective communities' (Halbwachs 1980). Such communities need what Assmann called 'hot memory', that is, memory that reflects the plurality and rivalries of today because it is created by the present for the present (Assmann 2004).

So the richest and most productive field of research conceived in this volume is, perhaps, the exploration of the deep interaction between religious and secular memory work. Most contemporary cases of collective memory either reveal combinations, whether relatively organic or rather uncomfortable, of religious and secular discourses and practices or reflect direct competition between them. In a secular age, religion is present either directly or, so to speak, in a hidden, or transformed way, because, as mentioned above, the very language of continuity, of the longue durée, of the sacralized past was borrowed by secular agents from religion, while the semiotics of the basic ritual performances of sacralization was borrowed by states and other secular agents from the religious repertoire.

Speaking specifically of today, it is worth adding yet another important reflection: the powerful rise of conservative sensibilities and reconstruction projects in various parts of the world has resulted in the activation of religious agency, discourses and rhetoric. Some (but not all) of these conservative reactions have included religious components. If Aleida Assmann's intuition is correct, and modernity's future-oriented temporal regime has indeed slowed down (Assmann 2013), and Pierre Nora's contention that there is now a greater demand for memory studies than futurology is also correct and we are indeed witnessing *l'avènement mondial de la mémoire* (the global upsurge of memory; Nora 2002), then religion is claiming back its rights and mobilizing its skills in preparation for its recreation and maintenance of 'the chain'.

Traumatic memory of the twentieth century through a religious optic (with a special focus on Eastern Europe)

Memory of the twentieth century has its own powerful singularity. In a very clear way, the twentieth century was squeezed between two grand narratives that, to use Bernhard Giesen's memorable opposition, may be conceived of as the narrative of triumph and the narrative of trauma (Giesen 2004). Today's collective memories are still defined by this opposition, which is at the very core of modernity's ambitions and failures. The hero and the victim are the two archetypical figures currently defining the collective memorial imagination. These narratives usually come together. In fact, the triumph, or heroica of the century, promoted by nation states (to support national pride) or by optimistic scientists and humanists (to save the reputation of 'progress') is inseparable from the memorialization of the trauma of massive human losses and anthropogenic disasters of the century.

One further clarification: when we compare triumphalist heroica with the trauma of victimhood, it becomes clear how the latter predominates in the collective imagination. In fact, the twentieth century tends to be perceived as a period full of catastrophic violence. This perception may be viewed as an aberration from an objective rational standpoint, given the progress of the sciences and the overall increase in softness and tolerance throughout the century. Yet when we view twentieth-century history in terms of collective memory based upon the 'lived' history still affecting us today – even though this memory may, in some cases, be *postmemory* of something that happened two or three generations ago, or even 'borrowed' memory (as Halbwachs called memory not experienced directly; Halbwachs 1980, 51) – we tend to register ferocity rather than developing softness, xenophobia rather than growing tolerance, persecutions rather than growing freedom and mass atrocities rather than mass celebrations.

Maybe it is our tendency to dramatize the past that makes the memory of violence more powerful than any other kind of memory? It is true that the Holocaust, the genocides, the two world wars and, generally, histories of loss and suffering have traditionally held a special place in memory studies (Linde 2009, quoted in Vasiliev 2012). However, it is harder to keep such topics within a cold, objective and neutral academic frame of reference. Moreover, traumas and emotional shocks, whether experienced individually or collectively, produce the strongest effects and leave the deepest traces in memory (van der Kolk 2007; Bremner 2016). This dark side of history still affects people in many regions of the world, and this is particularly noticeable in the part of Eastern and Central Europe that Timothy Snyder has called the *Bloodlands* (Snyder 2012).

When such memory traces of trauma are examined more closely, another strong connection between memory and religion becomes apparent: thinking about mass violence necessarily implies religious, or religiously inspired, references. There are several reasons for this. First, we know that particular acts of violence were religiously motivated or legitimized, openly or implicitly, as was the case with some acts of genocide and ethnic wars. Second, the twentieth century saw a proliferation of mass violence, which was, on the contrary, motivated by purposely *anti*-religious, 'godless' intolerance. Third, even beyond these direct yet oppositional historical connections, mass violence implies religious references simply because of religion's own special relationship with the ultimate issues that powerfully emerge amid the rampant violations of justice, dehumanization and dying that can occur in any of the traumatic moments known as a *Grenzsituation*.[2] Mass atrocities and biopolitical engineering created

34 Alexander Agadjanian

a huge *semantic disruption* in the rational explanation of history, and this led to a quest for a different kind of knowledge, explanation, justification, and indeed, reconciliation with the past. Here again, we have Halbwachs's classic opposition of schematic cold historical science (the Nietzschean 'historical sickness' mentioned above) and affective warm collective memory: when the former proves to be unable to grasp a sense of the past, the latter helps to provide this sense using non-rational means (Halbwachs 1980, 78ff.). The semantic disruption of inscrutable atrocities can be addressed using a variety of religiously connoted cognitive tools: blasphemous revolt; deep, metaphysical doubt; paradox and irony; apocalyptic fears; or stubborn faith. 'Triumph and trauma', as Giesen writes, 'represent ultimate breaks and ruptures in the construction of meaning' (Giesen 2004, 8). Religion can help to partially restore this process of meaning-building – at least for some, if not for all – by offering its language and symbolic resources as tools in the struggle to restore what Peter Berger would term as 'plausibility structures' against social (and cognitive) 'anomy' (Berger 1967).

The obvious inclination in today's memory to emphasize the dark side of history even affects the way we remember triumphalist heroica. Rather than bringing any radiance or joy, past triumphs are almost inevitably connected to trauma and victimhood. Despite their extreme complexity, twentieth-century trauma and victimhood can be broadly categorized as belonging to one of three types of tragedy. The first possibility is the tragedy of innocent suffering, which involves complete dehumanization and downgrading to the level of *la vita nuda*, or 'bare life', as Giorgio Agamben termed it (Agamben 1998). The second category is the tragedy of guilt, either that experienced by murderers or a collective guilt arising from being connected to murderers by family ancestry or shared nationality. Giesen refers here to Nazi Germany as a paradigm case, when heroes came to realize that they had actually been perpetrators (Giesen 2004, 3). The third possibility is the 'tragedy of the hero'. Here, Giesen is referring to a certain price that needs to be paid for the triumph, namely, the sacrifice – a quintessentially religious mythological archetype blended in collective imagination with the myth of heroes.

In Central and Eastern Europe, memory of the twentieth century appears to be crystal clear with regard to the innocent victims of the Holocaust or other genocides. In other cases, however, this memory becomes convoluted and intricate, or what Alexander Etkind called, in relation to memory of the Soviet political terror, 'warped mourning' (translated into Russian as *krivoe gore*, or 'distorted/awkward grief'; Etkind 2013). In such cases, there was no clear boundary between victims and perpetrators, victims and heroes, or innocence and guilt. This all creates an impossible tangle of moral judgments, which is aggravated by the imperfection of the legal system and ambiguities in the politics of memory, including the politics of forgetting (silencing). In Germany's case, the grief and trauma were also 'distorted', and *Vergangenheitsbewältigung* – or coming to terms with the past – could only make partial progress in purely legal terms because deep, emotional work, usually framed as repentance, was required. Indeed, as Pascal Bruckner has provocatively highlighted, *repentance* – despite being 'tyrannically' self-imposed sometimes – has become a keyword for dealing with hard, distorted memories of the past century (Bruckner 2006).

This keyword, like others such as sacrifice, suffering, innocence, guilt, mourning and repentance, definitely comes from the 'Abrahamic heritage' of the religious thesaurus. Of course, these words can intermingle with secular words and concepts, and these religiously associated terms may themselves even be used in a secular context and with a secular meaning. For example, the word *guilt* is a legal term, but when seen through the lens of moral 'Abrahamic memory', it carries the additional connotation of *sin*. A *sacrifice* could be made for a nation or revolutionary cause, and it could also be framed within militant atheism, but an instance of sacrificial death inevitably triggers archetypical images of *martyrdom*. The amount of mass violence that was perpetrated in the twentieth century created such a total and prolonged *Grenzsituation* that the ultimate questions of life and death have inevitably reactivated the old religious vocabulary.

In the final analysis, mass violence has raised a few fundamental questions in which religions have traditionally claimed expertise, but these questions have turned out to be barely resolvable for the religions themselves, irrespective of whether they are represented by official authorities or their common flock. One of those issues has been *human nature*: what can we say about it after everything that has happened? Is it divinely virtuous or originally sinful, or both? The second issue has been the *nature of the world order* as such, which can be reduced to the issue of providence and final redemption, the issue of goodness and the omnipotence of God and the classic question of theodicy. Finally, the sheer scale of the twentieth century's catastrophes beg another, much more radical question: is God really there, or was He really present when all this unfolded? The classic form of this doubt was the Nietzschean 'death-of-god' prediction and its continuation in some post-Auschwitz theologies, like Richard Rubenstein's covenant-rejecting theology (Rubenstein 1966). Others would start from a position of revolt and anger against God, like Elie Wiesel (Wiesel 2006). Within the European Christianities, including those functioning in Central and Eastern Europe, the trauma was manifold. Some felt a sense of complicity in the Holocaust most keenly, while others sensed they had been left behind and let down by God during the communist persecutions. Others still harboured doubts over the overall validity of God's benevolent providence. These doubts and even anger were coupled with massive secularization in Eastern Europe as well as the West. The combined impact of these developments was to demarcate limits for the participation of religions in the work of memory and raise questions about the validity of purely religious forms of commemoration and moral judgment.

Returning to the convoluted memory landscape of Central and Eastern Europe, the Holocaust can serve as a paradigm test. In Poland, the issue of complicity in the Holocaust has been widely discussed based on the case of the massacre that took place at Jedwabne (Gross 2001), but even beyond the direct discourse of complicity or guilt, religion has been deeply involved in shaping

36 *Alexander Agadjanian*

national memory, as the story of the 'crosses of Auschwitz' has shown (Zubrzycki 2006; see also Jarzyńska and Głowacka-Grajper in this volume). The situation in Lithuania exploded after the publication of Ruta Vanagaite's book *Our People* (*Mūsiškiai*), which examines the role ethnic Lithuanians played in the extermination of Jews during the German occupation. One of its most notable revelations was that the Catholic Church played an ambiguous role. However, although its prelates would not officially acknowledge the genocide, there are documented cases where individual priests made such an acknowledgement and assisted Jews (Vanagaite 2020).

The complexity of this memory, hard to grasp as it is, is further exasperated in this region by the experience of socialism/communism. In the middle of the twentieth century, these nations were squeezed between two totalitarian behemoths, Nazi Germany and the Soviet Union. Anti-Soviet heroes, partisans and resistance fighters could collaborate with the Nazis in the same way as anti-fascist fighters collaborated with the NKVD (the Soviet secret police), and thus both anti-Stalinists and anti-Nazis could be complicit either in the Holocaust or the Soviet terror, respectively. These confusions can be framed as the 'competition of victimhood', a phenomenon that produces a certain asymmetry of memories between different groups, and even entire nations (Lim 2010). This asymmetry can be seen in the manner in which most post-communist discourses, memorials and museums highlight the victims of communism and interpret forced or voluntary collaboration with the Nazis (a phenomenon certainly exemplified by the crosses at Auschwitz, as well as some policies of the conservative Polish governments in the 2010s).[3] The consequences of such competition can either be preferential treatment being conferred on *some* victimhood regarded as sacrificial or, as far as other victims are concerned, various strategies of forgetting – to use the fine Ricoeurian analysis – being applied through avoidance, evasion, and flight, or by omission, negligence and imprudence (Ricoeur 2006, 444–56). Forgetting attends to the construction of a moral discourse of accountability to which societies, in general, and religions, in particular, have been deeply involved.

Even beyond the issue of the traumatic memories of the Holocaust and communist repressions, a simple fact (already referred to above) should be kept in mind, notably the strong presence of dominant religions in the public memory discourse and infrastructure of Eastern European nations. Catholicism's powerful narrative of Polish history continues to shape national memory in Poland (Porter-Szucs 2011). This is also true, in a different configuration, for Romanian Orthodoxy (Stan and Turcescu 2007). Ukrainian collective memory in general and religious memory in particular are dramatically torn, unsettled and plural as such memory is still 'under construction' while the issue of ecclesiastic autocephaly continues to be passionately debated,[4] yet Ukraine's religions are constantly becoming involved in crucial identity debates (Marchenko 2017; Kalenychenko 2017). Religion has been central in post-Soviet collective memories in Georgia and Armenia (Serrano 2018; Agadjanian, Jödicke, and van der Zweerde 2015) and for the Muslim republics of the former Soviet

Union (Khaleed 2007; Hanks 2016). For religious minorities, religion has been an indispensable skeleton of identity. This has not only proved to be the case for the minority Uniate (or Greek Catholic Churches) in Hungary, Romania, Slovakia and Ukraine, but also for the Muslim and Protestant communities persecuted in the Soviet Union.

Religious and secular collective memory in Russia: a tissue of agendas, narratives and frames

In what follows, I will attempt to apply some of the general ideas formulated above to the complex palimpsest of collective memories represented by Russia. Anyone reflecting on Russia of the twentieth century will find it perfectly exemplifies the aforementioned memory dilemma between the 'narrative of triumph' and 'narrative of trauma', which, in this case, is developing around two cardinal foci: the Second World War and the Soviet communist project. The field of memory is structured within this cognitive grip.

Victory in the Second World War, specifically emphasized in Russia as a unique Soviet achievement, has become the cornerstone of the country's 'official memory' and Russia's current 'civil religion', with its repertoire of mythological narratives and commemorative ritual practices (Tumarkin 1994; Kahla 2014). Victory in the war – in this case, *the* Victory – has two functions in the field of memory. First, it is the foundational event of an official patriotism based on the imagining of imperial might and a cult of strong nation and strong state. In fact, it is the state that has been the central player in the field of memory. Speaking through Pierre Bourdieu's optic, the symbolic policies of the state, whose management of national memory is a 'resource of legitimation', has strongly defined the entire field of symbolic power (Bourdieu 1977). While the notion of the state playing a special role in the pragmatic use of military glory is not exceptional to Russia, in this particular case, this role grew out of an authoritarian, state-centric tradition, which was reproduced after a short power crisis at the end of the Soviet Union.

Second, the Victory tends to be seen as a sacrificial experience of global relevance, or the quintessential example of purposeful suffering. As was mentioned above, the idea of suffering is linked, and sometimes subordinate, to the idea of triumphant heroism. The trend towards triumphalist perceptions of V-Day growing at the expense of tragic perceptions of that holiday has been noted by researchers (Arkhipova et al. 2017, 112–13; Voronina 2018). The triumph of the Victory tends to be interpreted in terms of the redemption for all the sufferings of the century, including the atrocities of the Stalinist terror. The evils of the Gulag, Holodomor, Katyn, mass ethnic deportations, and so on all, seem to be redeemed through the victory over the *greater* evil of Nazism. The blood of the war heroes not only justified the war losses but also purified the nation's sins.

These discourses define the search for a 'usable past', as well as interpretation of the Soviet era as a whole. In the first post-Soviet years, the Soviet past

38 Alexander Agadjanian

(as an ideological project and social reality) was emphatically rejected, with a strong emphasis being placed on the victims of communist terror. Later, in the Putin era, this emphasis was downplayed as the official memory tended to 'split' the Soviet past into two parts: whereas the revolutionary tradition was seen as a historical deviation and therefore either stifled or treated as a harmful interruption, the Soviet experience as a whole was interpreted as a combination of sacrificial losses and glorious achievements.[5] The sacrificial losses included the victims of both the communist terror and the war, but the former were profiled much less than the latter.

Although overall, policies of memory have never attended to a deliberate coherent paradigm, a sort of official consensus was finally reached in the 2010s that revolutionary breaks are, by definition, traumatic and harmful, while the continuity of a strong order is fundamental. Hence the ambivalent attitude in Russia to the Soviet past: whereas avant-garde rebellion contains danger and risks, war-winning and space-winning glory is incontestable, as it links the Soviet era to the longue durée narrative of power and present-day need for order. There is no need for a Russian *Vergangenheitsbewältigung*: in an act of strategic (and selective) forgetting, the Soviet past could be 'disinfected' before being implanted into a chain of continuity.[6]

Continuity is, indeed, a keyword in this context. In a sense, official memory policy in Russia is in concordance with what Halbwachs saw as the work of collective memory as opposed to that of 'history': whereas history breaks the past into periods, collective memory connects all periods into one continuous stream (Halbwachs 1980, 81).[7] Post-Soviet collective memory works in this way, as it is trying to splice together various shards and splinters of former (Soviet) experience to create the illusion of 'no-interruption'. This illusion seems to be an intuitive antidote to complete identity disorder, so the official policy of gluing together old splinters can attract broad support.

Russian Orthodoxy has been referred to by many civil, academic and official voices as an important element of this continuity and the 'genome' from which Russian identity is coded.[8] Although its memory agenda diverges from state memory policy, the Russian Orthodox Church, for obvious reasons, faces similar dilemmas while negotiating the past. The Church, along with other previously repressed or forgotten images (empire, nobility, etc.) has made a quick return into the public imagination (Khmelevskaia 2004, 14). There has been a strong tendency to present the Russian Orthodox tradition as a millennial chain of continuity deeply intertwined with the chain of Russian statehood leading from Prince Vladimir, the tenth-century Baptizer of Rus' to Vladimir Putin. This has been made clear in many speeches and documents produced both by the Church and political leaders. It was also strongly stated in a pre-election propaganda documentary about Valaam, an old monastery on Lake Ladoga, where President Putin directly and unequivocally connected the triumph and the traumas of the Russian state with the flourishing and destruction of the Russian Orthodox Church (Valaam 2017). According to this logic, the 1917 Revolution was seen as a break, both political and religious, in the chain as well as a tragedy and catastrophe for the traditions of both Church and state. Yet the image of a strong Soviet state was somehow separated from its revolutionary origins. Such an interpretation makes it difficult to soberly assess the entirety of Soviet history, especially given the official political propensity to include the power of the Soviet state in the model of continuity.

A gigantic interactive exhibition project titled *Russia – My History*, which is currently being displayed in pavilions in about twenty cities across the country, is revelatory due to the extent to which religious and official political visions of Russian history, including the Soviet period,[9] intersect in it. The project's concept of history was designed by a well-known personality from the Church, Metropolitan Tikhon Shevkunov, in cooperation with patriotically driven historians. In the exhibitions, a harmonious continuity between Church and state is interwoven into the visual narrative, with revolution and anti-religious terror being interpreted as an unnatural, tragic break. The project is an interesting example of a 'meeting point' of religious and secular memories of the Soviet past. Without directly imposing religious meanings, and even *secularizing* the Orthodox reading of the revolution, the creators of the exhibit have incorporated the space of history into the religious perspective (Klimenko 2020, 7).

However, the mechanism used by the state to redeem collective sins/guilt through strategic (selective) forgetting cannot be accepted by a Church that was a direct victim of the totalitarian terror. For Russian Orthodoxy, as for all religious communities, the Soviet era was a tragic experience of precarious survival involving persecutions and resistance but also reluctant adaptation and collaboration with the regime. The massive loss of people, institutions and spiritual strength during the Soviet era undoubtedly affected today's Russian Orthodoxy. Since then, the Church memory's central project has been the creation of a hagiography of 'New Martyrs and Confessors' who were persecuted throughout the Soviet repressions but are now officially canonized as saints (see below). However, the Church has also inherited the big compromise of 1927, when the patriarchal deputy–*locum tenens* Metropolitan Sergius Stragorodsky declared the Church's loyalty to the Bolshevik regime. This compromise was never redressed, even amid the cruellest waves of persecution in the 1930s. In late Soviet times, the Church hierarchy was still tightly connected to the regime and cooperated with it. The Church's 'hard memory' of the past therefore has an ambivalent meaning.

Later, within the context of a close ideological partnership with Putin's regime, the Church has been trying to avoid direct confrontation with the state by using the official political memory agenda based on narratives of triumph, sacrifice for the sake of humanity, national continuity and perennial conservative values. Traces of the Patriarchal Church's partial collaboration and docility during the Soviet period, along with the partnership it has forged with the post-Soviet state in commemorative projects, have created ambiguities that are partly at odds with the discourse and practices involved in worshipping the New Martyrs. These practices can be fused with the commemoration of heroic victims of war who might also be imagined as martyrs, but in a different, non-confessional sense. In fact, as a Russian historian noted, 'the glorification of martyrdom [within the Church] can be seen as a memorial project complementing the main memorial project of the victory of the Great Patriotic War of the Soviet people' (Semenenko-Basin 2010, 185).

Overall, the Russian Church, which was once only a marginal player in the memory field, has definitely become, over two or three decades, a leading agent of historical politics (Voronina 2018, 101), second only to the state. This role is part of a general growth in the Church's public profile and ambient presence. As an institution that possesses, as we described above, professional symbolic resources of commemoration, the Church is a major agent in the business of creating the sacred loci through which commemoration is channelled.

While undertaking such work, the Church enters into direct relations with secular agents of memory. While the Putinist state, as we have seen, has taken a collaborative approach to the Church, certain public agencies and autonomous civil groups might be more competitive. One major example of this competition are the rivalries between public museums and the Church over the possession and use of heritage buildings and artefacts (Koellner 2010; Bernstein 2014; Stepanova 2019). More relevant to our discussion here is the Butovo phenomenon, named after the Moscow suburb that contains the site of mass executions during the Great Terror of 1937–38 – the first and paradigmatic instance of a place where the Church, civil society and the state have negotiated over the traumatic memory of political repressions. While retaining certain civil and pluralist openness through positioning itself as a memorial complex, the place has gradually developed an Orthodox infrastructure and increasingly inscribed itself into the religious discourse (Rousselet 2007, 2013; Christensen 2018).

It is worth taking a closer look at another example: the complicated relationship between the Church and the Memorial Society NGO (non-governmental organization), the major agent in the field of commemoration of the Soviet repressions. Both institutions have been active across the country and have often come into direct contact with each other, sometimes cooperating to an extent or working with parallel agendas and at other times directly competing with one another (Bogumił, Moran, and Harrowell 2015; Bogumił 2018). This interaction has occurred on three levels corresponding to what we have earlier described as religious forms of participation in memory work: ritual commemoration practice, symbolic expression and 'writing space', and the development of a normative discourse of the past.

The first level of interaction, commemoration, really began to gather momentum in 1989, when the Synodal Commission of canonization was created. By 2020, almost 1,800 named persons had been canonized as 'New Martyrs and Confessors of the Russian Orthodox Church'.[10] In 2000, the Church adopted a special holy day within its liturgical calendar, which was followed by the development of a special hymnography (an *Akathist* for the New Martyrs, approved in 2009, and other personal *Akathists* for particular saints) and iconography (see Bodin 2007, 231–50; Semenenko-Basin 2010; Christensen 2018; Burgess 2017, 122–63; see also Bodin in this volume).[11]

Religion and collective memory 41

The Memorial Society started its active research of the Soviet repressions at about the same time. It created its own secular commemorative ritual called 'The Return of the Names', an annual public invocation of the names of victims of repressions on 29 October, the eve of the official day devoted to their memory. The ritual was first staged in 2007 in downtown Moscow near the infamous Lubyanka secret services headquarters and former prison by a newly designed mnemotope: the Solovki stone, which had been brought to the centre of Moscow from the site of one of the first Soviet political camps. Since then, the action has spread through many cities in and even outside Russia. Although the secular ritual includes elements carrying religious connotations (candles and some commemorative wordage), the ritual script and style are radically different to religious forms of remembrance.

As for the second level of interaction, symbolic spatial presence, the Church's main activity has been the building of crosses, chapels and so-called churches-on-blood, such as the Church of All Saints in Ekaterinburg (opened in 2003), which was built at the site where the last tsar and his family were murdered; the Church of New Martyrs in Butovo (2007); or another important shrine with the same name at Lubyanka in downtown Moscow (2017); as well as a few smaller new churches across the country dedicated to New Martyrs. The construction of such shrines can be seen as a symbolic appropriation of the memory field (Dorman 2010). For its part, as we have seen, the Memorial Society has used the stone instead of the cross as a universal sign of the tomb and enduring memory (Bogumił 2010, 2012; Bogumił, Moran, and Harrowell 2015, 1425ff.). Exhibitions and museums, both in situ and elsewhere, and monuments together constitute a contested visual language in which religious and secular forms of expression have collided at many locations across the country (for a detailed analysis, see Rousselet 2007; Bogumił 2018).

At the third level of interaction, normative discourse, both the Church and the Memorial Society have been creating their own moral map of the past. Although both actors have used detailed archival research methods, they diverged from the beginning in terms of their objectives and ideology. The goal of the Church consisted of discerning those victims who had died for Christ or their Christian faith, with eventual canonization as the final objective.[12] The Orthodox historiosophy expressed in liturgical and general texts is based upon typical ideas of repentance, suffering-for-redemption and the blood of martyrs as 'the seed of the Church' (Emelianov 2010; Orlovsky 2016). The 'seed' trope is repeated a few times in the Akathist for the New Martyrs. The sites of their murders have often been called a (Russian) Golgotha. The eschatological bias of this redemptive topos, as mentioned before, has created a bridge for fusing victims of repressions with the victims of war and likening the glory of resurrection to the glory of victory in war (Christensen 2018, 211). In non-official, popular theologies, one can come across other explanations for the totalitarian anti-religious atrocities, from the most primitive conspiracy theories to more sophisticated explanations referring to God's providential plan for purification through suffering, the revolution being viewed as a sort of *flagelum Dei* (scourge of God), with a special emphasis on an eschatological interpretation of the murder of the royal family as an atoning sacrifice analogous to the Atonement of Jesus (Semenenko-Basin 2010, 209; Shtyrkov 2019, 153–58). In some reflections following this providential logic, a Holy Rus' purified through sufferings has been paradoxically conserved within a Soviet 'shell' from the corruption of liberal modernity that subdued the rest of the world (e.g. Birov 2013). This explains the tendency, at least in some popular Orthodox milieux, towards de-emphasizing the discourse of Soviet guilt and legitimizing the Soviet period within a historical continuity. The image of Russia as a global guardian of conservative morality and spirituality is found on both official and vernacular levels.

The Memorial Society's memory project resembles the Church's hagiography work in that the recovery of the names of specific victims from archival documents is of central importance (as the title of the Return of the Names ceremony would also suggest; see more in: Shcherbakova 2004, 184). However, there are a few clear differences to the Church's memory projects. First of all, the Memorial Society, as a secular institution, has always targeted all victims irrespective of their social or confessional belonging. Second, innocence, rather than sainthood or even a particular virtue, is expected from the victims of persecution who are to be remembered. (To be sure, the notion of innocence presumes not only legal but also moral and political predilections: those recognized as perpetrators who were later illegally executed could not be treated as innocent because of the crimes they had previously committed.) As far as memorial discourse is concerned, sacrifice and repentance motifs have been much weaker in the work undertaken by the Memorial Society. A distinction was also made between trauma caused by political terror and trauma caused by the Second World War, with the focus being placed on the former. National traumatic memory was placed outside the frames of redemptive victories or millennial continuity supported within the official policy of the state. Finally, in contrast to the primarily apolitical canonization work being carried out by the Church, the discourse of the Memorial Society emphasized the guilt of the Soviet regime and combined its research on the Soviet repressions with human rights activism addressed to both the Soviet and post-Soviet political regimes.

Overall, the activities of civil groups like the Memorial Society create a counter-memory opposed to both the official national narrative and the mainstream religious narrative. Although all these three agents sometimes share some textual, symbolic and performative elements from the intuitive repertoire of the human work of mourning and remembrance, the differences in their message and agenda are obvious. Interactions of agendas within the field of memory are common because of the multiplicity of collective memories. Besides Memorial, whose position is exceptional in the field, there are many social, familial, confessional, local and other memory actors that create a complex tissue containing intricate spaces of (strategic) remembrance and (strategic or imprudent) forgetting.

To illustrate this complex tissue, I would like to refer to another example: a 'holy spring' near Lozhok, a Soviet mass murder site fifty kilometres outside Novosibirsk. Investigation of this site reveals the intersection of various agendas and frames. The Church diocese that built here yet another church (finished in 2015) dedicated to New Martyrs clashed with local worshippers' vernacular practices that were seen as heterodox by canonical standards. The diocese's notion that *all* who died in the Gulag were Orthodox martyrs – an idea taking for granted the endemic Orthodoxy of all Russians, including pronounced atheists – contradicts the lofty criteria placed on the definition of 'new martyr' (nothing less than sainthood) by the Church Canonization Commission. The local metropolitan spoke of the 'bloodthirsty individuals' behind the repressions, without ever mentioning by name Stalin or anybody else involved in the murders in Siberia and without condemning the regime, as such, because he knew that memory of the victims is intermingled with nostalgic loyalty to the Soviet Union and high appraisal of Stalin in the minds of some of the locals. On top of this, the governor of Novosibirsk region was promoting the spring as a touristic heritage attraction while neglecting to mention either its tragic past or its sacral symbolism (Rouhier-Willoughby 2014).

Concluding overview

The above examples show, as indeed many others do, how religion is involved today in a network of entangled memory (and forgetting) agendas and narratives constructed around mnemotopes, monuments, museums, acts of commemoration and other events related to the turbulent history of the twentieth century. For a number of reasons elaborated at the beginning of this chapter, I assumed that religion retains a few tools and media compatible with and usable for the process of memory production. I also assumed that, for equally good reasons, religious legacies are appropriate specifically for coping with traumatic pasts that activate the language and practice associated with the transcendental justification of history. For the most part, the twentieth century, with its mass atrocities, represents such a *lieu de mémoire*, and it has indeed created what we referred to above as 'semantic disruptions'. These have made religious responses all but expected.

In sociological terms, what I have here called 'religious responses' have proved to be a complex phenomenon split into various layers, from official 'normative' voices to particular quasi-autonomous publics expressing vernacular 'hidden transcripts'. We should also remember those quasi-religious languages and techniques that have been borrowed, consciously or instinctively, by nonreligious commemorative agents. At the same time, we saw that the memory field has continued to be a space of appropriation contested by various agents. We have also seen how the manner in which complex religions have historically related to a traumatic past (either by exhibiting passivity or collaborating with totalitarian regimes) potentially lays them open to criticism and exposure, and

44 Alexander Agadjanian

also how the confessional memory discourse could potentially be rejected as being too particularistic and replaced with one that is more universalistic.

As I was attempting to apply my general observations to Russia, I identified two essential factors that typified this particular case. First, the combination of religion's high public profile and Russian society's strong secular habitus are making competition over memory particularly visible and controversial. Second, the state can be seen as a major player that is instrumentalizing the dominant (Russian Orthodox) religion within the official politics of memory, with an emphasis on conservative imperial continuity. Although such a patriotic liaison between the Church and the state can never be perfect, it does affect the tenor of how the catastrophic twentieth century is being remembered from a religious perspective and is intensifying the struggle over the past. Overall, it can be concluded that the role of religious forms of commemoration, spatial presence and normative deliberation will continue to be central, if not uncontested, well into the twenty-first century.

Notes

1 For more on this, see the classic work by Halbwachs (1941). Pierre Nora's fundamental project on spaces of memory presents a widening, secularizing perspective on Halbwachs's earlier work (see Nora 2011).

2 *Grenzsituation,* literally 'limit situation', was a term introduced by Karl Jaspers in his early psychological works in the 1930s that designated 'the moments, usually accompanied by experiences of dread, guilt or acute anxiety, in which the human mind confronts the restrictions and pathological narrowness of its existing forms' (Stanford Encyclopedia of Philosophy, https://plato.stanford.edu/entries/jaspers/).

3 The concept of 'competitive victimhood' was introduced in social psychology within the field of intergroup conflicts and reconciliations (see Noor, Brown, and Prentice 2008; Kelman 2008). It is mostly applied to ingroup/outgroup narratives of concrete conflicting groups but can be extended, in my view, to broader collective memory narratives.

4 The autocephaly, or the independence of the Ukrainian Church from the Moscow Patriarchy, was granted by the Ecumenical Patriarch of Constantinople in early 2019 in response to the needs of accelerated nation-building and initiated by the national political elite; however, it was not recognized by many other churches and was also contested from within.

5 An analysis of the 'usable past' was made in Malinova (2013); the idea of the 'splitting' of the Soviet past is my own. See also Kagarlitsky's similar discussion on the process of selective remembrance within public memory: 'a connection of the Sovietness to the 1917 explosion that brought it into being, has been artificially broken' (Kagarlitsky 2012, 14).

6 Selective forgetting can be partly explained in terms of inertia, or 'path dependency' – a syndrome that has produced conservative reactions when applied to the post-Soviet experience (see Afontsev 2010). The coexistence, and sometimes alternation, of horror of the past and nostalgia of the past has been reported to be a phenomenon not unusual in collective memory (Khmelevskaia 2004, 8). For the most comprehensive overview of Russian collective memory about the Soviet past, see Epplee (2020).

7 When referring to France's revolutionary experience, Halbwachs went on to claim that a crisis or revolution breaks down generations and times, but 'then, on the day after the crisis, everyone affirms that they must begin again at the point of interruption, that they must pick up the pieces and carry on. Sometimes nothing is considered changed, for

the thread of continuity has been retied. Although soon rejected, such an illusion allows transition to the new phase without any feeling that the collective memory has been interrupted' (Halbwachs 1980, 82).

8 In this chapter, I will not be addressing Russia's minority religions and their collective memories, which is a complex issue requiring special bespoke research.

9 For more on the exhibition, see https://myhistorypark.ru.

10 The very principle of meticulous documentation (based on secret service investigations) used by the Canonization Commission, and thus reliance upon the methods of secular historiography in drawing the criteria of sainthood, was an important novelty for the Church tradition. It showed how the new cultural conventions had been negotiated and adapted by this tradition. At the same time, many from the Church milieu felt uncomfortable with such a deviation from the old logic and imagery used in hagiographic texts (see discussion in Christensen 2018, 101–2). A particularly interesting controversy, going beyond my scope here, has been the heated argument within the Church about how the evidence found in archival documents should be interpreted in defining the moral criteria of sainthood and the very meaning of sainthood and martyrdom (Christensen 2018, 64–74).

11 The canonization of Soviet victims was impossible before the late Soviet liberalization, while the Russian Orthodox Church Abroad, administratively independent until 2007, started this work much earlier and created the very discourse of 'new martyrdom' of the communist era (Semenenko-Basin 2010, 118–32). For the main *akathist* of the New Martyrs and Confessors, see Akathist of New Martyrs and Confessors of the Russian Church.

12 Not all victims who died for their faith were seen as candidates for canonization: along with the Synodal Commission that presented almost 1,800 persons eventually officially canonized as martyrs and confessors, there was a group of Orthodox archivist-historians at the Moscow St Tikhon Orthodox University who created an online database titled 'Suffered for Christ', with up to 36,000 names (not only those who were murdered): http://rublev.com/novosti/bolee-36-tysiach-novomuchenikov-vnesli-v-bazu-dannykh-pstgu.

References

Afontsev, Sergey. 2010. Zavisimost' ot istoricheskogo puti, sotsial'noe deistvie I istocheskii protsess [Path Development, Social Agency and the Historical Process]. In *Sovetskoe nasledstvo. Otrazhenie proshlogo v sotsial'nykh I ekonomicheskikh praktikakh sovremennoi Rossii*, edited by L. Borodkin, K. Kessler and A. Sokolov, 21–36. Moscow: Rosspen.

Agadjanian, Alexander, A. Jödicke, and E. van der Zweerde, eds. 2015. *Religion, Nation and Democracy in the Southern Caucasus*. London: Routledge.

Agamben, Giorgio. 1998. *Homo Sacer: Sovereign Power and Bare Life*. Stanford, CA: Stanford University Press.

Akathist of New Martyrs and Confessors of the Russian Church. https://akafistnik.ru/akafisty-russkim-svyatym/akafist-novomuchenikam-i-ispovednikam-tserkvi-russkoj/.

Arkhipova, Alexandra, D. Doronin, D. Kirziuk, D. Radchenko, A. Sokolova, A. Titkov, and A. Yugai. 2017. Voina kak prazdnik, prazdnik kak voina [War as a Feat, Feats as a War]. *Antropological Forum* (33): 84–118.

Assmann, Aleida. 2013. *Ist die Zeit aus den Fugen? Aufstieg und Fall des Zeitregimes der Moderne*. Munich: Carl Hanser Verlag München.

Assmann, Aleida, and S. Conrad, eds. 2010. *Memory in a Global Age: Discourses, Practices and Trajectories*. Basingstoke: Palgrave Macmillan.

Assmann, Jan. 2004. *Cultural Memory and Early Civilization. Writing, Remembrance, and Political Imagination*. Russian Edition. Moscow: Yazyki slavianskoi kul'tury.

46   *Alexander Agadjanian*

———. 2006. *Religion and Cultural Memory: Ten Studies*. Stanford, CA: Stanford University Press.

———. 2008. Communicative and Cultural Memory. In *Cultural Memory Studies. An International and Interdisciplinary Handbook*, edited by A. Erll, A. Nünning and S. Young, 109–18. Berlin: De Gruyter.

Berger, Peter. 1967. *The Sacred Canopy. Elements of the Sociological Theory of Religion*. New York: Doubleday.

Bernstein, Anna. 2014. "The Impossible Object: Relics, Property, and the Secular in Post-Soviet Russia." *Anthropology Today* 30 (2): 7–11.

Birov, Eduard. 2013. "Ob otnoshenii pravoslavnykh k SSSR [On the Attitude of Christian Orthodox to the USSR]." *Rossiia Navsegda*. http://rossiyanavsegda.ru/read/1487/. Accessed May 5, 2020.

Bodin, Per-Arne. 2007. *Eternity and Time. Studies in Russian Literature and the Orthodox Tradition*. Stockholm: Stockholm University Press.

Bogumił, Zuzanna. 2010. "Kresty I kamni: Solovetskie simvoly v konstruirivanii pamiati o Gulage." *Neprikosnovennyi zapas* 71 (3).

———. 2012. "Stone, Cross and Mask: Searching for Language of Commemoration of the Gulag in the Russian Federation." *Polish Sociological Review* 177 (1): 71–90.

———. 2018. *Gulag Memories: The Rediscovery and Commemoration of Russia's Repressive Past*. New York: Berghahn Books.

Bogumił, Zuzanna, Dominique Moran, and Elly Harrowell. 2015. "Sacred or Secular? 'Memorial', the Russian Orthodox Church, and the Contested Commemoration of Soviet Repressions." *Europe-Asia Studies* 67 (9): 1416–44.

Bourdieu, Pierre. 1977. "Sur le pouvoir symbolique." *Annales Economie Societe Civilisation* #3: 405–11.

Bremner, Douglas. 2016. *Posttraumatic Stress Disorder: From Neurobiology to Treatment*. Hoboken, NJ: Wiley Blackwell.

Bruckner, Pascal. 2006. *La tyrannie de la pénitence: Essay sur le masochisme occidental*. Paris: Grasset & Fasquelle.

Burgess, John. 2017. *Holy Rus'. The Rebirth of Orthodoxy in the New Russia*. New Haven, CT: Yale University Press.

Christensen, Karin Hyldal. 2018. *The Making of the New Martyrs of Russia: Soviet Repression in Orthodox Memory*. London: Routledge.

Davie, Grace. 2000. *Religion in Europe: Memory Mutates*. Oxford: Oxford University Press.

Derrida, Jacques. 1999. "Le siècle et le pardon." *Le Monde des débats* (December).

Dorman, Veronika. 2010. "From the Solovki to Butovo: The Appropriation of the Memory of the Repressions by the Russian Orthodox Church." *Laboratorium* 2: 431–436.

Eliade, Mircea. 1987. *The Sacred and the Profane. The Nature of Religion*. San Diego: Harcourt Brace Jovanovich.

Emelianov, Nikolai. 2010. "Suffered for Christ in the Twentieth Century: The Blood of Martyrs as the Seed of the Church." An Interview (in Russian). *Pravmir*. www.pravmir.ru/za-xrista-postradavshie-v-xx-veke-krov-muchenikov-semya-cerkvi-2/.

Epplee, Nikolai. 2020. *Neudobnoe proshloe*. [Uncomfortable Past]. Moscow: NLO.

Etkind, Alexander. 2013. *Warped Mourning: Stories of the Undead in the Land of the Unburied*. Stanford: Stanford University Press.

Giesen, Bernhard. 2004. *Triumph and Trauma*. London: Routledge.

Gross, Jan. 2001. *Neighbors: The Destruction of the Jewish Community in Jedwabne, Poland*. Princeton, NJ: Princeton University Press.

Halbwachs, Maurice. 1941. *La topographie legendaire des evangiles en terre sainte*. Paris: Presses Universitaires de France.

————. 1980. *The Collective Memory* (Translated from French). New York: Harper & Row.

Hanks, Reuel. 2016. "Narratives of Islam in Uzbekistan: Authoritarian Myths and the Janus-State Syndrome." *Central Asian Survey* 35 (4): 501–13.

Hervieu-Léger, Danièle. 1993. *La Religion pour mémoire*. Paris: Cerf.

Kagarlitsky, Boris. 2012. "Zagadka sovetskogo sfinksa." [Enigma of the Soviet Sphinx]. In *SSSR: Zhizn' posle smerti*, edited by I. Glushchenko, B. Kagarlitsky and V. Kurennoi. Moscow: Higher School of Economics.

Kahla, Elina. 2014. "Civil Religion in Russia. A Choice for Russian Modernization?" *Baltic Worlds* 7 (2–3): 56–64.

Kalenychenko, Tetiana. 2017. "Public Religion During the Maidan Protests in Ukraine." *Euxeinos: Governance & Culture in the Black Sea Region* 24: 23–38.

Kelman, Herbert. C. 2008. *Reconciliation from a Social-Psychological Perspective*. In *The Social Psychology of Inter-Group Reconciliation*, edited by A. Nadler, T. E. Malloy and J. D. Fisher, 15–37. New York: Oxford University Press.

Khaleed, Adeeb. 2007. *Islam After Communism. Religion and Politics in Central Asia*. Berkeley: University of California Press.

Khmelevskaia, Yulia. 2004. "Vvedenie. O memorializatsii istorii i istoricheskoi pamiati." [Introduction. On memorialization and historical memory]. In *Vek pamiati, pamiat' veka. Opyt obrashcheniia s proshlym v XX veke*, 7–20. Cheliabinsk: Izdatel'stvo Kamennyi poia.

Klimenko, Ekaterina. 2020. "Building the Nation, Legitimizing the State: Russia – My History and Memory of the Russian Revolutions in Contemporary Russia." *Nationalities Papers* (February): 1–17.

Köllner, Tobias. 2010. "On the Restitution of Property and Making an 'Authentic' Landscape in Contemporary Russia." *Europe-Asia Studies* 70 (7): 1083–102.

Leontieva, Olga. 2011. *Istoricheskaia pamiat' i obrazy proshlogo v rossiiskoi kul'ture XIX – nachala XX vv*. [Historical Memory and Images of the Past in Russian Culture of the 19th and Early 20th century]. Samara: Kniga.

Lim, Jie-Hyun. 2010. "Victimhood Nationalism in Contested Memories: National Mourning and Global Accountability." In *Memory in a Global Age. Discourses, Practices and Trajectories*, edited by A. Assmann and S. Conrad, 138–62. Houndmills: Palgrave Macmillan.

Linde, Charlotte. 2009. *Working the Past: Narrative and Institutional Memory*. New York: Oxford University Press.

Malinova, Olga. 2013. "Problema politicheski 'prigodnogo' proshlogo i evolutsia ofitsial'noi simvolicheskoi politiki v sovremennoi Rossii" [The Problem of Politically Usable Past and Evolution of the Official Symbolic Policy in Today's Russia]. *Politicheskaia kontseptologiia* 1: 114–30.

Marchenko, Alla. 2017. "Religious Rhetoric, Secular State? The Public References to Religion by Ukraine's Top Politicians." *Euxeinos: Governance & Culture in the Black Sea Region* 24: 39–50.

Noor, Masi, Rupert Brown, and Garry Prentice. 2008. "Prospects for Intergroup Reconciliation: Social-Psychological Predictors of Intergroup Forgiveness and Reparation in Northern Ireland and Chile." In *The Social Psychology of Intergroup Reconciliation*, edited by A. Nadler, T. E. Malloy and J. D. Fisher, 97–114. Oxford: Oxford University Press.

Nora, Pierre. 2002. L'avènement mondial de la mémoire. *Transit. Europeische Revue* 22. Downloaded from eurozine.com (www.eurozine.com/lavenement-mondial-de-lamemoire/).

————. 2011. *Présent, nation, mémoire*. Paris: Gallimard.

Orlovsky, Fr. Damaskin. 2016. "Vvedenie" [Introduction]. In *Zhitia novomuchenikov i ispovednikov rossiiskikh XX veka* [Lives of Russian New Martyrs and Confessors of the 20th Century]. *Biblioteka Iakova Krotova*. http://yakov.works/libr_min/05_d/am/askin_tom_1.htm.

Porter-Szucs, Brian. 2011. *Faith and Fatherland: Catholicism, Modernity and Poland*. Oxford: Oxford University Press.

Ricoeur, Paul. 2006. *Memory, History, Forgetting*. Chicago: University of Chicago Press.

Rouhier-Willoughby, Jeanmarie. 2014. "Politics, Religion, and Memory. The Lozhok Holy Spring." *Russian Life* 57 (4): 54–58.

Rousselet, Kathy. 2007. "Butovo. La creation du lieu de pélérinage sur la terre des massacres." *Politix* 20 (77): 55–78.

———. 2013. *The Russian Orthodox Church and Reconciliation with the Soviet Past*. In *History, Memory and Politics in Central and Eastern Europe. Memory Games*, edited by Laure Neumayer and Georges Mink, 39–53. London: Palgrave Macmillan.

Rubenstein, Richard. 1966. *After Auschwitz: Radical Theology and Contemporary Judaism*. Indianapolis: Bobbs-Merrill.

Semenenko-Basin, Ilya. 2010. *Sviatost' v russkoi pravoslavnoi kul'ture XX veka. Istoriia personifikatsii* [*Holiness in the Russian Orthodox Culture of the Twentieth Century. A History of Personification*]. Moscow: RGGU.

Serrano, Silvia. 2018. *Orthodoxie et politique en Géorgie postsoviétique*. Karthala: Collection Meydan.

Shcherbakova, Irina. 2004. "Pamiat' Gulaga. Opyt issledovania memuaristiki i ustnykh svidetel'stv byvshykh uznikov" [Memory of the Gulag. An Essay of Memoirs and Oral Testimonies of Former Inmates]. In *Vek pamiati, pamiat' veka. Opyt obrashcheniia s proshlym v XX veke*, 168–85. Cheliabinsk: Izdatel'stvo Kamennyi poias.

Shtyrkov, Sergey. 2019. "Dukhovnoe videnie istorii kak diskursivnyi poriadok politicheskoi eskhatologii: ubiistvo sem'i Nikolaia II v posdne- i postsovetskoi pravoslavnoi istoriosofii" [The Spiritual Version of History as Discursive Order of Political Eschatology: The Murder of Tsar's Family in Late-Soviet and Post-Soviet Orthodox Historiosophy]. *Gosudarstvo, religiia, tserkov' v Rossii i za rubezhom* 37 (4): 130–66.

Snyder, Timothy. 2012. *Bloodlands. Europe Between Hitler and Stalin*. New York: Basic Books.

Stan, Lavinia, and Lucian Turcescu. 2007. *Religion and Politics in Post-Communist Romania*. Oxford: Oxford University Press.

Stanford Encyclopedia of Philosophy. https://plato.stanford.edu/.

Stepanova, Elena. 2019. "Competing Moral Discourses in Russia: Soviet Legacy and Post-Soviet Controversies." *Politics, Religion & Ideology* 20 (3): 340–60.

Tumarkin, Nina. 1994. *The Living and the Dead: The Rise and Fall of the Cult of World War II in Russia*. New York: Basic Books.

Valaam. 2017. A film by Andrey Kondrashov. https://valaam.ru/video/89580.

Van der Kolk, Bessel. 2007. "Trauma and Memory." In *Encyclopedia of Stress*, edited by G. Fink, 2nd ed., 765–67. Cambridge, MA: Academic Press.

Vanagaite, Ruta. 2020. *Our People: Discovering Lithuania's Hidden*. Holocaust. Rowman & Littlefield Publishers.

Vasiliev, Aleksey. 2012. "Memory Studies: Edinstvo Paradigm – mnogoobrazie ob'ektov" [Memory studies: One Paradigm, Many Objects]. *Novoe literaturnoe obozrenie* 5: 461–80.

Voronina, Tatiana. 2018. "From Socialist Realism to Orthodox Christianity: 'Blockade Temples' in St. Petersburg." *Laboratorium* 10 (3): 79–105.

Wiesel, Elie. 2006. *Night*. New York: Hill and Wang.

Zubrzycki, Genevieve. 2006. *The Crosses of Auschwitz. Nationalism and Religion in Post-Communist Poland*. Chicago: University of Chicago Press.

3 Sacred religio–secular symbols, national myths and collective memory

Geneviève Zubrzycki

The term 'sacred' is primarily associated with the religious (*sacred music, sacred texts*), while the profane is either (negatively) associated with blasphemy, the sacrilegious and the irreverent or – more neutrally – with 'the secular'. However, Émile Durkheim insisted in his canonical *Elementary Forms of Religious Life* (1995 [1912]) that the categories of the sacred and of the profane were based not on their content but on their form and functions. For Durkheim, the sacred is what is set apart from the profane (the everyday, mundane or ordinary) and is protected from it. Regardless of their content, sacred symbols and the rituals celebrated around them exist to reinforce social bonds by making collective representations and ideals feel real and close to the members of a group. Hence a totem, a cross or a rock can be a sacred symbol if it is a representation of the group and its beliefs, and if it is isolated and protected from the profane. We might readily accept that totems, crosses or rocks are sacred because these are all recognized symbols of established religious traditions. But a flag or a football jersey – both secular symbols – can be as sacred to members of the group they represent as what we traditionally consider to be 'properly religious' practices or symbols.

While this is well known in the sociology of religion (and has also been criticized for being too expansive a definition of religion[1]), I return to Durkheim's conceptualization here to break the 'sacred = religious' and 'profane = secular' false associations and, by extension, invalidate the spurious 'sacred versus secular' dichotomy. Breaking these problematic couplings and oppositions is especially important when studying the complex imbrications of religion and politics, a point the editors of this volume also make in their introduction. Uncritically associating politics with the realm of the profane may distort our understanding of the power of political speech, symbols and rituals – which are often sacred despite their putative secularity or which sometimes mix secular and religious traditions (Riesebrodt 2010). I am therefore arguing for greater caution to be applied when using these categories. As social scientists, our goal should be to ascertain the different configurations of the religious and the political and pinpoint when and why those are sacred or profane and when the religious is political (and vice versa). Another objective should be to identify the role of historical narratives, national mythology and collective memory

DOI: 10.4324/9781003264750-4

50 *Geneviève Zubrzycki*

in creating these amalgams. In this chapter, then, I examine how and why Christian rituals and symbols such as the cross acquired a political dimension in nineteenth-century Poland and how they came to embody and carry historical narratives, national myths and collective memory that have continued to shape national identity and inform political debates to this day. By doing so, I hope to show what we may gain by bringing the sociology of religion, nationalism studies and collective memory into dialogue.

The cross as a sacred religio-secular symbol

I have previously called the cross in Poland a sacred religio-secular symbol (Zubrzycki 2006, 2016). It is sacred not only because of its Christian signification but also because of its secular, national signification. It is the key symbol of Polish romantic nationalism.

Polish romanticism was articulated in the nineteenth century, when Poland had disappeared from the European map after being partitioned among Russia, Prussia and Austria (1795–1918). The most influential figures of this period were poets who equated the Partitions of Poland with its crucifixion. Poland, in the writings of Adam Mickiewicz (1798–1855), Juliusz Słowacki (1809–49) and Zygmunt Krasiński (1812–49),[2] was the 'Christ among nations': having been sacrificed for the sins of the world, it would be brought back to life to save humanity from Absolutism (Figure 3.1). This interpretation of the Partitions was coupled with the prophetic revelation of Poland's victory qua resurrection in poems, plays and other writings, such as Mickiewicz's *The Books of the Nation and the Polish Pilgrimage*, a national-biblical parable.[3] The eminent literary critic Maria Janion called this peculiar mix of philosophical ideals, political projects and religious metaphors the Polish nation's 'secular gospel' (Janion and Żmigrodzka 1978, 10). Sociologist Ewa Morawska referred to it as Poland's 'romantic civil religion' (1984), extending the Durkheimian framework to the Polish case.[4]

Within a context in which education, publishing and freedom of organization were seriously restricted and Polish was banned from public usage, religious worship and practices provided a significant space for Poles to affirm their sense of community (Morawska 1984; Olszewski 1996; Kłoczowski 1991; Zubrzycki 2006). Popular practices emerged around the metaphor of Poland as the Christ of Nations, which blended Catholic rituals with political national practices. Holy Week became an occasion to create Easter Sepulchres that commemorated Poland's 'crucifixion' and to pray for its 'resurrection', and Sunday Masses in churches throughout the lands of partitioned Poland concluded with the singing of religio-patriotic hymns. The Virgin Mary, as the mother of the crucified nation, accrued significance. Although the Church had neither created nor openly endorsed this fusion of Catholic symbols and practices with Romantic messianism – and in fact had actually condemned it – Catholicism became the 'carrier' of that 'romantic civil religion'.[5]

Sacred religio-secular symbols, myths 51

Figure 3.1 Popular postcard published circa 1891. The postcard commemorates major events in the life of the nation. In the background is Kraków's Wawel Castle (the panorama was sometimes changed to a view of Warsaw). A cloth draped around the cross bears the inscription 'The Time of Redemption Has Not Yet Come'. Poland is represented as both Jesus and his mother. The dates on Jesus's staff are those of the Partitions (1772, 1793, 1795), and the dates on the beam of the cross are those of the Centennial of the Constitution of May the Third (1791–1891). Hence Jesus represents the union of the nation and the state, crucified (by being repeatedly partitioned) but certain to rise again. The pages ripped from the nation's Bible, which appears against the background of Mary's cloak, mark key (failed) national uprisings. The Virgin appears to represent the nation mourning the loss of statehood; though presently in chains, she will one day be 'free' (i.e. regain independence).

Source: Reproduced from Kłoczowski (1991) with permission of Editions Spotkania.

52 *Geneviève Zubrzycki*

After the violent crushing of the January Uprising (1863–64), Polish society underwent a 'national ritual of martyrdom and death' (Janion and Żmigrodzka 1978, 549). Residents of Warsaw marched in funeral processions for the nation, and political protests were carried out at memorial sites, or even at cemeteries during burials. Noblewomen mourned the nation by wearing black gowns and so-called patriotic jewellery – which often included religious objects such as rosaries and crosses repurposed as bracelets and necklaces, or religious and secular symbols juxtaposed into a single piece of jewellery (e.g. crosses engraved with 'Poland' or crucified white eagle, pins containing the supplication 'God save Poland', brooches taking the form of a crown of thorns). Many of these symbols and practices popular in the late nineteenth century resurfaced with unusual intensity during World War II and under communism: Easter Sepulchres, for example, became popular again. The opposition, underground publishers and artists frequently used Paschal themes depicting Poland as Jesus (Rogozińska 2002). The use of these sacred religio-secular symbols created a language to express rebellion against the authorities that often acted as a protective shield against repression, as when protesters carried crosses during political demonstrations or when religious iconography was used to advocate for the struggle against the repressive communist regime (Figure 3.2).

Romantic messianism thus not only gave a narrative structure to the situation of Poles under the Partitions but a framework for interpreting Polish history in its entirety. According to this narrative framework, Poles are a chosen people, 'the spiritual leaders of mankind and the sacred instrument of universal salvation' (Walicki 1990, 30–31) and innocent sufferers at the hands of evil oppressors. The messianic vision of Poland as martyr and saviour became a core narrative, or what Victor Turner called a 'root paradigm', referring 'not only to the current state of social relationships existing or developing between actors, but also to the cultural goals, means, ideas, outlooks, currents of thought, patterns of belief which enter into those relationships, interpret them, and incline them to alliance or divisiveness' (1974, 64).

Messianic martyrology gave meaning to events and social relationships by offering an interpretive frame through which to make sense of them. It also provided what Tim Edensor, following Raymond Williams, calls a 'structure of feeling', 'a communal way of seeing the world in consistent terms, sharing a host of reference points which provide the basis for everyday discourse and action' (Edensor 2002, 19), while additionally serving as a semiotic centre for clustering religious and national symbols and articulating a script for collective rebellion (Kertzer 1988; Kubik 1994). This is how Catholicism became, in the 1980s, what José Casanova called a 'public religion' (1994).

Materiality and memory

Beyond their immediate significations, these religio-national symbols and material objects were also significant in that they often acted as what I call 'trans-temporal nodes' that compress layers of historical narratives, myths and collective memories into a single image or object, thereby providing specific

Sacred religio-secular symbols, myths 53

Figure 3.2 Postcard circulated in 1980. The tall cross is the sign of individual and collective liberation. A worker has broken his chains and spread his arms into the 'V' for victory shape that became the emblematic Solidarity gesture, following its use by Lech Wałęsa during the August strikes and throughout the 1980s. The cross is the 'cross of gratitude, symbol of the workers' strikes in July 1980 in Lublin'. It is dedicated by the Lublin Car Repair Workshop. At the top of the postcard, a quote from John Paul II: 'You are not a slave, you must not be a slave. You are a son'.

Source: KARTA Center, with permission.

interpretive frames to understand the present (Zubrzycki 2011). Crucially, it is both religious and secular dimensions that, when combined into a single object or practice, made the symbol even more potent: *more* sacred, not less. Given that Poland had to contend, at various times, with the loss of statehood, periods under occupation and foreign domination, religious symbols and practices

54 Geneviève Zubrzycki

acquired a political, secular signification that made them even more significant. That particular configuration arose in a specific political and institutional context and could be called into question and change in a different context, as I will discuss below.

Let us return briefly to Durkheim. Durkheim understood the totem or icon as sacred and powerful because it embodied and materialized collective representations. 'Collective ideals', he wrote, 'can only be manifested and become aware of themselves by being concretely realized in material objects that can be seen by all, understood by all, and represented to all minds' (2010, 49–50). It is by projecting ideals of its own creation onto an object – a totem, an idol or an icon – that a group becomes conscious of itself. While Durkheim recognized the importance of materiality, he regarded the actual materials of the symbol as irrelevant, a mere envelope, a shell: 'nothing but a block of stone or a piece of wood, things which in themselves have no value', he wrote. Conversely, the anthropologist Victor Turner argued in *The Forest of Symbols* (1967) that the power of sacred symbols resided in their specific material features, because it is the physical features of a given symbol that make possible, through the senses, the conjoining of a community's abstract ideas and ideals with the emotional, affective attachment of members to the group. For him, the emotions felt vis-à-vis certain symbols were related to the physiological functions that a particular symbol evoked. Turner argued that two central African trees, one with white sap and the other with red sap, were central in the rites of passage of the Ndembu tribe because their physical properties could be associated with those of humans, in particular puberty and reproduction, and life and death. While this was an improvement on Durkheim's conception of the ritual process and the role of symbols in them, I argue that the mobilizing power of symbols also resides in the *historical narratives* they evoke and the *collective memories* rituals around them they come to embody. And it is precisely because of those collective memories that certain symbols continue to be used.

Historical narratives, national myths and collective memory

So far, I have argued for the severing of the false associations between the sacred and the religious, and the profane and the secular. I now turn to an analysis of two significant conflicts in Poland over the presence of the cross in public space that show that the mobilizing power of symbols resides not only in their ability to embody collective ideals or the evocative power afforded by their material features, but also because they call to mind historical narratives, national myths and collective memories.

The war of the crosses at Auschwitz[6]

In 1997–98, self-defined 'Poles-Catholics' erected hundreds of crosses just outside the Auschwitz-Birkenau Museum in Oświęcim (Figure 3.3). The proximate cause of their mobilization was the rumoured removal of a large cross at the site, a cross nicknamed the 'Papal Cross' because it had been on the altar of a Mass celebrated by John Paul II at Birkenau in 1979 (see Huener 2003). The cross had been dismantled after the Papal Mass and stored, without attracting undue attention, in a local church basement for ten years until it mysteriously reappeared one night in the garden of the Carmelite convent just outside the Auschwitz-Birkenau Museum. The erection of the cross at that site occurred during a heated debate about the convent's relocation in 1989;[7] the gesture was therefore a political one, even though the religious signification of the symbol is not in question. Over several months in 1997–98, patriotic associations, youth groups and individuals came to the site to plant crosses.

Given the history of Auschwitz, the action quickly created a controversy of international proportions. My analysis of the case showed that one profound motivation for the cross action was the Poles-Catholics' desire to retain the memory of Auschwitz as a site of *Polish* martyrdom at a point when the history of the camp was being revised around the Holocaust, while *also* insisting on the continued validity of the association between Catholicism and Polishness just when that link was being questioned in the public sphere and constitutional debates (Zubrzycki 2001, 2006).

First, the memory of 'Oświęcim'.[8] The Auschwitz-Birkenau Museum was created in 1947 on the basis of a law 'on the remembrance of the martyrdom of the Polish Nation and other Nations'. As the name of that law suggests, although Poles were not the camp's sole victims, it was implied that they were its main martyrs. The museum was indeed squarely Polish from its inception,

Figure 3.3 The papal cross surrounded by smaller crosses in the summer of 1998.
Source: From the personal archives of Kazimierz Świtoń.

56 *Geneviève Zubrzycki*

even though the story was told in the socialist mode. In that narrative, 'Victims of Fascism' from Poland and from twenty-seven other nation states were exploited and exterminated at the camp before being liberated by the victorious and just Red Army, a narrative that fitted neatly with, and in many ways reinforced, the romantic martyrological one. Poles were thus portrayed as the camp's (and the war's) main martyrs. The socialist and nationalist appropriation of Auschwitz went hand in hand with the socialist narrative of World War II presented in history textbooks, official commemorations and monuments: people died during the war not because of their ethnic origins or 'race', as defined by Nazi ideology, but because they were opposed to 'fascism', an evil political and economic system. In that specific understanding of history and its telling, Jews and the Holocaust took a backseat or simply disappeared, folded into the Polish/socialist national narrative.

Following the fall of communism in Poland and the opening of Soviet archives after 1991, the Auschwitz-Birkenau Museum revised its narrative line. The museum dropped the socialist rhetoric and, most importantly, its guides and informational panels started stressing that Jews constituted 90% of the camp's victims (Piper 1992). For Poles, however, who for three generations had been socialized to the implied 'fact' that they had constituted the majority of prisoners and victims of the camp, and of World War II more broadly, and who often carried family memories of the camps, this revision of history was not easy to accept. When confronted by the museum's new narrative line, Poles were often stunned, and many saw the 'Judaization' of Auschwitz and the Holocaust takeover of World War II history as a profound rejection of a key tenet of their national identity.

As the numbers of victims of Auschwitz were revised, their ethnic and religious affiliation clearly stated, memorial plaques erased and reinscribed and commemorative events held (Young 1993), all of which now stressed that Jews had constituted the overwhelming majority of the camp's victims, Poles were disoriented and shocked. The opening of the Eastern Bloc to Western tourists and pilgrims and the popular annual Marches of the Living, as well as Steven Spielberg's *Schindler's List* (1993) – which was shot over several months in Kraków and later gave rise to a Schindler's List tourism industry – also brought Poles into contact with a very different narrative of World War II than the one in which they had been socialized for the previous fifty years, profoundly destabilizing the Polish myth of martyrdom.

Protesters used the cross to resist that trend and mark Auschwitz as a *Polish* site of collective suffering. The symbol was used primarily as a secular symbol of identity that marked the site as Polish in a debate over who owned the memory of Auschwitz. But the crosses were also erected there in that summer and autumn to insist that post-communist Poland was still Catholic and that Polishness was still indelibly linked with Catholicism at a time when many in Poland were debating the very identity of the nation, and questioning whether it was still appropriate, in a free and democratic Poland, to use the cross as a national symbol.

In both these dimensions, the cross was a religio-secular symbol. The symbol was no less sacred because the national and political semantics dominated. The fact that the cross was both a religious *and* a national, secular, political symbol actually added weight (and complexity) to the controversy. The key issue in the controversy was collective memory, in particular the memory of World War II and the memory of the fight against communism. Self-proclaimed Defenders of the Cross borrowed from a well-established repertoire of protest that evoked the aesthetics of August 1980 and other practices developed long before then, during the Partitions – processions, prayers to the nation, patriotic hymns, and so forth (Gach 1995). By doing so, the Defenders of the Cross were both inserting themselves in a long line of fighters for the nation and inscribing the protest in a well-known (and easily recognizable) national script.

It is precisely the historical associations of the cross with the fight for national independence that made it possible for protesters to use the symbol in that fashion. And it is based on such historical associations and collective memory that the court of appeals, a few months later, maintained a lower court's judgment that rejected the claim of a plaintiff in Łódź, who had filed a lawsuit against the presence of the cross at city hall because it infringed on his freedom of conscience. The court of appeals argued that in the Polish patriotic tradition, the cross has not only played a religious role but also expressed a specific set of moral and historical values:

> In addition to its religious signification, the symbol of the cross in the experiences of the Polish Nation . . . has also been inscribed in social consciousness as a symbol of death, pain, sacrifice, and as a way of honouring all those who fought and cared about freedom and independence in the struggle for national liberation. . . . For centuries [it] has designated the graves of ancestors and the place of national memory. In non-religious collective behaviour, this last meaning of the cross as an expression of respect for, and unity with, the liberators of the Fatherland even has precedence, since other universal means to express respect have not been developed. . . . Understood and felt in that way, the symbolism of the cross, independently from reference to an Absolute, is inscribed in the history of the country from its early dawn.
>
> (*Orzecznictwo sądów polskich* 1999, 488; my translation)

Historical narratives of war and oppression, and national myths of martyrdom and salvation, as well as personal and collective memories of suffering and resistance, are embedded in the symbol of the cross. Without paying attention to them, we risk missing that the secular, political meaning of the symbol weighs heavily on its sacrality. We might also miss the ways in which the secular dimension of the symbol can be used to tone down its religious – and more specifically Christian – semantics (as in the judgment of the court of appeals cited above). This process is not unique to Poland, of course. We observe it in many other places. In Canada, for example, a crucifix was affixed over the

58 *Geneviève Zubrzycki*

president's seat in the provincial parliament of Quebec because the object was deemed a historical and artistic artefact instead of a religious one (Zubrzycki 2016).

The war of the Smoleńsk Cross

The cross in its sacred religio-secular configuration became the object of another controversy in 2010, when a conflict erupted around the presence of the so-called Smoleńsk Cross by the Presidential Palace in Warsaw. While the context was very different from that of Auschwitz – being related to the commemoration of the tragic plane crash that killed the president of the republic and his wife, along with ninety-four dignitaries and crew – the debate again focused around the Catholicity of Poland, national mythology and collective memory.

Within hours of the crash, the tragedy was called a 'second Katyń', in reference to the very event and place where the VIP delegation was headed to commemorate the deaths of some 20,000 Polish officers murdered in 1940 by the Soviet NKVD.[9] A few days after the event, Cardinal Dziwisz, archbishop of Kraków, announced that the president and his wife would be buried in the cathedral of the Wawel Royal Castle in Kraków, where kings and the greatest national heroes lie in rest. The cardinal explained his announcement in a press conference as follows: 'Surely President Kaczyński deserves to be buried at Wawel since he died in exceptional circumstances – heroically even, one can say, *since he was flying to Katyń to honour the nation's martyrs in the name of the nation*' (TVN24, 13 April 2010; my translation and emphasis). Thus articulated, it was not President Kaczyński's life or presidency that made him worthy of a royal burial, but his *proximity* to Katyń, a key site and symbol of Polish martyrdom: *physical* proximity, as the plane crashed by the Katyń forest; *historical* proximity, as the president and the delegation were en route to Katyń to commemorate the 70th anniversary of the murders; and *ideological* proximity, as Kaczyński was a proponent of so-called historical politics, namely the political cultivation of historical consciousness as a tool for strengthening national identity. As part of historical politics, the president had organized a 'parallel' commemoration of the event, distinct from the official one celebrated jointly by the prime ministers of Poland and Russia a few days prior, to which Kaczyński had not been invited.

'Katyń', not just a place but an event, was a symbol of Polish martyrdom during World War II that was forced underground during fifty years of communism (Kosicki 2015). It had become, in the words of Prime Minister Donald Tusk, 'the founding myth of Free Poland', because it was finally possible to talk about that event after 1989. It is thus through his proximity to (and contagion by) the historical event turned sacred symbol of national martyrdom and freedom, and the narration of his death in that particular script, that the president attained the status of martyr himself. Despite the controversial nature of his presidency, low political capital and a questionable political legacy, Kaczyński was awarded the honour reserved to few exceptional historical figures, and none whose monumental status had not already been burnished over many years. But the power of Katyń itself also resides in the fact that the event fits neatly into a well-established national mythological script of messianic martyrdom, of which it had become the key twentieth-century instantiation. The plane crash and Katyń were thus layered onto each other and folded into the national mythological structure (Figure 3.4). However, this martyrologization of President Kaczyński was far from being widely accepted. In fact, it caused the first cracks in a rare show of national grief and unity, as loud protests were organized immediately after Cardinal Dziwisz's announcement of the Wawel burial.[10]

Throughout August 2010, several thousand young Poles gathered in the streets of Warsaw, this time to protest against the presence of the wooden cross in front of the presidential palace. It had been agreed by state and Church authorities that the cross erected by boy scouts in the days following the plane crash in April would be relocated on 3 August via religious procession to a nearby church. But the Defenders of the Cross aggressively prevented the church-led ceremonial relocation, which they understood as the profanation

Figure 3.4 Makeshift altars to the memory of President Kaczyński. These altars have become semi-permanent features of the Katyń crosses and monuments throughout Poland that provide visual indicators of the merging of the Smoleńsk tragedy into the martyriological structure of Katyń. Here, the Katyń cross in Kraków, by Grodzka street, in March 2011.

Source: Photo by Geneviève Zubrzycki.

60 *Geneviève Zubrzycki*

of the symbol *and* of the nation. Like the defenders of the cross at Auschwitz before them, this group was composed of loosely connected individuals united by their distrust of authorities (both secular and religious). The site quickly turned into a new 'war of the cross', as the discursive and symbolic folding of the tragic crash into the collective memory of Katyń – itself part of a long-standing narrative of martyrdom – further sacralized the Smoleńsk Cross.

The site provided a visible platform for proponents of the cross as a national symbol, but also a stage for protesting against the religio-nationalist and anti-Semitic Poland that the cross had come to signify for the Left in the years following the fall of communism. Organizers of the protests specifically asked the participants *not* to bring national flags or any religious items in order to desacralize the site and delegitimize the claims of the Defenders of the Cross. The area around the Presidential Palace became a theatre of the grotesque where small religious groups sang religio-patriotic hymns while protesters blasted 'disco-polo' hits and threw around a beach ball; some elderly Defenders of the Cross bound themselves to the cross with flags while young protestors mocked them by initiating a war-of-the-cross 'pillow fight'; and some protestors declared their willingness to die for the cross while others carried placards that joked 'where there's a cross, there's a party!'.

The 'stand-off' at the Presidential Palace, which lasted several weeks that summer, became the top news item in the media. Like the War of the Crosses at Auschwitz, the event was initiated by a group of marginal characters but generated vocal opposition and served as the prism through which social actors, politicians, the Church authorities and ordinary citizens – many of them in the 18–24 age group – discussed and debated the place of religion in Poland and what Poland is or should be. The wooden cross was removed and relocated later that autumn, but a small group who insists that the cross should be present continues to meet every night. They bring a wooden cross, build a makeshift altar and pray for the 'True Poland' to return (Figure 3.5).[11] The Law and Justice government also organizes official monthly commemorative events. In Kraków, flowers, candles and prayers are offered at the Wawel Castle Cathedral, where Lech Kaczyński and his spouse are laid to rest, and at the Katyń Cross at the foot of Wawel Hill, thereby ritually linking both national tragedies.

In this case again, the cross is acting as a sacred religio-secular hybrid, although one could argue that its religious semantics have been overshadowed by the political instrumentalization and politics of history being conducted by Law and Justice. The politics of history aims to shape collective memory in order to ossify a certain definition of Polishness that is intrinsically linked to conservative Catholicism. In both wars of the cross, religion, politics, memory and nationalism became intertwined in powerful ways.

This is not to say that all Poles agree with this dual signification of the cross. Self-proclaimed 'open Catholics', for example, reject that understanding of the symbol and argue for its depoliticization and for its return to the strictly religious sphere. Open Catholics are an elite group of clergy and intellectuals initially associated with personalist Catholic publications such as *Tygodnik Powszechny, Znak* and *Więź*, which in the last two decades have expanded their

Figure 3.5 As of 2018, a small group of self-proclaimed Defenders of the Cross continued to meet in front of the Presidential Palace every evening. They prayed for the return of the so-called Smoleńsk Cross, for light to be shed on the 'whole truth about the Smoleńsk murders' and for 'Poland to be Poland'.

Source: Photo by Geneviève Zubrzycki, June 2011.

reach to liberal secular outlets such as the daily *Gazeta Wyborcza*. For them, traditional Catholicism in Poland is associated with secular emotions to such an extent that it has become a political religion. They therefore warn against the conflation of nation and religion and stress instead the universality of Catholicism. Following the personalist tradition, they emphasize the need for a deepening and active internalization of faith.[12]

Others argue for getting rid of the cross altogether (Figure 3.6). Polish street artist Peter Fuss suggests, in a giant studded cross, that the symbol is not the source of national salvation but rather an instrument of torture for Poland.

Conclusion

What does the analysis of the Polish case contribute to our thinking about the sacred and memory?

The cross's force in mobilizing support to specific causes in Poland derives from the historical narratives, collective memories and national aesthetics that have accrued around it, notably Poland as the Christ of nations, or the cross as it was used in Solidarity's resistance to communism, or the cross as a protective

Figure 3.6 Studded *Cross*, metal, by Polish street artist Peter Fuss. The cross was completed after the war of the Smoleńsk Cross.

Source: Peter Fuss, with permission of the artist.

weapon against others. The ability of symbols to evoke and channel emotions depends on their location in historically compelling narratives, as these narratives are more or less successfully reactivated by political activists in the present. Sacred religio-secular symbols, because of their dual nature of being both religious and secular, are easily mobilized to make memory claims. Because of their dual sacredness, it is especially difficult to refute memory claims articulated around them – hence the fight among political actors for control over their definition.

This chapter also shows that the attribution of power to symbols is not totemic, as Durkheim suggested (i.e. the sacralization in a symbol, of society *as it is*) but rather *polemical*: the pressing of claims, through symbols, about how society *should* (or should not) be. Symbols serve to highlight, magnify and exaggerate particular features of national identity. These effects, in turn, allow social actors to contest given representations and narratives and articulate new ones.

Notes

1 This definition of the sacred leads to such a broad understanding of what religion 'is' or to what 'counts as' religion that many scholars have abandoned the Durkheimian framework (e.g. Smith 1998; Lincoln 2003). Sociologist of religion Martin Riesebrodt pointedly noted that adopting a Durkheimian definition of religion leads us to consider 'barbecues with guitar music, soccer games, shopping in supermarkets, or art exhibitions' as religious phenomena (2010, xi), draining religion of any analytical purchase.

Sacred religio-secular symbols, myths 63

2 They are called in Polish, the *Trzej wieszcze*, which means both the 'three bards' and, significantly enough, the 'three prophets'. Together, they are part of the national pantheon of founding fathers, martyrs and heroes.

3 The work was first published anonymously in 1832, shortly after the failure of the November Uprising in Russian Poland (1830–31). It appeared in the form of a missal commonly referred to as the 'Mickiewicz Homilies', and was widely distributed, free of charge, to émigrés/exiles who were new arrivals to Paris, where Mickiewicz himself lived. The work was condemned by papal edict for its use of religious motifs to justify the pursuit of what the Church considered a radical social programme (which included the abolition of serfdom and the declaration of universal civil rights extended to women and Jews).

4 The concept of civil religion, first elaborated by Jean-Jacques Rousseau in *The Social Contract* (1988 [1782]) and then by Émile Durkheim, underwent a renaissance in the sociology of religion when it was resurrected by Robert Bellah in his 1967 article 'American Civil Religion'.

5 Messianism was quite heterodox and even seen as heretical by some, because it promised an earthly incarnation of the divine (Porter 2000, 28). Moreover, as the Holy See had recognized the Partitions of Poland, Polish Catholics were instructed by the Church hierarchy to focus their thoughts on things eternal and to leave worldly affairs to the anointed authorities – in that case, the rulers of the partitioning powers (Żywczyński 1995; Porter 2000, 31).

6 This section is a condensed summary of the war of the crosses of Auschwitz in 1997 and 1998, which I analyze at great length in my book *The Crosses of Auschwitz: Nationalism and Religion in Post-Communist Poland* (Zubrzycki 2006).

7 For a discussion of the Carmelite convent controversy, see Zubrzycki (2006, 4–8); for detailed accounts, see Bartoszewski (1990), Głownia and Wilkanowicz (1998), Rittner and Roth (1991) and Klein (1991). Klein's account is especially valuable because he acted as the main Jewish negotiator with the Church authorities over the convent's relocation.

8 The symbolic representations of the site should not be conflated with the site itself. I therefore use quotation marks to emphasize the construction and porousness of 'Oświęcim' as a meaningful symbol. The names without quotation marks refer to physical sites: Auschwitz is the former camp and current museum, while Oświęcim is the town where Auschwitz is located. For a detailed analysis of the different layers of meaning Poles found in 'Oświęcim'/'Auschwitz' as symbols from the early 1940s until 2005, see Kucia (2005) and Zubrzycki (2006, 98–140). See also Tanay (1991), Webber (1992) and Goban-Klas (1995). For a recent analysis of the evolution of Polish understandings of Auschwitz, see Kucia (2019), and for the most recent survey data, see CBOS (2020).

9 On the collective memory of Katyń in Poland from 1943 until 2015, see Kosicki (2015). For analyses on how it is remembered in Poland, Ukraine, Belarus, the Baltic states and Russia, see Etkind et al. (2012).

10 Multiple Facebook pages protesting the burial plans and the mythologization of President Kaczyński appeared within hours of the announcement, which was described in comments by users, bloggers and editorialists as 'national hysteria'. Pages named 'Let's all get buried at the Wawel!' and 'Wawel is not Enough! Why not the Pyramids?' were especially popular, gathering tens of thousands of 'fans'. For links to multiple Facebook pages, see http://wiadomosci.gazeta.pl/Wiadomosci/1,80708,7771897,Facebook_Wawelem_podzielony.html?as=2&startsz=x. See also the important editorials from Polish public intellectuals in the *New York Times* that specifically address the 'traps' of national mythology and messianic martyrology (Wiktor Osiatyński, 'Polish Heroes, Polish Victims', and Olga Tokarczuk, 'Where History's March Is a Funeral Procession', both published on 15 April 2010).

11 The monthly commemorations of the Smoleńsk crash held in different cities are more structured and of greater significance ritualistically. See Golonka-Czajkowska (2018) for an analysis of Kraków's commemorations.

12 For a typology of Catholicisms within the Polish Catholic landscape, see Gowin (2000) and Zubrzycki (2006).

References

Bartoszewski, Władysław T. 1990. *The Convent at Auschwitz*. New York: George Braziller.

Bellah, Robert N. 1967. "Civil Religion in America." *Daedalus* 96: 1–120.

Casanova, José. 1994. *Public Religions in the Modern World*. Chicago: University of Chicago Press.

Centrum Badań Opinii Społecznej. 2020. *Auschwitz-Birkenau w pamięci zbiorowej – 75 lat po wyzwoleniu*. Warsaw: CBOS.

Durkheim, Émile. [1912] 1995. *The Elementary Forms of Religious Life*. Translated by K. Fields. New York: Free Press.

———. 2010. "Value Judgments and Judgments of Reality." In *Sociology and Philosophy*, translated by D. F. Pocock, 42–51. New York: Routledge.

Edensor, Tim. 2002. *National Identity, Popular Culture and Everyday Life*. Oxford: Berg.

Etkind, Alexander, Rory Finnin, Uilleam Blacker, Julie Fedor, Simon Lewis, Maria Mälksoo, and Matilda Mroz. 2012. *Remembering Katyn*. Cambridge: Polity Press.

Gach, Piotr Paweł, ed. 1995. *Otwórz swój skarbiec . . . Antologia modlitwy za ojczyznę*. Kraków: Wydawnictwo WAM.

Głownia, Marek, and Stefan Wilkanowicz, eds. 1998. *Auschwitz: Konflikty i dialog*. Kraków: Wydawnictwo Św. Stanisława.

Goban-Klas, Tomasz. 1995. "Pamięć podzielona, pamięć urażona: Oświęcim i Auschwitz w polskiej i żydowskiej pamięci zbiorowej." In *Europa po Auschwitz*, edited by Zbigniew Mach, 71–91. Kraków: Universitas.

Golonka-Czajkowska, Monika. 2018. "In the Shadow of the Sacred Bodies: The Monthly Smoleńsk Commemorations in Kraków." *Ethnologia Polona* 38: 107–23.

Gowin, Jarosław. 2000. *Kościół w czasach wolności 1989–1999*. Kraków: Znak.

Huener, Jonathan. 2003. *Auschwitz, Poland, and the Politics of Commemoration, 1945–1979*. Athens: Ohio University Press.

Janion, Maria, and Maria Żmigrodzka. 1978. *Romantyzm i historia*. Warsaw: Państwowy Instytut Wydawniczy.

Kertzer, David I. 1988. *Ritual, Politics, and Power*. New Haven, CT: Yale University Press.

Klein, Théo. 1991. *L'affaire du Carmel d'Auschwitz*. Paris: Éditions Jacques Bertoin.

Kłoczowski, Jan. 1991. *Dzieje chrześcijaństwa polskiego*. Paris: Editions du Dialogue.

Kosicki, Piotr H. 2015. "Forests, Families, and Films: Polish Memory of Katyń, 1943–2015." *East European Politics and Societies* 29(4): 730–60. https://doi.org/10.1177/0888325415594670.

Kubik, Jan. 1994. *The Power of Symbols Against the Symbols of Power: The Rise of Solidarity and the Fall of State Socialism in Poland*. University Park: Pennsylvania State University Press.

Kucia, Marek. 2005. *Auschwitz jako fakt społeczny: Historia, współczesność i świadomość społeczna KL Auschwitz w Polsce*. Kraków: Universitas. https://doi.org/10.1080/17504902.2019.1567658.

———. 2019. "The Meanings of Auschwitz in Poland, 1945 to the Present." *Holocaust Studies* 25(3): 220–47.

Lincoln, Bruce. 2003. *Holy Terrors: Thinking About Religion After September 11*. Chicago: University of Chicago Press.

Morawska, Ewa. 1984. "Civil Religion vs. State Power in Poland." *Society* 21(4): 29–34.

Olszewski, Daniel. 1996. *Polska kultura religijna na przełomie XIX i XX wieku*. Warsaw: Instytut Wydawniczy Pax.

Orzecznictwo sądów polskich. 1999. Position 177, 486–88. Warsaw: Wydawnictwa Prawnicze PWN.

Piper, Franciszek. 1992. *Ilu ludzi zginęło w KL Auschwitz: liczba ofiar w świetle źródeł i badań 1945–1990*. Oświęcim: Wydawnictwo Państwowego Muzeum w Oświęcimiu.

Porter, Brian. 2000. *When Nationalism Began to Hate: Imagining Modern Politics in Nineteenth-Century Poland*. New York: Oxford University Press.

Riesebrodt, Martin. 2010. *The Promise of Salvation: A Theory of Religion*. Chicago: University of Chicago Press.

Rittner, Carol, and John K. Roth, eds. 1991. *Memory Offended: The Auschwitz Convent Controversy*. New York: Praeger.

Rogozińska, Renata. 2002. *W stronę Golgoty: inspiracje pasyjne w sztuce polskiej w latach 1970–1999*. Poznań: Księgarnia Św. Wojciecha.

Rousseau, Jean-Jacques. 1988 [1782]. *The Social Contract*. Translated by GDH Cole. Amherst, NY: Prometheus Books.

Smith, Jonathan Z. 1998. "Religion, Religions, Religious." In *Critical Terms for Religious Studies*, edited by Mark C. Taylor, 269–85. Chicago: University of Chicago Press.

Tanay, Emanuel. 1991. "Auschwitz and Oświęcim: One location, Two symbols." In *Memory Offended: The Auschwitz Convent Controversy*, edited by Carol Rittner and John K. Roth, 99–112. New York: Praeger.

Turner, Victor. 1967. *The Forest of Symbols: Aspects of Ndembu Ritual*. Ithaca, NY: Cornell University Press.

———. 1974. *Dramas, Fields and Metaphors: Symbolic Action in Human Society*. Ithaca, NY: Cornell University Press.

Walicki, Andrzej. 1990. "The Three Traditions in Polish Patriotism." In *Polish Paradoxes*, edited by Stanisław Gomułka and Antony Polonsky, 21–39. New York: Routledge.

Webber, Jonathan. 1992. "The Future of Auschwitz: Some Personal Reflections." In *The First Frank Green Lecture*. Oxford: Oxford Centre for Postgraduate Hebrew Studies.

Young, James E. 1993. *The Texture of Memory: Holocaust Memorials and Meaning*. New Haven, CT: Yale University Press.

Zubrzycki, Geneviève. 2001. "'We, the Polish Nation': Ethnic and Civic Visions of Nationhood in Post-Communist Constitutional Debates." *Theory and Society* 30 (5): 629–69.

———. 2006. *The Crosses of Auschwitz: Nationalism and Religion in Post-Communist Poland*. Chicago: University of Chicago Press.

———. 2011. "History and the National Sensorium: Making Sense of Polish Mythology." *Qualitative Sociology* 34: 21–57. https://doi.org/10.1007/s11133-010-9184-7.

———. 2016. *Beheading the Saint: Nationalism, Religion, and Secularism in Quebec*. Chicago: University of Chicago Press.

Żywczyński, Mieczysław. [1935] 1995. *Watykan wobec Powstania Listopadowego*. Kraków: Universitas.

Part II

Postsecularity and politics of memory

4 The Armenian genocide

Extermination, memory, sacralization

Adam Pomieciński

On 23 April 2015 at 7:15 p.m., the bells rang out at the monastery in Etchmiadzin in Armenia to celebrate the conclusion of the ceremonial process of canonizing the victims of the genocide of Armenians committed 100 years before on the orders of the Ottoman authorities. The ringing bells in Armenia were not only simultaneously accompanied by the tolling of bells in churches serving the Armenian diaspora all over the world, but also by bells in Christian churches – from Moscow and Tbilisi, through Prague and Warsaw, to Vienna, Berlin, Paris and Madrid. On that day, the Armenian Apostolic Church announced that all the Armenians murdered in 1915 in Ottoman Turkey were saints. This was the largest-scale canonization not only in that Church but also in the entire history of Christianity.

For Armenians, the experiencing of genocide and collective massacre became a turning point in the history of their nation and the definition of their own identity. It caused intergenerational trauma that brought far-reaching consequences. Despite the fact that the crime was committed a century ago, memory of this genocide still exerts a significant influence not only on internal relations within Armenian society (consolidating a sense of community among Armenians living in the country and in the diaspora) but also on external relations, especially with Turkey, considered to be the perpetrator of the genocide (up to this day, the border between Armenia and Turkey remains closed). The canonization of the victims of the genocide became a spectacular event. The act of sacralizing thousands of victims of ethnic violence should be treated as a factor in the reinforcement of national memory of the genocide in intergenerational communication. It is also an act of solidarity from the Church and a gesture of support towards Armenian ethnic policy. When eyewitnesses to a genocide have already died, canonization is an important cultural reference that can transmit a genocidal narrative by transporting the memory of ethnic crime into the religious sphere. At the collective level, it expresses a need to demonstrate memory of the genocide, memory that is, in itself, an act of resistance towards all negationary attitudes or actors trying to erase the genocide from the past and from historiography.[1]

The Armenian genocide is often compared to the Holocaust of the Jews (Seppälä 2015; Sacks 2015). At the beginning of the twentieth century, when

DOI: 10.4324/9781003264750-6

the term 'genocide' was not in common use, the term 'Armenian Holocaust' was used to describe the massacre of the Armenians. The significance of the Armenian genocide for the Jewish Holocaust also arose from the fact that the term 'crime against humankind' was already being used publicly for the first time by the Allies during the First World War. Great Britain, France and Russia were using such language to condemn Turkish acts that they clearly viewed as atrocious. A similar situation occurred after the Nuremberg trials, at which Nazis had been accused of 'war crimes and crimes against humankind' (Dadrian 1998). The Jewish and Armenian nations are also both perceived, due to the atrocities and harm they experienced in the twentieth century, as 'neighbors of memory' (Marutyan 2014), while the two genocides are compared to each other because of the social consequences they shared, which included the need to deal with collective trauma, the existence of transnational memory of genocide and attempts at denial being made by the perpetrators (Dawoodi 2018). In the Armenian language, genocide is described using the term *Mec Jeghern*, which means 'great disaster' or 'great catastrophe', which is similar in essence to the Hebrew word *Shoah*, which means 'total destruction' or 'total annihilation'. Despite the various associations with, and comparisons between, these two events, the Armenian genocide and later the memory of it were shaped in specific socio-cultural, political and historical conditions. The main purpose of my elaboration in this chapter is to investigate the memory practices that constitute an important reference for Armenian identity. Particular attention is paid to the canonization of the victims of the genocide, which situates memory of the genocide within the scope of categories like Christian martyrdom or religious persecution. The canonization occurred during the commemoration of the 100th anniversary of the Armenian genocide and signified the recognition, by the Church authorities, that all the victims of Turkish massacres were saints. The questions of the experiencing of genocide and collective memory thus continue to be not only national, ethical and political issues but also religious ones. This is not without significance for contemporary processes shaping the Armenian identity. This chapter is part of a research trend referred to as 'anthropology after genocide' (de Lame 2007), which seeks to show societies going through reconstruction after great trauma. The continued existence of living memory of the genocide eloquently underlines the timeliness and great significance of the genocidal narrative, both in contemporary Armenian politics and in the cultural consciousness of the entirety of Armenian society, in Armenia itself and in the diaspora.

Mec Jeghern. The face of mass extermination

It is commonly believed that the extermination of Armenians carried out by the Ottoman authorities was the first genocide of the twentieth century.[2] The barbarism of that crime contributed to the reinforcement of the very notion of genocide in the international arena and in many legal acts. A particularly important contribution to this reinforcement was made by Raphael Lemkin, an American lawyer of Polish descent. While observing the behaviour of the Turks during the genocide, he was not only aware of the scale of the atrocities being committed towards Armenians but also of the consequences of actions aimed at nothing less than the systematic and total annihilation of the nation. The mass murder of Armenians, destruction of monuments of culture, acts of torture using crosses and forced conversions to Islam were acts that required appropriate naming and the instigation of legal proceedings and moral evaluation (Balakian 2013). Thus, the Armenian Holocaust became part of the origin of the very notion of genocide.

Armenians lived in the Ottoman Empire for centuries as one of many national minorities. Being Christians, they were also a religious minority. They mainly lived in eastern Anatolia. Although the Ottoman Empire was an Islamic state, it tolerated minorities for a long time and allowed them to maintain their cultural separateness and practice their religions. However, in the second half of the nineteenth century, these minorities stopped feeling safe. When the Ottoman Empire began to dissolve, moods and attitudes towards Armenians radically changed. After a war with Russia was lost in 1877–78, accusations appeared against Armenians calling them agents of Christian powers. The Ottoman authorities began to sanction and encourage their persecution. The wave of terror escalated in the mid-1890s, during the rule of Sultan Abdul Hamid II. At this point, many Armenians experienced violence and death, and these crimes are currently known as the 'Hamidian massacres' (Kurt 2018; Laderman 2019). However, these events were only a prelude to what was to come in the near future.

Less than two decades later, the First World War broke out, and battles between Turks and Russians resurfaced on the eastern border of the Ottoman Empire. The Ottoman leaders suspected that Armenians were collaborating with Russia. This was just a pretext for the commencement of the mass extermination of Armenians and organized destruction of native Christian communities.

Even in 1908, before the outbreak of war, a revolution had started in the Ottoman Empire, and power had been taken by nationalistically oriented politicians who aimed for the complete reorganization of the state. Soon, the so-called Young Turks formed a government headed by Minister of Internal Affairs Talaat Pasha, who was assisted by two other members: Minister of War Enver Pasha and Minister of the Navy Djemal Pasha. For nationalists, a multiethnic Ottoman state was doomed to failure. Their political ideals refused to sanction a nationally and religiously differentiated world. Christians living in the Islamic empire constituted a growing problem for them. The First World War gave Turkish nationalists greater freedom over the perpetration of violence against their enemies (Suny 2015). Those who were considered to be traitors were sentenced to death.

The year 1915 was marked in the history of the Armenian nation by the cruel slaughter of its population. The Young Turks government decided to introduce and implement their barbaric ethnic cleansing plan. On 24 April 1915, the

72 *Adam Pomieciński*

mass deportation and murder of the Armenian population began on the basis of previously issued governmental decrees. Every stage of the genocide was thoroughly planned: first, the Armenians in the Ottoman army were liquidated; then, all the leaders and intellectuals of Armenian community were captured and killed; and finally, 'deportations' were directed against the rest of the Armenian population (Sarafian 2010). They were mostly tortured and led through the Syrian desert. The exodus of the Armenians was brutal: under the supervision of Ottoman civilian and military officials, children, elderly people, women and men were killed. Those who were not murdered died from hunger, thirst, extreme exhaustion and illness. The desert became a mass grave for the Armenian population. As previously mentioned, many were also forced to convert to Islam, and children were given to Kurdish, Turkish and Arab families for their upbringing. By the end of the war, over 90% of Armenians had disappeared from the Ottoman Empire and their culture would never be reborn (Suny 2016). The policy of annihilating the Armenian nation was managed deliberately and only ended in the first years of the Turkish Republic established by Atatürk. The genocide of Christians served as the Islamization of Anatolia, and by the beginning of the 1920s, the Turkish state was ethnically almost homogeneous and mono-religious (Morris and Ze'evi 2019).

Apart from liquidating Armenians, the extermination that was carried out also had other consequences. The emigration it caused not only contributed to the formation of an Armenian diaspora in many countries of Europe, the Middle East and America, but also to changes in national and political relations in the Caucasus. Some of the survivors made it to the Russian Empire where, after the end of the First World War, the First Armenian Republic was formed (May 1918–December 1920). However, following its annexation by the Bolsheviks, the independent Armenian state quickly ceased to exist and became part of the Soviet Union (1920–91).

From suppressed memory to regained memory

After the establishment of Soviet rule in Armenia, the question of the Armenian genocide was pushed into the background. The leaders of the Soviet Union took care to maintain good relations with Turkey, as evidenced by the friendship treaties between those states that were already being signed in the 1920s and that stayed in force until 1945. Several years after the Second World War, in 1953, the Soviet Union also stated that it did not have any territorial claims over Turkey. This led to part of the former Armenian lands being located within the borders of the Turkish state.

Any Armenian–Turkish antagonism was successfully silenced, and the question of the genocide stopped being discussed. During Stalin's dictatorship, talking about or recalling the genocide was perceived as a sign of nationalism that was severely punished (Marutyan 2014). The communist authorities were shaping another model of history and memory. All the citizens of the Soviet Union, including Armenians, had to share common socialist ideals and refer

The Armenian genocide 73

to the 'heroic' past of communist Russia (Zakharova 2017). Stalin's repressions and the populism of his successors deprived Armenians, for many years, of the opportunity to openly express their memories of the massacres at the beginning of the twentieth century. This episode is often called the 'loss of national memory' or 'period of national amnesia' (Shushanyan 2013). However, these expressions do not precisely reflect the actual condition in which memory of the Armenian genocide could be found in the Soviet state. Despite such memory being erased from the public sphere and official discourse, it was transmitted within family circles and through oral testimonies (Pomieciński 2017). Under the surface of memory that was officially suppressed, living memories were still being kept and archived for the coming generations.

It is also worth mentioning at this juncture that the approach taken to the genocide was different in the diaspora, where the memory of the genocide was never censored. In fact, Armenians living outside the Soviet Union were often lobbying for the genocide to be recognized (Koinova 2017). One of the primary goals of many diasporal organizations that functioned in Western countries and in the Middle East but were barred from functioning in the Soviet Union was to publicize the Armenian genocide (Zolian 2015). Their efforts to publicize the crime were accompanied by various commemorative practices, including the construction of memorials or calls for the crime of 1915 to be recognized internationally. At times when Armenians were deprived of their sovereign motherland, the diaspora sought a strategy for building their national identity, and the question of the genocide began to create a bridge and ideological binder between the groups of Armenians dispersed around the world.

The situation in Soviet Armenia changed somewhat during Khrushchev's Thaw. Memories of the genocide that had been hidden up to that point began to be articulated publicly. In April 1965, several thousand Armenians rallied in Yerevan fifty years after the event to demand that the genocide committed on their Anatolian ancestors in the Ottoman Empire be recognized and commemorated (Papazyan 2019). This delayed commemoration supposedly arose from a need to break the silence about the terrible trauma that had been experienced by the Armenian nation. Apart from Khrushchev's Thaw, the publicization of the history of the Holocaust of the Jewish nation also created conditions favourable for the public articulation of demands for the Armenian genocide to be recognized and condemned.

Demonstrations involving thousands of people coming out onto the streets of Yerevan not only surprised the local authorities of the Armenian Socialist Republic but also the authorities in Moscow. The main role in these protests was played by young people and students, who left the buildings of their universities and went onto the streets. The protesters gathered in Lenin Square and then congregated in front of the opera building. As the young people and students marched, they were joined by others. The protesters gathered near the Yerevan opera called on the Armenian Communist Party to build a monument to the genocide and demanded pressure be put on the authorities of the Soviet Union to return the historical lands of the Armenian motherland that had

74 *Adam Pomieciński*

ended up, after the war, in Turkey and the Republic of Azerbaijan (Papazyan 2019). During the demonstrations, protestors clashed with the police and some of them were arrested.

These protests had a great significance for Armenians. First of all, they made the local authorities approach Moscow for permission to build a monument commemorating the Armenian genocide. They also provoked a discussion on national problems within the Soviet Union. Finally, the fact of the tragedy of the genocide being publicly articulated on the streets of Yerevan became the source for the formation of a collective national consciousness among the dispersed Armenian population, thereby shortening the distance between the Soviet Armenians and the Armenian diaspora around the world (Suny 2011). After the short political thaw in the Soviet Union, the authorities charted a more conservative course that blocked grassroots movements and social initiatives.

Nevertheless, the fact that the communist authorities had expressed their agreement to the idea of building a memorial to the Armenian genocide was an undoubted turning point in regard to the long struggle over the need to express 'the truth about the Armenian question'. The construction of the monument was also a form of institutionalized social memory of the mass crime against the nation. The Armenian Genocide Memorial Complex was erected on a Yerevanian hill called Tsitsernakaberd in 1967. However, the Soviet authorities attempted, in their own fashion, to appropriate the memory of the Armenians murdered in the Ottoman massacres by celebrating other events related to Soviet history next to the monument. The first ceremony in front of the monument to the Armenian genocide took place on 29 November 1967, which was the 47th anniversary of the Red Army's creation. According to the communist propaganda of the time, the genocide memorial complex was supposed to symbolize general memory relating to the victims of violence and the struggle against fascism (Darieva 2006), while the heroism of the Armenian nation was presented within the context of its rebirth under communism. Despite the previous concessions, such procedures were instigated by the authorities of the Soviet Union and the state apparatus when memory of the Armenian genocide in public space was subjected to censorship once again.

These conditions did not change until the 1980s, when the government was taken over by Mikhail Gorbachev, who introduced perestroika policies. The genocide was officially condemned by the state on 22 November 1986, when the Supreme Council of the Socialist Republic of Armenia adopted a law condemning the Armenian genocide and established 24 April as a National Day of Remembrance. Several years later, on 23 August 1990, the question of the genocide was also incorporated into the Armenian Declaration of Independence.

It is worth emphasizing that the process of regaining memory was occurring simultaneously in the diaspora, where the reality was very different from that prevailing in Soviet Armenia. The genocide was, to a large extent, the symbolic beginning of the modern Armenian diaspora. Therefore, memory of the genocide was, from the very beginning, also an important element of identity for those who had been forced to live in exile (Dawoodi 2018). In their host communities, Armenians were building Christian churches, creating their own

The Armenian genocide 75

educational centres, developing a sense of national unity and preserving family mementos that did not allow them to forget about their lost motherland and tragic past (Aleksanyan 2016). Over the years, memory of the genocide was an important building block that helped to create a sense of nationhood among subsequent generations of the descendants of those who had survived it. This is evidenced, at the very least, by the monuments erected at various sites around the world to commemorate the Armenian genocide. Some of the first memorials commemorating the killed Armenians were erected in Mexico City in 1930 (Antaramián 2010) and in Lebanon, where in Antelias, near Beirut, a small chapel honouring the victims of the Armenian genocide was built in 1938 (Papkova 2014, 177). Many memorials were created as a sign of solidarity with those protesting in Yerevan in 1965, or shortly after these events. These were the circumstances of the construction of the monuments to the genocide in, for instance, São Paulo in Brazil (1965), and Watertown (1965) and Montebello (1967) in the United States. In the 1970s and 1980s, further monuments were created in, among other countries, France (1973), Iran (1973 and 1975), Uruguay (1975), the United States (1978 and 1980) and Argentina (1983). After Armenia gained its independence, the number of memorials to the Armenian genocide began to increase quickly on a global level. According to recent estimates, several hundred of them have been erected so far in over thirty countries, including Argentina, Australia, Austria, Canada, Chile, France, Germany, Iran, Lebanon, Mexico, Poland, Ukraine, the United States, Switzerland, Syria, Uruguay and Venezuela.[3]

Regaining memory of the genocide became one of the most important components of a review process examining social and state identity in independent Armenia. Despite the difficult political situation in Armenia, and a war with Azerbaijan over Nagorno-Karabakh in the first half of the 1990s, the question of the genocide did not disappear from public discourse. In 1995, one year after the signing of an Armenian–Azerbaijani truce, celebrations of the 80th anniversary of the genocide were organized. The main point of these was to provide an opportunity for the opening of the Armenian Genocide Museum-Institute, which was on Tsitsernakaberd, close to the memorial built on that hill in 1967. Today, the monument towering over that site combines with the museum to create a homogeneous memorial-museum complex. In the museum building and its three exhibition rooms, a multilayered narrative about the Armenian genocide has been maintained. The first exposition room contains a large map of the Armenian plateau and neighbouring countries. The map also illustrates Armenian settlements in Western Armenia and other parts of the Ottoman Empire that existed until 1915, the year of the 'death marches'. The exposition comprises photographs, artefacts and data about the Armenian population in Ottoman Turkey that depict their everyday life before the genocide. The second room presents testimonies and documents concerning the slaughter and atrocities committed against Armenians. The photographs of victims and perpetrators and various records from 1915 to 1922 fill the entire space. The third room makes visitors realize the scale of the genocide by describing the number of deportees and deaths. A special part of the exposition includes original documents condemning the Armenian genocide issued by the parliaments of other states and international organizations. Crystal vases have been set into the floor and filled with earth from the historical regions of Armenia.

The monument and the Museum of Armenian Genocide in Yerevan is certainly an extraordinary place. Every year, on 24 April, a state event takes place there, which is broadcast live on Armenian television. The martyrological complex, which includes the monument as well as a museum, is also an obligatory destination during visits paid to Armenia by almost all foreign official delegations. It is also a site of 'pilgrimage' for numerous excursions taken by members of the Armenian diaspora from all around the world. The monument and the Museum of the Armenian Genocide serve as an institute containing a library and reading room, where lectures, conferences and educational lessons for young people are organized. The history of the genocide together with the memorial-museum complex are among the most important national symbols of Armenia.

In Armenia, the memory of the genocide has also become an important part of the school education provided to the youngest children. Information on this topic is conveyed through lessons, history textbooks, literature, the Armenian language, music and art (Mkrtchyan 2015). These practices form part of the field of so-called postmemory (Hirsch 1997), which is associated with particular acts and activities that deconstruct genocide in commemorative institutions, historical transmission, literary narratives, the erection of monuments and social education.

The discourse about the genocide in Armenia and the diaspora created a distinct opposition between victims and perpetrators, which served to determine the notions of historical truth, recognition and memorialization of the victims of the massacres. The complicated relations prevailing between Armenia and Turkey, and the two different models of national politics conducted by consecutive governments of those countries, have so far provided little leeway for official dialogue and reconciliation. Armenians were faced with a moral dilemma: how could they reach an accommodation between the trauma of the genocide and the need to seek reconciliation? On the other hand, a similarly thorny problem was faced by the Turkish state, which would have to somehow reconcile itself to its uncomfortable past and acknowledge the arguments being put forward by the Armenians. Despite these obstacles, in 2008, Armenia announced the beginning of talks on reconciliation with Turkey, and in the following year, both states signed protocols on the development of mutual relations. This was made possible both by internal conditions in Turkey and political changes that had occurred in Armenia. In Turkey, Recep Erdoğan's Justice and Development Party introduced the policy of 'zero problems with neighbours', while in Armenia, Serzh Sargsyan, after bloodily suppressing a demonstration by the opposition following the presidential election in March 2008, was soliciting the leaders of other states for international legitimization of his position. Talks between the two countries were also encouraged by the United States and were not discouraged by Russia. Public opinion in Armenia and Turkey learned about the plan to normalize Turkish–Armenian relations during qualification for the FIFA World Cup in 2010. The Armenian and Turkish teams found themselves in the same qualifying group. When the two teams met for their matches, the presidents of both countries sat in the stands, first Abdullah Gul in Yerevan, then Serzh Sargsyan in Turkish Bursa. However, the signed protocols could not be implemented in practice. Pressure exerted on the government in Ankara by Azerbaijan, which perceived the reconciliation process as a betrayal on Turkey's part, led to a stiffening of the Turkish position and the propounding of new, revised conditions. The most serious of these proposed conditions was a request for Armenian concessions in the peace negotiations over the conflict in Nagorno-Karabakh. For the government in Yerevan, that was tantamount to breaking the reconciliation process (Terzyan 2016). By 2010, these talks between Turkey and Armenia had already been suspended, and they eventually stalled (Shushanyan 2013). Further attempts to establish relations with Turkey on the basis of reconciliation over the question of the genocide being downgraded to a historical problem led to protests in the diaspora and strong criticism of the policies being pursued by the government in Yerevan (Mandaci 2014).

Clearly, memory of the genocide determines both internal and external politics. The pursuit of general acknowledgement of the genocide on a national level was transmitted into the arena of international relations, and an important role in this regard was also played by the Armenian diaspora. This consistent policy did in fact contribute to the development of the phenomenon of recognition of the genocide on the international arena. This became particularly evident in 2015. Owing to the 100th anniversary of the genocide, a global campaign was conducted seeking recognition for the Armenian genocide. On 21 April 2015, the Armenian National Assembly addressed a statement to the parliaments of all countries and international organizations calling for it to be officially recognized and condemned.[4]

With the 100th anniversary of *Mec Jeghern* approaching, the issue of sacralization of all the genocide's victims was incorporated into the official discourses of the articulation of memory. After a several-hundred-year break in the canonization processes, the Armenian Apostolic Church announced during a special liturgy that about 1.5 million Armenians who had lost their lives in the Ottoman Empire at the beginning of the twentieth century were saints. This was not only an act that both recognized and condemned the genocide, but it was also a manifestation of national identity. The Anatolian ancestors of modern Armenians were deemed to have died martyrs' deaths for both their faith and their motherland. Raising such a large group of people to the altar based on their ethnic identity and honouring their dignity through acts of public worship has so far constituted the apogee of deification of the Armenian nation. As Karekin II, Catholicos of All Armenians, said during the canonization ceremony:

> The canonization of the victims of the genocide brings new life, grace and blessing for our church and national life. We believe that we are weaving a crown of new rebirth of our people through canonization of the victims

78 *Adam Pomieciński*

of the Armenian genocide. Memory about our saint martyrs is not any longer a prayer required for sacrifice and the dead, but a triumphal hymn for victorious soldiers who died for faith and motherland.

(Danielyan 2015)

These words indicate that religion is an inherent element of Armenian identity that plays a significant role in the system of national bonds and relations between Armenians and their state. For Armenians, national belonging is equivalent to Christian belonging, or to be more precise, it is related to participation in the Armenian Apostolic Church as a national institution. Thus, canonization of the victims of the genocide may be interpreted in ethno-religious categories: the religious penetrates into the national, and the national penetrates the religious sphere and acquires a sacral character.

Canonization of the victims of the genocide and the sacralization of memory

The convergence of religious and national identity is nothing new for Armenians. Historical circumstances, such as the age-old confrontation with Islam or the Armenian Apostolic Church's isolated position within the Christian world have resulted, for a very long time now, in religion being interpreted within the context of national culture (Antonyan 2011). In 301, Armenia was the first state in the world to recognize Christianity as its national religion. Only two years later, St Gregory the Illuminator established a bishopric in Etchmiadzin. In 387, the Armenian kingdom was divided between the Eastern Roman Empire and Persia. In the territories subordinated to Persia, Armenians were persecuted for their faith and perceived as supporters of a hostile Byzantium, where Christianity had become the dominant religion. In the fifth century, the Armenian Church broke ties with the Byzantine Church and adopted the rules of Monophysitism, creating a separate national Church led by a patriarch based in Etchmiadzin who took the title Catholicos of All Armenians (Król-Mazur 2016). In the period between the ninth and fifteenth centuries, the seat of the Armenian Apostolic Church was transferred to Sis in Cilicia, and from 1199, the Kingdom of Cilicia, also known as Lesser Armenia, was established. The kingdom was invaded by Mongols and other peoples, which eventually led to the apostolic seat being moved back to Etchmiadzin. However, this decision caused divisions within the Armenian Church that are still visible to this day. As things stand, the spiritual leader is still the Catholicos of All Armenians based in Etchmiadzin. The title 'Catholicos', despite its lower rank than Catholicos in Etchmiadzin, is also used by the head of the Great House of Cilicia. Furthermore, the historical development of the Armenian Church resulted in the creation of two more patriarchal capitals, in Jerusalem and Constantinople. Besides the four aforementioned hierarchic Churches, there are church organizations functioning around the world, called dioceses, which have their own diocesan supervisors. The great majority of these dioceses, for instance those in the United States, France, Germany, Romania, Bulgaria, Argentina, Brazil and Australia, are subordinated to the Catholicos of All Armenians in Etchmiadzin. However, the dioceses in Lebanon, Syria, Iran and Cyprus are under the jurisdiction of the Catholicos of the Great House of Cilicia (Sahakyan 2018).

The Armenian Apostolic Church's peripheral location, its separation from the rest of the world, its doctrinal separateness from both Catholicism and the Orthodox Church and its development of autonomous organizational structures were the main reasons why it limited its activity to 'its own people'. In such circumstances, the centuries-old tradition of autocephaly created a special kind of attachment to the Church that, in situations of danger, would also become a mainstay for national values. Years of political turmoil, wars and the internal instability of the Armenian state also led to the Church being viewed as a strong source of support for Armenian identity. The religious resistance of Armenians towards invaders also always coincided with national resistance (Król-Mazur 2016). For the major part of its history, the Armenian Apostolic Church served as a tool for the survival of the Armenian nation, especially in those periods when Armenia lost its statehood. At these critical moments, it not only provided religious services but also took political responsibility for the Armenian communities dispersed around the world.

The twentieth century turned out to be the most tragic century of all both for Armenians themselves and the Armenian Apostolic Church. The Armenian genocide in the Ottoman Empire contributed to the almost total destruction of the Armenian Church in these territories. The Sovietization of Eastern Armenia was facilitated by the serious weakening of the Church's internal structures and the collapse of religious life. In spite of that, the Armenian Apostolic Church continued to be an important institution due to its role reinforcing the memory of the martyrdom of the nation. The first commemoration of the victims of the Armenian genocide took place on 24 April 1919 in Constantinople at the Holy Trinity Church. Those who survived the genocide participated in the event, which was organized by the patriarchy of that region. Following this historical commemorative event, 24 April was officially adopted as a day of mourning and remembrance devoted to the victims of the Armenian genocide (Payaslian 2006). The question of national genocide made such a large contribution to the history and memory of Christian martyrdom that it literally became part of the Armenian Apostolic Church.

Despite encountering many difficulties, the Armenian Apostolic Church, both in Armenia itself and in cooperation with the diasporic organizations, continued to commemorate the victims of the genocide. In 1938, for example, as mentioned earlier, a small chapel devoted to the Armenians who had lost their lives in 1915 was erected within the grounds of the monastery in Antelias in Lebanon, and in 1965, a monumental sculpture (a khachkar recalling the main places of the Armenian annihilation) was placed in the courtyard of the cathedral in Etchmiadzin. Furthermore, many churches of the diaspora contain chapels or sculptures dedicated to the memory of the Armenian martyrs

80 *Adam Pomieciński*

of 1915, either created on their own initiative or in cooperation with local Armenian communities.

A new chapter in the history of the Armenian Apostolic Church was opened once Armenia become independent. The Armenian Church quickly began to reinforce its status after years of communism. It secured a privileged position in the state, which was legally guaranteed. It obtained freedom of action, the formal status of a national Church and protection from a state that acknowledged the Church's mission in spiritual life and the crucial contribution it makes to the development of national culture and maintenance of the Armenian nation's identity. The Church began a 'new wave of evangelization' in independent Armenia. Ironically, even though the majority of Armenians consider themselves to be Christians, very few of them participate in the liturgies. Armenia's period of independence has also revealed many structural weaknesses in the Armenian Apostolic Church that have showed it was not ready for new challenges (due to insufficient human and material resources) and incapable of finding an effective remedy for the consequences of secularization and atheism inherited from the Soviet epoch (Tchilingirian 2016). All these conditions were not without influence on the potential canonization of the victims of the genocide, an idea which was being ever more loudly discussed in the atmosphere created by Armenia's independence. Even before the 75th anniversary of the genocide, both Catholicoses had issued statements on the canonization of the victims. However, internal divisions in the Church, the lack of canonization rituals and political problems and conflicts within the Armenian state itself all made it difficult to realize this enterprise. Questions were surfacing about the practical implications of canonizing 1.5 million people without a solid foundation enabling their sanctity to be proved. Meanwhile, bishops at specially convened synods were laboriously staking out a path that would enable the mass canonization of the victims. However, the imminent approach of the hundredth-anniversary celebrations ultimately encouraged the bishops to accelerate their efforts. In 2013, one of the bishops, Aris Shirvanian, who also happened to be director of ecumenical and foreign relations at the Armenian Apostolic Patriarchy in Jerusalem, said that reaching agreement on the question of the victims' canonization was of the highest priority. He added that 'we, the bishops and archbishops living today, are descendants of Armenian genocide' (Herszenhorn 2013). The canonization process therefore turned out to be a great challenge for the Armenian nation and Church.

In Christian churches, canonization is an official act that recognizes a deceased member, or members, of a community as deserving of public worship and legitimizes the recognition of that individual or group's sainthood. This sainthood is certified through specific legal and moral procedures applied by the Church (Zanet 2016). The most important general rules that need to be met for canonization to take place include evidence of martyrdom for one's faith and motherland; individual or collective behaviour of a holy nature; the presence of miracles at the time of life or death; and actions directed at spreading the faith. In the Eastern Churches, which include the Armenian Apostolic

The Armenian genocide   81

Church, canonization is more an announcement of sainthood accompanied by celebrations often referring to Armenian tradition than a complicated process such as that which takes place in, for instance, the Roman Catholic Church. It continues to be the last stage in the process of declaring sainthood and needs to be authorized by the official seals of the highest church officials. At this final canonization stage, it is believed that a person or a group of people share in the holiness of God and their lives evidenced the authenticity and truth of the Christian gospel (Manoukian 2015).

As was mentioned before, the question of the Armenian genocide and collective memory of these traumatic events continues to be a complex problem that first and foremost refers to national, ethnical and political factors. The collapsing Ottoman Empire carried out ethnic cleansing for the benefit of the new state that would emerge after the war. However, it was mostly Christians, and especially Armenians, that were targeted by that cleansing. Thus, the national extermination also had religious overtones. Clearly, in this case, religious, as well as national, ethnical and political factors, intertwined with one another.

In the Armenian Apostolic Church, the canonization of the victims of the genocide was taking place hundreds of years after the most recent canonization process. The last person to be incorporated by the Armenian Church into its group of saints had been Gregory of Tatev, a philosopher and theologian living at the turn of the fifteenth century. It is worth mentioning at this juncture that among those who lost their lives in the 'death marches' of 1915 were two clergymen, who are considered to be saint martyrs in the Roman Catholic Church. In 2001, Ignatius Maloyan, an Armenian archbishop, was beatified in the Vatican by John Paul II. Then, in 2015, Flavianus Michael Malke, an Assyrian bishop – who like Maloyan was executed by the Turks during the genocide for refusing to renounce his faith – was beatified in Lebanon by Cardinal Angelo Amato on behalf of Pope Francis. The Catholic Church's established and rigorous canonization procedures enabled it to ably incorporate them into its list of saints.

The issue of the canonization of the martyrs of the Armenian genocide was already being raised during the First Armenian Republic. In 1920, Armenian writer and social activist Vrtanes Mesrop Papazian addressed a letter to George V, Catholicos of All Armenians, requesting that 760 murdered leaders of the Armenian community be commemorated, including journalists, teachers, doctors, pharmacists, merchants, bankers and clergymen. He presented the same proposition to the parliament of the Republic of Armenia and the Minister of Education and Culture. Armenian Christians reacted to this appeal with a special encyclical addressed to the local diocesan councils in Yerevan, Baku, Tbilisi and Nagorno-Karabakh, recommending that they perform prayers for the memory of the 760 intellectuals and clergymen murdered in April 1915 in Constantinople and all the Armenian provinces (Manoukian 2015).

Armenian history was so turbulent that the issue of the canonization of the victims of the genocide had to be postponed for many years. The Armenian Church was significantly weakened under communism, and internal divisions did little to foster frequent meetings between bishops. This made it impossible to make common decisions and establish canonization procedures. The canonization issue only really returned when the Soviet Union was beginning to dissolve. On 29 April 1989, Vasken I, the Catholicos of All Armenians, and Karekin II, the Patriarch of the Great Cilician House, marked the occasion of the 75th anniversary of the genocide by proposing, in a common statement, that all activities preparing for the canonization of the victims of the genocide should be continued (Manoukian 2015). Discussions on this topic were conducted at various church commissions and in different clergy circles over the following decades. Finally, in 2014, the Armenian Apostolic Church made the final decision to canonize all the victims of the genocide and recognize them as saints on 23 April 2015 – the day before the 100th anniversary of the massacres in the Ottoman Empire. From this moment on, the canonization ceased to be a spiritually and morally unfulfilled obligation towards those who had lost their lives due to their Christian faith and Armenian identity. According to one of the bishops, Bagrat Galstanjan, the Armenian Apostolic Church were only recognizing 'the sainthood of the persons who in the memory and minds of Armenians already were saints' (Nikoghosyan 2015). From this perspective, the canonization became an important element in the sacralization of the memory of the genocide, something which the Armenian nation had been demanding for a long time. Memory of the 'death marches' through the Syrian desert began to be conceived as an 'Armenian Golgotha' of dying Armenians (Balakian 2010) and developed into the profound public worship of national martyrs who had fallen for their faith and their own culture. The Church thus confirmed the validity of the previous practices devoted to the sacralization of the memory of the genocide victims previously that were being performed in Armenia and the diaspora.

The actual ceremony during which 1.5 million victims of the genocide were canonized was sublime in character. It took place in Etchmiadzin, the spiritual capital of Armenia and most important place for the Armenian Apostolic Church. The ceremony was led by Karekin II, the Catholicos of All Armenians, and Aram I, the Catholicos of the Great Cilician House. They were accompanied by clergymen representing the four sister Churches of the Armenian Apostolic Church: the Coptic Orthodox Church, Assyrian Orthodox Church, Ethiopian Orthodox Church and Indian Assyrian Orthodox Church. During the canonization service, fourteen relics of saints were gathered, including the Geghard Holy Lance, which, according to tradition, was used by a Roman soldier to pierce Christ's side while he was hanging from the cross; the Right Hand of St Gregory the Illuminator, the most important clergyman and patron of the Armenian Apostolic Church, who in 310 made Christianity the national religion; and the Relic of the True Cross, which was, according to tradition, a small fragment of the cross on which Christ died. These were supplemented by relics of the victims of the Armenian genocide.

The prayers during the ceremony were enriched by special hymns and sacred chants known as Sharakan. Furthermore, texts about the history of the conversion of Armenian nation to Christianity were read out, and speeches were delivered that emphasized the suffering of the Armenian martyrs for their faith in Christ. Finally, there was a reading of the declaration of the victims' consecration that had been pre-approved by the bishops' synod. This declaration, dedicated to those 'who fell in love with the faith and motherland', announced that 24 April would henceforth be the Day of Remembrance of the Armenian Martyrs. According to Catholicos Karekin II, 'Today, the warm spirit of the martyrdom of our holy martyrs and warm spirit of patriotic love has spread from the Syrian desert to Holy Etchmiadzin and Tsitsernakaberd, to independent Armenia and the reborn Armenian world' (AGBU 2015). In the second part of the canonization ceremony, the icons of the victims of the genocide were anointed, and Catholicoses Karekin II and Aram I used special prayers to tell the story of the heroism of the consecrated. At the end of the ceremony, honour was paid to the victims of the genocide by the President of Armenia, Serzh Sargsyan. The consecration of the Armenian martyrs concluded with the ceremonial ringing of a hundred bells at 19:15 (7:15 p.m.), symbolizing the year 1915. At the same moment, bells in other churches of the Armenian diaspora and other Christian churches in various parts of the world also rang out.

The canonization of the martyrs of the Armenian genocide is still, at the time of writing, the largest-scale mass consecration of victims within the Christian Church. It was also one of the most important religious events in the history of the Armenian Church. Besides the Church hierarchs, other ceremony participants included representatives of the Armenian government, with President Sargsyan taking pride of place, and delegations from several other countries, including Georgia and Iran. The ceremony also served as a prelude to the main events forming part of the celebrations of the hundredth anniversary of the Armenian genocide in the Ottoman Empire. The next day, 24 April, the Presidents of Serbia (Tomislav Nikolic), Cyprus (Nicos Anastasiadis), Russia (Vladimir Putin) and France (François Hollande) arrived during the state celebrations in front of Tsitsernakaberd hill. The modest attendance at the celebrations among world leaders signalled that some caution was being exercised over the use of the term 'Armenian genocide' on the international arena and in political relations between the states.

The symbolic meaning of this canonization was telling, however. Victims of a genocide were transformed into victors of Christ in a process that did them justice. Although this justice was largely transcendent and based on a narrative that contradicted the opposing Turkish narrative of the same events, it not only confirmed the fact that the genocide had occurred but also recognized that the people who had been killed were regarded today as victorious martyrs for their faith (Winter 2017). In effect, the sacralization of the victims of a national catastrophe had changed the rank of historical events that had happened 100 years before by officially ennobling these events as religious testimonies. Therefore, the canonization, rather than seeking to contravene historical details, was actually more of a mythologizing act integrated into the collective identity of the Armenian nation.

Conclusions

Memory should be treated as the continuous art of representing the past in contemporaneity (O'Neill and Hinton 2009). Its 'production' has particular meaning not only for societies affected by genocide but also for those that are considered to be the 'perpetrators' of a tragedy. Contemporary Armenian society may be called a post-genocidal society for whom the memory of *Mec Jeghern* fundamentally influences many spheres of public life as well as internal and external politics, while also redefining the sense of ethnic community. After the genocide in 1915, the Armenian nation lived under strong censorship in an atmosphere of official denial of the mass extermination. The policy of recognizing the genocide, which manifested itself strongly after Armenia gained its independence, began to play an important role in understanding and expressing collective identity. Societies that, like the Armenians, have engaged with their memory of genocide make this memory an inherent element in the building of a sense of national community. Collective memory, officially manifested, began to be understood as the antithesis of falling into the trap of forgetting.

The Soviet Union and the Armenian republic that was part of it were, for many decades, effectively silencing the memory of the genocide by erasing it from the official discourse. In fact, the first museum devoted to the Armenian genocide was not established until eighty years after the historical date (1915) of the commencement of the genocide (Marutyan 2014). The process of regaining the memory – or, more correctly, bringing it back into the public sphere – was a component of the national awakening that started during the mass protests in 1965. It proved to be impossible for the Turkish authorities to silence the memory of the genocide by consistently pursuing the politics of negation and denial and trying to force through their own interpretation of the events. In the face of danger, the Armenian nation realized that it needed to fight to maintain that memory.

Nowadays, the memory of the genocide has been inherited by the descendants of the generation that lived through the mass crime. *Mec Jeghern* has become such a powerful part of the consciousness of subsequent generations that they feel it as their own. Moreover, it is constantly being updated and celebrated, the most spectacular example of this being the mass canonization of the victims of the genocide performed in 2015. Inherited memory of the genocide has become a kind of religious metanarrative, and the need to remember has become firmly grounded in the sacral sphere and symbolic practices. Much like other commemorative activities, the mass canonization of the victims of the genocide appears to form part of the complex and long-lasting process of rebuilding Armenian society after a great trauma. These practices organize the nation on various levels: from the emotional–psychological to the political–religious. They provide a posteriori evidence of the fact that it is impossible to cast aside the stigma of the past, because genocide always leaves visible traces and never disappears from memories. Memory overcomes the fragility of existence.

Notes

1 Turkey officially maintains that the 1.5 million Armenians killed by Ottoman soldiers during the First World War lost their lives due to domestic turmoil and civil war rather than a planned extermination. Despite considerable historical evidence to the contrary, Turkey denies the fact of the Armenian genocide and diminishes the number of victims. However, it is worth noticing that in spite of continued censorship and political pressure, there are numerous initiatives in Turkey, outside of the official sphere, that commemorate the Armenian genocide (Carikci 2016; Çelik and Öpengin 2016). This suggests a conflict between official state memory and the social memory of Turks and Kurds living in eastern Turkey (Üngör 2014).

2 However, some scholars indicate that the first genocide of the twentieth century took place not in the lands of Ottoman Turkey, but in German South West Africa (now Namibia), a colony annexed by the German Empire at the beginning of the 1880s. In 1904–07, Germans exterminated the native Ovaherero population and groups of Khoi-hoi who were revolting against them. All the purposeful activities conducted by the Germans at that time qualify this crime as a genocide (Gewald 1999; Steinmetz 2005).

3 The database of memorials devoted to the memory of the Armenian genocide is constantly being updated by the Armenian National Institute (ANI). It is available in an electronic version at www.armenian-genocide.org/memorials.html. It should be added here that there are several detailed elaborations devoted to the issue of memory of the genocide in the communities of the Armenian diaspora. These include the latest texts based on studies of the memory of the genocide in the diasporas comprising American Armenians (Paul 2000), French Armenians (Al-Rustom 2013) and Canadian Armenians (Kaya 2017).

4 So far, over thirty countries and several international organizations have recognized that the slaughter of Armenians in the Ottoman Empire was a genocide. In recent years, such resolutions were adopted by both houses of Congress of the United States (2019) and the parliament of Syria (2020). All these acts provoked diplomatic objections from Turkey.

Bibliography

AGBU (Armenian General Benevolent Union). 2015. "Հայոց ցեղասպանության զոհերի սրբադասման կարգ Մայր Աթոռ Սուրբ Էջմիածնում" [Order of Sanctification of the Victims of the Armenian Genocide in the Mother See of Holy Etchmiadzin]. www.agbu.am/am/archive/2015-02-05-13-25-23/news-2015-arm/2481-canonization-ceremony-arm.

Aleksanyan, Ashot. 2016. "The Impact of the Armenian Genocide on the Formation of National Statehood and Political Identity." *Armenological Issues* 2 (8): 22–43.

Al-Rustom, Hakem. 2013. "Diaspora Activism and the Politics of Locality. The Armenians of France." In *A Companion to Diaspora and Transnationalism*, edited by Ato Quayson and Girish Daswani, 473–93. Malden, MA: Blackwell.

Antaramián, Carlos. 2010. "Armenians in 1930's Mexico City." *Journal of the Society for Armenian Studies* 19 (1): 45–60.

Antonyan, Yulia. 2011. "Religiosity and Religious Identity in Armenia: Some Current Models and Developments." *Acta Ethnographica Hungarica* 56 (2): 315–32.

Balakian, Grigoris. 2010. *Armenian Golgotha: A Memoir of the Armenian Genocide, 1915–1918.* New York: Vintage Books.

Balakian, Peter. 2013. "Raphael Lemkin, Cultural Destruction, and the Armenian Genocide." *Holocaust and Genocide Studies* 27 (1): 57–89. https://doi.org/10.1093/hgs/dct001.

Carikci, Alaettin. 2016. *The Arts of Memory: The remembrance of the Armenians in Turkey.* Leiden: Leiden University Repository. https://openaccess.leidenuniv.nl/handle/1887/39674.

86   *Adam Pomieciński*

Çelik, Adnan, and Ergin Öpengin. 2016. "The Armenian Genocide in the Kurdish Novel: Restructuring Identity Through Collective Memory." *European Journal of Turkish Studies* (July 8). http://journals.openedition.org/ejts/5291.

Dadrian, Vahakn. 1998. "The Historical and Legal Interconnections Between the Armenian Genocide and the Jewish Holocaust: From Impunity to Retributive Justice." *Yale Journal of International Law* 23 (2): 504–59. https://digitalcommons.law.yale.edu/yjil/vol23/iss2/5.

Danielyan, Gayane. 2015. "The Victims of the Armenian Genocide were Consecrated." *Azatutyun.am*. www.azatutyun.am/a/26974750.html.

Darieva, Tsypylma. 2006. "Bringing the Sol Back to the Homeland. Reconfigurations of Representation of Loss in Armenia." *Comparativ* 16: 87–101.

Dawoodi, D. J. 2018. "The Aftermath of the Armenian Genocide and the Holocaust: A Comparative Study." *Social Crimonol* 6 (2). https://doi.org/10.35248/2375-4435.18.6.183.

de Lame, Danielle. 2007. "Anthropology and Genocide." In *SciencesPo. Mass Violence and Resistance – Research Network* (November 4). www.sciencespo.fr/mass-violence-war-massacre-resistance/en/document/anthropology-and-genocide.html.

Gewald, Jean-Bart. 1999. *Herero Heroes: A Socio-Political History of the Herero of Namibia 1890–1923*. Oxford: Ohio University Press.

Herszenhorn, David. 2013. "Armenian Church, Survivor of the Ages, Faces Modern Hurdles." *New York Times*, October 3. www.nytimes.com/2013/10/04/world/europe/armenian-apostolic-church-survivor-of-the-ages-faces-modern-hurdles.html.

Hirsch, Marianne. 1997. *Family Frames. Photography, Narrative, and Postmemory*. Cambridge, MA: Harvard University Press.

Kaya, Duygu. 2017. "Memory and Citizenship in Diaspora: Remembering the Armenian Genocide in Canada." *Citizenship Studies* 22 (4): 401–18. https://doi.org/10.1080/1362 1025.2018.1462503.

Koinova, Maria. 2017. "Conflict and Cooperation in Armenian Diaspora Mobilisation for Genocide Recognition." In *Diaspora as Cultures of Cooperation. Global and Local Perspectives*, edited by David Carment and Ariane Sadjed, 111–29. Cham: Palgrave Macmillan.

Król-Mazur, Renata. 2016. "Rola religii w konflikcie o Górski Karabach." In *Armenia. Dziedzictwo a współczesne kierunki przemian kulturowo-cywilizacyjnych*, edited by Paweł Nieczuja-Ostrowski, 225–55. Poznań: Fundacja na rzecz Czystej Energii.

Kurt, Ümit. 2018. "Reform and Violence in the Hamidian Era: The Political Context of the 1895 Armenian Massacres in Aintab." *Holocaust and Genocide Studies* 32 (3): 404–23. https://doi.org/10.1093/hgs/dcy048.

Laderman, Charlie. 2019. *Sharing the Burden: The Armenian Question, Humanitarian Intervention, and Anglo-American Visions of Global Order*. Oxford: Oxford University Press.

Mandaci, Nazif. 2014. "Reconciliation Under the Shadow of Diaspora Politics: Some Lessons from the Turkish-Armenian Reconciliation Commission." *Sosyal Bilimler Enstitüsü Dergisi* 16 (2): 235–57. https://doi.org/10.16953/deusbed.28144.

Manoukian, Abel. 2015. *New Saints. Canonizing the Victims of the Armenian Genocide in the Armenian Church*. Geneva: Books on Demand.

Marutyan, Harutyun. 2014. "Museums and Monuments: Comparative Analysis of Armenian and Jewish Experiences in Memory Policies." *Études arméniennes contemporaines* 3: 57–79. https://doi.org/10.4000/eac.544.

Mkrtchyan, Satenik. 2015. "The Memory of the Armenian Genocide as Taught in Armenian Schools: Textbooks, School Rituals and Iconography." *Heinrich Böll Stiftung Foundation Tbilisi*. https://ge.boell.org/en/2015/04/23/memory-armenian-genocide-taught-armenian-schools-textbooks-school-rituals-and-iconography.

Morris, Benny, and Dror Ze'evi. 2019. *The Thirty-Year Genocide: Turkey's Destruction of Its Christian Minorities 1894–1924*. Cambridge, MA: Harvard University Press.

Nikoghosyan, Alina. 2015. "Holy Recognition: Church to Canonize Genocide Victims." *ArmeniaNow.com.* www.armenianow.com/hy/genocide/60307/armenian_apostolic_church_genocide_holy_see_echmiadzin.

O'Neill, Kevin Lewis, and Hinton, Alexander, Laban. 2009. *Genocide: Truth, Memory and Representation.* Durham and London. Duke University Press. https://doi.org/10.2307/j.ctv11sn03j.

Papazyan, Sabrina. 2019. "The Cost of Memorializing: Analyzing Armenian Genocide Memorials and Commemorations in the Republic of Armenia and in the Diaspora." *International Journal for History, Culture and Modernity* 7: 55–86. https://doi.org/10.18352/hcm.534.

Papkova, Irina. 2014. "The Three Religions of Armenians in Lebanon." In *Armenian Christianity Today. Identity Politics and Popular Practice,* edited by Alexander Agadjanian, 173–95. Farnham and Burlington: Ashgate.

Paul, Rachel. 2000. "Grassroots Mobilization and Diaspora politics: Armenian Interest Groups and the Role of Collective Memory." *Nationalism and Ethnic Politics* 6 (1): 24–47. https://doi.org/10.1080/13537110008428586.

Payaslian, Simon. 2006. "The Destruction of the Armenian Church during the Genocide." *Genocide Studies and Prevention: An International Journal* 1 (2): 149–71. https://scholarcommons.usf.edu/gsp/vol1/iss2/6.

Pomieciński, Adam. 2017. "Od pamięci stłamszonej do pamięci odzyskanej: Pomnik i Muzeum Ludobójstwa Ormian w Erywaniu." *Our Europe. Ethnography – Ethnology – Anthropology of Culture* 6: 7–14. http://oe.ptpn.poznan.pl/wp-content/uploads/2019/11/OE-2017-007-014-Pomiecinski.pdf.

Sacks, Adam. 2015. "*On Ararat Alone, No Arc Can be Rest.* Beyond Morgenthau: Jews, Social Democrats, and Jewish Social Democrats: Alliances and Solidarity During the Armenian Genocide Epoch." *International Journal of Armenian Genocide Studies* 2 (1): 59–85.

Sahakyan, Armen. 2018. "The Role of Religion in the Fate of the Armenian People." *Humanistyka i Przyrodoznawstwo* 24: 347–57. https://doi.org/10.31648/hip.2624.

Sarafian, Ara. 2010. "The Absorption of Armenian Women and Children into Muslim Households as a Structural Component of the Armenian Genocide." In *In God's Name: Genocide and Religion in the Twentieth Century,* edited by Omer Bartov and Phyllis Mack, 209–21. New York: Berghahn Books.

Seppälä, Serafim. 2015. "Genocide Descending: Half-Jews in Poland and Half-Armenians in Turkey." *International Journal of Armenian Genocide Studies* 2 (1): 39–57.

Shushanyan, Zaruhi. 2013. *Between the Memories and the Present: On the Armenian Genocide.* The Hague: International Institute of Social Studies.

Steinmetz, George. 2005. *The First Genocide of the 20th Century and Its Postcolonial Afterlives: Germany and the Namibian Ovaherero.* http://hdl.handle.net/2027/spo.4750978.0012.201.

Suny, Roland. 2011. "Writing Genocide: The Fate of the Ottoman Armenians." In *A Question of Genocide: Armenians and Turks at the End of the Ottoman Empire,* edited by Roland Suny et al., 15–41. Oxford: Oxford University Press.

———. 2015. '*They Can Live in the Desert but Nowhere Else': A History of the Armenian Genocide.* New Brunswick, NJ: Princeton University Press.

———. 2016. "'They Can Live in the Desert but Nowhere Else': Explaining the Armenian Genocide. One Hundred Years Later." *Juniata Voices* 16: 208–29.

Tchilingirian, Hratch. 2016. "In Search of Relevance: Church and Religion in Armenia Since Independence." In *Religion et politique dans le Caucase post-soviétique,* edited by Bayram Balcı and Raoul Motika, 277–311. Istanbul: Institut français d'études anatoliennes.

Terzyan, Aram. 2016. "The Evolution of Armenia's Foreign Policy Identity: The Conception of Identity Driven Paths. Friends and Foes in Armenian Foreign Policy Discourse." In *Values and Identity as Sources of Foreign Policy in Armenia and Georgia,* edited by Kornely Kakachia and Alexander Markarov, 145–83. Tbilisi: Universal.

88 *Adam Pomieciński*

Üngör, Uğur. 2014. "Lost in Commemoration: The Armenian Genocide in Memory and Identity." *Patterns of Prejudice* 48 (2): 147–66. https://doi.org/10.1080/00313 22X.2014.902210.

Winter, Jay. 2017. *War Beyond Words. Languages of Remembrance from the Great War to the Present.* Cambridge: Cambridge University Press.

Zakharova, Larissa. 2017. "Soviet Public Spheres." *Politika.* www.politika.io/en/notice/soviet-public-spheres.

Zanet, Lodovica. 2016. *La Santità dimostrabile. Antropologia e prassi della canonizzazione.* Bologna: Edizioni Dehoniane.

Zolian, Mikael. 2015. "Remembering and Demanding: How Armenia and the Diaspora are Approaching the Centennial of the Armenian Genocide." *Heinrich Böll Stiftung Foundation Tbilisi.* https://ge.boell.org/en/2015/04/22/remembering-and-demanding-how-armenia-and-diaspora-are-approaching-centennial-armenian.

5 Building a patrimonial Church

How the Orthodox Churches in Ukraine use the past

Yuliya Yurchuk

Introduction

The religious situation in Ukraine is quite specific. From the collapse of the Soviet Union to 2018 there were de facto four main churches in Ukraine: the Ukrainian Orthodox Church of the Moscow Patriarchate (UOC-MP), which continued to be dependent on the Russian Orthodox Church (ROC); the Ukrainian Orthodox Church of the Kyiv Patriarchate (UOC-KP), which was established in 1992 by those members of the clergy who diverged from the UOC-MP; the Ukrainian Autocephalous Orthodox Church (UAOC), which originated in 1921 in parallel with Ukrainian aspirations in 1917–22 to build an independent state; and the Ukrainian Greek Catholic Church (UGCC), which formed as a result of the Brest Agreement of 1596 between the Holy See and the Ruthenian Orthodox Church (Denysenko 2018; Plokhy and Sysyn 2003). During Soviet times, only the ROC was permitted to function by the state. In practical terms, the UAOC and UGCC were banned (the UAOC was permitted up to 1930 and the UGCC was forced to unite with the ROC in 1947; most priests from these Churches were repressed by the Soviet regime and many moved to the United States or Canada, where they became active in the Ukrainian diaspora). When the UAOC and UGCC were re-established in Ukraine at the end of the 1980s and beginning of the 1990s, their revival was closely connected to the national revival (Brüning 2016; Wanner 2018; Wawrzonek 2015). The same can be said of the UOC-KP, which appeared as a consequence of the state declaring its independence. It would therefore be fair to say that the profile of all the Churches that have (re-)appeared in the territory of Ukraine since the beginning of the 1990s has been shaded with national undertones and closely associated with the processes of nation- and state-building. Taking this further, it can be stated that Church-building in Ukraine has been aligned with the processes of nation- and state-building since 1991. The UOC-MP held the strongest position during this period because it inherited the structures and parishes of the ROC. In the 1990s, all the newly (re)established Churches were competing with the Moscow Patriarchate to (re) gain both church property and churchgoers. In such a highly competitive environment, all the Churches took active standpoints in politics and used historical

DOI: 10.4324/9781003264750-7

narratives to legitimize their own place in society. The politics of memory pursued by the Churches within the context of nation- and state-building is the primary focus of my study. However, I narrowed down the empirical material by choosing to trace the uses of the past related to one concrete memory event: the celebration of anniversaries of the Christianization of Kyivan Rus'.

I have chosen the three decades from 1988 to 2018 as temporal axes for several reasons. I decided to start with the 1980s, as this was a time of religious revival during which religion started to be more visible and present in the social and political arena. It marked the beginning of the movement of religious actors into the political arena and the strengthening of the Church's position as a political actor (Agadjanian 2017; Elsner 2018). I then concentrate on the Churches' politics of memory and uses of the past in independent Ukraine from 1991 to 2018. I conclude with the year 2018, because at the very beginning of 2019, the Ukrainian Orthodox Church was granted a *tomos*, an official document recognizing the Church's independence. The granting of this document in effect marked the end of one long stage of the Church-building process and the beginning of a new one.

The main questions in this chapter are influenced by the ongoing discussion in memory studies about how different social actors use the past. First, I am interested in the role that historical legacies play in the formation of the specific religious situation in Ukraine. Second, I am interested in how and why the past is used by the different Orthodox Churches. Some studies of religions have already discussed how religious communities are constructed through memory (Hervieu-Léger 2000; Davie 2000). However, little attention has so far been paid within memory studies to uses of the past by religious actors. Some historians and sociologists have drawn attention to how important the usage of historical narratives is for understanding the religious situation in Ukraine (Brik 2019; Denysenko 2018; Fert 2020; Pankhurst 2020). My aim is to broaden this discussion by comparing the official discourses of Orthodox Churches related to the commemorations of the Christianization of Kyivan Rus' that took place from 1988 to 2018. Consequently, my study is concentrated on the politics of memory pursued by Orthodox Churches in response to the political and societal turbulence that influenced these politics. I concentrate on the UOC-MP and UOC-KP because these Churches have the highest number of believers in Ukraine. I have not included the UAOC due to the comparatively low number of believers it attracts and the limitations of the present study.

I argue that throughout the period I have analyzed, each Orthodox Church in Ukraine was attempting to position itself as the 'patrimonial Church', namely the most traditional and historically justified Church for Orthodox believers in Ukraine. I see the struggle of each Church to gain its unique place in society as part of a Church-building process that coincided with a parallel process of nation- and state-building. I call this process a patrimonializing process, by which I mean Church-building that intensively employs narratives about the past that represent a certain Church as the only bearer of authentic religious tradition in a given society.[1] In this process, religion as such is presented as part of a patrimony that in its own way forms part of national identity.

Building a patrimonial Church 91

The chapter starts with some theoretical reflections on memory and religion and on the concept of 'patrimonial Church'. After this, I briefly present the historical context. I then go on to develop my argument and analyze the ways in which each Church represents itself as the 'patrimonial Church'. I narrow down the empirical material by mainly concentrating on official discourses that are related to the history connected with the celebration of anniversaries of the Christianization of Kyivan Rus' in each consecutive decade: 1988–97, 1998–2007 and 2008–18. I end my chapter by discussing how the concept of 'patrimonial Church' can be used to better comprehend the role the Ukrainian Orthodox Churches play in national and geopolitical struggles in which the Church-building process runs in parallel with the nation- and state-building processes. My analysis is limited to the official discourses of the heads of the Churches and state leaders. An examination of responses from these Churches' believers would have greatly contributed to the present study, but because of the chapter's limited scope, I left the analysis of believers' perspectives for a future study.

The patrimonializing process as a conceptual framework

When Danièle Hervieu-Léger wrote her groundbreaking book *Religion as a Chain of Memory*, she specifically underlined the legitimizing role of religion in the building of tradition that holds together diverse members of a community (2000). Hervieu-Léger refers to contexts resembling the situation in France, where there is one majority religion represented by one Church (Roman Catholicism). What happens, though, when there is one majority religion, but it is represented by different Churches? How is the tradition that holds the community together created and sustained in such a context? As my study shows, in circumstances favouring the coexistence of several different Churches representing the same religion, chances are high that the 'legitimizing' potential of religion will not only be used for consolidating the group but also for splitting the group or fostering several groups within one country. In such a context, each Church tries to create its own specific tradition. This tradition may be adhered to by both believers and non-believers. The most important issue in this context is not the question of religious belief but rather the question of other elements forming this tradition that resonate with people's identity. This can be demonstrated by recent statistics on religious belonging in Ukraine.

Most people in Ukraine say that they are Christians: 71.7% of the population declare themselves to be believers; 67.3% of the population declare adherence to Orthodox Christianity (of these, 28.7% declare themselves to belong to the Kyiv Patriarchate, 12.8% to the Moscow Patriarchate and 0.3% to the UAOC, 23.4% declare themselves to be simply 'Orthodox' without indicating which patriarchate they belong to and 1.9% declare adherence to other types of Orthodoxy) and 7.7% of the population say they are 'Christian' with no declared denominational affiliation (Razumkov 2018, 22). Orthodox Christianity can therefore be regarded as the majority religion in Ukraine. These numbers do not show whether people go to church or not, but they do show how people want to

92 *Yuliya Yurchuk*

identify themselves. Compared to the findings of previous surveys undertaken before the Russian aggression against Ukraine started in 2014, these data demonstrate a dramatic decrease in the number of people answering that they belong to the UOC-MP (Razumkov 2013).[2] This suggests that it is not only a question of belief but also personal interpretations of politics and current affairs that matter when people declare to which Church they belong. This argument is strengthened by the results of another survey in which the respondents admitted that, for them, the UOC-MP was associated with aggressive Russian policies against Ukraine (Democratic Initiative Foundation 2015). In the same survey, most of the believers named the UOC-KP as 'the only church of the Ukrainian people' (Democratic Initiative Foundation 2015).

I argue that the historical narratives produced by Churches play an important role in shaping the cultural tradition they construct. Sociologist Tymofii Brik has proposed a historically driven approach to the intra-doctrinal competition between the Orthodox Church jurisdictions in Ukraine. He shows that historical narratives are often the main differential in how Churches present themselves to society (Brik 2019). In a situation in which there is one majority religion, it is history that provides Churches with an opportunity to present differentiating narratives about themselves. These narratives have the potential to resonate with societies and their collective identities. Clearly, adherence to a particular historical narrative can prove to be meaningful when believers choose a Church to belong to, especially when it is taken into account that the nature of religious belief itself does not vary much from individual to individual. In fact, sometimes the importance of one particular historical narrative can lead some individuals to sympathize with a Church even though they do not share that Church's religious beliefs at all. Taken to extremes, such an adherence to a certain narrative, unaccompanied by religious faith, can even bracket out the question of religion completely, only leaving space for adherence to a certain tradition. For instance, this is exactly what inspired some Muslims in Ukraine to celebrate the granting of the *tomos* to the Ukrainian Orthodox Church in 2019 by widely using the slogan 'I am a Muslim of the Kyiv Patriarchate' across social media networks. Through this gesture, Muslims have sought to underline the fact that they support the idea of the Church's independence, and of course, this has nothing to do with religious belonging, as such.

While conceptualizing religion as the bearer of a certain tradition, Hervieu-Léger underlined the 'heritage value' of a religious legacy in which religion is regarded as a 'common cultural good' transferred from the past (Hervieu-Léger 2015, 18). In a similar vein, Grace Davie approached religion as an evolutionary framework of memory (Davie 2000) and elaborated the framework of religion as a form of collective memory (Davie 2002, 14–18). This line of thought should be understood within the context of discussions on secularization in which both Davie and Hervieu-Léger suggest, through their focus on memory, that secularization theory has certain limitations. It is indeed important for the memory scholar to consider the conceptualization of religion as memory, as this helps to explain the mechanisms underlying the transmission of tradition as well as the power of religion to sustain communities and its vitality, which can transcend millennia of history. Hervieu-Léger explains these mechanisms of transition through the concept of patrimonialization. She argues that through patrimonialization, 'religion is constituted as a collective patrimony, theologically neutralized and capable of being claimed by one and all: it has become a set of markers rooted in a distant past' (2015, 19). As was already mentioned, Hervieu-Léger was writing about France and Britain, where, as she stated, the collective patrimony 'no longer defines a believing community' and where ' "cultural patrimonialization" allows the British and French to revisit their religious, and specifically Christian, heritage, while at the same time revealing how distant they have become from religion as an organizing framework of collective and individual life' (2015, 19).

In Ukraine, in contrast to France and Britain, there is no single predominant Church that represents the patrimonial religion. While most of the population subscribe to Orthodoxy, which we can conceptualize as a patrimonial religion, the question of belonging to a certain Church is still fluid. That is why the whole process of patrimonialization in Ukraine can be framed as a quest to establish a 'patrimonial Church' able to define different, believing communities within the boundaries of one state. Hervieu-Léger wrote that patrimonial religion 'nurtures the dream of a continuing shared identity able to survive the accelerating pace of change' (2015, 20). In Ukraine, each Orthodox Church constructs historical narratives that nurture this 'dream of a continuing shared identity'. Thus, we can assume that several different identities are being nurtured during the patrimonialization process in Ukraine.

The Christianization of Kyivan Rus' as a memory event

The narrative of the choice of faith in the tenth century by the Prince of Kyivan Rus' Volodymyr bears all the hallmarks of a legend: when faced with a choice between Judaism, Islam, and Christianity, represented by either Rome or Constantinople, the powerful ruler chose the faith of the most powerful state in the region, and this strategic choice resulted in Kyivan Rus' adopting Byzantine Christianity (Plokhy 2015, 34; Plokhy and Sysyn 2003). The year 988 became officially recognized as the year of the state's Christianization but in fact, the conversion to Christianity was a slow process so that year has a rather symbolic meaning. However, it is important to emphasize that it was because of this choice that the Kyivan Church became directly dependent on its Mother Church in Constantinople. Formally, the Kyivan Church was under the jurisdiction of the Ecumenical See in Constantinople until 1686, when it was transferred to the jurisdiction of Moscow. When, on 5 January 2019, the Ecumenical Patriarchate granted autocephaly to the Orthodox Church of Ukraine (OCU), it was the transfer of 1686 that had been annulled.

Interestingly, the Day of the Christianization of Kyivan Rus' was first introduced to the Russian Empire's calendar in 1776.[3] This day was mainly celebrated by the Church. After the 1917 Revolution, the meaning of the Day of the Christianization of Kyivan Rus' started to broaden, as Russian émigré circles in Europe began associating it with pre-revolutionary Russia and celebrating it not only as an ecclesiastical but also a patriotic event. In the Soviet Union, though, where the status of religion was so complicated, with state policy ranging from suppression and repression to moderate tolerance, the Day of the Christianization of Kyivan Rus' was mainly limited to church celebrations.

When perestroika started in the Soviet Union in the mid-1980s, the communist regime began looking for new myths and narratives about the past that could unite the nations within the USSR that were demanding transformations. The mythical narrative of the 1917 Revolution was no longer able to support the regime (Bogumił 2018; Smolkin 2018). Thus, the state turned to the religious narrative of the past and the 1000th anniversary of the Christianization of Kyivan Rus'. Consequently, this event acquired the status of an important site of Soviet memory. As I will discuss below, the state and the Church used this past for their own purposes.

The Christianization of Kyivan Rus' is a foundational event for all the main Churches in Ukraine and for the ROC, but for each Church this event has a different meaning. The ROC uses an image of Kyivan Rus' as a symbol of unity between all 'Rus's peoples': Russia, Ukraine, and Belarus (Suslov 2014; Burgess 2017). Moreover, since the 1990s, the ROC has been strengthening the narrative of 'Holy Rus'' to underline the unity of the people who found themselves dispersed across different countries and nations after the disintegration of the Soviet Union (Burgess 2017; Suslov 2016). In the 2000s, this narrative of Holy Rus' was merged to a larger degree with the ideological construct of the 'Russian world' (Russkiy Mir), which serves the Russian geopolitical agenda (Knorre 2019; Hovorun 2016; Suslov 2016, 2019; Turoma and Aitamurto 2019). Importantly, as will be seen in the analysis below, throughout the 1990s and beginning of the 2000s, the UOC-MP tried to formulate a historical narrative that would emphasize the potency of Orthodoxy in the Ukrainian lands while also underlining its unity with the ROC. By contrast, the UOC-KP used an image of Kyivan Rus' to underline the particularity of Kyivan Orthodoxy, stressing the fact that the Kyiv Metropolitan was under the jurisdiction of the Patriarch of Constantinople from the Christianization of Rus' to the year 1686.

Importantly, all these interpretations of Kyivan Rus' put forward Orthodoxy as a central element in both the Russian and Ukrainian national identities. Thus, Orthodoxy is presented as the patrimonial religion in both nations. Furthermore, these interpretations are in line with the official state-sanctioned interpretations of the legacy of Kyiv Rus' in both Russia and in Ukraine, which go back to the nineteenth-century historiography of the Russian historian Mikhail Pogodin and the Ukrainian historian Mykhailo Hrushevskyi, who laid the foundations for the national historiographies of Russia and Ukraine, respectively (Berežnaja 2009; Plokhy 2017). While Pogodin's interpretation was in use during Soviet times, as it served the purpose of emphasizing the unity of the East Slavic people, Hrushevskyi's interpretation, which emphasized that

Building a patrimonial Church 95

Ukraine had taken a separate historical path to Russia, was regarded as nationalist. Everything changed when Ukraine became independent in 1991 and Hrushevskyi's conceptualization was used for the formation of a historical master narrative. In such a way, the development of the historical narrative by the Churches went hand in hand with the development of the national historical narrative in the 1990s. It can be assumed that the active redefinition of national history that took place in Ukrainian society from the beginning of the 1990s (Yurchuk 2017) contributed to the public's readiness to accept the new narratives that resulted from these redefinitions.

The events of 1988 that set the stage for a religious revival

The most important development in the history of the Soviet Union in the 1980s regarding its relationship with religion and the Church was the revival of the societal role performed by the ROC. The state ideology propagating atheism was failing. The Soviet authorities saw this clearly and began to turn their gaze towards religion and the Church. The perestroika policies that had been introduced since 1985 allowed some freedom, including religious freedom, which was of mutual benefit to the Church and believers. In 1988 Gorbachev decided to support the celebration of the Christianization of Kyivan Rus' at a Soviet governmental level, thereby turning the celebration into 'a national celebration sanctioned by the Soviet state' (Smolkin 2018, 1). As the historian Natalia Shlikhta aptly commented, the celebration of the millennium of the Christianization of Kyivan Rus in 1988 'marked the last "honeymoon" in relations between the declining Soviet regime and the Russian Orthodox Church considered by many to be the "state" Church in the USSR' (2016, 124). Owing to the massive celebrations of the millennial anniversary in 1988, the day acquired its public status and the Church became a visible actor on the Soviet (and even the international) scene. The celebrations of the 1000th anniversary of the Christianization of Rus' were used by the Soviet authorities to demonstrate the strength and unity of a Soviet Union that was in fact falling apart.

The celebration of the Christianization of Kyivan Rus' became a watershed moment when the state authorities de facto publicly announced their appreciation of the Church as a state-builder. Thus, when state officials met with Church officials in 29 April 1988, Gorbachev took up the question of history and of state–Church relations in his official address as follows:

> Our meeting is taking place on the eve of the 1000th anniversary of the introduction of Christianity in Rus', which has not only religious but also social and political meaning as, it is a big step in the centuries-long development of our Fatherland's history, its culture and Russian statehood.
> (Gorbachev 1988)[4]

Thus, Gorbachev stressed the role of the Church as a bearer of culture and carrier of the identity of Russian statehood as well as the unity of Church and

96 *Yuliya Yurchuk*

state at that particular moment. Interestingly, in his long speech Gorbachev simply referred to Rus', without mentioning Kyiv. Seeing as Gorbachev directly equated Russian statehood, Russian culture and Russian history with the Fatherland, one might wonder where all the other nations of this Soviet Fatherland had disappeared to. In effect, Orthodoxy was being presented as the 'patrimonial' religion and the ROC as the 'patrimonial Church' of the Russian state. The statement made by Pimen, Patriarch of Moscow and All Rus', at the same meeting resonates with the statements made by Gorbachev:

> [One thousand] years have passed since the Christianization of Rus'. The Church has always combined its service with care for the unity of our Fatherland, protection from foreign encroachments and the strengthening of justice in society, in order to develop spiritual culture.
>
> (Pimen 1988)

There is a pronounced emphasis here on the unity between the Church and the state. Moreover, the head of the ROC also mentioned perestroika and socialism when addressing Gorbachev directly:

> on behalf of the bishops, clergy, nuns, monks, laypersons of our Church and the citizens of our socialist Motherland, I am expressing to you, the architect of perestroika and the herald of new political thinking, our full support for this benignant process [perestroika]. We, the priests, are adamantly praying for the success of this process and trying to do everything possible to aid its development. . . . It [perestroika] is being enthusiastically welcomed by the Churches of the world, and we are supporting it by explaining its nature to religious people in terms of the renewal of life in our society.
>
> (Pimen 1988)

The Church's support for the state policies facilitating perestroika is not surprising as perestroika policies allowed a certain degree of religious freedom, which had not been possible before. This demonstration of mutual support also shows that the Church and the state needed each other at this critical moment in history when the Soviet state was starting to disintegrate. It was not only the Soviet state, but also the ROC, which was faced with an existential threat, as every attempt by a Soviet Republic – Ukraine included – to gain its independence was followed by attempts to build an independent Orthodox Church separated from the ROC (Denysenko 2018). The emphasis on unity was so prominent in 1988 precisely because it was this very unity that was under serious threat.

Spaces of celebration: Kyivan Rus' scattered and reassembled

The celebrations of the Christianization of Rus' took place in many of the Soviet Union's cities. The biggest celebrations were in Moscow and in Kyiv.

Building a patrimonial Church 97

Because the focus of my study is Ukraine, I will be discussing the celebrations in Kyiv. The commemorative events dedicated to the anniversary took place in June and July 1988. All the ceremonies and memorial events in Kyiv were conducted by Filaret, the Metropolitan of Kyiv and Halychyna. The celebration included an official opening and two special concerts at the Taras Shevchenko Theater of Opera and Ballet, the reading of a liturgy at St Volodymyr's Cathedral, another liturgy on Saint Volodymyr Hill and a visit to the sacred places of Kyiv Pechers'k Lavra (Kyiv Monastery of the Caves) and St Sophia's Cathedral. The celebrations therefore took place in both ecclesiastical and non-ecclesiastical settings, which reflects both the sacred and profane dimensions of these events. Especially interesting in this regard is the fact that the celebrations in Kyiv included a ceremony near the Grave of the Unknown Soldier and the laying down of a wreath at the Eternal Flame.

This ceremony is the most telling example of the Church's appropriation of profane space. The sites of memory of the Second World War are the most patriotically laden sites in Soviet mnemonic culture (Tumarkin 1994). Some priests taking part in the ceremony had several rows of military medals on their clerical gear. Such a demonstration of their belonging to the culture of memory of the Second World War shows the lengths to which the Church was prepared to go to present itself as a bearer of patriotic values through adherence to the patriotic memory of society. Through their presence at these sites, the clergy not only positioned the Church within the realm of secular power but also imbued this space with sacred meanings. At the same time, by visibly occupying secular spaces, the Church was presented with a chance to demonstrate its own power and promote Orthodoxy as a popular religion. The celebrations in Kyiv clearly showed that already, by 1988, the official discourse of the Church differed from what was being said in Moscow or in Kyiv. The head of the Orthodox Church in Ukraine could not use the same rhetoric of 'Russian statehood' and 'Russian culture' as was being used by Gorbachev and Pimen, Patriarch of Moscow and All Rus'. In the Ukrainian Soviet Socialist Republic, there were already demonstrations at that time demanding national autonomy, and these could not be ignored by the Church as it strived to increase its popular appeal. Consequently, during the celebrations in Kyiv, the emphasis was not so much placed on unity between the state and the Church as unity between the Church and the people:

> The Orthodox Church has never separated itself from its people. We see our goal as the renewal and spiritual growth of the citizens of our country. Under the conditions of perestroika, in the struggle for peace, the Church will also act together with its people.
>
> (Filaret 1988)

Therefore, Metropolitan Filaret directed his speech in Kyiv towards unity between the Church and the people. It should be stressed that Filaret, who had been heading the Church in Ukraine since 1966, was never supportive of

98 *Yuliya Yurchuk*

the idea of an independent Ukrainian Church. But when he was confronted at the end of the 1980s with the looming possibility of the collapse of the whole Soviet system, he tried to act in accordance with the changing situation. Thus, the Church was trying to tailor its official discourses to the local circumstances. It was a difficult task to maintain a balance between growing demands for independence in Ukraine and the more stringent efforts by Moscow to hold the union together.

The 1990s: the search for a new motherland and the radical politicization of religion

Moving on to 1998, when discussing the 1010th anniversary celebration of the Christianization of Kyiv Rus', it is important to remember that many important events happened after the celebrations in 1988. The Soviet Union collapsed, the Soviet republics became independent states, the old Orthodox Autocephalous Church returned to Ukraine after decades of operating from abroad and a new Orthodox Church even appeared on Ukrainian territory: the UOC-KP (its creation is discussed in the next paragraph). But prior to the formal collapse of the Soviet Union, the Ukrainian Orthodox Church was granted 'independence in management' at the council of ROC bishops that took place on 25–27 October 1990. This Church is usually referred to in subsequent literature as the UOC-MP. Filaret, the Metropolitan of Kyiv, continued to serve as the Kyiv exarch. It should be added that Filaret harboured ambitions of becoming the Patriarch of the ROC in 1990, after the death of Pimen, Patriarch of Moscow and All Rus'. But Filaret was passed over in favour of Aleksy II. Some scholars believe that it was the thwarting of Filaret's ambitions that made him turn to the idea of an independent Ukrainian Church (Denysenko 2018; Hovorun 2020).

When Ukraine became independent on 24 August 1991, Metropolitan Filaret sent a request to the ROC to grant the Ukrainian Church total independence. This request was denied. On 27–28 May 1992, the council of bishops of the UOC-MP convened in Kharkiv without Filaret and elected a new Metropolitan of Kyiv, Volodymyr (Sabodan). Filaret, who formally ceased to be Metropolitan of the Ukrainian Orthodox Church, did not accept the council's decision, and on 25 June 1992 he convened the All-Ukrainian Orthodox Council, at which the UAOC under Patriarch Mstyslav (Skrypnyk) merged with a group of bishops from the UOC-MP that remained loyal to Filaret.[5] At this council, they established the UOC-KP. Mstyslav became the patriarch of this Church. He died in 1993, and Volodymyr (Romaniuk) took over as his successor. When Patriarch Volodymyr died in 1995, Filaret was elected as the patriarch of the UOC-KP. It should be said that the UOC-KP was not recognized by the rest of the world's Orthodox Churches and so failed to meet the main requirement for the Church to be canonical. The question of canonicity was a trump card used against this Church from the moment of its creation. The question of the Ukrainian independent Church's canonicity was only solved in 2019, when the *tomos* was granted by Constantinople.

Building a patrimonial Church 99

Socially and politically, the year 1998 was a time of deep crisis in Ukraine. To stay in power, the incumbent president, Leonid Kuchma, tried to establish a so-called manual democracy – a regime with a strong centre that delivered dictates to all levels of administration under the guise of democratic procedures (elections, representation, etc.). Manual democracy also included the oppression of freedom of speech, which led to a proliferation of persecutions against journalists (D'Anieri 2010). Public frustration culminated in the 'Ukraine without Kuchma' campaign, and in general the whole period of Kuchma's second presidency (1998–2003) was characterized by political and social frictions, which led many commentators to present the country as a 'divided' society.

From the very beginning of the 1990s, the Churches had an unequal position in society. The UOC-MP's lineage with the ROC, which had continued right through the Soviet period until Ukraine became independent, meant that it was in a dominant position in terms of the number of parishes it served. Taking into account that the belief and doctrine of all the Orthodox Churches are basically the same, the Churches had to be creative to draw believers to their parishes and identify certain factors that would make them stand out from one another. Such drawing power could be found in the Churches' positioning vis-à-vis the nation and the state and, in particular, in their narratives about the past and the manner in which they imagined the nation's future.

While the UOC-KP was mainly using the narratives of national revival to present itself to society as the 'patrimonial Church' – an independent Church in an independent country – the UOC-MP had to find a more complex way to present itself as the 'patrimonial Church' in an independent country without erasing its links to the ROC. The historian Andriy Fert argued, when commenting on the memory of the UOC-MP, that the Church was faced with two primary tasks when it came to form its historical narrative: on the one hand, it had to justify its subordination to Moscow without losing the emphasis on the 'national' dimension and, on the other, it had to present itself to believers whose historical memories sometimes contradicted the Church's own (2020). Obviously, this was not an easy task. The UOC-MP tried to solve it by applying two narratives: one focused on the history of 'Orthodoxy in Ukraine' and the other concentrated on the history of 'the Ukrainian Church', as Fert explains (2020).

The question of canonicity was the main argument the UOC-MP used against the UOC-KP (Brusanowski 2016; Hovorun 2020), but the 'uncanonical' UOC-KP managed to draw a great deal of believers, and already by the mid-1990s it was second only to the UOC-MP in terms of the number of believers and parishes it served. With the Kyiv Patriarchate becoming stronger, the Moscow Patriarchate became more defensive. Each Church attempted to defend its exclusive position in Ukraine by applying a 'divide-and-rule' strategy. This is very well articulated in the discourses of the celebrations of the 1010th anniversary of the Christianization of Rus' in 1998. It was against the background of the deep political crisis that was described above that the celebrations of the 1010th anniversary of the Christianization of Kyivan Rus' took place.

The anniversary also showed the divergent paths taken by the UOC-MP and the ROC in dealing with the specific political situation in Ukraine. It revealed that there were limits to the UOC-MP's dependency on the ROC and showed how much autonomy had been claimed by Metropolitan Volodymyr, head of the UOC-MP. The ROC presented Ukraine as a deeply split country. Drawing on the Huntingtonian notion of a civilizational divide running through Kyiv and splitting the world into Orthodoxy and Catholicism (Huntington 1996), the Patriarch of Moscow and All Rus' Aleksy II reiterated the image of Western Ukraine as a bedrock of hostility, exhibited not only by the Catholic Church but also by the Kyiv Patriarchate:

> At present, the people of Ukraine are split. There are a few who are in favour of the autocephaly of the Ukrainian Church, but there are also many who oppose it, especially in the eastern, northern and southern regions of Ukraine. The ecclesiastical term 'autocephaly' is considered by many who do not know the history of the Church or its canons to be a phenomenon that is connected to national independence. Such a reversal of the Orthodox essence of the Church through the question of national identity leads to severe and sometimes tragic consequences. Under such circumstances, a premature autocephaly leads to new schisms.
>
> (Aleksy 1998)

Therefore, in the view of the head of the ROC, the split was not only the consequence of tensions between people of opposing viewpoints. The split was presented as the reason for the impossibility of the Ukrainian Church ever being granted autocephaly. The emphasis on Orthodoxy as a part of national identity is prominent here. The Patriarch of Moscow underlined that it was erroneous to merge Orthodoxy with national identity in Ukraine. Metropolitan Volodymyr of the UOC-MP reiterated the stance that Ukraine was a split country but also mentioned the role of the Church in uniting society:

> Our common grief is that Orthodoxy in Ukraine is split. It is a large problem that pains us all. Our Church takes, and will take, an exclusively Orthodox position. The initiators of the schism and those who sympathize with them are not our enemies. They are our prodigal brothers who have lost their path and we pray for them to find a way back to truth with the help of God.
>
> (Volodymyr 1998)

By emphasizing the readiness of the Church to accept back the 'prodigal brothers', Metropolitan Volodymyr of the UOC-MP positions himself and his Church as a father who is ready to forgive and embrace those who have 'lost their path'. For him, it is also an indisputable fact that there is only one authentic patrimonial Orthodox Church in Ukraine and that is the UOC-MP, while the others are the 'initiators of the schism'. Furthermore, the UOC-MP is

Building a patrimonial Church   101

constructed as a patrimonial Church with strong links to its Mother Church in Moscow, which unites it with the other East Slavic peoples incorporated into the construction of the world's Orthodoxy.

When addressing the celebrations of 1998 in his speeches, Filaret, the head of the UOC-KP, referred to the Christianization of Kyivan Rus' as 'a powerful impetus for the development of new spirituality, the spirituality of a new testament' in Ukraine (Filaret 1998). Moreover, he also used the opportunity presented by the anniversary to speak about the prospect of the Ukrainian Orthodox Church being granted the autocephaly that would result from the unification of all the Orthodox churches in Ukraine:

> Is it impossible? . . . Yes. But who would have thought in the 1930s that St. Michael's Cathedral, which was destroyed at the time, would be rebuilt? An even more striking example is the historic collapse of the Soviet Union and blessed bloodless creation of the independent Ukraine. No long-term forecasts could have foreseen such events; there seemed to be no reasons.
>
> (Filaret 1998)

Clearly, the collapse of the Soviet Union and creation of the independent Ukraine are presented as deeds of God that were virtually impossible yet still happened. The same hopes are cherished for the unification of the Churches. But Filaret saw Metropolitan Volodymyr of the UOC-MP as too dependent on Russia, which excluded any possibility of mutual dialogue about a potential unification (suffice to say that it was only the UOC-KP under his own leadership that Filaret saw as a platform for such a unification): 'I do not think that we will start any negotiations with Metropolitan Volodymyr because he is completely dependent on Moscow and they know there that our dialogue could lead to the unification of the Ukrainian Church' (Filaret 1998).

Clearly, the UOC-KP had also adopted a divide-and-rule strategy and stressed that the division within the country had been caused by external powers (i.e. Russia). Whereas opponents of the UOC-KP were using its non-canonical status as the main argument against its legitimacy, the UOC-KP was using the canonical status of the UOC-MP when accusing it of serving a foreign power and its own non-canonical status as evidence of its independence and loyalty to the Ukrainian people alone. These arguments could not be reconciled, and each Church continued to celebrate the Christianization of Kyivan Rus' separately.

It should be stressed that throughout the 1990s and up to 2014, when the military conflict with Russia began, the state officials in Ukraine supported all the Churches and denominations without promoting any one particular Church. In such a climate of political support, the Churches had freedom of self-representation. Each Church used this opportunity to present itself to the public as a patrimonial Church. The UOC-MP presented itself as the 'patrimonial Church' with close ties to its 'Mother Church' in Russia, constructing, in such a way, a transnational imagined religious community of believers united

102 Yuliya Yurchuk

by faith and common history and values. By contrast, the UOC-KP presented itself as the 'patrimonial Church' in an independent country and even began constructing a narrative of its own specific spirituality.

The year 2008: the turbulence continues

The whole first decade of the 2000s in Ukraine was characterized by contestation between the Orthodox Churches that was even fiercer than in previous years. In 2004, as a result of mass protests against the rigged election that are commonly named the Orange Revolution (Wilson 2005), Victor Yushchenko became the third president of Ukraine. In his presidential campaign, Yushchenko promised to establish an independent and united Ukrainian Orthodox Church.

When the 1020th anniversary was approaching, Yushchenko issued a decree titled 'On the Celebration of the Christianization of Rus'-Ukraine'. The decree stated that a day of celebration was to be established to reflect 'the meaning of Orthodox traditions in the history and development of Ukrainian society' (Yushchenko 2008). The decree was a response to requirements from all three Orthodox Churches of Ukraine to establish such a special commemorative day. Thus 28 July – the Day of Volodymyr the Great, the Prince who baptized Rus' – became the official day for such a commemoration (Yushchenko 2008). In Russia, 28 July was also incorporated into the state calendar as the Day of the Christianization of Rus', two years later, in 2010. The ROC was also the initiator of this official recognition of the date. In both cases, by satisfying their Churches' requirements, the two states had demonstrated their support and underlined the significance of Orthodoxy in state-building both in Ukraine and Russia. Their support led to the patrimonial status of the Orthodoxy becoming institutionalized on a state level.

The 1020th anniversary of the Christianization of Kyivan Rus' was used by the Churches and state authorities in Ukraine as an opportunity to unify all the Orthodox churches. In 2008 Viktor Yushchenko had a meeting in Kyiv with the Ecumenical Patriarch of Constantinople Bartholomew I about the ongoing anniversary, at which they did indeed discuss the prospect of the Church gaining its independence. Although autocephaly was not granted to the Ukrainian church, it became clear that the ecumenical patriarch did not oppose the possibility of autocephaly being granted in the future when he confirmed Constantinople's historical rights in Ukraine and cast doubt on the idea that Moscow held the same rights there (Bartholomew 2008).

The UOC-MP promoted itself as a platform for a unification of the Orthodox Churches that would potentially lead to autocephaly (Hovorun 2020), but the ROC leadership did not support the idea of Ukrainian autocephaly. After 2008, there was a clear divergence on the question of autocephaly that affected relations between the ROC and the UOC-MP as well as relations inside the UOC-MP itself. By 2008, groups had formed around, on the one hand, Metropolitan Volodymyr, who supported the autocephaly, and on the other, around those in the UOC-MP who opposed that idea (Hovorun 2020; Richters 2013;

Suslov 2016). In response to the ecumenical patriarch's plans to visit the Ukrainian capital to celebrate the anniversary in 2008, the ROC convened a special synodal meeting on 24–29 June, where the special decree on unity was signed by all the metropolitans of the Churches under the jurisdiction of the ROC. Metropolitan Volodymyr of the UOC-MP also signed this decree, thereby demonstrating his view that even if autocephaly was to be granted to the Ukrainian Church, it should be in communion with the Moscow Patriarch.

The most significant events connected to the celebration in Kyiv in 2008 were the visits, in July of that year, of both the Patriarch of Constantinople Bartholomew I and Patriarch Aleksy II of the ROC. Aleksy II was in poor health, so it was a challenging endeavour for him to make a trip to Ukraine, but in the end he did come to Kyiv. He described his visit as a necessity, claiming that if he had not come, 'the Patriarch of Constantinople would have led the ceremony and taken all the responsibility on himself. . . . The mass media would have shown that Moscow has abandoned [the Orthodox believers in Ukraine]' (Aleksy 2008). In fact, the celebration was still led anyway by the Patriarch of Constantinople, who held a liturgy on 27 July 2008 on Saint Volodymyr Hill, a symbolic place where the celebration in 1988 had also been held.

The main stance reiterated by Aleksy in Kyiv was in line with the rhetoric of 1998. He stressed the split within Ukraine and the unity of all the Orthodox people. In his view, the split in Ukraine was not between people but between the state and the people: 'It [the unity of all the Orthodox people] may not be very pleasing for the authorities. This unity among God's people has shown once again with whom the people are' (Aleksy 2008).

Aleksy also commented on what he regarded as Yushchenko's political weakness: 'Having lost political support, he thought that he is an equal to Prince Vladimir, who can unite something which it is absolutely not possible to unite' (Aleksy 2008), by which he meant all the Orthodox Churches in Ukraine. Aleksy II time and again stressed the unity of all the Slavic peoples: Russians, Ukrainians and Belarusians (Aleksy 2008). Therefore, whereas the UOC-MP, in the person of Metropolitan Volodymyr, envisaged possible scenarios in which the UOC-MP would serve as a platform for the unification of all the Churches, the head of the ROC refused to accept such a possibility. Interestingly, the ROC's position remained unchanged despite changes of government in Kyiv. Although Kuchma and Yushchenko positioned themselves differently with regard to nation- and state-building in Ukraine, the position of the ROC to the questions of Ukrainian autocephaly remained the same whoever was in power. Thus, Metropolitan Volodymyr's efforts, undertaken since the early 1990s, to present the UOC-MP as the patrimonial Church had to strike a balance between, on the one hand, the state and the society the Church was serving and, on the other, the Mother Church in Moscow on which it formally depended. In this sense, the UOC-KP was in an easier position, in which its historical narrative coincided with the historical narrative of the independent Ukraine, the national revival was connected to a religious revival, and church independence was associated with national independence.

2018: a *tomos* as a gift for the 1030th anniversary?

There are many similarities but also many significant differences between the years 2008 and 2018. The similarities lie within the sphere of the political will of the incumbent presidents – Viktor Yushchenko and Petro Poroshenko, respectively – to gain independence for the Ukrainian Orthodox Church. The main differences are, of course, the situation in the country in general and the change of leadership in the UOC-MP. In 2014 Metropolitan Volodymr died and a new metropolitan, Onufrii, was installed as the head of the UOC-MP. He was a representative of the group in the UOC-MP that opposed the view that an independent Ukrainian Orthodox Church was a possibility. In spring 2014 Russia annexed Crimea and from the summer of the same year, Ukraine was in a military conflict with Russia-supported separatists in the eastern part of the country (Grant 2015; Wilson 2014; Yekelchyk 2015). The role of religion in this conflict is beyond this study, but it is important to mention that Orthodoxy has been used by separatist groups and the Russian paramilitary as part of the ideology they use to justify the war against the Ukrainians (Krawchuk and Bremer 2016; Clark and Vovk 2020; Knorre 2019). The long-lasting silence on the war in Donbas from UOC-MP officials, the use of Orthodoxy in the concept of the 'Russian world' (Suslov 2016; Hovorun 2016), the creation of the Russian Orthodox Army in Donbas, the persecutions of the believers of other religions and confessions in the territories not controlled by the Ukrainian government (Carras 2015; Gaufman 2020; Kokhan 2016; Kozlovsky 2020; Institute for Religious Freedom 2014) and the refusal of some ROC-MP priests to conduct funeral services for Ukrainian soldiers killed in the War in Donbas have all drawn the sympathies of many believers away from the Moscow Patriarchate. The main approach taken by the officials of the UOC-MP that the 'Church is outside of politics principle' (Shestopalets 2019, 46) did not seem to be popular among the population, which resulted in a decrease in the number of people associating themselves with the UOC-MP.

The weakening of the UOC-MP's position and strengthening of the Ukrainian authorities' political will created new possibilities for the creation of an independent Ukrainian Orthodox Church. It was the Church's independence that dominated preparations for and discussions on the 1030th anniversary of the Christianization of Kyiv Rus'. President Petro Poroshenko made autocephaly one of the targets in his political agenda. On several occasions, he promised to gain independence for the Church by celebrating the 1030th anniversary of the Christianization of Rus'. Being a churchgoer affiliated to the Moscow Patriarchate, Poroshenko envisaged that the new independent Church would be created on the foundation of all the Orthodox Churches in Ukraine. But for the UOC-MP this was not a solution, as the question of autocephaly was not on the agenda of the Church under the leadership of the new Metropolitan Onufrii. Thus, if in 1998 it was the UOC-KP that was categorically against unification, by 2018 it was the UOC-MP that opposed it.

The conflict between the state and the main Orthodox churches in Ukraine culminated in 2016 when, for the first time in post-independence Ukrainian history, the head of state openly condemned a Church and accused it of loyalty to a foreign power. This culmination took place during the celebration of the 1028th anniversary of the Christianization of Kyiv Rus'. Although this was not the 1030th anniversary, which was more 'festive', it is worth pausing at this juncture to examine this anniversary in more detail.

The celebrations of the anniversary by both Churches were divided in time. With the UOC-KP receiving greater support from the state, the UOC-MP directed its efforts at using the anniversary to demonstrate that despite the lack of support it received from the state, it enjoyed vast support from believers. The Moscow Patriarchate organized a procession that passed through several Ukrainian cities and concluded with the reading of the liturgy on Saint Volodymyr Hill in Kyiv on 27 July. The Kyiv Patriarchate held a liturgy at the same place on 28 July. President Poroshenko joined the UOC-KP's celebration. At this, he criticized the UOC-MP and argued that their procession was a provocation undertaken on behalf of the 'Russian world'. Poroshenko stated:

> We will not indifferently stand aside and watch how a foreign state is intruding in our church affairs, how it tries to use the feelings of some Ukrainian Orthodox believers to further its own interests. . . . Two and a half years ago, Moscow started a war against golden-domed Kyiv. This [the war] should be called by its name.
>
> (Poroshenko 2016)

In such a way, Poroshenko criticized the UOC-MP's position on the conflict. This led to the anniversary in 2016 becoming a watershed moment that severed the history of contemporary Ukraine into 'before' and 'after' periods. Whereas before 2016 the main discourse of the political authorities was based on acceptance of the coexistence of all the Churches, after that year the state openly declared that the UOC-MP was regarded as part of the ROC and the Russian state ideology of the 'Russian world'. This constituted de facto state support being granted to only one Church, which was regarded as the 'patrimonial Church', at the expense of another Church, which was presented as an enemy.

When the celebrations of the 1030th anniversary of Christianization of Kyivan Rus' took place, the question of autocephaly was presented as a fait accompli. It was only a matter of a couple of months before the document granting independence was handed to the head of the new Ukrainian Orthodox Church on 5 January 2019. The core of the independent Church was made up of the UOC-KP, the UAOC and just a couple of bishops from the UOC-MP who joined them. The newly established Church received a new metropolitan, Epiphanius I (b. 1979), the representative of a new generation of the UOC-KP, who had received his education at UOC-KP institutions (this is actually the first generation of Orthodox clergy to receive their education at academic institutions established by the UOC-KP). Filaret, who had, in one way or another, been part of the leadership of the Orthodox Church in Ukraine since 1966, aligning his policies and behaviour in response to societal and political

106 Yuliya Yurchuk

changes, lost his power.[6] A new page in the church history of Ukraine was turned. That history is already engulfed in conflicts and tensions, but those are far beyond the scope of the research upon which this chapter is based.

Conclusions

My analysis of the official memory policies of the two main Orthodox churches in Ukraine from 1988 to 2018 has led me to conclude that each of these Churches used the past to present itself as the 'patrimonial Church', namely, the most authentic and historically justified Church for the Ukrainian nation. I have called such a process of Church-building a 'patrimonializing process'. This process goes hand in hand in Ukraine with nation- and state-building. The official discourses of the past discussed above, and in particular those relating to the Christianization of Kyivan Rus', show how each Church presented its own views on the nation and its geopolitical place in the world. Each Church had to respond to ever-changing political and societal circumstances. Often the churches aligned themselves with different political actors and constructed different historical narratives to both address and shape separate communities of believers. While the UOC-MP stressed the unity of the Slavic peoples and tensions inside the Ukrainian state, the UOC-KP stressed the unity of the people in Ukraine and underlined the differences between Ukraine and Russia. As the Churches share one religion, narratives of the past became the main resource for formulating differences between them.

My study demonstrates that within a context in which there is one majority religion that is represented by different Churches transmitting different messages about the past, separate religious traditions are created. These traditions appeal to different communities. The case analyzed above shows that the 'legitimizing' potential of religion was often not so much used by the Churches to consolidate the wider community as to create smaller communities. Consequently, in Ukraine, rather than nurturing 'the dream of a continuing shared identity able to survive the accelerating pace of change', a description that Hervieu-Léger applied to another context (2015, 20), the patrimonial religion represented by the conflicting Churches – Orthodoxy – actually perpetuated the differences born out of such an accelerating pace of change that started with perestroika and has continued to the present.

Notes

1 For more on the question of authenticity, national identity and religion, see Raudvere, Stala, and Stauning Willert 2012.
2 According to a Razumkov Center survey undertaken in 2013, 27.7% responded that they belonged to the Moscow Patriarchate and 25.9% to the Kyiv Patriarchate (Razumkov 2013, 26). Cf. respective figures of 12.8% and 28.7% from 2018 (Razumkov 2018).
3 Moskovskii lubopytnyi mesiatseslov na 1776 god (Pechatan pri Moskovskom Universitete, 1776). The author is grateful to Andreas Schönle for his generous sharing of this information with her.
4 All translations from Russian and Ukrainian in this chapter are made by the author.

5 Not all the attendees of the UAOC agreed to unite with Filaret's group in 1992. The participants that did not form the UOC-KP continued as the UAOC and elected a new Patriarch, Dmytro (Yarema), in 1993. When he died in 2000, the Church decided not to elect a new patriarch, establishing a metropolitan instead. Currently, this Church is headed by Metropolitan Makarii (Maletych). For more, see Denysenko 2018; Hovorun 2020.

6 Patriarch Filaret was a target of criticism for many, even believers who belonged to the UOC-KP. His way of managing the Church according to the politics of the moment was often regarded as a reflection of his own ambitions for power, which in turn caused him to change his principles and behaviour. Suffice to mention that during the period of Soviet rule, Filaret fiercely opposed any steps towards the Ukrainization of the Church, including the use of the Ukrainian language in services (Denysenko 2018; Hovorun 2020).

References

Agadjanian, Alexander. 2017. "Tradition, Morality and Community: Elaborating Orthodox Identity in Putin's Russia." *Religion, State & Society* 45 (1): 39–60. https://doi.org/10.108 0/09637494.2016.1272893.

Aleksy. 1998. "Relihiia I suspil'stvo." *Den* (23) (February 7): 4.

Aleksy. 2008. "Moskva. Patriarh Aleksii: Vzvesiv vse ya reshyl yehat v Kiev." *Pravoslavie v Ukraine*, December 12. Accessed May 21, 2020. http://arhiv.orthodoxy.org.ua/uk/tserk-ovni_hroniki/2008/12/12/21058.html.

Bartholomew. 2008. "Cited in: Ecumenical Patriarch Bartholomew Delivers Speech to the Ukrainian Nation During 1020th baptismal anniversary of Kiev-Rus." *Order of Saint Andrew the Apostle.* July 26. Accessed November 3, 2021. https://www.archons. org/-/ecumenical-patriarch-bartholomew-delivers-speech-to-the-ukrainian-nation-during-1020th-baptismal-anniversary-of-kiev-russia

Berežnaja, Lilija. 2009. "Der Kiewer Kirchenstreit." *Osteuropa* 59 (6): 171–88.

Brik, Tymofii. 2019. "When Church Competition Matters? Intra-doctrinal Competition in Ukraine, 1992–2012." *Sociology of Religion* 80 (1): 45–82. https://doi.org/10.1093/ socrel/sry005.

Bogumił, Zuzanna. 2018. *Gulag Memories: The Rediscovery and Commemoration of Russia's Repressive Past.* New York: Berghahn Books.

Brüning, Alfons. 2016. "Orthodox Autocephaly in Ukraine: The Historical Dimension." In *Churches in the Ukrainian Crisis*, edited by Andrii Krawchuk and Thomas Bremer. New York: Palgrave Macmillan, 79–102.

Brusanowski, Paul. 2016. "Autocephaly in Ukraine: The Canonical Dimension." In *Churches in the Ukrainian Crisis*, edited by Andrii Krawchuk and Thomas Bremer. New York: Palgrave Macmillan, 47–78.

Burgess, John P. 2017. *Holy Rus': The Rebirth of Orthodoxy in the New Russia.* New Haven, CT: Yale University Press.

Carras, Iannis. 2015. "Can Ukraine's Divided Church Help Heal the Divided Country." *Open Democracy*, January 15. Accessed October 5, 2019. www.opendemocracy.net/en/ odr/can-ukraines-divided-church-help-heal-divided-country/.

Clark, Elizabeth A., and Dmytro Vovk. 2020. *Religion during the Russian-Ukrainian Conflict.* New York: Routledge.

D'Anieri, Paul. 2010. *Orange Revolution and Aftermath: Mobilization, Apathy, and the State in Ukraine.* Baltimore: Johns Hopkins University Press.

Davie, Grace. 2000. *Religion in Modern Europe: A Memory Mutates.* Oxford: Oxford University Press.

———. 2002. *Europe, the Exceptional Case: Parameters of Faith in the Modern World.* Darton: Longman & Todd.

Democratic Initiative Foundation. 2015. "Bilshist' naselennia Ukrainy vidnosyt sebe perevazhno do Pravoslavnoii Tserkvy Kyivs'koho Patriarhatu." Accessed May 18, 2020. https://dif.org.ua/article/bilshist-naselennya-ukraini-vidnosit-sebe-perevazhno-do-pravoslavnoi-tserkvi-kiivskogo-patriarkhatu.

Denysenko, Nicholas E. 2018. *The Orthodox Church in Ukraine. A Century of Separation.* DeKalb: Northern Illinois University Press.

Elsner, Regina. 2018. *Die Russische Orthodoxe Kirche vor der Herausforderung Moderne. Historische Wegmarken und theologische Optionen im Spannungsfeld von Einheit und Vielfalt.* Wurzburg: Echter.

Fert, Andriy. 2020. "Equivocal Memory: What Does the Ukrainian Orthodox Church of the Moscow Patriarchate Remember?" In *Religion During the Russian-Ukrainian Conflict*, edited by Elizabeth A. Clark and Dmytro Vovk, 192–210. New York: Routledge.

Filaret. 1988. "Z nahody 1000-littia hreshchennia Rusi." *Literaturna Ukraina* (25) (June 19).

Filaret. 1998. "Relihia i suspil'stvo", Den' (116) (21 June).

Gaufman, Elizaveta. 2020. "Come All ye Faithful to the Russian World: Governmental and Grassroots Spiritual Discourse in the Battle Over Ukraine." In *Religion During the Russian-Ukrainian Conflict*, edited Elizabeth A. Clark and Dmytro Vovk, 54–68. New York: Routledge.

Gorbachev, Mikhail. 1988. *Pravda* (121 (25473), April 30).

Grant, Thomas. 2015. *Aggression Against Ukraine: Territory, Responsibility, and International Law.* New York: Palgrave Macmillan.

Hervieu-Léger, Daniele. 2000. *Religion as a Chain of Memory.* (Translated from *La religion pour mémoire* by Simon Lee.). New Brunswick, NJ: Rutgers University Press.

———. 2015. "Religion as Grammar of Memory: Reflections on the Comparison Between Britain and France." In *Modernity, Memory, and Mutations: Grace Davie and the Study of Religion*, edited by Abby Day and Mia Lövheim. London: Routledge.

Hovorun, Cyril. 2016. "Interpreting the 'Russian World'." In *Churches in the Ukrainian Crisis*, edited by Andrii Krawchuk and Thomas Bremer, 163–72. New York: Palgrave Macmillan.

———. 2020. "The Cause of Ukrainian Autocephaly." In *Religion During the Russian-Ukrainian Conflict*, edited Elizabeth A. Clark and Dmytro Vovk, 180–91. New York: Routledge.

Huntington, Samuel. 1996. *The Clash of Civilizations and the Remaking of World Order.* New York: Simon & Schuster.

Institute for Religious Freedom. 2014. *Chronicle of Terror: Religious Persecution by Pro-Russian Militants in East Ukraine*, August 19. Accessed April 30, 2019. www.irf.in.ua/eng/index.php?option=com_content&view=article&id=421:1&catid=34:ua&Itemid=61.

Knorre, Boris. 2019. "The Culture of War and Militarization Within Political Orthodoxy in the Post-Soviet Region." In *Religion, Expression, and Patriotism in Russia: Essays on Post-Soviet Society and the State*, edited by Sanna Turoma, Kaarina Aitamurto and Slobodanka Vladiv-Glover, 25–56. Stuttgart: Ibidem.

Kokhan, Natalia. 2016. "Shaping Ukrainian Identity: The Churches in Socio-Political Crisis." In *Churches in the Ukrainian Crisis*, edited by Andrii Krawchuk and Thomas Bremer, 105–22. New York: Palgrave Macmillan.

Kozlovsky, Ihor. 2020. "The Orthodox Identification of Militants Is an Element of Their Understanding of the *Russkiy mir*." Interview in *Religion during the Russian-Ukrainian Conflict*, edited Elizabeth A. Clark and Dmytro Vovk, 213–18. New York: Routledge.

Krawchuk, Andrii. 2016. "Redefining Orthodox Identity in Ukraine After Euromaidan." In *Churches in the Ukrainian Crisis*, edited by Andrii Krawchuk and Thomas Bremer, 175–202. New York: Palgrave Macmillan.

Krawchuk, Andrii, and Thomas Bremer. 2016. *Churches in the Ukrainian Crisis*. New York: Palgrave Macmillan.

Pankhurst, Jerry G. 2020. "History, Ecclesiology, Canonicity, and Power: Ukrainian and Russian Orthodoxy After the Euromaidan." In *Religion During the Russian-Ukrainian Conflict*, edited Elizabeth A. Clark and Dmytro Vovk, 159–79. New York: Routledge.

Pimen. 1988. *Pravda* (121) (25473, 30 April 30).

Plokhy Serhii. 2017. *Lost Kingdom: The Quest for Empire and the Making of the Russian Nation*. New York: Basic Books.

Plokhy, Serhii. 2015. *The Gates of Europe: A History of Ukraine*. New York: Basic Books.

Plokhy, Serhii, and Frank E. Sysyn. 2003. *Religion and Nation in Modern Ukraine*. Edmonton: CIUS Press.

Poroshenko, Petro. 2016. Cited in Chervonenko, Vitalii. "Poroshenko na shliakhu vid Moskovskoho patriarkhatu." *BBC Ukraine*. Accessed October 5, 2019. www.bbc.com/ukrainian/society/2016/07/160712_church_orthodox_procession_vc.

Raudvere, Catharina, Krzysztof Stala, and Trine Stauning Willert. 2012. *Rethinking the Space for Religion: New Actors in Central and Southeast Europe on Religion, Authenticity and Belonging*. Lund: Nordic Academic Press.

Razumkov Center. 2013. *Relihiia I vlada v Ukraiini: problem vzaiemovidnosyn*. Accessed June 5, 2020. www.irs.in.ua/files/publications/2013.04.23_Razumkov_Center__Religion_and_Authority_irs.in.ua.pdf.

———. 2018. *Report on Religion in Ukraine*. Accessed May 18, 2020. http://razumkov.org.ua/uploads/article/2018_Religiya.pdf.

Richters, Katja. 2013. *The Post-Soviet Russian Orthodox Church: Politics, Culture and Greater Russia*. London: Routledge.

Shestopalets, Denys. 2019. "The Ukrainian Orthodox Church of the Moscow Patriarchate, The State and The Russian-Ukrainian Crisis, 2014–2018." *Politics, Religion & Ideology* 20 (1): 42–63.

Shlikhta, Natalia. 2016. "Eastern Christian Churches between State and Society: An Overview of the Religious Landscape in Ukraine (1989–2014)." *Kyiv Mohyla Humanities Journal* 3 (3): 123–42.

Smolkin, Victoria. 2018. *A Sacred Space Is Never Empty: A History of Soviet Atheism*. Princeton, CT: Princeton University Press.

Suslov, Mikhail. 2014. "'Holy Rus': The Geopolitical Imagination of the Contemporary Russian Orthodox Church." *Russian Politics and Law* 52 (3): 67–86.

———. 2016. "The Russian Orthodox Church and the Crisis in Ukraine." In *Churches in the Ukrainian Crisis*, edited by Andrii Krawchuk and Thomas Bremer, 133–62. New York: Palgrave Macmillan.

———. 2019. "The Russian Orthodox Church in Search of the Cultural Canon." In *Religion, Expression, and Patriotism in Russia: Essays on Post-Soviet Society and the State*, edited by Sanna Turoma, Kaarina Aitamurto and Slobodanka Vladiv-Glover, 57–92. Stuttgart: Ibidem.

Tumarkin, Nina. 1994. *The Living and the Dead: The Rise and Fall of the Cult of World War II in Russia*. New York: Basic Books.

Turoma, Sanna, and Kaarina Aitamurto. 2019. "Contesting Cultural and Religious Identities in Russia: An Introduction." In *Religion, Expression, and Patriotism in Russia: Essays on Post-Soviet Society and the State*, edited by Sanna Turoma, Kaarina Aitamurto and Slobodanka Vladiv-Glover, 7–24. Stuttgart: Ibidem.

Volodymyr. 1998. "Rozkolote pravoslavia – nash spilnui bil." *Ukraina I svit siohodni* (2) (August 22–28): 10–11.

110 *Yuliya Yurchuk*

Wanner, Catherine. 2018. "Public Religions After Socialism: Redefining Norms of Difference." In *Religion, State & Society* 46 (2): 88–95. https://doi.org/10.1080/09637494.2018.1465245.

Wawrzonek, Michal. 2015. *Religion and Politics in Ukraine: The Orthodox and Greek Catholic Churches as Elements of Ukraine's Political System*. Cambridge: Cambridge Scholars.

Wilson, Andrew. 2014. *Ukraine Crisis: What It Means for the West*. New Haven, CT: Yale University Press.

———. 2005. *Ukraine's Orange Revolution*. New Haven, CT: Yale University Press.

Yekelchyk, Serhy. 2015. *The Conflict in Ukraine: What Everyone Needs to Know*. Oxford: Oxford University Press.

Yurchuk, Yuliya. 2017. "Reclaiming the Past, Confronting the Past: OUN-UPA Memory Politics and Nation-Building in Ukraine (1991–2016)." In *War and Memory in Russia, Ukraine, and Belarus*, edited by Julie Fedor, Markku Kangaspuro, Jussi Lassila and Tatiana Zhurzhenko, 107–37. New York: Palgrave Macmillan.

Yushchenko, Viktor. 2008. "Pro Den Khreshchennia Kyiivs'koii Rusi-Ukraiiny." In *Zakonodavstvo Ukraiiny*. Accessed May 18, 2020. https://zakon.rada.gov.ua/laws/show/668/2008.

6 'God is in truth, not in power!'

The re-militarization of the cult of St Alexander Nevsky in contemporary Russian cultural memory

Liliya Berezhnaya

On 10 September 2019, Patriarch Kirill of Moscow and All Russia participated in a meeting of the organizational committee responsible for preparing celebrations for the 800th anniversary of Alexander Nevsky's birth. The meeting took place at the Cathedral of Christ the Saviour in Moscow. In his speech, the patriarch emphasized Prince Alexander's military and diplomatic achievements while highlighting his virtues as a wise ruler and pious Christian. He made clear that St Alexander's example should inspire 'young people to live according to God's Commandments and help to promote patriotic education and spread the moral ideals of love and mercy among them' ('Vystupleniye' 2019).[1]

In these and many other recent official speeches and ceremonies, St Alexander Nevsky (1221–63; canonized in the Russian Orthodox Church in 1547; feast days 23 November and 30 August) is presented as a heavenly defender of Russia. Apart from that, he is not only a patron saint of Saint Petersburg, the Russian diplomatic corps and the Russian army's ground troops and marines, but also of Russia's Federal Security Service (FSB). His cult apparently demonstrates not only religious but also political and military features. In fact, Nevsky is one of a few canonized rulers in Russian history who fulfil the criteria for an all-Russian saintly hero. The commemoration of St Alexander Nevsky is, to quote Frithjof Benjamin Schenk, 'a crystallization point of collective memory and identity' (Schenk 2004, 13). His opinion is also shared by Mariëlle Wijermars, who affirms that

> Nevskii has come to represent a new strand of state patriotism that carries an Orthodox overtone. His memory is connected to an understanding of Russia as a civilisational stronghold within a globalising and secularising world, and Orthodox Russians as benevolent *primi inter pares* within the Russian state.
>
> (Wijermars 2018, 119)

DOI: 10.4324/9781003264750-8

112   *Liliya Berezhnaya*

Yuriy Krivosheev and Roman Sokolov, two Russian historians of Nevsky's heritage, go even further, asserting that prevailing attitudes to the phenomenon of St Alexander can be used as 'a litmus test for major changes' in Russian society (Krivosheev and Sokolov 2013, 53; Krivosheev and Sokolov 2009).

St Alexander Nevsky's prominent role in Russian cultural memory is determined by his image as an outstanding military commander and ideal ruler whose figure embodies continuities in Russian history and a pursuit for a 'golden age'. In what follows, I set out to investigate how the image of St Alexander Nevsky has transformed in Russian cultural memory over the course of the past decade. I argue that St Alexander Nevsky is one of a number of religious *lieux de mémoire* in post-Soviet Russia that not only symbolize the sacralized politics of memory but also the patriotization of this politics and the general Russian anti-Western geopolitical orientation. What is more, the image of St Alexander Nevsky as a warrior saint has recently undergone re-militarization connected with the pluralization of his memories on regional, national and international levels.

St Alexander Nevsky as a military saint

Alexander Nevsky served as Prince of Novgorod, Grand Prince of Kyiv and Grand Prince of Vladimir. Shortly before his death, he took monastic orders under the name Alexiy. This was one of the earliest such examples involving local ruling dynasties (Sirenov 2017, 369). As Prince and ruler, Alexander halted the eastward drive of the Germans and Swedes. He also maintained close relations with the powerful Golden Horde while also agreeing to pay them tribute, thus forestalling the imposition of Mongol rule over Kyivan Rus'. His defeat of a Swedish invasion in the North at the confluence of the Rivers Izhora and Neva (1240) won him the name Nevsky. Prince Alexander is also known for his victory over the Teutonic Knights who had invaded Kyivan Rus's northern territories. Alexander defeated the Knights in the famous 'Battle on the Ice' (1242) on a narrow channel linking Lakes Chud (Peipus) and Pskov.

Historians debate the scale of Prince Alexander's personal contribution to these military events as well his impact upon Kyivan Rus's relations with the Golden Horde (Torkunov, Kudryavtsev, and Ukolova 2010; Pronina 2008). There is also little unanimity between historical interpretations of Alexander's confrontations with his brother Andrey when they were fighting for control of the princely throne (Schenk 2004; Nazarenko and Kvilvidze 2000).

However, practically no historians manage to avoid mentioning a single extract from St Alexander's *Vita*. This description of Prince Alexander's earthly life and posthumous miracles was composed shortly after his death and has existed in numerous editions (Lurye 1997; Begunov 1995; Isoaho 2006). The author of the first edition was most probably a clergyman from the Theotokos Nativity Monastery in Vladimir (where St Alexander was buried) who came from the inner circle of Metropolitan Kirill of Kyiv (1250–81). It is supposed that the chronicler himself and/or Metropolitan Kirill were personally acquainted with Prince Alexander, and the *Vita* was based upon real historical events (Schenk 2004, 60; Likhachev 1947). One passage from the first edition of *Vita* depicts St Alexander preparing to combat the invasion of the Swedes as follows:

> Leaving the church, he wiped away his tears and began to encourage his regiments, saying: 'God is in Truth, not in power (*Ne v sile Bog, no v pravde*)'. Let us remember the psalmist who said: 'Some came with weapons and some on horses, but we called upon the Lord God for our help and they were defeated and fell, but we rose up and stood straight'.
> (Zhitiye 1995, 191; Mansikka 1913, 3; Isoaho 2006, 43)

For the medieval chronicler, the key concept in the depiction of St Alexander Nevsky as an ideal ruler and warrior was the notion of 'truth' (*pravda*) juxtaposed with earthly 'power' (*sila*, which could also be translated as 'force'). Of these two words, *pravda* has the most complex meaning. It falls into the category of 'untranslatables', that is, words that are almost impossible to render precisely in foreign languages, largely because it designates 'not only truth but also justice. The accent falls chiefly on the latter meaning when we examine words that have the same root: *pravo* . . . (law), *spravedlivost'* . . . (justice, equity), *pravosudie* . . . (justice, correct judgment)' (Sigov 2014, 813).

The last few decades have witnessed ongoing scholarly interest in the history of the notions of 'truth', 'law' and 'justice' in different European cultures (Prodi 2003; Plotnikov 2019). Different interpretations of *pravda* within the context of a ruler's image and the concepts of law and justice in premodern and modern Russian history have turned out to be of particular importance (Brüning 2020; Plaggenborg 2018). It is not only 'truth' and 'justice' that are deemed to be the key duties of a monarch, but also a 'certainty in the invisible', that is, the ability to follow the harmony of the divine order (Danilevskiy 2018, 43; Brüning 2020, 33). The ruler should serve 'with faith and order' (*veroyu i pravdoyu*; Yurganov 1998, 81), a notion that Stefan Plaggenborg argues in his most recent study was 'part of the economy of salvation'. *Pravda* presumed the duty of a ruler was 'to serve the folk that live here in fear of the Lord, as an *imitatio Christi*' (Plaggenborg 2018, 53, 62). It is therefore hardly surprising that the abovementioned fragment from the *Vita* of St Alexander Nevsky was often interpreted not only as a testimony to Prince Alexander's sanctity but also as a message to secular rulers: 'The figure of Aleksandr Yaroslavich was created from an ideal of Christian behaviour and piety which was an essential feature of a ruler, assuring him of divine favour on the battlefield and in government' (Isoaho 2006, 41). Or, as the famous Russian émigré philosopher, Nikolay Berdiyayev, put it, 'the tragedy of the Russian people is that the Russian powers did not follow these words' (Berdiyayev 2008, 62; Semenkov 2014).

There were some later editions of the *Vita* depicting Prince Alexander as a pious ruler and the forefather of Muscovite princes in which he is designated by the epithets 'the Great', 'the Brave' and 'Nevsky' (Okhotnikova 1987, 354–63; Sirenov 2017, 370). Other editions of the *Vita*, including the one composed by Iona Dumin (archimandrite of the Theotokos Nativity Monastery in Vladimir, 1591–94), were based on fragments of the *Great Menaion* (*Velikiye Cheti Minei*) and the *Book of Degrees* (*Stepennaya Kniga*; Pokrovskiy and Lehnhoff 2007, 25). These and several other editions compiled after Alexander's canonization contain elements that were supposed to point to the sacral character of his life and princely rule, but also to the miraculous action of his relics. Alexander was canonized as a miracle worker (*chudotvorets*) under the name 'Monk Alexiy', signifying that his cult was mostly based upon evidence of him granting posthumous assistance with various everyday needs. Schenk argues that such examples testify to a shift in the reasoning behind the construction of his image as the saint, a transferral from a 'worldly ruler to a miracle-working monk' (Schenk 2004, 92). This shift is important for understanding the multifaceted character of memories of St Alexander Nevsky, regardless of whether they formed during the period of his canonization or are being created today. For instance, the edition of the *Vita* composed by Dumin contains a description of the posthumous assistance St Alexander Nevsky granted over the course of the Battle of Kulikovo (1380) against the Golden Horde and during a fire in the city of Vladimir (1491) (Schenk 2004, 97). The *Vita* also lists eleven sick people (including several blind women and Istoma Golovin, a gravely ill boyar scion) who were cured with the merciful help of St Alexander (Mansikka 1913, 103–13). The image of St Alexander Nevsky as an ideal Christian warrior and ruler and as a merciful heavenly intercessor was also applied in the liturgical canon (*sluzhba*) composed in 1547 by the monk Mikhail. The text of the *sluzhba* contains phrases like 'a great shield and fortress of the Russian land', 'a real help for believers in their fight . . . with passions', but also 'a humble monk' (Rogov 1967; Schenk 2004, 98). These aspects of the cult of St Alexander Nevsky (as a military ruler and miracle worker helping believers to provide for their everyday needs and overcome spiritual temptations) classify him as a military saint (*svyatoy voin*), or *miles Christi*.

Military saints, also variously known as warrior saints, warrior martyrs or soldier saints, represent a particular type of patron saint familiar since the reign of the Emperor Diocletian (284–305) (Restle 1991). The cult of military saints was connected with processes entailing the 'Christianization of warfare' and 'militarization of the Christian'. It presupposed that a ruler had a particular role to play in the defence and extension of *christianitas* as well as the gradual mobilization of ecclesiastical institutions to meet the needs of war (Scharff 2004, 478–79; Sarti 2013; Berezhnaya 2020, 29–30). The militarization of saints is one of the features of a militarized society, namely,

> a society in which there is no clear distinction between soldier and civilian, nor between military officer and government official; . . . where the symbolism of warfare and weaponry is prominent in official and private life, and the warlike and heroic virtues are glorified.
>
> (James 1997, 19)

'God is in truth, not in power!' 115

The representation of saints as *milites Christi*, that is, soldiers conducting both earthly and spiritual wars, is part of a transferral of processes in which different language forms, images and rituals are used to exemplify parallels between saints' lives and serving in the military (Scharff 2004, 480; Gübelc 2018, 222–25). Their cults were widespread across medieval and early modern Europe as well as the Middle East. Various amulets depicting saints on horseback battling with dragons and snakes were particularly popular among pregnant women and the sick in the Byzantine Empire (Walter 2003, 33–38).

Clearly, St Alexander Nevsky fulfilled the criteria of a military saint in a militarized society of that time. His cult was based upon the notion of an ideal Orthodox ruler able to protect the population against both earthly and other-worldly enemies. St Alexander was also venerated because of the power of his incorrupt miraculous relics to help those who were ill or in danger.

However, when the early iconography of St Alexander Nevsky is taken into account, the reason for his attribution as a military saint does not seem that clear. The ambiguity of presenting the prince as a saint was grounded in the peculiarity of his cult. St Alexander, as mentioned before, was canonized as 'a saint, the right-believing (*blagoverny*) Prince Alexander, Alexiy in the monastic schema'.[2] It is therefore hardly surprising that the first iconographic images were of Alexiy as a schema-monk of muscular stature in black robes (Shlyapkin 1915, 8; Begunov 1995, 172–73). On the iconographic level, Prince Alexander's military credentials were not so essential. St Alexander Nevsky was displayed at that time as a holy ruler, the 'root of the Muscovite state' (Sukina 2019) and a pious monk, but not as a soldier.

The memorialization of St Alexander Nevsky during the period preceding the reign of Peter the Great (1682–1725) reveals a tension between the initial Christian idea of refraining from the use of violence and the protective function of military saints, an opposition that remained intact in the Orthodox tradition of that time (White 2013; Berezhnaya 2020). In the case of St Alexander Nevsky, 'a two-pronged cultural memory was formed, encompassing a religious and a state-oriented component' (Wijermars 2018, 85–86). Military memorialization played a very subordinate role in this construction.

The ambiguity inherent in the memorializing of St Alexander Nevsky as a warrior saint survived until the beginning of the eighteenth century, a period that marked the beginning of the 'statification' period in the history of memory of St Alexander (Schenk 2004, 125–67). In 1721 the Russian Emperor Peter I concluded the Nystad Peace Treaty with Sweden and decided to transfer St Alexander Nevsky's relics from Vladimir to the new northern capital, Saint Petersburg. On 30 August 1724, they were placed in the Holy Trinity Cathedral of the Alexander Nevsky Lavra monastery complex. Archimandrite Gavriil Buzhinsky (1680–1731) wrote a new special service in remembrance of the Nystad Peace, which he combined with a service dedicated to St Alexander Nevsky. From this time on, St Alexander became an official patron saint of the new Russian capital. With the completion of the Trinity Cathedral of the Alexander Nevsky Monastery in 1790, the shrine and relics were transferred there, where they remained until 1922. St Alexander was recognized as a defender of Russian imperial glory and the capital city, so he became a military symbol of the new Russian state. The image of humble schema-monk Alexiy was of no use within this context, and the liturgical service dedicated to St Alexander Nevsky lost its monastic memorializing elements. Moreover, on 15 April 1724 the Holy Synod had issued a decree prohibiting the iconographic portrayal of St Alexander in monastic robes. Thenceforth, only images of St Alexander as the Great Prince were allowed (Shlyapkin 1915, 18; Nazarenko and Kvilvidze 2000; see Figure 6.1). The transformation of St Alexander into the imperial military saint was also manifested in the introduction of the Imperial Order of St Alexander Nevsky (1725).

Figure 6.1 St. Alexander Nevsky Southern Russia, Trubchevsk. End of 18th century. Ikonen Museum Recklighausen. Inv. No. 721. Photo Jurgen Spiler

'God is in truth, not in power!' 117

The new wave of militarization of the St Alexander Nevsky cult coincided with the period of nationalization in the Russian Empire at the turn of the twentieth century. This transformation was implemented amid the rise of anti-Western, anti-Catholic elements in the memorialization of the saint and at a time when new protective functions were being attributed to his cult. On the eve of the October Revolution, St Alexander was not only venerated as a defender of the Russian Empire, its capital city and the ruling dynasty, but also of 'Russianness' (language, culture and folklore) and of military forces in general. His iconography was also being transformed: the image of the Western-style ruler was being replaced by the figure of a warrior in traditional Russian princely attire with his hand on his sword (Schenk 2004, 168–217).

This tendency fitted into a general trend of that time. During the process of nation building the 'bracket between state, monarchy and people' (Samerski and Zach 2007, 4) was reorganized with the help of national-oriented historical narratives based upon the cults of national patrons (Rohdewald 2014). Saints like Alexander Nevsky, who are often stylized as religious *lieux de mémoire*, are constructing blocks of cultural memories (Wünsch 2013, xxviii).

Situations of danger and instability often coincided with periods of 'belligerent upheaval' (Leonhard 2008) accompanied by the nationalization of the old *antemurale christianitatis* myth that served the popularization of the idea of a nation as the last bastion of Christianity (Berezhnaya and Hein-Kircher 2019). Military saints were often perceived as bulwarks of the faith, fatherland, and nation. It is not by chance that most foreign churches devoted to St Alexander Nevsky were constructed during this period (Krivosheev and Sokolov 2009, 202–4; Sorokin 2017).

The image of Nevsky as a military talent and protector of Russian lands resurfaced under Stalin after a period of deconstruction following the October Revolution. Importantly, it was one of Sergey Eisenstein's most acclaimed films, *Alexander Nevsky* (1938), with a score by Sergey Prokofiev, that made a significant contribution to the construction of the 'Soviet version' of memory of St Alexander Nevsky (Schenk 2004, 266–435). This version accentuated the outstanding accomplishments of the prince as ruler and military commander but suppressed any references to his sainthood. In this way, the memory of St Prince Alexander was completely desanctified (Wijermars 2018, 86).

After the fall of the Soviet Union, the memory of the saint prince entered a 'pluralization' phase. Schenk traces the differing elements coexisting within post-Soviet memory of St Alexander Nevsky in Russia: the patriotic general, the prince and the local patron saint (Schenk 2004, 436–69; see also Wijermars 2018, 87). He also emphasizes the importance of the renaissance of interpretations of St Alexander stemming from pre-revolutionary times as well as narratives formed by the diaspora. According to Schenk, in contrast to the Soviet period, Nevsky nowadays appears less as a military hero, and more as a miracle worker and protector of Russia. Schenk defines this 'postmodern bricolage' as a fluctuation between the re-sacralization and profanization of the saint's memory (Schenk 2007). All these fragments fit into the general picture of an entangled cultural memory. In what follows, I suggest that, at least since

118 *Liliya Berezhnaya*

2008, several additional elements have been observed in the pluralist image of St Alexander Nevsky, namely, the re-militarization of memory and the diversification of veneration practices on local, national and international levels. Over the past decade, the military and patriotic image of St Alexander Nevsky has acquired new dimensions and overtones. One of these is connected with changing perceptions of Russia's civilizational path.

St Alexander Nevsky as a symbol of the 'Russian civilizational code' in contemporary cultural memory

It was not by chance that Patriarch Kirill was personally involved in the organization of the abovementioned festivities to celebrate the 800th anniversary of Alexander Nevsky's birth. Back in 2008, Kirill, then Metropolitan of Smolensk and Kaliningrad, had taken part in a Rossiia TV Channel media event titled *The Name of Russia*. The viewers had the opportunity to vote for and elect the greatest Russian of all time. The final twelve candidates selected on the basis of the votes cast included St Alexander Nevsky, whom Metropolitan Kirill presented to the general public. At the end of the contest, St Alexander Nevsky was elected by TV viewers as the greatest Russian historical personality. Wijermars, who studied the interactivity of the *Name of Russia* programme within the context of Russia's memory politics, emphasizes that '2008 was a watershed year in the (re)popularization of Nevskii with the general public' (Wijermars 2018, 119). Importantly, this year also marked the end of the period defined by Alexey Miller as an 'escalation of historical politics' in Russia (2003–08). This period was notable for attempts to introduce standardized history textbooks, regulate interpretations of history via legislation and establish politically engaged institutions (Miller 2012, 255–63). *The Name of Russia* was one such initiative within the framework of the new Russian politics of memory. Metropolitan Kirill made a crucial contribution to its success by reactivating the memory of St Alexander Nevsky. In his video presentation. He stressed Nevsky's importance as 'the saviour and builder of Russia. . . . A leader, moreover, who does not require rehabilitation or defending . . . since all the stories about his feats known to the Russian people are laudatory . . . without him Russia and its "civilisational code" would not exist today'. Furthermore, Metropolitan Kirill quoted the abovementioned passage from St Alexander's *Vita* about *pravda* being the greatest virtue of a ruler and saint, while also asserting that 'if Russian history had seen a larger share of saintly rulers, its course would have been markedly different' (Imya Rossii 2011; Wijermars 2018, 114).

The major lines of this argumentation favouring St Alexander Nevsky were reasserted by Metropolitan Kirill on multiple occasions (Wijermars 2018, 71). In this sense, the head of the Russian Orthodox Church functions as a mnemonic actor, a political force so 'interested in a specific interpretation of the past' (Kubik and Bernhard 2014, 4)[3] that he mediates the image of St Alexander Nevsky as a pious warrior and ideal ruler.

The theme of a 'civilizational code' peculiar to Russia equivalent to a kind of 'genome' appears as a constant refrain in the Patriarch's public addresses on St Alexander Nevsky. The application of this term should be generally regarded within the context of a 'civilizational turn' that has taken place in Russian political discourse and memory politics over the last decades (Linde 2016). Marlène Laruelle and Jean Radvanyi assert that '"civilization" has become a catchall term in Russia, used and abused by the media as well as the government'. This presumes the existence of 'Russia's "civilizational codes", of Russia as a separate *civilization* with its own cultural and moral foundations'. However, it is not quite clear what is meant by that term: 'References to Russia – whether as a European civilization, a distinct Orthodox civilization, or a Eurasian civilization oriented toward a Euro-Asian equilibrium – can be found scattered through Russian official discourse as both context and reference point' (Laruelle and Radvanyi 2018, 64; Yakhshiyan 2019).

Yet the term 'civilizational code' is often correlated with the concept of the 'Russian world' (*russkiy mir*), a specific form of civilizational unity associated with Russian culture. This has both ideological and practical applications within and beyond Russia. As Daniel P. Payne elaborates, Vladimir Putin created the Russian World Foundation in 2007 to strengthen 'the Russian culture and language as well as for helping deliver domestic stability, restore Russia's status as a world power, and increase her influence in neighboring states" (Payne 2015). Vyacheslav Nikonov, the executive director of the foundation, has repeatedly pointed out the commonalities in meaning between the notions of the 'Russian world' and Russia's 'own civilisational code' (Nikonov 2015; Kazharski 2020, 28).[4] According to Stephen White and Valentina Feklyunina, such a 'vision implied that Russia's differences from the rest of Europe did not make it a bad or an underdeveloped Europe; they simply made it different' (White and Feklyunina 2014, 107).

For the hierarchs of the Russian Orthodox Church, however, the 'Russian world' is more 'a religious concept, not a political or cultural term' (Payne 2015, 66). This difference is obvious in the interpretation Patriarch Kirill elaborated in 2009. According to him, the 'Russian world' rests on several pillars: Eastern Orthodoxy, Russian culture, common historical memory and common views on social development. Patriarch Kirill has paid special attention to the figure of St Alexander Nevsky within this context. For him, St Prince Alexander is one of a number of paradigmatic examples of saints common to the Russian lands that cannot be defined in national terms. Or, as Patriarch Kirill expressed it himself: 'Therefore we have to keep the unity of the Russian Church, venerate the common saints, and visit the holy sites of the Russian World' (Vystupleniye 2020; Wawrzonek 2016). In Patriarch Kirill's opinion, the *Russkiy mir* is a spiritual community based upon common sacral memory. St Alexander Nevsky's appeal across this Russian world is so broad that he has become one of its integrating factors. Patriarch Kirill has continually emphasized that the 'Russian world' is a 'notion of civilization' that has nothing to do with politics,

120   *Liliya Berezhnaya*

and that 'those who state otherwise are trying to use the concept for "their own political interests"' (Wawrzonek 2016, 38).

In fact, one of the actors in contemporary Russia that brings up the memory of St Alexander Nevsky in connection with geopolitical, civilizational and military doctrines is the famous Russian neoconservative think tank, the Izborsk Club. Founded in 2012, it brings together experts in the fields of politics, culture and the humanities. As aptly noted by Marlène Laruelle, 'the Club's ideological stance' is 'Russia's historical continuity and its fundamental mission as a fortress against Western influences', which 'are two sides of the same coin. When political changes cause Russia to lose its sense of temporal unity, it becomes vulnerable to external attacks'. Laruelle scrutinizes the doctrine of the Izborsk Club, which combines 'two different doctrinal traditions, the "Soviet empire" and political Orthodoxy' (Laruelle 2019, 141, 138).

The members of the Club and experts affiliated to it have represented a 'conservative turn' in Russian intellectual and political discourse over recent years (Engström 2014). Several of them have repeatedly addressed the memory of St Alexander Nevsky to illustrate the idea of the continuity of Russia's civilizational path and the need to strengthen Russian military power and oppose attempts of Western countries to destroy Russia and the Orthodox Church. For instance, Yuriy Trifankov, a history professor at the Briansk State Technical University, affirms that

> we should remind ourselves that after the destruction of Orthodox Byzantium, the West proposed . . . the total physical annihilation of all Orthodox Russians as 'barbarians'. As we know, they did not manage to fulfil their plans due to the rightful and powerful politics of Alexander Nevsky. In Western schoolbooks our saint Alexander Nevsky, the saviour of Russia who occupies first place among the greatest Russians according to sociological surveys, is depicted as the major enemy of the West and a wild barbarian.
>
> (Trifankov 2016)

Similar conclusions are drawn by another history professor, Vardan Bagdasaryan, in his expert paper on sacral history as a basis of national self-consciousness. Bagdasaryan mentions St Alexander Nevsky as one of the 'key figures of Russian sacral history', while also pointing out that 'not only the military achievements, but also the new anti-Western civilizational choice of Alexander Nevsky classifies him' as belonging to this category (Bagdasaryan 2018). Alexander Prokhanov, the chair of the Izborsk Club, also brings up the name of St Alexander in connection with Russian geopolitics, sacral history and defence strategies. Prokhanov 'evokes his fetish theme of the "Russian weapon" . . . that embodies Russian cultural characteristics' (Laruelle 2019, 146) in order to illustrate the prominent role the saint has played in sacral Russian military history:

> The Russian weapon is the holy weapon; it is the weapon of the Russian Dream. Modern submarines, tanks and fighter planes contain . . . the

metal from the sword used by Prince Alexander Nevsky in the 'Battle on the Ice'.

(Prokhanov 2019)

The writings and activities of the Izborsk Club may seem dubious and marginal within the polyphonic orchestra of memories about St Alexander Nevsky in contemporary Russia. Besides the hierarchs of the Russian Orthodox Church and expert communities, there are numerous other mnemonic actors, including Russian diplomats, the media and policymakers or cinema producers, who are contributing to the image of St Alexander as a prominent warrior and embodiment of the Russian civilizational path (Wijermars 2018, 97–107; Curanović 2018, 200; Nakhimova 2010). There are also some critical stances to be found in this chorus, most of which come from historians and the political opposition (Schenk 2004, 454–69, Schenk 2020). One of the most recent examples was a documentary titled *Alexander Nevsky – On a Razor's Edge* (2020, dir. by Oleg Stas Vitvitskiy), which was aired by the Russian TV channel *Kultura* on 6 December 2020, the Russian Orthodox Church's Day of Remembrance for St Alexander. The film aims to dismantle some popular myths about the Prince. Several prominent Russian historians attempt to give an answer to the question of whether St Alexander 'was a hero or a cunning despot'. The documentary ends with a general conclusion about the outstanding contribution the prince made to the formation of Russian statehood. On the whole, the position taken by expert communities such as the Izborsk Club is indicative of a wide-ranging surge of interest in the figure of St Alexander Nevsky among actors engaged in a common search for the kind of 'usable past' mentioned by Alexander Agadjanian in his chapter (see also Malinova 2019). The image of St Alexander Nevsky is paradigmatic when there is a need to exemplify continuities that occurred within Russian history in spite of post-revolutionary periods containing semantic breaks when religion was 'deprived of memory' (Hervieu-Léger 2000, 123–40).

The return of a military saint

It is St Alexander Nevsky's almost unique character as a symbol of historical continuity that has virtually never fallen into oblivion that has determined the peculiar place he occupies in the sacralized, politicized and apparently re-militarized variant of contemporary Russian politics of memory. This is most noticeably exemplified by the abovementioned festivities marking the occasion of the 800th anniversary of the birth of Prince Alexander Nevsky. The organizational plan was confirmed by the Russian Minister of Culture, Vladimir Medynsky, in 2017 upon the basis of an executive order of Vladimir Putin titled 'On the Celebration of the 800th Anniversary of the Birth of Alexander Nevsky' (2014). Notably, neither in the executive order nor in the organizational plan was there any mention of Alexander Nevsky's sainthood. Instead, he was presented as an 'outstanding statesman and army commander'. The plan to organize celebrations to mark the anniversary in 2021 was justified

122 *Liliya Berezhnaya*

by a need 'to retain the military, cultural and historical heritage, to strengthen the unity of the people of Russia' (Executive Order 2014). This demonstrates an apparent attempt by the Russian state authorities to regulate the memorialization of the St Alexander Nevsky cult in its quasi-Soviet form. In terms of the politics of memory, such initiatives are clearly 'rooted in the past', whereas 'its illocutionary content, that is, the desired communicative effect of these discourses, is motivated by contemporary political considerations' (Verovšek 2016, 530). While interpreting the past in the public sphere, secular leaders in contemporary Russia have opted for a single version of history in which the cult of St Alexander Nevsky as a patriot and military hero plays a crucial role.

Nevertheless, in contrast to the Soviet period, religious memory is very much present in such initiatives. The major executive powers assigned to the planning for the anniversary celebrations include various ministries, cultural institutions, local government agencies, businesses and non-governmental organizations. But the patriarchy plays a significant role in their realization as well. Although the title of the organizational plan does not mention Alexander Nevsky's sainthood, its content presupposes quite a clear strategy for the revitalization of the religious cult. Numerous exhibitions, contests, conferences and publications will be conducted under the aegis of the Russian Orthodox Church (Plan 2017). Moreover, Patriarch Kirill himself chairs the 'Alexander Nevsky' programme launched in 2009 by the Ural Mining and Metallurgical Company and the Foundation of St Andrew the First-Called (led by Vladimir Yakunin). The programme is regarded as the preliminary stage in the realization of the plans for the festivities. Its major aims are defined to emphasize the merits of the 'right-believing Prince as a pious Christian, outstanding military commander, wise ruler and skilful diplomat' (Plan 2017). Within the framework of the programme, the Foundation of St Andrew the First-Called is organizing an annual display of St Alexander Nevsky's relics for veneration in various eparchies and metropolitans both within and outside Russia. Furthermore, the programme envisages regional 'Alexander Nevsky Days' aimed at schoolchildren and students who would be expected to take part in numerous lectures, summer camps and re-enactments of historical battles featuring training sessions in the martial arts. One of the important initiatives is the construction of churches in honour of St Alexander Nevsky in the Russian borderlands. They are meant to form a symbolic cross to provide Russia with spiritual protection against foreign invasions.[5] Such plans are providing a new impetus to memory of St Alexander Nevsky conceived as a symbol of *antemurale christianitatis*, or a national bulwark of Christianity.

The festivities marking the occasion of the 800th anniversary of St Alexander's birth also encompass numerous events at the 'Russia – My History' multimedia exhibition parks that are located all over Russia. These parks were jointly developed in 2013 by the state and the Russian Orthodox Church (Bogumił 2018, 197), with secular expert communities making a further contribution to their conceptualization and popularization (Kazmina 2020; Krasilnikova and Valdman 2019). The parks provide a platform for the interweaving and dissemination of religious and secular memories of St Alexander Nevsky.[6] Apart from this, the Moscow Patriarchate supports the activities of the 'Heirs of Alexander Nevsky' All-Russian historical-patriotic society, which promotes 'patriotism among the young generation based on the example set by an outstanding military commander and state ruler Alexander Nevsky and his followers, and aims to glorify the heroism of our people' (Lapin 2020, 85).

The combined efforts of the upper echelons of the Russian Orthodox Church's leadership, the state and historical expert communities to uphold patriotic and militarized narratives are well-studied (Torbakov 2014; Laruelle 2020; Rousselet 2013). These politics go hand in hand with praising military achievements, military service and giving up one's life for one's country on the battlefield. This value system yields a 'militaristic approach to national pride' and 'military piety' (Richters 2013, 73; Knorre and Zygmont 2020), both of which are popularized by some Church hierarchs. It also reveals the general rise of militaristic sentiments (or 'militarized patriotism', an apt term coined by Valerie Sperling [2009]). Although contemporary Russian society could not, of course, be classified as fully militarized (according to the abovementioned definition by Edward James), militarized narratives evidently play a considerable role in its cultural memory.

The veneration of Alexander Nevsky also fits well into this narrative framework because it reconciles the collective memories of pre-revolutionary and Soviet times. Patriotism continues to be a key argument binding together these two periods. Apparently, since the late 2000s, St Alexander Nevsky has turned out to be one of the major symbolic figures of the Russian continuous past. The re-militarization of his cult serves the same purpose: to emphasize the past victories of the Russian and Soviet armies and to sacralize current military achievements. St Alexander Nevsky is regarded as a heavenly protector of the Russian army and fleet. His memory is commemorated in numerous 'navy churches' erected in pre-revolutionary times and the modern day (Seleznev and Tsarev 2005). One recent example is the depiction of St Alexander Nevsky on the walls of the Resurrection of Christ Cathedral to be built in the 'Patriot' park in the Moscow Region. This cathedral is devoted to the Armed Forces of the Russian Federation and contains four altar corners bearing the names of warrior saints. St Alexander Nevsky is presented as a heavenly protector of the Russian army field forces. Moreover, the cathedral's dome is meant to 'resemble the helmet of Alexander Nevsky so that the body of the temple will mirror the image in the icon of the faithful saint prince' (Knorre and Zygmont 2020).

Notably, the militarized memory of St Alexander is not only commemorated in churches and cathedrals but also in the Russian army: a gun cruiser and a nuclear submarine bear his name. What is more, the syncretic memory of St Prince Alexander has been recently promoted and visualized in the form of new monuments 'that spring up like mushrooms' (Laruelle 2020, 128) all over the country. Monuments, stone busts and crosses devoted to St Alexander Nevsky are often placed near churches or other sanctuaries, but also on battlefields. They symbolize 'the Church in the service of a country in combat'

(Rousselet 2015, 52, 58). But even more importantly, they mark local identities and local patriotism and signify a search by regional elites for their roots (Filyushkin 2017, 390, 395) as well as the diversification of veneration practices.[7] Clearly, not only the central authorities and Church leaders, but also local politicians and regional intellectuals, are disseminating religious, political and military memories of the saint.

The memory of St Alexander Nevsky has recently been revitalized not only in the Russian provinces, but also in several contested border areas outside of Russia. For example, the Church of the St Right-Believing Alexander Nevsky was reopened in 2011 close to the Bender fortress in Transnistria. To mark the occasion of Patriarch Kirill's visit to the region in 2013, a sculpture bust of St Alexander was erected close to that church (Voronovich and Felker 2020, 585–86). Furthermore, an image of St Alexander Nevsky was used to decorate Luhansk, the capital of the unrecognized Luhansk People's Republic, during preparations for the 2017 Victory Day. As Elena Babkina has asserted, such symbols testify to the combination of 'Soviet' and 'Russian imperialistic' military elements in 'Novorossiya's' memorial landscape (Babkina 2020, 600). Consequently, the 'internationalization' of memory of St Alexander has religious, secular and military aspects, but it is the military aspect that reconciles the other two.

Importantly, memory of St Alexander Nevsky connects institutional and individual forms of militarized patriotism. The veneration of St Alexander is not only transforming the kind of official 'Kremlin-backed' patriotism being promoted by the Church leadership, but also individual and collective practices. Appropriated patriotism from below (Rousselet 2015; Daucé et al. 2015, 1) encompasses forms of veneration of St Alexander Nevsky that could aptly be described as what Grace Davie would term as 'mediated memory': 'late-modern individuals . . . can and do reestablish themselves in the form of virtual discussion groups, including religious ones. New communities form just as others disintegrate, formations which depend very largely on the instant exchange of information' (Davie 2000, 184, 98–114).

One good example of such a virtual discussion group associated with the cult of St Alexander Nevsky and patriotism is a forum on the VK (originally VKontakte) social media network titled 'Alexander Nevsky – Glory, Spirit, and the Name of Russia', which was launched in 2013 upon the initiative of the Gorodets eparchy of the Russian Orthodox Church. The group unites young people, who send their creative works to the forum and initiate different patriotic events. It currently has 4,253 subscribers (Molodezhnyy 2019). Another example of 'patriotic and military appropriation' of St Alexander Nevsky's memory on a popular level is the military-patriotic Brotherhood of Alexander Nevsky youth club, which is based in Yuzhno-Sakhalinsk and combines studies of church history and theology with social ministry and training sessions in the martial arts (Obshchestvennaya 2020).[8]

The diversification or pluralization of memory of Alexander Nevsky as a military saint has another side. This tendency, fittingly described by Schenk as post-Soviet 'profanization' and 'trivialization' (Schenk 2007), is being implemented

'God is in truth, not in power!' 125

in a variety of forms. A few recent examples are the Prince Alexander Nevsky housing complex in Saint Petersburg, a number of popular computer games (Wijermars 2018, 88) and a luxury 'Tsar-version' Alexander Nevsky mobile phone designed for military personnel. The phone is made from gold and onyx and features engraved extracts from the Novgorodian chronicle and a portrait of the saint prince (Portret 2020). The majority of these brands regard St Alexander as a symbol of Russian military glory. However, such appropriations occasionally end up causing conflicts involving the Church authorities or Church-affiliated institutions. For instance, the Union of Orthodox Citizens officially protested in 2008 against the use of St Alexander Nevsky's image in an advertisement for crispbread bites made for the company that produces them, 'Khrustim' (Kto 2008; for earlier protests by Metropolitan Kirill on similar occasions, see V Russkoy 2007).

The pluralization of memory of St Alexander Nevsky has also led to diversification in his iconography. Dmitriy Mironenko defines four historically embedded types of contemporary St Alexander Nevsky iconography: 'venerable (*prepodobnyy*), princely, imperial and military'. The borders between these iconographical types are blurred: the 'venerable (monk) type' is often supplied with an inscription about the saint's princely origin, while the 'princely type' bears the symbols of the 'military' one. In general, 'Alexander Nevsky is presented as a physically strong and energetic' saint. One of the distinctive features of his iconography from early times onwards has been a praying gesture, an emblem of his intercessory mission (Mironenko 2020; for secular depictions of Alexander Nevsky, see also Reginskaya and Tsvetkov 2010; Gerasimenko and Saenkova 2008, 227–29).

St Alexander Nevsky as a heavenly protector in times of crisis

The 'personal' or 'intercessory' side of memory of St Alexander Nevsky is sometimes forgotten amid the official patriotic and military grandeur connected with his name. It is important to mention that St Alexander Nevsky's cult is not only associated with military parades and geopolitical strategies but also with personal veneration practices in contemporary Russia. Tens of thousands of pilgrims, aptly defined by Zhanna Kormina as 'Orthodox nomads' (Kormina 2019), arrive every year to venerate St Alexander's relics at the St Trinity Alexander Nevsky Lavra in Saint Petersburg.[9] As has been the case for centuries, Orthodox believers ask the merciful saint for help with their everyday needs. In July 2019, a naval religious procession carrying the relics of St Alexander Nevsky and St Apostle Andrew the First-Called was conducted in the Kerch Strait to pray for the successful construction of the Crimean bridge (Pod Krymskim mostom proshel morskoy krestnyy khod 2019). During the times of uncertainty and danger associated with the coronavirus, many believers have addressed the original meaning of St Alexander Nevsky's cult. They ask him, in his role as military saint and schema monk, to protect them against 'the deadly infection' and to pray for those who are ill or continue working despite the threat posed by the coronavirus. Such prayers were intoned by several priests and bishops of Volgograd who conducted an aerial religious procession by helicopter in April 2020 in which they flew the relics of St Alexander Nevsky and Theotokos icons over the city (Vozdushnyy 2020). Similar prayers were recently heard during a religious procession at the six churches of the St Trinity Alexander Nevsky Lavra in Saint Petersburg (Svyashchenniki 2020). As far as the realm of memory politics is concerned, such practices might be signs of the 'ontological insecurity' (Rumelili 2018) associated with the coronavirus. The feelings of danger and fear it is causing are bringing about ruptures between the state's militarized 'historical self-understanding' (Mälksoo 2015, 225) and individual experiences. When performing its role as a mnemonic actor, the Russian Orthodox Church is also not speaking with a single voice (Torbakov 2014), and some hierarchs and parishioners are choosing to revive the image of St Alexander Nevsky not only as a military commander but also as a heavenly protector in times of pandemic and instability.

Conclusion

Recent years have witnessed a radical surge of interest in the figure of St Alexander Nevsky in Russian cultural memory. Whereas the upper echelons of the Church hierarchy have been the most active participants in this process, it has also involved a variety of other mnemonic actors, from historians and secular politicians, through diplomats and cinema makers, to computer game producers and businessmen. Sometimes their views on St Alexander Nevsky's do not correlate with each other, but very often they are making a joint contribution to the image of St Alexander as a symbol of the continuity of Russia's geopolitical orientation and military history. After the fall of the Soviet Union, the return of memory of Prince Alexander as a military saint meant that his image as a heavenly protector of Russian statehood was mediated in a militarized form. The 'statist' component of the Nevsky cult contributed to the sacralization and patriotization of his memory (Schenk 2020). The 'military' aspect of his image regained a new importance, mainly after 2008, when the official historical narrative achieved a sort of consensus. As a military saint venerated at regional, national and international levels, St Alexander Nevsky has turned into one of the prominent symbols of the Russian civilizational path and the 'Russian world', as well as the embodiment of an *antemurale christianitatis*. Over the past decade, 'militarized memory' of St Alexander Nevsky was pluralized in various forms, contributing to the commercialization of his image. At the same time, the veneration of St Alexander has recently regained its original meaning when expressed in the form of prayers for intercession in times of danger and insecurity. There is no doubt that the commemoration of St Alexander Nevsky as a military saint and Russia's heavenly patron will be kept alive over the coming years.

Notes

1 The author of this chapter has included her own translations of quotations from the following sources in the text: Patriarch Kirill's speeches (Vystupleniye 2019, 2020; Plaggenborg 2018; Trifankov 2016; Bagdasaryan 2018; Prokhanov 2019; Lapin 2020).
2 Although he had been elevated by 1381 to the status of a local saint, there were practically no iconographic depictions before his canonization in the sixteenth century.
3 See also the chapter by Naum Trajanovski in this volume.
4 Despite similarities, there are differences in usage and the purpose attached to both terms. Fabian Linde draws attention to the fact that in contrast to the 'civilizational code', 'the "Russian world" concept was co-opted by the Russian government as a means of reaching and attracting the Russian diaspora. It was also part of an effort to enhance its soft power in the near abroad' (Linde 2016, 621 n. 48).
5 The outposts of the Orthodox Christianity will be built in Sakhalin, Osetia, Kaliningrad, and Solovetsky Islands (Fond Andreya Pervozvannogo).
6 For instance, in 2018 the Saint Petersburg park organized the screening of the Soviet film *Alexander Nevsky* (Alexander Nevsky v programme 2018), while the Volgograd park combined a screening of the same film with an excursion themed on the great battles of the Rurik dynasty (V istoricheskom parke 2018). A year later, the Volgograd park organized a themed museum class titled 'Portrait of Alexander Nevsky', which brought together a presentation on icons, churches and monuments devoted to St Alexander Nevsky and a performance by the Shatun Historical Club featuring medieval weapons and the military lifestyle (Istoricheskiy park 2019).
7 For similar examples related to St. Olga's cult in the region of Pskov see Donovan 2018.
8 For more on patriotic Church-affiliated clubs, see Rousselet (2015).
9 There are approximately 60,000–70,000 tourists a year, according to Lavra's Abbot Nazariy, Bishop of *Kronstadt* (Novyye 2017).

References

Alexander Nevsky v programme "Film vykhodnogo dnya." 2018. https://myhistorypark.ru/poster/aleksandr-nevskiy-v-programme-film-vykhodnogo-dnya-/?city=ros.

Babkina, Elena. 2020. "Ideologiya 'Novorosii' v kontektse istoricheskoy politiki samoprovozglashennykh respublik Donbassa." In *Politika pamyati v sovremennoy Rossii i stranakh Vostochnoy Yevropy: instituty, aktory, narrativy*, edited by Alexey Miller and Dmitriy Yefremenko, 591–609. Saint Petersburg: Izdatelstvo Yevropeyskogo Universiteta.

Bagdasaryan, Vardan. 2018. "Sviashchennaya istoriya – osnova natsionalnogo samosoznaniya." https://izborsk-club.ru/16331#_ftn1.

Begunov, Yuriy. 1995. "Zhitiye Alexandra Nevskogo v russkoy literature XIII-XVIII vekov." In *Kniaz Alexander Nevsky i yego epokha*, edited by Yuriy Begunov and Anatoliy Kirpichnikov, 163–71. Saint Petersburg: Dmitry Bulanin.

Berdiyayev, Nikolay. 2008. *Russkaya ideya*. Saint Petersburg: Azbuka-Klassika.

Berezhnaya, Liliya. 2020. "Soldaten und Märtyrer: Zum Prozess der Militarisierung der Heiligen im östlichen und westlichen Christentum." In *Die Militarisierung der Heiligen in Vormoderne und Moderne*, edited by Liliya Berezhnaya, 9–58. Berlin: Duncker & Humblot.

Berezhnaya, Liliya, and Heidi Hein-Kircher. 2019. "Introduction. Constructing a Rampart Nation. Conceptual Framework." In *Rampart Nations. Bulwark Myths of East European Multiconfessional Societies in the Age of Nationalism*, edited by Liliya Berezhnaya and Heidi Hein-Kircher, 3–30. New York: Berghahn Books.

Bogumił, Zuzanna. 2018. *Gulag Memories: The Rediscovery and Commemoration of Russia's Repressive Past*. New York: Berghahn Books.

128 *Liliya Berezhnaya*

Brüning, Alfons. 2020. "Symphonia, kosmische Harmonie, Moral. Moskauer Diskurse über gerechte Herrschaft im 16. und 17. Jahrhundert." In *Gerechtigkeit und gerechte Herrschaft vom 15. bis zum 17. Jahrhundert. Beiträge zur historischen Gerechtigkeitsforschung*, edited by Stefan Plaggenborg, 23–52. Oldenburg: de Gruyter.

Curanović, Alicja. 2018. "Guided by a 'symphony of views'. The Russian Orthodox Church's role in building Russia's symbolic capital." In *Orthodox Religion and Politics in Contemporary Eastern Europe: On Multiple Secularisms and Entanglements*, edited by Tobias Köllner, 195–213. New York: Routledge.

Danilevskiy, Igor. 2018. *Istoricheskaya tekstologiya*. Moscow: High School of Economics.

Daucé, Françoise, Marlene Laruelle, Anne Le Huérou, and Kathy Rousselet. 2015. "Introduction: What Does It Mean to Be a Patriot?" *Europe-Asia Studies* 67: 1–7.

Davie, Grace. 2000. *Religion in Europe: Memory Mutates*. Oxford: Oxford University Press.

Donovan, Victoria. 2018. "Militarized Memory: Patriotic Re-Branding in Post-Soviet Pskov." In *Russia's Regional Identities. The Power of the Provinces*, edited by Edith W. Clowes, Gisela Erbslöh and Ani Kokobobo, 73–95. New York: Routledge.

Engström, Maria. 2014. "Contemporary Russian Messianism and New Russian Foreign Policy." *Contemporary Security Policy* 35 (3): 356–79.

Executive Order on Celebrating 800th Birthday Anniversary of Alexander Nevsky. 2014. http://en.kremlin.ru/acts/news/46050.

Filyushkin, Alexandr. 2017. "Kogda i zachem stali stavit pamyatniki istoricheskim personazham Drevney Rusi?" *Drevnyaya Rus: Vo vremeni, v lichnostyakh, v ideyakh* 7: 382–97.

Fond Andreya Pervozvannogo. Alexandr Nevsky. O programme. http://fap.ru/programs/aleksandr-nevskiy.

Gerasimenko, Nadezhda, and Elena Saenkova, eds. 2008. *Ikony svyatykh voinov. Obrazy nebesnykh zashchitnikov v vizantiyskom, balkanskom i drevnerusskom iskusstve*. Moscow: Interbook Business.

Gübele, Boris. 2018. *Deus vult, Deus vult. Der christliche heilige Krieg im Früh- und Hochmittelalter*. Ostfildern: Jan Thorbecke Verlag.

Hervieu-Léger, Danièle. 2000. *Religion as a Chain of Memory*. Cambridge: Polity Press.

Imya Rossii: Mitropolit Kirill o Alexandre Nevskom. 2011. www.youtube.com/watch?v=Frz-WQ4HjFE.

Isoaho, Mari. 2006. *The Image of Aleksandr Nevskiy in Medieval Russia. Warrior and Saint*. Leiden: Brill.

Istoricheskiy park „Rossiya – Moya istoriya" poznakomit volgogradtsev s zhiznyu Svyatogo Knyazya Alexandra Nevskogo. 2019. *Rossiya – Moya istoriya*. https://myhistorypark.ru/poster/istoricheskiy-park-rossiya-moya-istoriya-poznakomit-volgogradtsev-s-zhiznyu-svyatogo-knyazya-aleksan/.

James, Edward. 1997. "The Militarisation of Roman Society, 400–700." In *Military Aspects of Scandinavian Society in a European Perspective AD 1–1300*, edited by Anne N. Jørgensen and Birthe L. Clausen, 19–24. Copenhagen: National Museum.

Kazharski, Aliaksei. 2020. "Civilizations as Ontological Security?" *Problems of Post-Communism* 67 (1): 24–36.

Kazmina, Viktoriya. 2020. "Istoricheskiye parki 'Rossiya – moya istoriya' kak otrazheniye transformatsiy institutsionalnogo izmereniya rossiyskoy politiki pamyati." In *Politika pamyati v sovremennoy Rossii i stranakh Vostochnoy Yevropy: instituty, aktory, narrativy*, edited by Alexey Miller and Dmitriy Yefremenko, 172–87. Saint Petersburg: Izdatelstvo Yevropeyskogo Universiteta.

Knorre, Boris, and Aleksei Zygmont. 2020. "'Militant Piety' in 21st-Century Orthodox Christianity: Return to Classical Traditions or Formation of a New Theology of War." *Religions* 11 (1): 2. www.mdpi.com/2077-1444/11/1/2.

'God is in truth, not in power!' 129

Kormina, Zhanna. 2019. *Palomniki. Etnograficheskiye ocherki pravoslavnogo nomadizma*. Moscow: High School of Economics.

Krasilnikova, Yekaterina, and Igor Valdman. 2019. "Praktiki politiki pamyati: park-muzey 'Rossiya – moya istoriya' v sisteme institutsionalnykh protivorechiy". *Vestnik Tomskogo gosudarstvennogo universiteta* 444: 72–82.

Krivosheev, Yuriy, and Roman Sokolov. 2009. *Alexander Nevsky: epokha i pamyat. Istoricheskiye ocherki*. Saint Petersburg: Izdatelstvo Sankt Peterburgskogo Universiteta.

———. 2013. "Phenomen natsionalnogo geroya v obshchestvennom soznanii i ideologii (na primere Alexandra Nevskogo)." *Trudy Istoricheskogo fakulteta Sankt-Peterburgskogo universiteta* 15: 43–57.

"Kto ostanovit koshchynnikov i khokhmachey?" 2008. *Russkaya Narodnaya Liniya*. https://ruskline.ru/news_rl/2008/06/12/kto_ostanovit_kowunnikov_i_hohmachej.

Kubik, Jan, and Michael Bernhard. 2014. "Introduction." In *Twenty Years After Communism. The Politics of Memory and Commemoration*, edited by Michael Bernhard and Jan Kubik, 1–6. Oxford: Oxford University Press.

Lapin, Vladimir. 2020. "Rossiyskoe istoricheskoe obshchestvo (RIO) i Rossiyskoe voenno-patrioticheskoe obshchestvo (RVIO) kak instrument istoricheskoy politiki pervoy chetverti XXI veka." In *Politika pamyati v sovremennoy Rossii i strankakh Vostochnoy Yevropy: instituty, aktory, narrativy*, edited by Alexey Miller and Dmitriy Yefremenko, 74–95. Saint Petersburg: Izdatelstvo Yevropeyskogo Universiteta.

Laruelle, Marlène. 2019. *Russian Nationalism. Imaginaries, Doctrines, and Political Battlefields*. New York: Routledge.

———. 2020. "Politika pamyati Russkoy pravoslavnoy tserkvi: reabilitiruya, perekhvatyvaya, vozvrashchaya." In *Politika pamyati v sovremennoy Rossii i strankakh Vostochnoy Yevropy: instituty, aktory, narrativy*, edited by Alexey Miller and Dmitriy Yefremenko, 122–43. Saint Petersburg: Izdatelstvo Yevropeyskogo Universiteta.

Laruelle, Marlène, and Jean Radvanyi. 2018. *Understanding Russia: The Challenges of Transformation*. Lanham, MD: Rowman & Littlefield.

Leonhard, Jörn. 2008. *Bellizismus und Nation. Kriegsdeutung und Nationsbestimmung in Europa und den Vereinigten Staaten 1750–1914*. Munich: Oldenburg Verlag.

Likhachev, Dmitriy. 1947. "Galitskaya literaturnaya traditsiya v Zhitii Alexandra Nevskogo." *Trudy Otdela Drevnerusskoy Literatury* 5: 36–56. Saint Petersburg: Russian Academy of Sciences.

Linde, Fabian. 2016. "The Civilizational Turn in Russian Political Discourse: From Pan-Europeanism to Civilizational Distinctiveness." *The Russian Review* 75: 604–25.

Lurye, Yakov. 1997. "Kizucheniyu letopisnoy traditsii ob Alexandre Nevskom." In *Trudy Otdela Drevnerusskoy Literatury*, Vol. 17, 387–99. Saint Petersburg: Russian Academy of Sciences.

Malinova, Olga. 2019. "Constructing the 'Usable Past': The Evolution of the Official Historical Narrative in Post-Soviet Russia." In *Cultural and Political Imaginaries in Putin's Russia*, edited by Niklas Bernsand and Barbara Törnquist-Plewa, 85–104. Leiden: Brill.

Mälksoo, Maria. 2015. "'Memory Must Be Defended:' Beyond the Politics of Mnemonical Security." *Security Dialogue* 46 (3): 221–37.

Mansikka, Viljo Johannes. 1913. *Zhitiye Alexandra Nevskogo. Razbor redaktsiy i tekst*. Saint Petersburg: No publisher.

Miller, Alexei. 2012. "The Turns of Russian Historical Politics, from Perestroika to 2011." In *The Convolutions of Historical Politics*, edited by Alexei Miller and Maria Lipman, 253–78. Budapest: Central European University Press.

Mironenko, Dmitriy. 2020. *Obraz Alexandra Nevskogo v russkom iskusstve XVI- nachala XXI vekov*. Sankt Peterburg: Izdatelstvo Sviato-Troitskoy Alexandro-Nevskoy Lavry.

130 *Liliya Berezhnaya*

Molodezhnyy mezhregionalnyy proekt 'Alexander Nevskiy – Slava, Dukh i Imya Rossii'. 2019. *V Kontakte*. https://vk.com/imya_rossii.

Nakhimova, Elena. 2010. "Mifologema 'Alexandr Nevskiy v sovremennoy massovoy kommunikatsii." *Politicheskaya lingvistika* 3 (33): 105–8.

Nazarenko, Alexandr, and Nina Kvilvidze. 2000. "Alexandr Yaroslavich Nevskiy." In *Pravoslavnaya entsyklopediya*, Vol. 1, 541–44. Moscow: Tserkovno-nauchny tsentr Pravoslavnaya Entsiklopedia.

Nikonov, Vyacheslav. 2015. *Kod tsivilisatsii. Chto zhdet Rossiyu budushchego?* Moscow: Eksmo.

Novyye ekskursionnye programmy predstavila Alexandro-Nevskaya Lavra. 2017. *Palomnicheskiy tsentr Alexandro-Nevskoy Lavry*. http://palomnik-lavra.ru/464/.

Obshchestvennaya organizatsiya "Bratsvo Alexandra Nevskogo" g. Yuzhno-Sakhalinsk. 2020. *Baza dannykh po sotsialnomu sluzheniyu Russkoy Pravoslavnoy Tserkv*. http://social.diaconia.ru/service/2582.

Okhotnikova, Valentina. 1987. "Povest o zhitii Alexandra Nevskogo." In *Slovar knizhnikov i knizhnosti Drevney Rusi*, Vol. 1, 354–63. Leningrad: Nauka.

Payne, Daniel P. 2015. "Spiritual Security, the Russkiy Mir, and the Russian Orthodox Church: The Influence of the Russian Orthodox Church on Russia's Foreign Policy Regarding Ukraine, Moldova, Georgia, and Armenia." In *Traditional Religion and Political Power: Examining the Role of the Church in Georgia, Armenia, Ukraine and Moldova*, edited by Adam Hug, 65–70. London: Foreign Policy Centre.

Plaggenborg, Stefan. 2018. *Pravda. Gerechtigkeit, Herrschaft und sakrale Ordnung in Altrussland*. Paderborn: Wilhelm Fink.

Plan osnovnykh yubileynykh meroproyatiy po podgotovke i provedeniyu prazdnovaniya 800-letiya so dna rozhdeniya knyazya Alexandra Nevskogo. 2017. http://archives.ru/sites/default/files/plan-2017-2021-aleksandr-nevsky.pdf.

Plotnikov, Nikolaj. 2019. "Kulturen der Gerechtigkeit. Zum Konzept einer interkulturellen Gerechtigkeitsforschung. Einleitung des Herausgebers." In *Gerechtigkeit in Russland. Sprachen, Konzepte, Praktiken*, edited by Nikolaj Plotnikov, 1–19. Paderborn: Wilhelm Fink.

Pod Krymskim mostom proshel morskoy krestnyy khod. 2019. Kerch.com.ru. www.kerch.com.ru/articleview.aspx?id=84378&utm_source=yxnews&utm_medium=desktop&utm_referrer=https%3A%2F%2Fyandex.ua%2Fnews.

Pokrovskiy, Nikolay, and Gail D. Lehnhoff, eds. 2007. *Stepennaya Kniga tsarskogo rodosloviya po drevneyshim spiskam*, Vol. 1. Moscow: Yazyki Slavyanskoy kultury.

Portret Alexandra Nevskogo poyavilsya na rossiyskom Tsar-telefone. 2020. *Caviar Royal Gift*. https://caviar-phone.ru/news-ru/portret-aleksandra-nevskogo-poyavilsya-na-rossiyskom-car-telefone-bez-kamery-dlya-rossiyskih-voennosluzhaschih.

Prodi, Paolo. 2003. *Eine Geschichte der Gerechtigkeit. Vom Recht Gottes zum modernen Rechtsstaat*. Munich: C. H. Beck.

Prokhanov, Alexander. 2019. "Putin – russkiy mechtatel." *Izborskiy Klub*. https://izborskclub.ru/16446.

Pronina, Nataliya. 2008. *Alexandr Nevskiy: Natsionalnyy geroy ili predatel?* Moscow: Yauza.

Reginskaya, Natalya, and Sergey Tsvetkov. 2010. *Blagovernyy kniaz pravoslavnoy Rusi – svyatoy voin Alexandr Nevskiy*. Saint Petersburg: Blitz.

Restle, Marcell. 1991. "Kriegerheilige." In *Lexikon des Mittelalters*, Vol. 5, edited by Gernot Giertz, 1528. Munich: Artemis-Verlag.

Richters, Katja. 2013. *The Post-Soviet Russian Orthodox Church: Politics, Culture and Greater Russia*. New York: Routledge.

Rogov, Alexandr. 1967. "Alexandr Nevskiy i borba russkogo naroda s nemetskoy feodalnoy agressiyey v drevnerusskoy pismennosti i iskusstve." In *"Drang nach Osten" i istoricheskoye razvitiye stran Tsentralnoy, Vostochnoy i Yugo-Vostochnoy Yevropy*, 32–58. Moscow: Nauka.

'God is in truth, not in power!' 131

Rohdewald, Stefan. 2014. *Götter der Nationen. Religiöse Erinnerungsfiguren in Serbien, Bulgarien und Makedonien bis 1944*. Köln: Böhlau Verlag.

Rousselet, Kathy. 2013. The Russian Orthodox Church and Reconciliation with the Soviet Past." In *History, Memory and Politics in Central and Eastern Europe. Memory Games*, edited by Laure Neumayer and Georges Mink, 39–53. Basingstoke: Palgrave Macmillan.

———. 2015. "The Church in the Service of the Fatherland." *Europe-Asia Studies* 67 (1): 49–67.

Rumelili, Bahar. 2018. "Breaking with Europe's Pasts: Memory, Reconciliation, and Ontological (In)security." *European Security* 27 (3): 280–95.

Samerski, Stefan, and Krista Zach. 2007. "Einleitung." In *Die Renaissance der Nationalpatrone. Erinnerungskulturen in Ostmitteleuropa im 20./21. Jahrhundert*, edited by Stefan Samerski and Krista Zach, 1–9. Köln: Böhlau Verlag.

Sarti, Laury. 2013. *Perceiving War and the Military in Early Christian Gaul (ca. 400–700 A.D.)*. Leiden: Brill.

Scharff, Thomas. 2004. "Karolingerzeitliche Vorstellungen vom Krieg vor dem Hintergrund der romanisch-germanischen Kultursynthese." In *Akkulturation: Probleme einer germanisch-romanischen Kultursynthese in Spätantike und frühem Mittelalter*, edited by Dieter Hägermann, Wolfgang Haubrichs and Jörg Jarnut, 473–90. Oldenburg: de Gruyter.

Schenk, Frithjof Benjamin. 2004. *Aleksandr Nevskij. Heiliger-Fürst-Nationalheld. Eine Erinnerungsfigur im russischen kulturellen Gedächtnis (1263–2000)*. Köln: Böhlau Verlag.

———. 2007. "Alexander Newskij. Ein russischer Heiliger zwischen Resakralisierung und Profanierung." In *Die Renaissance der Nationalpatrone. Erinnerungskulturen in Ostmitteleuropa im 20./21. Jahrhundert*, edited by Stefan Samerski and Krista Zach, 41–61. Köln: Böhlau Verlag.

———. 2020. "Alexander Newski – Russlands unsterblicher Held." *Ost-West. Europäische Perspektiven* 3: 210–18.

Seleznev, Alexander, and Boris Tsarev. 2005. "Flotskiye i grazhdanskiye khramy vo imya Sv. Blagovernogo velikogo kniazya Alexandra Nevskogo." *Morskoy Vestnik* 1 (13): 102–8.

Semenkov, Vadim. 2014. "'Ne v sile Bog no v pravde'. Kommentariy k izvestnomu vyskazyvaniyu Aleksandra Nevskogo." *Vestnik Russkoy khristianskoy gumanitarnoy akademii* 15 (3): 183–89.

Shlyapkin, Ilya. 1915. *Ikonografiya blagovernogo knyazya Alexandra Nevskogo*. Petrograd: Tipografiya M. A. Alexandrova.

Sigov, Constantine. 2014. "Pravda." In *Dictionary of Untranslatables: A Philosophical Lexicon*, edited by Barbara Cassin, 813–19. Princeton, NJ: Princeton University Press.

Sirenov, Alexey. 2017. "Alexander Nevskiy v culture Rossii srednevekovya i novogo vremeni." In *Trudy otdeleniya istoriko-filologicheskikh nauk, 2016*, 368–80. Moscow: Nauka.

Sorokin, Piotr. 2017. *Okresnosti Peterburga. Iz istorii izhorskoy zemli*. Saint Petersburg: Tsentrpoligraf.

Sperling, Valerie. 2009. "Making the Public Patriotic: Militarism and Anti-Militarism in Russia." In *Russian Nationalism and the National Reassertion of Russia*, edited by Marlène Laruelle, 218–71. New York: Routledge.

Sukina, Liudmila. 2019. "Alexandr Nevskiy – 'koren Russkogo gosudarstva' v knizhnosti v izobrazitelnom iskusstve XVII v." In *Aksiologicheskoye prostranstvo russkoy slovesnosti: traditsii i perspektivy izucheniya*, edited by M. Mikhaylov, 219–24. Moscow: Izdatelskiy tsentr MGIK.

Svyashchenniki Peterburga proveli krestnyy khod dlya izbavleniya ot virusa. 2020. *Interfax*. www.interfax.ru/russia/701399.

Torbakov, Igor. 2014. "The Russian Orthodox Church and Contestations Over History in Contemporary Russia." *Demokratizatsiya* 22 (1): 145–70.

132 *Liliya Berezhnaya*

Torkunov, Anatoliy, Oleg Kudryavtsev, and Valentina Ukolova, eds. 2010. *Alexandr Nevskiy. Gosudar, diplomat, voin.* Moscow: R. Valent.

Trifankov, Yuriy. 2016. "Salralnoye znacheniye davleniya Zapada na Rossiyu." In *Izborskiy Klub.* https://izborsk-club.ru/11118.

V istoricheskom parke sostavyat portret Alexandra Nevskogo. 2018. *Rossiya – moya istoriya.* https://myhistorypark.ru/poster/v-istoricheskom-parke-sostavyat-portret-aleksandra-nevskogo/?city=ros.

V Russkoy Pravoslavnoy Tserkvi rezko vystupayut protiv prevrashcheniya imen svyatykh v kommercheskie brendy. 2007. *Interfax-Religion.* www.interfax-religion.ru/?act=news&div=20549.

Verovšek, Peter J. 2016. "Collective Memory, Politics, and the Influence of the Past: The Politics of Memory as a Research Paradigm." *Politics, Groups, and Identities* 4 (3): 529–43.

Voronovich, Alexandr, and Anastasiya Felker. 2020. "V poiskakh proshlogo: memorialnyy landshaft nepriznannoy PMR." In *Politika pamyati v sovremennoy Rossii i stranakh Vostochnoy Yevropy: instituty, aktory, narrativy,* edited by Alexey Miller and Dmitriy Yefremenko, 572–90. Saint Petersburg: Izdatelstvo Yevropeyskogo Universiteta.

Vozdushnyy krestnyy khod protiv koronavirusa proveli v Rossii. 2020. *Uralinform.* www.uralinform.ru/news/society/325538-vozdushnyi-krestnyi-hod-protiv-koronavirusa-proveli-v-rossii/?utm_source=yxnews&utm_medium=desktop&utm_referrer=https%3A%2F%2Fyandex.ru%2Fnews.

Vystupleniye Svyateyshego Patriarkha Kirilla na torzhestvennom otkrytii III Assamblei Russkogo mira. 2020. *Official site of the Moscow Patriarchate.* www.patriarchia.ru/db/text/928446.html.

Vystupleniye Svyateyshego Patriarkha Kirilla na zasedanii Orgkomiteta po podgotovke i provedeniyu yubileynykh meropriyatiy, posvyashchennykh 800-letiyu so dnya rozhdeniya kniazya Alexandra Nevskogo. 2019. www.patriarchia.ru/db/text/5497869.html.

Walter, Christopher. 2003. *The Warrior Saints in Byzantine Art and Tradition.* Aldershot: Ashgate.

Wawrzonek, Michał. 2016. "'Russkiy mir': A Conceptual Model of the Orthodox Civilization." In *Orthodoxy Versus Post-Communism? Belarus, Serbia, Ukraine and the Russkiy Mir,* edited by Michał Wawrzonek, Nelly Bekus and Mirella Korzeniewska-Wiszniewska, 37–70. Newcastle-upon-Tyne: Cambridge Scholars.

White, Monica. 2013. *Military Saints in Byzantium and Rus, 900–1200.* Cambridge: Cambridge University Press.

White, Stephen, and Valentina Feklyunina. 2014. *Identities and Foreign Policies in Russia, Ukraine and Belarus: The Other Europes.* Basingstoke: Palgrave Macmillan.

Wijermars, Mariëlle. 2018. *Memory Politics in Contemporary Russia: Television, Cinema and the State.* New York: Routledge.

Wünsch, Thomas. 2013. "Einleitung: Religiöse Erinnerungsorte in Ostmitteleuropa." In *Religiöse Erinnerungsorte in Ostmitteleuropa. Konstitution und Konkurrenz im nationen- und epochenübergreifenden Zugriff,* edited by Joachim Bahlcke, Stefan Rohdewald and Thomas Wünsch, xv–xxxiii. Berlin: Akademie Verlag.

Yakhshiyan, Oleg. 2019. "Russkiy kulturny (tsivilizatsionny) kod. Identchnost i politika." *Vestnik Universiteta* 10: 52–58.

Yurganov, Alexey. 1998. *Kategorii russkoy srednevekovoy kultury.* Moscow: Miros.

"Zhitiye Alexandra Nevskogo. Pervaya redaktsiya. 1280-e gody. Rekonstruktsiya teksta Povesti o zhitii i o khrabrosti blagovernogo i velikogo knyazya Oleksandra." 1995. In *Kniaz Alexander Nevsky i yego epokha,* edited by Yuriy Begunov and Anatoliy Kirpichnikov, 190–203. Saint Petersburg: Dmitry Bulanin.

7 The martyrdom of Jozef Tiso

The entanglements of the sacred and secular in post-war Catholic memories

Agáta Šústová Drelová

Martyrs and the processes that make them constitute an important part of post-war Catholic memory and history. Recent cases of martyrs being canonized or beatified (a form of recognition that smooths the path for their public veneration) have generated much public as well as scholarly interest (Woodward 1990; Peterson 1997; Leemans and Mettepenningen 2005; Royal 2006; Blacker and Fedor 2015; Caridi 2016; Cunningham 2005; Middleton 2020; Rodriguéz 2017). The post-socialist era saw a particularly pronounced increase in the popularity of the public veneration of saints, not only those who were already established, but also others, including New Martyrs, who were deemed to be victims of the communist state (Samerski 2007; Bogumił and Łukaszewicz 2018; Kolstø 2010; Christensen 2017). Despite this growing interest in the study of officially sanctioned martyrdom, comparatively little attention has been dedicated to the study of the veneration of those who are not (yet or at all) considered fit for beatification or canonization. So far, the focus has been on the practice of veneration (i.e. the commemoration of canonized martyrs) rather than, more generally, commemoration of Catholic historical figures. Moreover, the few studies that have been completed have mostly concerned non-Catholic, especially Orthodox, conceptualizations of martyrdom (Ciobanu 2018; Conovici 2013).

While official and unofficial 'saints' differ in the extent to which their celebration is allowed in the public spaces of the Church, the commemorative cultures created around both kinds of saint offer equally interesting windows into the dynamics of Catholic memory or, more specifically, windows into the entanglements between the secular and sacred, religious and political, and elite and popular. The saint-making projects, successful or not, have been enveloped by nonreligious contexts and influences, making it impossible at times to draw a clear line between the sacred and secular. In fact, it makes sense to think about martyrdom (official or unofficial) in more general terms as a 'key node within a cluster of semantically rich and interlinked concepts – victimhood, sacrifice, persecution – all of which can be used to mount compelling claims to legitimacy and authority, especially in the absence of alternative channels for

DOI: 10.4324/9781003264750-9

134 Agáta Šústová Drelová

political expression' (to use the definition formulated by historians of memory Ulieam Blacker and Julie Fedor 2015, 198).

An especial place among these 'saintly' figures has been held by those associated with attempts to 'renew nations' and nation states. In countries where the communist era was almost immediately preceded by a pro-Nazi regime (as was the case in Slovakia), the commemoration of these individuals has been greatly influenced by the memories of both previous political systems. Such attempts were often informed by a desire to return to the pre-communist past, a time when, the promoters of these figures typically argue, these nations were independent and more in contact with their presumably Christian character (Kolstø 2011).

This chapter explores the making of Jozef Tiso's martyrdom and, more specifically, which actors were able to create and maintain this unofficial martyr within official post-war (and especially post-communist Catholic) discourse, when and how they did this and to what extent they achieved this. Tiso was a Roman Catholic priest who was also the first and only president of the 1939–45 Nazi-satellite Slovak Republic. His was a presidency during which more than 70,000 Slovak Jews were deported to and died at Auschwitz (Ward 2013, 8). After the end of the Second World War, Tiso was tried by a Communist-dominated national court for collaboration, treason and crimes against humanity. Found guilty on all charges, he was hanged on 18 April 1947. Tiso's supporters, many of whom were one-time members of Hlinka's Slovak People's Party, the ruling party in the wartime state, and who had therefore fled Slovakia before the advancing Soviet army, subsequently viewed Tiso as a martyr. In the late 1970s they made their first attempts to promote Tiso's beatification, and these continued after 1989 in Slovakia, when they sought to have Tiso beatified and commemorated not only as a 'martyr for faith' but also as a 'martyr for nation', in effect demanding a title not recognized by the Church. Their initiative, which portrayed Tiso as a martyr of communist persecution, was possible largely thanks to the continuous appeal of anti-communism in the public discourse of the Cold War–era Western democracies. The appeal of anti-communism survived the fall of state socialism and gained new relevance in post-communist societies. In post-1989 Slovakia, it was the Catholic hierarchy that significantly contributed to the maintenance of Tiso's memory as an unofficial martyr, first indirectly, by participating at commemorations organized by those seeking Tiso's beatification, and later directly, especially by celebrating requiem mass services. After 1989, memory of Tiso as a 'martyr for faith and nation' was kept alive by the specific anti-communist, nationalist and clerical focus of post-communist Catholic memory. At the centre of this memory was an image of the Roman Catholic Church as the chief victim of the Communist persecution, which was anchored in a broader national narrative in which the Slovak nation figures as the victim of suppression by other nations, especially the Hungarians and Czechs (Panczová 2020).

Martyrdom in official and popular Catholic memory

Martyrs and their stories of martyrdom are historically an important part of Christian, and especially Roman Catholic, memory. Viewed from a theoretical angle grounded in social or collective memory, beatification and canonization can be understood as the authorization or recognition of particular Catholic figures and their lives for the purposes of collective commemoration, more precisely, for veneration. Memory is central to the making of martyrs. Recognized memory is anchored in ritual veneration that is often part of the liturgy and closely resembles commemoration of the Passion of Christ (Caridi 2016; Woodward 1990). Recognition by the Church thus means not only authorizing a memory for commemoration, but also confirming the compatibility of a personal story with the larger historical narrative of persecution for faith.

Canonization, generally speaking, is a decree that allows public and universal ecclesiastical veneration of an individual. Although, as Kenneth Woodward points out in his study on the practice of making saints, the Roman Catholic Church has never issued a dogmatic definition of martyrdom, the early Church did develop a 'classical model' of the martyr as 'an innocent victim who dies for the faith at the hands of a tyrant who is opposed to the faith' (Woodward 1990, 130). This model of martyrdom clearly centres on faith. The centrality of faith was further reinforced by the post-Reformation pope, Benedict XIV, who, according to Woodward's summary, established strict criteria according to which 'advocates of a cause must show that the victim died for the faith . . . they have to prove that the "tyrant" was provoked into killing the victim by the latter's clear and unambiguous profession of faith'. They therefore need to provide evidence and produce witnesses affirming that 'a profession of faith took place, that the tyrant acted in *odium fidei* (hatred of the faith), and that the victim's motives, if not unalloyed, are clearly religious' (Woodward 1990, 129).

The 1980s and the papacy of John Paul II brought a breakthrough in the definition of martyrdom. Having already gained a reputation for canonizing and beatifying more candidates than any of the previous popes (Higgins 2006; Bennett 2011), John Paul II made it his personal cause to canonize Maximilian Kolbe, a Catholic priest killed by the Nazis at Auschwitz. Although a Vatican commission ruled that it could not be proved that Kolbe was killed for his faith and therefore, he could not be canonized as a martyr, John Paul II canonized Kolbe in 1982 not only for his heroic virtue (another qualification for sainthood), but also as a 'martyr of charity'. The pope's action introduced the category of 'martyrs of charity', signalling, argues Anna L. Peterson, that 'a person can die a martyr's death for one element of Christian belief rather than for the faith or the church in general' (Peterson 1997, 94). This conceptualization was buttressed by Jesuit theologian Karl Rahner in his famous call for a redefinition of martyrdom that would 'involve the entirety of the Christian message' (Rahner 1983, 9). As Peterson clarifies, 'in this light, a believer who willingly dies for an aspect of the faith, such as charity, justice, or peace, can be considered a martyr "for the faith"' (Peterson 1997, 95). This conceptualization of

136   *Agáta Šústová Drelová*

martyrdom was not entirely new. Indeed, the thirteenth-century philosopher Thomas Aquinas asserted that 'dying for the common good could be considered martyrdom from a theological perspective' (Peterson 1997, 94). These shifts, as well as the end of Communist rule in Central Eastern Europe, created space for emergence of new unofficial martyrs. Martyrs whose death could not, and cannot, be clearly established as martyrdom for faith or, for that matter, charity (Hlavinka and Kamenec 2014). Indeed, as will be elaborated later, the Aquinasian definition of martyrdom was referred to in early claims for Tiso's beatification. Yet, scholars of religious, and in particular Catholic, memory have largely overlooked these cases.

This omission, in part, is owing to the fact that early theoretizations of religious memory followed traditional Church history, and especially its understanding of religion being isolated from the outside (secular) world and its focus on ecclesiastical elites. For example, for Maurice Halbwachs, whose works on memory were largely written with the Catholic Church in mind, religious memory was characterized by normativity which 'is inherent in the structure of the religious group, mostly in the unequal relationship that binds the simple believers – ordinary believers in ritualized remembrance – to the authorized producers of collective memory' (Hervieu-Léger 2006, 125–26; Davie 2000, 31–33).

However, in popular religiosity, which has historically played a crucial role in the maintenance of the cults of saints and martyrs, recognized memory of canonized or beatified figures can very easily get reconstructed according to popular cultural needs (Spalová 2012). Indeed, as argued by Oliver Bennett, the twentieth-century papacy itself played an important role in this 'popularization' of saints. Pope John Paul II promoted popular sanctity through a 'sustained programme' of 'strategic canonization', that is, by propagating carefully chosen 'models of sanctity that conveyed very clear social and political messages' (Bennett 2011, 438). The same applies to the making of unofficial martyrs. Unrecognized memory, too, has not infrequently been maintained by authorized producers of memory, such as bishops. To an extent this is a matter of the specific role they perform in the beatification process, where they play a central role at the local stage: it is they who decide whether or not a cause will be sent to Rome for consideration. But alongside guarding 'purity of faith', their role is also to represent the Church in the secular world. In short, bishops also seek to promote martyrs and saints who reflect very specific social and political messages.

More generally, Catholic memory is always interacting with non-Catholic collective memory. As Elizabeth Castelli points out, memory work done by early Christians on the historical experience of persecution and martyrdom was a form of culture-making whereby Christian identity was profoundly marked by collective memory (Castelli 2004, 4). More specifically, as Kenneth Woodward argues with regard to boundaries between religious and political memory, 'once the church itself gained temporal as well as spiritual authority over her subjects, the line between political and religious martyrdom became more difficult to draw' (Woodward 1990, 127).

This blurring of lines is evident in the impact nationalism has had on Catholic memory. The rise of nationalism, whether religious or secular, has altered the boundaries between officially recognized and unrecognized memory. Indeed, the nineteenth century saw the papacy struggling to control many of its faithful who were too readily succumbing to the trend for nationalization. But as the Church gradually accepted the modern nation state, and local churches began to search for ways to strengthen their legitimacy, nationally minded Catholics, who by this time included hierarchs, began to nationalize Catholic memories and Catholicize national memories. Given their great mobilizing power, the cults of saints and martyrs were widely used, often turning them into national patrons and patronesses and integrating them into national historical narratives. This state was enabled and reinforced by a number of developments. First, religion remained closely tied to politics. Although the Church had lost most of its political power by the early twentieth century, by the middle of the century its clergy remained variously connected to political power. Second, the Catholic laity were empowered, mainly thanks to party politics, into becoming active, if unauthorized, producers of Catholic memory. All these Catholic actors integrated officially recognized saints into unrecognized collective memories, and the boundaries between recognized and unrecognized memories became less clear. All the while, the Church's magisterium remained silent on the subject of nation (Llywelyn 2010, 2) and the relationship between Catholicism and nationalism.

This is not to suggest that recognized memory has lost its role. On the contrary, beatification and canonization continue to set limits to the Catholic production of collective (including national) memory. Indeed, even as 'tyrants' change, martyrs should be similar in death; martyrdom for faith integrates their story into the universal narrative of persecution, even as the forms of commemoration change. But the official process of making saints is far from being the only process through which Catholic memory is being created. This complexity in the making of Catholic memory is evident in the making of one unofficial martyr: Jozef Tiso.

Tiso's life and death

The life and death of the Catholic priest and politician Jozef Tiso was in many ways emblematic of twentieth-century entanglements between the sacred and secular, ecclesial and political, and national and supranational; entanglements that helped to create, maintain and legitimize Tiso's martyrdom. As maintained by the author of Tiso's most recent biography James Mace Ward, Tiso's life and histories can be understood as expressions of three 'theologies', two of which are especially pertinent to this study:

> The first is a Catholic theology in which vices and virtues are clearly delineated, in which priests function as moral experts, and in which God is the final object of man's exile on earth. The second is modern vision of

138 *Agáta Šústová Drelová*

morality in which notions of progress supplant religion. Rather than God, the object of man's activities becomes various understandings of 'the people', be they nation, the working class, or the electorate.

(Ward 2013, 289)

These theologies were at the centre of Tiso's life as well as the ideology and politics of Hlinka's Slovak People's Party, his political home. It was these theologies that interlaced in the making of Tiso's martyrdom, both during his lifetime and after his death.

Tiso began his political career in 1918, the year when Austria-Hungary collapsed and Czechoslovakia was created. Tiso joined the Slovak People's Party (colloquially referred to as the *Ľudáci* (Ľudáks), which had been founded in 1913 by Andrej Hlinka, a Catholic priest, while Slovakia was still part of Austria-Hungary. During the interwar period, Tiso rose from among the leaders of the Slovak People's Party and became one of the most ardent proponents of Slovakia maintaining its autonomy within a Czechoslovak framework. After 1925, the Ľudáks were the largest party in Slovakia.

The party ideology centred on Catholicism and nationalism, gradually blending the two into a form of Catholic nationalism. The Ľudáks, who sought to achieve and maintain political autonomy or independence for the Slovak nation, were increasingly disposed against ethnic and ideological others (especially Czechs, Hungarians, Jews and Communists, with their worst enemies of course being imagined groups that combined more than one of the categories, such as 'Judaeo-Bolsheviks'). With Catholic priests comprising over a third of the party membership, Ľudák ideologues worked with Catholic teachings and theologies, which they typically nationalized and, in some cases, fascisized (Szabó 2018, 2019). The nationalization of Catholicism grew in extent and intensity as the party radicalized. By the early 1930s, the party was divided among radicals who openly admired Nazi Germany and moderates who sought to build a national ideology inspired by current Catholic social teaching and 'national traditions'. The clashes with increasingly self-confident radicals did not stop and Tiso began to perceive and portray his role in internal politics as that of sacrifice.

This sense of (self-)sacrifice was further reinforced by international developments. Tiso, argues Ward, found it increasingly hard to resist the internationalization of Slovak politics and eventually fully succumbed to the influence of Nazi Germany. The circumstances of the establishment of the wartime Slovak Republic, the state itself and Tiso's role in it constitute an important episode in Tiso's imagined martyrdom. When Hlinka died in 1938, Tiso quickly consolidated his control over the party, becoming its chairman in autumn 1939. In October 1938, Nazi Germany annexed and occupied the Sudetenland, the German-speaking parts of Czechoslovakia. Afterwards, the Slovaks declared their autonomy within Czechoslovakia. Tiso, as leader of the Hlinka Slovak People's Party (HSĽS), became prime minister of the autonomous Slovak region, with HSĽS introducing an authoritarian one-party rule. German representatives tried, as part of their plan to dismantle the remaining Czechoslovak state, to persuade Tiso in February 1939 to declare Slovakia independent. Tiso agreed only after Hitler threatened that in the event of Tiso's refusal, Germany would allow Hungary (and to a lesser extent Poland) to annex Slovakia's remaining territory. The Slovak parliament was convened on 14 March and unanimously declared the independence of Slovakia, which in effect became a German satellite (Felak 1994; Ward 2013; Kamenec 2013).

Tiso's apologists have sought to portray Tiso's fate in Nazifying Slovakia as one of everyday martyrdom for the nation, thereby shoring up the 'Christian' character of the state. They seek to extricate Tiso from Slovakia's Nazification and its tragic consequences (see e.g. Vnuk 1967; Sutherland 1973; Ďurica 1992, 2017), asserting that Tiso remained a consistent moderate and, in fact, protected the Slovak nation from the Nazifying influence of the radicals in his own party. They often interpret his position as one of principled opposition to the Nazification of Slovakia along Christian lines. This interpretation is most notable in their widespread tendency to credit him with principled opposition to the Jewish Code and the deportations (see e.g. Ďurica 1957, 1964). This, however, is mere hagiography. The moderates, and Tiso among them, showed inclinations towards anti-Semitism. Already by the end of the First World War, the priest Jozef Tiso was warning against the rise of communist ideas and the 'supremacy of the Jews in public and political life' (Kamenec 2013, 33). Tiso's anti-Semitism became fully apparent in his approach towards the Jews during his time as President of the Slovak Republic. Although papal encyclicals required Tiso, as a Roman Catholic priest, to oppose the racial basis of the Jewish Code, he did so only superficially, argues Ward. In his 15 August 1942 speech in the Slovak town of Holíč, he openly defended the state's anti-Semitic policy, equating it with a divine order to 'get rid of our parasite' (Fabricius and Hradská 2007, 492). Furthermore, apart from his anti-Semitism, Tiso likely viewed tacit and open cooperation with the deportations as instrumental in gaining German support against the radicals (Ward 2002, 224–41).

Non-Jews in Slovakia also suffered under Tiso's rule, especially during the suppression of the anti-Nazi Slovak National Uprising and the subsequent occupation of Slovakia by its Nazi patrons until spring 1945 (Ward 2013, 8). Tiso saw the Uprising as a conspiracy of Czechs, Jews and 'Slovak traitors', namely, forces 'alien' to the 'Christian' Slovak nation. Subsequently, he did not hesitate to hand over captured participants of the Uprising as well as their co-nationals (in the case of Jews) to the Germans, this time with active help from the paramilitary Hlinka guards. As Ward maintains, through these secular policies Tiso clearly gave priority to nationalist over Catholic concerns (Ward 2013, 286).

Tiso left Slovakia in early spring 1945, fleeing before the advancing Red Army across the territories of the crumbling Third Reich and hiding in monasteries in Austria's Kremsmünster and Bavaria's Altötting. After being captured by the American authorities, he was tried by a communist-dominated National Court in the Second Czechoslovak Republic for collaboration, treason and

140 *Agáta Šústová Drelová*

crimes against humanity and found guilty on all charges. Tiso was hanged on 18 April 1945. His final statement reveals that he was convinced that he was dying a martyr for his faith and for the Slovak nation at the hands of the Bolsheviks. The statement, which would become the centrepiece of his later glorification, included the following:

> I proclaim that I feel innocent. In politics I did only what the well-being and interest of the Slovak nation dictated. What I have done I have done according to my best judgement (conscience and consciousness), that is for the wellbeing and profit of the Slovak nation, being always led by moral rules, both in my understanding of the nation, and in the discernment of the means for its accomplishment; I have always and in many ways avoided evil and I have given way to it only if the nation was threatened with a greater evil, to avoid this evil.
>
> (Skala 1987)[1]

Despite the fact that nation was clearly his main priority, and the reason for his 'sacrifice', Tiso saw his death also in terms of faith. In a message he wrote to the Slovak nation before his execution, he stated that he understood himself to be a 'martyr for God's law . . . and a martyr for the defence of Christianity against Bolshevism' (Čulen 1992, 537). These words, especially the fact that Tiso identified 'Bolshevism' as the ideology beyond his execution would become an important fuel not only for the cause of his beatification but also more broadly for his commemoration in the late socialist and early post-socialist era.

The origins of Tiso's martyrdom among Slovak exiles

The beginnings of the cult of Tiso as a national martyr date to the late 1940s and beginning of the 1950s (Čulen 1992; Lacko 2019). At this time, émigrés who had escaped Slovakia out of fear of Soviet retaliation maintained the cult as part of a broader agenda promoting the renewal of independent Slovak statehood (Pešek and Vondrášek 2011; Lacko 2019). The understanding of Tiso as martyr for faith and nation was effectively a continuation of pre-war and wartime Catholic nationalism. The leitmotif of Tiso's martyrdom was sacrifice for the faith and the nation; the two were always mentioned together in evocations of his death.

The émigrés did not see martyrdom for 'faith and nation' as going against the classical model of Catholic martyrdom, a viewpoint they justified by referring to those (officially recognized) martyrs who represented political aspects of historical martyrdom. Jozef Papin, a theologian of Slovak origin who left Slovakia for the United States in 1946, taking up posts at the University of Notre Dame and later Villanova University, claimed that Tiso could be rightfully considered a martyr according to the Aquinasian definition of martyrdom. Papin argued that Tiso was a martyr for the common good and for a political cause. Such a conceptualization made his case appear similar to those of Thomas Becket, Thomas More or Joan of Arc (Papin 2014).

The distinctly anti-communist conceptualization of Tiso's martyrdom made the memory culture acceptable and even won support from some notable émigré anti-communists within and outside the Church. Anti-communism was one of the central rallying ideologies in the post-war Catholic Church. Pope Pius XII was a consistent fighter against communism and was followed by a generation of anti-communist clergy and bishops (Luxmoore and Babiuch 1999, 52–68). To this day, the émigrés claim that Fulton Sheen, a New York cardinal and Catholic celebrity, allegedly 'proclaimed before journalists several times, that Dr. Tiso was a true martyr, because he died in defence of God's and national truth' (Papin 2014). Although unconfirmed, the émigrés clearly believed the claim and spread it among themselves and after 1989 in Slovakia as well. Such proclamations not only left the cult unchallenged but added more strength to its justification and appeal.

This idolizing and uninformed approach to Tiso by some noted Catholic anti-communists was further reinforced as religion became part of a symbolic warfare during the Cold War. Historian of the Cold War Philip Muehlenbeck mentions a 'religious cold war', arguing that 'its main adversaries saw it that way, and to a certain extent framed their rivalry in religious terms' (Muehlenbeck 2012, xiii). In the Cold War context, religion (or religious affiliation) was seen in a patently positive light, as a 'prerequisite to democratic freedom' and as 'a weapon to wage the Cold War, for faith had a unique capacity to undermine irreligious (usually Communist) dictatorial regimes' (Muehlenbeck 2012, xiv). This understanding of religion (and, relatedly, religious figures) may thus work to overshadow the fact that some noted anti-communist Catholics collaborated with the Nazis.

The first organized campaign promoting Tiso as a candidate for beatification as a martyr began in the late 1970s (Kirschbaum 1999). In 1979, Paris-based Jesuit priest Jozef Kováč began what he presented as a 'nationwide prayer campaign' for the beatification of Jozef Tiso. The cause was promoted by émigré periodicals known for their nationalism, such as *Kanadský Slovák, Slovák v Amerike, Ave Maria, Slobodné Slovensko,* and others (Nesnadný 1978; Bor-Žatko 1980, 1984; *Kanadský Slovák* 1983; *Slobodné Slovensko* 1983). As Kováč argued, 'Slovaks all over the world are steadfastly convinced that the first [Slovak] president is a true martyr, his death was the death of a true saint' (Kováč 1980). He created a special prayer, which was distributed among Slovak exiles. This was not a standard way of starting a beatification process and was given by the fact that starting this process in Slovakia was out of the question.

The prayer revealed two persistent agendas: separatist nationalism and anti-communism. In the thanksgiving part of the prayer, Tiso was described as 'accepting a martyr's death for his faith and his nation', as 'a defender of faith and martyr for God and for nation'. In the intercession, in particular, the nationalist component was reinforced by a strong anti-communist one. They asked God to 'grant the Slovak nation . . . our lost freedom and convert those who persecute our nation and our faithful people'. But they also asked for 'conversion of all those, who blindly sow and spread godless communism.

142 *Agáta Šústová Drelová*

Make it so that the atheistic and inhumane communism is to be overcome as soon as possible, so that you defeat it soon and definitively'.[2]

The organizers of the initiative were able to secure some organizational support from representatives of the Church. The prayer was given an imprimatur (i.e. a license to be published) by Msgr. Joseph T. O' Keefe, vicar general of the New York archdiocese. In addition, a group of Ľudák émigrés were allowed to organize an annual pilgrimage to one of the most significant German Marian pilgrimage sites in Altötting, Bavaria (beginning in 1979).

Officially unhindered, the Slovak émigrés in Canada gathered in the Canadian Slovak League were increasingly active. Their periodical, *Kanadský Slovák* (Canadian Slovak), was packed with articles about Jozef Tiso and advocacy for his beatification *(Zahraniční Slováci a ich činnosť za slovenskú štátnosť. Svedectvá pravdy III. Diel* 1999). But support for such promotion of Tiso as a 'martyr for faith and nation' was not universal among the Slovak émigrés.

The attempts to promote the cause of Tiso's beatification were opposed by a number of moderate exiles, some of whom worked for Radio Free Europe (RFE). At RFE, they acquired a good knowledge of Western foreign policies, something the first wave of Ľudák émigrés had never had. They were fully aware that despite the persistent appeal of anti-communism, especially in the conservative circles in the West, there was little chance for the acceptance of separatist Slovak nationalism, in particular in its Ľudák form. This second wave of Ľudák émigrés continued to support the cause of greater Slovak independence but were aware that the cause could not derive its legitimacy from the wartime Slovak Republic. For example, when in the 1950s they attempted to persuade RFE to establish a separate Slovak section, they were turned down (Šramek 1991). RFE, which, as Arch Puddington writes, was known as a 'general rule to favour those groups which best reflected Western democratic values as opposed to those of nationalist or populist stripe' (Puddington 2000, 268), was not willing to make any concessions on this point, either then or during the late-socialist period. Within this context, the campaign for Tiso's beatification was only adding insult to injury.

Seeking to halt the Ľudák émigrés, these moderates contacted some Slovak exiles in Rome because they were the closest to the papacy. They expected them to confirm that there was no real chance of starting the process (Braxátor 1992, 160–63). In fact, the Rome-based Bishop Dominik Hrušovský, who was the clerical leader of the Slovak Catholic émigrés, was not willing to endorse the cause and tried to stop pilgrimages to Altötting (Cagáň 2014). This, however, did not mean that he wished Tiso to be forgotten. The Rome-based exiles confirmed that beatification would not be possible but did not see the case as hopeless. Instead of gaining an ally in their efforts to thwart the beatification campaign, the moderate émigrés found out that the cause had more supporters among the Rome émigrés.

These Rome-based émigrés did not refuse the cause as such; they simply advised a change of strategy. They pointed out that there was little chance at the time that the Vatican would be in favour (the Vatican had only recently published a volume of diplomatic documents from the Second World War, which included documents confirming Tiso's refusal to heed the Vatican's protests against the discrimination and eventual deportation of Jews from Slovakia).[3] In addition, they saw further obstacles in Slovakia. The Church in Slovakia was controlled by the state and according to these émigrés, there was not the slightest chance that the bishop currently presiding over the Banská Bystrica Diocese, where Tiso had spent most of his life, would promote the cause in the Vatican. Indeed, Bishop Jozef Feranec was a loyal supporter of the Communist Party and its rule (Zúbek 1984). Yet these current circumstances, they argued, were not unchangeable. Moreover, much could be done to help the cause even before the actual process was officially started. A writer for *Slovenske Hlasy z Ríma*, a periodical read by Slovak, mostly clerical, émigrés in Rome, came up with a rather long list of what could be done to further this cause in the meantime. He suggested that prayers should be said for the cause. In doing so, the faithful would contribute to maintaining *fama sanctitatis*, namely, the reputation of sanctity that, if well established, can contribute to furthering the process of beatification.

Regardless of whether the Slovak nationalist émigrés followed this advice, or whether they identified their agenda of Slovak independence as important, most of them celebrated Tiso as a statesman. For those who did strive for Tiso's beatification, the fall of state socialism, which brought the state control of the Church to an end, marked a new chance to relaunch the cause. For these nationalists, Tiso's beatification made perfect sense, especially after forty years of a communist regime that Tiso and his followers opposed.

Tiso's martyrdom and Catholic activists in Slovakia

Catholics in Slovakia did not follow up on the Ľudák attempts to start the beatification process. The year 1987, which was the fortieth anniversary of Tiso's execution, saw the publication of a single brief account of Tiso's life and death (Skala 1987). In general, the coverage of Tiso was limited for several reasons.

First, Catholic activists nipped any potential interest in Tiso in the bud to avoid attacks from the official authorities. The communist one-party state identified itself as the inheritor of the anti-fascist traditions, especially the tradition of the Slovak National Uprising that significantly helped bring Tiso's Slovak state to an end (Jablonický 2009, 46–48). The official authorities readily labelled and prosecuted any activities of Catholic activists as if they were all related in some way to the wartime Slovak state (*Pravda* 1988, 11–12 February), despite the fact that most of these activities were focused on the promotion of greater religious freedom (Šimulčík 1997, 2000). Even once the interest in Tiso had started to appear by the late 1980s, Catholic activists sought to present their main focus of interest as serious historical research, and often considered both official and unofficial sources. The accounts that did emerge were purely reactions to official attacks. The best-known response of that kind was a letter addressed by the clerical leader of Catholic underground church Bishop Ján Chryzostom Korec to Czechoslovak TV reacting to a series titled *Crucifix in the Snares of Power*, which portrayed the Catholic Church as fully

144   *Agáta Šústová Drelová*

supporting Tiso's state and Tiso himself as a pro–Nazi Catholic (*Príloha Rodin-ného spoločenstva* 1989; *Katolícky Mesačník* 1989). The younger generation of Catholics also avoided Tiso in an effort to create a modern national ideology that could be used in a new democratic system (see e.g. the writings of Ján Čarnogurský 1997).

The communist state thus, on the one hand, contributed to the creation of an image of Tiso as a victim of communism by making him a 'victim' of official forgetting, and on the other, kept Catholics away from the influence of émigrés promoting Tiso's beatification. Some of these reasons for avoiding the com-memoration of Tiso disappeared with the fall of state socialism. Tiso's death could then potentially become an example of the suffering of the Catholic Church over the forty years of the communist regime.

Martyrdom, the Catholic Church and Catholics after 1989

After the fall of state socialism, which in Czechoslovakia began in Novem-ber 1989, a number of Catholic activists assumed top political and ecclesial positions. Ján Chryzostom Korec was ordained the bishop of the Nitra diocese and was later appointed cardinal. The hierarchy itself went from being incom-plete and fully dependent on the socialist state to being fully staffed and more or less independent. Many former members of the underground church joined the Christian Democratic Movement (KDH) established in February 1990 and led by the Catholic activist Ján Čarnogurský.

The Christian Democrats, together with the hierarchy, spearheaded or co-organized an increasing number of pilgrimages, commemorations and public events. Although some of these Catholic elites got involved in maintaining the memory of Jozef Tiso by participating at various commemorative events organized by Tiso's apologists (Jablonický 2009; *Zamlčaná pravda o Slovensku* 1997), others overlooked these events or opposed them. These differing atti-tudes to Tiso and the cause for his martyrdom typically reflected the Catholic elites' stance on the issue of Slovakia's political independence.

With the political future of Slovakia, and the Czechoslovak federation more generally, becoming one of the key topics in post-socialist Slovak politics, the cause of Tiso's martyrdom quickly became entangled with contemporary poli-tics. The cause of Slovak independence was advocated by separatist nationalists. They promoted the cause of Slovak independence as a struggle for either Slo-vak sovereignty (*zvrchovanosť*) or Slovak self-determination (*sebaurčenie*). Both of these terms signified the fast-tracked exit of Slovakia from the common state. These nationalists were recruited from ex-communist nationalists – who domi-nated the *Matica Slovenská* heritage organization and Slovak National Party – and from among separatist Ľudák émigrés.

The Ľudák advocates of Tiso's beatification hoped to find support for both immediate independence and the rehabilitation of Tiso and the Slovak state among ex-dissident Catholics. However, their appeal for support was met with a mixed reaction. They turned to František Mikloško, a former Catholic activist – who was by then a leading member of the first and largest pro-democratic

The martyrdom of Jozef Tiso 145

movement, the Public Against Violence (VPN), and the chairman of the Slovak parliament – with an appeal for Tiso's rehabilitation (interview with the author, 13 July 2011). Instead of heeding Tiso's apologists, Mikloško organized a conference that brought together both critics and defenders of Tiso (Bystrický 1992). The Ľudáks did not fare much better with the related cause of immediately attaining Slovak independence.

The Christian Democratic leaders, in particular, steered clear of the beatification cause. The Ľudáks were present at the first congress of the KDH in 1990, where they suggested that Slovak independence should become the movement's central goal. Ján Čarnogurský, the leader of the movement, thought otherwise. As he asserted, the Christian Democrats endorsed 'the Czechoslovak federation, and at the same time [envisioned] Slovakia's [future] position as an independent subject in any future supra-state integration, whether within Central Europe or within Europe' (Čarnogurský 1990). Čarnogurský affirmed the 'right to self-determination'. But, as he elaborated, he did not derive this right from 'the existence of the Slovak state in 1939–1945' but 'from international law' and from the existence of the Slovak people as 'an independent nation' (*Smena* 1990, 11 October). In this respect, the Christian democratic approach resonated more with the late 1980s attitude of moderate émigrés. Čarnogurský also rejected the Ľudák sites of memory, particularly Altötting, as he was seeking a democratic historical grounding for his self-determination project, a grounding that would seem feasible to the international community (Cagáň 2014).

Tiso's apologists and their cause for Tiso's martyrdom was more successful with the Catholic hierarchy. At that point, the ex-dissident Bishop Ján Ch. Korec, widely considered a symbol of resistance against 'totalitarianism', took part in a commemoration of Jozef Tiso organized by émigrés in July 1990 in support of Slovakia's independence. On the émigrés' initiative, a plaque dedicated to Tiso was installed on the façade of the former Teaching Academy in Bánovce nad Bebravou, Western Slovakia. Tiso had been the dean of the Bánovce parish from 1924 until 1945, which included his time in office as president of the Slovak state. In 1934, he had established this local Roman Catholic Men's Teaching Academy in the town. In a clear reference to Slovak state ideology, the organizers referred to Tiso as 'successor to Svätopluk' (according to nationalist narratives, the first king of the first Slovak Kingdom, ninth-century Great Moravia). Beneath this title, the plaque displayed Tiso's motto: 'Faithful to ourselves, forward together' (*Bojovník* 1990). At the end of the ceremony, a Catholic hymn of praise and gratitude, the *Te Deum*, was sung, giving the event the air of solemn Catholic ritual.

Korec's participation at the event was subjected to a barrage of criticism in the media. His presence was interpreted by some critics as 'moral support' for the political project of Slovak independence (Kocúr 2009, 225). In fact, Korec would later become an ardent supporter of the separatist nationalists. But in the summer of 1990, he was not yet giving any open support to independence or any of the other ultranationalist projects. At that time, Korec argued that he had not noticed the inscriptions and was simply there to acknowledge 'Tiso's contribution to Slovak culture', a notion which, in his view, had been

146   *Agáta Šústová Drelová*

supressed by the previous regime (*Národná obroda* 1990). At this stage, Korec's main motivation may well have been anti-communism. But nationalism soon began to play an equally important role.

Even though the persecution of the Church was stopped in 1989, some Catholics understood criticism of Tiso as an instance of anti-clericalism reminiscent of the communist regime. The criticism that followed in the wake of the plaque installation mobilized Korec's fellow bishops into displaying both private and public support for Jozef Tiso and endorsing his martyrdom. Bishops Alojz Tkáč of Košice and Eduard Kojnok of Rožňava wrote immediately to the Slovak National Assembly (SNR). Bishop Tkáč wrote on behalf of all the priests of the Košice diocese, claiming that 'bishops, priests, and religious as well as non-religious, truth-loving people are outraged by how the media are being misused' (Tkáč 1990). He wrote: 'we object to the understanding of the Slovak state and its president Dr. Jozef Tiso; [this understanding] is not at all different from the evaluation that had been given by Marxist historiography for the past 45 years'. Indeed, the bishops were clearly most appalled by the fact that some of the criticism came from historians who had worked unhindered during the communist regime. Clearly, they claimed, the persecution of the Church had not really ceased in 1989; it had merely changed its form. Korec also lamented what he presented as 'continuing attacks on the Church', arguing that even 'in times of freedom it is still not possible to obtain the whole truth about president Tiso'. But what was 'this whole truth about Tiso'?

Over the following months and years, some bishops embraced the nationalist Ľudák narrative, perceiving and portraying Tiso as a martyr, even as his martyrdom remained officially unrecognized by the Church. According to Bishop Kojnok, who wrote to the SNR on behalf of the priests from his diocese, 'Slovaks are convinced that the trial of Dr. Jozef Tiso was unfair'; adding that 'our fathers went to the SNP [Slovak National Uprising] to fight for Tiso' (Kojnok 1990). In short, if these Catholic Bishops in Slovakia were primed by anti-communism to support the cause for Tiso's martyrdom, it was nationalism that kept them engaged in the cause.

As the debate about the future status of Slovakia culminated in the proclamation of Slovak sovereignty in July 1992 and the eventual breakup of the federation (1 January 1993), some hierarchs, especially those who had sympathized with the advocates of Slovak independence, aligned themselves beyond the newly founded state. To be precise, not all the bishops supported the ruling Movement for Democratic Slovakia (the HZDS) and its leader Vladimír Mečiar, who advanced the cause of Slovak sovereignty. But most of the hierarchy did mobilize the Catholic past towards building the state's official memory.

Shortly after the declaration of sovereignty at the Slovak National Council, *Katolícke Noviny*, the major Catholic weekly controlled by the hierarchy, published an article by ex-communist historian turned ardent nationalist Anna Magdolenová on Tiso's thoughts on nation: 'The goal of politicians should be service to God and nation in the interest of convergence towards higher spiritual civilization'. According to Magdolenová's interpretation, Tiso understood nation as a 'community created by the Creator from biological roots in the process of ethnogenesis' (Magdolenová 1992). According to Tiso, the assertion of national liberty and independence was 'reverence and fulfilment of God's will'. In his understanding of the meaning of the history, nations are called upon to contribute to human progress directed towards spirituality; their political independence is a necessary prerequisite to attaining this goal.

It followed that dying for Slovak independence equalled dying for faith in a national form. Work for the nation was thus work for the realization of faith. According to another *Katolícke Noviny* article written by the émigré historian Milan S. Ďurica, the leading advocate of Tiso's beatification and rehabilitation, Tiso's martyrdom gave 'witness to Christ, his Church and the Slovak nation' (*Katolícke Noviny* 1992). These articles clearly echoed Tiso's own understanding of the relationship between nationalism and Catholicism. Both Tiso and his advocates understood nation, informed by religion, as the main driving force of history.

By publishing Magdolenová's and Ďurica's articles, the *Katolícke Noviny* gave voice to this separatist nationalism inspired by Tiso's thought. In sum, nations cannot fulfil their calling and contribute to human spiritual progress unless they form a separate state: struggling for independence thus means fulfilling God's will.

Within this context, some hierarchs began to see Tiso and his 'martyrdom' as part of the story of the Slovak 'struggle for independence' in its distinctively nationalist version, directed, as it was, against the Czechs. Importantly, some bishops went as far as to claim their revival of Tiso's martyrdom to be in line with Catholic teaching. An enthusiastic reader of Tiso's chief apologist Milan Ďurica, Alojz Tkáč, bishop of Košice and a former Catholic dissident, was one of the most outspoken supporters of Tiso (interview with the author, 12 November 2013). In September 1993, he used the commemoration of the anniversary of the death of the interwar leader of the Slovak People's Party and autonomist Andrej Hlinka to talk about Tiso. In his sermon, which was later published in *Katolícke Noviny*, Tkáč presented his 'personal view', while at the same time claiming this view to be in accord with Catholic teaching (Tkáč 1993). As he stated in the sermon, he was 'convinced about his [Tiso's] innocence' and saw his 'death as martyrdom for the nation'. Yet, as he informed the congregation, Tiso will never be beatified. Why? Because Tiso was Slovak, 'a priest and a politician at the same time' (Tkáč 1993). In short, the Czechs and the Marxists would not have allowed it. Tkáč did not explain how exactly these two groups could have influenced a possible future beatification process.

Despite speaking in his capacity as bishop and explicitly claiming compliance with the Church's teaching, Tkáč did not refer to the Church's official understanding of martyrdom, nor did he see it as necessary to explain the category of 'martyrdom for nation' (Tkáč 1993). Rather than presenting the teachings of the Church, the sermon thus revealed the extent to which Tkáč's understanding of that teaching and of his own role in its promotion was influenced by Ľudák nationalism in its contemporary guise. Interestingly, such a liberal interpretation of the Church's teaching and promotion of unrecognized memory was left largely unsanctioned.

148 *Agáta Šústová Drelová*

The re-emergence of memory of Tiso within official Church spaces in the early 1990s did not provoke any intervention from the Vatican. The Vatican kept silent on the matter and Tiso's apologists fully exploited that silence. The more adventurous of them even sought to establish links between Tiso, the cause for Slovak independence and the incumbent pope, John Paul II. The 1980s and 1990s evocation of this idea of nation as a spiritual entity was buttressed by a specific reading of John Paul II's theology of nation, which for the first time presented nation as a theological category (Llywelyn 2010, 159–66). Štefan Polakovič, a one-time ideologue of the Slovak state, wrote in the introduction to one of several memoiristic accounts of Tiso's life and times that were reprinted in Slovakia after 1989: 'Dr. Tiso in the position of President of the Republic embodied and presented before the world the fundamental sovereignty of the Slovak nation, which John Paul II emphasized in . . . his speech at the UN in Geneva in 1980' (Polakovič 1991, 8). The oft emphasized papal appreciation of nation as a theological category clearly allowed a rather liberal interpretation in this case.

Strictly speaking, the contribution of Catholic elites to the maintenance of the memory of Tiso was a matter of individual initiative, and such initiatives were not organized by the Church hierarchy as such. Nevertheless, by partaking in the maintenance of this memory, these Catholics and the hierarchs who had suffered persecution during the communist regime buttressed the memory through their position as symbols of persecution. In doing so, they helped reproduce the myth of Tiso as the victim of Communist persecution.

The interest in Tiso among Catholics was reignited in the mid-1990s. An important factor was the launching of the process of beatification of Ján Vojtaššák, bishop of the Spiš diocese, who was in office during wartime Slovak Republic and was later persecuted by the communist regime (Hlavinka and Kamenec 2014). Vojtaššák's story, especially his death following years in communist prison, was mentioned by John Paul II during his visit to Slovakia in 1995 (Kernová 2006). At this point, even those bishops who had criticized Slovak nationalists during the independence debates began to show an interest in commemorating Tiso within the Church. Most notably, Rudolf Baláž of Banská Bystrica, a former Catholic dissident who had been one of the most consistent critics of the separatist nationalists, commented in relation to the opening of Tiso's memorial house in Bytča, that

> [a] memorial house for Doctor Tiso as President of the Slovak state is nothing special. He was an exceptional and great personality both for our nation and our state. Why should he not have a memorial hall now when almost anyone can have one? He deserves it.
>
> (*SME* 1996, 18 October)

Baláž clearly saw giving honours to Tiso as a matter of justice and a way of reckoning with the communist regime's injustices.

Requiem masses for Jozef Tiso

On the fiftieth anniversary of Tiso's death in 1997, the Church hierarchy found a way of commemorating Tiso: requiem masses. None of the bishops passed the anniversary by without paying any attention to it. The difference between the individual approaches nonetheless makes it possible to see the various ways in which this method of commemorating Tiso could be used either to promote or to restrict memory of Tiso as a martyr.

Cardinal Korec used the anniversary to instruct his priests about Tiso, the meaning of his legacy and his death. He wrote in his instruction: 'this is the only case of an execution of a priest in a thousand years. Dr. J. Tiso went to his execution with exceptional faith and dignity and understood his death as a sacrifice' (*Acta Curiae Episcopalis Nitriensis*, 1997). Korec encouraged priests to say mass for Tiso; he himself said a mass at the diocesan cathedral for 'Tiso and for the Slovak nation' (*Acta Curiae Episcopalis Nitriensis*, 1997). Although Korec emphasized that the commemoration should be confined to the mass only, he had already used this instruction to promote the memory of Tiso as a martyr.

Bishop Baláž acted with more restraint. In an instruction to the priests of his diocese, he recommended saying a mass for 'the first Slovak president Jozef Tiso and for the Slovak people, so that they would live in mutual understanding and love' (*Acta Curiae Episcopalis Neosoliensis* 1997). Similarly to Korec, Baláž made it clear that Tiso was considered the first Slovak president, but he avoided any comments about Tiso's death. In general, there were no public statements resembling those of the 1993 sermon by Bishop Tkáč.

This was most probably linked to intervention from the hitherto largely silent Vatican that came ahead of the anniversary. The Vatican's nuncio to the Slovak Republic instructed the Slovak hierarchy to keep the commemoration low-key (Baláž 1997, 1). He began to take action once concern about Tiso's glorification was voiced by the archbishop of Passau, in whose diocese annual pilgrimages to Altötting were taking place. Prompted by this appeal, the nuncio turned to the Slovak bishops, urging that 'the fiftieth anniversary should not be emphasized too much, so that it does not cause any unnecessary controversies. It would be useful if those in charge encouraged and assisted historical research with the goal of knowing Tiso's life' (Baláž 1997, 2). This recommendation was understood differently by different members of the hierarchy, but none of them let Tiso's anniversary pass by without a requiem mass. In fact, the interpretation of the nuncio's appeal created tensions among the members of the hierarchy (Baláž 1997, 1–4). Clearly, the Church hierarchy in Slovakia was not going to restrict its way of commemorating Tiso any further, and the Vatican did not seem to take much interest in the case either.

Throughout the 2000s, these bishops would regularly take part at requiem masses for Tiso. These were, however, never organized on a nationwide level. The most active of these bishops was Archbishop Sokol of Trnava, who also spoke in the media on various occasions in favour of Tiso and the Slovak state

(*SME* 2008, 11 June). He became known for what he presented as his own experience of the Slovak state bringing material 'abundance' to the Slovak nation (*Hospodárske Noviny* 2007, 4 January).

In 2007, the national assembly of the hierarchy of bishops known as the Conference of Slovak Bishops (the KBS) presented a stance in which it maintained that the bishops did not see any problem with the requiem masses, which, he claimed, 'could be served in memory of anyone' ('Sokol slúžil omšu'). Although this comment was essentially accurate as far as mass intentions were concerned, it glossed over the fact that the masses for Tiso were, at the same time, being offered for the Slovak nation, thus expressing a special relationship between Tiso and the nation.

The interest in commemorating Tiso within the Church through church rituals supported by the Church hierarchy disappeared with the passing of the first generation of post-socialist bishops. Since these bishops retired, the anniversary has been celebrated by a handful of neo-Nazis and traditionalist Catholics who celebrate Tiso as symbol of the marriage between altar and throne.[4] The Catholic participation in the maintenance of memory was sustained by the character of post-socialist memory, at whose core were figures who suffered or were deemed to have suffered during communism. In a sense, the commemoration of Tiso was influenced by memory culture associated with a particular generation of bishops who had suffered during communism.

The bishops who succeeded them did not show much interest in these commemorations. Theirs is a much more detached approach. In a recent newspaper interview, one of these hierarchs, Bishop Jozef Haľko, suggested that much of the discussion about Tiso had been fuelled by the fact that Tiso was a Catholic priest. As he said,

> If Tiso were not a priest, the attitudes towards him would be less radical. Some seek to defend him because they would not be able to bear the responsibility (for the crimes) that are ascribed to him. Others seek to denigrate him precisely because he was a priest. They can then hardly see the whole problem in its complexity.
>
> (Hanus 2015)

Archbishop Sokol's successor, Archbishop Bezák, went even further, asking rhetorically how Tiso could have remained passive during the deportations of Jews. He also criticized Archbishop Sokol's supportive comments about Tiso and the Slovak state, arguing that Archbishop Sokol could hardly give an authentic and accurate account of what it was like to live in a Slovak state because he was a child during this time (Čobejová 2009).

Currently, commemorations of Jozef Tiso happen outside official Catholic spaces. For example, although the organizers of the annual Tiso memorial continue to emphasize that this is a 'Catholic pilgrimage', that pilgrimage is no longer accompanied by memorial mass services and no hierarchy members are present (*VII. Ročník*, 2015).

Conclusion

Although Jozef Tiso was never recognized as a Catholic martyr, and the cause to have him officially beatified did not manage to attract any significant following, the memory of Jozef Tiso as a 'martyr for nation' thrived among the nationalist exiles and, after the fall of state socialism, in nationalist Catholic circles in Slovakia. The participation of Catholics, especially the Catholic hierarchy, in the maintenance of this memory was facilitated by the specific character of post-socialist cultures of Catholic memory, which especially focused on martyrs and priests. The fact that these bishops who embodied the memory of the Catholic Church as the victim of the communist regime (making them 'martyrs', as it were) endorsed and commemorated Tiso confirmed his image as a martyr. Revealing just how much this image of Tiso was related to this generation of bishops, and by extension Catholics, the hierarchy's interest in Tiso's martyrdom began to wane as the generation of dissidents-turned-bishops retired. As far as the accessible materials are concerned, the Vatican played a rather passive role, interfering only once the matter had expanded beyond the Church in Slovakia.

Tiso's martyrdom was made and remade in a variety of different temporal, geographical and geopolitical contexts, religious and nonreligious, global and local, and immediate post-war, post–Cold War and post-communist. All of these deeply influenced who promoted Tiso's martyrdom and how they did this as well as the meanings this martyrdom took on. In all these meanings, Tiso's martyrdom was interlinked with issues of national identity and Slovak political and cultural sovereignty and independence, as well as the political and societal standing of the Roman Catholic Church in Slovakia and globally. In sum, this case shows how much the making of Catholic memory, both officially recognized and unrecognized, depends on the historical context and stems from the encounters and negotiations between the sacred and secular, and the religious and political.

Notes

1 All the translations from Slovak to English were made by the author.
2 The prayer for Tiso's beatification included the following: 'Prayer for the beatification of Joseph Tiso, Slovak martyr, and for the liberation of the Slovak nation . . . As a priest he was a true shepherd, and as President of the Slovak nation he was a wise and just ruler who governed his country and guided it safely through most difficult times. Slovenský mučeník Jozef Tiso' (New York: Osada sv. Jána Nepomuckého, 1981).
3 *Actes et documents du Saint Siege relatifs a la Seconde Guerre Mondiale*, typically abbreviated as Actes or ADSS. The documents were published in eleven volumes and are available online at www.vatican.va/archive/actes/index_en.htm.
4 See e.g. "*Memoriál mučeníka Jozefa Tisu*," accessed 12 June 2020, http://jozeftiso.sk/memorial.

Bibliography

Primary sources

VII. Ročník memoriálu mučeníka Jozefa Tisa. April 19, 2015. Accessed June 11, 2020. www.jozeftiso.sk/memorial.

152   Agáta Šústová Drelová

Acta Curiae Episcopalis Neosoliensis. 1(1997).

Acta Curiae Episcopalis Nitriensis. 2(1997).

Baláž, Rudolf. 1997. Correspondence to František Rábek, June 5, 1997, MS-Document not numbered, Box Personal Correspondence of Bishop František Tondra, Folder KBS, Bishop František Tondra fond, Spiš Diocese Archive, Spišská Kapitula, Slovakia.

Bojovník. 1990. "Nezodpovedené otázky." July 21.

Bor–Žatko, Ján, E. 1980. "Msgr. Dr. Jozef Tiso: president a mučeník." Slovák v Amerike, April.

———. 1984. "Exil nezabúda na Dr. Jozefa Tisu." Slovák v Amerike, July.

Cagáň, Igor. 2014. "K histórii najväčšej pravidelnej náboženskej a politickej manifestácie za slovenskú štátnu samostatnosť. Slovenské národné púte za mučeníka Jozefa Tisu do Altöttingu." Jozef Tiso- mučeník viery katolíckej a národa slovenského, January 29. Accessed March 23, 2021. https://jozeftiso.sk/jt/ludovy-kultus/altotting/218-k-historii-najvacsej-pravidelnej-nabozenskej-a-politickej-manifestacie-za-slovensku-statnu-samostatnost.

Čarnogurský, Ján. 1990. "Federácia, konfederácia alebo samostatný štát, Zo záverečného prejavu Jána Čarnogurského na zjazde v Nitre." Bratislavské Listy, March 7.

———. 1997. Videné od Dunaja. Bratislava: Kalligram.

Čobejová, Eva. 2009. "Nový arcibiskup a Tiso." June 5. www.tyzden.sk/nazory/18090/novy-arcibiskup-a-tiso/.

Čulen, Konštantín. 1992. Po Svätoplukovi druhá naša hlava. Partizánske: Garmond; Priatelia prezidenta Tisu v cudzine a na Slovensku.

Dobrý, Andrej (pseudonym). 1988. "Kto je Pavol Čarnogurský, Tajná cirkev' v službách antikomunizmu." Pravda, February 11.

———. 1988. "Náš ľud rozpozná svetlo od tmy." Pravda, February 14.

Ďurica, Milan S. 1957. Dr. Joseph Tiso and the Jewish Problem in Slovakia. Middletown: Jednota Press.

———. 1964. Dr. Joseph Tiso and the Jewish Problem in Slovakia. Padova: Stamperia Dell'Universita.

———. 1992. Jozef Tiso-Slovenský kňaz a štátnik. Martin: Matica Slovenská.

———. 2017. Jozef Tiso, Životopisný profil. Bratislava: Lúč.

Hanus, Martin. 2015. "Jozef Tiso a čas na rozsudok." Pravé Spektrum, April 19. www.prave-spektrum.sk/print.php?518.

Hospodárske Noviny. 2007. "Arcibiskup chválil Tisa aj jeho štát." January 4. https://slovensko.hnonline.sk/124310-arcibiskup-chvali-tisa-a-jeho-stat.

Kanadský Slovák. 1983. "Tiso sa vracia na Slovensko." June 18.

Katolícke Noviny. 1992. "Hľadáme pravdu?" August 16.

Katolícky Mesačník. 1989. "Kríž v osídlach moci." October n.d.

Kernová, Mirka. 2006. "Ján Vojtaššák: mučeník či kontroverzná postava? Proces blahorečenia trvá už desať rokov." SME, January 19. www.sme.sk/c/2551213/jan-vojtassak-mucenik-ci-kontroverzna-postava-proces-blahorecenia-trva-uz-desat-rokov.html.

Kirschbaum, Jozef M. 1999. "Slovenská emigrácia a Dr. Jozef Tiso." In Zahraniční Slováci a ich činnosť za slovenskú štátnosť (Svedectvá pravdy), 12–19. Trnava: Optima.

Kojnok, Eduard. 1990. Correspondence to the Slovak National Assembly, July 18, 1990, MS: 126090–1212, Box: Personal Correspondence of Bishop František Tondra, Folder: KBS, Bishop František Tondra fond, Spiš Diocese Archive, Spišská Kapitula, Slovakia.

Kováč, Jozef. 1980. "Celonárodná kampaň modlitieb za blahorečenie Jozefa Tisu." Slobodné Slovensko, February n.d.

Magdolenová, Anna. 1992. "Idea slovenského národa v politickom úsilí Dr. Jozefa Tisu (I)." Katolicke Noviny, August 16.

Národná Obroda. 1990. "Korec obhajuje Tisa." July 14.

The martyrdom of Jozef Tiso 153

Nesnadný, Viktor. 1978. "Nezabúdajme na prezidenta Slov. Republiky Dr. J. Tisu." *Kanadský Slovák*, April 29.

———. 1980. "Msgr. Dr. Jozef Tiso: Prezident a mučeník." *Slovák v Amerike*, April 9.

Papin, Jozef. 2014. "Prezident Tiso mučeníkom v súlade s učením sv. Tomáša Akvinského." In *Memoriál Mučeníka Jozefa Tisu MMXIV*, edited by Igor Cagáň. Prešov: Nové Slobodné Slovensko.

Polakovič, Štefan. 1991. "Úvodné Slovo." In *Spomienky a Svedectvo*, edited by Karol Murín. Trenčín: Priatelia Prezidenta Tisu.

Príloha Rodinného Spoločenstva. 1989. "List otca biskupa J. Ch. Korca cs. Televizii k relácii Kríž v osídlach moci." March n.d.

Prítomný. 1983. "Slovenský exil sľubil vernosť Tisovi." *Slobodné Slovensko*, May–June n.d.

Skala, Martin. 1987. "40. Výročie Tisovej smrti." *Náboženstvo a súčasnosť* (2) (n.d.): 7–11.

Slobodné Slovensko. 1983. May–June.

Slovák v Amerike. 1984. "Exil nezabúda na Dr. Jozefa Tisu." July n.d.

SME. 1996. "Biskup Baláž 'Tiso bol výnimočná osobnosť.'" October 18. www.sme. sk/c/2093967/biskup-balaz-tiso-bol-vynimocna-osobnost.html.

Smena. 1990. "Rozhovor s Jánom Čarnogurským." October 11.

Šramek, Jozef. 1991. "Slobodná Európa a česko-slovenský syndróm." *Slovenský denník*, January 24.

Sutherland, Anthony Xavier. 1973. *Jozef Tiso and Modern Slovakia*. Diss. Columbus: The Ohio State University.

Tkáč, Alojz. 1990. Letter to the Slovak National Assembly, July 20, 1990, MS-125990–1211, Box Personal Correspondence of Bishop František Tondra, Folder KBS, Bishop František Tondra fond, Spiš Diocese Archive, Spišská Kapitula, Slovakia.

———. 1993. "Nestratiť svedomie národa." *Katolícke Noviny*, September 5.

Zahraniční Slováci a ich činnosť za slovenskú štátnosť. Svedectvá pravdy III. Diel. 1999. Trnava: Optima.

Zamlčaná pravda o Slovensku, Prvá Slovenská Republika, Prvý Slovenský prezident Dr. Jozef Tiso, Tragédia Slovenských Židov podľa nových dokumentov. 1997. Partizánske: Garmond.

Zúbek, Teodorik J. 1984. "Pripad Mons. Jozef Tisu, Prezidenta Slovenskej Republiky," *Hlasy z Ríma*, October 10.

Secondary sources

Bennett, Oliver. 2011. "Strategic Canonisation: Sanctity, Popular Culture and the Catholic Church." *International Journal of Cultural Policy* 17 (4): 438–55.

Blacker, Uilleam. 2015. "Martyrdom, Spectacle, and Public Space: Ukraine's National Martyrology from Shevchenko to the Maidan." *Journal of Soviet and Post-Soviet Politics and Society: 2015/2: Double Special Issue: Back from Afghanistan: The Experiences of Soviet Afghan War Veterans and: Martyrdom & Memory in Post-Socialist Space* 1 (2): 257–92.

Blacker, Uilleam, and Fedor, Julie. 2015. "Soviet and Post-Soviet Varieties of Martyrdom and Memory1." *Journal of Soviet and Post-Soviet Politics and Society: 2015/2: Double Special Issue: Back from Afghanistan: The Experiences of Soviet Afghan War Veterans and: Martyrdom & Memory in Post-Socialist Space* 1 (2): 197–215.

Bogumił, Zuzanna, and Łukaszewicz, Marta. 2018. "Between History and Religion: The New Russian Martyrdom as an Invented Tradition." *East European Politics and Societies* 32 (4): 936–63.

Braxátor, František. 1992. *Slovenský exil 68*. Bratislava: Lúč.

Bystrický, Valerián, ed. 1992. *Jozef Tiso, Pokus o politický a osobný profil Jozefa Tisu*. Bratislava: SAV.

154 *Agáta Šústová Drelová*

Caridi, Cathy. 2016. *Making Martyrs East and West: Canonization in the Catholic and Russian Orthodox Churches.* Ithaca, NY: Cornell University Press.

Castelli, Elizabeth A. 2004. *Martyrdom and Memory, Early Christian Culture Making.* New York: Columbia University Press.

Christensen, Karin Hyldal. 2017. *The Making of the New Martyrs of Russia: Soviet Repression in Orthodox Memory.* Abingdon: Routledge.

Ciobanu, Monica. 2018. "Criminals, Martyrs or Saints? Romania's Prison Saints Debate Revisited." *Cultures of History Forum,* February 19.

Conovici, Iuliana. 2013. "Re-Weaving Memory: Representations of the Interwar and Communist Periods in the Romanian Orthodox Church After 1989." *Journal for the Study of Religions and Ideologies* 12 (35): 109–31.

Cunningham, S. Lawrence. 2005. *A Brief History of Saints.* Oxford: Blackwell.

Davie, Grace. 2000. *Religion in Modern Europe, a Memory Mutates.* Oxford: Polity Press.

Fabricius, Miroslav, and Katarína Hradská, eds. 2007. *Jozef Tiso. Prejavy a články (1938–1944).* Bratislava: AEP.

Felak, James Ramon. 1994. *At the Price of the Republic: Hlinka's Slovak People's Party, 1929–1938.* Pittsburgh, PA: University of Pittsburgh Press.

Haľko, Jozef, ed. 2000. *Päťdesiat rokov od 50tych rokov.* Bratislava: RKCMBF.

Hervieu-Léger, Danièle. 2006. *Religion as a Chain of Memory.* Cambridge: Cambridge University Press.

Higgins, Michael W. 2006. *Stalking the Holy: The Pursuit of Saint Making.* Toronto: House of Anansi.

Hlavinka, Ján, and Ivan Kamenec. 2014. *The Burden of the Past: Catholic Bishop Ján Vojtaššák and the Regime in Slovakia (1938–1945).* Bratislava: Dokumentačné Stredisko Holokaustu.

Hruboň, Anton. 2017. "Budovanie kultu Jozefa Tisa." *Kultúrne dejiny* 8 (2): 213–39.

Jablonický, Jozef. 2009. *Fragment o histórii.* Bratislava: Kalligram.

Jelinek, Yeshayahu. A. 1976. *The Parish Republic: Hlinka's Slovak People's Party, 1939–1945* (Eastern European Monographs, No. XIV). Boulder: Eastern European Quarterly (Distributed by the Columbia University Press).

Kamenec, Ivan. 2013. *Tragédia politika, kňaza a človeka.* Bratislava: Premedia.

———. 2009. *Spoločnosť, politika, historiografia.* Bratislava: Historický ústav SAV.

Kocúr, Miroslav. 2009. "For God and Nation: Christian National Populism." In *National Populism in Slovak-Hungarian relations in Slovakia, 2006–2009,* edited by Kálmán Petöcz, 221–42. Šamorín: Forum Minority Research Institute.

Kolstø, Pål. 2010. "Bleiburg: The Creation of a National Martyrology." *Europe-Asia Studies* 62 (7): 1153–74.

———. 2011. "The Croatian Catholic Church and the Long Road to Jasenovac." *Nordic Journal of Religion and Society* 24 (1): 37–56.

Lacko, Martin. 2019. "Dr. Jozef Tiso v pamäti národa. Náčrt problematiky." *Združenie slovenskej inteligencie KORENE,* December 19. Accessed March 3, 2021. https://zsi-korene.sk/dr-jozef-tiso-v-pamati-naroda-nacrt-problematiky/#_ftn28.

Leemans, Johan, and Jürgen Mettepenningen, ed. 2005. *More than a Memory: The Discourse of Martyrdom and the Construction of Christian Identity in the History of Christianity.* Leuven, Paris and Dudley, MA: Peeters Publishers.

Letz, Róbert. 2001. "Prenasledovanie kresťanov na Slovensku v rokoch 1948–1989." In *Zločiny Komunizmu na Slovensku 1948–1989,* 267–335. Prešov: Vydavateľstvo Michala Vaška.

Llywelyn, Dorian. 2010. *Toward a Catholic Theology of Nationality.* Lanham and Plymouth: Lexington Books.

Luxmoore, Jonathan, and Jolanta Babiuch. 1999. *The Vatican and the Red Flag: The Struggle for the Soul of Eastern Europe.* London: Geoffrey Chapman.

Middleton, Paul, ed. 2020. *Wiley Blackwell Companion to Christian Martyrdom*. Hoboken: John Wiley & Sons.

Moss, Candida R. 2012. *Ancient Christian Martyrdom: Diverse Practices, Theologies, and Traditions*. New Haven, CT: Yale University Press.

Muehlenbeck, Philip Emil, and Philip Muehlenbeck, eds. 2012. *Religion and the Cold War: A Global Perspective*. Nashville, TN: Vanderbilt University Press.

Panczová, Zuzana. 2020. "The Victims, the Guilty, and 'Us'." In *Conspiracy Theories in Eastern Europe: Tropes and Trends*, edited by Anastasiya Astapova et al. London: Routledge.

Pešek Ján, and Michal Barnovský. 1999. *Pod kuratelou moci, Cirkvi na Slovensku v rokoch 1953–1970*. Bratislava: SAV.

———. 2004. *V zovretí normalizácie, Cirkvi na Slovensku 1969–1989*. Bratislava: SAV.

Pešek Ján, and Václav Vondrášek. 2011. *Slovenský povojnový exil a jeho aktivity 1945–1970*. Bratislava: VEDA.

Peterson, Anna L. 1997. *Martyrdom and the Politics of Religion. Progressive Catholicism in El Salvador's Civil War*. Albany: State University of New York Press.

Puddington, Arch. 2000. *Broadcasting Freedom: The Cold War Triumph of Radio Free Europe and Radio Liberty*. Lexington: University Press of Kentucky.

Rahner, Karl. 1983. "Dimensions of Martyrdom: A Plea for the Broadening of a Classical Concept." *Concilium* 163: 9–11.

Rodriguéz, Rubén Rosario. 2017. *Christian Martyrdom and Political Violence, a Comparative Theology with Judaism and Islam*. Cambridge: Cambridge University Press.

Royal, Robert. 2006. *The Catholic Martyrs of the Twentieth Century: A Comprehensive World History*. Chestnut Ridge: Crossroad.

Samerski, Stefan, ed. 2007. *Die Rennaissance der Nationalpatrone: Erinnerungskulturen in Ostmitteleuropa im 20./21. Jahrhundert*. Köln: Böhlau.

Šimulčík, Ján. 1997. *Svetlo z podzemia, Z kroniky Katolíckeho samizdatu 1969–1989*. Prešov: Vydavateľstvo Michala Vaška.

———. 2000. *Zápas o Nádej, Z kroniky Tajných kňazov 1969–1989*. Prešov: Vydavateľstvo Michala Vaška.

Spalová, Barbara. 2012. *Bůh ví proč. Studie paměti a režimů moci v křesťanských církvích v severních Čechách*. Brno: Centrum pro studium demokracie a kultury.

Szabó, Miloslav. 2018. "'For God and Nation' Catholicism and the Far-Right in the Central European Context (1918–1945)." *Historický časopis* 66 (5): 885–900.

———. 2019. *Klérofašisti*. Bratislava: Slovart.

Vnuk, František. 1967. *Dr. Jozef Tiso. President of the Slovak Republic*. Sydney: The Association of Australian Slovaks.

Ward, James M. 2002. "'People Who Deserve It' Jozef Tiso and the Presidential Exemption." *Nationalities Papers* 30 (4): 574–75.

———. 2013. *Priest, Politician, Collaborator: Jozef Tiso and the Making of Fascist Slovakia*. Ithaca, NY: Cornell University Press.

Woodward, Kenneth. 1990. *Making Saints, Inside the Vatican: Who Become Saints, Who Do Not, and Why*. London: Chatto and Windus.

Zahraniční Slováci a ich činnosť za slovenskú štátnosť. Svedectvá pravdy III. Diel. 1999. Trnava: Optima.

8 Remembering and enforced forgetting

The dynamics of remembering Cardinal József Mindszenty in the Cold War decades

Réka Földváryné Kiss

There are few spheres of academic discourse that so aptly capture the evolution of the spiritual profile of post-war Europe as the development of the culture of remembrance and the multidisciplinary field of memory studies. This statement rings especially true when applied to the analysis of the complex interactions between memory and religion. However, while memory studies, or the study of individual and collective attitudes towards the past, has led to a paradigm shift within European academic forums in general, it would appear that research on the correlations between memory, religious communities and ecclesiastical institutions has taken different directions in Western and Eastern Europe.

Until recently, research was largely governed by the hypothesis of secularization (Pollack and Rosta 2017; Tomka 1998; Stark 1999; Berger 1999; Swatos and Christiano 1999; Görföl 2014), according to which modernization necessarily reduces the role of religion and religiousness. Moreover, it was presumed that this reduction had already been completed.[1] This approach inevitably caused research to move away from examining the societal impact of religious actors and processes, which meant that even a field such as memory studies has rarely focused on the role of religion. Meanwhile, the former satellite states of the Soviet Bloc, after several decades of religion being oppressed, are experiencing a new renaissance in research on religion, Church history and anthropology, which was paradoxically facilitated by communist regimes that had not actually regarded the Churches and religion as uninteresting or irrelevant. In fact, these regimes acknowledged the prominent position held by the Churches and religion in social, cultural and political processes, regardless of whether they were presented as enemies to be crushed or opponents to be brought under control.

In the decades before the fall of the Iron Curtain, public discourse within the Socialist Bloc considered the role of religion in shaping society as self-evident, though religion was predominantly discussed in a negative context. This 'quasi-consensus' on the cultural and social role of religion has survived the collapse of the communist regimes and is now being studied from a plurality of perspectives. In this regard, research on memory and sites of memory (*lieux de memoire*) did not emerge in a vacuum, but within the wider context

DOI: 10.4324/9781003264750-10

of religion, and as such it had a positive impact on renewed interest in the history and anthropology of religion. It is no coincidence that it was in East-Central Europe that a comprehensive volume of studies dedicated specifically to religious sites of memory (titled *Religiöse Erinnerungsorte in Ostmitteleuropa*) was recently published. One of the most important conclusions drawn in this volume was that in the historically deeply rooted, multi-ethnic and multiconfessional societies of East-Central Europe, the relationship between national and religious memory and identity is much deeper and tighter than previous research had presumed (Bahlcke, Rohdewald, and Wünsch 2013). The volume also highlights one of the most important focal points of renewed academic interest, namely, the main approaches to and intersections between regional research on memory and research on Church history, both of which are centred on the paradigm of confessionalization (or *Konfessionalisierung*) and the development of the modern nation state.

The complex processes of the first and second confessionalization periods[2] and of the development of modern nation states – which were already riddled with conflict due to their occurrence along constantly shifting religious, political, ethnic, territorial and cultural dividing lines – were forced into a new channel by the openly anti-religious and anti-Church policies of the Soviet-type regimes of East-Central Europe. Having seized power with the support of Soviet forces, the confessedly atheistic communist parties pursued a policy of exerting control over the Churches, exploiting the social and cultural positions of the Churches and using religious channels of communication to reaffirm the legitimacy of the regime. This policy was pursued in accordance with the social and denominational circumstances of the given state and the momentary political and strategic interests of the ruling communist party. This of course led to the implementation of rather ambivalent strategies that both persecuted and instrumentalized the Churches, thus leading to the simultaneous emergence and clash of different strands of anti-religious yet religiously coded policies of remembrance.

The present study aims to contribute to academic discourse on the processes of religion and memory within the context of the communist dictatorships by examining changes in memory, and the layers of meaning attributed to a symbolic figure of the era, the incumbent head of the Hungarian Catholic Church, Cardinal József Mindszenty, as well as his political trial, which took place in 1949. In the following sections, then, I shall examine the development of the discourse and memory surrounding the figure of Cardinal Mindszenty as the head of the Hungarian Catholic Church both in the decades of communist rule and in the period following the collapse of the dictatorial regime.

In the first section of this study, I shall trace the ways in which the image of Cardinal Mindszenty became ideologically charged, and then instrumentalized, in order to achieve communist political aims. I respond to two key questions: What elements did the ruling communist party use to construct its own negative image of Mindszenty and how did it create the language necessary to promote this negative image? How was the image of Mindszenty concurrently

158 *Réka Földváryné Kiss*

manifested in political discourse beyond the Iron Curtain, and how did the cult of Mindszenty develop in Hungarian emigrant circles?

In the second section of this study, I shall examine how the period after the Hungarian Revolution of 1956 brought significant changes in the evolution of Cardinal Mindszenty's image. During the revolution, the cardinal was liberated from prison, but after a few days of freedom and activity, he was forced to seek refuge at the US embassy in Budapest. In the wake of the events of 1956, Mindszenty had once again become a subject of political discourse, but in the roughly fifteen years he had spent in confinement, the figure of the elderly cardinal eventually faded from the forums of public consciousness controlled by the communist party. In this section, I also address two crucial questions: How did the official remembrance policy towards Mindszenty's legacy develop and change within the one-party state? What strategies and instruments of power did the communist regime use in an attempt to banish the figure of Cardinal Mindszenty from public discourse and cast him into collective oblivion? Last, I would like to consider how successful these dictatorial policies of (forced) forgetting were.

In the final section of this study, I shall provide a brief overview of the period following the political system change and examine how Cardinal Mindszenty has become a prominent figure in ecclesiastical and political spaces. In the words of Margit Balogh, the author of a critically objective and comprehensive academic monograph on Mindszenty:

> He was not simply a prelate, but the archetype of a political or public figure. Even in twenty-first-century Hungary, his name is a serious clarion call that is generally, though not unanimously, heeded by society: he was a missionary, a plebeian conservative, overwhelmingly patriotic, unwavering anti-Nazi and an anti-dictatorial prelate with a historicizing worldview, who had simultaneously become a persecuted victim of communism and a diplomatic sacrifice on the altar of communism. Ever since, his recognition and afterlife have been fluctuating between the extremes of uncritical canonization and stigmatizing diabolization.
>
> (Balogh 2015, 15)[3]

In light of the above, the question arises of how previously developed structures of memory were preserved and then mobilized in rival communities of memory. The first question that needs to be asked is, how did Mindszenty become a symbolic figure of the traumatic past, a martyr personifying religious faithfulness and resistance against totalitarian dictatorships, an anti-communist icon and a symbol of the victims of communism? The second question I examine in this chapter is, what processes of remembrance policy led to Mindszenty becoming a divisive political symbol in debates surrounding policies of remembrance?

In summary, the present study aims to offer a comprehensive picture of the complex processes of remembering, forgetting and forced forgetting from the

Remembering and enforced forgetting   159

recent past to the present by examining interactions between religious and political communities of different value systems through actors in various positions of (political) power.

Historical context: the trial of Cardinal József Mindszenty

On 26 December 1948, the second day of Christmas, the communist political police arrested the head of the Hungarian Catholic Church and archbishop of Esztergom, Cardinal József Mindszenty. A few months later in February 1949, the head of the Hungarian communist party, Mátyás Rákosi, directly orchestrated a political trial in which the cardinal, who had been subjected to severe mental and physical torture in prison, was made to confess his guilt and then sentenced to life imprisonment by the court. It is worth noting that Mindszenty had spent less than four years in office as cardinal, and yet his charismatic personality promised such greatness that he had turned into a symbol from the very beginning.

After long and extensive preparations, the head of the Hungarian Catholic Church was arrested in December 1948 as part of a carefully planned political operation that was preceded by an intensive anti-Church press campaign. It is important to note that the timing of his arrest was no coincidence. Following the Soviet occupation of Hungary in 1945, it was only at the end of 1948, by which point it had eliminated its political opponents, that the Hungarian Communist Party had seized enough power to begin dismantling the institutions of the democratic system and to systematically eliminate social, economic and cultural pluralism. The final phase of this process was to declare an attack on the last significant public and social actor opposing the monolithic regime, the Hungarian Catholic Church, and to arrest József Mindszenty himself, whose status and personality made him extremely suited to victimhood and martyrdom.

Mindszenty was relatively unknown at the time of his appointment as head of the Hungarian Catholic Church. For twenty-five years, he had served as the parish priest of a small town until, on 4 March 1944, a mere two weeks before the German occupation of Hungary, Pius XII appointed him as the bishop of Veszprém. A few months later, Mindszenty was imprisoned by the extreme right Arrow Cross regime, which had joined forces with the occupying Germans. Upon his release, Mindszenty spent less than six months in his office as bishop of Veszprém because, in October 1945, he was appointed to the vacant archiepiscopal seat in Esztergom. In this manner, the Hungarian Catholic Church received a leader who consciously chose to actively participate in religious life as well as public and political life during the period of the gradual Sovietization of Hungary, when the communist party was redoubling its efforts to forcefully expand its power. This made a confrontation between the communist party and the Churches seem inevitable.

From the perspective of the Churches, the year 1945 marked a period of post-war reflection that highlighted the possibility as well as the necessity of

160   *Réka Földváryné Kiss*

theological and institutional renewal. This renewal was manifested in spectacular, impulsive mass religious demonstrations, the likes of which the Hungarian Catholic Church had never seen before. With his charismatic and novel approach to pastoral duty, Mindszenty successfully utilized these democratic mass movements to his advantage. He managed to recognize the opportunities inherent in modern mass communication and was extremely effective in mobilizing the Catholic faithful. His efforts culminated in a series of events celebrating the Marian Year of 1947–48, some of which managed to attract several hundreds of thousands of participants.

From Cardinal Mindszenty's perspective, the policies of the communist party constituted a clear attack on the Churches and religion. Mindszenty responded, from 1945 onwards, by making an obvious commitment to enter into open confrontation with the communist party, which led to considerable changes in multiconfessional Hungary. In the interwar period, one of the most defining social conflicts in the country was the rivalry between the Catholic and Protestant denominations. After 1945, however, the openly anti-Church and anti-religious policies of the communist party caused the leaders of these Churches to set aside their differences and cooperate with one another. Moreover, Mindszenty's commitment to defending religion and opposing the communist regime was able to mobilize the religious masses, even across denominational boundaries.

Mindszenty's actions were especially effective because, unlike his predecessors, the cardinal could actively mobilize the patriotic masses at a time when Hungary's national sovereignty and independence had been lost once again, and by doing so, he offered a new and very novel role and identity to Hungarian Catholicism (Klimó 2010). According to the national historical canon, which crystallized in the nineteenth century and became deeply rooted in Hungarian cultural memory, the Hungarian Catholic clergy catered to the imperial aspirations of Habsburg Catholicism, whereas the Protestant Churches had been advocating for freedom of religion and national sovereignty for centuries (Brandt 1996; Kiss 2014). During the Hungarian Revolution of 1848, in addition to its obvious Protestant undertones, this national historical canon was also coloured by bourgeois and liberal nuances, and, in contrast to these deeply rooted constructs of memory, Mindszenty managed to introduce new and radical notions. On the one hand, he was the first head of the Hungarian Catholic Church in modern Hungarian history to strongly and openly commit to national independence by combining the issue of national sovereignty with the issue of freedom of religion; on the other, of the public figures 'still standing' in the wake of religious persecution, he was the most prominent representative of the public protest against the expansion of communism and the continuing violation of human rights. These factors combined to create a paradoxical situation where the figure of a fundamentally conservative Catholic who had actually distanced himself from ecumenism managed to transcend denominational boundaries and become one of the most important symbols of resistance against the communist dictatorship.

Even during the cardinal's lifetime, his contemporaries were aware of the possibility of Mindszenty becoming a symbol and icon. As renowned Hungarian writer Sándor Márai, who had been forced into exile by that time, noted in his diary, 'They have arrested Mindszenty. The former parish priest of Zalaegerszeg has grown into his role and fate to a frightening degree, which is clearly the fate of Hungarians today' (Márai 1968). In this succinct statement, voiced by one of the cardinal's contemporaries, Márai was expressing a collective contemporary experience or view that became one of the most important pillars of emerging memory of Mindszenty, and, as such, was not exclusive to the narrative of Catholic communities, notably, the view that the martyrdom of the head of the Hungarian Catholic Church embodied the martyrdom of the Hungarian nation itself.

The instrumentalization of the Mindszenty trial

Creating a specific image of Cardinal Mindszenty was by no means a unidirectional process: from the very beginning, conflicting remembrance policy goals and different narratives created by various communities of memory were set in play. Beyond the Iron Curtain, a narrative of victimhood was emerging, while in Hungary, where the communist party had turned the persecution of the Churches into a policy programme, the political leadership began to formulate its own ideologically charged image of Mindszenty, which could then be put to the service of its political aims.

In order to lay the foundations of the prospective accusations against Mindszenty, the trial of the cardinal was preceded by a coordinated anti-Church propaganda campaign in which the centrally organized propaganda machine used all means of mass communication at its disposal – including the printed press, brochures, pamphlets, newsreels, mass demonstrations and operative measures – to systematically construct a new image of the enemy. At an internal affairs forum, the incumbent Minister of the Interior János Kádár outlined the role to be played by press propaganda in this process as follows:

> When Mindszenty was arrested, nobody gave a damn, when just three years ago, he managed to beguile 50,000 hysterical people who were kissing his clothes [at the mass religious celebrations held during the Marian Year in 1947 and 1948]. This was because before he was arrested, Our Party spent years exposing him in front of the people. Even the religious masses knew that he was a collaborator and enemy. . . . There is only one medicine here, and that is mass agitation.
>
> (Kádár 1950)

We can best reconstruct what Reinhart Koselleck refers to as the conceptual structures and discursive practices of conceptualizing the enemy (Koselleck 1985) through contemporary press materials and communist party materials, as they document the introduction of certain concepts into public discourse that

162 *Réka Földváryné Kiss*

would become the discursive building blocks of the communist party's anti-Church culture of remembrance policy. In this context, the most often used umbrella term was 'reaction', often preceded by the adjective 'clerical', and 'the struggle against the reaction' became one of the cornerstones of the communist party's programme.

After its introduction, the concept of 'reaction' went through multiple rapid changes and expansions of meaning. Originally, in the literature of the workers' movement, the term meant 'opposition to social progress', but in public discourse, it soon became a synonym for 'anti-democratic attitude', and by 1946, József Révai, the chief ideologue of the communist party and chief editor of the party's newspaper, even ventured so far as to argue that

> *a reactionary is anti-communist*, someone who considers the fact that the Communist Party has become the great party of the Hungarian working people and a prominent factor in national and state life to be a greater misfortune than the wartime defeat of the country. . . . Those who work on politically isolating the Communist Party are *reactionary* and *anti-popular*, because the Communist Party is the great party of the Hungarian working class and the Hungarian working people, and represents millions of the masses.
>
> (*Szabad Nép*, [*Free People*][4] 22 July; emphasis mine)

As seen in this excerpt, Révai defined 'anti-communism' as 'reactionary' and proceeded to equate being 'reactionary' with being 'anti-popular'; in other words, to be anti-communist was to be anti-popular as well as anti-democratic, because discourse on the reaction had become closely intertwined with discourse on democracy. In this context, the communist party monopolized the quality of being 'democratic' and attempted to intellectually and politically isolate its ideological and political opponents by labelling them as 'anti-democratic'. According to a contemporary newspaper article, 'in this country, from the church pulpit to the chief executive officer's desk, lethal weapons are being sharpened everywhere against democracy' (*Népszava*, [*Word of the People*] 12 January 1946).[5] By expanding the semantic range of the term 'reactionary' even further, 'reactionary' also became quasi-synonymous with 'fascist' and 'anti-Semite'. As the writer of the article, József Révai put it in another article of his, 'fascism and anti-Semitism are the brainchildren, weapons, and ideology of the reaction. One is inseparable from the other, and who here would give refuge and cover to the reaction, and consequently to fascism?' (*Szabad Nép*, 4 August 1946). The question posed at the end was answered by a previous article, which argued that 'those who had cheered for Mindszenty in Parliament were covertly pledging their support to the spirit of Szálasi and Imrédy' (*Népszava*, 5 March 1946).[6]

Thanks to its carefully devised language policy offensive, the Hungarian Communist Party managed to introduce the concept of 'reactionary' into public discourse in a manner that rendered the term highly fluid and undefinable.

On the one hand, this allowed the party leadership to expand the category of 'enemy' indefinitely, and on the other, it enabled them to weave a web of negative connotations around a term laden with the implied accusation that the person or organization at which it was directed was anti-progressive, anti-democratic or pro-fascist. The last accusation had such severe repercussions that it could lead to its target's moral and political annihilation, even in cases where the charge was unproven or had no criminal consequences, as it was well-nigh impossible to dispute it in a public sphere dominated by the communist party. In the hands of the dictatorial one-party state, the concept of 'reactionism' had thus become an effective tool for intensifying discursive terror (Keep 1995), as it not only served to designate persons or groups as the enemy, but also to lay the foundations for the libel and defamation of the enemy by inspiring negative attitudes towards them by association (Edelman 1988; Todorov 2003).

The next phase of the communist party's language policy offensive was to take the previously introduced concept of 'reaction' and combine it with the adjective 'clerical' in order to create the discursive framework necessary for the persecution of the Churches. As General Secretary Rákosi, the leader of the communist party, put it:

> Based on fifteen months of experience in democracy, we can safely say that we cannot eliminate the reaction if we continue to tolerate the clerical reaction! . . . If we want to carry out a thorough attack against the reaction, then this attack must include the struggle against the clerical reaction as well.
>
> (*Szabad Nép*, 26 March 1946)

As a language construct, the term 'clerical reaction' served two functions: on the one hand, the adjective 'clerical' positioned the Churches as solely political actors, which meant that any conflicts at all between the communist party and the Churches became political by default, and on the other hand, the term 'reactionary' mobilized the negative connotations of, and emotions associated with, being anti-popular and anti-democratic. In other words, the communist party created a linguistic code that identified the Churches as a meeting place for anti-popular and anti-democratic elements within the arena of the political struggle, regardless of the subject of any given debate. By following this strategy, the communist party leadership managed to force political discourse into a semantic framework where debates on Church policy and ideology could only be interpreted in one way, namely, as a clash between progress and reaction, or between democracy and anti-populism, all of which can be viewed as 'asymmetrical counter-concepts' in the sense used by Koselleck (Koselleck 1985).[7] This interpretation was explicitly articulated in a report published in the party newspaper on the heated cultural policy debate surrounding the nationalization of schools: 'in the question of the nationalization of schools, the conflict is not between religion and irreligion, but between the reaction and democracy' (*Szabad Nép*, 6 June 1948).

164 *Réka Földváryné Kiss*

Based on contemporary media coverage, the term 'clerical reaction' inherited every negative attribute associated with the concept of 'reaction'. Consider the following examples:

> The clerical reaction collaborates with the imperialists and hopes for another war that would restore the old blood-sucking system and its own privileged position.
>
> (*Tiszántúli Néplap*, 7 December 1949)

> Just as in Korea, so too in Hungary, the clerical reaction wanted to see houses destroyed by bombs, factories reduced to smouldering ruins, and peaceful workers and peasants, old people and innocent children slaughtered en masse.
>
> (Magyar Dolgozók Pártja 1951–52)

> while the opposition of democratic transformation . . . hides behind the cassock of the clerical reaction to carry out its divisive machinations.
>
> (*Szabad Nép*, 11 January 1946)

According to the communist party, Cardinal Mindszenty donned the cassock of the clerical reaction (or 'dark' or 'black' reaction, according to another turn of phrase) every day and had thus become 'the patron saint of murderers and marauders' (*Népszava*, 20 January 1946). As the propaganda campaign progressed, more and more accusations were levelled against the cardinal, including all the obligatory tropes associated with political trials, such as treason, conspiracy against the democracy, espionage for the Americans and foreign currency manipulation. The communist leadership also attempted to accuse him of being fascist and anti-Semitic, but Mindszenty's professed anti-Nazi stance and his past imprisonment by the extreme right Arrow Cross Party (which had collaborated with the occupying Germans) meant these accusations proved to be less effective.

The strategy and language policy offensive designed to present Mindszenty as an enemy of the people made it impossible to properly evaluate or debate the cardinal's public statements, Church policy decisions, achievements, alleged or actual mistakes and pastoral activity, despite the fact that even before his arrest, Cardinal Mindszenty's public and political views and statements had become a subject of debate in communist as well as non-communist political circles. His followers lauded his consistently humanitarian stance against disenfranchisement and injustice and viewed Mindszenty as a brave defender of democracy against the expanding communist dictatorship and a prelate who brooked no compromise and was even prepared for religious martyrdom. Meanwhile, his critics viewed the cardinal as an anti-modern, conservative, legitimist prelate who brooked no compromise because he sought to protect the anachronistic public position of authority formerly enjoyed by the Churches.

It is indisputable that Cardinal Mindszenty's personality and participation in public matters provided ample munition to both his cult and anti-cult. Drawing upon an extensive repertoire of anti-Mindszenty clichés, the communist party leadership attempted to appeal to the masses by repeatedly presenting the cardinal as a retrograde, conservative and feudal prelate. As long as their propaganda was based around these tropes, they retained their impact as the most pervasive elements of the communist image of Mindszenty. A journalist writing for the newspaper *Szabad Nép* offered the following succinct explanation of the message the communist policy of remembrance addressed to the general public: 'Mindszenty attempted to bring back the odious reign of the Habsburgs and with it the landlords, the Middle Ages, and the era of darkness' (*Szabad Nép*, 30 December 1948).

One crucial factor in the process of discrediting Cardinal Mindszenty's character was that the spirit of the prelate had been so thoroughly broken in prison that he even admitted to the most absurd accusations against him; naturally, his admission of guilt was then used by the propaganda machine to ridicule and verbally humiliate the cardinal. As a commentator from *Szabad Nép* said after the announcement of the verdict on 9 February 1949: 'at the hearing, Mindszenty was a spineless and pitiful dwarf, the embodiment of human wretchedness' (*Szabad Nép*, 9 February 1949).

From the perspective of the communist party, the trial of Cardinal Mindszenty acquired the utmost significance, not only because it presented them with the means for eliminating the head of a system of ecclesiastical institutions that constituted the last autonomous ideological and political opponent of the communist regime, but also because it had become a defining chapter in communist identity politics. As Tzvetan Todorov's analysis of the characteristics of totalitarian dictatorships pointed out, twentieth-century totalitarian regimes were unique inasmuch as they waged war not only on civilian populations but also on memory (Todorov 2003).

The communist party expected the trial of Cardinal Mindszenty to become the metanarrative of their legitimacy: in February 1949, at a restricted session of the Political College of the Ministry of the Interior, Minister of the Interior Kádár openly discussed the function the Mindszenty trial could perform in the communist policy of remembrance.

Once the communist party had devised its own theoretical construct, the only question was to what extent they would be able to sear their own image of Mindszenty into the collective memory of Hungarian society using everything under their control and at their disposal. This included every means of mass communication as well as censorship, which not only blocked absolutely any public attempts to offer an alternative interpretation but also covered up the human rights violations and mental and physical abuse committed against Mindszenty.

The contemporary press campaign sought to deliver a simplified message of party leadership to every stratum of Hungarian society. According to Todorov's description of the operating mechanisms of policies of remembrance pursued by totalitarian dictatorships, the regime made arduous attempts to eradicate the very memory of human rights abuses by suppressing memory by intimidation, destroying evidence, and generating an alternative narrative (especially through

166 *Réka Földváryné Kiss*

the manipulation of language), which was then enforced as the only 'true' memory (Todorov 2003).

Apart from stressing the need for Hungarian society to passively receive party propaganda, the communist party also emphasized how important it was for the masses to actively participate and occupy public venues; to this end, before and after the trial, mass demonstrations were organized across the country to denounce Mindszenty, which the media then reported in great detail. The general public was not only informed that the Hungarian people were attending 'hundreds and thousands of mass demonstrations' to express that they had 'had enough of Mindszenty and the prowling of the black reaction' (*Szabad Nép*, 30 December 1948), but an impression of authenticity and familiarity was maintained by ensuring that citizens received daily updates on how local communities (e.g. the workers of the Mauthner Leather Factory or the residents of the virtually unknown village of Letkés) were protesting against Mindszenty's machinations.

As the one-party state propaganda machine announced the separation of Church and state and the secularization of the Hungarian state, the public sphere was simultaneously flooded with intensive anti-religious and anti-Church propaganda, which often forced the population to actively participate in staged mass events. One notable subgenre of these mass events was the organization of staged protests involving intimidated and manipulated religious and Church communities, especially children attending religious schools. The aim of such protests was to demonstrably create divisions among Catholics as a community of memory and intimidate social groups that could have countered the communist policy of remembrance by constructing counter-remembrance practices of their own. Contemporary press reports interpreted these staged mass events as follows:

> The working Catholic masses have had enough of the anti-popular instigations of Cardinal and Archbishop Mindszenty. The Catholic high school students of Budapest marched to Rózsák [Roses] Square, and under the leadership of their cleric teachers, the students demanded that the Hungarian Catholics be led by a prelate that follows the teachings of the Gospel and works for the people, not for the counts and barons.
>
> (Tüntetés Mindszenty bíboros ellen 1948)

On 8 February 1949, a court of first instance sentenced Cardinal József Mindszenty, the head of the Hungarian Catholic Church, to lifetime imprisonment. By the summer of the same year, the court of second instance had confirmed the verdict, which marked the end of the trial, but this by no means brought an end to the struggle revolving around Mindszenty's memory. The communist party soon launched a new language policy turn of phrase, declaring war on 'Mindszentyism' and the 'local Mindszentys'. By using an already existing enemy construct, the party created a new image of the enemy in the struggle against the Churches, thereby ensuring that the image of Mindszenty that had been so meticulously crafted by the communist party would remain on the political agenda.

The remembrance of Cardinal Mindszenty within the context of the Cold War

While the diabolized image of Cardinal Mindszenty became a basic component of the Hungarian Communist Party's identity politics, beyond the Iron Curtain a similarly intensive cult was emerging that flatly contradicted the party line. According to this cult, Mindszenty's commitment to open confrontation with the communist regime and his subsequent imprisonment paved the way to his becoming a symbol of the resistance against communism and an anti-communist icon (Balogh 2015; Betts 2016). In order to maintain this alternative memory of Mindszenty, the Hungarian political émigré community – which had significantly increased in number by the Cold War – contributed extensive literature on the subject in an attempt to counterbalance the defamatory propaganda campaign of the Hungarian communist government. Discourse on Cardinal Mindszenty was a crucial factor in the development of the Hungarian emigrant community's cultural memory, as the community constituted a discursive space that was not dominated by the communist regime, and where the formulation of non-communist narratives and the narration, interpretation and memory of traumatic experiences under the communist dictatorship were possible (Assmann 2012). In the predominantly anti-communist conservative circles of the Hungarian ecclesiastical and political émigré population of the 1950s, Cardinal Mindszenty soon became nothing short of a cult icon, a position supported by the proliferation of Hungarian emigrant literature on Mindszenty presenting him as a martyr who had been unjustly and illegally persecuted in his struggle for the faith and the freedom of the Churches. These publications were also supported by other means used to promote the Mindszenty cult, such as commemorative plaques, statues, collective remembering and commemorative ceremonies.

It is important to note that the Hungarian emigrant population was not the only community that closely followed Cardinal Mindszenty's case: even by today's standards, his trial had received enormous global media attention. *Life* magazine published a special issue on the trial, *Time* magazine put Mindszenty on its front cover and daily newspapers continuously reported on developments in the trial. According to publishing statistics, the *New York Times* dedicated some eighty articles to the Mindszenty case, while *Le Monde* published close to a hundred. Additionally, the international Catholic world erupted in a wave of protests. At Saint Peter's Square, Pope Pius XII condemned the political trial in front of approximately 300,000 of the faithful, while in the United States, Cardinal Francis Spellman 'thundered that the USA needed to unite in prayer and protest for the imprisoned cardinal' and a Catholic author referred to the trial as 'the crucifixion of mankind' (Betts 2016, 284).

Church leaders such as Cardinal Spellman were joined in their support of the imprisoned Catholic prelate by many leading politicians, including the president of the United States, and while tens of thousands protested in Paris, around 150,000 people had gathered to protest in Dublin. Mindszenty's

168 *Réka Földváryné Kiss*

imprisonment soon inspired a play and two movies as well: in 1950, a year after the trial, Hollywood released a movie titled *Guilty of Treason*, and five years later, in 1955, the United Kingdom released *The Prisoner*, starring Alec Guinness and Jack Hawkins (Glant 2016). As the speedy response of the movie industry shows, in the developing Cold War world, the trial of Cardinal Mindszenty was of such symbolic importance to the West that it transcended the context of the persecution of religion and the Churches and elevated the trial of the cardinal to a struggle between good and evil. Cardinal Mindszenty thus entered public discourse as the defender of fundamental democratic values, human rights and freedom of expression, and he became one of the first international symbols of the victims of post-war totalitarianism. The typical Cold War–era movies produced about Mindszenty basically functioned as sites of memory that not only reinforced this narrative of remembrance but also preserved and transmitted memory of Mindszenty as an anti-communist and anti-Soviet martyr.[8]

As Peter Betts has pointed out, one notable aspect of the process whereby Mindszenty became a symbolic figure was that communist terror and violence were thematized and presented through the fate of the prelate. In other words, it was the fate of Cardinal Mindszenty that caused Western public opinion to wonder what sort of physical and mental torture could have led to the breaking of the spirit of such a steadfast man, and what new scientific discoveries were being used by the Soviet Union to force him to admit to even the most absurd of accusations. People following Mindszenty's fate were confronted by the brutality of the communist regimes; according to Betts, 'the widespread Cold War anxiety about "brainwashing" had its origins in the Mindszenty trial' (Betts 2016, 286).

The moment Cardinal Mindszenty was arrested on 26 December 1948, the US ambassador to Hungary, Selden Chapin, recognized the possibility of the cardinal becoming a symbol of communist terror and how his status as a symbol could be utilized within the context of the Cold War. In his report issued as early as the end of December, Chapin informed his superiors of how and why the case of József Mindszenty should be utilized in the global political struggle, claiming that to the people of Eastern Europe, the cardinal embodied the same spirit of freedom as that represented by the United States (Balogh 2015). This human rights perspective and the narrative of the Soviet communist attack on the fundamental values of the West were also voiced by an editorial in *Life* magazine titled 'The Mindszenty Case: The sentencing of a Hungarian prelate imperils the Western idea of human rights', according to which

> no matter what the surface indications may show, in sentencing Mindszenty the Hungarian court was not only undermining the rights of Catholics, it was also cutting at the philosophical view of life that is the very basis of the American republic.
>
> (*Life*, 26 (1949), 30)

Enforced forgetting: the development of the communist image of Mindszenty in the Kádár regime after 1956

As discussed above, two radically different cultures of remembrance emerged around Cardinal Mindszenty, one behind and one beyond the Iron Curtain, but these two cultures did not cross paths in Hungary until 1956, when the Hungarian Revolution saw Mindszenty's liberation from prison. Though the cardinal enjoyed less than a week of freedom, he once again became the subject of political and public attention. Following his liberation, every public gesture made by Mindszenty was viewed as symbolic in and of itself, as he embodied the suffering of Hungarian society that had culminated in an uprising against the Soviet regime. Cardinal Mindszenty had essentially become a living site of memory; at the same time, his strong political statements added new fuel to the debate around his person for decades to come. Based on the interviews he gave during his brief period of freedom, both his followers and his opponents came to view Mindszenty as the embodiment of the conservative Christian political and public tradition and as a quasi-political actor, but they then proceeded to interpret this image in very different ways. These differing interpretations then became key points of reference for rival communities of memory constructing their own image of Mindszenty.

Following the repression of the Hungarian Revolution of 1956, Cardinal Mindszenty sought asylum at the US embassy in Budapest, where he spent the next fifteen years in confinement; meanwhile, in accordance with a decision made by the Moscow leadership, János Kádár was appointed the head of the Hungarian government. This was the same politician who had once been in charge of the communist regime's anti-Church campaign and personally oversaw the preparation of the indictment against Mindszenty. Following his appointment, he remained in power for the next thirty years (Somorjai and Zinner 2013). As the former Minister of the Interior, Kádár was not only familiar with the system of anti-clerical tropes used to defame Mindszenty, but after 1956, he actively participated in revisiting these tropes and reintroducing them into official political discourse. Once the Soviet forces had reinstated communist party rule and the government had consolidated its power enough to symbolically demonstrate it, the ruling communist party organized its first tightly controlled mass gathering on 1 May 1957. At this event, First Secretary Kádár used the remembrance policy constructs formerly devised by General Secretary Rákosi to outline the communist regime's metanarrative of the events of 1956. According to this, the archbishop of Esztergom had joined the ranks of the enemy once more: 'The capitalists, landlords, bankers, princes, and counts have once again entered the stage of politics at the instigation of Mindszenty' (Kádár 1957). Consequently, the cardinal, who had only regained his freedom in the last few days of the Hungarian Revolution, had once again become the most important political enemy in the dominant and exclusive narrative created by the communist party:

> The counterrevolutionary revolt united every domestic enemy of the Party and the People's Republic as symbolized by their leaders, Mindszenty, et cetera. These [enemies], the majority of whom were well-known

170 *Réka Földváryné Kiss*

capitalists, infamous reactionaries, and traitors, had pushed the hitherto unexposed Imre Nagy into the foreground, and kept their real goals secret for a long time.

(Kádár 1959)

According to Kádár's interpretation, the 'counterrevolution' of 1956 was the result of two groups collaborating against the worker and peasant government: the anti-progressive conservative right wing led by Mindszenty, and communists who had denounced their loyalty to the communist party and the Soviet Union and became traitors under the leadership of Prime Minister Imre Nagy, who was consequently sentenced at a political trial and executed. The ideological mechanisms of the Kádár regime had thus created a new image of the enemy by connecting two personalities and political traditions that had mutually positioned each other as rivals and ideological and political opponents during the revolution. These two groups viewed each other as the 'heirs to the fallen system' – the only difference being the 'fallen system' they were referring to. According to the logic of the identity politics of the Kádár era, however, the conservative prelate Mindszenty and the 'treasonous communist' Imre Nagy were on the same 'remembrance policy platform', while the political communities that viewed them as their leaders and symbols did not share a common platform at all. Nevertheless, until the political system change, it was impossible to debate these different traditions or their memory of the events of 1956 in the Hungarian public sphere ruled by the communist party, which meant that discourse on the remembrance of 1956, including the memory of Mindszenty, was only possible in the forums of the Hungarian émigré community.

Following the execution of wide-scale, comprehensive reprisals and political retribution affecting every stratum of Hungarian society, the Kádár government began to focus on the long-term establishment or consolidation of the regime, which entailed the redefinition of the party's Church policy and, by extension, the issue of Cardinal Mindszenty. It is quite telling that by the 1960s, a new motto was chosen to represent the Kádár regime's Church policy and the changes in the exercise of power. It was a paraphrased quote from the Bible: 'Whoever is not against us is for us' (Kádár 1961). Having learned its lesson from the Hungarian Revolution of 1956, the communist regime's biggest priority was to mitigate social tension, which in Church policy terms meant that open and violent oppression was abandoned in favour of the gradual disruption, manipulation and exploitation of legal institutional structures through the veiled use of discrimination and operative and propaganda methods (Tabajdi 2019).

Concurrently with the changes in the communist regime's Church policy, the position of the Churches in society had also undergone considerable changes. The general secularization and modernization processes of the era were exacerbated by the fact that in the years following the Hungarian Revolution of 1956, the regime managed to complete the forced collectivization of traditional rural society, which meant that having lost their lands and

Remembering and enforced forgetting   171

livelihood, the last existentially independent social group in Hungary had also become dependent on the communist state to such an extent that it was forced to migrate to urban areas en masse. These radical changes in the lifestyle of the traditional peasantry constituted a taboo social trauma in communist Hungary that not only impacted individual lives but also dismantled old frames of reference and identity and created a radically new situation for Church communities, because their traditional religious milieu and natural cultural environment had suddenly shrunk and was gradually being rendered obsolete (Horváth 2018). This situation also presented new challenges for secularized society, which the limited or prohibited operation of Church institutions was unable to successfully address, especially in metropolitan areas, and because of this, the means of cultivating an alternative religious memory in small communities, parishes and families became very limited as well (Bögre 2004).

The political pragmatism and revised Church policy goals of the Kádár government and the transformation of Hungarian society also altered the regime's official memory of Cardinal Mindszenty: instead of fostering an active anticult against him, the identity politics and remembrance policy of the 'mature' Kádár era focused on the active forgetting of the past, where the new policy of remembrance was manifested in public silence.

The task of forgetting the past was not about forgetting per se.[9] If the task of remembering the past is to strengthen and mobilize a community through its ability to identify and connect with the past, then forced forgetting serves to take away the ability of a given community to strengthen and mobilize itself by identifying and connecting with the past (Gyáni 2017). In other words, rather than seeking to mobilize the masses, the new memory policy of the Kádár regime attempted to make it impossible for the Mindszenty cult to mobilize them. It essentially sought to deprive rival communities of memory and prevent them from engaging in collective remembering or creating their own interpretations and reference narratives (Connerton 2008) or reflecting on and providing adequate answers to debated questions about Mindszenty's ecclesiastical career. This strategy ultimately served to weaken Hungarian collective identity in a way that suited the interests of the regime; as Kádár put it in a speech on Church policy issues, 'the race for souls is still ongoing, after all' (Kádár 1983).

The Kádár government gained the upper hand in the 'race for souls' in Hungary by devising a new strategy that involved responding to any mention of Mindszenty in public discourse by emphasizing internal divisions in the Catholic Church and then claiming that Mindszenty had essentially prevented the communist party from reaching an agreement with the Catholic Church. This strategy and the way it positioned Mindszenty was an integral part of the Kádár regime's Church policy, which centred on the subversion of the Churches. According to their interpretation, Mindszenty was no longer the organizer of the reactionary masses and the leader of the enemy, but he was still an obstacle to harmonious cooperation between the Catholic Church and the communist regime and someone who represented no one's interests but his own. As Kádár

172 *Réka Földváryné Kiss*

put it in 1977 at an international press conference organized during a visit he paid to Pope Paul VI:

> Cardinal Mindszenty greatly contributed to the fact that the relationship of the Hungarian state and the Hungarian Roman Catholic Church had become so complicated and difficult. Perhaps this was the reason why we were only able to settle our relationship with the Catholic Church last. Nevertheless, two years ago our relationship returned to normal, which we consider a very important and good development.
>
> (Kádár 1977)

The communist regime's new remembrance narrative not only served to position Cardinal Mindszenty as an exclusively political actor and create a sense of emotional detachment, but it also provided the ideological basis for an agreement to resolve the Mindszenty issue by releasing him from the US embassy in Budapest. After all, if the figure of the cardinal no longer carried any symbolic weight nor represented anything other than his own 'reactionary and anachronistic' views, then allowing him to leave the country also had no political significance nor posed any remembrance policy risks.

Settling Mindszenty's situation ultimately turned into an extremely prolonged and complicated diplomatic and political chess game played out between the United States, the Vatican and the Hungarian government (supervised by the Moscow leadership), in which the fate of the cardinal and his evolving memory was greatly influenced by an international thawing of relations and the announcement of the Vatican's *Ostpolitik* (Fejérdy 2015; Somorjai and Zinner 2013). Instead of being an active agent in the process, Mindszenty had essentially become a pawn, as the covert political negotiations were no longer about an imprisoned defender of human rights but rather the settlement of an unpleasant issue that was getting in the way of attempts at creating dialogue. As a result of confidential diplomatic agreements, Mindszenty left the building of the US embassy in Budapest in 1971 and crossed the Iron Curtain despite his disappointment at the new political situation and the decisions made about his fate. A few years into his exile, it was especially difficult for him to accept Paul VI's decision in 1974 to declare the archiepiscopal seat of Esztergom vacant; nonetheless, Mindszenty obediently accepted the pope's decision.

Once he arrived abroad, Mindszenty soon regained his spirits and, until his death in 1975, he devoted himself to actively touring the Hungarian diaspora scattered across the globe and pastoring the Catholic faithful. Though he no longer participated in Church policy debates, his pastoral activity became a very strong collective experience among the Hungarian emigrant community. In the process, Mindszenty also managed to publish his *Memoirs*, which he intended as a powerful plea against the decades of slander heaped upon him by the Rákosi and Kádár regimes. Following the publication of his memoirs, his cult among the conservative Hungarian emigrant communities gained newfound momentum, and a new element was added to the web of remembrance surrounding his person: his defence of the faith was no longer considered a matter of communism versus Christianity, for it had also became a symbol of 'faith-centredness' (Lénárd 2006). This was one of several possible ways in which the Church leadership could have responded to the challenges of the communist regime. Depending on the interpretive framework, the opposite of faith-centredness was unprincipled collaboration or prudent compromise with the dictatorial regime.

As discussed above, Mindszenty went from symbolizing the resistance of *the* Catholic Church to symbolizing *a* Church leader's typical mode of conduct; at the same time, different interpretations of Mindszenty's character began to emerge within the Catholic Church. While the dramatic twists and turns of Mindszenty's life became a renewed and exceptionally strong symbol of uncompromising faithfulness and defending the faith, his steadfastness not only became the antithesis of the communist regime, but also posed continuous questions to alternative Church governments seeking a modus vivendi with the dictatorship, a state of affairs that reflects the success of the subversive politics of the Kádár regime. It is no coincidence that First Secretary Kádár attempted to present the settlement of the Mindszenty case as a success story of the communist regime's diplomatic Church policy:

> Indeed, this Mindszenty case shows the merits of internal affairs and the merits of our policies. If only we were able to solve every issue as well as we resolved this one, where the conclusion of this matter was that the West declared that this figure [i.e. Mindszenty – author's note] was obsolete, and in reality they were facing the Vatican and not the Hungarian People's Republic when they were negotiating the Mindszenty issue.
>
> (Kádár 1974)

Whether József Mindszenty is an 'obsolete figure' or a prelate who fought uncompromisingly for freedom (because he understood the operation of the dictatorship better than his contemporaries) has been the subject of continuous debates about him and his remembrance since the political system change. While the system of political tropes devised by the Rákosi and Kádár regimes still persists regardless of the presence or absence of its original source, and new political actors have since joined the debates, we are also experiencing the institutionalization of the hitherto silenced and non-official cult of Mindszenty and his cultural memory, a defining but still unfinished chapter of which is the pending process of Mindszenty's canonization.

In conclusion, the image of Mindszenty, which transformed multiple times, was formed by the opposing remembrance policy aims and narratives of different communities of memory. The communist party, which made Church persecution a political programme, initially hoped the master interpretation of its own legitimacy would come from the trial of the cardinal. The party used a media campaign and the language policy offensive centred around the trial to fix structures of thinking that developed into a basic language set for the communist party's anti-Church and anti-religious culture of memory and became the only frame of interpretation in the public discourse. The communist party forced a language code and frame of interpretation into public discourse that only allowed the struggles of Church policy and differing worldviews to be interpreted within the framework of two possible dichotomies: progressive versus reactionary or democratic versus anti-popular. At the same time, the ideological formation of Mindszenty's image and its instrumentalization for the purposes of the maintenance of communist power made it impossible to have a real debate about the cardinal's public and pastoral activities.

Meanwhile, the image of Mindszenty was diabolized by the communists in Hungary beyond the Iron Curtain. Mindszenty became an international martyr of the heroic struggle against communism, a kind of anti-communist icon in the West whose fate could represent the brutality of the communist regime as well. The discourse centred around Mindszenty contributed significantly to the development of the Hungarian emigrant communities' collective memory as well, because this was a milieu of communication where a non-communist narrative could be formed publicly and the traumas caused by the communist dictatorship had the space to develop.

After the crushing of the 1956 revolution, the Kádár regime redefined the formation of Mindszenty's image, focusing on the long-term preservation of the political system. A change of aims in state policy towards the Church and transformations in the social milieu also brought a radical turn in the regime's memory of Mindszenty. After settling the 'Mindszenty question', the regime placed collective enforced forgetting at the centre of its remembrance policy. It had no further intention of mobilizing the masses. It just wanted to prevent them from being mobilized by, and identifying themselves with, the Mindszenty cult. The regime achieved this by exerting its power, in this case, by banishing the cardinal's character from the territory of public discourse. By suppressing the evocation of common memories, they hoped to deprive the remembering religious communities of the possibility of creating their own interpretation. And whenever the topic of Mindszenty's character did actually come up, the new communist remembrance policy tried to deepen the fault lines within the Church by emphasizing that Mindszenty had in fact made it impossible for the communist party to come to terms with the Church. This new type of approach towards Mindszenty was an organic part of the Church policy pursued by the Kádár regime, whose key phrase was disintegration. At the same time, the development of new directions in the state policy towards the Churches in the Kádár era were accompanied by a new frame of interpretation being added to Mindszenty's image by religious communities. The cardinal's most eventful life became a symbol of renewal expressing uncompromising loyalty and faith, a symbol that not only served as the antithesis of the communist system but also challenged those alternative Church governance policies that established a modus vivendi with the system.

Since the fall of communism, the cardinal's character has become the primary focus of Church and political memory debates once again. However, despite

Remembering and enforced forgetting 175

the existence of different interpretations, the figure of József Mindszenty has become a defining site of memory in Hungarian history and an important component of the identity of Catholic communities seeking to process the past.

Notes

1 For rethinking the secular and postsecular thesis, see Casanova (1994) and Habermas and Ratzinger (2007).
2 For the concept of confessionalization and second confessionalization, see Blaschke (2000) and Schilling (1999).
3 All citations in the chapter were translated by the author.
4 *Szabad Nép* (Free People) was the official daily newspaper of the Communist Party until 1956, from when it was published under the name *Népszabadság* (People's Freedom).
5 *Népszava* (Word of the People) was the daily newspaper of the Social Democratic Party.
6 Ferenc Szálasi was the leader of the extreme right Arrow Cross Party and Béla Imrédy was prime minister of Hungary from 1938 to 1939.
7 According to Koselleck, 'It is characteristic of counterconcepts that are unequally antithetical that one's own position is readily defined by criteria which make it possible for the resulting counterposition to be only negated' (Koselleck 1985, 163).
8 The movies had such a profound impact that two decades later, Mindszenty prefaced his *Memoirs* with corrections and comments on *The Prisoner* (Glant 2016).
9 For the mechanisms and dynamics of social amnesia or collective forgetting and the various types of forgetting, see Assmann (2012), Connerton (2008), Ricoeur (2004), Gyáni (2017) and Keszei (2017).

References

Assmann, Aleida. 2012. "To Remember or to Forget: Which Way Out of a Shared History of Violence?" In: *Memory and Political Change*, edited by Aleida Assmann and Linda Shortt, 53–71. Basingstoke: Palgrave Macmillan.
Bahlcke, Joachim, Stefan Rohdewald, and Thomas Wünsch, eds. 2013. *Religiöse Erinnerungsorte in Ostmitteleuropa. Konstitution und Konkurrenz im nationen- und epochenübergreifenden Zugriff*. Berlin: Akademie Verlag.
Balogh, Margit. 2015. *Mindszenty József (1892–1975) I-II*. Budapest: MTA Bölcsészettudományi Kutatóközpont.
Berger, Peter L., ed. 1999. *The Desecularization of the World*. Washington, DC: Erdmans.
Betts, Paul. 2016. "Religion, Science and Cold War Anti-Communism: The 1949 Cardinal Mindszenty Show Trial." In *Science, Religion and Communism in Cold War Europe*, edited by Paul Betts and Stephen A. Smith, 274–307. New York: Springer, Palgrave Macmillan UK.
Blaschke, Olaf. 2000: "Das 19. Jahrhundert: Ein Zweites Konfessionelles Zeitalter?" *Geschichte und Gesellschaft* (26): 38–75.
Bögre, Zsuzsanna. 2004. Vallásosság és identitás. Élettörténetek a diktatúrában (1948–1964) [Religiosity and Identity. Life-stories in the Dictatorship (1948–1964)]. Budapest: Dialog Campus Kiadó.
Brandt, Juliane. 1996. "Protestantismus und Gesellschaft im dualistischen Ungarn." *Südost-Forschungen* (55): 179–240.
Casanova, José. 1994. *Public Religions in the Modern World*. Chicago: University of Chicago Press.
Connerton, Paul. 2008. "Seven Types of Forgetting." *Memory Studies* 1 (1): 59–71.
Edelman, Murray. 1988. *Constructing the Political Spectacle*. Chicago: University of Chicago Press.

176 *Réka Földváryné Kiss*

Fejérdy, András, ed. 2015. *The Vatican "Ostpolitik" 1958–1978. Responsibility and Witness during John XXIII and Paul VI.* Rome: Bibliotheca Academiae Hungariae.

Glant, Tibor. 2016. "Cardinal Mindszenty and the 1956 Hungarian Revolution on Film in the West, 1950–59." https://ieas.unideb.hu/admin/file_6692.pdf.

Görföl, Tibor. 2014. "Posztszekuláris társadalom? A kereszténység nyilvános jelenlétének megítélése Jürgen Habermasnál." [Postsecular Society? Public Religion in Jürgen Habermas's Thought.] *Sapientiana* (7): 33–52.

Gyáni Gábor. 2017. "A felejtés mint politikai mítosz." [Forgetting as Political Myth]. *Korall* (67): 5–21.

Habermas, Jürgen, and Joseph Ratzinger. 2007. *The Dialectics of Secularization: On Reason and Religion.* San Francisco: Ignatius Press.

Horváth, Gergely Krisztián. 2018. "Communist Agricultural Policy and Two Waves of Collectivization in Hungary." In *NEB Yearbook 2016–2017,* edited by Zsolt Horváth and Réka Kiss. Budapest: NEB. https://neb.hu/asset/phpp4fkoo.pdf.

"Igazságos ítélet." 1949. ['A Just Verdict']. *Szabad Nép,* February 9.

"Kádár János belügyminiszter beszéde a minisztérium politikai kollégiumában. Jelentés. Budapest, 1949. február 14." ["Speech by Minister of the Interior János Kádár at the Political College of the Ministry of the Interior. Report. Budapest, February 14, 1949"]. Historical Archives of the Hungarian State Security (Állambiztonsági Szolgálatok Történeti Levéltára, ÁBTL), 2.1. XI/8.

"Kádár János beszéde a budapesti Hősök terén, 1957. május 1." ["Speech by János Kádár at the Heroes Square in Budapest, May 1, 1957"]. *Népszabadság,* May 1.

"Kádár János előadása 'A magyar reakciónak és külföldi segítőinek szervezeti és munkamódszerei és az ellene való harc' címmel a Magyar Dolgozók Pártja pártfőiskoláján, 1950. március 25." ["Lecture by János Kádár titled 'The organizational and working methods of the Hungarian reaction and its foreign supporters, and the struggle against them' at the Party College of the Hungarian Working People's Party, March 25, 1950"]. National Archives of Hungary (Magyar Nemzeti Levéltár Országos Levéltára, MNL OL), M-KS 276. f. 75. cs. 30. ő. e.

"Kádár János felszólalása a Belügyminisztérium parancsnoki értekezletén, 1974. december 13." ["Speech by János Kádár at the command meeting of the Ministry of the Interior, December 13, 1974"]. Archives of Political History and the Trade Unions (Politikatörténeti és Szakszervezeti Levéltár, PIL), 765. f. 43. ő. e., 20–22.

"Kádár János felszólalása a Hazafias Népfront Országos Tanácsának ülésén, 1961. december 8." ["Speech by János Kádár at the Congress of Patriotic People's Front, December 10, 1961"].

"Kádár János felszólalása az MSZMP VII. kongresszusán, 1959. November 30." ["Speech by János Kádár at the Seventh Congress of the Hungarian Socialist Workers' Party, November 30, 1959"].

"Kádár János felszólalása egyházpolitikai kérdésekről az MSZMP KB ülésén, 1983. február 15." ["Speech by János Kádár on Church policy questions at the session of the Central Committee of the Hungarian Socialist Workers' Party, February 15, 1983"].

"Kádár János sajtókonferenciája Rómában." 1977. ["János Kádár's Press Conference in Rome"]. In *Magyar Külpolitikai Évkönyv* ["Hungarian Foreign Policy Yearbook"], 128-30. Budapest.

Keep, John L. H. 1995. *Last of the Empires: A History of the Soviet Union.* Oxford: Oxford University Press.

Keszei, András. 2017. "Felejtés, társadalom, történelem. In: Forgetting, Society, History." *Korall* 2017 (67): 5–21.

Kiss, Réka. 2014. "National and Congregational Identity in the Shadow of Dictatorship." In *Confessionality and University in the Modern World: 20th Anniversary of "Károli" University. (Studia Caroliensia, 2013 Yearbook of Károli Gáspár University of the Reformed Church in Hungary)*, edited by Enikő Sepsi, Péter Balla and Márton Csanády, 227–36. Budapest: Károli Gáspár University of the Reformed Church in Hungary and L'Harmattan Publishing.

Klimó, Árpád. 2010. "Catholic identity in Hungary – The Mindszenty Case." *Hungarian Studies* 24 (2): 189–213.

Koselleck, Reinhart. 1985. *Futures Past; on the Semantics of Historical Time.* Cambridge, MA: MIT Press.

Lénárd, Ödön, Ágnes Tímár, Gyula Szabó, and Viktor Attila Soós. 2006. *Utak és útvesztők. [Roads and Mazes].* Budapest: Kairosz.

Life 26 (1949): 30.

Magyar Dolgozók Pártja [Hungarian Working People's Party]. 1951/1952. "A klerikális reakció – népi demokráciánk ellensége." ["The Clerical Reaction – The Enemy of Our People's Democracy"], Budapest.

Márai, Sándor. 1968. *Napló (1945–1957).* [Diary (1945–1957)]. Washington: Occidental Press.

"Mindszentynek felelni kell." ['Mindszenty Must Be Held Accountable']. *Szabad Nép*, December 30, 1948.

Népszava, January 12, 1946.

Népszava, March 5, 1946.

Pollack, Detlef, and Gergely Rosta. 2017. *Religion and Modernity. An International Comparison.* Oxford: Oxford University Press.

Révai, József. 1945. "A demokrácia támadásban." ["Democracy on the Offensive"]. *Szabad Nép*, July 22, 1945.

———. 1946. "Párizs és Miskolc" ["Paris and Miskolc"]. *Szabad Nép*, August 4, 1946.

Ricoeur, Paul. 2004. *Memory, History, Forgetting.* Chicago: University of Chicago.

Schilling, Heinz. 1999. "Das konfessionelle Europa. Die Konfessionalisierung der europäischen Länder seit der Mitte des 16. Jahrhunderts und ihre Folgen für Kirche, Staat, Gesellschaft und Kultur." In *Konfessionalisierung in Ostmitteleuropa. Wirkungen des religiösen Wandels im 16. und 17. Jahrhundert in Staat, Gesellschaft und Kultur*, edited by Joachim Bahlcke and Arno Strohmeyer, 13–62. Stuttgart: Franz Steiner Verlag.

Somorjai, Ádám, and Tibor Zinner (compiler). 2013. *Do Not Forget This Small Honest Nation: Cardinal Mindszenty to 4 US Presidents and State Secretaries 1956–1971 as Conserved in American Archives and Commented by American Diplomats.* Bloomington: Xlibris Corporation.

Stark, Rodney. 1999. "Secularization, RIP (Rest in Peace)." *Sociology of Religion* (60) 4: 249–73.

Swatos, William H. Jr., and Kevin J. Christiano. 1999. "Secularization Theory: The Course of a Concept." *Sociology of Religion* 60 (3): 209–28.

Szabad Nép, January 11, 1946.

Szabad Nép, March 26, 1946.

Szabad Nép, June 6, 1948.

Szabó, István. 1946. "A hercegprímáshoz" ["To the Prince Primate"]. *Népszava*, January 20, 1946.

Tabajdi, Gábor. 2019. *Bomlasztás. Kádár János és a III/III.* [Disruption. János Kádár and the III/III.] Budapest: Jaffa.

Tiszantúli Néplap, December 7, 1949.

Todorov, Tzvetan. 2003. *Hope and Memory: Lessons from the Twentieth Century.* Princeton, NJ: Princeton University Press.

178 *Réka Földváryné Kiss*

Tomka, Miklós. 1998. "Contradictions of Secularism and the Preservation of the Sacred: Four Contexts of Religious Change in Communism." In *Secularization and Social Integration*, edited by Rudi Laermans, Bryan Wilson and Jaak Billiet, 177–89. Leuven: Leuven University Press.

"Tüntetés Mindszenty bíboros ellen" ["Protest Against Cardinal Mindszenty"]. 1948. *Filmhíradó [Newsreels]* 40 (December). Accessed October 15, 2020. Source: https://filmhiradokonline.hu/watch.php?id=6980.

Part III
Post-conflict memories

9 Evocation and the June Fourth Tiananmen candlelight vigil

A ritual-theological hermeneutics

Lap Yan Kung

On 4 June 1989, the Chinese authorities ordered the army to clear Tiananmen Square by opening fire on the protestors who were occupying it. According to a newly released source from Alan Donald, the British ambassador to China at that time, more than 10,000 civilians were killed (Tao 2017). The Chinese authorities condemned the protest movement for undertaking revolutionary activity, while the protestors defended it as a non-violent civil rights movement campaigning against corruption and bureaucracy (Calhoun 1997; Lim 2014; Shen and Yen 1998; Unger 1991). Those who seek to emphasize the killing of protestors on the night of June Fourth have named the incident the Tiananmen Square Massacre. By naming the incident the Massacre, it is easier to arouse public sentiment, but the weakness of such an approach is that it may dilute any concern over the incident's civil rights implications. Because this study focuses on the June Fourth candlelight vigil, I will follow this convention and refer to the incident as the Massacre. The date of 4 June 1989 has become a taboo in China's everyday life since then. There is no detailed reference to the Massacre in any history textbooks in China. Attempts to discuss and commemorate the incident are met with aggressive censorship (Citizenlab 2019). For instance, in 2016, four people who designed a wine poster and bottle label containing the number 8964 (the date of the Massacre) were detained for three years before finally being convicted in April 2019 for disturbing the social order and sentenced to three years of imprisonment (Voice of America 2019). Around the Fourth of June, people from the Tiananmen Mothers, a group comprising the parents, friends and relatives of victims of the Massacre, are not allowed to visit their children's gravesites. Ding Zilin (丁子霖), a spokesperson for the Tiananmen Mothers and the author of a book titled *In Search of the Victims of June Fourth, 1989–2005* (2005), wrote an open letter to President Xi Jinping (習近平) in 2018, which contains the following grievance: 'Each year when we would like to commemorate our loved ones, we are all monitored, put under surveillance, or forced to travel' (Tiananmen Mothers 2018).[1] The attempts being made by the Chinese authorities to fully erase traces of the Massacre from people's everyday lives are nothing new, because the Chinese authorities are fully aware that 'remembrance of the past may give rise to dangerous insights' (Marcus 1964, 98). Remembering the Massacre poses a threat to the official

DOI: 10.4324/9781003264750-12

182　*Lap Yan Kung*

narrative. Hong Kong and Macau are the only places on Chinese soil at which open vigils remembering the Massacre have been held yearly since 1990. We are not sure that the Tiananmen commemoration would be an illegal activity under the National Security Law imposed on Hong Kong in July 2020. The June Fourth candlelight vigils in both Hong Kong and Macau are very symbolic. They form a barometer reflecting how the Chinese authorities are honouring the promise of 'one country, two systems'.[2] This chapter focuses on the candlelight vigil taking place in Hong Kong, adopting a ritual-theological hermeneutics to explore the religious/spiritual dimension of the vigil and reflect on how religious/spiritual resources contribute to memory of the Massacre and how the Massacre itself affects how religion interprets itself.

The June Fourth candlelight vigil as a sign of collective memory

The June Fourth candlelight vigil is not the only annual event remembering the Massacre. In fact, it is the culmination of a series of remembrance events that start in early April. These include symposiums, exhibitions, the flying of kites for democracy and a patriotic democratic parade. The candlelight vigil is organized by the Hong Kong Alliance in Support of Patriotic Democratic Movements of China (hereinafter the Alliance), which comprised 146 affiliated organizations at its peak. Both the Chinese authorities and the Hong Kong government remain tolerant of the Alliance and its organized activities because the freedom to hold the candlelight vigil is a significant sign showing the world the success of 'one country, two systems'. The freedoms of expression and assembly are protected, and the freedom to hold the candlelight vigil continued after 1997 (the Chinese authorities resumed the exercising of sovereignty over Hong Kong on 1 July 1997).

The Massacre has left a strong emotional imprint on the people of Hong Kong. For instance, on 21 May 1989, more than a million people – one-fifth of the population – joined the rally in Hong Kong supporting the students protesting in Beijing. On the same day, the Hong Kong Alliance in Support of Patriotic Democratic Movements of China was established. On 27 May 1989, HK$12 million was raised to support the democratic movement in Beijing. After the Massacre on 4 June 1989, Operation Yellow Bird in Hong Kong was launched to assist protestors to escape from China and take refuge in other countries (Lo 2010, 23–26). The Massacre has destroyed dialogue between the Chinese government and pro-democracy groups in Hong Kong from then until now. The candlelight vigil has been held in Victoria Park without interruption since 1990. Collective memory gives people a sense of how they become who they are, builds solidarity and sometimes challenges the present (Connerton 1989; Schudson 1992). The Massacre has become the people of Hong Hong's collective memory (Lee and Chan 2016). However, this memory has at least as much, if not more, to do with legitimating the present needs and mores of our societies as representing an accurate record of what actually happened. It is the dominant needs of present society that dictate how and what human societies remember (Connerton 1989, 3). What makes the people of Hong Kong persist in remembering the Massacre? Has there been any change in the needs and mores of Hong Kong society over the last thirty years?

First, the people of Hong Kong at that time were not very suspicious of their Chinese identity and shared the protestors' concern over China's future. They saw themselves as patriotic, but in the eyes of the Chinese government, patriotism had to comply with any demands made by the leadership of the Chinese Communist Party. The protestors primarily focused on calling for an end to official corruption and for political and economic reform. Students in Beijing, China, announced the Hunger Strike Declaration on 13 May 1989, which stated:

> This country is our country,
> These people are our people,
> This government is our government,
> If we do not cry out, who will?
> If we do not act, who will?

> Though our shoulders are still fragile, though death still seems too great a burden for us, we are ready to leave you. We could not but go. History asks this of us. . . .
> We do not want to die; we want to live, to live fully, for we are at life's most promising age. We do not want to die; we want to study. Our motherland is so impoverished, it feels as if we are abandoning her to die. Yet death is not what we seek. But if the death of one or a few people can enable more to live better, and can make our motherland prosperous, then we have no right to cling to life.[3]

Second, the people of Hong Kong understand very well that the protection of human rights in Hong Kong will not be respected if there is no democratization in China. This is a pragmatic concern (Cheng 2011, 180–83). Third, the people of Hong Kong are not bystanders to the Massacre; they are witnesses to the killing. In particular, those who were in Beijing during the Massacre consider that they have a responsibility to victims and survivors to bear witness to the killing to the world (Hong Kong Journalists Association 2019). Irrespective of their differing political views, both the pro-Chinese government and the democratic camps in Hong Kong stood as one at that time to condemn the Chinese authorities. However, this unified sense of condemnation only lasted a few years. Some people who had originally condemned the Chinese authorities no longer wished to maintain a relationship of constant tension with them and so gradually moved towards a more pragmatic compromise position. These people consider that any insistence on truth-seeking and justice after the Massacre would be futile, not only because such effort would have no impact on Chinese politics but also because the relationship with the Chinese government would be further worsened. They contend that people should not be focusing on the Massacre or amplifying it. Instead, people should be living for the future rather than the past and focusing on China's economic prosperity. Furthermore, the human rights situation in China has been improving greatly in comparison with previous times, so the Chinese authorities should be given the time and space to improve it further. In the ongoing struggle over memory, 'Don't want to remember, dare not forget' (不想回憶，未敢忘記) has become an important catchphrase associated with the June Fourth candlelight vigils. As a whole, the Massacre has led to a substantial transformation in Hong Kong's political culture. Many people in Hong Kong see the Massacre as the point of their political awakening (Lee and Chan 2011).

Police statistics show that the annual attendance for the candlelight vigil over the last thirty years has been between 12,000 and 110,000, while the statistics from the organizer claim between 35,000 and 180,000 (HKUPOP 2018). On the thirtieth anniversary (2019), the organizer said there were 180,000 participants, while the police figure was 37,000. According to the Public Opinion Programme at the University of Hong Kong, in 2018, about 70% of the participants were aged thirty or older. There are fewer people aged thirty or younger because the generation born after 1989 does not have first-hand experience of the Massacre. With a view to informing this post-1989 generation about the Massacre, the Alliance and other groups have organized different commemorative activities. For instance, since 2009, artist Him Lo (盧樂謙) has initiated This Generation's June Fourth (這一代的六四), an event that openly invites artists to present performances on 3 June every year. These artists have been seeking to engage the public in a more personal approach by contextualizing the Massacre within the current situation and everyday life in Hong Kong, and relating it to the younger generations who did not directly experience it.[4] However, the meaning and appropriateness of the candlelight vigil has been seriously challenged by the rise of Hong Kong localism since the early 2010s. This is a very different scenario from the results of the study done by Francis Lee and Joseph Chan in 2010 (Lee and Chan 2013). Their research aimed to explain why participating in the candlelight vigil had risen in popularity among the young generation. In 2016, the Hong Kong Federation of Students withdrew its membership from the Alliance. The withdrawal of the student organization not only resulted in a decline in the numbers of young participants but also threatens the collective identity that emerged from collective memory of the Massacre (Cheng and Yuen 2019). The first criticism made by young people is that the vigil promotes a form of Chinese nationalism that has fallen out of sync with the younger generation. Many young people tend to have a much stronger local identity (Hong Kongers) than Chinese identity. They argue that they do not hold any responsibility for China. Even if they choose to commemorate the victims, this should be done out of respect for human rights rather than nationalistic sentiment. The second criticism focuses on the form assumed by the vigil. They contend that the vigil has been too ritualistic and that these rituals are largely drawn from an old-fashioned repertoire. They therefore serve no more than a symbolic purpose and have no actual impact on either the Chinese government or Hong Kong's democratization progress. Third, the Alliance is too easily satisfied with the number attending the candlelight vigil, and the vigil itself has become more of an illusory healing process. It may be meaningful to the Tiananmen Mothers and people involved, but it has no meaning for the new generation (Cheng and Yuen 2019; Ho 2016). They have different views on the candlelight vigil and challenge the monopolization of the Massacre commemoration by the Alliance, but there is no dispute over the content of the memory itself. This consensus makes a significant contribution to the process of memory mobilization, because 'memories of past struggles, as well as the conservative mobilizing choices by leaders, who aim to work within the experiences of their people, may severely constrain the range of possible choices of the form' (McCarthy 1995, 150). In addition, the candlelight vigil should be a kind of communicative memory. The participation of a group in communicative memory is diffuse and there are no specialists in informal, communicative memory (Assmann 1995). Therefore, challenges from localists and young people should be positively received and assessed even though such challenges may threaten collective identity.

The candlelight vigil is the only remembrance activity on Chinese soil to challenge the Chinese government's discourse of the Massacre. There are always a small number of participants from mainland China. Most of them are shocked after attending the candlelight vigil. This is their first experience of listening to a version of the Massacre that differs from the Chinese government's version. Crystal Xu, a 22-year-old student, came to Hong Kong in 2014 to study journalism in the wake of the seventy-nine-day protest that had galvanized the city, and she wanted to know more about social movements in China. Her reading led her to the Massacre: 'I don't know if my friends know about this. Nobody on the mainland would talk about June Fourth, and nobody told me about June Fourth before'. She decided to brave the censors to help educate her friends and posted a collection of links to articles and interviews about the Massacre on WeChat (Time 2019). Another student from mainland China, R. Sun, says the only time he heard the mysterious term 'June Fourth' was during a high school history class in China. The teacher briefly mentioned the date, explaining that this part of history was not in the textbook because it was deliberately erased. Then in 2009, Sun moved to Hong Kong and noticed posters around his university campus announcing memorials for the twentieth anniversary of the Massacre. The posters' reference to 4 June 1989 reminded him of a date he had almost forgotten. 'I've been told lies', he said on realizing that he had been fed propaganda. Every year, he now commemorates June Fourth in some way or other, such as fasting, taking part in vigils or creatively using the numbers 8, 9, 6 and 4. He says, 'June Fourth has shaped [me], and is a part of who I am today' (*Time* 2019).

There have been differences in emphasis on the candlelight vigil over the last thirty years due to socio-political changes, but the goals of commemorating those killed in the Massacre, showing solidarity with the survivors, demanding

186 *Lap Yan Kung*

truth and justice, ending one-party rule and establishing a democratic China have remained the same. The recent concerns of the candlelight vigil are not confined to those killed in the Massacre but also extend to issues relating to the violation of human rights in China, such as *weiquan* (right protection) and Charter 08 (a manifesto signed by Chinese dissident intellectuals and human rights activists). Because the candlelight vigil is the only remembrance activity on Chinese soil to expose the ruthlessness of the Chinese government, the organizer consciously makes use of its capacity to arouse the issue of human rights violations in China without diluting the significance of the Massacre itself.

On the night of June Fourth, the commemoration vigil starts at 8:00 p.m. and ends at 9:30 p.m. Taking the year 2019 as an example, the programme rundown was as follows: a video of Hong Kong people's June Fourth, the laying of flowers, a eulogy, a moment of silence, a video from the Tiananmen Mothers, a song, a witness to the June Fourth Massacre, a second song, a video and a moment of shared reflection, a third song, a sharing of experience, a fourth song, the manifesto of the Alliance, the burning of books of condolence, the chanting of slogans, and a fifth song. It is performed as a Chinese funeral ceremony. Participants are dressed in black or white, and they are asked to bow three times to the statue of condolence, which is a standard custom practised at Chinese funerals as a sign of respect to the spirits of the dead, the spirits of the ancestors of the dead and the spirits of heaven and earth. It does not have any explicit religious ritual and symbols, but in Chinese culture it can easily be seen as a ritual of *zhaohun* (招魂, evocation). *Zhaohun* is originally a Chinese folk religious practice that involves calling upon or summoning the wandering spirits of the dead in order that they can be comforted and guided to *yin* (陰), the place where the dead belong, which is also their ancestral home. This is especially for people who did not die a good death (Jiang 2019, 57–61). *Zhaohun* is also applied to the living. Daoist belief considers that one of the reasons that a person may be sick is because one of their spirits/souls has left them, and so *zhaohun* is used to call and bring back the missing spirit/soul to whom it belongs. Rather than sharing the Daoist practice of *zhaohun*, Confucians talk about the experience of communion with the dead using the idea of *zhenqing tong youming* (真情通幽冥). Christians share the practice of *zhenqing tong youming*, but they interpret it differently, as the communion of saints. The candlelight vigil marks the moment in *zhaohun* at which the spirits of the dead are comforted, the living are healed and the living and the dead are in communion. In the following section, I will articulate the religious dimension in the candlelight vigil.

Chaodu (超渡) and rest in peace

Chaodu is a religious belief and practice found in both Buddhism and Daoism. As far as it relates to the spirits of the dead, *chaodu* constitutes the ritual of their progression towards salvation (Palmer and Liu 2012, 87). Buddhists focus on the

Evocation and the Tiananmen vigil   187

individual spirit through the stages of rebirth to the stage of nirvana, while the Daoists focus on the injustice and loneliness experienced by the spirits of the dead. One of the major focuses of Daoist *chaodu* is to resolve feelings of moral outrage caused by injustice.

Chinese tradition believes that if the spirit of someone who has died does not rest in peace, it not only affects their own fate after death but also brings adversity to the living world. What makes a person unable to rest in peace? First, a person dying at an inappropriate age would not be able to rest in peace. In fact, *yingnian zuoshi* (英年早逝, too young to die) is a very common Chinese saying. *Yingnian* (英年) refers to people aged between twenty and forty. So a person dying at the age of forty or younger has not died a good death. By contrast, a person dying at the age of sixty or older is called *xiaosang* (笑喪), which means dying with satisfaction. Second, a good death takes place when a dying person does not need to suffer for a long time or experience a great deal of pain. This is more related to the Greek idea of euthanasia (εὐθανασία). Third, a good death occurs when a person has died of natural causes. On the other hand, if someone has been murdered or killed by accident or violence, this is definitely not a good death. The spirit, rather than being able to go to *yin* (陰), the abode of the spirits of the dead, would instead wander around *yang* (陽), the place where the living exist. Furthermore, the wandering spirit may create troubles for the living. In order to let the spirit of the dead rest in peace, a proper burial should be arranged, a regular commemoration should be held and justice for the dead should be pursued.

According to Daoist belief and practice, *chaodu* is performed for the spirits of the dead on any one of these three occasions. First, *chaodu* is for the spirits of the dead who are still being punished in *yin*. Through the power of the priests and the merits of their relatives, the spirits of the dead can be redeemed from punishment and suffering. Second, *chaodu* is for the spirits of the dead who have been killed. Their feelings of moral outrage and grievance make them remain in *yang*. They are not able to rest in peace. *Chaodu* is performed to comfort them and even to bring justice for them. Third, *chaodu* is for the spirits of the dead who have not regularly received offerings from their descendants. They are the spirits left behind and forgotten, who are called *guhun* (孤魂). *Chaodu* is not confined to the funeral moment but it is also a practice performed at *zhongyuan jie* (中元節, the festival of the Middle Season), which falls in August. This is also commonly known as the festival of the hungry ghosts, or *Yue Lan* festival. (*Yue Lan* is derived from the Sanskrit *Ullambana* [DeBernardi 2009, 156–81; Orzech 1996] and is an example of integration between Buddhism and Daoism.) During the festival, Daoist priests perform *chaodu* for spirits being released from *yin* at this time. Ordinary people make offerings to appease the wandering spirits in order to ease their sufferings and maintain harmony between the realms of *yang* and *yin* (Graham 2017). Their actions are based on the Daoist belief of *pudu* (universal salvation and love), which seeks to save others through ritual means (Pregadio 2008, 792–95). *Chaodu* is primarily for the spirits of the dead, but it also comforts the survivors because

188 *Lap Yan Kung*

the survivors can be relieved when they know that the spirits of the dead they love are resting in peace.

One does not need to be a Buddhist or a Daoist to understand *chaodu*, because the belief and practice of *chaodu* are embedded in Chinese culture and expressed at the *zhongyuan jie* or *Yue Lan* festival. The festival is more commonly known as *Yue Lan* in Hong Kong. It is not a public holiday in Hong Kong but the two weeks over which it is celebrated in public space have left a deep impression on the everyday life of the people. In 2011, the *Yue Lan* festival was included on the list of China's intangible cultural heritage. Since 2015 the organizers, with the support of the Hong Kong government, have actively promoted the culture of the *Yue Lan* festival. People in Hong Kong may not share a belief in *chaodu*, but *chaodu* is not alien to their experience.

On what basis can we say that the June Fourth candlelight vigil is a kind of *chaodu*? There is no explicit religious ritual practice in the candlelight vigil, but the ritual of the burning of books of condolence is in itself a very typical Daoist, rather than Buddhist, practice. According to Daoist practice, offerings are burnt to transmit the offerings to the dead by transforming them through fire. Books of condolence are burnt at the vigil to offer condolences to the people killed in the Massacre. It is never regarded as a disrespectful act to people who have signed a book of condolences that is to be burned. Besides, most of the civilians killed in the Massacre died relatively young and suffered violent deaths. Some of them did even not have a proper burial. They need to be able to rest in peace. The candlelight vigil is not a *chaodu* but it can serve as a *chaodu*, comforting the spirits of the dead, resolving their feelings of moral outrage and even bringing the missing spirits/souls of those who survived back to them. Zhang Xianling (張先玲), a member of the Tiananmen Mothers, marked the thirtieth anniversary (2019) with the following written statement:

> On behalf of the Tiananmen Mothers, we would like to convey our deepest respect and heartfelt gratitude to you. For the past thirty years, the candlelight of Victoria Park has accompanied the Tiananmen Mothers along the rocky road and warmed our hearts.[5]

Though the candlelight vigil focuses on the Massacre, it may serve the purpose of something like *pudu* in the *Yue Lan* festival. It is a *chaodu* for the people who were being killed by the Chinese government during the campaigns to suppress counter-revolutionaries (1950–53), the Tibetan Uprising (1959), the Cultural Revolution (1966–76) and others, because the spirits of the dead are *guhun*.

Participants, not confined to Buddhists and Daoists, would find the candlelight vigil comforting to them, but the candlelight vigil is not necessarily an illusory healing, as critical localists have claimed, because the practice of *chaodu* serves as an annual reminder that the dead are not able to rest in peace. Although *chaodu* does not resolve the grievances of the dead, their grievances, paradoxically, are retold at every *chaodu*. The *chaodu* at the vigil is a performative act that exposes the injustice done to the dead and challenges the oppressors by making it clear that their accountability for the Massacre will not be forgotten.

Zhenqing tong youming (真情通幽冥) and communion in truthfulness

Buddhism, Confucianism and Daoism have their own belief systems and practices, but these cannot be separated when an attempt is being made to understand Chinese religious belief and practice, philosophy, arts and social structures. They are called the *Sanjiao Heyi* (the unity of the Three Teachings, 三教合一; Brook 1993). I would like to turn to Confucianism first.

Classical Confucianism has no interest in exploring life after death. One well-known Confucius saying goes: 'We do not as yet understand life; so how can we understand death?' Traditionally, Confucianism focuses on this life and the living. Chun-I Tang (唐君毅, 1909–78), who was one of the significant figures associated with neo-Confucianism, was one of the very few Confucius scholars to explore the meaning of death in Confucian tradition (Ng 1998). He argued that it was very natural for humans to talk and think about death, simply because humans have feelings about their own death and the deaths of others. Any refusal to talk about death was inhuman. He went on to contend that such concern for the meaning of death was not confined to religion. Religion had a contribution to make to the articulation of the meaning of death because religion had emerged from the pursuit of perfection (Tang 1988, 439–40). Because humans were in the process of pursuing goodness, such a pursuit would continue till eternality. This was a sign of humans' inner transcendence (Makeham 2003, 142). Tang therefore suggested that a person, rather than vanishing completely after their death, would exist in a different way. Thus, dying did not equate to the death of a person's spirit. Instead, it meant the liberation of a person's spirit from their body through death so that their spirit could continue the pursuit of goodness (Tang 1975, 74).

Because a dead person's spirit continues to exist, Tang considered that the spirit of a dead person could be in communion with the living in a mysterious way. People who live apart yet love each other deeply can be united in a mysterious way. He called this *zhenqing tong youming* (Tang 1993, 97–107). *Zhengqing* (真情) means truthful affection and love emerging from a person's pure or truthful heart. *Tong* (通) is about 'feeling and knowing an object or situation and penetrating it with one's empathetic response' (Ng 1998, 293). *Youming* (幽冥) is a place where the spirits of the dead reside. The phrase *zhenqing tong youming* means that it is the love and true affection of people that can break through the boundary between the living and the dead, and as a result, the living and the dead come together in an affective presence before each other. Tang related his personal experience of this. During a commemorative service, he felt strongly connected with the spirits of the saints. Tang described this mysterious union as very natural. It is not restricted to people with religious discipline; rather, it is the natural experience of being human. He goes

190 *Lap Yan Kung*

beyond what classical Confucianism says about immortality in terms of one's virtues, teachings and accomplishments. He introduces a fourth dimension of immortality, namely, the immortality of spirit (Tang 1955, 583). However, it is important to note that in Tang's explanation, human transcendence is still closely allied to the Confucian emphasis on virtues.

Tang's idea of *zhenqing tong youming* has provided the cultural background for interpreting the candlelight vigil. The obituary for those who died in the Massacre at the candlelight vigil on the thirtieth anniversary of June Fourth said:

> Thirty years ago, in mid-April, you and your classmates exited the school gates and walked halfway across Beijing. You openly opposed the Party's official line and showed the world that the Chinese people would not comply.
>
> Thirty years ago, in May, you and your neighbours used your bodies to block military vehicles attempting to enter the city and gently convinced the soldiers to show the world love and courage. . . .
>
> But the revolution you started has not ended; your spark still shines the way to those who have come after you. . . .
>
> We more fondly remember your goodness, your hopes and dedication, your courage and persistence. We remember that because of you, the world became a different place that early summer. We remember, and then we go on. . . .
>
> You have gone, but you are still here.
>
> In every candle in Victoria Park this evening, in every act of resistance in this land, in the hearts of all who still pursue democracy, you live on.

First, the people killed in the Massacre were witnesses to the Confucian highest virtues of *shesheng chengren* (捨身成仁, to die for the sake of humaneness or benevolence) and *shasheng quyi* (殺身取義, to die for the sake of righteousness or rightness). Mencius (372–289 BC) said,

> I like fish, and I also like bear's paws. If I cannot have the two together, I will let the fish go, and take the bear's paws. So, I like life, and I also like righteousness. If I cannot keep the two together, I will let life go, and choose righteousness. I like life indeed, but there is that which I like more than life, and therefore, I will not seek to possess it by any improper ways. I dislike death indeed, but there is that which I dislike more than death, and therefore there are occasions when I will not avoid danger.

Mencius's spirit is fully reflected in the May 13 Hunger Strike Declaration (1989). The phrase 'martyrs of democracy live in eternity' (民主烈士永垂不朽), which is engraved on the statue of condolence at the candlelight vigil, reflects the Confucian value of *ren* (humanness). In the Confucian view, these martyrs of democracy are saints. Second, even though they were killed, their spirits keep human life flourishing because they have exemplified virtues in

Evocation and the Tiananmen vigil 191

their lives. This is the classical Confucian understanding of immortality. Third, some people may existentially feel the presence of the spirits of the martyr-saints and they feel a connection with them during the candlelight vigil ceremony. According to Tang, both the dead and the living are encountered in truthfulness. People are inspired, encouraged and empowered in their communion with the dead. A young participant at the vigil said,

> It is raining at the candlelight vigil, and we are holding umbrellas. When we sing the song, *Freedom of Flower*, a strong passion comes from my heart, and tears which can't be stopped are running down. I feel union with the people killed in the Massacre. This is an unforgettable experience. It brings me to reflect on what I should hold on to, and what I should pursue.[6]

A mysterious union between the living and the dead is experienced at the candlelight vigil. This is a transcendental experience.

The Confucian values of *ren* and *yi* are reflected in the lives of the dead. The pro-government camp in Hong Kong keep their silence on the candlelight vigil because there is no other virtue that can override the Confucian highest values of *ren* and *yi*. They can only ask people to leave the memory behind and move on. The mysterious experience of union between the living and the dead at the candlelight vigil emboldens the participants to uphold the virtues of *ren* and *yi*. There is always a debate over whether Confucianism is a conservative force that tends to maintain law, order and the status quo due to its emphasis on *li* (禮, proper conduct for sustaining social and cosmic order). However, it can also be argued that *li* is a transformational force for change that can change the world according to its moral idealism. The stories of the dead and survivors (told by the Tiananmen Mothers) continuously expose the falsehood of a *li* built on violence, lies and the government's desire for power.

Crucified people and hope at death

The candlelight vigil does not have an explicitly Christian component, but Christianity is the only religion in Hong Kong that is actively engaged in remembering the Massacre. The Hong Kong Christian Alliance in Support of the Chinese Patriotic and Democratic Movement and Association of Catholic Organizations in Support of Patriotic Democratic Movements in China were founded in 1989, around the same time as the founding of the Alliance. The Christian Alliance holds seminars, organizes a commemorative service and prepares a public prayer in remembrance of the Massacre every year. Likewise, the Catholic association organizes exhibitions, seminars, prayer meetings and Masses for the Massacre. Their activities are included in the Alliance's propaganda poster. What makes Christians keep on remembering the Massacre?

Apart from a sense of justice and the shared destiny of being Chinese, these Christians are united by one of the defining characteristics of their Christian faith: the remembrance of suffering. In Christian scripture, Christians

192   *Lap Yan Kung*

remember the slavery of the Hebrews in Egypt, the exile of Israel in Babylon, the massacre of the Holy Innocents, the crucifixion of Jesus and the suffering of the early Christian martyrs. However, the Christian tradition always only remembers these sufferings in relation to the hope-filled promises of the Exodus, the return from exile, the Incarnation and the Resurrection. Thus, Christian memory of suffering is always linked to hope for, and the promise of, a future in which suffering will be no more. This is fully reflected in the Christian practice of the Eucharist. Christians are nurtured to adopt a perspective of suffering and solidarity with sufferers.

Latin American liberation theology has a good articulation of solidarity with sufferers. In Latin America, poverty often equates to death rather than being a mere matter of inadequacy. Theologically, Latin Americans are the crucified people. This concept is derived from a mutual analogy between the crucifixion of the people and the death of Jesus. The crucified people are those who 'are denied a chance to speak and even to call by name, which means they are denied their own existence' (Sobrino 2008, 4). To be crucified does not mean simply to die but rather to be put to death. There are victims and there are executors. The crucified people personify the reality that the sin in the world continues to violate human dignity, and that the powerful of this world continue to rob the poor, the marginalized and the defenders of human rights. The crucified people are the actualization of Christ crucified, the true servants of Yahweh, because throughout history, Jesus was there wherever suffering people were to be found. Suffering under injustice is not just the sufferers' story; it is Jesus's story as well as God's story. The story of Jesus reminds us that 'God makes Godself present in these crosses, and the crucified peoples become the principal sign of the times. This sign (of God's presence in our world) is always the historically crucified people' (Sobrino 1990, 122). The crucified people will not be forgotten because the Spirit of God who resurrects Jesus from death will resurrect them as well. The crucified people are no longer just the people being killed, but they are the bearers of salvation, for God's salvation will come upon them, and the executors are called to repent. Ignacio Ellacuria writes, 'The accent is not on what Jesus and the people are, but on what they represent for the salvation of humankind' (Ellacuria 1986, 258). The crucified people are the light of the nations and bringers of salvation because God promises that they will not be forgotten. The crucified people are the losers in history, but in God's history they are winners because God's resurrection comes upon them. The Christian belief in Jesus's resurrection leads to the emergence of the idea of a fellowship of solidarity beyond time and death (Lochman 1985, 210–16). Every Christian memorial service is a moment of communion between God, the dead and the living, and a promise of resurrection.

The people killed in the Massacre are the crucified people. Their death is a consequence of a deliberate inhumane decision. Besides, they are deprived of the right to be remembered. The Chinese authorities use all means to cover up the truth and prohibit any form of public mourning, but what they have done is futile because the cries of the crucified people reach God, and God promises

Evocation and the Tiananmen vigil   193

to deliver their resurrection. There is always a future for the dead because the new life and creation illustrated in Jesus is offered to them. Therefore, memory of suffering is not simply a matter of looking backward archaeologically but also embracing future-oriented, forward-looking memories in which we also remember the promises made by God and the hopes that are experienced as a result of those promises. Remembering the crucified Jesus and the crucified people is a way of resisting the power of violence and lies. Jesus's resurrection is a definite 'yes' to the people committed to justice and peace, and an unambiguous 'no' to the power of violence.

In what ways do Christian engagements contribute to the candlelight vigil? First, the Christian community are aware of the debate on the candlelight vigil between the Alliance and the localists. However, they prefer to keep organizing commemoration practices (such as Masses) for the Massacre. This helps to shield the original purpose of commemorating the Massacre from potential distractions. Second, slightly over 40% of primary and secondary schools in Hong Kong are run by churches. The Christian community can nurture in its members the values expressed by the protestors in the Massacre, that is, *ren* and *yi*, and this message can be passed on to the young generation through its schools. Third, the Christian notion of hope revealed in Jesus's resurrection reveals that the candlelight vigil is more than a moment of mourning. It is a liberating hope that transcends any anticipation of the form that deliverance would take, and is open to the objection that, in many cases, the hoped-for deliverance does not take place. This is a spirituality of resistance to fatalism as well as fantasy.

Liminality and religious symbols

The participants in the candlelight vigil experience a social relation different from what they are used to. This social relation is articulated through a sense of communion with the dead, a challenge to the Chinese government's discourse and a quest for identity. This is what Victor Turner means by *communitas* emerging from the liminal state. '*Communitas* is spontaneous, immediate, concrete – it is not shaped by norms, it is not institutionalized, it is not abstract' (Turner 1974, 272). At such a liminal state, people are beyond the boundaries of the normal social structure and its values, norms and obligations. Van Gennep describes this liminal experience as sacred, not in a religious sense but in the sense that it arises from a disruption to the social order caused by a movement or change in a state of an individual, group or even the natural world (van Gennep 1960, 12–13). The liminal state is not only notable for its isolation from hardened structures but also the potentialities it contains for forming alternative structures. Turner describes the liminal as 'a realm of pure possibility whence novel configurations or ideas and relations may arise', as 'a state of reflection' and as 'the realm of primitive hypothesis' which opens up 'a certain freedom to juggle with the factors of existence' (Turner 1967, 93–111). Returning to the primary concerns of this chapter, how do religious symbols articulate the liminal experience of the participants in the candlelight vigil?

194 *Lap Yan Kung*

How do the religious symbols fuel imagination of the future? To what extent does this liminal experience contribute to post-liminality?

In the case of the Massacre, the Chinese authorities heavily rely on the tactic of destroying and controlling the victims' memories. They do this by wiping out evidence of their own crimes, intimidating or eliminating those who could potentially bear witness, employing euphemisms in place of the plain truth and asserting outright falsehoods. This manipulation culminates in the erasure of memory, especially the memory of suffering, in order to effect the total domination of individuals, communities and whole peoples. The mood and tone of the candlelight vigil is set for a funeral and *zhaohun*. Daoist belief and the practice of *chaodu* emphasize that there will be no peace if justice is not restored for the people killed in the Massacre. This is a strong message repeatedly recited in the candlelight vigil. The spirits of the dead will keep on disturbing and accusing the oppressors, and the only way the government can escape from their entreaties is by granting them justice. The people killed in the Massacre have personified the highest virtues in Confucian thought, namely, *shesheng chengren* and *shasheng quyi*. Telling the stories of those who were killed in the Massacre not only emboldens those who remain to pick up the standards and agendas of those who were killed and advance them once more, but it also provokes a transcendental moment of communion between the living and the dead, namely, *zhenqing tong youming*. Finally, the crucified Jesus in Christianity reveals that the killings in the Massacre were deliberate, inhumane acts. Their stories will not be forgotten, because God will remember the killed, and the resurrection of Jesus will bring them to life. People are empowered by hope in their struggle for justice. Confucianism and Daoism are very different from Christianity, but all three help to articulate the experience of injustice in a non-exclusive way. Christians do not feel that there is a religious barrier preventing them from attending the candlelight vigil. Likewise, believers devoted to Buddhism, Confucianism and Daoism do not feel that there is religious barrier to them attending Christian activities for the commemoration. It is the suffering and injustice of the people that transcends the differences between these four faiths. To use Pope Francis's term, this is the ecumenism of blood. The vigil participants are united in suffering and commitment to justice and peace. These four faiths reject any attempt to seek a trade-off between *yi, ren* and solidarity with sufferers on the one hand, and economic prosperity, social stability and personal fortune on the other. Remembered suffering bolstered by religious symbols has the subversive power to interrupt received narratives about the way things are, subvert official versions of the past and uncover the reality for what it truly is. At the same time, it expresses concern for how society should (or should not) be. The interruption effected by remembered suffering forces individuals and communities to unlearn their received understandings of reality, and in particular those understandings that legitimate the domination wielded by those who hold positions of power. This is particularly true to people from mainland China who attend the candlelight vigil.

Evocation and the Tiananmen vigil 195

Max Horkheimer comments that the otherworldly elements of religion are 'a longing for something other than this world', a longing that can help to open and keep the human imagination alive to the possibility that what presents itself as the natural order of things is not the fullness of what might be (Horkheimer 2013, 50). Religious belief and practices may serve to interrupt this closed system: 'Such a concern for truth beyond the immediately given cannot as such be separated from theism' (Horkheimer 2013, 47). Christianity plays a more conscious role by organizing a series of events remembering the Massacre, such as Masses and seminars, but the Confucian and Daoist communities, like the Buddhist community, do not organize any activities devoted to the Massacre. The limited role played by Buddhists, Confucianists and Daoists in the recent social movements in Hong Kong (the Umbrella Movement in 2014 and the Anti-extradition Bill Movement in 2019) would indicate that they are inclined to comply with the government, but this is not the case with Christians. Despite this, religious symbols are not monopolized by religious communities. They are embedded in the culture, and people can employ them freely. It could be said that the Massacre, to a certain extent, retrieves the liberating dimension of religions. Religious symbols are polemical rather than totemic.

One of the themes shared by these four religions is the virtue of forgiveness and reconciliation. Daoism considers that forgiveness not only enables the self to heal but also frees one from karmic dynamics so that one is released from pain and suffering and has peace (Eppert 2012, 73). In fact, *chaodu* itself is a process for resolving enmity. Confucianism talks about *shu* (恕) and how it is part of *ren* (仁). '*Shu* asks us to put ourselves in the shoes of the other person, and once we see that we too are capable of the same wrongdoing, our compassion calls on us to forgive' (Lewis 2018, 108; Holmgren 2012, 220). The Lord's Prayer in Christianity says 'forgive us our trespasses, as we forgive those who trespass against us'. Jesus's resurrection is not a message of retaliation but a message of reconciliation. As Arendt claimed:

> Forgiving, in other words, is the only reaction which does not merely re-act but acts anew and unexpectedly, unconditioned by the act which provoked it and therefore freeing from its consequences both the one who forgives and the one who is forgiven.
>
> (Arendt 1958, 241)

In 2012, Chai Ling (柴玲), one of the foremost student leaders at the 1989 Tiananmen Square protests and a two-time Nobel Peace Prize nominee, said:

> Because of Jesus, I forgive them. I forgive Deng Xiaoping and Li Peng. I forgive the soldiers who stormed Tiananmen Square in 1989. I forgive the current leadership of China, who continue to suppress freedom and enforce the brutal One Child Policy. . . . I understand such forgiveness is countercultural. Yet it is only a small reflection of the forgiveness that Jesus

gave, and I was filled with peace when I followed him in forgiving. When forgiveness arises, a lasting peace can finally reign.

(Chai 2012)

Rather than earning words of appreciation, Chai Ling's forgiveness has attracted severe criticism. She has been accused of betraying the victims and survivors. The theme of forgiveness is absent from the candlelight vigil, because the survivors and the organizers do not consider this is the right moment to talk about forgiveness. No religious symbol expressing forgiveness and reconciliation is employed at the candlelight vigil. In fact, the Chinese authorities continue to deny the survivors and the public the right of public mourning, the right to truth and the right to justice. Encouraging the victims to forgive the oppressors, as Chai Ling did, is not the main issue. The most important task is to prepare an environment characterized by respect for human dignity and equality that makes forgiveness and reconciliation more possible.

Finally, to what extent is the liminal experience at the candlelight vigil carried on at the post-liminal stage? This is the precise concern of the localists and the reason for their critique of the candlelight vigil. They find it has no practical impact on either China's or Hong Kong's democratization process. But is this the only criterion to evaluate the significance of the candlelight vigil? In fact, some expect the role of the candlelight vigil should be to show solidarity with the victims. The Tiananmen Mothers expressed their gratitude for the candlelight vigil in 2019 as follows: 'On behalf of the Tiananmen Mothers, we would like to convey our deepest respect and heartfelt gratitude to you. For the past thirty years, the candlelight of Victoria Park has accompanied the Tiananmen Mothers along the rocky road and warmed our hearts'.[7] Some are satisfied that the candlelight vigil functions as a heterotopia to expose human rights violations by the Chinese authorities and yet subvert them. Such differences in expectation create a fissure in the memory repository and this may have an impact on the collective identity of the people of Hong Kong that has been built on the Massacre (Cheng and Yuen 2019). A fissure in the memory repository is common in memory, especially in communicative memory. Seeing as memory is created by the present and for the present, plurality and rivalry between competing memories seems unavoidable. The contemporary political scene in Hong Kong has changed tremendously due to the experiences shared by participants in the Umbrella Movement (2014) and the Anti-extradition Bill Movement (2019–20). This does not necessarily mean that the role of the Massacre in the formation of the people of Hong Kong's collective identity is declining, but it does mean that the people of Hong Kong are in a better position to share more about the suffering experienced in the Massacre. The most pressing issue is not so much how to deal with the split in the memory repository, but whether the Hong Kong government will allow a candlelight vigil to be held in 2021 in the conditions imposed under the National Security Law given that the Chinese authorities condemn the Tiananmen Incident as revolutionary activity. It is possible that the advocates for the Alliance and the localists could be tempted to leave aside their differences when they discover that the real threat they are potentially facing does not really stem from their different expectations over the content of the memory repository. Actually, the main threat they face is being denied the right to hold a public commemoration.

Conclusion

Broadly speaking, religious symbolism is the use of religious acts, artwork and events to articulate and communicate human aspiration. Thus, religious symbols are not confined to insiders. Outsiders can also find religious symbols meaningful to their experience, though there are different interpretations of religious symbols among insiders and outsiders. Religious symbols carry the power to explain or interpret experience, the power to communicate experience and the power to explore what is possible. I have illustrated the kind of religious symbols used in the candlelight vigil, which include *chaodu, zhaohun* and crucified people. I have also shown how these religious symbols from Christianity, Confucianism and Daoism provide participants with the language to express their grievances, the vision to interpret their experience and the faith to sustain their hope in the pursuit of justice and truth. In the case of the candlelight vigil, religious symbols play a subversive role, empowering the victims and challenging the power structure instead of maintaining and legitimizing the status quo.

Notes

1 Translated by the author.
2 *"One Country, Two Systems"* is a fundamental policy of the Chinese authorities designed to accomplish the peaceful reunification of China by resolving the sovereignty questions of Hong Kong, Macau and Taiwan, all of which have arisen from a complicated historical background. In Hong Kong, it emphasizes the principle that the Hong Kong people should be running Hong Kong with a high degree of autonomy.
3 https://chinadigitaltimes.net/2019/05/30-years-ago-students-declare-hunger-strike/ (accessed on 4 December 2020).
4 www.youtube.com/watch?v=6iB85r-S6Yo (accessed on 4 December 2020). This is an interview with Mr Him Lo.
5 www.scmp.com/news/hong-kong/politics/article/3013115/hong-kong-keeps-tiananmen-crackdown-memory-alive-record (accessed on 4 December 2020).
6 Translated by the author.
7 www.scmp.com/news/hong-kong/politics/article/3013115/hong-kong-keeps-tiananmen-crackdown-memory-alive-record (accessed on 4 December 2020).

References

Arendt, Hannah. 1958. *The Human Condition*. Chicago: University of Chicago Press.
Assmann, Jan. 1995. "Collective Memory and Cultural Identity." *New German Critique* 65: 125–33.
Brook, Timothy. 1993. "Rethinking Syncretism: The Unity of the Three Teachings and Their Joint Worship in Late-Imperial China." *Journal of Chinese Religions* 21 (1): 13–44.
Calhoun, Craig. 1997. *Neither Gods nor Emperors*. Berkeley: University of California Press.

198 *Lap Yan Kung*

Chai, Ling. 2012. "I Forgive Them: On the 23rd Anniversary of the Tiananmen Square Massacre in 1989." Accessed December 4, 2020. www.huffpost.com/entry/tiananmen-china_b_1565235.

Cheng, Edmund W., and Samson Yuen. 2019. "Memory in Movement: Collective Identity and Memory Contestation in Hong Kong's Tiananmen Vigils." *Mobilization: An International Quarterly* 24 (4): 419–37.

Cheng, Joseph. 2011. "The Tiananmen Incident and the Pro-Democracy Movement in Hong Kong." In *The Impact of China's 1989 Tiananmen Massacre*, edited by Jean-Philippe Béja, 179–93. New York: Routledge.

Citizenlab. 2019. "Censored Commemoration." Accessed December 4, 2020. https://citizenlab.ca/2019/06/censored-commemoration-chinese-live-streaming-platform-yy-focuses-censorship-june-4-memorials-activism-hong-kong/.

Connerton, Paul. 1989. *How Societies Remember.* Cambridge: Cambridge University Press.

DeBernardi, Jean Elizabeth. 2009. *Penang: Rites of Belonging in a Malaysian Chinese Community.* Singapore: National University of Singapore Press.

Ding, Zilin. 2005. *Xunfang Liusi Shounanzhe, 1989–2005 (In Search of the Victims of June Fourth, 1989–2005).* Hong Kong: Kai Fang. (Written in Chinese).

Ellacuria, Ignacio. 1986. "The Crucified People." In *Systematic Theology: Perspectives from Liberation Theology*, edited by J. Sobrino and I. Ellacuria, 258–70. London: SCM.

Eppert, Claudia. 2012. "Walking the Talk: East-West Reflections on the Wisdom of Remembrance, Forgiveness and Forgetting." In *Reconciliation and Pedagogy*, edited by Pal Ahluwalia et al., 65–94. New York: Routledge.

Graham, Fabian Charles. 2017. *Visual Anthropology: A Temple Anniversary in Singapore.* Gottingen: Max Planck Institute for the Study of Religious and Ethnic Diversity.

HKUPOP. 2018. "Combined Charts of June 4 Vigil Over Years." Accessed December 4, 2020. www.hkupop.hku.hk/chinese/features/june4/chart/june4_chart.html.

Ho, K. Yuen. 2016. "June 4 Commemoration: Why Are the Youth Localists discontented? What are Their Misunderstandings?" (In Chinese). Accessed December 4, 2020. https://theinitium.com/article/20160606-opinion-ky-64/.

Holmgren, Margaret R. 2012. *Forgiveness and Retribution: Responding to Wrongdoing.* Cambridge: Cambridge University Press.

Hong Kong Journalists Association. 2019. *I am a Journalist: My June Fourth Story* (DVD, In Chinese). Hong Kong: Hong Kong Journalists Association.

Horkheimer, Max. 2013. *Critique of Instrumental Reason.* New York: Verso.

Jiang, S. Z. 2019. *Study of Religion and Art* (宗教藝術論). Taipei: Showwe (Written in Chinese).

Lee, Francis L. F., and J. M. Chan. 2011. *Media, Social Mobilization, and Mass Protests in Post-Colonial Hong Kong.* London: Routledge.

———. 2013. "Generational Transmission of Collective Memory About Tiananmen in Hong Kong: How Young Rally Participants Learn about and Understand 4 June." *Journal of Contemporary China* 22 (84): 966–83.

———. 2016. "Collective Memory Mobilization and Tiananmen Commemoration in Hong Kong." *Media, Culture and Society* 38 (7): 997–1014.

Lewis, Court D. 2018. *Repentance and the Right to Forgiveness.* London: Lexington.

Lim, Louisa. 2014. *The People's Republic of Amnesia: Tiananmen Revisited.* Oxford: Oxford University Press.

Lo, Sonny H. 2010. *Competing Chinese Political Visions.* Santa Barbara, CA: Praeger.

Lochman, Jan. 1985. *The Faith We Confess.* Edinburgh: T. & T. Clark.

Makeham, John, ed. 2003. *New Confucianism: A Critical Examination.* New York: Palgrave Macmillan.

Marcus, Herbert. 1964. *One Dimensional Man*. Boston, MA: Beacon Press.

McCarthy, John D. 1995. "Constraints and Opportunities in Adopting, Adapting and Inventing." In *Comparative Perspectives on Social Movements*, edited by D. McAdam, John D. McCarthy and Mayer N. Zald, 141–51. Cambridge: Cambridge University Press.

Mencius. Accessed December 4, 2020. https://ctext.org/mengzi/gaozi-i.

Ng, William. 1998. "Tang Chun-I on Transcendence: Foundations of a New Confucian Religious Humanism." *Monumenta Serica* 46: 291–322.

Orzech, Charles. 1996. "Saving the Burning-Mouth Hungry Ghost." In *Religions of China in Practice*, edited by Donald S. Lopez, 278–83. Princeton, NJ: Princeton University Press.

Palmer, David, and Xun Liu, ed. 2012. *Daoism in the Twentieth Century: Between Eternity and Modernity*. Berkeley: University of California Press.

Pregadio, Fabrizio, ed. 2008. *The Encyclopedia of Taoism*. New York: Routledge.

Schudson, Michael. 1992. *Watergate in American Memory*. New York: Basic Books.

Shen, Tong, and Marianne Yen. 1998. *Almost a Revolution*. Ann Arbor: University of Michigan Press.

Sobrino, Jon. 1990. "The Crucified Peoples: Yahweh's Suffering Servant Today." In *The Voice of the Victims*, edited by L. Boff and V. Elizondo, 49–57. London: SCM.

———. 2008. *No Salvation Outside the Poor*. Maryknoll, NY: Orbis.

Tang, Chun-I. 1955. *The Re-establishment of the Spirit of Humanism*. (人文精神之重建) Hong Kong: New Asia Research Center (Written in Chinese).

———. 1975. *Heart and Life*. (心物與人生). Taipei: Students Press (written in Chinese).

———. 1988. *Essays on the Comparative Study Between Chinese and Western Philosophy* (中西哲學論文比較文集) Taipei: Students Press (Written in Chinese).

———. 1993. *Human Experience*, Vol. II. (人生之體驗續編) Taipei: Students Press (Written in Chinese).

Tao, Anthony. 2017. "No, 10000 Were Not Killed in China's 1989 Tiananmen Crackdown." Accessed December 4, 2020. https://supchina.com/2017/12/25/no-10000-not-killed-in-tiananmen-crackdown/.

Tiananmen Mothers. 2018. "An Open Letter to Xi Jinping from Tiananmen Mothers." Accessed December 4, 2020. www.tiananmenmother.org/TiananmenMother/29%20years/m20180604001.htm.

Time. 2019. "I've Been Told Lies." Accessed December 4, 2020. https://time.com/5600385/tiananmen-june-4-1989-china-30th-anniversary-censorship/.

Turner, Victor. 1967. *The Forest of Symbols: Aspects of Ndembu Ritual*. Ithaca, NY: Cornell University Press.

———. 1974. *Dramas, Fields and Metaphors*. London: Cornell University Press.

Unger, Jonathan. ed. 1991. *The Pro-Democracy Protest in China*. New York: Routledge.

Van Gennep, Arnold. 1960. *Rites of Passage*. Translated by Monika B. Vizedom and Gabrielle L. Caffee. Chicago: University of Chicago Press.

Voice of America. 2019. "The Case of June Fourth Wine." Accessed December 4, 2020. www.voacantonese.com/a/tiananmen-1989-wine-trial/4860014.html.

10 Religious echoes of the Donbas conflict

The discourses of the Christian, Muslim and Jewish communities in Ukraine

Nadia Zasanska

Introduction

Over the last decade, religious organizations in Ukraine have increased their visibility and presence in public discourse through the digitalization of religious media. New information technologies have increased the religious actors' potential to reach their followers, participate in political discourse and express their attitudes to domestic and international affairs, as well as to shape perceptions of the present or past events. Religious leaders enjoy the highest level of trust within a Ukrainian society[1] whose members distrust political institutions and seek the safe space of a community with common values, history, traditions and beliefs.

The study of religious discourse in Ukraine has become even more significant within the context of the ongoing conflict in the east of Ukraine. Although the Donbas conflict has been widely addressed in media research (Taradai 2019; Klymenko 2019), political studies (Landwehr 2019; Malyarenko and Wolff 2018) and identity and nationalities studies (Ilchuk 2016; Sasse and Lackner 2018; Mitchnik 2019), the latest research on the role of the religious factor in the conflict focuses specifically on Christian organizations based in Ukraine (Denysenko 2014; Krawchuk and Bremer 2016; Shestopalets 2019). Such a research focus, does not, however, fully take account of the religious diversity of Ukraine, where Christians, Jews and Muslims have lived together for many centuries.

This study addresses religious discourse, conceived as 'a form of social practice which both constitutes the social world and is constituted by other social practices' (Jørgensen and Phillips 2002), to investigate how different religious institutions in Ukraine have been narrating the conflict in East Ukraine. Approaching religious discourse as a social practice that both reflects and shapes knowledge about reality, identity and social relations (Fairclough and Wodak 1997; Van Dijk 2006) will enable me to outline how the Donbas conflict has influenced the content and structure of religious discourse in Ukraine, and also how religious actors are mediating the conflict within their communities and beyond.

The narrative of conflict is a primary concern of memory research that approaches language as a universal constructor and mediator of memory.

DOI: 10.4324/9781003264750-13

As 'the most elementary and the most stable framework of collective memory' (Halbwachs 1992, 45), language reconstructs the past and communicates it to new generations (Assmann 2008). The reconstruction of memory is inextricably bound to social interaction, as memories not only emerge from verbal stimuli associated with the past but also through various social conventions attached to these memories. Only when they are part of a society do people 'recall, recognize, and localize their memories' (Halbwachs 1992, 38). Within this social context, communicative memory is 'a willful agreement of the members of a group as to what they consider their own past to be' (Welzer 2008, 285).

As a cognitive and socio-cultural space, language interacts with religion and memory through a 'meaning about the past' that it creates and reconstructs from the standpoint of the present. Consequently, that meaning also brings certain expectations for the future (Straub 2008). While communication builds on ongoing processes of encoding and decoding information, the formation of memory depends to a great extent on the process of its verbalization, the social context and the communicative intentions of its participants (Echterhoff 2008). In other words, verbalization may predetermine such components of the recollection process as what is retrieved, what is omitted, and how recollections are remembered. Different interpretations of the past lead to differing memories, and this in turn enables power institutions to write a 'common history', create national myths and re-visualize the problematic past.

Drawing on the notion of the communicative construction of memory, Metzger (2018) defines three modes, mediating its relations with religion: religious language, symbolical practices and narratives. Accordingly, the sacralization of religious language is the main mechanism behind the transition of a religious community's memory into broader public spaces that gradually modify religious memory into a complex, multi-layered and intertextual construction. Rituals mediate memory through performance, re-visualization, veneration and commemoration. Symbolical practices create a relation of transcendence when the invisible becomes sensually communicable and visible. Finally, narratives of memory integrate religious and national discourses of the past to produce a 'confessionalization of the nation' (Metzger 2018, 341–42).

The Donbas conflict has been intensively covered by media outlets from various social, political and religious backgrounds. This chapter discusses six narratives of the conflict presented in media outlets run by organizations identifying as Christian (Ukrainian Orthodox Church of the Kyiv Patriarchate [UOC-KP], Ukrainian Orthodox Church of the Moscow Patriarchate [UOC-MP], and Ukrainian Greek Catholic Church [UGCC]), Jewish (the Association of Jewish Organizations and Communities [VAAD]), and Muslim (Spiritual Administrations of the Muslims of Ukraine [DUMU and DUMU-Umma]). My hypothesis is that each religious organization in Ukraine uses a different lexicon and rhetorical strategies to frame the common themes of the conflict, thereby promoting an interpretation of the conflict to its own community that diverges from the interpretations of the other religious organizations. Consequently, such religious narratives have developed into a number of differing memories of the Donbas conflict that coexist within one country, which makes it more challenging to develop a coherent vision of the collective traumatic past in Ukrainian society. Two pertinent research questions emerge: Are religious organizations highlighting or backgrounding specific themes in their narratives of the Donbas conflict? What rhetorical strategies do religious organizations apply to interpret the conflict? I answer these questions by applying corpus-based lexical analysis (Scott 2018) and ideological discourse analysis (Van Dijk 2006) to the systematic study of sermons, interviews, articles and news published by religious organizations during 2014–18 for references to themes from the Donbas conflict. The chapter begins by focusing on religious memory as a source to sacralize present events and actors, and then goes on to conduct a comparative case study of the religious discourses of the aforementioned six religious institutions based in Ukraine. Finally, the chapter discusses how religious actors are mediating the Donbas conflict within their communities and beyond.

Methodology

This corpus-based study relies on lexical and ideological analyses of 1,890 articles published by religious organizations during 2014–18. First, I analyzed the articles in terms of word frequency, keywords and typical collocations (Scott 2018). Then, I studied each discourse as a structure expressing such themes as (1) situation (how religious organizations define the conflict); (2) place (is the conflict addressed as local, European, or international?); (3) actor 1 (how religious institutions represent the Ukrainian army); (4) actor 2 (how religious organizations portray the confronting side); (5) society and (6) state authorities (how religious institutions define the role of the Ukrainian society and authorities during the conflict); and (7) resolution (how religious organizations address the conflict's potential resolution). Finally, I applied ideology analysis (Van Dijk 2006) to the analysis of statements made by six religious leaders by using a *we–they* frame, which allowed me to determine the basic rhetorical strategies they were using to narrate the Donbas conflict.

Interreligious dialogue in Ukraine

The religious landscape in Ukraine has been shaped under complex historical and political conditions. After being framed into the Christianity of the Eastern tradition in 988, the religious situation developed under the major influence of Poland, Russia and Austria (Krawchuk and Bremer 2016). Although Orthodox Christianity remained the dominant religion in the area, the influence of the Catholic Church was significant in the western parts of Ukraine, where the Greek Catholic Church emerged in the sixteenth century. Ukraine's centre of Christianity, the Kyiv Metropoly, lost its leadership under the growing influence of the Russian Empire in the seventeenth century, when it was absorbed by the Russian Orthodox Church (ROC). In 1992, after Ukraine declared its independence, a number of religious leaders declared the Metropoly's autonomy from the ROC, which intensified Orthodox rivalry in Ukraine between those religious authorities who remained under the ROC's jurisdiction and those who did not. However, in 2018, the Ukrainian Orthodox Church was granted the *tomos* of autocephaly by the Ecumenical Patriarch of Constantinople Bartholomew.[2] Seeing as the ROC has never granted its approval for the autocephaly, the atmosphere of rivalry has continued to develop unabated.

Today the majority of Ukrainians identify as Christians, and the largest proportion of these (34% of all Ukrainians) belong to the Orthodox Church of Ukraine (known as the UOC-KP up until it was granted autocephaly in 2019). Other Ukrainian Christians either belong to the UOC-MP (13.8%), the UGCC (8.2%), Protestant Churches (0.7%) or the Roman Catholic Church (0.4%). In addition, 27.6% of respondents consider themselves to be Orthodox Christians without belonging to either of the two Orthodox Churches. Believers of other confessions make up 0.6% of the total.[3]

Despite differing theological and spiritual traditions, in 1996, the religious organizations of Ukraine founded the Ukrainian Council of Churches and Religious Organizations (UCCRO), an interreligious union that articulates the shared visions of Ukrainian religious institutions on religious and social values, public policy, legislative matters, relations with the state and the common good of Ukraine. Krawchuk (2014, 278) evaluates the UCCRO as 'a unique and unprecedented forum for working towards interreligious consensus in Ukraine' because it provides a venue for those religious institutions that may not favour each other's activities in religious contexts but are prepared to collaborate with each other under the auspices of the council. This common discursive space allows the UCCRO to position itself as a unified body of influence on the state by promoting social values that transcend boundaries between religions. Remarkably, another one of the shared domains of the interreligious discourse handled by the UCCRO is Ukraine's past (Krawchuk 2014). The historic past is interpreted within the framework of religious values as a practical resource for cherishing new consciousness, social transformation and continuity with tradition. Collective references to shared memory allow the UCCRO to benefit from its diverse religions, histories and ethnicities by making it possible for Ukrainian religious institutions to realize their moral responsibilities in present-day society (Krawchuk 2014).

A shared commitment to social values triggers interreligious discourse that transcends any boundaries to cooperation between the various members of the UCCRO. That comes into view whenever the member organizations' values are at risk. During 2013–14 at Maidan, or the Revolution of Dignity,[4] when thousands of demonstrators protested in Kyiv against the brutality of Yanukovych's pro-Russian presidency, many religious organizations demonstrated spiritual union with the protesters, coming together as one voice in support of justice, freedom and dignity. Maidan signified the emergence of civil society in post-Soviet Ukraine. Fylypovych and Horkusha (2016) stress that Maidan became a communicative platform based on mutual aspirations for a shared purpose, collective consensus and dialogue. The Maidan discourse, which incorporated diverse religious meanings, was coherent and integral because it was grounded in such 'axiological categories as dignity, truth, person, life, responsibility, justice, freedom, conscience, civil rights, co-action, and mutual respect' (Fylypovych and Horkusha 2016, 89).

However, the interreligious discourse in Ukraine lacks unity and consensus when addressed from theological perspectives. With the majority of Ukrainians identifying themselves as Orthodox Christians, the 'historically original' Orthodox and Greek Catholic Churches consider themselves in a position of primacy over other minor religious institutions (Krawchuk 2016). What is also notable is that there is no meaningful dialogue between the Orthodox Churches themselves: the UOC-MP, which is affiliated to the ROC, considers the Orthodox Church of Ukraine uncanonical and schismatic. This religious dissonance has political shades: the ROC is an ideological supporter of the authoritarian regime in Russia (Stoeckl 2016; Lutsevych 2016; Curanović and Leustean 2015); the Church denies that Russia acted aggressively in Ukraine and that Crimea was annexed.

Collective memory – from sacred past to sacred present

In memory studies, religion is conceived as a realm of active cultural memory represented in texts, images, symbols, places, architectural spaces, liturgical rites and practices. However, this perspective narrows memory in religion down to a static, archival mode that presents religious memory as a source for the secular sacred activated through its relations with nation, identity, tradition and history (see the introduction by Bogumił and Yurchuk). The dynamic characteristics of memory processing enable it to be approached as a space of selection whose parts are constantly being selected, modelled and transformed before they materialize in verbal and non-verbal form (Metzger 2018). Much like memory is an ongoing process of knowledge (re-)construction, religion is a system involving the ongoing formation of meaning that disseminates its values through communicative spaces.

Religions use the oldest forms of memorization, which are based on the repetition of rituals, regular retrieval of knowledge and collective practices (Assmann 2008; O'Collins and Braithwaite 2015). Such practices of anamnesis provide a 'lineage of belief' – a source for continuity, connection with history and self-definition (Hervieu-Léger 2000). Through the normative and creative characteristics of collective memory, religion incorporates believers into a 'chain of memory' – a symbolic unity of the past and present (Hervieu-Léger 2000). Although it has maintained its popularity, Halbwachs's interpretation of 'collective memory' needs significant reconceptualization (Gensburger 2016), and this term has been most frequently addressed in recent studies of social memory (Olick 1999), community (Feldman 2015), history (Hilton and Liu 2017), shared social resources (Irwin-Zarecka 1994) and social practices (Huang 2018). Interpreting collective memory through the modes of culture and communication (Assmann 2006) shows how religious memory may incorporate features of both. Religious memory shares such significant functions of memory as identity formation, reconstruction of the past, the institutionalization of collective knowledge, establishing communicative practices and the systematization of values (Assmann 1995), yet it also displays more specific attributes that distance it from other forms of collective memory. Religious memory relies on the concept of the sacred being actualized through the meanings of authority, sin and loss.

Religious memory is a source of sacred meaning, holy knowledge and a transcendent connection to a supreme deity. Sacredness is one of the most crucial attributes of religious memory and a structure of innate and universal meanings that transcend changes of time and place (Hervieu-Léger 2000). The sacred is so universal that any religion may be addressed as a 'way of tying together multiple experiences and memories of the sacred into a single system of belief and practice' (Fenn 2007, 6). When a religious community regularly refers to specific memory anchors of the past – such as historical events, myths, characters and texts, all of which are changeable due to the fluidity of time – a frame of sacredness grants unity to all memory anchors, making them meaningful to the present lives of individual believers. Once the past has been sacralized, memory achieves a higher level of significance in a group where sacred knowledge obliges all its members to remember, preserve significant memories for the coming generations and maintain the religious uniqueness of the group. The holy status of religious memory turns it into a truthful and reliable channel of knowledge which, as a result, prevents sacred memories from being transformed and 'desecrated'.

Religious ceremonies reveal the most important attributes of a charismatic situation: a festive atmosphere, a break with the habitual and autonomy from institutionalized forms of social relations. Through reconnecting with the past in the form of festive rituals, charismatic situations provide a basis for shaping the religious identity of the community. Assmann (2011) stresses, when considering the opposition between the festive and ordinary, that 'collective identity needs ceremony – something to take it out of the daily routine'. Festivals and rituals, as the primary forms of memory storage, compensate for the imperfectness of the material world by expanding it into the realm of the cosmic and the ideal, where it is independent of time or space (Assmann 2011).

Along with the central role of authority – represented by God, holy personalities, a supernatural power and sacred texts – religious discourse is significantly imbued with an appeal to the emotions. Religious communication evokes sensual and aesthetic associations, which make it possible to address religious memory in terms of implicit memory based on feelings, in contrast to explicit memory based on knowledge and facts (Sutton 2014). Accordingly, the specific settings of charismatic situations intensify the emotional involvement of a person in collective practices through appealing to private feelings and experience. Moreover, because the concept of a sinful human nature predominates in many faiths, religious discourse recruits memory as a channel for reconnecting with God, coming back to an ideal home and finding salvation and eternity. In this light, religious memory serves as a personalized moral

206 *Nadia Zasanska*

guardian when remembrance of sins in the past may prevent believers from committing sins in the present. Thus, memory is addressed through its moral agency, and in particular its ability to transmit a system of ideals, moral norms, commitments and values (Miller 2009).

Although time is traditionally viewed in diachrony, memory proves to be synchronic. Religious discourse, as emotionally loaded communication, personalizes religious memory by creating multimodal scenes for each participant to relive in the present. When in structural terms religious discourse builds on myths, metaphors and symbols of the past, these elements contribute to a specific understanding of the present. Having been individualized and adapted, the conventional forms of the past receive new meanings relevant to the social reality of community. This ability of religious memory to stay relevant in form due to the plurality of personalized meanings resonates with Assmann's idea of two modes of cultural memory: potentiality and actuality. When some parts of accumulated knowledge of the past become highlighted in the current context, the others remain backgrounded (Assmann and Czaplicka 1995).

What is happening in the east of Ukraine?

The majority of religious organizations in Ukraine (but not the UOC-MP and DUMU) define the situation in the east of Ukraine as *Russia's war against Ukraine*. The theme of the conflict is the most well-represented lexically in the discourses of the UOC-MP and UGCC (25% and 20%, respectively), while the other institutions use a similar proportion of conflict-themed lexis (UOC-KP, 11%; DUMU, 11%; DUMU-Umma, 11%; VAAD, 9%). The interpretation of the conflict ranges from it being symptomatic of the global threat posed by Russia to the political order and international law (UOC-KP) or a chance for Ukrainian society to test its civil maturity (UGCC) to it being a moral ordeal that needs to be overcome for a new Ukraine to be built (VAAD and DUMU-Umma), a hardship (DUMU) or a civil war threatening the Orthodox unity of Ukrainians and Russians (UOC-MP).

The discourses of the UOC-KP and UGCC define the conflict in Donbas as Russia's war against Ukraine, describing it as *conquering, invading, aggressive, hybrid* and *undeclared*. In their speeches, two church leaders, Patriarch Filaret, the head of UOC-KP, and Sviatoslav, the head of UGCC, stress the global dimension of the Russian aggression that is undermining the whole foundation of human rights in the world. Within this context, the religious authorities are demonstrating their very clear position on the conflict, which stands in opposition to the position of the Ukrainian state authorities, who have never officially declared the armed confrontation with the Russia-backed troops as a 'war'.

> We were attacked. It is a war – we have to declare that! . . . Evil has to be called evil and has to be punished. I don't mean revenge, but justice. If the evil is neither pronounced, nor punished, it will spread further.
>
> (Head of the UGCC Sviatoslav Shevchuk)[5]

The narratives of the UGCC account for the war by bringing up the historical clash between the Soviet past and European present in Ukraine, on the one hand, and Second World War ideology in Russia on the other (the most fruitful basis for rebuilding an aggressive policy and replanting propaganda and Soviet myths in Ukrainian society).

The most significant feature of the UOC-MP's discourse is its framing of the conflict as a civil war. Such a position mirrors the official position of the Russian Federation and Russian Orthodox Church, whose official documents have an imperative character for the UOC-MP. Patriarch Kirill, in his first speech on the events in Ukraine in 2014, defined the conflict as 'an internecine war in the eastern areas of historical Rus".[6] The emphasis on the brotherhood of Ukrainians and Russians resonates well with Patriarch Kirill's vision of the ROC as 'the Church of spiritually undivided Rus' [that] cannot divide the one people of God based on political, national, social or any other principles'.[7] With such a focus on the spiritual and historical unity of Ukrainians and Russians, the narratives present the war as a clash between Orthodox Christian values and European values that are 'inimical' to the mentality of people in Eastern Ukraine. Consequently, in the rhetoric of the UOC-MP, Euromaidan is depicted as an eruption of nationalistic ideology that imposed the Ukrainian language, culture and history specific to Western Ukraine on the citizens of East Ukraine.[8] As the data I collected for this research showed, the other 'threats' to the UOC-MP associated with Euromaidan are Catholicism and the growing influence of the UOC-KP in Ukrainian society. Overall, the discourse of the UOC-MP stresses the cultural, political and religious differences between the Ukrainians of the East and the West, and these are framed as the main reasons for the Donbas conflict.

Moreover, the UOC-MP defines participating in the conflict as committing the mortal sin of fratricide. While Orthodox Christian doctrine justifies righteous war in cases when there is a clear need to mount a defence against aggression, the UOC-MP rhetoric largely accentuates the moral commitment, 'Thou shalt not kill'. By doing this, the UOC-MP backgrounds the Christian meaning of defence, while promoting the message of showing humility and obedience to aggressors.

The discourses of the Islamic organizations, the DUMU and DUMU-Umma, display considerable differences in their portrayals of the conflict. The DUMU-Umma refers to the defence of the motherland as 'the civil duty of a Muslim that maintains an interest in defending his honour, property, and family'.[9] The document also explains the position of the DUMU-Umma on the conflict in the East of Ukraine:

> The Muslims of Ukraine, having suffered from the consequences of the Crimean and Donbas occupation, are in solidarity with their coreligionists in these Ukrainian territories and stand for the swiftest restoration of justice and, in particular, of the territorial integrity of Ukraine.
>
> (*The Social Concept of the Muslims of Ukraine*)

208 *Nadia Zasanska*

While the DUMU-Umma signifies the Donbas conflict as a *war, occupation* and *aggression*, the DUMU adheres to politically neutral lexemes: *situation, events,* and *condition*. The leader of the DUMU, Sheikh Ahmed Tamim, underlines the religious mission and non-political position of the organization, so the DUMU's rhetoric places more emphasis on religious and social issues, while the political life of Ukraine remains backgrounded. For instance, the theme of the Donbas conflict emerged in 107 (19%) out of 567 news articles during 2014–18. According to the data I collected for this study, the DUMU addresses the conflict in religious terms (as a difficulty, life challenge and hardship), which significantly raises the emotionality of the discourse. Overall, the DUMU avoids evaluating the Donbas conflict with all its tragic consequences (e.g. the casualties, internally displaced persons and occupation).

The narratives of the Jewish organization VAAD refer to the conflict in Eastern Ukraine as a *war* (37%), *military operation* (12%), *situation* (12%), *aggression* (9%), *conflict* (9%), and *ATO* (anti-terrorist operation, the official name for a military operation in Donbas used by the Ukrainian government) (6%). In 2014, the chairman of the VAAD of Ukraine, Joseph Zissels, addressed the Donbas conflict at the World Jewish Congress in Berlin:

> For half a year, Ukraine has been in a war provoked by Russia to prevent the fulfilment of Ukraine's European choice. While we are holding the Congress in Berlin, seven civilians have been killed in an artillery shelling because the pro-Russian forces are violating the ceasefire.[10]

A dominant feature in the discourse of the VAAD is a recurring parallel drawn between Ukraine and the State of Israel. The narratives stress the similar experience both countries shared of suffering under the oppression of a neighbouring country as well as the relatively short period of time that has elapsed since they gained their independence and their ongoing struggle for peace. Within this context, the Donbas conflict is compared with the conflict in the Gaza Strip. The State of Israel is presented as a 'military guru' for Ukraine, a model state with advanced technologies and military experience.

The Ukrainian army: heroes or villains?

The theme of 'the Ukrainian Army' emerges most frequently in the discourses of the UOC-KP (20%) and the UGCC (14%), and displays a similar level of lexical representation in organizations affiliated to the UOC-MP (11%), DUMU-Umma (7%) and VAAD (9%). In the DUMU's discourse, the theme of the army is backgrounded, constituting only 1.5% of the whole lexicon. Rather than focusing on the frequency of words illustrating this theme, it is more important to define *how* religious institutions frame the Ukrainian Army in their rhetoric on the conflict.

As the data I collected for this research showed, the UOC-KP and the UGCC address the Ukrainian Army as heroes and defenders of the motherland.

A narrative of victimhood for the sake of a new Ukraine is a significant feature in both corpora. By glorifying heroes, the narratives evoke the cult of martyrdom for fallen soldiers, as well as the Heroes of the Heavenly Hundred (the activists killed at Euromaidan in 2014) and volunteers. The narratives of the UGCC emphasize the national commitment of Ukrainians to honouring the memory of the warriors' self-sacrifice as the highest expression of love for the mother-land and the purest example of a merciful Christian life. Within this context, the phrase *Heroes never die*, a slogan created for Euromaidan in 2014, shows the Christian understanding of the heroic death.

> Hatred for one's enemies will never make someone a hero, for only love for the Motherland, family and the most precious and holiest things in our hearts will suffice And the person whose heart is full of heroic love never dies. Since that love is from God, it is more powerful than death.
>
> (Head of UGCC Sviatoslav)[11]

Moreover, the religious glorification of heroes has also materialized in the public commemorative practices of the UOC-KP. In 2015, the institution introduced its own decoration known as the 'For Sacrifice and Love for Ukraine' medal, which it awards to activists, soldiers and volunteers for acts of heroism during Euromaidan or the Donbas conflict.

Similarly to the UOC-KP and UGCC, the Islamic DUMU-Umma signifies the Ukrainian Army as defenders of Ukraine, although its narratives underline the role performed by Muslim soldiers in the defence. By doing this, the DUMU-Umma is challenging stereotypes about Islam in Ukrainian society and addressing the religious diversity of Ukraine as a significant precondition for victory.

> We are of different nationalities and different religions, but Ukraine can work miracles: we have united and intensified each other's strength, courage and experience. Together we are fighting for our Ukraine!
>
> (Mufti Said Ismagilov)[12]

The DUMU-Umma appreciates the role the Ukrainian Army has played in the conflict and decorates Muslim warriors with 'For Serving Islam and Ukraine' medals. One significant feature of the discourse is the portrayal of a new image of the Muslim woman. Within this context, the name of Amina Okueva, a famous activist, doctor and soldier, not only stands for a defender of Ukraine but also portrays a Ukrainian Muslim woman from a new perspective – as a charismatic leader, public person, warrior and devoted believer.

Although the Ukrainian Army theme emerges in the discourse of the UOC-MP, it has different levels of lexical representation in formal and informal discourses. In news resources, the Ukrainian Army is depicted with the neutral words *soldiers, military forces* or *servicemen*, whereas in interviews with religious leaders, the army is portrayed as a *participant in a fratricidal war*. Another noticeable attribute of this theme is that the narratives stress the responsibility of the state authorities of Ukraine (those in power during 2014–18) for a conflict in which 'Cain kills Abel'. In this light, the UOC-MP downplays the image of the Ukrainian soldier by portraying him and his comrades as puppets in the hands of Ukrainian state power.

Who is the enemy?

The UOC-KP, UGCC, DUMU-Umma and VAAD define Russia and pro-Russian forces as the aggressors in the conflict, whereas the DUMU completely omits the theme of 'enemy' in its discourse. The enemy narrative is the most well represented lexically in the discourses of the UOC-KP (18%) and VAAD (15%) (compared to the UGCC [8%], DUMU-Umma [7%] and UOC-MP [4%]). The enemy theme builds on numerous lexical signifiers: (1) the state-aggressor (*Russia, Russian Federation, Russian Empire, neighbouring country, northern neighbour*); (2) state authorities (*Putin, Kremlin, Moscow, Russian power*); and (3) the military forces of Russia (*Russian military/forces/generals/soldiers/officers*).

In this study, the enemy theme reveals another confrontation, the rivalry between Ukraine's two main Orthodox Christian institutions, the UOC-KP and UOC-MP. Their discourses portray various forms of confrontation within Ukrainian society: between the former and current state authorities (and their respective supporters in society), between public aspiration for a European future and nostalgia for the Soviet Union, or the battle for Orthodox supremacy between the UOC-KP and UOC-MP. The narratives of both institutions build on the ideological *we–they* frame.

> They (the Moscow Patriarchate) talk about civil war; they pray for peace. So do we. We are against the war. But what kind of peace are they praying for? And what kind of peace are we praying for? They are praying for peace under Russia. If Ukraine accedes to Russia, peace would be achieved but along with the slavery in which we have lived for more than 300 years. So do we need such peace? We want a just peace in an independent country.
> (Head of the UOC-KP Patriarch Filaret)[13]

The corpora of the UGCC contain the concept of *Christian patriotism*, conceived as 'having no hatred for any of our brothers of the other nations and obeying Christ's wish to love all peoples of the world as our neighbours'.[14] Christian patriotism is also revealed in collective prayers for the Ukrainian authorities, enemies, army, victims of the conflict and unity of Ukraine. Thus, the UGCC stresses the need for reconciliation through overcoming hatred and cherishing love in society.

As long as the UOC-MP declares its 'supra-political' peacemaking position, the narratives avoid labelling any side of the conflict as an 'enemy'. At the lexical level, the collocations *fratricidal war* and *civil war* emphasize the UOC-MP's notion of internal conflict. In their rhetoric, the Church accentuates the significance of humbleness, reconciliation and patience (with such words as *forgiveness, repentance, dialogue, unity, brothers*). Such simplification and distortion of the events in the east of Ukraine mirrors the official interpretation of the conflict by the Russian Orthodox Church as a civil war.

Similarly, the *we–they* frame emerges in the discourse of the DUMU, which positions itself as the main Islamic organization for Ukraine's Muslims. Despite its active cooperation with other Muslim communities and organizations in Eastern countries, its narratives background the themes of Crimea, the Crimean Muslims and Crimean Tatars. Moreover, the DUMU distances itself from the other Islamic organizations in Ukraine and labels them as extremist threats. However, this mutual confrontation is rooted in ideological differences relating to the understanding of Islam among Ukraine's different Muslim communities. Thus, in 2018, at the 6th Congress of Ukraine's Muslims in Kyiv, Sheikh Ahmed Tamim criticized the other Muslim organization, the DUMU-Ummu, for attempting to unite Ukraine's Muslims under the *Charter of Ukraine's Muslims* and *the Social Concept of the Muslims of Ukraine*, the first documents designed to declare the position of the DUMU-Umma's community on political, economic, social, cultural and religious processes in the country.

> To serve the Ukrainian society, we do not need any mere declarations, statements, concepts or charters. All those are worth no more than the paper they are written on. We have been serving our people and our country for 26 years without any declarations, and we will continue to serve them. And when all these declarations come to pass, we will still serve our society and our unity.
>
> (Sheikh Ahmed Tamim)[15]

A society in conflict: a future of unity and reconciliation

The theme of 'society' was addressed through a focus on verbal signifiers used to refer to individuals and groups affected by the conflict (e.g. volunteers, people, patriots, the community). As the data collected for this research showed, the high frequency of lexis illustrating this theme is a shared feature of all the compared discourses (UOC-KP, 21%; UOC-MP, 16%; UGCC, 23%; DUMU, 69%; DUMU-Umma, 48%; VAAD, 16%). The studied religious institutions have drawn on moral and civil expectations from society as well as their own role during the conflict.

Analysis of the society theme shows how the religious leaders of the UOC-KP, UGCC and DUMA-Ummu portray the future of Ukraine – in victory and peace – and call for unity, patriotism, mutual support and sacrifice. Prayers for victory and peace have also been officially incorporated into the liturgies of Ukraine's Christian Churches, and their leaders have issued statements on reading collective prayers for peace. For example, in 2014, Patriarch Filaret

212 *Nadia Zasanska*

called for regular readings of the *Prayer for the Victory over the Aggressor and Establishment of a Righteous Peace in Ukraine* at the liturgies of all of the UOC-KP's churches.

In the discourse of UGCC, the society theme evokes the metaphor of a struggle between good and evil, in which Ukraine defends the truth – the spiritual weapon of Christians against their enemies:

> Fear not! Christ has won. In Him is our victory!
>
> (Synod of Bishops 2016)[16]

A significant place in the UGCC's discourse is occupied by the meaning of Euromaidan – the Revolution of Dignity in 2014 (Fylypovych and Horkusha 2016). The narratives frame Euromaidan as a new sacral concept of the fearless and righteous struggle for truth, trust in God and readiness to build a better country. Euromaidan is depicted as the historical moment in the development of Ukraine when national dignity resurrected and united people in their struggle against the violation of rights, corruption and the authoritarian regime. Thus, 'Euromaidan' has become the epitome of the moral revolution that started in 2014 and, according to the UGCC, continues in the Donbas areas and all over Ukraine.

Much like the UGCC's narratives, the narratives of the DUMU-Umma emphasize the significance of civil commitment to Ukraine, linking it with a need for moral transformations within Ukrainians themselves.

> Love, value and defend Ukraine! Let us build a new Ukrainian society without corruption, hatred and lies; a new society with the rule of law, dignity, justice and peace.
>
> (Mufti Said Ismagilov)[17]

Moreover, the DUMU-Umma reconstructs memory of the mass deportation of Crimean Tatars in 1944. In the new context, it is paralleled with the forced displacement of people from the east of Ukraine. This reference to a collective traumatic past evokes the sacral concept of 'home', denoting places where one may return after many years of exile.

The DUMU's narratives put forward the concept of Ukraine's citizenship, society and community. In this corpus, Ukraine is framed as a common home for Ukraine's diverse nationalities and ethnic minorities. Thus, the narratives appeal for national unity as the vital basis for overcoming conflicts and peace. The DUMU stresses the value of Ukraine's citizenship as a common ground for reconciliation and setting aside religious or ethnic self-identification. By appealing for reconciliation and 'our common home', the DUMU is not only referring to citizens of the West and East of Ukraine but also to Christians and Muslims. However, such an appeal for unity and integrity among Ukrainians simplifies the Donbas conflict, ultimately framing it as a domestic problem caused by ethnic or religious diversity that can be solved by setting common national goals for the state's development and prosperity.

The discourse of the UOC-MP develops the society theme with an emphasis on the victims of the Donbas conflict. With the notion of 'civil war' appearing in official statements by the UOC-MP, the narrative of the conflict is emotionally overloaded and replete with appeals for reconciliation with the Orthodox Christians on the confrontational side. By highlighting the suffering of the civilians affected by a conflict, including children, orphans, mothers, widows, and the elderly, sick and injured, the UOC-MP intensifies the rhetoric emphasizing the futility of the war, guilt of the Ukrainian state authorities for the deaths and destruction of Donbas, betrayal of Orthodox brotherhood and the 'sinfulness' of the Ukrainian Army.

Similarly, the society theme emerges in the narratives of the VAAD within the context of victimhood. By focusing on the problem of the Jewish community in the occupied areas, the organization addresses the issues of humanitarian aid, repatriation and volunteering. Another feature of the discourse is an attempt to highlight Israel's aid to Ukraine and the work of Jewish volunteer organizations.

Religion, state and conflict resolution

In the discourses of 2014–18, religious organizations either (1) support the state authorities (UOC-KP, VAAD, DUMU-Umma); (2) distance themselves from the state authorities (UGCC, DUMU); or (3) blame/demonize the state authorities (UOC-MP).

The UOC-KP's discourse frames Ukraine as a peaceful country that gave up its nuclear weapons after signing the Budapest Memorandum on Security Assurances in 1994. At the outbreak of the conflict, Patriarch Filaret addressed the officials of European states and the United States to warn them about the possibility of a new world war:

> On behalf of millions of Ukrainians, I appeal to the United States of America to provide security assurances under the terms of the Budapest Memorandum by applying all necessary means, and to help Ukraine stop the aggressor and restore our state's sovereignty within its internation-ally recognized borders. Today, by defending peace in Ukraine, you are defending peace in the United States and the whole world.
>
> (Head of the UOC-KP Patriarch Filaret)[18]

Within the discourse of the UOC-MP, the state authorities of Ukraine are framed as being solely responsible for resolving the conflict. According to the leader of the Church, Archbishop Onufriy, the authorities need to be more 'flexible in this conflict'.[19] Such rhetoric from the UOC-MP resonates with the provocative slogan: 'Kyiv does not hear Donbas' (where Kyiv stands for state authorities), which stoked up confrontation and hostility within the

214 *Nadia Zasanska*

country in 2014. By doing this, the UOC–MP is acting in compliance with an address by the Episcopal Council of the Russian Orthodox Church:

> The borders of the Church are not defined by political preferences, ethnic differences, or even by state borders. The Church protects its unity despite all changeable conditions.
>
> (Episcopal Council, 19 March 2014)[20]

By downplaying the significance of national values and international law while accentuating the 'canonic values' of the Russian Orthodox Church, the UOC–MP has positioned itself as a peacemaker for the people of Crimea and Donbas whose areas continue to fall under their religious jurisdiction following the annexation of Crimea and aggression in the east of Ukraine: 'Our Church, only our Church has not divided Ukraine; we are still controlling Crimea, the east of Ukraine and Donbas – all these territories are under the jurisdiction of our Church'.[21]

In its discourse, the UGCC focuses on the mission of the political elite of Ukraine during the conflict and appeals for unity, compassion and solidarity with the citizens of Eastern Ukraine. The Church draws attention to the responsibilities of the authorities in times of war and appeals to Ukrainians to overcome their inner enemy, corruption, which is defined as the primary hindrance to achieving victory over the external aggressor, Russia. Overall, the UGCC's narratives frame the authorities as the servants of people who have 'power from God, but must obey Christ's laws'.[22]

The DUMU-Umma supports the resolution of the conflict through the complete de-occupation of Ukraine. The leader, Mufti Said Ismagilov, has appealed for moral commitment to be shown to the innocent people who are suffering in the occupied areas of Ukraine and to the memory of all Ukrainians who have fallen in the war. This idea also activates the concept of Ukraine's betrayal of the citizens in Crimea when the Ukrainian authorities failed to prevent the occupation and annexation of the peninsula by Russia in 2014: 'We will never yield to the shameful compromises over refusal to withdraw from our occupied territories. That is out of the question. So, I do believe that we will gain back our Crimea and Donbas. . . . The struggle for the unity of Ukraine will continue into the future!'[23] The DUMU's leader, Sheikh Ahmed Tamim, calls for unity within Ukrainian society, and for the state authorities to set common goals for everyone. The integrity of society is interpreted as the highest expression of the people's patriotic love for Ukraine despite their political, religious and linguistic diversity:

> The solution to any conflict depends on whether there is cohesion in society. A citizen who lives in the east of Ukraine should have the same feeling of love for Ukraine as those who live in the West, North, or South. I cannot criticize the authorities, but I can only wish for them to look at Ukraine as a single organism.
>
> (Sheikh Ahmed Tamim)[24]

Rhetorical strategies in the narrative of the Donbas conflict

	Rhetorical Strategy	UOC-KP	UOC-MP	UGCC	DUMU-Umma	DUMU	VAAD
WE	Positive self-presentation	+	+		+	+	+
	Simplification of the conflict		+		+		
	Warning		+		+		
	Victimization	+	+	+	+		+
	Glorification of heroes	+		+	+		
	Glorification of nation	+			+		
	Consensus		+			+	
	Victory focusing	+		+	+		
	Compassion moves		+	+			
	Sacralization	+	+	+	+		
THEY	Distancing from authorities			+		+	
	Polarization with authorities		+				
	Norm violation			+		+	
	Negative other religious institution	+	+			+	
	Enemy blaming	+	+	+	+		+
	Negative lexicalization		+				

Discussion

The purpose of this comparative study was to define what dominant themes and rhetorical strategies Christian, Muslim and Jewish organizations have applied to the narration of the conflict in the east of Ukraine. This task was achieved through (1) corpus-based lexical analysis of seven structural themes of the narrative (*situation, place, Ukrainian army, authorities, victims, enemy, society*) and (2) ideological analysis of statements made by religious leaders. With regard to the first research question, the study has demonstrated that the Donbas conflict has been lexically mirrored in all the religious discourses under consideration, but the religious organizations' references to the conflict have varied in terms of the level of their lexical representation. While the themes of 'society' and 'place' demonstrate lexical similarities in all the compared discourses, such themes as *victims, Ukrainian army* and *enemy* are represented differently. For example, the DUMU and UOC-MP background these themes in contrast to the UOC-KP and the UGCC, which develop the topics of defenders, heroes and aggressors.

The representation of the 'Ukrainian army' and 'enemy' themes significantly differ in each religious discourse. For example, while the majority of the religious organizations (UOC-KP, UGCC, DUMU-Umma and VAAD) portray Russia as the aggressor in the conflict, the UOC-MP, being under the jurisdiction of the ROC, avoids direct polarization with the Russian Federation by promoting the idea of internecine or civil war. Consequently, their rhetoric of victimization refers to the civilians affected by the conflict, specifically children, mothers and widows, which emotionally recharges the discourse. Although the 'pro–Ukrainian' religious organizations frame the Russian Federation as the aggressor, they tend to present Ukraine as a defender of its independence rather than a victim or martyr. Besides, there is a sense of mutual confrontation in the narratives of the Orthodox Churches, which blame each other for the conflict: the UOC-MP is presented as the traitor and Kremlin's agent in Ukraine, while the UOC-KP is criticized by their opponents for promoting the conflict and supporting the state authorities.

As for the second research question, the data showed that the concept of Euromaidan can be addressed as a *tertium comparationis* in this study because the religious discourses demonstrate similar themes and rhetorical strategies in relation to their attitude to Euromaidan as the starting point of the conflict. In this study, religious organizations stress their own role in the resolution of the conflict through the rhetorical strategy of 'positive self-presentation'. This strategy, along with the strategy of 'negative other presentation', is revealed in the discourses of the Christian organizations (UOC-MP and UOC-KP) in competition with each other within Ukrainian society.

First of all, the diverse rhetoric of the Donbas conflict shows how religious organizations are accommodating memory of their communities' past to narrate the Donbas conflict in the present. This feature is specifically revealed in the discourses in which religious leaders refer to present events through reflections on the past either drawn from sacred texts or 'official' history. For example, the leaders of the UOC-MP frequently refer to the personality of Prince Volodymyr the Great, who baptized the barbaric tribes of Kyivan Rus' in the tenth century and paved the way to a new phase of cultural development in Eastern Europe. By stressing the peacemaking mission of Volodymyr the Great, the official leaders of the UOC-MP are drawing a parallel between his role and the current mission of their Church in the conflict, thereby positioning themselves as peacemakers and conciliators in contrast to the other Christian churches.

Thus, through the reinterpretation and recontextualization of familiar forms of religious knowledge, such as symbols, metaphors, characters, myths and practices, religious discourse mediates new layers of religious meaning. This resonates with Assmann's (1995) notion of two modes of cultural memory: potentiality and actuality. While the first mode stands for the accumulation of knowledge as archives of human experience, the second one refers to the flexibility of memory and its ability to stay relevant in contemporary contexts. A similar idea is found in a study on nostalgia by Oushakine (2007), who argues that influential symbols of the past, due to the familiarity of their old shapes, grant 'a positive structuring effect', which enables them to function in new contexts.

Second, the study demonstrates that in times of conflict, religious memory may serve as a significant tool for religious and ethnic self-identification actualized by such strategies as 'positive self-presentation', 'hero glorification' and 'nation glorification'. For example, in the discourses of the Muslim DUMU-Umma and DUMU, a strategy of positive self-presentation is employed to raise awareness of the collective history shared by Ukrainians and Islamic culture, thereby helping to create new positive images of Islam in Ukraine. By drawing attention to the religious plurality of Ukraine, Muslim communities help overcome traditional views of Ukrainian identity as being solely Christian. Moreover, the occupation of Crimea and the conflict in Donbas have urged Ukrainian Muslims to strive for a new level of civil and ethnic connectedness in the country, and to rethink their vision of Ukraine and their role in it. This has resulted in the development of the first documents produced by Ukraine's Muslims to demonstrate their positions on political, economic, social, cultural and religious processes in Ukraine, notably the *Charter of the Muslims of Ukraine* and *Social Concept of the Muslims of Ukraine.*

In the corpora, religious memory is also evoked through the sacralization of significant events, actors, places and practices. For example, the discourse of the UGCC presents the new concepts of *The Heavenly Hundred* (heroic martyrdom) and *Euromaidan* (the moral struggle for justice and dignity). The DUMU-Umma's narratives sacralize Ukraine, and in particular Crimea, as the only home for Crimean Tatars. The UOC-MP discourse defines the unity of Kyivan Rus' as 'sacred Rus'' for Ukrainians, Russians and Belarusians. Furthermore, the narratives of the UOC-MP link the Donbas conflict to another sacred concept, that of Orthodox brotherhood. The latter helps frame the situation in the east of Ukraine as the 'sin of fratricidal murder'. As this study has showed, religious communities not only tend to sacralize their past associated with religious knowledge, authorities and traditions, but they also tend to imbue the recent past or present with sacred meaning.

This study's lexical analysis of the Islamic discourse demonstrated that the religious organizations of Ukraine's Muslims are undergoing complex institutional transformations. The significant differences in the rhetoric on the Donbas conflict produced by the two main institutions is another sign of the numerous ideological controversies (over Islamic traditions, national identity, civil involvement and relations with the authorities) that continue to divide the DUMU and Umma. These findings resonate with research on the domestic diversity of Islam within Ukraine, for instance, the role of the local authorities in shaping 'Islamic tradition' (Yarosh and Brylov 2011), the politicization of Islam (Yakubovych 2010), the traditionalism and reformism of Islamic organizations (Brylov 2018) and the transformation of Islamic institutions after the annexation of Crimea and Donbas conflict in 2014 (Muratova 2019).

Finally, this study shows how memory may be recruited by religious institutions to shape certain opinions and attitudes. The UOC-MP discourse mediates the ideology of the ROC regarding the common history of the Slavic peoples, Orthodox values and a shared future for the 'brother nations' in the 'sacred Rus''. This finding accords with numerous studies on state–Church relations in Russia in which the ROC is addressed as a tool of Russia's soft power (Lamoreaux and Mabe 2019), the guardian of traditional values (Curanović and Leustean 2015; Stoeckl 2016; Zasanska 2019) and an agent of the 'Russian world' promoting Russian values (e.g. language, culture, historical memory, and Orthodox Christianity) that are common to Ukrainians, Belarusians and Russians (Lutsevych 2016).

218 *Nadia Zasanska*

Acknowledgements

I am very thankful to the European Network Remembrance and Solidarity for providing me with an opportunity to present an earlier draft of this chapter at the 8th Genealogies of Memory conference (Warsaw 2018). I would also like to express my deep gratitude to the anonymous reviewers of this volume and its editors, Zuzanna Bogumił and Yuliya Yurchuk, for their constructive comments, which helped me to improve the chapter.

Notes

1 Social survey "Religious and Church Self-Identification of Ukrainians: Tendencies 2010–2018," accessed September 2019, https://risu.org.ua/ua/index/all_news/community/social_questioning/70946/.
2 See more in the chapter by Yulia Yurchuk in this volume.
3 Social survey "Religious Affiliation of Ukrainians," accessed January 2020, http://razumkov.org.ua/napriamky/sotsiologichni-doslidzhennia/konfesiina-ta-tserkovna-nalezhnist-gromadian-ukrainy-sichen-2020r.
4 See more about Maidan on the website "National Memorial to the Heavenly Hundred Heroes and Revolution of Dignity Museum," accessed September 2019, https://maidanmuseum.org/en/node/319.
5 Interview with head of the UGCC Sviatoslav Shevchuk (my translation), 2014, accessed July 2018, http://ugcc.ua/official/head.ugcc/zmi/publikatsii_2014/blazhenn%D1%96shiy_svyatoslav_tse_nasha_%D1%96_vasha_borotba_za_svobodu_71482.html.
6 Patriarch Kirill's address to the Episcopal Council of the Russian Orthodox Church, June 2014 (my translation), accessed July 2018, www.patriarchia.ru/db/text/3675015.html.
7 Patriarch Kirill's address to the Episcopal Council of the Russian Orthodox Church, June 2014 (my translation), accessed July 2018, www.patriarchia.ru/db/text/3675015.html.
8 The Orthodox Journalists Union, accessed July 2018, https://spzh.news/ua/zashhita-very/39189-chomu-upts-molitsya-pro-pripinennya-mizhusobnoi-brani.
9 The Social Concept of the Muslims of Ukraine, accessed July 2018, https://umma.in.ua/ua/node/1890.
10 Joseph Zissels's address at the World Jewish Congress, 15 September 2014 (my translation), accessed July 2018, http://vaadua.org/news/vystuplenie-predsedatelya-vaada-ukrainy-iosifa-ziselsa-na-zasedanii-soveta-upravlyayushchih.
11 Address of the Head of GCCO Sviatoslav Shevchuk on the commemoration of the Second World War, May 2015 (my translation), accessed July 2018, http://ugcc.ua/documents/lyubov_ponad_use_73714.html.
12 Mufti of Ukraine Said Ismagilov's address on the Defender's Day, 14 October 2016 (my translation), accessed July 2018, http://islam.in.ua/ru/novosti-v-strane/ukrainskie-voiny-zakalili-sebya-v-boyah-s-agressorom-i-stali-nastoyashchimi.
13 Interview with Archbishop Filaret, January 2017 (my translation), accessed July 2018, www.5.ua/interview/sviatiishyi-filaret-rizdviane-interviu-135560.html.
14 Archbishop Guzar's reference to Metropolitan Sheptytskyi, November 2013 (my translation), accessed January 2018, https://www.pravda.com.ua/columns/2013/11/8/7001772/
15 Sheikh Ahmed Tamim's address, November 2018 (my translation), accessed July 2018, https://islam.ua/publikatsii/novosti/obrashhenie-verhovnogo-muftiya-ukrainy-shejha-ahmeda-tamima-k-musulmanam-i-vsemu-ukrainskomu-narodu/.
16 The Synod of Bishops address to citizens of Ukraine, affected by the occupation of Crimea and Donbas, September 2016 (my translation), accessed July 2018, http://velychlviv.com/stavshy-vygnantsyamy-na-svoyij-zemli-virte-shho-vy-nikoly-ne-budete-pokynutymy-chy-zabutymy-bogom-zi-zvernennya-synodu-yepyskopiv-ugkts/.

17 Interview with Mufti of Ukraine Said Ismagilov, 14 March 2018 (my translation), accessed July 2018, http://islam.in.ua/ru/mnenie/said-ismagilov-davayte-vmeste-stroit-novoe-ukrainskoe-obshchestvo-gde-budut-gospodstvovat.
18 Archbishop Filaret's address to leaders of EU and USA, October 2014 (my translation), accessed July 2018, www.religion.in.ua/news/vazhlivo/27107-glava-upc-kp-zvernuvsya-do-glav-derzhav-parlamentiv-ta-narodiv-yevropi-iz-zaklikom-zupiniti-rozpalennya-iii-svitovoyi-vijni.html.
19 Interview with Archbishop Onufriy about the war in Donbas, 2015, accessed July 2018, www.youtube.com/watch?v=RiDKHZqQBa4.
20 Patriarch Kirill's address to the Episcopal Council of the Russian Orthodox Church, June 2014 (my translation), accessed July 2018, www.patriarchia.ru/db/text/3675015.html.
21 Interview with Archbishop Onufriy, accessed July 2018, http://news.church.ua/2014/03/13/mitropolit-onufrij-to-chto-proisxodit-sejchas-ispytanie-nashej-lyubvi-k-bogu-i-blizhnemu/.
22 Interview with Liubomir Guzar, former head of UGCC, 21 May 2015 (my translation), accessed July 2018, https://zaxid.net/10_porad_blazhennishogo_lyubomira_guzara_ukrayintsyam_n1352241.
23 Interview with Mufti of Ukraine Said Ismagilov, 23 January 2017 (my translation), accessed July 2018, http://islam.in.ua/ru/tochka-zreniya/nas-i-v-dalneyshem-ozhidaet-borba-za-edinstvo-i-sobornost-ukrainy-said-ismagilov.
24 Interview with Sheikh Ahmed Tamim, April 2016 (my translation), accessed July 2018, https://ukraine.segodnya.ua/ukraine/muftiy-ukrainy-nash-dzhihad-eto-truditsya-dlya-blaga-vsego-obshchestva-710815.html.

References

Assmann, Aleida. 2008. "Canon and Archive." In *Media and Cultural Memory: An International and Interdisciplinary Handbook*, edited by Astrid Erll and Ansgar Nunning. Berlin: Walter de Gruyter.

Assmann, Jan. 2011. *Cultural Memory and Early Civilization: Writing, Remembrance, and Political Imagination*. Cambridge: Cambridge University Press.

———. 2006. *Religion and Cultural Memory: Ten Studies*. Stanford, CA: Stanford University Press.

Assmann, Jan, and John Czaplicka. 1995. "Collective Memory and Cultural Identity." *New German Critique* (65): 125–33. https://doi.org/10.2307/488538.

Brylov, Denis. 2018. "Islam in Ukraine: The Language Strategies of Ukrainian Muslim Communities." *Religion, State and Society* 46 (2): 156–73. https://doi.org/10.1080/0963 7494.2018.1456766.

Curanović, Alicja, and Lucian Leustean. 2015. "The Guardians of Traditional Values: Russian and the Russian Orthodox Church in the Quest for Status." *Transatlantic Academy Paper Series* (1).

Denysenko, Nicholas. 2014. "Chaos in Ukraine: The Churches and the Search for Leadership." *International Journal for the Study of the Christian Church* 14 (3): 242–59. https://doi.org/10.1080/1474225X.2014.925261.

Echterhoff, Gerald. 2008. "Language and Memory: Social and Cognitive Processes." In *Media and Cultural Memory: An International and Interdisciplinary Handbook*, edited by Astrid Erll and Ansgar Nunning. Berlin: Walter de Gruyter.

Fairclough, Norman, and Ruth Wodak. 1997. "Critical Discourse Analysis." In *Discourse Studies: A Multidisciplinary Introduction*, edited by T. van Dijk, Vol. 2, 258–84. London: Sage.

Feldman, Anat. 2015. "In the Realms of Ethnicity, Religion and Emigration: New Communities of Memory in Israel." *Review of Religious Research* 57 (2): 171–89. www.jstor.org/stable/43920096.

220 *Nadia Zasanska*

Fenn, Richard K. 2007. "Editorial Commentary: Religion and the Secular; the Sacred and the Profane: The Scope of the Argument." In *The Blackwell Companion to Sociology of Religion*, edited by Richard K. Fenn. https://doi.org/10.1002/9780470998571.part1.

Fylypovych, Liudmyla, and Horkusha Oksana. 2016. "Voice of the Church: Axiological Dimensions of Religious Rhetoric at Maidan in 2013–2014." *Philosovska dumka* (4).

Gensburger, Sarah. 2016. "Halbwachs' Studies in Collective Memory: A Founding Text for Contemporary 'Memory Studies'?" *Journal of Classical Sociology* 16 (4): 396–413. https://doi.org/10.1177/1468795x16656268.

Halbwachs, Maurice. 1992. *On Collective Memory*. Translated and edited by Lewis A. Coser. Chicago: University of Chicago Press.

Hilton, Denis J., and James H. Liu. 2017. "History as the Narrative of a People: From Function to Structure and Content." *Memory Studies* 10 (3): 297–309. https://doi.org/10.1177/1750698017701612.

Hervieu-Léger, Daniele. 2000. *Religion as a Chain of Memory*. New Brunswick, NJ: Rutgers University Press.

Huang, Ke-hsien. 2018. "Restoring Religion Through Collective Memory: How Chinese Pentecostals Engage in Mnemonic Practices After the Cultural Revolution." *Social Compass* 65 (1): 79–96. https://doi.org/10.1177/0037768617747506.

Ilchuk, Yuliya. 2017. "Hearing the Voice of Donbas: Art and Literature as Forms of Cultural Protest During War." *Nationalities Papers* 45 (2): 256–73. https://doi.org/10.1080/00905992.2016.1249835.

Irwin-Zarecka, Iwona. 1994. *Frames of Remembrance: The Dynamics of Collective Memory*. New Brunswick: Transaction.

Jørgensen, Marianne, and Louise Phillips. 2002. *Discourse Analysis as Theory and Method*. London: Sage Publications.

Klymenko, Lina. 2019. "Understanding the Donbas War in Terms of World War II: A Metaphor Analysis of the Armed Conflict in Eastern Ukraine." *Ethnopolitics*: 1–18. https://doi.org/10.1080/17449057.2019.1608064.

Krawchuk, Andrii. 2014. "Constructing Interreligious Consensus in the Post-Soviet Space: The Ukrainian Council of Churches and Religious Organizations." In *Eastern Orthodox Encounters of Identity and Otherness*, edited by Krawchuk Andrii and Bremer Thomas. New York: Palgrave Macmillan.

Krawchuk, Andrii, and Thomas Bremer, eds. 2016. *Churches in the Ukrainian Crisis*. Palgrave Macmillan. https://doi.org/10.1007/978-3-319-34144-6.

Lamoreaux, Jeremy, and Michael Mabe. 2019. "The Kremlin's Strategy vis-àvis the Baltic States: A Role for Orthodoxy." *International Journal for the Study of the Christian Church*. https://doi.org/10.1080/1474225X.2019.1678374.

Landwehr, Jakob. 2019. "No Way Out? Opportunities for Mediation Efforts in the Donbas Region." *East European Politics* 35 (3): 291–310. https://doi.org/10.1080/21599165.2019.1647532.

Lutsevych, Orysia. 2016. *Agents of the Russian World: Proxy Groups in the Contested Neighbourhood*. Chatham House. www.chathamhouse.org/sites/default/files/publications/research/2016-04-14-agents-russian-world-lutsevych.pdf.

Malyarenko, Tatyana, and Stefan Wolff. 2018. "The Logic of Competitive Influence-Seeking: Russia, Ukraine, and the Conflict in Donbas." *Post-Soviet Affairs* 34 (4): 191–212. https://doi.org/10.1080/1060586X.2018.1425083.

Metzger, Franziska. 2018. "Devotion and Memory – Discourses and Practices." *Kirchliche Zeitgeschichte* 31 (2): 329–47. https://doi.org/10.2307/26742810.

Miller, Richard B. 2009. "The Moral and Political Burdens of Memory." *Journal of Religious Ethics* 37 (3): 533–64. https://doi.org/10.1111/j.1467-9795.2009.00399.x.

Mitchnik, Igor. 2019. "Making Donbas, Breaking Donbas: The Impact of Conflict Experience on Identity Shifts in the East of Ukraine." *Ethnopolitics*: 1–21. https://doi.org/10.10 80/17449057.2019.1613059.

Muratova, Elmira. 2019. "The Transformation of the Crimean Tatars' Institutions and Discourses After 2014." *Journal of Nationalism, Memory & Language Politics* 13 (1): 44–66. https://doi.org/10.2478/jnmlp-2019-0006.

O'Collins, Gerald, and David Braithwaite. 2015. "Tradition as Collective Memory: A Theological Task to Be Tackled." *Theological Studies* 76 (1): 29–42. https://doi.org/10.1177/0040563914565300.

Olick, Jeffrey K. 1999. "Collective Memory: The Two Cultures." *Sociological Theory* 17 (3): 333–48. https://doi.org/10.1111/0735-2751.00083.

Oushakine, Serguei. 2007. "We're Nostalgic but We're Not Crazy. Retrofitting the Past in Russia." *Russian Review* 66 (3): 451–82.

Sasse, Gwendolyn, and Alice Lackner. 2018. "War and Identity: The Case of the Donbas in Ukraine." *Post-Soviet Affairs* 34 (2–3): 139–57. https://doi.org/10.1080/10605 86X.2018.1452209.

Scott, Mike. 2018. *WordSmith Tools Help*. Stroud: Lexical Analysis Software. Accessed July 2020, https://lexically.net/wordsmith/

Shestopalets, Denys. 2019. "The Ukrainian Orthodox Church of the Moscow Patriarchate, the State and the Russian-Ukrainian Crisis, 2014–2018." *Politics, Religion & Ideology* 20 (1): 42–63. https://doi.org/10.1080/21567689.2018.1554482.

Stoeckl, Kristina. 2016. "The Russian Orthodox Church as Moral Norm Entrepreneur. Religion." *State and Society* 44 (2): 132–51. https://doi.org/10.1080/09637494.2016.1194010.

Straub, Jürgen. 2008. "Psychology, Narrative, and Cultural Memory: Past and Present." In *Media and Cultural Memory: An International and Interdisciplinary Handbook*, edited by Astrid Erll and Ansgar Nunning. Berlin: Walter de Gruyter.

Sutton, John. 2014. "Memory Perspectives." *Memory Studies* 7 (2): 141–45. https://doi.org/10.1177/1750698013518131.

Taradai, Daria. 2019. "Who Is Ukraine's Enemy: Narratives in the Military Communication Regarding the War in Donbas." *Russian Journal of Communication* 11 (2): 141–56. https://doi.org/10.1080/19409419.2019.1622196.

Van Dijk, T. A. 2006. "Politics, Ideology, and Discourse." In *Encyclopedia of Language & Linguistics*. https://doi10.1016/B0-08-044854-2/00722-7.

Welzer, Harald. 2008. "Communicative memory." In *Media and Cultural Memory: An International and Interdisciplinary Handbook*, edited by Astrid Erll and Ansgar Nunning. Berlin: Walter de Gruyter.

Yakubovych, Mykhaylo. 2010. "Islam and Muslims in Contemporary Ukraine: Common Backgrounds, Different Images." *Religion, State and Society* 38 (3): 291–304. https://doi.org/10.1080/09637494.2010.499287.

Yarosh, Oleg, and Denis Brylov. 2011. "Muslim Communities and Islamic Network Institutions in Ukraine: Contesting Authorities in Shaping of Islamic Localities." In *Muslims in Poland and Eastern Europe: Widening the European Discourse on Islam*, edited by K. Górak-Sosnowska, 252–65. Warsaw: University of Warsaw.

Zasanska, Nadia D. 2019. "New Producers of Patriarchal Ideology: Matushki in Digital Media of Russian Orthodox Church." *ESSACHESS – Journal for Communication Studies* 12 (2(24)): 99–128. Accessed December 2019. http://essachess.com/index.php/jcs/article/view/466.

11 Official quests, vernacular answers

The Macedonian Orthodox Church – Ohrid Archbishopric (MOC-OA) as a memory actor in the post-conflict Republic of North Macedonia (2001–19)

Naum Trajanovski

Introduction

It could easily be claimed that the major socio-political developments of late have rounded off a critical cycle in the recent history of the Republic of North Macedonia's domestic and foreign politics.[1] The former southernmost federal unit of Yugoslavia declared its independence from that state in September 1991. Even though the newly established state avoided the bloodshed of the early stages of the Yugoslav wars (1991–95), the univocal mediascape, the so-called Greco-Macedonian name dispute and the Greek trade embargo on North Macedonia (1994), which was followed by the Kosovo crisis (1995–99), have 'further undermined the internal fragile inter-ethnic balance' within the country (Spaskovska 2011, 2; also see Lewis 2001; Hozić 2014; Ramet 2017). The escalating inter-ethnic cleavages culminated in a nine-month armed conflict between the Macedonian forces and the ethnic Albanian radicals (January–November 2001). The insurgence was settled by the Ohrid Framework Agreement (OFA; 13 August 2001), a peace treaty that institutionalized the state's multicultural reality (see Brunnbauer 2002; Dimova 2006; Bieber 2008).

In 2006, a coalition led by the rightist Internal Macedonian Revolutionary Organization – Democratic Party for Macedonian National Unity (VMRO-DPMNE) seized power, and in the aftermath of a Greek veto in 2008 against Macedonia being granted full NATO membership status, it launched a set of ethno-nationalistic memory policies as the state's top political priority (for more, see Popovska 2015; Graan 2016; Cvitković and Kline 2017; Trajanovski 2020b). A major wiretapping scandal in mid-2015, which involved a number of VMRO-DPMNE affiliates, triggered a massive protest wave culminating in snap governmental elections in 2016. This plebiscite and the local and presidential elections in 2017 and 2019 established the centre-left Social Democratic Union of Macedonia (SDSM) as the main political factor in the Macedonian political camp. In brief, the initial SDSM period of

DOI: 10.4324/9781003264750-14

Official quests, vernacular answers 223

governance was marked by a set of proactive bilateral policies resulting in the Bulgarian-Macedonian Friendship Treaty (BMFT) from August 2017 and the Greco-Macedonian Name Agreement (GMNA) from June 2018.[2] The ruling coalition has also adopted the Law on the Use of the Languages (January 2019), which elevates the Albanian language to the status of a second official state language, and put forward the National Strategy for the Development of the Concept One Society and Interculturalism, a policy initiative aiming to 'reduce divisions and increase trust among the communities in North Macedonia' (N/A 2019b).

This chapter discusses the mnemonic discourses and practices of the Macedonian Orthodox Church – Ohrid Archbishopric (MOC-OA) in post-2001 North Macedonia. I approach the MOC-OA's agency by analyzing two paradigmatic events: the commemorations of the predominant state holiday, Republic Day, also known as Ilinden; and the so-called Mara Buneva commemorations, an annual, Skopje-based one-day event that has been taking place in early January since 2001. Even though several accounts of the MOC-OA as a 'social actor' or 'political actor' have emerged in academic scholarship over the last two decades (see e.g. Kostovski 2003; Risteski 2009; Vangeli 2010; Matevska 2011; Zdravkovski and Morrison 2014; Angelovska and Cacanoska 2020), the role of the Church as a secular 'memory actor' or an 'agent of memory' has heretofore not been researched (this is developed in the next section). I therefore argue that one should examine the agency of the MOC-OA to better understand the dynamics of (1) Macedonian memory politics in the post-conflict setting, (2) intrastate mnemonic struggles across partisan lines and (3) the MOC-OA's reception of the recently ratified bilateral settlements.

Furthermore, the 'mnemopolitical' positions that the MOC-OA has taken up in the wake of the most recent Macedonian bilateral developments have yet to be subjected to a close reading and critical analysis.[3] In late 2017, the MOC-OA sought the 'paternal authority' of the Bulgarian Orthodox Church after a five-decade-long dispute with the Serbian Orthodox Church over its ecclesiastical independence (more in Blaževska 2017; Stankovik 2017). The Macedonian Orthodox Church was re-established as autonomous in 1959, after preliminary talks over the need for a separate national Church in the early 1940s (for more on the Macedonian post-war nation-building, see Troebst 1997). By the same token, the MOC-OA proclaimed its autocephalous status on 17 July 1967, the 200th anniversary of the abolishment of the Ohrid Archbishopric in 1767 (Dimevski 1965, 1989; Ilievski 1972; Trajanovski 2008; Cepreganov and Shashko 2010; Gjorgjevski 2017; Čairović 2018).[4] After the demise of Yugoslavia, the MOC-OA was introduced in 17 November 1991 into the Macedonian Constitution, and since then it has acted as the largest Orthodox Church in North Macedonia and claimed ecclesiastical jurisdiction over Macedonian Orthodox Christians and the ethnic Macedonian diaspora (Cepreganov, Angelovska-Panova, and Zajkovski 2014; Irwin 2019; see Krindatch 2002 for an overview of the Church's activities in the United States).

Theoretical background and methodological design

It has become a scholarly commonplace for contemporary memory studies to shift its research focus from the Halbwachsian societal representations that used to dominate the field to the agency and discursive practices of social actors (see Gensburger 2016 for an overview of this argument; for a different take on the religious institutions in memory studies, see Assmann 2008). The aforementioned assumption can be illustrated by the appearance of a novel wave of research on 'mnemonic actors' (for an overview, see Kubik and Bernhard 2014a, 2014b), 'memory entrepreneurs' (e.g. Kaiser 2012) or 'memory agents' (e.g. Zelizer 2014). In Central and Eastern European scholarship, Jan Kubik and Michael Bernhard have developed a theoretical model of 'memory regimes' as interplay between 'mnemonic actors' in a given national synchrony. According to this model, 'mnemonic actors' are defined as 'political forces that are interested in a specific interpretation of the past' (2014a, 4).[5] In the concluding, comparative chapter of their book, Kubik and Bernhard recognize 'Churches' as one of a number of agents including 'governments, political parties, schools, families, museums and so on', which

> work hard to reproduce both the *themes* (cultural heroes, myths of origin, narratives of greatness, etc.), that are defined as constitutive units of one or more specific visions of 'national heritage', and *scripts* or *scenarios of action* that together amount to what is often defined as (a version of) the 'national character'.
>
> (Kubik and Bernhard 2014b, 286)

Trencsényi also notes the role played by religions and religious actors as being focal in the emerging memory wars in Central and Eastern European post-communist space. He also stresses that, within the aforementioned geographical context, 'there is a common sentiment of the legitimizing and organizing power of religion, and, in some ways, the erupting *Kulturkampf* is also about the repositioning of the Church in society' (Trencsényi 2014, 151).

Within the Balkan setting, there is a clear emphasis on an additional, 'highly political' development in the 'post-conflict' constellation (Katzenstein 2014) that has arisen from the traumatic and violent experiences of the aforementioned Yugoslav wars, Kosovo crisis and the 2001 Macedonian conflict.[6] Scholarly discourse on the region has heretofore recognized the role of the Orthodox Church as the 'core of the national mythologies' (Leustean 2008; see also Iveković 2002; Buchenau 2005; Payne 2007; Hilton Saggau 2018), while the national Orthodox Churches have been approached as 'political actors' in post-2001 Serbia (Vukomanović 2008; Barišić 2016; also see Subotić 2019) and as institutions 'involved in significant developments' in post-communist Bulgarian politics (Broun 2004). This chapter maps the MOC-OA's agency through the diachrony of almost two decades of Ilinden and Mara Buneva commemorations. The commemorations will be reconstructed by triangulating media

Official quests, vernacular answers   225

outlets, institutional discourses and political rhetoric. The two case studies are unarguably the most representative official and vernacular commemorations in contemporary North Macedonia (for the official/vernacular dichotomy, see Bogumił and Głowacka-Grajper 2019). Media outlets were analyzed at three Skopje-based libraries, while the institutional discourses and political rhetoric were mapped using the relevant parties' official organs.[7] Finally, I will provide a brief context, or prehistory, for both commemorations, thereby situating them within the relevant scholarship and public and political debates.

The Ilinden commemorations

Setting the scene

It is commonplace for 'Ilinden' to be used as a keyword for Macedonia of the twentieth century.[8] The 1903 Ilinden Uprising was organized by activists affiliated to the Internal Macedonian-Adrianople Revolutionary Organization, which had the revolutionary goal of securing political autonomy for Macedonian territory. The uprising broke out on the Orthodox Christian holiday of the prophet St Elijah (*Ilija, Ilinden*) – 20 July, according to the Julian calendar, and 2 August, according to the currently valid Gregorian calendar. One of the major military successes was the liberation of the town of Kruševo from Ottoman rule and the formation of the so-called Kruševo Republic and the proclamation of the 'Kruševo Manifesto'. Even though the Republic only lasted for ten days, and the rebellion was stifled within a month, the events unarguably contributed to a significant political realignment in the region. Moreover, in the aftermath of the Second World War, the Tito-led Partisan movement deliberately chose the date of 2 August 1944 – the 41st anniversary of the 1903 Ilinden Uprising – to officially proclaim the formation of the Anti-Fascist Assembly of the National Liberation of Macedonia (AANLM), a pseudo-governing body dating from the wartime period that was transformed into the first Macedonian government. Consequently, Ilinden was immediately inaugurated as Republic Day in the new political unit known as Democratic Federal Macedonia. The notion of a 'symbolic chain' that linked the socialist revolution to the 'unfinished business' (Brunnbauer 2004, 178) of the late nineteenth-century Macedonian revolutionaries was originally instigated by partisan military units inspired by the writings of the interwar Macedonian intelligentsia, but it was completed by the postwar generation of Macedonian historians, assisted by the Macedonian Church, which also endorsed the 'two Ilindens' trope.[9]

Despite this progress, it took several decades to develop the Ilinden legacy as a 'sacred place' of Macedonian nationhood (see e.g. Brown 2000, 2003; Majewski 2015). By the late 1960s and early 1970s, the majority of the 1903 revolutionaries had passed away, taking their communicative memory of the uprising with them, so it was the state that had to reimagine Kruševo as Ilinden's 'symbolic epicenter' (Brown 2003, 2) and the foundation of the still-ongoing Ilinden commemorative ritualogy. On the one hand, this political

226   *Naum Trajanovski*

project is exemplified by such initiatives as Tito's visit to Kruševo in 1969 (Soldić 2012), the *Makedonium* memorial complex (opened to the public in 1974; for more, see Marinkoviḱ 1974) and the inauguration of a monument in Sliva, in the vicinity of Kruševo. On the other hand, the venue for the first session of the AANLM, the Orthodox Christian monastery of St Prohor Pčinjski, was also re-envisioned as a *lieu de mémoire* during the same period. The monastery hosted the official Republic Day commemorations from August 1969 after an agreement was reached between the monastery's governing body and the Socialist Republic of Macedonia's State Secretariat for Education, Science and Culture (26 May 1969). The agreement authorized the Macedonian side to use the facilities of the monastery, which was in the Serbia-Macedonia borderlands, in return for a certain financial compensation (Džikov and Todorovski 1990, 14–15), while in 1974 a road to the monastery from the Macedonian town of Kumanovo was finished and opened to the public (Pačkov 1974). Seeing as the official commemoration strategy was fabricated around two sites of memory, the political actors moved from one place to another year by year.

Moreover, Ilinden's symbolic richness was also a significant factor throughout the Yugoslav dissolution, with the Macedonian post-socialist elite appropriating the phrase 'Third Ilinden' from the Macedonian political diaspora as a political framework for Macedonian independence.[10] Despite this, the controversy over the Ilinden commemorations and the St Prohor Pčinjski Monastery came to epitomize the post-Yugoslav Macedonian–Serbian political contestations that began in the 1990s.[11] In 1990, the memorial plaque in the monastery's AANLM memorial room, now part of the constituent state of the Federal Republic of Yugoslavia – the Republic of Serbia – was demolished by Serbian radical groups, while the police 'brutally stopped the commemorative activities' (Georgievski 2001, 23–24). The following year, the AANLM memorial room was relocated by the Serbian authorities without prior announcement, a move which was reported as a 'desecration' of Macedonian history (Risteski 1991). Otherwise, the initial Macedonian post-Yugoslav decade did not witness a serious shift from the Ilinden commemorative model established in the 1970s. Nevertheless, the period was marked with the first attempts to discontinue the symbolic link between the two Ilindens by attributing an ethnocentric tone to the Ilinden commemorative narrative and the partisan interpretation of events. For example, the former state president Kiro Gligorov, a member of the AANLM, was criticized for 'choosing the AANLM instead of Ilinden' in 1999 (N/A 1999), while in 1998 the incumbent leader of one of the major Albanian parties of the time in North Macedonia, Abdurahman Aliti, was pushed into answering a media question on 'his arrival in Kruševo' (Mihajlovski 1998).

The MOC-OA and the Ilinden commemorations in the 1990s and early 2000s

The role performed by the MOC-OA during the Ilinden commemorations of the 1990s and early 2000s should be viewed within the context of escalating intrastate tensions and Macedonian–Serbian bilateral contestations (for an overview, see Ilievski 2012). The major illustration of the MOC-OA's stance on intrastate tensions is the opposition it expressed to certain constitutional changes projected by the OFA. The projected amendments concerned Article 19 of the 1991 Macedonian Constitution, which up until 2001 had mentioned that the MOC-OA and 'the other religious communities and groups' were 'separate from the state and equal before the law' (Macedonian Constitution 1991, art. 19). The new proposal to name the 'other religious communities and groups' in the Constitution – instead of mentioning them as collective nouns – provoked a set of 'public exchanges' between the MOC-OA and the Islamic Community of Macedonia over the course of 2001 (Latifi 2001), which culminated in the Islamic Religious Community, Catholic Church, Evangelical Methodist Church and the Jewish Community all being included in the constitutional Amendment VII of 2001 (Macedonian Constitution 1991, amend. VII).[12] As for the latter issue, the bilateral contestations between North Macedonia and Serbia, which were of a clerical and political nature, appeared to be triggered by the so-called Niš Agreement, a failed attempt in 2002 to settle a dispute between the MOC-OA and Serbian Orthodox Church (SOC) that would shortly afterwards be harshly criticized by the Macedonian side. The failure to settle this ecclesiastical dispute resulted in the so-called Vraniškovski Affair in the mid-2000s, an attempt to establish a Serbian-backed Orthodox Church in North Macedonia operating in parallel with the MOC-OA (Morée 2005; Aleksov 2010; Paszkiewicz 2016). The MOC-OA reacted to the challenges it faced in the early 2000s by employing the Ilinden commemorations as an instrument for politicizing both the intrastate multi-confessional tensions and the ecclesiastical Macedonian–Serbian dispute.

In other words, the Ilinden commemorations and the bilateral quarrel over the monastery were used as platforms to raise the Church's profile on the political agenda in the early 2000s. In 2003, the centennial anniversary of the first Ilinden, the SOC refused to mount a memorial plaque dedicated to the AANLM in the St Prohor Pčinjski monastery without receiving a public rationale, while the disputed Archbishop Jovan (Vraniškovski), leader of the short-lasting Serbian-backed church in North Macedonia, was invited to conduct the Ilinden liturgy at the same monastery (Kuzmanovska 2003). The MOC-OA responded to what it viewed as a provocation by issuing an official statement denoting the developments over the monastery as a high-level 'state issue' (Vasilevska 2003). This bilateral dispute escalated again during the 2004 Ilinden commemorations. The VMRO-DPMNE, which was in opposition at the time, scapegoated the second SDSM government for 'holding secret meetings with Serbian representatives'. The VMRO-DPNME also criticized the MOC-OA: Archbishop Stefan's position on the sporadic but active clerical negotiations was reported to be 'unsatisfactory' (N/A 2004). The MOC-OA responded by boycotting the Ilinden ceremonial speech by Ljupčo Jordanovski, the incumbent speaker of Parliament, who was affiliated to the SDSM. The dispute over the

228 *Naum Trajanovski*

commemorations at the St Prohor Pčinjski monastery was resolved by a decision to implement a Macedonian project that established an AANLM memorial centre in Pelince, which was only a few kilometres away from the monastery but on Macedonian territory. The ongoing clerical issue over the MOC-OA's autocephality has not only determined the status of ecclesiastical relations between the two neighbouring states over the last two decades but also, to a large extent, the dynamics of political bilateral relations in toto.

The mid-2000s rightist turn

An electoral change in 2006, which brought the VMRO-DPMNE back into power, contributed to the MOC-OA playing a more active role in the annual Ilinden commemorations. I have argued elsewhere that the initial post-conflict years of the early 2000s can be viewed as a joint political effort to establish a reconciliatory commemorative narrative on Ilinden (Trajanovski 2020a). The state-sponsored Ilinden commemorations of 2007 and 2008 are illustrative of pending modifications to the Republic Day's commemorative model. This discursive shift was moulded across the two partisan visions of the Ilinden legacy, or in other words, the complementarity between the two Ilinden risings. In brief, the SDSM governments of the 1990s and early 2000s nurtured the continuity of Socialist Macedonian interpretations of the twentieth century, with a singular stress on AANLM's institutional legacy. Conversely, the VMRO-DPMNE, being the party which claimed legacy over the initial revolutionary organization, accentuated the 1903 uprising as the focal point in Macedonian history for the 1990s. The partisan narrative of late modern Macedonian history evolved into a teleological discourse in the mid-2000s that highlighted the rightist interwar wings of the organization opposed to the wartime Yugoslav partisan struggle and the anti-communist political diaspora from the post–Second World War period. This discourse would belittle the role of the anti-fascist struggle, showing favour instead to the martyrdom of the local ethnic Macedonian anti-communists and the émigré dissidents. This narrative structure is most visible in a major mnemonic project depicting the Macedonian twentieth century under the second VMRO-DPMNE government – the state-sponsored Museum of the Macedonian struggle for Sovereignty and Independence – which was envisioned in the mid-2000s and opened in 2011 (Trajanovski 2020b). Thus, the two major political camps' positions on the Ilinden legacy in the late 2000s can be viewed as a competitive endeavour to establish an interpretative framework for Macedonian statehood and national identity – in stark contrast to the post-conflict quest for a consensus mnemopolitics.[13]

What was the MOC-OA's position in this newly polarized environment? On the one hand, one can argue that the MOC-OA contributed to this discursive shift over Ilinden's legacy from 2006 and the formation of the second VMRO-DPMNE-led governmental coalition. This positioning is most obviously traceable from the official commemorative statements (*Ilindenski poslanija*) the MOC-OA issued on the occasion of Ilinden commemorations.

In 2006, the MOC-OA's official Ilinden statement did not contain a single reference to the AANLM, while also syncretizing Ilinden as a 'national holiday of the Macedonian people, state and Church' (N/A 2006a). This was the first annual MOC-OA statement containing no reference to the AANLM. Moreover, the convergence between the respective positions of the MOC-OA and VMRO-DPMNE eventually culminated in an attempt to redefine the Ilinden commemorative ritualogy – an initiative that materialized when the second VMRO-DPMNE government was at the peak of its popularity. By way of illustration, from 2011 onwards, the city of Skopje hosted the major Ilinden commemorative activities, which often lent legitimacy to the so-called Skopje 2014 project – an umbrella term for the 137 memorial objects erected in the capital city's centre over the course of the second VMRO-DPMNE government's tenure – and ensured that the religious authorities were the central agents of the ceremonies. Two events are significant enough to be mentioned in these respect: the official opening of the Millennium Cross in Skopje, which was announced as a 'contribution to the commemoration of Ilinden' (N/A 2007a); and the opening of the Orthodox Church of St Prophet Elijah in Skopje on Ilinden (2 August), which was attended by high officials of both the governmental and Orthodox Christian religious bodies and promoted as the major Ilinden event of the year (N/A 2007b).

On the other hand, even though the MOC-OA participated in this discursive redefining and its practical outcomes, the Church strove to present a more inclusive historical storyline while leaving the more radical historical interpretations for local clergy and clerics in the diaspora. Yet the format of the annual Church statements issued annually by the MOC-OA's archbishop remained unchanged and continued to touch on broad socio-political issues. After the public and media reacted negatively to the MOC-OA's failure to mention the AANLM in its first annual statement (for an overview, see N/A 2006a, 2006b), the Church included a reference to the second Ilinden and the AANLM in subsequent official Ilinden statements, but only in passing (see the commemorative speeches listed as N/A 2010, 2013a, 2015, 2017, 2018). Moreover, the MOC-OA oftentimes employed this discursive platform to address various mnemopolitical stances, which were frequently aligned to the dominant VMRO-DPMNE memory policy of the time. So in 2013, for example, the MOC-OA was critical of the 1913 Bucharest Treaty, a crucial event for the partitioning of the Macedonian territories instrumental within rightist partisan narratives (see the Ilinden speech marking the hundredth anniversary of the Treaty of Bucharest, N/A 2013a). Over the past decade and a half, the Ilinden mnemonic discourse of the other MOC-OA authorities has been similar in tone to the MOC-OA archbishop's statements and speeches, and on certain occasions, contained more radical historical interpretations. By way of illustration, in his 2016 Ilinden speech, Metropolitan Petar, head of the MOC-OA Diocese of Australia and New Zealand, linked the Ilinden struggle to the 'ongoing' political 'war' in the national setting, with the protagonists being the affiliates of the political party in power (N/A 2016).

230 *Naum Trajanovski*

However, in the most recent period, a clear political break can be traced with the mnemonic discourses promoted by the second VMRO-DPMNE government. After the latest governmental change and especially after the BMFT friendship treaty with Bulgaria, the SDSM government has promoted Ilinden by stressing its value as a national holiday for Macedonian citizens (which is in line with the aforementioned strategy on interculturalism) and by highlighting its potential as a reciprocal Macedonian–Bulgarian historical legacy (in line with the BMFT and the bilateral project for joint commemorations of events revered in both states).[14] Post-2017, the MOC-OA's Ilinden speeches can be interpreted as a minor reapproval of the aforementioned developments. The 2017, 2018 and 2019 speeches have stressed the 'spiritual' dimension of the 1903 Ilinden Uprising, while the 2018 speech placed an accent on the Orthodox Christian passages in the Kruševo Manifesto (N/A 2018). The 2019 Ilinden speech also contained a particular formula for the MOC-OA to endorse the second Ilinden that interpreted the AANLM as an event that had 'opened the possibility' to establishing a Macedonian Church (N/A 2019a).

The Mara Buneva commemorations

A Skopje-based assassination

The shifting MOC-OA discourse on the Ilinden commemorations illustrates the Church's alignment with the official memory policies in contemporary North Macedonia. Moreover, as discussed, during the second VMRO-DPMNE government, the MOC-OA not only followed the dominant political memory but also contributed to a certain recreation of the late socialist and early post-Yugoslav commemorative model of the Ilinden commemorations. However, even though the early 2000s Ilinden commemorations were identified as particular attempts to raise the ecclesiastical issues on the state agenda, one has to look at local mnemonic developments in North Macedonia to better understand the MOC-OA's stances on the contested historical points in recent Macedonian history. The relatively small, Skopje-based commemorations of Mara Buneva, which have taken place from 2001 onwards, present a perfect research opportunity for analyzing these dynamics.

Since 2001, almost every 13 January, a commemorative plaque dedicated to Mara Buneva has been mounted – and demolished, on several occasions – in the very city centre of Skopje. Buneva (1902–28), who was affiliated to the interwar Internal Macedonian Revolutionary Organization's (IMRO's) right wing, is famous for her assassination of Velmir Prelić (1883–1928), a high-ranking representative of the Kingdom of Serbs, Croats and Slovenes (Kingdom of SCS) on the territory of today's North Macedonia. Buneva committed suicide immediately after the assassination, while Prelić died in the local hospital just a few hours after the assault (N/A 1928). Coming from a wealthy family from Tetovo, a city located in northwest North Macedonia, Buneva was raised in the Bulgarian Exarchate spirit and managed to establish contact with the IMRO through one of her older brothers, who served as a military trainer at the organization.[15] A memorial plaque has been set every year at the point where Buneva committed the assassination, on the right bank of the River Vardar, which flows through the centre of Skopje, as a finale to the one-day commemorative ceremony. Even though this event is of a partisan character, it has continued to provoke reactions among the Macedonian public. A recent development, however, has led to a turnaround in Buneva's posthumous status. After being the subject of a counter-mnemonic practice for almost two decades, she has now been officially recognized as a national martyr. In this section, I look at the role the MOC-OA has performed in the socio-political developments over Buneva's commemorations and her historical role in the Macedonian historical and mnemonic canon.

After the ill-fated 1903 Ilinden Uprising, the cleavages within the revolutionary organization deepened, contributing to its demise on the eve of the First World War. In the aftermath of the war, an activist network emerged in Petrich/Pirin Macedonia (part of today's Republic of Bulgaria), which called itself the IMRO and claimed its right to the legacy of the pre-Ilinden organization, thereby managing to consolidate a strong regional core. However, in the aftermath of the First World War, what is North Macedonia today become part of the post-Versailles Kingdom of SCS. The kingdom fostered the process of integrating the local population into the Serbian *ethnie* and the new South Slav (Yugoslav) *politie*. However, the governing mode of the Serbian authorities in the new 'South Serbian' territories was de facto colonial, so cultural differences were suppressed and repressive police measures introduced (for an overview, see Boškovska 2017). In the 1920s, the first youth counter-hegemonic groups started to appear, often operating with the institutional support, and within the underground network, of the Petrich-based IMRO. Despite its ephemerality, the Macedonian Youth Secret Revolutionary Organization (MYSRO), one of the first groups of its kind, won wider recognition after a state purge followed by 'brutal' legal proceedings against its members (Todorovski 1998; see also Gyuzelev 1942 for a direct account). This legal process should be read as a focal point for the assassination carried out by Mara Buneva, as the IMRO issued a 'death penalty' against Prelić, the main prosecutor in the legal proceedings, and Buneva was 'instructed and sent by the IMRO' to execute the punishment (Trajanovski 2015).

The oblivion and memory of Mara Buneva

Ivan (Vančo) Mihajlov (1896–1990), who headed the IMRO from 1924 until 1934, acts as the key dramatis persona in the narrative of the political assassination. Mihajlov had immediately endorsed the assassination carried out by Buneva and claimed responsibility for the event. This endorsement was a direct outcome of the IMRO's activism under Mihajlov's leadership. During the period of his tenure, the Petrich region 'became virtually autonomous', and it was from this base that the 'IMRO launched raids into Greece and Yugoslavia' (Hall 2014, 187–88). Mihajlov also managed to eliminate the intra-organizational

232 Naum Trajanovski

ideological wings and consolidate his power through a 'regime of terrorism', which resulted in a series of assassinations of both 'unsuitable' party members and the IMRO's enemies (for more, see Frusetta 2003). The interwar terrorism and anti-regime activism had further developed into a pro-occupational stance by the time of the Second World War. Thus, in the 1940s, Mihajlov was claimed to be an informal advisor to the Independent State of Croatia's (NDH) Ante Pavelić (Banac 1993), a friendship which can be traced back to the MYSRO trials, during which the latter served as the group's attorney (Kisić Kolanović 2003). Therefore, after the establishment of the post–Second World War Macedonian state within the Second Yugoslavia, Mihajlov's name became one of the most contentious in Macedonian late modern history.[16] Consequently, post-war Macedonian historiography treated Mihajlov's anti-communist activism, his terrorist modus operandi and his network of associates as a 'symbolic pollution' of the national canon (Brown 2004).[17] Mara Buneva and the memory of her act were only present in the wartime martyrology of Mihajlov's IMRO. At the same time, a monument to her was erected in Skopje by the Bulgarian authorities. In the aftermath of the war, the monument was immediately demolished, and local memory of Buneva was thus 'sentenced to oblivion' (Bechev 2009, 35).

In the post–Second World War period, Buneva's historical legacy was endorsed by the politically active pro-Mihajlovist diaspora (see Andonovski 2003). After the fall of the communist regimes in the Balkans, a Bulgarian-based political party titled the Internal Macedonian Revolutionary Organization – Union of Macedonian Association (VMRO-UMA), which appealed to 'Bulgarians of Macedonian origin' (Frusetta 2003, 119; Nedeva and Kaytchev 2001), started to claim the right to Mara Buneva's legacy. A women's organization titled 'Mara Buneva' emerged under the aegis of the VMRO-UMA in the early 1990s, while the party also published a 16-page brochure on Buneva as one of their first publishing endeavours (Gosheva 1994).[18] There is no doubt that in North Macedonia there were no social actors cultivating the memory of Buneva in the first post-Yugoslav decade. Moreover, it is also hard to trace any change in public perceptions of interwar rightist activism in the initial Macedonian post-Yugoslav historiography. However, in the 2000s, two developments led to a shift in the mnemopolitical treatment of Buneva in North Macedonia. On the one hand, an association of 'Bulgarians in Macedonia' titled Radko (Mihajlov's pseudonym) was established in the Macedonian city of Ohrid in 2000. It was the members of this association who initiated the very first post-socialist commemoration of Mara Buneva in Skopje in 2001.[19] On the other hand, one can trace a significant shift in the VMRO-DPMNE's mnemopolitical stance on the eve of the 2006 governmental elections. The partisan call to promote rightist 'therapeutics', or in other words to accentuate the 'movement's own victims' (Sarkanjac 2011, 115), can be read as a rationale for the aforementioned process, which eventually sent major tremors through Macedonian memory politics during the second VMRO-DPMNE government's tenure (2006–16).

Official quests, vernacular answers 233

The religious service and the political message

Returning to the Buneva commemorations, it is crucial to mention that the commemorative events in Skopje followed a pattern instigated by Mihajlov himself. In his memoirs and interviews, Mihajlov pleaded for an annual Skopje-based commemoration of Buneva by Bulgarian patriotic youth, who were 'supposed to lay fresh flowers at the assassination spot' (Andonovski 2003). This initiative was picked up and further developed by VMRO-UMA affiliates. In the early 1990s, for instance, Ekaterina Gosheva advocated the recreation in Skopje of the 'missing' religious service dedicated to Buneva. Consequently, the first commemorative ritual commenced in 2001 with a religious service at the Skopje-based Orthodox Church of St Demetrious, which was near the assassination site. This was followed by an act honouring the assassinator herself, which was carried out at the actual assassination spot. From 2002 onwards, the commemorating group also mounted a memorial plaque at the same spot – a ritualogy that was actively performed until the most recent commemorations. This ritualogy of recreating the 'missing religious service' dedicated to Buneva can be viewed as a quest to establish an 'accountability' process which, according to Katherine Verdery, involves dead bodies in efforts to 'determine the historical truth, which many accuse socialism of having suppressed' (1999, 38). However, the Macedonian public struggled to endorse the Skopje-based Buneva commemorations in the 2000s. For instance, in 2002 and 2003, the commemorative plaque was demolished just hours after the commemorative events (Popovski 2002). Moreover, although the public discourse against the early 2000s commemorations stressed the crucial contribution the Church of St Demetrious had made by facilitating the event, few commentators noticed that this contribution went against ecclesiastical rules forbidding the provision of a religious service for a person who had committed suicide (for more, see Trajanovski 2015). On the other hand, in the aftermath of the 2001 conflict, several voices of concern were raised about the informal, partisan 'worshipping' of historical figures. It was argued that the 'Buneva case' set a precedent for future mnemonic activities by 'other minority groups' (N/A 2001).

The annual ceremony's public reception during the 2000s was marked by a strict discursive line of division between the intruders commemorating Buneva in Skopje and the opposition to the commemorative events. This juxtaposition was mostly created by the Macedonian media and public intellectuals who aligned their arguments with earlier interpretations of Buneva's role in the local historical context (see Trajanovski 2015). A build-up of tensions came to a head in 2007, when the group commemorating Buneva clashed with a group opposing the commemorative event, culminating in approximately fifteen people being injured and an official note from the Bulgarian embassy in Skopje. These occurrences overlapped with the VMRO-DPMNE's second period of government which, as mentioned, attempted to condemn the Macedonian national canon in the mid- to late 2000s. The Mara Buneva commemorations, their mobilizing potential and the media attention they provoked in the course of the 2000s acted as a trigger for the political reimagination of the IMRO's rightist interwar activism, leading to their instrumentalization within the domestic constellation of political power. The political operation of reimagining Buneva's historical role also drew upon the work of a new, rightist-leaning generation of Macedonian historiographers who started in the early 2000s to promote the thesis of an 'unscientific' division between the two ideological camps of the interwar Macedonian political activism, thus rewriting the assassination carried out by Mara Buneva in 1928 as the 'highest moral act, a heroic deed' (the key text here is Todorovski 2008). Furthermore, the assassination, as a contextual framework, was relegitimized as 'a segment of IMRO's terrorism against the Serbian occupational government', with the focus being placed on the act's bravery and how it encompassed the political credo of the Mihajlovist IMRO (Todorovski 2008). This discursive reshuffling from the late 2000s and early 2010s resulted in a more structured approach to the 'Bulgarian provocateurs' in 2014 and their religious service dedicated to Buneva in 'Macedonian churches' (N/A 2014). As of 2015, the major Buneva commemorations have been organized by rightist ethnic Macedonian non-governmental organizations that would be instrumental in the protests against the replacement of the VMRO-DPMNE-led government in 2017, while a separate commemorative event was organized by the 'Bulgarian Cultural Club' in Skopje.

The MOC-OA played a key role in facilitating the shift in attitude towards the Buneva commemorations in Skopje, their public perception and official endorsement. The MOC-OA, unarguably, followed its institutional agenda in the case of the Buneva commemorations in a rather clearer manner than it had with the Ilinden commemorations. More precisely, the MOC-OA hosted the religious services dedicated to Buneva that were organized by the various sets of commemorative groups and mnemonic communities, highlighting, as such, its opposition to the national historical canon established in socialist Macedonia. From a historiographic perspective, the MOC-OA's perception of Buneva as an antagonist to its clerical archenemy, the communist regime, created the symbolic base required to reclaim her deed as the act of a national Christian martyr, thereby legitimating the religious services in Skopje. Furthermore, the MOC-OA contributed to this narrative shift by allowing, or to a lesser degree, not reacting to, the media's use of religious discourse regarding the Buneva commemorations. The religious service dedicated to Buneva (along with the commemorative event as a whole) was depicted as a *Parastos* up until the mid-2000s, while from 2007 onwards it was defined as a *Panikhida* (more in Trajanovski 2015). Even though recent Macedonian Orthodox Christian literature tends to present the Parastos and Panikhida as synonymous, one crucial *differentia specifica* is traceable when the two concepts are transplanted to the public–private axis. Parastos, in this context, implies a smaller gathering, usually reserved for a nuclear family ('relatives and close family members'). Conversely, Panikhida suggests a rather public ceremony suitable for commemorating renowned and public figures (see e.g. the official interpretation by the MOC-OA's St Annunciation Church in Prilep in N/A 2013b).

Finally, in line with the MOC-OA's approach to the post-2001 Ilinden commemorations, the Church's role in the Buneva commemorations was amplified during the second VMRO-DPMNE government. Even though the MOC-OA has actively held religious services dedicated to Buneva (attended by various groups) in the past two decades, MOC-OA priests have only led participants in the commemorations from the Church of St Demetrious to the assassination spot in recent years, thus setting the tone for the commemorative event in toto. When asked if it was aware of the scope and implications of these activities, the MOC-OA responded in an official statement from 2014 as follows:

> the Church does not have a right to refuse such a demand. Our task is to pray for everyone. We do not have a right to judge the past or politics. We are not interested in that. The Church is above all politics, all parties, all nations. We are indeed unhappy about this event's politicization. We are not happy that this temple is being called a "Bulgarian church", but our task is to treat every Christian equally. The Christian Church is open to everyone.[20]
>
> (Stankovik 2014)

Concluding remarks

This chapter mapped two developments in the memory politics of post-2001 North Macedonia – the official state Ilinden commemorations and the Mara Buneva commemorations – to determine the role played by the MOC-OA as a 'memory actor' in both these remembrance events. The common denominator in the MOC-OA's mnemonic engagement is its positioning as an agent promoting an ethno-centred historical reading of the Macedonian twentieth century, oftentimes hostile not only to the leftist figures and events from this particular period but also to the actual national canon established in the two post–Second World War Macedonian decades. However, the MOC-OA has rarely issued openly divisive statements or comments, tending instead to underline its role as an all-encompassing institution in contemporary Macedonian society. This discursive inclusivity has not always translated into practice, as shown by the discussion on the MOC-OA's approach to the post-2001 history of the Ilinden and Mara Buneva commemorations. In this case, the local Buneva commemorations were identified as a ceremony that brought to light the Church's opposition to Macedonian society's dominant segment, which was unsympathetic to the commemorative event in the 2000s. Moreover, following the political endorsement of both Buneva's historical role and the event commemorating her, the Church's affiliates got more involved in the commemorations, not only facilitating the religious ceremony, but also leading the cohort of participants to the assassination spot, thus, at the very least extrapolating the religious dimension of the event to the field of the ongoing political struggle. The post-2001 Ilinden commemorations were discussed in this chapter as another example of the MOC-OA's discursive amplification and political realignment within the recent Macedonian context. In the early 2000s, the MOC-OA used Ilinden as

236 *Naum Trajanovski*

a platform to address bilateral and ecclesiastical issues. As soon as the VMRO-DPMNE took power in 2006, the MOC-OA assumed a more active role in the state-sponsored annual commemorations.

Notes

1 The new name for the state and the subsequent ethnic and national adjectives came into use following the 2018 Greco-Macedonian Name Agreement.

2 Both treaties, as part of their commitment to bilateral partnership, seek to enhance cooperation between neighbouring states through the joint revision of history textbooks and public memorials.

3 I employ 'mnemopolitical' as a construct denoting the present-day political interpretations of a particular historical event, enabling me to focus on 'the past as it is remembered' within the political space (more in Tamm 2015).

4 The prehistory of the MOC-OA dates back to the ninth century, a period when the Orthodox Church operated as an autonomous entity under the tutelage of the Ecumenical Patriarch of Constantinople (1019–1767). The abolishment of the Church was announced by decree of Sultan Mustapha III, at the request of the Ecumenical Patriarch of Constantinople. More in Trajanovski (2001).

5 Kubik and Bernhard identify four types of mnemonic actor (warrior, pluralist, abnegator and prospective) and, depending on the actors prevailing in the present constellation, three memory regimes (fractured, pillarized and unified).

6 The authors of the introductory chapter to a book on post-conflict studies introduce the notion of 'memorialization' as one of four processes or modalities seen to be 'operating both continuously *within* post-conflict periods, and simultaneously *upon* the very periodization of conflict and post-conflict as discontinuous'. Memorialization along these lines is denoted as a 'form of missionization carried out by the local actors that focus on memory' (Gagnon, Senders and Brown 2014, 9). The resemblance between the aforementioned construct and 'memory entrepreneur' activism can be suggested within this context, even though the authors do not develop their argument in this direction.

7 The library depositories used in the writing of this chapter are the Braka Miladinovci City Library in Skopje, the St Kliment of Ohrid National and University Library and the Library of the Macedonian Academy of Sciences and Arts.

8 Ilinden was also proposed as a potential solution to the Greco-Macedonian dispute in 2018 over the naming of the state. The regional media came up with the name 'Republic of Ilinden Macedonia' as a compromise solution reached on the sidelines of the EU–Western Balkans summit in Sofia in May 2018. However, Athens officially condemned the proposal shortly after the summit, while the Macedonian oppositional camp criticized the initiative, highlighting the constitutional changes contained within the proposed agreement (more in Kokkinidis 2018).

9 See the writings of Dimo Hadži Dimov and Krste Petkov Misirkov, publications by the Macedonian émigrés' circles in Sofia in the 1920s, the first studies by Hristo Siljanov, Kosta Veselinov and Angel Dinev in the 1930s and the literary interpretations by Nikola Kirov Majski.

10 A brief look at the party programmes from the 1990s shows that almost all ethnic Macedonian political entities had Ilinden or the so-called Ilinden ideal on their political agendas (for more, see Timovski and Stefanovski 1990).

11 The monastery saga's prehistory holds a peculiar place in the border demarcation debates from 1946 until the termination of the agreement for using the monastery's facilities for commemorative purposes in 1986 (for more, see Džikov and Todorovski 1990; Džikov 2004).

12 The full 2001 Amendment VII to the Macedonian Constitution reads: '(1) The Macedonian Orthodox Church, as well as the Islamic Religious Community in Macedonia, the Catholic Church, Evangelical Methodist Church, the Jewish Community and other Religious communities and groups are separate from the state and equal before the law.

Official quests, vernacular answers 237

(2) The Macedonian Orthodox Church, as well as the Islamic Religious Community in Macedonia, the Catholic Church, Evangelical Methodist Church, the Jewish Community and other Religious communities and groups are free to establish schools and other social and charitable institutions, by way of a procedure regulated by law. (3) Item 1 of this amendment replaces paragraph 3 of Article 19 and Item 2 replaces paragraph 4 of Article 19 of the Constitution of the Republic of Macedonia' (Macedonian Constitution 1991, amend. VII).

13 The incompatibility between the two opposing positions was clearest when the VMRO-DPMNE's Ivica Bocevski, a governmental spokesman, responded to accusations of party-centred Ilinden rhetoric and politicized mobilization during the Ilinden commemorations by stressing that 'the time when the national holidays were within a single subject's domain' was 'long gone' (Gorǵevski 2007).

14 In 2018, the Kruševo event was led by the parliamentary speaker, Talat Xhaferi, himself an ethnic Albanian, who stressed the 'multicultural and multiconfessional constant' of the two Ilindens, while the VMRO-DPMNE official boycotted the ceremony.

15 Her other brother lived in Serbia and was reported to be loyal to the Kingdom of SCS's regime (for more, see Todorovski 1998; Ačkoska and Žežov 2004, 250–86; Cvetanoski 2012, 291–309).

16 Mihajlov was offered the opportunity to establish an independent Macedonian state by Nazi Germany in the final phases of the Second World War. His communication with the Nazi authorities and his visit to Skopje in 1944 are well noted in Macedonian historiography (see Troebst 2002).

17 Buneva, for instance, is neither mentioned in the writings of the Macedonian Institute of National History in the Yugoslav period (the first edition of the 1969 three-volume *History of the Macedonian People* may serve as a reference point) nor specialized publications on the wartime assassinations (see e.g. Ciriviri 1969).

18 The party was renamed the VMRO-Bulgarian National Movement in 1998. Nowadays, the VMRO-BNM is a member of the European Conservatives and Reformists group and, as part of the United Patriots political alliance, has been a member of the Bulgarian governing coalition since 2017.

19 The association was banned the following year (March 2001) after a scandal which occurred at the inaugural event (N/A 2009). In 2009, the European Court of Human Rights ruled in favour of the association. Vladimir Pankov, the erstwhile head of Radko stated, in the wake of the decision, that 'the Bulgarians can never be a minority to some so-called Macedonians' (N/A 2009).

20 Translated from Macedonian to English by the author of this chapter.

References

Ačkoska, V., and N. Žežov. 2004. *Predavstvata I atentatite vo makedonskata istorija*, 250–86. Skopje: Makavej.

Aleksov, B. 2010. "The Serbian Orthodox Church: Haunting Past and Challenging Future." *International Journal for the Study of the Christian Church* 10 (2–3): 176–91.

Andonovski, V. 2003. *Sto godini segašnost*. Skopje: Kultura.

Angelovska, M., and R. Cacanoska. 2020. "The Macedonian Orthodox Church and the Crossroads Between the External Denials and Internal Challenges." *Occasional Papers on Religion in Eastern Europe* 40 (5): 96–107.

Assmann, A. 2008. "Transformations Between History and Memory." *Social Research* 75 (1): 41–72.

Banac, I. 1993. *The National Question in Yugoslavia: Origins, History, Politics*, 307–28. Ithaca, NY: Cornell University Press.

Barišić, S. 2016. "The Role of the Serbian and Russian Orthodox Churches in Shaping Governmental Policies." In *The Warp of Serbian Identity: Anti-Westernism, Russophilia,*

238 *Naum Trajanovski*

Traditionalism . . ., edited by S. Biserko, 105–28. Belgrade: Helsinki Committee for Human Rights.

Bechev, D. 2009. *Historical Dictionary of the Republic of Macedonia*, 35. Lanham, Toronto and Plymouth: The Scarecrow Press.

Bieber, F. 2008. "Power-Sharing and the Implementation of the Ohrid Framework Agreement." In *Power-Sharing and the Implementation of the Ohrid Framework Agreement*, edited by S. Dehnert and R. Sulejmani, 7–41. Skopje: Friedrich Ebert Stiftung.

Blaževska, K. 2017. "MPC blagodarna na Majkata-Crkva BPC." *Deutsche Welle – North Macedonia*, November 27.

Bogumił, Z., and M. Głowacka-Grajper. 2019. *Milieux de mémoire in Late Modernity: Local Communities, Religion and Historical Politics*, 15–48. Berlin: Peter Lang.

Boškovska, N. 2017. *Yugoslavia and Macedonia before Tito: Between Repression and Integration*. London: I. B. Tauris.

Broun, J. 2004. "The Bulgarian Orthodox Church: The Continuing Schism and the Religious, Social and Political Environment." *Religion, State and Society* 32 (3): 209–45.

Brown, K. S. 2003. *The Past in Question: Modern Macedonia and the Uncertainties of Nation*. Princeton, NJ: Princeton University Press.

———. 2004. "Villains and Symbolic Pollution in the Narratives of Nations. The Case of Boris Sarafov." In *Balkan Identities: Nation and Memory*, edited by M. Todorova, 233–53. New York: New York University Press.

———. 2000. "A Rising to Count On: Ilinden Between Politics and History in Post-Yugoslav Macedonia." In *The Macedonian Question: Culture, Historiography, Politics*, edited by V. Roudometof, 143–72. New York: Columbia University Press.

Brunnbauer, U. 2002. "The Implementation of the Ohrid Agreement: Ethnic Macedonian Resentments." *Journal on Ethnopolitics and Minority Issues in Europe* 1 (1): 2–25.

———. 2004. "Historiography, Myths and the Nation in the Republic of Macedonia." In *(Re)Writing History. Historiography in Southeast Europe after Socialism*, edited by U. Brunnbauer, 165–200. Münster: LIT Studies on South East Europe.

Buchenau, K. 2005. "What Went Wrong? Church-State Relations in Socialist Yugoslavia." *Nationalities Papers: The Journal of Nationalism and Ethnicity* 33 (4): 547–67.

Čairović, I. 2018. "The Role of Vicar Bishop Dositej (Stojković) at the Beginning of the Church Schism in Macedonia in 1958." *Istorija 20. veka* 36 (2): 155–86.

Cepreganov, T., M. Angelovska-Panova, and D. Zajkovski. 2014. "The Macedonian Orthodox Church." In *Eastern Christianity and Politics in the Twenty-First Century*, edited by L. N. Leustean, 426–39. London: Routledge.

Cepreganov, T., and P. Shashko. 2010. "The Macedonian Orthodox Church." In *Eastern Christianity and the Cold War, 1945–91*, edited by L. N. Leustean, 173–88. London: Routledge.

Ciriviri, K. 1969. *Političkite ubistva vo Makedonija*. Preševo: Progres.

Cvetanoski, V. 2012. *VMRO Slava I Raskol*, 291–309. Struga: IRIS.

Cvitković, S., and M. Kline. 2017. "Skopje: Rebranding the Capital City through Architecture and Monuments to Remake the Nation Brand." *Sociologija I prostor* 55 (1): 33–53.

Dimevski, S. 1965. *Crkovna istorija na makedonskiot narod*. Skopje: Makedonska pravoslavna crkva.

———. 1989. *Istorijata na Makedonskata pravoslavna crkva*. Skopje: Makedonska kniga.

Dimova, R. 2006. "Rights and Size: Ethnic Minorities, Nation-States and the International Community in the Past and Present Macedonia." *Zeitschrift für Ethnologie* 131 (2): 277–99.

Džikov, S. 2004. "Zošto e premolčano prisvojuvanjeto na manastirot?" *Dnevnik*, July 31.

Džikov, S., and G. Todorovski. 1990. "Makedonskiot manastir Prohor Pčinjski: Dokumenti I argument." *Treta Programa Radio Skopje* 44: 11–36.

Frusetta, J. 2003. "Bomb-Throwers and Cookie-Pushers: American Diplomats, the Macedonian Question and the Perceptions of Violence, 1919–1941." *Balkan Studies* 4 (1): 3–17.

Gagnon, C., S. Senders, and K. Brown. 2014. "Introduction." In *Post-Conflict Studies: An Interdisciplinary Approach*, edited by C. Gagnon and K. Brown, 1–16. London: Routledge.

Gensburger, S. 2016. *National Policy, Global Memory. The Commemoration of the "Righteous" from Jerusalem to Paris, 1942–2007*, 35–81. New York: Berghahn.

Georgievski, Lj. 2001. *Ostvaruvanje na vekovniot son*. Skopje: NIP Nova Literatura.

Gjorgjevski, Gj. 2017. "Macedonian Orthodox Church in the Context of Balkan and European Orthodoxy." *Occasional Papers on Religion in Eastern Europe* 37 (4): 1–17.

Gorgevski, B. 2007. "SDSM go obvini Gruevski deka se otkažal od ASNOM." *Dnevnik*, July 31.

Gosheva, E. 1994. *Mara Buneva: Zhivot I Delo*. Sofia: VMRO-SMD.

Graan, A. 2016. "The Nation Brand Regime: Nation Branding and the Semiotic Regimentation of Public Communication in Contemporary Macedonia." *Sign and Society* 4 (S1): S70–S105.

Gyuzelev, D. 1942. *Zhertvite na skopskiya studentski proces*. Skopje: Kraynichanec.

Hall, R. C. 2014. *War in the Balkans: An Encyclopedic History from the Fall of the Ottoman Empire to the Breakup of Yugoslavia*. Santa Barbara: ABC-CLIO.

Hilton Saggau, E. 2018. "Unblocking the Sacred: New Perspectives on the Religious Revival in South Eastern Europe." *Religion and Society in Central and Eastern Europe* 11 (1): 39–55.

Hozić, A. A. 2014. "It Happened Elsewhere: Remembering 1989 in the Former Yugoslavia." In *Twenty Years After Communism: The Politics of Memory and Commemoration*, edited by J. Kubik and M. Bernhard, 233–61. Oxford: Oxford University Press.

Ilievski, B. 2012. "The Macedonian-Serbian Church Conflict from 1945 to the Present." In *Re-Sakralisierung des öffentlichen Raums in Südosteuropa nach der Wende 1989?* edited by A. Ivanišević, 133–45. Berlin: Peter Lang.

Ilievski, D. 1972. *Avtokefalnosta na Makedonskata pravoslavna crkva*. Skopje: Nova Makedonija.

Irwin, Z. T. 2019. "The Macedonian Orthodox Church in the New Millennium." In *Orthodox Churches and Politics in Southeastern Europe: Nationalism, Conservativism, and Intolerance*, edited by S. P. Ramet, 167–97. London: Palgrave Macmillan.

Iveković, I. 2002. "Nationalism and the Political Use and Abuse of Religion: The Politicization of Orthodoxy, Catholicism and Islam in Yugoslav Successor States." *Social Compass* 49 (4): 523–36.

Kaiser, W. 2012. "The European Parliament as an Institutional Memory Entrepreneur." In *A Value-Driven European Future*, edited by L. Bekemans, 113–24. Brussels: European Interuniversity Press.

Katzenstein, P. 2014. "Foreword." In *Post-Conflict Studies: An Interdisciplinary Approach*, edited by C. Gagnon and K. Brown, xi–xiii. London: Routledge.

Kisić Kolanović, N. 2003. *Zagreb-Sofija: Prijateljstvo po mjeri ratnog vremena 1941–1945*, 91–122. Zagreb: Hrvatski Državni Arhiv.

Kokkinidis, T. 2018. "Greece Rejects 'Republic of Ilinden Macedonia' Proposal." *Greek Reporter*, May 20.

Kostovski, S. 2003. "Church and State in Macedonia." In *Law and Religion in Post-Communist Europe*, edited by S. Ferrari and W. C. Durham, 197–214. Leuven, Paris and Dudley, MA: Peeters.

Krindatch, A. D. 2002. "Orthodox (Eastern Christian) Churches in the United States at the Beginning of a New Millennium: Questions of Nature, Identity, and Mission." *Journal for the Scientific Study of Religion* 41 (3): 533–63.

Kubik, J., and M. Bernhard. 2014a. "A Theory of the Politics of Memory." In *Twenty Years After Communism: The Politics of Memory and Commemoration*, edited by J. Kubik and M. Bernhard, 7–37. Oxford: Oxford University Press.

240 *Naum Trajanovski*

———. 2014b. "The Politics and Culture of Memory Regimes. A Comparative Analysis." In *Twenty Years After Communism: The Politics of Memory and Commemoration*, edited by J. Kubik and M. Bernhard, 7–37. Oxford: Oxford University Press.

Kuzmanovska, M. 2003. "Srpskata nota se izgubi na patot Belgrad-Skopje: Vistinata skriena pod mantija." *Večer*, July 25: 3.

Latifi, V. 2001. "Religious Strife Fuels Macedonian Conflict." *IWPR's Balkan Crisis Report* 262 (1).

Leustean, L. N. 2008. "Orthodoxy and Political Myths in Balkan National Identities." *National Identities* 10 (4): 421–32.

Lewis, P. G. 2001. *Political Parties in Post-Communist Eastern Europe*, 1–60. London: Routledge.

Majewski, P. 2015. "Kruševo – Pomiędzy Świętym Miastem Macedońskiego Nacjonalizmu a Pierwszym 'Ethnomiastem' w Europie." *Lud* 99: 161–84.

Marinkoviḱ, S. 1974. "Vrz Gumenje kaj Kruševo: Hram na slobodata." *Nova Makedonija*, July 27: 12–14.

Matevska, D. 2011. "The Relationship Between the Political and Religious Elite in Contemporary Macedonian Society." *Politics and Religion Journal* 5 (1): 129–40.

Mihajlovski, G. "Šengen filozofija." *Dnevnik*, August 8.

Morée, P. 2005. "Identity, Religion and Human Rights in the Balkans. The Macedonian Case of Archbishop Jovan in Its Broader Context." *Helsinki Monitor* 16 (4): 287–96.

N/A. 1928. "Atentat na Prav. Ref. G. Prelića." *Stara Srbija*, January 14: 2.

———. 1999. "Gligorov go odbra ASNOM mesto Ilinden." *Večer*, July 28: 2.

———. 2001. "Panihida I istoriski čas za Mara Buneva." *Večer*, January 15.

———. 2004. "SPC ḱe dozvoli poseta na Prohor Pčinjski pod tri uslovi." *A1*, July 31.

———. 2006a. "Bunt protiv nepravdata." *Vreme*, August 1.

———. 2006b. "Ilindensko poslanie." *Makedonska Pravoslavna Crkva*, July 21.

———. 2007a. "Naroden sobir vo crkvata Sv. Prorok Ilija vo Aerodrom." *Dnevnik*, August 1.

———. 2007b. "Otvoren i osveten patot kon Mileniumskiot krst." *Vreme*, August 1.

———. 2009. "Makedonija go zagubi sporot so bugarofilite od Radko." *A1*, January 15.

———. 2010. "Ilindensko poslanie." *PreminPortal*, August 2.

———. 2013a. "Ilindensko poslanie." *MPC.org*, July 26.

———. 2013b. "Slovo za parastosite." *Blagovesti – Oficijalen blog na crkvata Sv. Blagoveštenie Prilep*, April 25.

———. 2014. "Iskršena spomen pločata za Mara Buneva." *Deutsche Welle – Macedonia*, January 13.

———. 2015. "Ilindensko poslanie." *Prespansko-Pelagoniska Pravoslavna Eparhija*, August 2.

———. 2016. "Ilindenskoto poslanie na Mitropolitot Prespansko-pelagoniski Petar." *Mocdanz.org*, August 6.

———. 2017. "Ilindensko poslanie." *MPC.org*, July 26.

———. 2018. "Ilindensko poslanie." *Makedonska pravoslavna crkva Ohridska arhiepiskopija Tetovsko-gostivarska eparhija*, July 31.

———. 2019a. "Ilindensko poslanie." *Pokajanie*, July 30.

———. 2019b. "Concept of One Society and Inter-Culturalism Focus of OSCE-Supported High-Level Conference in Skopje." *OSCE Mission to Skopje*, October 3.

Nedeva, I., and N. Kaytchev. 2001. "IMRO Groupings in Bulgaria After the Second World War." In *The New Macedonian Question*, edited by J. Pettifer, 167–84. Basingstoke: Palgrave Macmillan.

Pačkov, T. 1974. "Intenzivna izgradba na patot za Prohor Pčinjski." *Nova Makedonija*, July 26.

Paszkiewicz, J. 2016. "Polityczne aspekty sporu o status Macedońskiej Cerkwi Prawosławnej (MCP) (1991–2014)." *Poznańskie Studia Slawistyczne* 10 (1): 227–41.

Official quests, vernacular answers 241

Payne, D. P. 2007. "Nationalism and the Local Church: The Source of Ecclesiastical Conflict in the Orthodox Commonwealth." *Nationalities Papers: The Journal of Nationalism and Ethnicity* 35 (5): 831–52.

Popovska, D. 2015. *Spomenikot, memorijata I identiteto*. Skopje: Institut za Nacionalna Istorija.

Popovski, K. 2002. "Anonimen povik do Utrinski vesnik: Kavadarčanec tvrdi deka ja skršil pločata na Mara Buneva." *Utrinski vesnik*, January 17.

Ramet, S. 2017. "Macedonia's Post-Yugoslav Reality: Corruption, Wiretapping, and Stolen Elections." In *Building Democracy in the Yugoslav Successor States: Accomplishments, Setbacks, and Challenges Since 1990*, edited by S. Ramet and C. M. Hassenstab, 287–320. Cambridge: Cambridge University Press.

Risteski, Ǵ. 1991. "Ušte eden atak vrz manastirot Prohor Pčinjski: Srpska kujna preku trpezarija." *Večer*, July 23.

Risteski, Lj. 2009. "Recognition of the Independence of the Macedonian Orthodox Church (MOC) as an Issue Concerning Macedonian National Identity." *EthnoAnthropoZoom* 6 (1): 145–85.

Sarkanjac, B. 2011. *Doma – Idejata na konzervativizmot*. Skopje: Makavej.

Soldić, M. 2012. "Ilinden: Linking a Macedonian past, present and future." In *Transforming National Holidays. Identity Discourse in the West and South Slavic Countries, 1985–2010*, edited by Lj. Šarić, K. Gammelgaard and K. R. Hauge, 1912–13. Amsterdam: John Benjamins.

Spaskovska, Lj. 2011. "Macedonia's Nationals, Minorities and Refugees in the Post-Communist Labyrinths of Citizenship." *CITSEE Working Paper Series* 5: 1–27.

Stankoviḱ, S. 2014. "Nova spomen-ploča za Mara Buneva." *Voice of America – Macedonia*, January 12.

———. 2017. "BPC ḱe bide posrednik I ḱe ja zastapuva MPC." *Voice of America – Macedonia*, November 27.

Subotić, J. 2019. "The Church, the Nation, and the State: The Serbian Orthodox Church After Communism." In *Orthodox Churches and Politics in Southeastern Europe: Nationalism, Conservativism, and Intolerance*, edited by S. P. Ramet, 85–110. London: Palgrave Macmillan.

Tamm, M., ed. 2015. *Afterlife of Events: Perspectives on Mnemohistory*. Basingstoke: Palgrave Macmillan.

Timovski, V., and S. Stefanovski. 1990. *Političkite partii vo Makedonija*. Skopje: POS Sistem.

Todorovski, Z. 1998. *Vnatrešnata Makedonska Revolucionerna Organizacija 1924–193*. Skopje: IP "ROBZ".

———. 2008. *Id Ego Sum: Makedonski istoriski refleksii*. Skopje: Makedonska reč.

Trajanovski, A. 2001. *Crkovnata organizacija vo Makedonija I dviženjeto za vozobnovuvanje na Ohridskata arhiepiskopija od krajot na XVIII I vo tekot na XIX vek – do osnovanjeto na Vnatrešnata makedonska revolucionerna organizacija*. Skopje: Institut za Nacionalna Istorija.

———. 2008. *Vozobnovuvanje na Ohridskata arhiepiskopija kako Makedonska pravoslavna crkva I nejziniot šematizam: 50 godini od vozobnovuvanjeto na Ohridskata arhiepiskopija kako Makedonska pravoslavna crkva 1958–2008*. Skopje: Institut za Nacionalna Istorija.

Trajanovski, N. 2015. "Komemoracijata na Mara Buneva vo Skopje, verzija 2015: Diskurs analiza na makedonskite I bugarskite mediumi." *Politička misla* 49 (1): 55–67.

———. 2020a. "The Three Memory Regimes of Ilinden Commemorations (2001–2018): A Prolegomenon to the Study of the Official Memory in North Macedonia." *Southeastern Europe* 44 (1): 28–52.

———. 2020b. *Operacija Muzej: Muzejot na makedonskata borba I makedonskite politiki na seḱavanje*. Skopje: Templum.

242   *Naum Trajanovski*

Trencsényi, B. 2014. "Beyond Liminality? The Kulturkampf of the Early 2000s in East Central Europe." *Boundary* 2 (41): 135–52.

Troebst, S. 1997. "Yugoslav Macedonia 1943–1953: Building the Party, the State, and the Nation." In *State-Society Relations in Yugoslavia, 1945–1992*, edited by M. K. Bokovoy, J. A. Irvine and C. S. Lilly, 243–66. New York: St. Martin's Press.

———. 2002. " 'Führerbefehl!' – Adolf Hitler und die Proklamation eines unabhängigen Makedonien (September 1944): Eine archivalische Miszelle." *Osteuropa* 52 (4): 491–501.

Vangeli, A. 2010. "Religion, Nationalism and Counter-Secularization: The Case of the Macedonian Orthodox Church." *Identity Studies* 2 (1): 79–97.

Vasilevska, Ǵ. 2003. "Po sekoja cena, li, Sv. Prohor Pčinjski." *Večer*, July 29: 2.

Verdery, K. 1999. *The Political Lives of Dead Bodies: Reburial and Postsocialist Change*. New York: Columbia University Press.

Vukomanović, M. 2008. "The Serbian Orthodox Church as a Political Actor in the Aftermath of October 5, 2000." *Politics and Religion* 1 (2): 237–69.

Zdravkovski, A., and K. Morrison. 2014. "The Orthodox Churches of Macedonia and Montenegro: The Quest for Autocephaly." In *Religion and Politics in Post-Socialist Central and Southeastern Europe*, edited by S. P. Ramet, 240–62. London: Palgrave Macmillan.

Zelizer, B. 2014. "Memory as Foreground, Journalism as Background." In *Journalism and Memory*, edited by B. Zelizer and K. Tenenboim-Weinblatt, 32–50. Basingstoke: Palgrave Macmillan.

12 Negotiating the sacred at non-sites of memory. The religious imaginary of post-genocidal society

Karina Jarzyńska

The ongoing discussions about memory of the Holocaust in Poland rarely consider the religious factors influencing the formation and contemporary revisions of that memory (Leder 2013; Dobrosielski 2017; Żukowski 2018), and even when they do, they concentrate on the impact of the Catholic Church on this matter (Leociak 2018). This tendency could not only be understood as a consequence of the predominantly secular model of memory studies and the extremely few tools it has at its disposal for incorporating religion into the scope of its interest (see the introduction to this volume), but also as a symptom of wider problems with the interpretation of the history of religion in Poland after the Second World War. In this chapter, I will address both those issues on the basis of recent research that has been conducted as part of a larger project.[1]

The genocidal practices committed in 'the Bloodlands' in 1939–45 (Snyder 2010; Feierstein 2014) provoked various outcomes that affected the religious imaginaries that function in this region (Taylor 2007; Dieleman 2012). These outcomes, which were also caused by shifting political borders and the mass migration of people associated with particular denominations, were an important though not exclusive factor influencing changes in the habitus of the residents of Polish territory before and after the Second World War. Quantitative changes in the denominational structure of the state intersected with qualitative changes resulting from new territorial and hierarchical relations between religions, as well as from the theological and existential challenges that individuals and institutions faced after the anthropogenic catastrophe of the war. The most easily quantifiable consequence of these changes was the new position Roman Catholicism found itself in, mainly because of the dramatic decline in the number of followers of Judaism and, to a lesser extent, members of the Orthodox and Protestant Churches. However, the centralized nature of the Catholic Church, and its inclination to present itself as historically unchanged and internally coherent, continue to inhibit efforts to understand how the experience of genocide has influenced contemporary religious imagination and social practices in Poland.

Qualitative research proves to be of great help in exploring such problems, especially when it is conducted on a small scale and focused on specific locations and individuals. Such a project has been recently undertaken by Polish

DOI: 10.4324/9781003264750-15

244   *Karina Jarzyńska*

researchers, who elected to concentrate on non-sites of memory as a valuable diagnostic field. Roma Sendyka, the head of the project, has defined these phenomena as sites that experienced ideologically motivated violence that left its material trace in the form of human remains, yet at the same time, these sites were unmemorialized and barely visible. Despite this, they play a vital role in identity formation processes and fashioning attitudes towards the past; as such, those sites only appear to have been removed from social and cultural circulation (Sendyka 2015).

Non-sites of memory often occur when human remains that are present there belong to members of an ethnic group different to those currently living in the vicinity of the burial ground (Sendyka 2016). The scale and nature of genocidal violence, and the ethnic and religious diversity of its victims, make living near such places a challenge and their status usually remains liminal, oscillating between memory and forgetfulness and – as I attempt to show in this text – between the sacred and the profane. From the perspective of the functionalist theory of religion, the status of holiness is conferred on objects, persons or units of time and space as a consequence of social consensus legitimized by a broader frame of beliefs and practices guaranteed by religious institutions (Durkheim 2008; Boddy and Lambek 2013, 20–24). This essentially conservative mechanism does not preclude the modification of existing ritual-mythical complexes by individuals, sometimes accepted by a larger group, which may result in reformative or revolutionary changes. The stimulus for change can be individual or collective experience and/or a change in the values recognized by the group. The sacred – understood by functionalists to be derived from the community's ideas about itself and legitimized by the institutions it educates – disappears along with the community that created it. A social construct exists only insofar as there is a society to maintain it. In post-genocidal societies, therefore, far-reaching changes can be expected in what is considered sacred (Zawiła 2019, 15, 45–51; Zubrzycki 2006). Another reason for this is the wide spectrum of violence used by the perpetrators that brought about psychological states and attitudes, such as grief and trauma, which had traditionally been the preserve of religion (see Agadjanian in this volume). However, when faced with events that were unprecedented in both their scale and nature, individuals and groups decided to resort to a variety of innovative tactics in response.

There are several arguments for interpreting events and objects observed in the vicinity of non-sites of memory as religious. The first is how they are interpreted by the actors living in this context, who often reach for religious images and scripts of behaviour in spaces of post-genocidal burials. Second, this choice of interpretative framework accords with the observation of phenomenologists of religion that human remains and death are often valorized as sacred, because they provoke a questioning of relations between what is human and non-human (Leeuv 2014). That is also one of the premises for considering human remains as agential, an idea developed by Ewa Domańska using the notion of *necros*, which was designed to destabilize the dichotomy between the dead and living matter and perceive the history of human remains as a complicated process of

Negotiating the sacred at non-sites   245

'unbecoming human' (Domańska 2019; Latour 2005; Laqueur 2015). As long as this process is still ongoing, the *necros* is the object/subject of a potential sacralization. Yet, if the remains in question belong to a former member of the religious group that is now absent from the area of its burial, it is less likely that a memory actor of a different faith will treat them as sacred.

According to Mary Douglas, unmemorialized genocide sites should be considered anomalies in the conventional spatial order (Douglas 1966). Owing to the violent transgression of social norms that took place there, and the absence of any ritual that could have neutralized this, they can be perceived as impure. Their troublesome nature is reinforced by the already mentioned ethnic otherness of the victims in relation to the contemporary habitants of the area. As such, these places are considered dangerous and demand to be marked, isolated and 'familiarized' through the order of myth and ritual (Eliade 1961). An alternative strategy for dealing with their potential sacredness is their profanation, understood as a violation of the boundaries between the sacred and the secular to destroy the former and restore the object into the sphere of everyday life. As far as the examined sites are concerned, one would expect that strategy to be chosen more often, the greater the threat the local community perceives in a given location. The 'alien' *sacrum* may undermine the identity of the community and, as such, be perceived as unwanted. Yet, the well-recognized ambivalent logic of the sacred should encourage memory scholars to keep their minds open to the wide spectrum of individual responses to such phenomena (Otto 1970).

It is local, small-scale observations that can, I believe, enable researchers to see and describe subtle shifts in the post-genocidal, contaminated landscape of contemporary Poland (Pollack 2014) and ultimately ask questions about the function religion performs in the memory culture of the societies living there (see also Bogumił and Głowacka-Grajper 2019). Inspired by Agnieszka Pasieka, I am primarily interested in the experienced religion of individuals and small groups, for whom the doctrine and practices codified by official institutions merely provide a context (Pasieka 2015). While researching non-sites of memory, our team conducted conversations with members of the respective communities and observed their practices (both commemorative and otherwise), but we also paid close attention to the material qualities of the sites themselves, treating them as legitimate actors of memory culture (Schuppli 2020). I believe the network of interrelations between various human and non-human subjects can be better understood by adopting the notion of 'religious imaginary', as developed by Thomas Csordas. This notion is particularly useful for capturing the individual religiosity resulting from the process of embodiment of the contact with sacred space. Csordas also emphasizes the influence of charismatic people, who interpret the individual experience (Csordas 1990; Lubańska 2018).

The gathered material provoked many questions, but I would like to concentrate on three: How do members of local communities deal with the ambivalence characteristic of non-sites of memory? How does the religious identity of the victims buried in non-sites of memory influence the texts, objects and behavioural scripts created in relation to them? What factors influence the

246 *Karina Jarzyńska*

(potentially sacred) valorization of human remains when there is an identity shift in a community that could consider them worthy of protection?

A trans-religious sacrum

Radecznica is a large village near Lublin, Poland, where a significant Jewish community lived before 1939. This community was later destroyed by the Nazi genocidal policy, mainly through on-site executions (the 'Holocaust by bullets'; see Desbois 2010). Today, it is known as a destination for pilgrims wishing to visit the Sanctuary of St Anthony of Padua, which is located there. Recently, the Sanctuary has also become a space for the display of various artefacts commemorating local partisans and other actors important for the identity of the Radeczniczans (Szczepan, Sendyka and Kobielska 2020). One of the main actors in Radecznica memory culture is Stanisław Zybała (1930–2014), a librarian, chronicler and author of many publications who has devoted a large part of his work to securing a peaceful rest for his Jewish schoolmate, Raźla Honig, and her family.

Stanisław co-authored a book with his wife, Marianna, titled *That's How I See You, Radecznica* (Zybała and Zybała 2013), which they characterized as a form of 'photo-scribbling' (*fotoskrybanie*) due to the parallelism between the photography and text on each of the book spreads. This feature, combined with the presence of the map and the walking route proposed in the text, makes the project more closely resemble a guidebook. Yet, unlike the classic examples of the genre, the Zybałas' guide does not so much present a space that is new to the reader as encourage people who already know a space to change their perceptions of it and, ultimately, transform that space's public status.

The book opens with the dreamlike vision of Stanisław – a witness to the holocaust where he lived and the main narrator of this particular guide – in which a Certain Illustrious Lady asks him to point out the place 'where no one sings Salve Regina, and no one recites the Kaddish'. Zybała remarks that this task was difficult, but he possessed 'steely motivation', and the Lady 'sent rays of power into him' that he might succeed (Zybała and Zybała 2013, 5). This rhetorical opening explicitly reveals the religious character of the impulse that pushed the author to undertake the commemoration of the victims of genocide. Implicitly, it also indicates that this kind of memory activism needs to be religiously legitimized to engage Zybała's readers. On the one hand, Zybała bolsters his argument and increases the efficacy of his instructions by calling upon the authority of a transcendent phantom: in fact, he suggests to his readers that by following the guide's instructions, they will be performing God's will. On the other hand, he supports his effort with a 'power' that could help him overcome his fear of the hardships presented by the task, which he hypostasizes by giving it the material form of a character with the attributes of holiness. The source of the Illustrious Lady's power is not directly revealed, but a female apparition with a mission is a characteristic embodiment of the Catholic Mother of God, a powerful figure in the Polish imaginarium. Stanisław

Negotiating the sacred at non-sites 247

Zybała, being a linguistically inventive local history expert, decided to merely suggest the identity of the apparition that sought the fulfilment of Jewish rituals for the deceased, and make her Catholic identity less evident.

The guidebook leads its target readership (the inhabitants of Radecznica) to, inter alia, seven 'non-Kaddish graves' (*bezkadiszowe groby*) and encourages them to walk along certain paths and say specific prayers: El Male Rachamim, Yizkor or Kaddish de-Rabannan. As we know from Marianna Zybała, the couple developed and practised this custom themselves and, as the years passed, they replaced the Catholic prayers familiar from their youth with Jewish prayers that they came to learn. From a Halakha perspective, none of the choices they made is ritually valid (recitations of Yizkor and the Kaddish require the presence of at least ten Jewish adults, a minyan, to have any performative power). The Zybałas' proposal draws from existing ritual scenarios to meet the needs of a particular itinerary. They seem somewhat careless about the theological accuracy of their work, yet they quote in extenso the texts of three Jewish prayers, exposing readers to the beauty of a tradition that they are in effect being invited to recognize as their own heritage. The practice that the guide's authors develop and invite the other members of their community to participate in crosses the boundaries between Catholicism and Judaism, and religious and secular culture, expanding the spectrum of available necro-rituals. In a similar way, the motivation of their work is not easily accommodated within any theological framework.

There is a similar trans-religious quality in the visual works of Stanisław Zybała, who was also a sculptor. For example, he made symbols to mark out the location of his school friend Raźla's hideout, the place that was later to be the site of her execution and burial – she was murdered, together with her family, in December 1942, in a forest gorge – the so-called Drugie Doły (Szczepan, Sendyka and Kobielska 2020). Zybała heard the execution take place and saw the traces of a fresh burial. At first the symbols he chose to mark it with were crosses, the first of which was placed on the vertical line formed by a natural split in the trunk of a tree. Later on – out of a sense of propriety, according to Marianna – he carved a Star of David on a neighbouring tree. The symbol of Judaism was slightly altered, however, by his untrained hand: the lines of the star only sometimes cross in the right way. The new, idiosyncratic form that resulted was later replicated by Zybała in, among other places, his map of Radecznica, as a way of marking uncommemorated sites related to the Holocaust. He sent that map to various institutions, including the Rabbinical Commission for Jewish Cemeteries, which financed a gravestone at Raźla's burial site in 2016, placing on it the symbol Zybała had created. The decision from the Jewish side to reuse and thereby recognize the modified version of the Magen David indicates their willingness to communicate using a local, vernacular language, one developed out of the need to speak of the Holocaust as a witness. This gesture amounted to a departure from the letter of Jewish rules so as to, I believe, show respect to a particular witness by going some way towards reciprocating his efforts to commemorate his Jewish neighbours, and also

248 *Karina Jarzyńska*

by involving the general public from the area to a greater extent by showing more openness to Polish voices about their common heritage. This compromise on religious customs was also born out of an awareness that the continued memory of Raźla and those she was closest to very much depends on the Christian inhabitants of Radecznica.

For the same reason, I would argue, the Zybałas provide arguments in their guidebook to Radecznica with which to convince their neighbours to join them in the commemoration. Besides emphasizing the spiritual nature of their mission, they use a peculiar kind of blackmail: marking the beginning of the route at a place where legend has it that ghosts haunt those who travel alone. They paint a vivid picture of the wraiths that so effectively torment the wanderers passing by that point that they never return (Zybała and Zybała 2013, 4). This indirectly suggests that neglecting one's duties towards the deceased can inhibit one's safe passage through the area. Another argument comes at the end of the book in the form of a reproduction of an image of Christ, unexpectedly appearing between pictures of Radecznica, accompanied by the remark: 'After all he was from among them'. This (unelaborated) comment reveals the fact that the intended readership of the book are Christians unwilling to acknowledge that Jewish remains are a part of their own heritage and that caring for them may be their obligation.

The modification of Judaic symbols was an important element of the artistic means used and developed by Zybała. Another example is his *Menorka* (the Polish diminutive of *menorah*), a sculpture made of wood taken from the vicinity of Raźla's death, thereby creating an indexical reference to the site of the genocide. It displays many differences to the traditional menorah it is based on, including the metal chain that entwines the whole, which is meant to symbolize Jewish suffering (Figure 12.1). The artist's family would place this unique candleholder on the table during Christmas as a way of performing a meeting of Judaism, Christianity and memory of the Holocaust. The latter, rather secular, referential field of the *Menorka* both separated and united other religious references. Like the walks past the non-Kaddish graves, this ritual seems to be a private commemorative exercise and at the same time part of a wider public activity symbolizing the search for a common language for the communities of the living and the dead, a language that would serve in the difficult circumstances they have encountered and continue to encounter in their shared territory.

Religious references in Zybała's sculptures were not limited to aspects of Judaism and Christianity. He also incorporated particular elements of a cosmic and pre-Christian imaginary into his art and self-identification. A prominent place in the Zybałas' apartment is occupied by a group of sculptures composed of a pair comprising local deity Rod and his maid (Figure 12.2) and a peculiar lunar calendar containing symbols of the waxing and waning moon aimed in opposite directions, both of which are set into an oval base into which a complex figure made of intersecting circles is carved (Figure 12.3).

Negotiating the sacred at non-sites 249

Figure 12.1 Stanisław Zybała, *Menorka* ('Little Menorah').
Source: Photo by Karina Jarzyńska (June 2019); courtesy of Marianna Zybała.

Zybała placed a similar form on the verso of the *Cemetery Symbol* – a round, double-sided bas-relief – and this one is easier to identify: it is a hexapental star known in many cultures under various names (Figures 12.4–5). In the pre-Christian culture of the Slavs, this star was associated with the god Perun and, more generally, with the sun and life; being a magical object, it has been used (and still is, sometimes) for apotropaic functions protecting people and objects against evil powers, destruction and death. The *Cemetery Symbol* is Zybała's complex statement on the effects of genocidal violence in Radecznica.

Figure 12.2 Stanisław Zybała's sculptures (untitled).

Source: Photo by Karina Jarzyńska (June 2019); courtesy of Marianna Zybała.

It combines religious and national symbols with indexical references, as he used wood and a pinch of soil from Drugie Doły to create it. The work represents the topological relationship between time (1942–43), space and community, making violence and death its decisive variable. In addition to strictly Judaic symbols, it uses covenant tablets with Roman numerals corresponding to the Ten Commandments, a symbol also important for Christians. The tablets are broken around the fifth commandment ('Thou shalt not kill') by some (presumably Nazi) shoe. The sculpture represents the destruction of the moral laws of religious sources along with the destruction of the community. The pre-Christian symbol on the verso seems to have been placed there to protect what remained of the author's land after the period of destruction – a magical defence against the repetition of history.

Zybała's works can be interpreted as a field of codification of memory language, written in various media, rooted in the experience of a Holocaust witness and a frequent, performatively engaged visitor to Drugie Doły. Given its personal nature, it is ultimately designed for the community of Christian and Jewish residents of Radecznica. When mediating between them, it does not subordinate itself to the rules of either faith taken individually. Yet it is not simply a 'Judaeo-Christian memory language', as it reaches beyond the two denominations (a characteristic feature not only of Zybała's work but also of his

Figure 12.3 Stanisław Zybała's sculpture (view from above).
Source: Photo by Karina Jarzyńska (June 2019); courtesy of Marianna Zybała.

personal choices, as they transgressed institutional norms and the boundaries set by tradition).[2] In response to the radical undermining of moral norms – implicit in suffering being inflicted intentionally on innocent people – Zybała involves himself in the process of these norms' restitution. He recognizes the religious imaginary and practices as allies in his artistic quest to reduce the 'semantic hole' produced by twentieth-century anthropogenic catastrophes (Agadjanian 2022). The sacred value of his work gains its legitimacy through the creative and respectful manner in which it constantly moves between the symbolic universes of Judaism, Catholicism and other religious traditions, transforming him into a trans-religious negotiator of a post-traumatic mnemoscape. He may also be perceived as an activist for a postsecular society, a society open to its members learning from each other, wherein both secular and religious attitudes interact within the framework of a modern democracy (Habermas 2008).

A suppressed sacrum

Wierzbica and Siedliska, two small villages in Miechów County located about twenty kilometres apart, were the two other cases incorporated into the project's research. During the Second World War, both became locations of unsuccessful attempts to rescue Jews, culminating in all those involved being

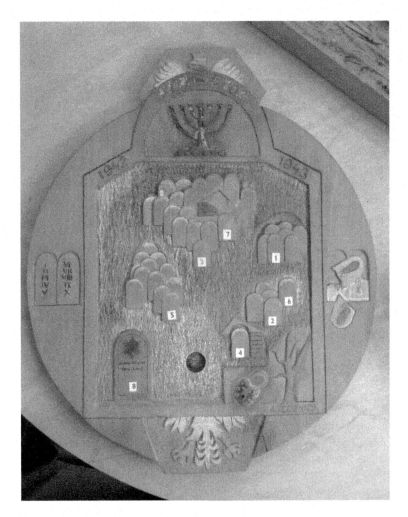

Figure 12.4 Stanisław Zybała, *Cemetery Symbol* (recto).
Source: Photos by Karina Jarzyńska (2017); courtesy of the Jewish Historical Institute in Warsaw.

executed; subsequently the villages became the burial spaces of these victims. The joint efforts made by Jewish and non-Jewish Polish citizens to oppose the Nazi policy of genocide could have strengthened the sense of solidarity that probably formed the basis of these humanitarian actions. Such a community, knitted together by the experiencing of violent death inflicted by the same hands and at the same place and time was not, however, directly extended through the memory of the survivors or their descendants living in the area.

The first execution took place in Wierzbica in January 1943, when four members of the Książek family and two Jews in hiding (probably related to the Wandersman family) were murdered (Jarzyńska and Muchowski 2020). After

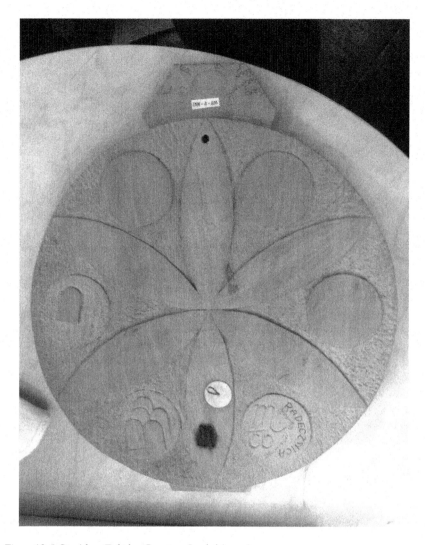

Figure 12.5 Stanisław Zybała, *Cemetery Symbol* (verso).
Source: Photos by Karina Jarzyńska (2017); courtesy of the Jewish Historical Institute in Warsaw.

this tragedy, the farm was abandoned, but when the relatives of the Catholic Poles returned from the war, they erected a gravestone at the corpses' place of burial. However, the gravestone did not mention the Jewish victims and little is known about their identity (Florek 2016). In 2017, a relative of the Książek family who had been tending to their grave pointed, while speaking to us, to some nearby bushes to indicate that this was where the Jewish victims had been buried (Conversations with S.M. 2017). It is unlikely, however, that whoever was digging the graves in the January frost after the execution would have

254 *Karina Jarzyńska*

bothered to create two separate holes for the dead a few metres apart merely to separate the victims on the basis of their ethnicity and/or religious denomination. What we do know for sure is that the victims were separated in local memory culture: their shared fate has nearly been forgotten.

The reasons for this situation are probably complex, but they in all likelihood include (1) the fact that family histories were not being transferred through the generations due to the simultaneous deaths of most relatives and (2) weakened ties with Jews of the younger generation who, because they grew up after the war, did not have the opportunity to share in the local sense of community with them, but also possibly (3) antipathy being shown towards this group, resulting either from cultural prejudices or from the circumstances surrounding the execution. Some witnesses claim that the hideout was denounced by one of those in hiding, Paweł Wandersman, who was captured, tortured and eventually killed by the Germans. Hence the inscription on the grave: 'They saved Jews, because of whom they were exposed and murdered by Germans' (the inscription on the grave is in Polish and was probably placed there in the 1970s; see Jarzyńska and Muchowski 2020). The biblical lexicon used on the tombstone suggests an active role was being played by the stereotype of the 'Jew the traitor' – formed on the basis of the figure of Judas Iscariot, by whom Christ was 'betrayed' (*wydany*; see Biblia Tysiąclecia Online 2003).

Less than two months later, in nearby Siedliska, five members of the Baranek family were killed along with four Jews they had been hiding – probably the Gotfrieds. This time, the bodies of the Catholic victims were buried in the Catholic cemetery in Miechów, whereas the Jewish victims were buried in agricultural fields next to the site of the execution. One of our interviewees told us that ten years later that place was still visible to the eye, as the wheat grew differently there (Conversation with M.B. 2018). The neighbours of this non-site of memory claim, however, that the bodies were exhumed a few years after the war 'by some Jewish organisation' (Conversations with E.Ś and S.Ż. 2018), yet there is no documentation of such an intervention in the archives.[3]

The absence of memory of the burial site of Jewish victims in Siedliska is reflected in their weak presence in the discourse about the crime that happened there. The Baranek family is presented as the main, if not the only, hero of the event, mirroring the approach taken to their counterparts in two similar stories – the Ulma and Kowalski families – which together co-create a self-affirmative narrative of the Polish rescuing of Jews, which is further presented and reinforced at the Ulma Family Museum of Poles Saving Jews in World War II in Markowa (Kobielska 2016, 365–68; for the differences in the collective memory of each of these families, see Bogumił and Głowacka-Grajper 2019, 233–43). The paradigmatic status of these families in the Polish memory of the rescuing of Jews is strengthened by emphasizing their Catholic identity as the main motivation for them to help (Website of the Ulma Family Museum). The Baraneks' story fits neatly into this narrative scheme.

A watershed moment favouring the presence of Siedliska in the regional and national discourse occurred in 2012, when the Baranek family was honoured with the title of Righteous Among the Nations. Since then anniversary celebrations have been organized, combining in various proportions religious rituals, political events and family meetings. As time has passed, one can also witness changes in the intensiveness and character of the references to the Jewish victims of the murder. Additionally, an apparently fixed element of those celebrations, a Holy Mass at the cemetery in Miechów, leaves the officiants with some room for interpretation.

The first of the anniversary masses was celebrated by Bishop Piotr Skucha, a relative of the Baraneks. He is a biblical scholar educated in Jerusalem and a promoter of the position of Vatican II on Judaism. In one of his articles, he declares that 'an encounter with Jesus Christ is already a meeting with Judaism' and strongly advocates against anti-Semitism (Skucha 2012, 479–80). The consequence of such an understanding of the relationship between the two religious traditions is a typological interpretation of the Bible that emphasizes the similarities between the Old and New Testaments and recognizes Jews as a 'type', a prefiguration of Christians. This practice can be traced through Skucha's sermons published in the *Uwierzcie Ewangelii* (*Believe the Gospel*) collection. In one of these, he refers to a passage from the book of Exodus – the same that the lectionary provided for reading during the celebrations on 15 March 2012, when Skucha gave the sermon (Exodus 32:7–14; John 5:30–47). Here is how he interprets the passage in his book:

> the desert witnesses the Nation's birth and upbringing. The educational process took place through the rebellion of the Israelites, who vehemently expressed their frustration with the discomforts of sojourning in the desert. . . . the memory of a historical sojourn in the desert is understood by the liturgy as a call to listen to God and serve him with faithfulness. Thus, the liturgy transfers past events into the present.
>
> (Skucha 2012, 444–45; trans. K. Jarzyńska)

The exact same readings were scheduled for 15 March 2018, the day I attended the Mass and listened to the sermon of another clergyman, Fr Stanisław Latosiński, a local priest, religious publicist and regional historian (Latosiński 2017), yet he interpreted the biblical passages in a completely different manner. Here is how he comments on Exodus:

> As we know, the Jews are a people chosen and loved by God, and yet causing so much trouble. Even after being released from Egyptian slavery, they could not trust in God and show their gratitude; similarly, after the covenant on Mount Sinai, as we heard in the reading a moment ago, God complains to Moses that this is a hard-necked nation, and his anger flared up against them. . . . God allowed them to follow their own path, which quickly led them to captivity in Babylon. . . . Then God fulfilled the prophets' announcements: the expected Messiah, Jesus Christ, came. The Jews, however, did not accept him, and treated him as the greatest

256 *Karina Jarzyńska*

villain, forcing Pilate to crucify him. That was the moment when the old covenant ended. Christ, by calling the Apostles, created a new covenant, i.e. the Church. The Jews, however, were dispersed.

> (Transcription of audio recording of the Holy Mass, Miechów, 15 March 2018; trans. K. Jarzyńska)

Not only did Latosiński not track the analogy between the old and the new covenant, but he went on to imply the radical separation of the groups they cater for. The infidelity towards God that the Jews showed in the desert is prolonged by their cruelty towards Jesus and – in a later part of the sermon – the ingratitude they have showed towards their host nations in the modern age:

> Most of them reached the countries of Western Europe. When there, they also became a problem and got expelled . . . they settled in Poland – a friendly place in which they felt safe for centuries. . . . The Second World War has revealed the true face of who is really who. When Poland came under the occupation of Nazi Germany and Soviet Russia, Jews did not show loyalty to Poles, their neighbours.
>
> (Transcription of audio recording of the Holy Mass, Miechów, 15 March 2018; trans. K. Jarzyńska)

Here, Jews and Poles are placed in opposition to each other based on their respective abilities to show loyalty, a trait that acquires essentialized features within the context of the whole sermon: Jews are always treacherous, and Poles are faithful. This logic was built on an admixture of anti-Semitic and anti-Judaic prejudices fuelled by the discourses of ethnic nationalism in politics and the 'Closed Church' in religion, as Joanna Michlic has diagnosed:

> The formation of the Closed Church, which, in many respects, stands against the present Vatican positions concerning Jews and Judaism can be evaluated as an obstacle in the implementation of the concept of dialogue with Jews and Judaism on a broader social level, and the elimination of anti-Jewish prejudices in the Catholic community. Furthermore, this is the formation in which anti-Jewish prejudices, belonging to the ethno-nationalist political and cultural heritage are acceptable to varying degree and intensity.
>
> (Michlic 2004, 479)

The origins of this ecclesiastical formation can be seen during the period of the Polish Partitions (1795–1918), when religion became a buttress for ethnonationalist attitudes and a Polish-Catholic complex developed that was associated with the sacred valorization of the nation (see Zubrzycki in this volume). The ambiguity of the word *ofiara* in Polish (corresponding to both the English 'victim' and 'sacrifice') favoured those killed while fighting the occupiers being recognized as martyrs (see also Lim 2010, 138–63). The same cultural habitus is activated by Latosiński, who used the surname of the Polish victims (Baranek, which is Polish for 'lamb') as a rhetorical framework for his sermon. The lamb is the paradigmatic sacrificial animal from the Bible, a symbol of Jesus himself. This made it easy for those listening to the sermon to associate the redemptive death of Christ with the death of the Baraneks (the Lambs) and therefore conceive of the family as martyrs whose blood might have a redemptive power for the community. Jews, on the other hand, were, for Latosiński, traitors who were complicit in the Nazi persecutions that also befell the Polish people, in analogy to the role of Judas. The priest went so far as to claim that the Jews in their treacherousness broke the covenant between God and themselves. This was why the new covenant was initiated with a new partner, the Christians. Indeed, in Latosiński's understanding, Jews and Christians are essentially separable groups. The last words of his sermon were:

> Brothers and sisters, we do not have to be ashamed of our history, a Catholic is not an anti-Semite, as many would like us to be . . . that is why I think I will not be making a theological error when I say that by praying for the Baranek family, we can also boldly ask them to intercede with God for us and ask Him for necessary favours.
> (Transcription of audio recording of the Holy Mass, Miechów, 15 March 2018; trans. K. Jarzyńska)

Despite the absence of theological grounds for believing in the redemptive power of the Baraneks' blood, there are two premises that provoke the preacher to take risks: the already discussed argument derived from the homonymous connotation of the surname and the fact that another family murdered for helping Jews (the Ulmas from Markowa) had already gained the status of servants of God, allowing the preacher to ask for their intercession. The grace that they could obtain from God would be the peace needed by the community accused of anti-Semitism. However, Latosiński's anti-Judaic interpretation of the Holy Scriptures and his tendency to sacralize the national community leads Latosiński to the very errors that he claims to be trying to avoid.[4]

In the cases discussed above (Wierzbica and Siedliska), although Jewish remains are not protected through the marking of their place of burial, one can still observe subversive forms of activation of their sacred potential. The trait of holiness is attributed to non-Jewish actors associated with past events: they are perceived as martyrs deserving canonization. The sacrum of the Jewish *necros* is suppressed, and its symbolic energy seems to be transferred to the Catholic imaginarium. This mechanism works on a similar principle as classic repression, which is one of the factors responsible for anti-Semitic elements appearing in the discourse about unsuccessful attempts to assist Jews rescuing themselves.

A sacrum negotiated

The Chodówki forest (in Miechów County), which hides a mass grave of Holocaust victims, has become a space of multidirectional memory work over the past decade (Rothberg 2009). Józef Jarno – a witness to war executions carried out there on Jewish and also non-Jewish inhabitants of the surrounding villages (mostly partisans) – cooperated with the local authorities to move the former site commemorating the murdered Jews from a nearby field to a location by the edge of a main road, near a Catholic cross. A new tablet was created containing a text connecting the memory of various groups of victims, and an opening ceremony was organized (Jarzyńska and Muchowski 2020). Although these activities seemed to meet the needs of the activist and his allies, they did not respond to the religious demands of the Jewish community, as it is forbidden by Halakha to exhume the bodies from the place where they rest; this ground is therefore perceived as sacred. In 2014, some members of the Jewish community acting as representatives of the Zapomniane ('Forgotten') Foundation entered the forest to identify the exact spot of the grave and mark it in a unique way.

The foundation has practised 'guerrilla grave placing' (Ellis 2018), which involves its activists erecting 'temporary' wooden *matzevot* in previously unmarked, but still identifiable, graves of the victims of the Holocaust, to protect them and make them more visible to the local community (Figure 12.6). Such a form of intervention enables relatively quick action on a large scale, as it is cheap and ephemeral, and so does not require many formalities to be met. Its simplicity leaves a space for negotiation with its neighbours on what form of commemoration they would like to build on each site in the future. The foundation claims that one of its goals is to 'support local communities in accepting the past and dealing with the difficult heritage of World War II' (website of the

Figure 12.6 'Temporary' *matzevot* for burials of victims of the Holocaust erected by the Zapomniane ('Forgotten') Foundation in Chodówki forest, Poland.

Source: Photo by Karina Jarzyńska, February 2018.

Negotiating the sacred at non-sites 259

Zapomniane Foundation; see also Janus 2020). Introducing religious symbols into spaces that witnessed genocidal violence and have not yet been publicly recognized exposes the underlying conflict between memories but also starts the process of their negotiation.

A similar yet more violent process is taking place in Borzęcin (Brzesko County), where representatives of the Romani people are struggling to commemorate the Samudaripen (Romani genocide). Their religious identity, Roman Catholic, simplifies the process in relation to the victims of the Shoah, as it is shared with the majority of Poles living in this area (Kapralski 2012). Romani bodies can be exhumed and buried in Catholic cemeteries. This is what happened in Borzęcin, where the bodies of twenty-eight Romani people murdered in 1942 by the Nazis in a nearby forest were transferred to the parish cemetery in 1959 (Szczepan and Posłuszny 2020). In 2011, the Romani community also felt the need to memorialize the site of the execution itself, and this came to pass by means of a wooden sculpture by Małgorzata Mirga-Tas (Gancarz 2016, 136). The sculpture did not refer directly to the sacred: it neither contained any religious symbols nor marked the place of the remains. I am writing about it in the past tense because it was destroyed by anonymous offenders in 2016. Soon afterwards, thanks to the financial support of the authorities and private donors, the monument was restored, but the artist took the remains of the first memorial with her. They became the subject of her new sculptural series, in which she exposed the violence the monument had gone through by displaying some of its damaged elements moulded in wax to emphasize their fragility, while also drawing symbolical analogies with the human body (Szymański 2020).

Simultaneously, a new gravestone was unveiled at the aforementioned parish cemetery, the resting place of the victims' bodies. The relationship between these two objects was interestingly thematized by placing the outline of Mirga-Tas's sculpture on the pedestal of the gravestone. What is more, during the 18th International Romani Caravan of Memory, in the presence of its participants, local authorities and the local priest, the inside of the outline was filled in with the sign of the cross. That the ceremony took such a course suggests the sacralization of the marked object, although the designation of the ritual is not clear: it might be about the bodies of the victims (whose resting place was marked with a tombstone), the tombstone itself or the statue created by Mirga-Tas whose destruction gave the impetus for the tombstone's renewal. The latter eventuality is interesting, as it clashes with the artist's intention to avoid religious connotations. If taken seriously, the gesture of sanctifying a representation of a destroyed monument could well be seen as a reaction to violence interpreted as an act of profanation. The need for such a gesture testifies to the Roma community's recognition that the site of their forebears' execution is sacred. Perhaps this recognition only dates from the devastation of the monument, which paradoxically and retroactively sanctified Mirga-Tas's sculpture. Defining the aforementioned ritual as a restitution of the sacred would therefore be the most justified response to the need to preserve the memory of the Roma Holocaust itself, the value

260   *Karina Jarzyńska*

of which was undermined by vandals. Nevertheless, the observed actions and artefacts seem to be part of an ongoing memory-negotiation process in which religion is one of the most important arguments.

Conclusion

The analysis of artefacts and practices related to the non-sites of memory in Radecznica, Siedliska, Wierzbica, Chodówki and Borzęcin allows us to outline the spectrum of possible tactics in the use of the religious imaginary within the framework of post-genocidal culture. Most of these artefacts and practices are inventive in comparison to the existing traditions, which in this case are mostly rooted in Catholicism or Judaism. The actors involved in the memory work discussed in this chapter are combining these traditions to create a language of communication between the living and dead by either sharing the same space (a trans-religious sacrum) or modifying one of the traditions in such a way as to deal with a difficult past in the interests of the community with which they identify. In the case of the negotiated sacrum, religiously motivated representatives of genocide victims are often the initiators of an uneasy process that enables all the parties involved to present their interests in the symbolic and political field. The long-lasting unmemorialized presence of human remains belonging to representatives of a different denomination than the contemporary residents of a certain area can also result in the suppression of their potential sacrum. Yet this sacrum is sometimes subversively activated, as in cases like the anniversary celebrations of the war victims associated with these remains (in Siedliska, this mechanism resulted in an anti-Semitic interpretation of the Bible and a vernacular attempt to canonize the Baranek family).

The tactics presented above underline that no single traditional denomination is, in itself, capable of framing the collective memory of the traumatic past. The memory of the genocide that destroyed the religious diversity in Poland is being built through difficult negotiations between the parties involved, a process accompanied by a weakening or strengthening of their denominational identification. We thus observe cases of discursive or physical violence typical of fundamentalist religiosity (Kepel 1994). One of the factors enabling that violence is the popularity of mythical frameworks enabling societies to build their own image. In the case of the ethnocentric nationalism functioning in Poland, this framework makes it more likely that Jews will be pushed into a position of opposition, while also impeding the recognition of their theology, the sanctity of their corpses or the seriousness of their suffering, as well as contributing to their weak position in memory culture and the absence of gravestones over their remains. It is worth remembering, however, that this mechanism is working in opposition to the doctrine of the Second Vatican Council, so it mostly circulates locally and unofficially rather than at the level of official documents or ceremonies. Finally, some observable trans-religious practices are based on an awareness of the inevitability of religious and secular entities cooperating

Negotiating the sacred at non-sites 261

with one another in the public sphere to make memory culture as inclusive as possible, and as such closer to a postsecular sensibility.

Bibliography

Primary sources

Conversation with E. Ś. Miechów, 19.06.2018 (with I.F., M.F., A.G., K.J., P.M., J.M., and A.S.).
Conversation with M. B. Miechów, 1.02.2018 and 15.03.2018 (with K.J., and J.M.).
Conversations with S. M. 2017, Wierzbica, 14.06.2017 (with K.J., J. M. M.F., P.M., and A.N.).
Conversation with S. Ż. Siedliska, 19.06.2018 (with I.F., M.F., A.G., K.J., P.M., J.M., and A.S.).
Ellis, Yehoshua. 2018. "Presentation During the *Memory and Religion. Central and Eastern Europe in a Global Perspective* Conference." Warsaw 16–18.10.2018 (organizer: European Network for Remembrance and Solidarity).
Latosiński, Stanisław. 2017. *Miechów na nowo odkryty.* Miechów: Czuwajmy.
NN (Grzywnowicz, Wioletta). 2013. *Żelazny Krzyż.* typescript.
Skucha, Piotr. 2012. *Uwierzcie Ewangelii. Księga jubileuszowa księdza biskupa Piotra Skuchy w 25. rocznicę sakry biskupiej.* Sosnowiec: Wydział Duszpasterstwa Ogólnego Kurii Diecezjalnej.
Transcription of audio recording of the Holy Mass in Miechów, 15.03.2018 (by K.J.).
Website of the Ulma Family Museum of Poles Saving Jews in World War II. Accessed January 13, 2020. https://muzeumulmow.pl/en/.
Website of the Zapomniane Foundation. Accessed January 14, 2020. https://zapomniane.org/miejsce/las-chodowki/.
Zybała, Marianna, and Stanisław Zybała. 2013. *Tak cię widzę, Radecznico. Ścieżkami, drogami, miedzami, po krzakach i zaroślach łąk, pól i lasów.* Radecznica: Urząd Gminy Radecznica.

Notes

1 This chapter is a result of my work within the research project, Unmemorialized Genocide Sites and Their Impact on Collective Memory, Cultural Identity, Ethical Attitudes and Intercultural Relations in Contemporary Poland (Polish Ministry of Science and Higher Education, the National Programme for the Development of Humanities, 2016–20).

2 Raised as a Roman Catholic, Zybała left the Church long before his death, donated his body to science and did not want a cross on his tombstone. The sculpture of Rod seems to be his self-portrait, and his nickname (Rozwar) can be seen as a sign of his affirmative stance on magical thinking. As Zybała explained, this neologism (which could be roughly translated as 'split up') refers to the fact that his finger had been sliced off by a mechanical saw in his youth. He buried it in the building where it happened and since then it has been separated from himself (Smoter-Grzeszkiewicz 2019, 25).

3 Based on the result of a query placed with the Polish Red Cross Archives in Warsaw. The story may be a legend told to soothe concerns caused by the thought of ritually uncleansed Jewish bodies lying on 'our' land, a worry perhaps exacerbated by ignorance of Halakha, which is disinclined to permit this kind of exhumation at all (see Gordon 2009, 108).

4 Another example of such an interpretation is a short story titled *Żelazny krzyż (The Iron Cross)* that was anonymously distributed during anniversary celebrations on 15 March 2013 (but I identified the author as Wioletta Grzywnowicz, a local writer). This is a hagiographical legend about Łucja Baranek, portrayed as a devoted believer, mother and wife, whose martyrdom is being annunciated to her by God via visionary dreams (NN [Grzywnowicz] 2013).

262 Karina Jarzyńska

References

Agadjanian, Alexander. 2022. "Religion and Collective Memory of the Last Century: General Reflections and Russian Vicissitudes." In *Memory and Religion from a Postsecular Perspective*, edited by Zuzanna Bogumił and Yulia Yurchuk. London: Routledge.

Biblia Tysiąclecia Online. 2003 Accessed November 2, 2021. https://biblia.deon.pl/index.php

Boddy, Janice, and Michael Lambek, eds. 2013. *A Companion to the Anthropology of Religion*. Malden, MA: Wiley-Blackwell.

Bogumił, Zuzanna, and Małgorzata Głowacka-Grajper. 2019. *Milieux de Mémoire in Late Modernity. Local Communities, Religion and Historical Politics*. Berlin: Peter Lang.

Csordas, Thomas J. 1990. "Embodiment as a Paradigm for Anthropology." *Ethos* 18 (1) (1990): 5–47. Accessed June 9, 2020. www.jstor.org/stable/640395.

Desbois, Patrick. 2010. *Holocaust by Bullets. A Priest's Journey to Uncover the Truth Behind the Murder of 1.5 Million Jews*. Basingstoke: Palgrave Macmillan.

Dieleman, Karen. 2012. *Religious Imaginaries: The Liturgical and Poetic Practices of Elizabeth Barrett Browning, Christina Rossetti, and Adelaide Procter*. Athens: Ohio University Press.

Dobrosielski, Paweł. 2017. *Spory o Grossa. Polskie problemy z pamięcią o Żydach*. Warsaw: Instytut Badań Literackich PAN.

Domańska, Ewa. 2019. "The Environmental History of Mass Graves." *Journal of Genocide Research*. https://doi.org/10.1080/14623528.2019.1657306.

Douglas, Mary. 1966. *Purity and Danger: An Analysis of Concepts of Pollution and Taboo*. London: Routledge.

Durkheim, Émile. 2008. *The Elementary Forms of Religious Life*. Translated by Carol Cosman. Oxford: Oxford University Press.

Eliade, Mircea. 1961. *The Sacred and the Profane: The Nature of Religion*. Translated by Willard R. Trask. New York: Harper Torchbooks.

Feierstein, Daniel. 2014. *Genocide as Social Practice. Reorganizing Society Under the Nazis and Argentina's Military Juntas*. Translated by Douglas Andrew Town. New Brunswick, NJ: Rutgers University Press.

Florek, Marcin. 2016. "Społeczność ziemi miechowskiej/powiatu miechowskiego w akcji pomocy Żydom 1939–1945." In *Pomoc świadczona ludności żydowskiej przez Polaków w latach 1939–1945 ze szczególnym uwzględnieniem Kielecczyzny*, edited by Jerzy Gapys and Agnieszka Dziarmaga. Kielce: Kappadruk Drukarnia.

Gancarz, Natalia. 2016. "*I stanie się on częścią tego miejsca. Jak pomnik staje się pomnikiem*." *Studia Romologica* 9.

Gordon, Ewa. 2009. *Modlitwy na cmentarzu I zwyczaje pogrzebowe*. Kraków and Budapest: Austeria.

Habermas, Jürgen. 2008. "Secularism's Crisis of Faith: Notes on Post-Secular Society." *New Perspectives Quarterly* 25. https://doi.org/10.1111/j.1540-5842.2008.01017.x.

Janus, Aleksandra. 2020. "Wernakularna pamięć I wspólnoty uwikłania." In *Nie-miejsca pamięci (2). Nekrotopologie*, edited by Roma Sendyka, Aleksandra Janus, Karina Jarzyńska and Kinga Siewior. Warszawa: IBL PAN.

Jarzyńska, Karina, and Jakub Muchowski. 2020. "Nie-miejsca pamięci Ziemi Miechowskiej. Przesunięcie I uznanie w lokalnej sieci pamięci." In *Nie-miejsca pamięci (1). Nekrotopografie*, edited by Roma Sendyka, Maria Kobielska, Jakub Muchowski and Aleksandra Szczepan. Warszawa: IBL PAN.

Kapralski, Sławomir. 2012. *Naród z popiołów Pamięć zagłady a tożsamość Romów*. Warsaw: Scholar.

Kepel, Gilles. 1994. *The Revenge of God: The Resurgence of Islam, Christianity and Judaism in the Modern World*. Cambridge: Polity Press.

Kobielska, Maria. 2016. "Polska pamięć autoafirmacyjna." *Teksty Drugie* 6. https://doi.org/10.18318/td.2016.6.21.

Laqueur, Thomas W. 2015. *The Work of the Dead: A Cultural History of Mortal Remains.* Princeton, NJ: Princeton University Press.

Latour, Bruno. 2005. *Reassembling the Social: An Introduction to Actor-Network-Theory.* Oxford: Oxford University Press.

Leder, Andrzej. 2013. *Prześniona rewolucja. Ćwiczenia z logiki historycznej.* Warsaw: Wydawnictwo Krytyki Politycznej.

Leeuv, Gerardus van der. 2014. *Religion in its Essence and Manifestation.* Translated by Ninian Smart and John Evan Turner. Princeton, NJ: Princeton University Press.

Leociak, Jacek. 2018. *Młyny Boże. Zapiski o Kościele I Zagładzie.* Wołowiec: Czarne.

Lim, Jie-Hyun. 2010. "Victimhood Nationalism in Contested Memories: National Mourning and Global Accountability." In *Memory in a Global Age. Discourses, Practices and Trajectories,* edited by Aleida Assmann and Sebastian Conrad. Houndmills: Palgrave Macmillan.

Lubańska, Magdalena. 2018. "Postmemory of Killings in the Woods at Dębrzyna (1945–6): A Postsecular Anthropological Perspective." *Ethnologia Polona* 38.

Michlic, Joanna B. 2004. "'The Open Church' and 'the Closed Church' and the discourse on Jews in Poland Between 1989 and 2000." *Communist and Post-Communist Studies* 37.

Otto, Rudolf. 1970. *The Idea of the Holy.* Translated by John W. Harvey. New York: Oxford University Press.

Pasieka, Agnieszka. 2015. *Hierarchy and Pluralism: Living Religious Difference in Catholic Poland.* London: Palgrave Macmillan.

Pollack, Martin. 2014. *Skażone krajobrazy.* Translated by Kris Niedenthal. Wołowiec: Czarne.

Rothberg, Michael. 2009. *Multidirectional Memory. Remembering the Holocaust in the Age of Decolonization.* Stanford, CA: Stanford University Press.

Schuppli, Susan. 2020. *Material Witness. Media, Forensics, Evidence.* Cambridge, MA: MIT Press.

Sendyka, Roma. 2015. "Prism: Understanding Non-Sites of Memory." Translated by Jennifer Croft. *Teksty Drugie* 2.

———. 2016. "Sites That Haunt: Affects and Non-sites of Memory." *East European Politics and Societies* 30(4). https://doi.org/10.1177/0888325416658950.

Smoter-Grzeszkiewicz, Regina. 2019. "Pan Kleks." In *Stanisław Zybała (bibliotekarz I regionalista),* edited by Marianna Zybała. Self-published. Szczebrzeszyn.

Snyder, Timothy. 2010. *Bloodlands. Europe Between Hitler and Stalin.* New York: Basic Books.

Szczepan, Aleksandra, and Łukasz Posłuszny. 2020. "Bielcza I Borzęcin. Ustanawianie I uśmierzanie pamięci o romskiej Zagładzie." In *Nie-miejsca pamięci (1). Nekrotopografie,* edited by Roma Sendyka, Maria Kobielska, Jakub Muchowski and Aleksandra Szczepan Warszawa: IBL PAN.

Szczepan, Aleksandra, Roma Sendyka, and Maria Kobielska. 2020. "Radecznica. Sieciowanie nie-miejsc pamięci." In *Nie-miejsca pamięci (1). Nekrotopografie,* edited by Roma Sendyka, Maria Kobielska, Jakub Muchowski and Aleksandra Szczepan. Warszawa: IBL PAN.

Szymański, Wojciech. 2020. "Curatorial commentary for the Małgorzata Mirga-Tas exhibition *Ćwiczenia ceroplastyczne.*" *Chapel Gallery in the Centre of Polish Sculpture in Orońsko.* Accessed June 9, 2020. www.rzezba-oronsko.pl/index.php?aktualnosci,1572,malgorzata_mirga_tas_29._cwiczenia_ceroplastyczne.

Taylor, Charles. 2007. *The Secular Age.* Cambridge, MA: Harvard University Press.

Zawiła, Małgorzata. 2019. *Dziedziczynienie przedwojennych cmentarzy na terenach postmigracyjnych Polski.* Kraków: Wydawnictwo Uniwersytetu Jagiellońskiego.

Zubrzycki, Geneviève. 2006. *The Crosses of Auschwitz. Nationalism and Religion in Post-Communist Poland.* Chicago: University of Chicago Press.

Żukowski, Tomasz. 2018. *Wielki retusz. Jak zapomnieliśmy, że Polacy zabijali Żydów.* Warsaw: Wielka Litera.

Part IV

Media and postsecular memory

13 The Crimean Tatars' memory of deportation and Islam

Elmira Muratova

Introduction

The Crimean Tatars owe their formation as a people to a long process of ethnogenesis that took place in the Crimean Peninsula[1] from the thirteenth to the sixteenth centuries. Representatives of the various ethnic groups that inhabited Crimea at different times participated in this process. These included Khazars, Cumans (Polovtsi), Greeks and Mongols. The Crimean Tatars consider themselves descendants of all these ethnic groups and one of the three indigenous peoples of Crimea.[2] Their native language belongs to the Turkic group, and they profess Sunni Islam. For more than three centuries (1441–1783), the Crimean Tatars had their own state, known as the Crimean Khanate, where they were the state-forming ethnic group. After the fall of the Crimean Khanate, the Crimean Tatars continued to inhabit Crimea, although their number as a proportion of the peninsula's total population was constantly decreasing. They gradually become a minority group in Crimea following several waves of Crimean Tatar emigration to the Ottoman Empire in the late eighteenth and early twentieth centuries and the settlement of the peninsula by natives of other Russian provinces (Williams 2000). By the end of the 1930s, the Crimean Tatars accounted for only about 20% of the total population[3] of Crimea (Ediev 2003, 242), which was by then an autonomous republic within the Russian Soviet Federated Socialist Republic of the USSR.

Islam and the customs and traditions associated with it occupied an important place in the identity and culture of Crimean Tatars. Islam was a unifying factor in the process of ethnogenesis that resulted in the appearance of the Crimean Tatar people (Ismailov and Muratova 2013, 83). For centuries, it was Islamic norms that determined the Crimean Tatars' way of life, worldview and values. The Crimean Khanate was an Islamic state in which Islam was the dominant religion. However, Islam's position within the state was significantly weakened by the spread of Russian, and later Soviet, culture through Crimea. The need to survive in an alien cultural environment forced the Crimean Tatars to borrow from the culture and values of other peoples and abandon some of their own religious traditions. An anti-religious campaign by the Soviet state in the 1920s and 1930s outlawed religion altogether. On the eve of the Second World War, almost all of Crimea's mosques and Muslim schools had been closed, and imams

DOI: 10.4324/9781003264750-17

268 *Elmira Muratova*

were not able to openly carry out religious ceremonies (Kondratyuk 2018, 33–34). In May 1944, the entire Crimean Tatar people were deported from Crimea on charges of collaborating with the enemy and resettled in Uzbekistan, the Urals, and other republics and regions of the USSR. Most Crimean Tatars were not able to return to Crimea until the late 1980s and early 1990s. Despite these cataclysmic events, the Crimean Tatars managed to preserve their religion and greeted the collapse of the Soviet state firm in their conviction of their Muslim identity. The post-Soviet period was marked by a religious revival that allowed the Crimean Tatars to intensify their religious life (Muratova 2008).

The collective memory of the Crimean Tatars includes an Islamic component appealing to their Muslim past. This past is mainly associated with the Crimean Khanate, regarded as the golden age of the Crimean Tatar people. This chapter attempts to reveal the role Islam has played in the Crimean Tatars' collective memory of one of the most significant events in their history: their forebears' 1944 deportation from Crimea. The genealogy of collective memory of the deportation passed through several stages. During the Soviet period, the Crimean Tatars were unable to openly talk about the deportation or commemorate its victims. The collective trauma remained within the community as it had no escape route. Opportunities to talk about the trauma and commemorate it only opened up after the collapse of the USSR, when the Crimean Tatar people were repatriated to Crimea, which by that time was already a republic in independent Ukraine. The post-Soviet period in Crimea was marked by the development of various media outlets devoted to the memory politics of the deportation. The Crimean Tatars' construction of memory of the deportation was paralleled by a similar process among Ukrainians wishing to work through the trauma of their communist past. Finally, post-2014 Crimea, which is de facto under Russian control, has seen attempts by the Russian authorities to regulate the memory politics of the deportation by means of state-approved forms of commemoration. Differing attitudes among Crimean Tatars towards Russia's control over Crimea have resulted in growing criticism of the discourse on the deportation formed by a religious institution loyal to Russia. The specific political context prevailing in post-2014 Crimea has resulted in this criticism turning into discussions between the secular and religious parts of the Crimean Tatar population.

Most of the data used in this chapter was collected in 2012 and presented earlier in a study titled 'The Past, Present and Future of the Crimean Tatars in the Discourse of the Muslim Community of Crimea' (Kouts and Muratova 2014). The study was based on interviews with thirty-seven informants, each of whom belonged to one of the four Islamic groups/organizations in Crimea – either the Spiritual Administration of Muslims of Crimea (SAMC), the Spiritual Center of Muslims of Crimea (SCMC), the Alraid Association or the Hizb ut-Tahrir Islamic Party. Even though the study mainly included Crimean Tatars who practise Islam (or are observant), its results, with certain reservations, can be extrapolated to the entire Crimean Tatar people. Other materials used in this chapter were obtained as a result of a post-2014 Crimean media discourse analysis.[4] I also rely on conclusions drawn from my own (sometimes participant) observations as a permanent resident of Crimea and member of the Crimean Tatar community.

The chapter consists of four parts. The first part deals with the concepts of collective memory and trauma as they were introduced into the social sciences by Halbwachs, Assmann, Olick, Bieler and others. I then go on to elaborate on the notion of deportation and its meaning for the Crimean Tatars. Next, I consider the politics of memory of the deportation in post-Soviet Crimea, revealing its religious dimension. The chapter concludes with an analysis of the Crimean Tatar discourse on the deportation, with a special focus on the features related to the Crimean Tatars' religious identity.

Collective memory and trauma

The founder of the study of collective memory, sociologist Maurice Halbwachs, argued that memory has social frames, which he understood to be the impact of society (through family, neighbourhood, ethnic and religious groups, etc.) on what and how an individual remembers. He believed that frames serve as a tool to recreate those images of the past that align with the dominant ideas of society at a given moment (Halbwachs 2007, 30). In other words, collective memory contains and reproduces those events of the past that are in tune with the aspirations and needs of a particular group in the present moment.

Further developing the theory of Halbwachs, Jan Assmann identified two types of collective memory: communicative and cultural. He associated both types with the mode of time. Communicative memory, according to the researcher, 'covers memories that are associated with the recent past. These are the memories that people share with their contemporaries' (Assmann 2004, 51). As an example of communicative memory, Assmann cites the memory of individual generations. This kind of memory is acquired by the group historically: 'This memory arises in time and passes together with it, more accurately, with its carriers. When the carriers that embodied it die, it gives way to new memory' (Assmann 2004, 53–54). Cultural memory, unlike communicative memory, is directed at certain fixed moments in the past. This memory, for Assmann, is sacred, mythologized and objectified in various forms, in particular through texts and commemorative practices. According to the author, all participants in a social group are involved in communicative memory, forming and supporting it: 'in this informal tradition, there are no specialists and experts, although some individuals can remember more and better than others' (Assmann 2004, 56). By contrast, cultural memory implies limited involvement and special intermediaries, such as teachers, scientists and writers.

Some researchers of collective memory mainly associate it with culture and note its role in the formation of group identity. The sociologist Jeffrey Olick understands collective memory as a separate and independent aspect of culture that generates consensus and a sense of collective identity (Olick 2007, 8). He believes that collective memory reflects a group's image of its past and finds expression in different forms, in particular, through monuments, music, poetry or sacred texts.

Scholars agree that collective memory actualizes different events of the past that tend to be significant. These often include tragic events involving collective violence. In this case, memories often take the form of collective trauma. Trauma refers to an engagement with the past in the aftermath of an event of over-whelming violence in which the actual horrific event cannot be recalled and cannot be brought into consciousness. This inaccessible event however returns and haunts the survivors in ways that cause new suffering.

(Bieler 2011, 50)

The field of trauma studies suggests that a healing ritual cannot take place unless a trauma story is being told. Acting as a witness to a trauma narrative provides a victim with the supportive context within which they can express the unspeakable (Stroinska, Szymanski, and Cecchetto 2014, 13).

When whole communities suffer atrocities, the collective trauma lingers within the fabric of individual families, communities and societies for genera-tions. Just as individual victims may need many years before they feel able to tell their personal stories of the trauma and begin to recover and return to life, the narrative of community trauma may only begin to be told in subse-quent generations (Audergon 2004, 20–21). Arlene Audergon believes that this process may often take fifty or even a hundred years. In her view, collec-tive trauma is often accompanied by a split in society, when one part of society (often an ethnic minority) has suffered an atrocity which they constantly refer to, while another part of society (as a rule, the dominant group) declares that it is time to move on. In post-Soviet Crimea, such a split in society was observed between the dominant group (in this case, Russians and Ukrainians) and the Crimean Tatar minority. Whereas Crimean Tatars called for justice and the restoration of the rights they had enjoyed before 1944 deportation, the major-ity of the population believed it was a time to forget past grievances and start all over again. Scholars suggest that for a traumatic event to become socially recognizable, it needs to pass through several levels of creation: an individual or a collective of people should start constantly recycling the issue within public space. According to Jeffrey Alexander, 'by allowing members of wider publics to participate in the pain of others, cultural traumas broaden the realm of social understanding and sympathy, and they provide powerful avenues for new forms of social incorporation' (Alexander 2012, 28). This process needs time and for a benevolent attitude to be shown by at least a proportion of the dominant group. The Crimean case is an interesting example of how this process develops in practice.

Research on the Crimean Tatars' memory of the deportation harmonizes with a growing body of studies on memories of injustices and traumatic moments (from the abuse and denial of human rights to deportation, starvation and death) caused by communist regimes. There is plenty of research dealing with memory in Ukraine (Yurchuk 2017; Törnquist-Plewa and Yurchuk 2017; Nikolko 2018; Myshlovska 2019) and other East European countries (Kucia, Duch-Dyngosz, and Magierowski 2013; Marschall 2013; Mitroiu 2015; Zubr-zycki 2006). All of these studies are contributing in a significant way to the reassessment of a past that was previously ideologized and the formation of national, ethnic and religious group identities.

The deportation and collective memory

There have been several events in the history of the Crimean Tatars that have radically changed the course of their lives and are therefore deeply rooted in their collective memory. The aforementioned 'Past, Present and Future' study (Kouts and Muratova 2014) showed that the Crimean Tatars highlight two events in their history: the annexation of Crimea by the Russian Empire in the late eighteenth century and the 1944 deportation. In the Crimean Tatars' discourse, the annexation and deportation act as events that negatively affected the lives of the people and determined the existence of various problems in their present development. The personal background of the respondents who participated in the study determined their preoccupation with religious issues. Thus, the main emphasis was placed on explaining the consequences of the annexation and deportation to the religious sphere. It would appear that the main consequences of these two events were the Crimean Tatars abandoning their religion, their traditions falling into oblivion, a general loss of spirituality and cultural assimilation (Kouts and Muratova 2014, 33–34). At the same time, it is the deportation that acts as a reference point, or a kind of boundary line that characterizes events in the Crimean Tatars' ethnic history on the basis of whether they occurred before or after that traumatic event. The deportation, as noted by Nikolko, who used Gilles Deleuze and Alain Badiou's theoretical concept of the 'Event' to flesh out his ideas, is one of the most important episodes in the twentieth-century development of Crimean Tatar ethnic identity, a collective trauma that provoked the creation of new discourses and significantly influenced the group's self-presentation (Nikolko 2018, 77).

The deportation of the Crimean Tatars took place on 18 May 1944, after the Soviet army liberated Crimea from the Nazi troops who had been controlling the peninsula from November 1941 to May 1944. As a result of a special operation carried out by the People's Commissariat of Internal Affairs (NKVD), more than 183,000 Crimean Tatars were deported from Crimea to various regions of the USSR. The official reason given for this was that the Crimean Tatars had been accused of mass collaboration with the enemy during the German occupation.[5] Once the Crimean Tatars reached their places of exile, they were forced to live in special settlements subject to a certain regime of restrictions. In March 1956, accusations of collaborating with the enemy were dropped, and the Crimean Tatars were rehabilitated, with many of their civil rights, although this did not include the right to repatriation or the right to restitution. In 1967, the Parliament of the Soviet Union officially recognized the injustice of the Crimean Tatars having been deported under Stalin's orders yet still prevented the Crimean Tatars from returning to their Homeland (Nikolko 2018, 73). According to Crimean Tatar activists, during the deportation and the first years of their exile, about 46% of the deportees died of hunger and disease (Uehling 2015, 3). As Uehling has argued, in addition to this bodily destruction, efforts were made to cleanse all traces of the victims from the Crimean landscape and to ensure the assimilation of survivors into their places of exile (Uehling 2004, 4). In the 1960s, the Crimean Tatars formed a national movement in their places of exile that sought permission from the authorities for their return to their Homeland in Crimea by using different methods (including petitions and appeals to the country's leadership, and pickets and rallies in the Central Asian republics and Moscow). It was at that time, as Nikolko notes, that the subjectivity of the Crimean Tatar people, which had been denied after deportation, became increasingly visible (Nikolko 2018, 72). The mass return of the Crimean Tatars to Crimea only became possible in the late 1980s and early 1990s following the weakening of the central government in Moscow and subsequent collapse of the USSR.

The memory of the deportation has become a constitutive narrative for the Crimean Tatars' national identity as well as one of the key distinctive features by which the majority of outgroups in Crimea identify them (Bezverkha 2017, 133). The importance of the deportation in the collective memory of the Crimean Tatars is determined by several main considerations. First, it is a relatively recent event in their ethnic history. Some of the people who were the direct victims of this tragedy are still alive, though they were all children at the time of the deportation. Second, the conditions of the deportation itself led to a significant number of victims. Almost every family has stories of relatives who either died during the forced displacement itself or during the first years of their lives in exile. Third, the deportation symbolized the separation of a people from their Homeland, the loss of their territory, and even statehood, and the transformation of the Crimean Tatars into a rogue nation of 'traitors', a label that became a kind of collective trauma that has still not healed.

Memory of the deportation is widespread among several generations of Crimean Tatars. It is remembered personally by the oldest generation, the witnesses to the tragedy who passed their memory to their children born in exile. It is remembered by the next generation, the children born in exile who passed through the regime of special settlements and experienced the difficulties of settling in a new place. The deportation is also remembered by the third generation of Crimean Tatars, the grandchildren of those who were exiled. Stories heard from their grandparents about their trials and nostalgia for their Homeland are all deeply rooted in the minds of this generation. The Crimean Tatars who were born in Crimea after the mass repatriation in the early 1990s, also remember the deportation (though to a lesser extent in relative terms). Their cultural memory has been formed by the politics of memory widely and variously represented in post-Soviet Crimea.

The politics of memory of the deportation

The Crimean Tatars returned to Crimea with a deep sense of rediscovering the Homeland that had been unjustly taken away from them by the Soviet authorities, a feeling that was consolidated by their collective memory of the deportation and its tragedy. This emotional upheaval was so powerful that it inspired thousands of Crimean Tatars to move back to Crimea despite the fact that they were leaving behind an established way of life and the stability of their places of exile. Naturally, driven by a sense of justice, the Crimean Tatars sought to pay tribute to the memory of deportation, honour its victims and recall the scale of the tragedy that had befallen the local (mainly Slavic)[6] population and especially the leadership of Crimea. Independent Ukraine, the state in which Crimea found itself after the dissolution of the USSR, made some effort to confront its Stalinist past and cultivate memories of the repression. As Uehling has argued, there were opportunities in post-Soviet Crimea to write the 1944 deportation back into the history books, replace the minarets on the mosques and erect multiple public monuments to commemorate Crimean Tatar military heroes and cultural leaders (Uehling 2015, 5). Consequently, the politics of memory of the 1990s and 2000s was dominated by the deportation, which occupied one of the key places in the Crimean Tatars' collective memory and identity. The Crimean Tatar media, historians and public figures used the personal memories of survivors of the deportation as an argument favouring the construction of an alternative memory of the Second World War that presents its true face and its consequences for the small ethnic groups of deportees in the USSR (Bezverkha 2017, 133). It is important to recognize the extent to which the Crimean Tatars were able, while the process was still far from complete, to reinstate their rightful presence on the peninsula and reinscribe their history on the landscape they hold sacred (Uehling 2015, 5).

The memory studies field suggests that there are four main types of 'media of politics' dedicated to the memory of a group that has become a victim of violence (Bieler 2011, 47). The first of these is affective media, which includes political or religious festivals, anniversaries, or holidays of remembrance intended to induce emotions that seek to serve a sense of collective identity and integration. One interesting example of this media of politics is the all-Crimean mourning rally that takes place on the annually celebrated Day of the Deportation of the Crimean Tatars. This rally makes evident the close interaction in Crimea between secular and religious actors in commemoration practices. The second type is aesthetic expressive media, which includes monuments, works of art, autobiographical and other writings, paintings and images. This type of media of politics dedicated to the deportation has been widely distributed in various forms across Crimea and is most vividly expressed, in movie form, in *Haytarma* (2013). This movie, which was dedicated to the deportation, became a landmark event in the lives of Crimean Tatars that also shows the interplay between the secular and religious in Crimean Tatar society. The third type of media of politics is instrumental cognitive media, represented by the creation of historical archives, books and documentaries. There is a growing body of historical literature available in Crimea on the deportation. The main focus of these works is on the publication of archival documents containing the official justification for the deportation and procedural instructions on how it should be conducted (Bekirova 2004; Bekirova 2017), statistical data on the Crimean Tatars who fought in the Red Army and guerrilla groups, and information about the awards and exploits of the Crimean Tatars during the Second World War (Kurtseitov

274 *Elmira Muratova*

2015; Polyakov 2013). Finally, the fourth type of media of politics, according to Bieler, is political moral media. This includes victim appeals for the perpetrators to be punished, reparation demands and calls for the establishment of truth and reconciliation commissions tasked with providing justice, rehabilitation or integration. Political moral media has not been used in Crimea, mainly because the main culprit in the tragedy of the Crimean Tatars (the Soviet state) did not exist anymore by that point. It should be added that the Crimean Tatars, neither in the years of their exile nor after their return to Crimea, did not put forward demands for the punishment of the perpetrators or the return of, or compensation for, the property that had been taken from them. Instead, they sought political rehabilitation and the permission to return to Crimea and called upon the authorities to assist in their socioeconomic development and the restoration of their political rights.[7] Given that the focus of this chapter is on the religious component of the commemoration practices in Crimea, I will address the first two types of media of politics dedicated to the deportation, notably affective and aesthetic expressive media, and reflect further on the all-Crimean mourning rally and the aforementioned movie *Haytarma*.

Public commemorations and religion

One of the most notable and effective methods of commemorating the deportation was the traditional all-Crimean mourning rally-march held annually on 18 May, the Day of the Deportation of the Crimean Tatars, in the central square in the capital of Crimea, Simferopol. This rally gathered up to tens of thousands of people from all over the peninsula and for many years was one of the most important events in the lives of the Crimean Tatar people. From the early 1990s to 2014, it was organized by the *Mejlis* of the Crimean Tatar people, an executive body formed by the Congress of the Crimean Tatars (*Qurultai*). The gathering took the form of public speeches by leaders of the *Mejlis*, the SAMC and representatives of the authorities and also served as a traditional venue for the airing of topical issues relevant to the Crimean Tatars and grievances about the authorities' tardy response to the resolution of the more pressing issues. It also performed an integrative function by actualizing the topic of the deportation within the collective memory of the Crimean Tatars and legitimizing the *Mejlis*, thereby demonstrating its mobilization capabilities to the authorities. This allowed the *Mejlis* to act as one of the influential political players in Crimea, forcing the Crimean and Ukrainian authorities into reckoning with its opinion. Over the entire post-Soviet period, the *Mejlis* were the leading secular actor in the politics of memory dedicated to the deportation in Crimea, and its vision for this politics has inspired Crimean Tatar journalists, artists, writers, historians and others.

The SAMC was the main religious actor in the Crimean politics of memory dedicated to the deportation. It is a centralized institution formed in 1992 to coordinate the Islamic revival in Crimea (Muratova 2008). It consistently performed the role of co-organizer of the mourning rally on the Day of the Deportation. The mufti who headed the SAMC was a regular speaker at the event, at which he addressed the public from the rostrum together with the leaders of the *Mejlis*. It was his duty to recite a prayer for the victims of the deportation. Besides these public prayers, the imams of all the 300 or so Crimean mosques controlled by the SAMC read a special sermon (*khutbah*) that also remembered the tragedy and commemorated the dead during the Friday prayers on the eve of the anniversary of deportation.

Islam is such an important part of Crimean Tatar identity and culture that it has become one of the main tools of commemoration. It is very difficult in post-Soviet Crimea to find a purely secular Crimean Tatar public commemoration of the deportation. Even ceremonies involving the laying of flowers at the memorial signs established throughout Crimea to mark the occasion of the deportation or the opening of exhibitions of paintings or other items devoted to the deportation are accompanied by religious rituals. They always take place in the presence of imams who recite prayers for the victims. Because the *Mejlis* and the SAMC have been allies in the promotion of the Crimean Tatar ethnic and political agenda in Crimea, the *Mejlis* has tried to use Islam to legitimize the 1944 deportation as the main event in the construction of Crimean Tatar identity. Ethnic narratives of the Crimean Tatars are basically constructed around a 'We' (the victims calling for justice) and 'They' (non-Crimean Tatars indifferent to our tragedy) dichotomy. This explains why secular and religious ceremonies go hand in hand in all commemorations devoted to the deportation.

Trauma, its artistic representations and religion

Since the mass repatriation to Crimea, a large array of aesthetic expressive media dedicated to the deportation of the Crimean Tatars have been created. These include monuments and memorials, paintings, billboards, collections of memories, stories, poems and songs. They are mainly created by (but not exclusively by) Crimean Tatars who sought to convey the pain of the tragedy through their use of such resources. When faced with a tragedy so large in scale that it was impossible to remember each victim separately and, crucially, with the absence of victim remains that could be buried and honoured, the Crimean Tatars decided to create means of remembrance that tended to be quite symbolic and were addressed to all victims at the same time.[8]

The example of aesthetic media that I have chosen to focus on is the feature film *Haytarma*, which was shot in 2013 by the Crimean Tatar director Akhtem Seytablaev. The film is named after a famous Crimean Tatar dance, which means 'return' and symbolizes the continuity of life. The film is dedicated to the deportation and shows the lives of Crimean Tatars on the eve of and during that tragedy. It came to mediate collective memory on the deportation and visualized multiple personal experiences in cinematic form (Zubkovych 2019, 53). The film is structured around the life of a half-Crimean Tatar fighter pilot, Amet-Han Sultan, who was a historical figure twice honoured as a hero of the USSR. It follows the protagonist through his period of service, when he was stationed in Crimea. The major turn in the plot comes when Amet-Han Sultan is given leave to see his family on the eve of the deportation. He and two friends find themselves in Amet-Han's home village on the night of the mass deportation (Uehling 2015, 7).

276 Elmira Muratova

A distinctive feature of the film is its crowd scenes involving ordinary Crimean Tatars, some of whom were direct victims of the deportation themselves. The film is based on personal histories and reflects Crimean Tatars' collective perceptions of the deportation and their customary manner of describing that event. The film contains scenes and symbols that are reproduced in the stories of the Crimean Tatars regardless of the victims' place of residence at the time of their deportation, their age or membership of a particular subgroup of the Crimean Tatar people.[9] These include religious symbols. For example, the film contains a scene showing how an elderly Crimean Tatar woman, on leaving her home to be sent to a place of exile, decides she has no need for any food or clothing and only takes the Holy Book of the Muslims, the Qur'an, saying that this book contains everything that is needed in this life. This scene reflects the story, widespread among the Crimean Tatars, of their trust in God at that critical moment, a motif that they often repeat when describing how the deportation took place. This motif has become an ever-present part of the collective discourse on the deportation. The young generation of Crimean Tatars who practice Islam like to cite this scene as an example when pointing out that people at that time were more devout than their contemporaries.

Thus, during the post-Soviet period of Crimea, numerous media of politics devoted to memory of deportation were created. These became a part of the cultural memory of the Crimean Tatars and ensured that the topic of the deportation would even be found in the collective discourse shared by those Crimean Tatars actually born in Crimea rather than any of the places of exile.

Politics of memory of the deportation from after 2014

The politics of memory dedicated to the deportation in post-2014 Crimea, which is de facto under the control of the Russian Federation, has been developing within the framework of state-controlled forms. Scholars believe that post-Soviet Russia only made limited efforts to confront its Stalinist past, seeming to prefer instead to suppress memories of repression and support the prevalence of the state-sponsored narrative over the victims' counter-histories (Adler 2012, 328). As a result of such a policy, the Day of the Crimean Tatars' Deportation has been depoliticized and generalized as a commemoration day for victims of the deportation of all Crimean peoples (Nikolko 2018, 88–89).

In 2014, the Crimean Tatars were allowed to hold small commemorations near the monuments to the victims of deportation and an all-Crimean rally in one of the suburbs of Simferopol. The following year, permission for the all-Crimean rally was refused altogether. In the rhetoric employed by the Crimean authorities, this decision was explained by their reluctance to 'politicize the day of mourning' (Nikiforov 2015). By 'politicization', officials meant that they wished to prevent the rally from becoming a place for Crimean Tatars' political statements and the expression of grievances against the authorities. Moreover, government officials also stressed that 18 May is not only the day of the Crimean Tatar deportation but also that of all the other peoples deported from Crimea during the Second World War (the Armenians, Greeks, Germans, etc.).

All public commemorations in post-2014 Crimea must be approved in advance by the authorities; otherwise they may be regarded as unauthorized rallies and punished under Russian law. In practice, only those organizations and people loyal to the authorities can secure such approval. Seeing as the *Mejlis* was banned in Russia as an extremist organization in 2016, its members are no longer able to organize any public commemorations. By contrast, the SAMC managed to develop working relations with the authorities and has become one of the most influential Crimean Tatar institutions in post-2014 Crimea. This, in turn, led to its legitimacy being questioned by certain groups among the Crimean Tatars, particularly those close to the *Mejlis*. It also forced the SAMC to reframe its discourse on the deportation developed during the previous period because it became problematic within the new political context and, as the next paragraph will show, caused discussions between the secular and religious parts of the Crimean Tatar population.

A deeper understanding can be gained of the context within which the media of deportation politics has been developing post-2014 by noting the desire of the Russian authorities not only to depoliticize and generalize the Day of the Deportation but also to minimize its impact on the Crimean Tatars' identity. This is how Crimean Tatars interpreted statements by officials on the need to stop calling them a 'deported people' as a way of ensuring that they are not enjoying special status (Ioffe . . . 2018). The same dispute was notable for a decision by the authorities to rename a committee, answerable to the Council of Ministers, which is responsible for building relations with the Crimean Tatar community. During the Ukrainian period of post-Soviet Crimea, it was called the Committee for Nationalities and Deported Citizens and was primarily engaged in promoting the integration of Crimean Tatars and other deported citizens into Crimean society. In 2019, the word 'deported' was removed from its title, and the committee became known as the Committee on Interethnic Relations (Nikiforov 2019).

The discourse of deportation and religion

While some unanimity can be found in the Crimean Tatars' discourse on the course and consequences of the deportation, there are certain differences of opinion regarding the causes of the tragedy between the observant and secular[10] Crimean Tatars. Observant Crimean Tatars, as shown by the 'Past, Present, and Future' study, tend to explain the causes of the tragedy by 'the will of God'. For them, this is an obvious conclusion to draw, which naturally follows from their religious consciousness, in which there is a clear understanding that everything that occurs in the world and the life of each person is according to God's will. And this opinion is shared by representatives of the different Islamic groups and movements interviewed in the course of the study, even though they have their differences on many other issues:

> From the point of view of religion, we can ask: why did God punish us? There were probably some violations.
>
> (male, 50, SAMC)[11]

Muslims will say that it is all by the will of God.

(female, 34, SCMC)[12]

I know it was predestined. . . . We had to go through it to be able to understand how we live and how we should live.

(female, 49, Alraid)[13]

When explaining the possible reasons for God's 'punishment' of the Crimean Tatars by God, the informants usually talked about the fact that their people, over many years of living under the Russian Empire and the Soviet government, had departed from Islam and forgotten their religion:

First of all, because Islam was not put into practice as a system of life.

(female, 28, Hizb ut-Tahrir)[14]

In 95 or even 98 per cent of the incidents that happen to people, according to the general understanding of Islam, a person should pay attention to his actions. . . . Responsibility should not only be placed on the leaders, I believe. . . . People themselves are to blame. They were passive.

(male, 35, SAMC)[15]

At the same time, the interviewees did not ignore the external causes of the deportation and pointed to the cultural/ideological differences between the Crimean Tatars and the rest of the population of Crimea, as well as the authorities' intention to 'purge' the peninsula of the 'other' population. However, in their view, the unfriendly intentions of external forces became a reality only because God wanted to 'punish' the people for their religious indifference.

Such an interpretation of the reasons for the deportation is still widespread among observant Crimean Tatars. For many years, it determined the content of the sermons read by the imams in the Crimean mosques on the eve of the anniversary of the deportation. And this interpretation was also typically adhered to by the imams at mosques controlled by the SAMC, which maintained close links with the *Mejlis*, a nationalist-oriented body, the main secular actor in the politics of memory of the deportation in Crimea. After 2014, many SAMC imams continued to read the sermons containing the same interpretation of the causes of the deportation. However, the changed political context has led many of the (mostly secular-oriented) Crimean Tatars who took a critical stance towards the SAMC's pro-Russian position to question whether such an interpretation accurately reflects the reality. They particularly strongly disagree with the contention that the tragedy was caused by 'God's punishment' of the people for their retreat from Islam. The very idea that the people themselves were guilty of the tragedy seems blasphemous to them. In May 2018, the Crimean Tatar newspaper *Avdet* published an article titled 'Are We Really to Blame for the Tragedy?', in which the author was inspired to raise that issue by a sermon in a mosque:

We are asked to consider whether the terrible events of 1944 were our people's punishment for their retreat from the true path, for the fact that people began to forget the name of their Lord. And today it should serve as a warning to us not to repeat the same mistakes.

(Zinedin 2018)[16]

The author makes clear that such statements, from his point of view, contradict common sense as well as the words the imam had pronounced at previous sermons. He draws particular attention to the inherent contradiction in these words being uttered by an imam who had previously said that Allah has endowed people with the mind and ability to think and he did this so that they could understand how the world works; angels sit on the shoulders of each person and write down all their good and bad deeds; and nothing will pass by and be forgotten and everyone will be rewarded on the day of judgment (Zinedin 2018). Furthermore, the author asks the question:

Why then, were the whole people indiscriminately subjected to such suffering? Why were the copybooks of each person's life not examined to determine a fair punishment [for each individual]? . . . There is a great deal of evidence that our ancestors were, in general, much more religious and God-fearing than we are. But all of them alike, each and every one of them indiscriminately, were sent to their deaths without trial.

Naturally, the article caused a heated discussion in social networks and received the support of representatives of the secular part of the Crimean Tatar population. Some of the social media comments were even harsher than the author's conclusions. For example, one of the participants in the discussion on Facebook said the following:

It is necessary to reject this malicious idea, regardless of who it comes from! If necessary, we will mobilize all the people against this lie! This is a Stalinist lie, designed for morons! All our troubles are from the country which destroyed our statehood only because historically it appeared in a more favourable situation. And to talk about the punishment of our people by God is not historical and is harmful to the national consciousness.[17]

Thus, contemporary Crimean Tatar discourse on the deportation contains many intersection points but also displays many significant differences in viewpoint depending on the place Islam occupies in the lives of different Crimean Tatar groups. After 2014, a new dividing line was added, which to a certain extent overlapped with the division into secular and observant Crimean Tatars. These two groups were also divided in terms of their opposing attitudes to Russia's control over Crimea.

Concluding remarks

The deportation has occupied one of the key places in the collective memory of the Crimean Tatars for many years. And if at first, to use Assmann's

280 Elmira Muratova

typology, it was a key topic in communicative memory, and was therefore discussed by the generation who were direct victims of the deportation as well as their children and grandchildren, it also gradually become one of the fundamental themes in the cultural memory of the Crimean Tatar people. Indeed, this theme was ultimately also shared by those who were born in post-Soviet Crimea and had therefore not experienced the consequences of deportation and had not even seen the places of their forebears' exile. The formation of cultural memory of the deportation was made possible in the Ukrainian period of post-Soviet Crimea by the emergence of a wide range of emotional aesthetic and instrumental media of politics dedicated to memory of the deportation. Taken together, they constitute a consolidated discourse on the deportation capable of explaining the course, scale and consequences of the tragedy. This unified discourse is shared and supported by representatives of different generations of Crimean Tatars, who tell similar stories about the deportation.

Religion plays an important role in the Crimean Tatars' collective memory of the deportation. This is evident from the involvement of religious organizations and individuals in the politics of memory as well as the presence of religious themes in the discourse on the deportation (as demonstrated by the story from the Qur'an in the film *Haytarma*) and the presence of discussions about the reasons for the deportation and its influence on the current situation. Religiously oriented Crimean Tatars appeal to history in the belief that their people should learn from the tragedy that has befallen them, reflect on their way of life and become more religious. For the religious institutions of the Crimean Tatars, the memory of deportation serves as a convenient tool for the realization of their agenda.

Although the religious leaders of the Crimean Tatars' perception of the causes of the deportation have remained unchanged throughout the post-Soviet period, it began to become problematic after 2014. Russia's arrival in Crimea changed the balance of power in a Crimean Tatar community within which the secular *Mejlis* previously used to be the most influential institution and the SAMC had simply followed its decisions. The banning of the *Mejlis* in 2016 automatically made the SAMC the only legitimate Crimean Tatar body and the latter could only survive by coming under the total control of the Russian authorities. Thus, the sermons given at mosques on the eve of the Day of the Deportation, which blame the Crimean Tatars themselves for the 1944 tragedy rather than mentioning the persecuting state (the USSR), have provoked discussions which were almost absent before 2014. These discussions consider the SAMC's dependence on the Russian authorities and its intentional avoidance of any mention of the Soviet state in order to prevent the strengthening of historically strong anti-Soviet/Russian sentiments among the Crimean Tatars.

Notes

1 The Crimean Peninsula is located in the south of Ukraine, where it is washed by the Black and Azov Seas. It has an area of 27,000 square kilometres.
2 The two other peoples are the Karaites and the Krymchaks.

3 According to the 1939 All-Soviet Union Census in the Crimean Autonomous Socialist Republic, the actual number of Crimean Tatars was 218,879.

4 The author has mainly analyzed materials from the Crimean Tatar newspaper *Avdet* (Return) and the Crimean Tatar segment of the Facebook social network.

5 Other peoples, including Armenians, Greeks, and Bulgarians, were expelled from Crimea on the same charge. In total, 225,000 people were expelled from Crimea (Williams 2001).

6 At the time of the mass return of the Crimean Tatars, the local population was still under the influence of Soviet propaganda, which positioned the Crimean Tatars as traitors. This only served to reinforce the Crimean Tatars' already heightened sense of justice at having been wronged.

7 This involved recognizing the status of the Crimean Tatars as an indigenous people of Crimea, which would give them the right to occupy senior positions in government and determine political and other agendas in Crimea.

8 Other groups that have been victims of collective violence have followed the same path. For more, see Sion (2011, 63).

9 There are three main subgroups of Crimean Tatars – the coastal (*yalyboylu*) group, the mountain (*tats*) group and the steppe (*nogaylar*) group – which differ from each other by virtue of their anthropological features, language dialects, etc.

10 Here, 'secular' refers to those Crimean Tatars who consider themselves Muslims because of their people's historical and cultural traditions, and thus they may not practice the basic norms of Islam, such as prayer, fasting, abstinence from alcohol, etc. According to a sociological study of 2009, such Muslims make up about 80% of the Crimean Tatar population (Muratova 2009, 10).

11 The interview quotes were translated from Russian by the author.

12 The SCMC was established in 2010 as an alternative structure to the SAMC. After 2014, it was renamed 'Tavrichesky Muftiyat' and continued its activities in Crimea.

13 Alraid is an association of public organizations established in 1997 to promote the development of Islam in Ukraine. The organization was created by Arab students who attended Ukrainian universities and had settled in Ukraine. After 2014, the Crimean branch of the association was renamed 'Creation' and received official registration following the passing of the relevant Russian legislation.

14 Hizb ut-Tahrir is an international, pan-Islamist political organization, which describes its ideology as Islam and its aim as the re-establishment of the Islamic Khilafah (Caliphate) or Islamic state in order to resume the Islamic way of life. It was established in 1953 in Palestine. In Crimea, the organization has been operating since the second half of the 1990s. In Russia, the party is officially regarded as terrorist and banned. In recent years, more than sixty Crimean Tatars accused of maintaining ties with this party have been persecuted in Crimea.

15 The quotes were translated from Russian by the author.

16 The quote was translated from Russian by the author.

17 The article was posted on Facebook on 19 May 2018, by which point it had attracted almost sixty comments from users either supporting or opposing its main arguments. It is interesting that, following pressure from the secular part of Crimean Tatar society, representatives of the SAMC began to deny that such thoughts could be heard during sermons.

References

Adler, Nanci. 2012. "Reconciliation with – or Rehabilitation of – the Soviet Past?" *Memory Studies* 5 (3): 327–38. https://doi.org/10.1177/1750698012443889.

Alexander, Jeffrey. 2012. *Trauma: A Social Theory*. Cambridge: Polity Press. https://doi.org/10.1111/1478-9302.12041.

Assmann, Jan. 2004. *Kul'turnaya pamyat': pis'mo, pamyat' o proshlom I politicheskaya identichnost' v vysokikh kul'turakh drevnosti* [Cultural Memory: Writing, Memory of the Past and

Political Identity in the High Cultures of Antiquity]. Translated by M. M. Sokol'skaya. Moscow: Yazyki slavyanskoi kul'tury.

Audergon, Arlene. 2004. "Collective Trauma: The Nightmare of History." *Psychotherapy and Politics International* 2 (1): 16–31. https://doi.org/10.1002/ppi.67.

Bekirova, Gulnara, ed. 2004. *Krymskotatarskaya problema v SSSR (1944–1991)* [The Crimean Tatar Problem in the USSR (1944–1991)]. Simferopol: Odzhak.

———. 2017. *Pol veka soprotivleniya: krymskie tatary ot izgnaniya do vozvrasheniya (1941–1991 gody)* [A Half-Century of Resistance: Crimean Tatars from Exile to Return (1941–1991)]. *Ocherk politicheskoi istorii.* Kiev: Kritika.

Bezverkha, Anastasia. 2017. "Reinstating Social Borders Between the Slavic Majority and the Tatar Population of Crimea: Media Representation of the Contested Memory of the Crimean Tatars' Deportation." *Journal of Borderlands Studies* 32 (2): 127–39. https://doi.org/10.1080/08865655.2015.1066699.

Bieler, Andrea. 2011. "Remembering Violence: Practical Theological Considerations." In *After Violence: Religion, Trauma and Reconciliation*, edited by Andrea Bieler, Christian Bingel and Hans-Martin Gutmann. Leipzig: Evangelische Verlagsanstalt GmbH.

Ediev, Dalkhat. 2003. *Demograficheskie poteri deportirovannykh narodov* [Demographic Losses of Deported Peoples]. Stavropol: Agrus.

Halbwachs, Maurice. 2007. *Sotsial'nye ramki pamyati* [Social Frames of Memory]. Translated by S. N. Zenkin. Moscow: Novoe izdatel'stvo.

"Ioffe predlojil otkazat'sya ot ponyatiya 'deportirovannyi' v pol'zu spravedlivogo razvitiya Kryma [Ioffe proposed to abandon the concept of 'deported' in favour of the fair development of the peoples of Crimea]." *KrymInform*, April 6, 2018. www.c-inform.info/news/id/63765.

Ismailov, Ayder, and Elmira Muratova, eds. 2013. *Islam v istorii I kul'ture Kryma* [Islam in the History and Culture of Crimea]. *Textbook.* Simferopol: Tavrida.

Kondratyuk, Grigoriy. 2018. "Etnokonfessional'naya politika v otnoshenii musulman Kryma v medzvoennyi period (20–30-e gg. XX veka). [Ethnic and religious policy regarding Muslims of Crimea in the interwar period (20–30s of XX century)]." *Krymskoe istoricheskoe obozrenie* 1: 27–39.

Kouts, Natalya, and Elmira Muratova. 2014. "The Past, Present, and Future of the Crimean Tatars in the Discourse of the Muslim Community of Crimea." *Anthropology & Archeology of Eurasia* 53 (3): 25–65. https://doi.org/10.1080/10611959.2014.1024066.

Kucia, Marek, Marta Duch-Dyngosz, and Mateusz Magierowski. 2013. "The Collective Memory of Auschwitz and World War II among Catholics in Poland." *History & Memory* 25 (2): 132–73. https://doi.org/10.2979/histmemo.25.2.132.

Kurtseitov, Refik. 2015. "Krymskie tatary vo Vtoroi mirovoi voine I posle. Geroi Sovetskogo Soyuza – nagradzdennye I otvergnutye. Bor'ba za chelovecheskoe dostoinstvo [Crimean Tatars during the Second World War and After. The Heroes of the Soviet Union – Rewarded and Rejected. The Fight for Human Dignity]." *Krymskoe istoricheskoe obozrenie* 2: 84–131.

Marschall, Sabine. 2013. "Collective Memory and Cultural Difference: Official vs. Vernacular Forms of Commemorating the Past." *Journal of South African and American Studies* 14 (1): 77–92. https://doi.org/10.1080/17533171.2012.760832.

Mitroiu, Simona. 2015. "Introduction." In *Life Writing and Politics of Memory in Eastern Europe (collective volume)*, edited by Simona Mitroiu. London: Palgrave Macmillan.

Muratova, Elmira. 2008. *Islam v sovremennom Krymu: indicatory I problemy protsessa vozrodzdeniya* [Islam in Contemporary Crimea: Indicators and Problems of Revival]. Simferopol: Elinio.

———. 2009. *Krymskie musul'mane: vzglyad iznutri (rezul'taty sotsiologicheskogo issledovaniya)* [The Crimean Muslims: A Look from Inside (the results of a sociological survey)]. Simferopol: Elinio.

Myshlovska, Oksana. 2019. "Delegitimizing the Communist Past and Building a New Sense of Community: The Politics of Transitional Justice and Memory in Ukraine." *International Journal for History, Culture and Modernity* 7: 372–405. https://doi.org/10.18352/hcm.561.

Nikiforov, Vadim. 2015. "Vlasti Kryma opravdalis' za zapret krymskotatarskogo mitinga I shestviya. Chinovniki dovol'ny, cho godovschina deportatscii proshla bez politiki [The Crimean authorities justified the ban on Crimean Tatar rally and march. Officials are happy that the anniversary of the deportation passed without politics]." *Commersant*, May 19, 2015. www.kommersant.ru/doc/2729800.

———. 2019. "Iz mejnatsional'nykh otnosheniy ubrali deportirovannykh [The Deported Were Removed from Interethnic Relations]." *Commersant*, October 16, 2019. www.kommersant.ru/doc/4126881.

Nikolko, Milana. 2018. "Collective Trauma, Memories, and Victimization Narratives in Modern Strategies of Ethnic Consolidation: The Crimean Tatar Case." In *Crisis and Change in Post-Cold War Global Politics. Ukraine in a Comparative Perspective*, edited by Erica Resende, Dovilė Budrytė and Didem Buhari-Gulmez. Palgrave Macmillan. https://doi.org/10.1007/978-3-319-78589-9.

Olick, Jeffrey. 2007. *The Politics of Regret: On Collective Memory and Historical Responsibility*. New York: Routledge.

Polyakov, Vladimir. 2013. *Partizanskoe dvidzenie v Krymu 1941–1944 gg*. [The Partisan Movement in Crimea 1941–44]. Simferopol: IT "ARIAL".

Sion Brigitte. 2011. "Missing Bodies, Conflicted Rituals: Performing Memory in Germany, Argentina, and Cambodia." In *After Violence: Religion, Trauma and Reconciliation*, edited by Andrea Bieler, Christian Bingel and Hans-Martin Gutmann. Leipzig: Evangelische Verlagsanstalt GmbH.

Stroinska, Magda, Kate Szymanski, and Vikki Cecchetto. 2014. "Introduction: We need to Talk about Trauma." In *The Unspeakable: Narratives of Trauma*, edited by Magda Stroinska, Vikki Cecchetto and Kate Szymanski. PL Academic Research. https://doi.org/10.3726/978-3-653-04423-2.

Törnquist-Plewa, Barbara, and Yuliya Yurchuk. 2017. "Memory Politics in Contemporary Ukraine: Reflections from the Postcolonial Perspective." *Memory Studies* 12 (6): 699–720. https://doi.org/10.1177/1750698017727806.

Uehling, Greta Lynn. 2004. *Beyond Memory: The Crimean Tatars' Deportation and Return*. New York: Palgrave Macmillan. https://doi.org/10.1162/jinh.2007.37.3.457.

———. 2015. "Genocide's Aftermath: Neostalinism in Contemporary Crimea." *Genocide Studies and Prevention: An International Journal* 9 (1): 3–17. https://doi.org/ 10.2307/20034393.

Williams, Brian Glyn. 2000. "Hijra and Forced Migration from Nineteenth-Century Russia to the Ottoman Empire." *Cahiers du monde russe* 41 (1): 79–108. https://doi.org/10.4000/monderusse.39.

———. 2001. *The Crimean Tatars*. Leiden, Boston and Cologne: Brill.

Yurchuk, Yuliya. 2017. "Reclaiming the Past, Confronting the Past: OUN – UPA Memory Politics and Nation Building in Ukraine (1991–2016)." In *War and Memory in Russia, Ukraine and Belarus*, edited by Julie Fedor, Markku Kangaspuro, Jussi Lassila and Tatiana Zhurzhenko. Palgrave Macmillan. https://doi.org/10.1007/978-3-319-66523-8_4.

Zinedin, Dilyaver. 2018. "My sami vinovaty v etoi tragedii? [Are We to Blame for This Tragedy?]." *Avdet*, May 19. Accessed November 25, 2019. https://avdet.org/ru/2018/05/19/my-sami-vinovaty-v-etoj-tragedii.

Zubkovych, Alina. 2019. "Politics of Cinematic Representation of Crimean Tatars in Ukraine: 2003–2018." *Euxeinos – Culture and Governance in the Black Sea Region* 9 (28): 47–64.

Zubrzycki, Geneviève. 2006. *The Crosses of Auschwitz: Nationalism and Religion in Post-Communist Poland*. Chicago: University of Chicago Press. https://doi.org/10.1086/651993.

14 The Soviet past in contemporary Orthodox hymnography and iconography

Per-Arne Bodin

Up to 1917, historians of the Russian Church were only familiar with a few martyrs. However, the Soviet persecution of religion totally changed the picture (Caridi 2015, 46–99). Since the fall of the Soviet Union, the Church has canonized approximately 2,000 martyrs for sacrificing their lives for their Christian faith. They are officially known as the New Martyrs, or *novomucheniki*. Vitae and hymns have been written to commemorate these saints, and icons have been painted to depict their deeds. In the vitae, the stories of their lives and details from their biographies are collected and presented according to the rules of the vita genre. Photographs have been published, most of which were taken by the secret police as a record of the future martyrs' faces.[1]

In this chapter, however, the focus will be placed on the liturgical texts and icons commemorating the New Martyrs rather than their vitae and biographies. The aim will be to analyze the artistic means used to describe the Russian Revolution and its immediate consequences for the Church, in particular the arrest of the newly elected patriarch, the murder of the Romanov family, the murder of two bishops and a number of attacks on religious processions. Art forms from the Middle Ages are being reused in modern memory making. Attention will be drawn to the relation between these ecclesiastical forms of art and their broader Soviet cultural context. The texts and the images will be analyzed as a single variety of religious memory. The use of these texts and images will be seen both as an attempt to reconsider the Soviet past and reach a reconciliation with it.

This chapter will analyze religious memory with a special focus on ritual memory or, when this is set into a Christian context, liturgical memory of the New Martyrs. Ritual memory is one of the most robust forms of memory making (Halbwachs 1992, 116). Jan Assmann points out that 'religious rituals are without doubt the oldest and most fundamental medium of bonding memory' (Assmann 2006, 11). This statement is especially relevant to the Orthodox Church's declarations on the permanence of its ritual practices. Christianity has broadly been defined as a 'memory religion' (Feistner 2003, 259) whose worship combines both linear (the salvation history) and circular (the church calendar) time. One of the most important aspects of the Eucharistic celebration is the anamnesis represented by the words 'do it in remembrance of me'.

DOI: 10.4324/9781003264750-18

In Orthodox worship, the commemoration of Christ's death and resurrection is expanded to incorporate the *memoria* of the Mother of God, the saints and the remembrance of virtually all the dead and living.[2] In Orthodox practice, this remembrance is realized both sacramentally in the Eucharist and in the mentioning of the names of the saints throughout the service in prayers as well as in the veneration of icons and the singing of hymns.

Brian A. Butcher notes, when elaborating on memory practices in the Orthodox Church, that such ritual memory expresses the core value of a religion:

> Inasmuch as the events commemorated by the liturgy can be considered also as 'limit-experiences', it would seem that the ritual process that serves for the preservation of the Church's collective memory must similarly constitute, in some sense, a final court of appeal.
>
> (Butcher 2018, 206)

In other words, ritual memory selects the most important and relevant parts of collective memory within its domain.

God and the double addressee

The remembrance process has a pedagogical function, what might be called a 'liturgical paideia', which operates within and between generations (Butcher 2018, 197). An important characteristic of liturgical or ritual commemoration is its repeatability. In fact, it is reproduced more or less exactly every year in each church. Saints also perform a function through their intercession between the Church and God. It is crucial for liturgical memory that the ritual, which in practice takes the form of texts, song, images and movement, does not only have the congregation as its addressee, but also God. This is stressed by Paul Ricoeur in his book *Essays on Biblical Interpretation* (1980, 88–89).

Thus, two sorts of memory exist in religious memory making in the Orthodox Church: the first of these is memory of man in history, within one generation and between generations, individually or collectively, and the second is God's memory of man and mankind. This is clearly illustrated in the last words of the Orthodox burial service: 'Eternal Memory'. This expression plays the same liturgical role as 'eternal rest' in the Western tradition, so is not only understood as historical remembrance, or a summons to remember the deceased, but also God's remembering of man. The Russian religious philosopher Pavel Florensky elaborates on these two meanings in *The Pillar and Ground of the Truth* (1997, 144).

All remembrance in the Orthodox tradition is addressed to God, who is the ultimate arbiter of remembering, forgiving or forgetting. During the Eucharistic service, the words of the good thief are always quoted: 'But like the thief, I confess to You: Remember me, Lord, in Your Kingdom'.

The icons have the same double addressee. Beyond their pedagogical meaning and mystical imagery, they perform the role of praising God. The French philosopher, Jacques Lacan, neatly elaborates on this and emphasizes that icons exist to please God. God is their primary addressee:

> What makes the value of the icon is that the god it represents is also looking at it. It is intended to please God. At this level, the artist is operating on the sacrificial plane – he is playing with those things, in this case images, that may arouse the desire of God.
>
> (Lacan 2018, 113)

This is the theological foundation for the liturgical celebration of the Russian New Martyrs. In this chapter I will scrutinize the mechanisms of this memory celebration against the background of an overview of the functioning of religious and ritual memory in the Orthodox tradition. I will also consider the role played by ritual memory in Russia in the secular world that has followed on from the Soviet atheistic period. I will be seeking answers to three questions. First, is it possible to integrate the Soviet Gulag experience into liturgical memory making, and if so, how is this done? Second, have there been any changes to or renewals within this robust memory making system? And finally, what happens to this special form of memory making as it is refracted through new media that not only offer new possibilities for the distribution of texts, visual representations and music but that also present new opportunities for this message to be manipulated?

With a few exceptions, before Soviet times, no martyrs were recognized by the Russian Church. However, throughout the seventy years following 1917, the Church was persecuted to the point where it nearly collapsed. Many bishops, priests, monks, nuns and other servants of the Church, and even laymen, were arrested and executed or died in prison camps because of their faith. As part of the canonization process, a special commission was assembled to collect material on martyrs from across Russia, and specific criteria, and even anti-criteria, for canonization were established to formalize the process of designating a new saint (Hyldal Christensen 2018).

Material and purpose

In this chapter I will focus on the *Assembly of New Martyrs* icon and its depiction of the revolutionary events from 1917 through to the Great Terror in the 1930s. It is a collective and cumulative icon in which the painters sought to capture the entire traumatic experience of the Soviet era. I will also investigate the hymnographical texts that relate to it: first, the *sluzhba*, which is hymns and prayers pertaining to all divine services for that day; and then the *akathistos*, a semi-liturgical type of hymn popular in Russian Orthodox practice. I will consider the textual and visual means used in them to depict the revolution and its immediate consequences for the Church. The hymnographic texts (the service texts were approved by the Church in 2002 and the akathistos in 2009) and the icon both date from around the year 2000 (Zhurnal 2002). The Assembly of the New Martyrs is celebrated annually on the nearest Sunday to 25 January, according to the Old Calendar. I will also refer to some other hymnographic texts pertaining to other New Martyrs, and in particular, to the tsar's family. Some other pieces of art will occasionally be drawn into the analysis for illustrative purposes.

The liturgical texts dedicated to the Assembly of the New Martyrs have a collective authorship, as is often the case with Orthodox hymnography, but one author in particular is mentioned in them: Bishop Afanasy of Kovrov. Given that he was confined to Soviet prison camps for eighteen years, some of his texts could thus be viewed as autobiographical, his own testimony, as it were, from the Gulag.[3] His texts are, however, devoid of any biographical details of his experience there.

The liturgical celebration contains text, icons, rituals and music that combine to form what the Russian religious philosopher Pavel Florensky defined as a synthesis of all arts (Florensky 2002, 95–112). My intention is thus to study the dual role of memory, both historical and sacramental, in these texts and images. The aim of the analysis is to consider liturgical memory within the context of the Soviet and post-Soviet realities.

Liturgical texts and Soviet history

All liturgical texts devoted to the New Martyrs are written in Church Slavonic and use Byzantine genres of hymnography. The melodies are the same as those traditionally used in divine services and are based on the Byzantine system of eight tones. Words referring to the modern world are absent from the Church Slavonic language, so the experiences of the revolution and the harassments in Soviet times must be translated into common Christian and medieval categories. This generalizing trait is, however, typical of Christian ritual practice as a whole. When listening to the singing of these hymns in church, the worshipper must then either retranslate the words back to the revolution and Soviet contexts or understand them as timeless expressions of good and evil independent of historical context.

There are different reasons for the application of this encoding method. The genre, as such, shuns details and the Church Slavonic language is devoid of any words for modern realia. Moreover, as some of the hymns were written in Soviet times, they had to be encoded or generalized to avoid censorship. This political encoding and decoding is a special case of what in Russian culture is called the Aesopian language, a literary language used in times of censorship, and one in which both the author and the reader (and sometimes even the censor) understand or are supposed to infer the hidden meaning (Sandomirskaja 2013, 188–98).

The crucial point, however, is that the liturgical memory of saints in the Orthodox tradition is characterized by its impersonality. It contains praises and a petition (Schmemann 1975, 146), but only the most important messages are left in these texts for their simultaneous addressees: the congregation and God.

288   *Per-Arne Bodin*

This tendency towards generalization is well exemplified by the following hymn, which describes the revolution; the forced abdication, internment and murder of the tsar and his family; and the civil war, foreign intervention and emigration, viewed through the prism of a service dedicated to the Romanov family, who are officially designated as passion-bearers. Despite the intervention being mentioned of several countries during the civil war, the burden of guilt is placed on the shoulders of the Russians themselves in almost all cases:

> When many of our kinsmen departed from God, turned away from God's commandments and rose up against the Lord and His anointed, then God's wrath came over the land of Russia and the love of many withered. The blood of our brethren was shed, the people of Russia were spread all over the face of the earth, our shrines were defiled, hunger, invasion of foreigners affected us, and we were ridiculed by all peoples.
>
> (*Sluzhba sviatym tsarstvennym strastoterptsam*)

The main idea in Orthodox hymnography in general is the use of a typological interpretation of holy history that compares the New Testament or recent events with episodes and characters that are mostly taken from the Old Testament, thereby weaving together the old and the new.

A good example of this interpretation is the utilization of the biblical tale of the murder of Abel, Adam and Eve's son, by his envious brother Cain. In the hymns, a parallel is drawn between Abel's murder and the Russian civil war which followed the revolution: 'It is for our sake that we, unworthy ones, beseech you, our holy relatives, not to forget your earthly fatherland because of the sin of Cain's fratricide, the desecration of shrines and godlessness burdened by our unlawfulness' (*Akafist*).[4]

The name of the god Baal is often used in the hymns to represent the foreignness of Marxism and the revolution: 'I beweep our blinded generation; do not abandon us in the wild madness of passions and sins and veneration of a foreign Baal' (*Akafist*). Baal is a heathen God from the Old Testament, persecutor of the righteous and rival to Yahweh. God says, according to Saint Paul (Romans 11:4, referring to 1 Kings 19:18): 'Yet I have reserved seven thousand in Israel, all whose knees have not bowed to Baal, and every mouth that has not kissed him'. This is the view of the Church: the New Martyrs were among these 7,000 righteous. This use of Baal is also significant in that this allusion is not only borrowed from the Bible and Orthodox hymnography. It was also one of the favourite mythical allusions used by Marx to refer to the capitalists (e.g. in his description of the stock exchange as the 'Temple of Baal').[5] In the Orthodox hymnography, Marx, along with Lenin, turns out to be a disciple of Baal, or even Baal himself.

The country where the martyrs lived, and for which they gave their lives to defend, is not named the Soviet Union, and normally not even Russia either. Instead, it is referred to as a sacred space called *Holy Rus'*. The ancient toponymy represents a special holy space that is inhabited by the saints inside the Soviet Union, but is not identical to the state. The toponomy of Rus' also

Soviet past in hymnography and iconography 289

has truly Soviet origins. The official title of the leader of the Russian Orthodox Church is the Patriarch of Moscow and all Rus'. The use of this ancient title was renegotiated between the Church leader of that time, Metropolitan Sergei, and Stalin during their meeting in 1943, when the Church was permitted to act more freely and to consecrate a new patriarch (Dickinson 2000, 337–46).

It is also significant that in these hymnographic texts dedicated to the New Martyrs that the country is often personified, and the people are viewed as a single entity. The guilt of the people, viewed collectively and not only that of sinners, is a special trait in these hymns. The hymns often use the first-person plural. A collective 'we' indicates collective guilt, and an exclusive 'we' is used for the believers standing against the common enemy of the Communist Party and the Soviet government. This use of pronouns is a method for generalizing the Soviet experience that imbues it with a common Russian or Christian meaning. Viewed from a political and contemporary perspective, this may also be understood as a way of blurring the guilt while also evading individual responsibility and avoiding the need to reckon with the Soviet past. Both interpretations are equally applicable.

The time denoted in these hymnographic texts is not 1917, the year of the revolution, or a later Soviet time, but the 'last hours' or the 'cruel time' as understood in the Slavic book of Psalms. There is an apocalyptic tone to the language used throughout all the hymnographic texts. Prison guards are referred to as the demonic host and the prison camps are compared to the Babylonian captivity, and at the same time they are described as worse than the Egyptian yoke – two other parallels to the Old Testament.

Such comparisons to the world of the Old Testament are especially important in a traditional hymnographic genre called the canon, in which a depicted event is compared to an eternally reoccurring set of biblical events. In the first ode of this genre, the sacred event is likened to the Jews' crossing of the Red Sea (Wellesz 1999, 123–245). This is also the case in the canon to the New Martyrs. The blood of the martyrs drowns the godless (symbolizing the revolutionaries or the Bolsheviks) in the same way as the Egyptians were drowned in the Red Sea: 'You drowned the godless tormentors with your blood, as in the Red Sea' (*Sluzhba novomuchenikom*). Another typological parallelism is Christ's suffering and Christ's blood.

One more typological parallel in the text pertains to the Three Young Men in the Furnace (Daniel 3:1–30). This compares the revolution and the harassment of believers that followed it to Nebuchadnezzar's torture of these young men. Such an allusion is often drawn in the hymnography, notably as a recurring image or antitype in odes seven and eight of the canon, but this is very suited to and common in all texts about the New Martyrs from Soviet times:

> The children in Babylon are not afraid of the flames, and the New Martyrs of Russia, and they likewise reckoned for nothing the persecution of the godless, and now we sing according to them: blessed be thou, Lord God our father.
>
> (*Sluzhba novomuchenikom*)

290   Per-Arne Bodin

Such comparisons also have a special Russian significance. The 'furnace play', which depicts this event in the Old Testament, was a unique theatrical performance performed in Russian cathedrals up to the time of Peter the Great, who forbade it (DiMauro 2006). Sergei Eisenstein used it in one of the most famous episodes of the second part of his historical film *Ivan the Terrible*. This scene, which is set in Uspensky Cathedral in the Kremlin, shows the refusal of the Metropolitan Philip to bless Ivan the Terrible while the furnace play is performed in the foreground. At this point, the performers are singing hymns of the canon genre about the unjust ruler. Stalin seems to have grasped the parallel to himself, and the film was swiftly forbidden. It did not receive its premiere until the time of the Thaw, although the script was published as early as 1944 (Eisenstein).

At this point in the analysis, it would be useful to create a lexicon of words and notions from the hymns that can be translated back into the Soviet reality:

The temptation of a false worldly paradise	Communism
The foreign Baal	Marx
People fighting against God and breathing murder	Communists
Cain's fratricide	The civil war
Cruel time	Soviet time
Cruel works, bitter works	Forced prison camp labour
The Babylonian captivity	The Gulag
The Egyptian yoke	The Gulag
Holy Rus'	The Soviet Union
Nebuchadnezzar	Lenin, Stalin
The three men in the furnace	The New Martyrs
The demonic host	Prison guards
Fear	The Stalinist Terror

The word 'today' often replaces the Biblical 'in that time'. In Schmemann's understanding of Orthodox liturgical theology, 'the whole meaning of the Feast Day is to give us a vison of the eternal "this day"' (1975, 136). This word substitution can be seen in the text of the *Sluzhba novomuchenikom*: 'Today, the church is rejoicing', 'Today the New Martyr of Russia in white robes is coming to the Lamb of God'.

The mechanism works as follows: the events are generalized so that a declining number of future generations will remember the actual facts. What will be left is the moral message of good and evil, bravery and cowardliness, and eventually just the icon and the chapter in the hymnbook: the *Assembly of New Martyrs*. All sins will be forgiven, as indicated in one of the hymns addressed to the Mother of God: 'Blessed Virgin, our land is devastated by deplorable and godless attacks. For this cause, we pray to You now: forgive the people who have sinned and save Holy Rus' (*Sluzhba novomuchenikom*).

The New Martyrs are celebrated on both the date of the feast of the Assembly of the New Martyrs and on the individual days dedicated to each martyr, who in principle have their own individual icons and individual hymnographic texts. There is therefore a huge demand for hagiographic and hymnographic material which cannot always be satisfied. Such a multitude of texts already exist that a kind of saturation point has been reached. Now that the times have changed, the canonization process seems to have halted. A few of the New Martyrs are still popular among the believers, but some of them have been forgotten already. The enormous amount of memorial days devoted to them has paradoxically led to their oblivion.

There are many icon painters in Russia, so producing icons of the New Martyrs does not seem to be a problem, but the challenge of finding skilful hymnographers is much more difficult to solve. There are so few of them partly because the hymnographic tradition was broken after the revolution much more definitively than in the case of icon painting. Despite the ongoing creation of new texts, parishes often have to use the so-called *General Menaia*, which is a handbook of hymns devoted to different categories of saints that only contains formulas into which a priest can insert whatever name is needed (Mother Mary and Ware 1969, 540). These texts were collected long before the revolution. The lack of texts or books in each church also has practical consequences for the concept of collective martyrdom. The liturgical process is coping with the Soviet experience by erasing all individuality from the liturgical act. This is also contributing to the reduction of any need to handle the question of personal guilt by transforming it into collective memory.

Another significant factor is that in most cases there is no site for the martyr's body and no relics, both important prerequisites for canonization. The saints were executed by the Soviet authorities and buried in mass graves such as those at Butovo on the outskirts of Moscow (Hyldal Christensen 2018; Bogumił and Łukaszewicz 2018, 936–63). The relation between the body of the saint and his or her veneration is lost. The anonymous mass graves pose an obstacle to the development of the devotion of the New Martyrs. Butovo is one example of an attempt being made to create a site of collective memory for a mass murder.

The *Assembly* icon

The *Assembly* (or *Synaxis*) *of the New Martyrs* (Figure 14.1) icon was revealed and venerated at a large solemn divine service on 20 August 2000 that functioned, in a sense, as the apogee of the canonization process of the Russian New Martyrs. The generalization that occurs in liturgical celebration texts is also applied to the painting of icons. In a commentary published by the Church itself, it is clear that a pre-existing model was being used, notably that of 'Assembly icons' depicting saints with a church positioned in the centre of the image (*Opisanie*). The church chosen for this icon was not, as one might have expected, one of the Kremlin cathedrals. Instead, it was the Christ Saviour Church that was selected. This church in the southern part of central Moscow possesses a special significance within this context because it was torn down during the Stalinist era, then rebuilt in the early post-Soviet period as an important symbolic act

Figure 14.1 The *Assembly (or Synaxis) of New Martyrs* icon.
Source: With permission of the St Tikhon Orthodox Theological Institute.

indicative of the Church's rebirth. The building itself stands out as a victim and a martyr, as stressed by the commentary the Church provides for this icon: 'The Church of Christ the Saviour was chosen to be depicted due to its obvious symbolic and factual connection both with the sufferings of the Russian Church and with Her rebirth in our day' (*Opisanie*).

Stylistically, the painters have clearly been inspired by icons from the sixteenth century, especially those by artists of the Moscow school who were mentored by the icon painter Dionisy. Consequently, the icon's style does not accord with that of icon painting dating from the period immediately before the revolution. The uppermost part of the icon depicts a traditional *Deesis* composition with Christ seated on the throne in the centre, where he is surrounded by Theotokos and John the Baptist, as well as the archangels and Peter and Paul, supplemented by the addition of many Russian saints from earlier times including the Grand Prince Vladimir, Boris and Gleb, the Metropolitans Peter and Alexy, Sergey and Serafim, and so on. This composition creates a link between the New Testament and Russian ecclesiastical history and a connection between Old Russia, the revolution, the Soviet epoch and modern times. This makes it possible to comprehend the continuity between the saints of Soviet times and their predecessors.

The Church's intention in creating this icon was to venerate a collective holiness and a collective martyrdom, which explains the multitude of characters depicted in the icon. It can be compared to, and viewed alongside, a painting that was much discussed at the time, the famous artist Ilia Glazunov's *The Eternal Russia*, a work created in 1988 that attempts to summarize Russian history by depicting hundreds of figures (Figure 14.2). Glazunov's painting can be viewed as a demarcation point both signalling the end of socialist realism and heralding the beginning of post-Soviet monumental nationalistic art. Both the icon and Glazunov's painting reproduce well-known figures from different epochs of Russian history. Furthermore, both Glazunov and the icon painters behind the *Assembly* are both looking for and creating a historical continuum in Russia.

Figure 14.2 Ilia Glazunov, *The Eternal Russia* 1988. Painting.

Source: https://upload.wikimedia.org/wikipedia/commons/1/1f/Photo_of_Ilia_Glazuov%27s_paint_%22Timeless_Russia%22_.jpg (accessed 25 January 2021).

294 *Per-Arne Bodin*

The remembrance of the martyrs is reproduced in the upper part of the centre of the icon by halos with no faces beneath them. The commentary explains: 'In accordance with ancient tradition, the multiplicity of unknown ascetics is indicated by the halos rising above the upper row of depicted hierarchs' (*Opisanie*).

This is the Church's way of remembering the martyrs and saints known only to God. The principle of impersonality is taken here to an extreme: the saints have no name, no image and no biography. Whereas in the Soviet Union, names were erased and their use was prohibited, in the icon the saints without any faces are reassigned their celestial identity.

Traditional forms of martyrdom are depicted in miniatures that run along all four sides of the icon. These miniatures are called *kleima* and reflect a practice often used in biographic icons showing the life of a holy person. They demonstrate incidents of harassment that took place in different parts of the country and at different times, but mainly date from the years immediately following the revolution. These small images map the Soviet Christian Martyrdom to form a sort of iconic historical narrative that traces the revolution, the murder of the tsar and his family (Figure 14.3), the closing and destruction of the Trinity monastery, the show trial against Metropolitan Veniamin of Petrograd and the confinement of the newly elected patriarch Tikhon (Figure 14.4). It employs the same artistic principles and formulas as in the old icon paintings, but here they are used to present the Soviet reality.

Very occasionally, Soviet realia can be seen in the compositions. For example, the guards depicted in these images wear *budenovki*, the special hats worn by Red Army soldiers. The small pictures constantly refer to the lives and martyrdom of earlier saints in the history of the Christian church. Clearly, these small pictures and the suffering depicted within them are modelled on the repertoire of torment that the martyrs of the ancient Church were subjected to.

Two features of the official commentary to the *kleima* published by the Church are particularly notable. First, the text very often operates within a general harmony–chaos opposition, with the Church representing order and the Soviet world representing chaos. Second, the text draws attention to how colours are used in the icon to convey certain messages. For example, the holiness of the martyrs and the demonic character of their opponents are stressed with the aid of a contrast being drawn between bright colours representing the martyrs and murky ones the tormentors. This is the way the Russian Orthodox Church tells its story of the Soviet past. In the following part of this chapter, I will focus more closely on some of the *kleima*.

One miniature shows the murder of the two bishops, Andronik and Ermogen, just a couple of years after the revolution (Figure 14.5). Andronik was buried alive and Ermogen was chained to a stone and thrown into the River Tobol.

The martyrs are depicted as if they were in icons from Medieval Russia, and as if they were wearing their episcopal robes rather than prison clothes when they were killed. The drowning of the martyr has its equivalent in the previously mentioned metaphor of martyrs drowning the enemies of the Church in

Soviet past in hymnography and iconography 295

Figure 14.3 The murder of the tsar and his family. Miniature from the *Assembly* icon.
Source: With permission of the St Tikhon Orthodox Theological Institute.

their own blood. The stories told about the New Martyrs are, as noted earlier, reminiscent of the narratives about the early Christian martyrs. Details of more modern forms of horror and torture are eliminated from the depictions in the icons. Such details would be incongruous with the medieval aesthetics and inessential according to the generalizing conventions of ritual memory making.

Two *kleima* depict the fate of the Romanov family. Nicholas II has been canonized with all his family, which has aroused much discussion and criticism, because the extent to which they adhered to the Christian way of life and especially the righteousness of the rule of the tsar himself have been called in question.

Figure 14.4 Patriarch Tikhon in confinement. Miniature from the *Assembly* icon.
Source: With permission of the St Tikhon Orthodox Theological Institute.

The canonization commission discussed the Tsar's suitability at length and the Metropolitan Yuvenaly, chairman of the canonization committee, explained that the tsar's responsibility had never been confirmed for the massacre that took place on 22 January 1905, known as Bloody Sunday, when hundreds of workers were killed at a peaceful demonstration for better working conditions (*Kanonizatsiia* 1999, 186–203). The tsar's involvement in Bloody Sunday was an important accusation levelled against him throughout the Soviet period and was also used as an argument against his canonization. The Metropolitan Yuvenaly also tried to diminish the tsar and his consort's guilt for giving Rasputin

Figure 14.5 The murder of Andronik and Ermogen. Miniature from the *Assembly* icon.
Source: With permission of the St Tikhon Orthodox Theological Institute.

such influence in Russia by explaining that they behaved in such a manner out of concern for their ailing son Alexei. He issued a document resembling a certificate that attests to the tsar and his family's Christian life (Rousselet 2011, 146–67). In the *Assembly of New Martyrs* icon, the tsar is standing beneath the church with his family. He is dressed as a Byzantine emperor although he never wore such attire during his lifetime. Such embroidering of the truth forms part of the Byzantinization of Russian history in post-Soviet Russia, a process whereby politicians and thinkers are increasingly referring to Byzantium's importance in relation to the development of Russia throughout history

298   Per-Arne Bodin

(Ivanov 2009). The typological parallel being drawn here is between Byzantium and Russia. One *kleimo*, which is also highly stylized, shows the murder of the tsar and his family.

The life of Patriarch Tikhon, who was elected as the first post-revolution primate in autumn 1917, is portrayed in one of the miniatures in the *Assembly* icon. He is represented as being under house arrest at Donskoy Monastery. Guards stand in front of and behind the patriarch, and a group of believers have gathered alongside him to be blessed by him (Figure 14.4).

Tikhon was also depicted earlier, in 1923, in a mock icon presented in the Bolshevik journal *Bezbozhnik* (1923 18:1). This depiction consists of the patriarch in his vestments seated on his throne in the centre. Rather than being encircled by miniatures depicting his life, he is surrounded by objects of devotion, an allusion to his reluctance to donate such objects to the campaign against the famine in Soviet Russia in 1921–22. In his hand, he holds the tip of a scroll containing his appeal directed against the secular authorities (Figure 14.6). This refusal to submit to their demands was one of the reasons for his arrest. In this case, the principles of icon painting are being used for an atheistic purpose. The mock icon motif was then transformed eighty years later into a real icon depicting him as an officially canonized saint. The close relationship between the mock icon and its real counterpart is certainly not a case of the former directly influencing the latter. Instead, it naturally arose from the deep religious structures and memory-making practices functioning in both the atheistic cartoon and the post-Soviet icon painting. The artist behind the cartoon was also personally sharing the memory of the sort of icon he was lampooning with the public who would consume this work.

One miniature in the icon depicts a religious procession taking place under Soviet fire in the town of Astrakhan in 1919 (Figure 14.7). In the years following the revolution, the Church and the Bolsheviks competed to organize processions and large street demonstrations. The street demonstration is a favourite theme in socialist realist Soviet propaganda art, the most common motif being a political demonstration being attacked by the tsarist regime. Any viewers accustomed to Soviet visual culture will recognize this and interpret the miniature of the procession as a bold inversion of the Soviet-era theme: a religious procession is being attacked by the Red Army.

The Church of Christ the Saviour and the question of fake icons

The Church (or Cathedral) of Christ the Saviour depicted in the centre of the icon was, as previously mentioned, also a victim of persecution. It was built in the nineteenth century and then destroyed in 1931 on the orders of Lazar Kaganovich, one of Stalin's closest associates.[6] On the same site, a palace and monument were to be built. However, that design for a Palace of the Soviets was never implemented for a number of reasons. Eventually, a swimming pool was built on the site after the Second World War, which was in turn destroyed

Soviet past in hymnography and iconography 299

Figure 14.6 Caricature of Patriarch Tikhon from the journal *Bezbozhnik*.

in 1991 for the cathedral to be re-erected. The importance of this church is evident in the *Assembly* icon and emphasized even more strongly in a later icon painted by the contemporary artist Sergei Kurakin: The *Novorussian Mother of God* icon (probably dating from 2011) depicts all the stages in the church's history from its foundation up to its reconstruction (Figure 14.8).

The artist has explained that he named the icon following a vision of the Mother of God that he himself experienced and on the basis that it was created for the new twenty-first century and 'for a new Russia' (Kurakin). The historical use of the toponymy 'New Russia' for the land north of the Black Sea and its current use in the conflict with Ukraine were not relevant to the icon's naming,

Figure 14.7 The Red Army attacks a religious procession. Miniature from the *Assembly* icon.
Source: With permission of the St Tikhon Orthodox Theological Institute.

and the pejorative use of the same words to describe rich Russians also exerted no influence on the artist's choice. The Church clearly reacted rather negatively to the enterprise. The artist received a letter signed by the patriarch that stressed that the icon could only be used for 'private prayers' (see the *Novorussian Mother of God* icon). The Church has criticized the lack of correspondence between the centre of the icon and the miniatures: in their view, the church ought to have been in the centre. There are extensive commentaries, produced

Soviet past in hymnography and iconography 301

Figure 14.8 The *Novorussian Mother of God* icon.

Source: https://upload.wikimedia.org/wikipedia/commons/b/b0/Икона_Новорусская_Богоматерь.jpg (accessed 30 May 2020).

by Kurakin himself, on all the *kleima*. These commentaries are so meticulous in their detail that it is difficult to know if they should be treated seriously or regarded as the whimsical endeavour of a well-known artist. His long text seems to mirror or, at the very least, be inspired by the Church's comments on

302   *Per-Arne Bodin*

the *Assembly of New Martyrs* icon, and he could perhaps be mocking it. There are examples in the artist's commentaries of Soviet history being translated into biblical and medieval categories, but these are actually brought to the point of absurdity, as in the following example of the Tower of Babel. The following quotations are from the English home page of the icon:

Scene X Construction of the Tower of Babel, 1931–1941

Left – a symbolic place exploded temple – blue lake, 'brimstone, where the beast and the false prophet' (Revelation. 20.10). The lake – sailing spirit of the Temple of the Saviour. The edges of the lake – the boundary of God's patience, the boiling waves – the waters of wrath. The asymmetry of the architecture – a sign reminding of the tragedy of the Earth, the explosion of December 5, 1931.

To the right, the new ruler of Russia is stepping towards the new construction, it is the apostase, in whose image is meant Stalin. On his left-hand side – The Tower of Babel – a symbol of the new government. Six turns on the tower – a sign of Satan.

(The *Novorussian Mother of God* icon)

Stalin and Kaganovich are seen as devils (Figure 14.9). The first Five-Year Plan (1928–32) is understood to be a parallel enterprise to the erection of the tower of Babel and viewed in relation to the unsuccessful attempt to build the Palace of the Soviets before the Second World War. This, in turn, is paralleled by (and may even be an allusion to) a sermon given by Patriarch Tikhon to mark the new year in 1918, in which he provided a summary of the revolutionary year of 1917: 'Last year was the year of the construction of the Russian State. But alas! Does this not remind us of the sad experience of the construction of the tower of Babel?' (Tikhon 2009, 187).

Kurakin is thus following norms when using the typological interpretation, but there is something too detailed or exaggerated both in the icon and in the explanation.

Miniatures show the reconstruction of the cathedral, with Boris Yeltsin, Mayor of Moscow Yury Luzhkov and Vladimir Putin looking on, though they are not provided with halos (Figure 14.10). This icon can be understood in three different ways: as a holy image, an ordinary work of art that uses the aesthetics of icon painting or a work of art designed to mock icon painting.

Kurakin's icon is a manifestation of a new post-Soviet phenomenon: the vast flood of icons that are being produced and reproduced as functional art objects and then distributed across the Internet. As has been demonstrated in different contexts, the use of reproductions diminishes the aura of an original picture. This statement goes back to Walter Benjamin's oft-quoted article (Benjamin 1969, 1–26). One reproduction method that was not possible in Benjamin's time was the broad manipulation technique of Photoshopping, which makes it even more difficult today to assess the seriousness or the authenticity of a work

Figure 14.9 The Tower of Babel. Miniature from the *Novorussian Mother of God* icon.
Source: www.novorusskaya-bogomater.ru/scene-x (accessed 25 January 2021).

of art (Justiniano 2013). What seems to be happening in the online world rings true with Walter Benjamin's article on the work of art in the age of mechanical reproduction. It is impossible to know if the depiction of Soviet history in Kurakin's icon ought to be taken at face value, or whether the icon should be understood as a fake or an attempt of some kind to mock icon painting in general. Following Benjamin's line of reasoning, the icons being distributed online are possibly not authentic. In fact, it seems even more likely they are fake or mock icons.

Some of these mass-produced icons depict Ivan the Terrible or Stalin. Perhaps the influence of these numerous pseudo-icons is spilling over into (more or less) authentic church art, rendering all manner of memories of Soviet times, or indeed any period, as 'fake' in some sense. This development is posing a

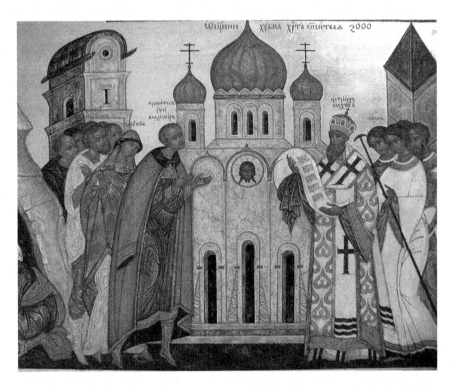

Figure 14.10 The consecration of the Cathedral of Christ the Saviour. Miniature from the *Novorussian Mother of God* icon. Putin on one side of the church, Patriarch Alexy II on the other. In reality, the president was not present on that occasion.

Source: www.novorusskaya-bogomater.ru/scene-xi-c6na (accessed 25 January 2021).

problematic challenge to both Russia and world culture in general. For the Church, this challenge is even threatening to dismantle the role liturgical memory has traditionally played as the 'final court of appeal', to quote Butcher (2018, 206) once again. 'Mock' liturgical texts have actually existed, though to a lesser extent than mock liturgical texts, since the days of Old Russia, but now cheap printing techniques and the Internet have totally transformed the situation.

The aesthetics of icon painting, socialist realism and the Internet, taken together, are telling a special, somewhat intriguing, somewhat whimsical and somewhat true story of the horrors of the revolution and Soviet times.

Conclusion

Liturgical memory is utilized to its fullest capacity in the celebration of the New Martyrs, a series of ritual practices that are ideally suited to liturgical memory's capabilities. The most important feature of the role liturgical memory plays in this process is its strong tendency to generalize, or strive for 'impersonality', as

Schmemann terms this phenomenon. There is, and needs to be, an opportunity to understand the underlying historical facts, yet the details of most of these are hidden through the use of general liturgical formulas. Another method used in abundance is typological memory making, which bonds together different periods and times. Studying the devotion of the New Martyrs provides us with an opportunity to view ritual memory-making in practice.

The Soviet realities sometimes correlate with and sometimes contrast with the liturgical commemoration of the New Martyrs. The new possibilities presented by the Internet pose a new challenge relating to the issue of authenticity, in particular the problem of fake icons, fake liturgical texts and other fake representations of all kinds.

The generalization and impersonal character of the commemoration practices discussed above are partially dictated by the conventions of the genre of Orthodox liturgical creation, which incorporates the production of liturgical texts written in Church Slavonic and the artistic principles of icon painting. The practical reality of there being an acute shortage of hymnographs following the destruction wrought during the Soviet era has played a role in the way the trauma of the Soviet experience has been processed in recent years. This shortage has not only influenced the remembering of details but has also attempted to make connections between the atrocities (and the bravery of those who opposed them) and the grand scheme of history and eternity. This component of ritual memory operates in parallel with all notions of secular forgetting or denial and the lack of lustration in Russia after the fall of the Soviet Union. Handling memory of the suffering of Soviet times in such a manner ultimately permits a situation in which such traumatic events are not commemorated by people themselves but by God instead.

Ritual memory is one of the facets of religious memory. I have, in this case, included visual representations in the form of icons because of the tight connection between liturgical performance and icon devotion in the Orthodox tradition. In the case of the *Assembly of New Martyrs* icon, this connection is even more direct: the motif is the same in the text as in the icon, and they were created by the Church as a single entity.

Ritual memory or liturgical memory interacts with hagiography, expressed through vitae texts that also represent an important component of Orthodox religious memory. I consciously excluded vitae from my reflections at the beginning of this chapter due to space considerations and the fact that this component of religious memory has been rather comprehensively studied already. In addition to the role played by vitae in memory making, an important contribution is also made by biographies in a more general sense and visual representations other than icons dedicated to the martyrs. All these components combine to form religious memory. The veneration of the New Martyrs is by no means a marginal phenomenon within the context of the remembrance of Soviet times. In fact, it is one of the components of what is a complex process. The *Assembly of New Martyrs* icon is also a showcase for how religious, and especially ritual, memory generally operates in relation to the secular and postsecular world, both explicitly and implicitly.

306 *Per-Arne Bodin*

And one final point: as is always the case in Orthodox practice, after New Martyrs have been canonized, they are no longer remembered in the aforementioned 'Eternal Memory' summons. Instead, they are elevated to a new category in the conviction that they are now remembered by God.

Notes

1 For the best introduction to this theme, see Hyldal Christensen (2018) and also Bodin (2009).
2 For more on the development of the veneration of saints in Orthodox tradition, see Schmemann (1975, 141–46).
3 For more on the bishop's life story, see *Sviatitel'*.
4 The translations of the Church Slavonic and Russian texts in the chapter are my own.
5 'Zuerst waren die scharfsichtigen Beobachter an der Londoner Börse nicht ganz abgeneigt, Napoleons Neujahrsstreich als ein Spekulationsmanöver ihres erhabenen Verbündeten zu betrachten. Tatsächlich, sobald die französischen Wertpapiere zu fallen begannen, stürzten sich die Leute Hals über Kopf in Baals Tempel, um Staatsobligationen, Credit-mobilier- und Eisenbahn-aktien um jeden Preis loszuschlagen' (Marx and Engels 1961, 169).
6 For more on the history of the church, see Haskins 2009, 25–62.

References

Akafist vsem novomuchenikom I ispovednikom rossiiskim. https://akafistnik.ru/akafisty-russkim-svyatym/akafist-novomuchenikam-i-ispovednikam-tserkvi-russkoj/.
Assmann, Jan. 2006. *Religion and Cultural Memory: Ten Studies*. Stanford, CA: Stanford University Press.
Benjamin, Walter. 1969. "The Work of Art in the Age of Mechanical Reproduction." In *Illuminations*, edited by Hannah Arendt, translated by Harry Zohn, from the 1935 essay, 1–26. New York: Schocken Books.
Bezbozhnik. 1923. No 18. Moscow: Akts. izd. obshchestvo "0Bezbozhnik."
Bodin, Per-Arne. 2007. *Eternity and Time: Studies in Russian Literature and the Orthodox Tradition*, 231–50. Stockholm: Stockholm University.
Bogumił, Zuzanna, and Marta Łukaszewicz. 2018. "Between History and Religion: The New Russian Martyrdom as an Invented Tradition." *East European Politics and Societies* 32 (4): 936–63.
Butcher, Brian A. 2018. *Liturgical Theology after Schmemann: An Orthodox Reading of Paul Ricoeur*. New York: Fordham University Press.
Caridi, Cathy. 2015. *Making Martyrs East & West: Canonization in the Catholic and Russian Orthodox Churches*. DeKalb: Northern Illinois University Press.
Dickinson, Anna. 2000. "A Marriage of Convenience? Domestic and Foreign Policy Reasons for the 1943 Soviet Church-State 'Concordat'." *Religion, State & Society* 28 (4): 337–46.
DiMauro, Giorgio G. 2006. "The Church and the Cult of Imperial Humility: Icons and Enactment of the Muscovite Furnace Ritual." *Harvard Ukrainian Studies* 28 (1/4): 415–28.
Eisenstein, Sergei. 1944. *Ivan Groznyi*. Moscow: Goskinoizdat.
Feistner, Edith. 2003. "Imitatio als Funktion der Memoria. Zur Selbstreferentialität des religiösen Gedächtnisses in der Hagiographie des Mittelalters." In *Kunst und Erinnerung: Memoriale Konzepte in der Erzählliteratur des Mittelalters*, edited by Ulrich Ernst and Klaus Ridder, 259–76. Köln: Böhlau Verlag.

Soviet past in hymnography and iconography   307

Florensky, Pavel. 1997. *The Pillar and Ground of the Truth: An Essay in Orthodox Theodicy in Twelve Letters*. Princeton, NJ: Princeton University Press.

————. 2002. *Beyond Vision: Essays on the Perception of Art*. London: Reaktion Books.

Halbwachs, Maurice. 1992. *On Collective Memory*. Chicago: University of Chicago Press.

Haskins, Ekaterina V. 2009. "Russia's Postcommunist Past: The Cathedral of Christ the Savior and the Reimagining of National Identity." *History and Memory* 21 (1): 25–62.

Hyldal Christensen, Karin. 2018. *The Making of the New Martyrs of Russia: Soviet Repression in Orthodox Memory*. Abingdon: Taylor & Francis Group.

Ivanov, Sergei. 2009. "Vtoroi Rim glazami Tret'ego: Evoliutsiia obraza Vizantii v rossiiskom obshchestvennom soznanii." https://polit.ru/article/2009/04/14/vizant/.

Justiniano, Silouan, FR. 2013. "The Degraded Iconicity of the Icon: The Icon's Materiality and Mechanical Reproduction." *Orthodox Arts Journal*. www.orthodoxartsjournal.org/author/fr-silouan-justiniano/.

Kanonizatsiia sviatykh v XX veke. 1999. Moscow: Izdatel'stvo Sretenskogo monastyria.

Kurakin, Sergei. "Rabota nad Novorusskoi Bogomater'iu." *Proza.Ru*. https://proza.ru/2012/09/08/1824.

Lacan, Jacques. 2018. *The Four Fundamental Concepts of Psycho-Analysis*. London: Routledge.

Marx, Karl, and Friedrich Engels. 1961. *Werke Band 13*. Berlin: Dietz Verlag.

Mary, Mother, and Kallistos Ware, eds. 1969. *The Festal Menaion: Orthodox Eastern Church – Liturgy and Ritual*. London: Faber and Faber.

The *Novorussian Mother of God* icon, Novorusskaia ikona Bogomateri. www.novorusskaya-bogomater.ru/history-of-creation.

Opisanie ikony sobora sviatykh novomuchenikov I ispovednikov. www.pravmir.ru/opisanie-ikony-sobora-svyatyx-novomuchenikov-i-ispovednikov-rossijskix/.

Opisanie ikony sobora sviatykh novomuchenikov I ispovednikov rossiiskikh. www.pravmir.ru/opisanie-ikony-sobora-svyatyx-novomuchenikov-i-ispovednikov-rossijskix.

Ricoeur, Paul. 1980. *Essays on Biblical Interpretation*. Philadelphia, PA: Fortress Press.

Rousselet, Kathy. 2011. "Constructing Moralities Around the Tsarist Family." In *Multiple Moralities and Religions in Post-Soviet Russia*, edited by Jarrett Zigon, 146–67. New York: Berghahn Books.

Sandomirskaja, Irina. 2013. "Bez stali I leni: Aesopian Language and Legitimacy." In *Power and Legitimacy – Challenges from Russia*, edited by Per-Arne Bodin, Stefan Hedlund and Elena Namli, 188–98. London: Routledge.

Schmemann, Alexander. 1975. *Introduction to Liturgical Theology*. 2nd ed. London: Faith Press.

Sluzhba novomuchenikom I ispovednikom rossijskim. http://days.pravoslavie.ru/rubrics/canon282.htm?id=282.

Sluzhba sviatym tsarstvennym strastoterptsam. https://azbyka.ru/days/worship/645. The *Novorussian Mother of God* icon. www.novorusskaya-bogomater.ru/history-of-creation.

Sviatitel' Afanasii Kovrovskii. www.fudel.ru/personalia/afanasij_kovrovskij_svt/.

Tikhon, Patriarch. 2009. '*V goidnu gneva Bozhiia': Poslaniia, slova I rechi*. Moscow: Pravoslavnyi Sviato-Tikhonovskii gumanitarnyi universitet.

Wellesz, Egon. 1999. *A History of Byzantine Music and Hymnography*. Oxford: Clarendon Press.

Zhurnal zasedanii Sviashchennogo Sinoda ot 12–13 marta 2002 goda. https://mospat.ru/archive/page/synod/2002-2/449.html.

15 Whose Church is it?

The nonreligious use of religious architecture in Eastern Germany

Agnieszka Halemba

Oskar Verkaaik starts his edited volume on religious architecture with the observation that though many religious traditions explicitly underplay the significance of religious buildings, it is remarkable how much time, energy and financial resources are put into the construction of new religious buildings as well as the restoration of old ones (Verkaaik 2013, 7). This statement could, on the one hand, be attributed to the author's Protestant bias, a factor that has undoubtedly affected the way in which some researchers have approached religion. After all, Protestantism has been regarded as seeing the essence of religion in belief, conceived as the internal conviction of the individual believer, while simultaneously downplaying the importance of the material aspects of religious worship, including religious architecture (Robbins 2007; Cannell 2005, 2006). On the other hand, in recent decades, the importance of religious materiality has been repeatedly demonstrated for many religious communities, including those professing traditional Protestantism (Houtman and Meyer 2012). Nevertheless, most anthropological works on religious materiality focus on the so-called problem of presence, that is, the ways in which the transcendent sacred, as well as religious ideals and values, become tangible or perceivable for believers through the use of objects, bodily postures, smells and sounds, but also technical equipment and architecture. Every religious tradition produces specific materiality, which corresponds to its semiotic ideology, understood to be a network of ideas concerning existence, agency and communication between various kinds of entities (Keane 2003; Meyer 2010). In brief, particular objects, senses and surroundings help believers to experience the presence of the sacred in particular social and historical circumstances.

What is interesting, however, especially with regard to contemporary Europe, is that religious materiality is also important outside a given religious community, because it also appears in contexts locally defined as secular, where 'the problem of presence' cannot be a central concern. Religious buildings are becoming tourist attractions, liturgical music fascinates nonreligious music lovers and church bells are rung in European cities for secular occasions. One could of course claim that religious materiality has always had various social, political or economic functions. Still, at present, this materiality is important for, and appreciated by, people who often see themselves as being situated outside the

DOI: 10.4324/9781003264750-19

Whose Church is it? 309

religious field, or even explicitly opposed to any presence of religion in the public sphere. Even in those regions of Europe considered to be most secularized (e.g. eastern Germany, the Czech Republic or Estonia; Pollack 2003), religious buildings are being used, maintained or even reconstructed by actors defining themselves as secular. In this chapter, I look at examples of the nonreligious and postreligious use of Protestant church buildings in eastern Germany – examples of religious architecture situated in space recognized as secular.

Religion, nonreligion, postreligion

The concept of religion, as it is used in the social sciences, is central to at least two rich fields of meaning. The first field refers to human relationships with phenomena and entities that transcend everyday individual lives; the second one refers to the relationship between the religious and the secular as a concrete historical process (see Bloch 2008). While in the first understanding religion is seen as a universal phenomenon, in the second case it can never be defined in universal terms, as it only exists through its relation to the secular, a relation that is in constant flux. In this second understanding, knowledge of what religion is and where it is located can only be gained at a specific time in a given place. Still, when this term is actually used in speech and writing, it is often assumed that religion does refer to a specific realm within which humans create relations with what goes beyond the everyday and individual lives. This conflation of the two very different ways in which the concept of religion is used in social science makes discussions concerning the presence of religion in secular space especially complex.

Talal Asad (1993, 2003) has been a prominent advocate of an understanding of religion based on its relation to the secular. In his approach, the history of relations between the secular and the religious is also the history of their mutual definition. His approach also involves the analysis of the processes of describing and categorizing certain things, people and events as 'religious' or 'belonging to the religious sphere', and others as 'secular' or 'belonging to the secular sphere'. Every time phenomena in which researchers, participants in events or other commentators see a religious aspect are analyzed, a category of religion is essentially being created anew. Any researchers wishing to follow Asad's perspective should therefore adopt a monistic approach as their starting point and develop research questions capable of answering why, how, and according to which principles the difference between the secular and religious is created in a given situation.

At any historical moment where the secular and the religious are differentiated in a particular way, it is also possible to witness the production of material objects whose physical existence sometimes outlives the given configuration of relations between the secular and the religious. Moreover, while those relations are in a state of flux, material objects are still frequently associated with the religious sphere in social memory despite the considerable changes taking place in the relations between the secular and the religious. Consequently,

310 *Agnieszka Halemba*

church buildings in contemporary Europe are socially recognized as religious places even though the relations between the religious and the secular are now different than at the time they were built. Such buildings can be appreciated and identified as important for a variety of reasons that transcend religion. For example, they may be regarded as objects of national and local heritage, monuments of architecture, the sites of individual memories, or buildings that make urban and rural landscapes aesthetically pleasing, outstanding or, conversely, typical. It seems that although, in some cases, the religious function (understood here as creating relations with the sacred) of such places might fade into the background, the fact that those places are, in one way or another, related to religion is important for secular actors. In order to describe and thereby better understand the place of religious architecture in contemporary Europe, a nuanced analytical vocabulary is required. In this chapter, I am going to use the concepts of the nonreligious and postreligious with regard to the use of Protestant Churches in the northern part of Brandenburg in eastern Germany.

The notion of nonreligiosity has a long history, especially in sociological research (see Wohlrab-Sahr and Kaden 2014). It is most often used to refer to *nones*, that is, people who, when asked about their 'religion' in sociological or statistical research questionnaires, mark the answer 'not applicable'. However, in this chapter I propose to utilize the adjective 'nonreligious' and the scalar concept of 'nonreligiosity', in accordance with Johannes Quack's definition (2014), which diverges from previous usage by applying the term to those phenomena that are considered not to be religious but nevertheless related to 'religion' in important ways. As I understand it, the most important manifestation of Quack's notion of nonreligiosity is the relationship between, on the one hand, a person or group of persons who at a given place and time define themselves as not belonging to a religious field and, on the other, a phenomenon, object or person perceived by the former as belonging to this field. In this approach, nonreligiosity, rather than being a permanent feature of a person, object or phenomenon, can be understood as a relationship between what is historically defined and recognized as religious and what is self-determined as secular. In other words, this term can be used to refer to a whole range of positions that are located, or locate themselves, at any particular historical moment outside the religious field, yet are connected to that field in important ways. Nonreligiosity differs from religious indifference (Quack and Schuh 2017) in that for the former, religion is an important point of reference that may be viewed as an opponent, but also an inspiration or, for example, a provider of aesthetic impressions. The activity of humanist societies might, for example, aptly be described as 'nonreligious' (Engelke 2014), as might unbelievers expressing their fascination with religious music or, as in this chapter, using church architecture for secular purposes in full awareness that the character of these buildings is religious in some particular sense.

The 'postreligious', on the other hand, is a term inspired by the works of the German theologian Hans Joachim Höhn (2006), which he uses to refer to a specific form of presence of religion in the contemporary world. In Höhn's

Whose Church is it? 311

opinion, in recent decades, there have been certain observable changes in how religion is perceived in Europe. It is no longer perceived as a metaphysical social binder or a reservoir of answers to questions about the meaning of life or the origin of the world. It is also not necessarily regarded as being about the establishment of contact with a transcendent god. Instead, he thinks that religion is mainly present in its aesthetic dimension and as a creator of moods. Such a presence is termed the 'postreligious'. Importantly, both the actions of people who describe themselves as religious and the nonreligious can be described as postreligious. To sum up, postreligiousness refers to the specific manner in which elements recognized in social memory as religious are present in a given relationship in ways that emphasize the potential of the materiality that is produced by historically defined religions to arouse aesthetic experiences and heightened moods. Unlike Höhn, I have chosen not to use this term as a generalized description of the state of religion in contemporary Europe. Instead, I aim to re-establish it as an analytic term referring to the particular relation between the religious and the secular.

Religious life in Eastern Germany

Observers of the religious situation in Germany agree that the areas formerly occupied by the German Democratic Republic (GDR), and especially the northern and north-eastern parts, are among the most secularized regions of Europe, both in terms of the residents' affiliation to religious organizations and participation in religious practices, and their personal beliefs (Pollack 2002; Pollack and Pickel 2000; Wohlrab Sahr 2011; Wohlrab Sahr, Karstein, and Schmidt-Lux 2009). According to the 2017 European Values Study,[1] about 90% of people interviewed in the states of Mecklenburg-Vorpommern and Brandenburg answered that religion is 'not important' or 'not at all important' in their lives. However, there are signs that religion still maintains a continuous presence in these states: religious organizations are responsible for running schools, retirement homes, kindergartens and counselling services; religion is often part of the school curriculum; and (even more importantly as far as the current study is concerned) church towers shape the architectural landscape and ringing church bells commemorate important occasions, whether they are religious or not. Some authors also note that although the communities of practising and religiously engaged people are small, they are very active (Peperkamp and Rajtar 2010; Hafner, Völkening, and Becci 2018).

When I started my research on the Polish–German borderland in 2016, I did not expect that religious issues would hold my research attention for long. Our first research team's focus was Polish–German transborder relations, and I did not expect to encounter many initiatives involving religious elements.[2] I started my research by talking to members of religious communities and pastors from the Evangelical Church in Germany (EKD), which is predominant among religious German inhabitants in this region, asking them, above all, what shape religious life had been in when the region was part of the GDR and

312 *Agnieszka Halemba*

also about the changes that had followed the reunification of Germany. The issue of German–Polish relations came up in my conversations with members of local religious communities and appeared in the observations I made, most of which applied to the use of church buildings. After Poland's accession to the European Union, and especially to the Schengen Area, many Polish families began to settle on the German side of the border, primarily attracted by lower property prices but also by a desire to live away from the commotion of the city and the opportunity to educate their children in two languages (Balogh 2013; Rutkowska 2019). One of the side effects of this phenomenon is the increased presence of Catholics in the area. Although it cannot be said that religious life is a priority for Poles crossing over to the German side of the border, many of them are, at least culturally, Catholics, so they want to have their children baptized and send them to their First Holy Communion, and newlywed couples want to be blessed in church. Some of the Poles who moved across the border are openly critical of the Catholic Church, while others are deep believers. Importantly, religion is nevertheless a meaningful point of reference for many of them, irrespective of whether they participate in religious practices, or conversely, openly criticize the Catholic Church. In my opinion, the appearance of people who have a clear attitude towards religion and the Church, whether as practitioners or as critics, has made religion more visible in a region not so much inhabited by Protestants as by Germans who are nonreligious, or even indifferent, towards religion (see Halemba 2019; Quack and Schuh 2017).

The German–Polish Memorial for Flight, Expulsion and a New Beginning

The German–Polish Memorial for Flight, Expulsion and a New Beginning is located in a church building in the middle of the small village of Rosow, which is just two kilometres from the German side of the Polish–German border. Sometimes activists simply call it a memorial (*Gedenkstätte*), and at other times people refer to it as a remembrance church (*Gedächtniskirche*). These designations are not always used interchangeably, as the question of whether this is actually a church or a secular building with memorial functions continues to occupy at least some of the people involved in the organization of events in that building or its maintenance. According to the German Wikipedia website: 'this building is a monument, but still offers the opportunity to hold religious services for the local religious community in Rosow'.[3] In front of the entrance to the church grounds is a small obelisk containing a larger inscription in German and a smaller one in Polish. Both read, 'In memory of the millions of Polish and German refugees of World War II' (Figure 15.1).

The building itself dates from the thirteenth century, and the village in which it is located celebrated its 775th anniversary in 2018 (Lau et al. 2018, 11). The medieval stone church with its unusual openwork steel tower dominates the village landscape. The building was partially destroyed during the last days of the Second World War. Nevertheless, until the early 1970s, it served as a place of prayer for the local Protestant religious community. Only then was

Whose Church is it? 313

Figure 15.1 The church in Rosow with its openwork steel tower.
Source: Photo by Agnieszka Halemba, March 2017.

it closed, apparently due to its poor state of repair. The faithful moved to the parish house and the church building slowly fell into ruin. Despite the decreasing number of parishioners, the local pastor made efforts in the mid-1980s to rebuild the church with the support of a befriended West German parish. However, nothing came of these plans and consequential talks on rebuilding this church did not start until after 1990.

Shortly after the reunification of Germany, the elderly daughter of a pastor who had served in this church between 1905 and 1932 came for a visit. One of her grandsons told me[4] that she expressed a strong wish that the church be

314   *Agnieszka Halemba*

rebuilt. This request motivated a diverse group of her relatives and other former and current inhabitants of Rosow to act. It should be noted that many churches were restored in former GDR territory after the collapse of the Berlin Wall. However, this particular church, probably due to the small number of believers in this particular village, as well as its dilapidated state, was not included in any of the church reconstruction programmes. It was only in 2002 that a secular association called Support Circle (*Förderkreis*) for the Memorial Church in Rosow, which mainly included members of old Rosow families and their friends, was founded and started to negotiate with the church authorities about its restoration. In effect, the church building was leased for twenty-five years to the association, which would undertake to rebuild it, carry out cultural activities there and, importantly, make it available for religious services if necessary. The status of the building thus became quite complicated: it was to be outside the jurisdiction of the church authorities for at least a quarter of a century, and its use was to be decided on by a secular association; at the same time, however, the association was obliged to manage the building and develop its interior in such a way that it could easily be used for religious worship.

The key question was, of course, financing. As the village is located in the Euroregion Pomerania, EU funding was seen as a real possibility. In the end, most of the renovation was carried out with the support of the European Union's financial aid programmes, and this fact had an instrumental significance for the establishment of the church as a Polish–German Memorial.

The idea of creating such a place in the church building was born from the need to adapt the aims of the association, for which the renovation of the building was the most important goal, to meet the existing grant regulations for the Euroregion Pomerania. The association had to develop a so-called *Nutzungskonzept* (a concept of use) that would transcend religious issues and show potential sponsors the social and cultural importance of investing in that place. Initially, it was decided that the church could be rebuilt as a Memorial for Flight, Expulsion and a New Beginning, a title that took into account the history of the village itself: many pre–Second World War inhabitants had left Rosow before the Red Army reached the village and their houses were taken over by Germans expelled from regions that had become Polish territory. However, when the association applied for EU support through the Euroregion Pomerania, the funding was withheld due to the protests of Polish partners in the Euroregion. It should be remembered that this was happening in the first years of the twenty-first century, at a time when the Polish media were writing a great deal about the activities of the Federation of Expellees in Germany (*Bund der Vertriebenen*) and the contested construction of the Centre Against Expulsions (Röger 2016; Zaborski 2007).[5] The initiators of the association were informed that the issue of commemorating the expulsions had to be presented from both a Polish and a German perspective. For the association, this was a new idea, but they fully accepted it. After all, Rosow's location right on the Polish–German border made the inclusion of the Polish experience sound sensible. Since then, the association has been obligated to carry out work concerning the memorialization of both the Polish and the

Whose Church is it? 315

German experience of fleeing their homes, being expelled from their countries and making a new beginning for themselves after the Second World War. The members of the association have collected interviews with people who experienced forced migration after the war and made extracts from transcriptions of these conversations available to the public in the form of a permanent exhibition in the church, while additional materials are also accessible for study in an archive located in the church's choir.

In 2007 the renovated church was opened. Interestingly, the church tower was given the form of an openwork steel structure (Figure 15.2). On the one

Figure 15.2 Obelisk in front of the church in Rosow. The obelisk bears the following inscription in German and Polish: 'In memory of the millions of Polish and German refugees of World War II'.

Source: Photo by Agnieszka Halemba, March 2017.

316 *Agnieszka Halemba*

hand, this was an economic choice, because the reconstruction, or rather the construction, of a new medieval tower exceeded the association's means. On the other hand, the openwork construction was supposed to indicate that what was at stake was not so much the reconstruction of the old church in an attempt to return to the past, but rather the creation of a place that looked, through remembrance, into the future. On the association's recently renewed website, one can read an interpretation explaining why the church building is suitable as a memorial site with a flight and expulsion theme:

> We initiators claim that a church is a good, an appropriate place for the presentation of and an encounter with this theme. We even think that a church is a particularly suitable place for this, as a symbolic place of suffering and hope. A 'protection' against unwanted zeal and an offer of trust for interested supporters of our project. This topic cannot be adequately presented in any other sponsored institution in our region – either at horse ranches or in folklore or technology museums.[6]

According to the association's website, around ten major events per year are currently organized at this church. These are generally concerts and celebrations of particular anniversaries. Roughly half of these have a clear religious component, such as a prayer led by an invited pastor or a religious service. Officially, this church does not have a pastor (it is not a so-called *Predigtstelle*) as it belongs to a secular association. Hence, each time the association wants to have a pastor to celebrate a service, it must ask for the consent of the provost responsible for the area. This presents a paradox of sorts, as the presence of religious activity is, after all, enshrined in the agreement between the association and the EKD,[7] which leased the building for twenty-five years. However, if the association wants to hold a service in the church, it must ask for permission, but if it wants to organize a concert or an exhibition, such permission is not necessary.

There are also smaller events organized locally or spontaneously (e.g. visits by tourist groups or art exhibitions), but also smaller prayer meetings and school or university visits. Those visits often have a Polish–German and sometimes also a religious character. The village of Rosow is one of those places where, in recent years, Polish citizens have started to buy houses after moving from the neighbouring city of Szczecin. One of these new arrivals is a Polish priest who is a theology professor at the University of Szczecin. He lives in a former restaurant building directly facing the Memorial Church in Rosow. He has quickly become a leading figure at the Polish–German events organized at the church. His presence and engagement are influencing the dynamics of activities centred around the Polish–German Memorial Church in Rosow.

The priest can collect the key to the church at any time and organize meetings there (including prayer meetings) or show visitors around the church. However, so far there have only been very preliminary discussions, or rather tentative suggestions, regarding the possibility of the building being regularly used by Catholic Poles. For years, locally based Poles who have wanted to take part in Catholic services have had to travel to nearby Polish parishes in

Whose Church is it? 317

and around Szczecin. Many of them still do so, but the priest from Rosow has decided that it is his duty to provide pastoral care on the spot. He has prepared a makeshift chapel in the dining hall of the former restaurant, where he now celebrates Holy Mass every Sunday. As he told me, he understands that although the church building is rarely used for religious purposes by local German inhabitants, it would be difficult to ask for permission for its regular use by Polish Catholics. One could say that the church building, though rarely used, stands for a vision of the village community rooted in the past. As the new permanent presence of Polish inhabitants has already greatly influenced the region in many respects, the granting of such permission could make the German inhabitants feel as if they are giving up their village entirely. It is difficult, or maybe even impossible, to tell what the dominant nexus of identity in this perspective is. Could this be national identity? Or maybe it is religious differences or a clash between younger, mobile, success-oriented newcomers and deeply interconnected long-term older residents who are rooted to the locality?

Is the church in Rosow still a 'church'? Is the former restaurant a religious place? Where should religious worship take place? Seeing as the _Nutzungskonzept_ underlines that the building has to be available for religious use, should this availability also be extended to non-Protestant denominations, or maybe even non-Christian religions? How about secular funerals or other celebrations? Should these be permitted? With regard to the last question, I had an interesting conversation with the provost (_Propst_) responsible for this region. According to his interpretation, this building cannot be regarded as a church because it is leased to a secular association and can be used nonreligiously for cultural activities. Still, in his opinion, the building should not be used 'postreligiously', in the sense Höhn (2006) understands the term, that is, it should not serve to create a mood or atmosphere as a side effect of its religious historical origins. For example, the provost is opposed to the organization of secular marriage and funeral ceremonies in this building. In his opinion, a personal renunciation of religion should also entail the renunciation of religious materiality, including religious architecture's power of attraction. He pointed out that in this region, 'people have not only forgotten their faith, but they have also forgotten that they have forgotten'. Still, young couples participating in a secular marriage ceremony often stop in front of the local church to take a picture. The provost judges such behaviour as an unauthorized appropriation of religious materiality. It would be fair to claim that his approach is modernist through and through, as he insists that the borders between the secular and the religious should be clearly set.

The relationship between religious and nonreligious use is also a complex question for the inhabitants of Rosow. For example, in 2017 a newcomer from another region suggested opening a café for tourists in the Memorial Church in the summer months. Despite the fact that the idea was given initial consideration by the association, as such a café would help to maintain the building financially in the long run, it was ultimately rejected because of protests on the part of the Rosow inhabitants who neither belong to any religious community nor to the association. They want the church to remain a church even if they

318 *Agnieszka Halemba*

themselves do not use it for religious worship and are aware of the building's controversial status.

Is Christmas Eve in a church a religious feast?

Since 2014, the celebration of Polish–German Christmas Eve on the Oder has been organized in a small medieval church in Mescherin, which is situated just across the Oder River from the Polish town of Gryfino. This church is a functioning religious site, with services being celebrated once or twice a month by a pastor residing in the nearby town of Gartz. Like other churches in the region, it is also regularly used as a concert hall. However, concerts are held there relatively often. In fact, the small municipality of Mescherin was already a tourist destination before the First World War, especially as a place for short trips from nearby Stettin (today's Szczecin). In GDR times, the holiday character of this village was preserved, and since the beginning of the 1990s, the picturesque location has attracted both visitors and new residents wishing to live permanently in beautiful surroundings.

The Polish-German Christmas Eve on the Oder is one of the most popular events taking place at the church. It is organized as a collaborative project by several local organizations: the Municipality of Mescherin; the *Pokolenia Pokoleniom (From Generations to Generations)* association from Gryfino; and RAA Perspektywa, a non-governmental organization based in Löcknitz. Notably, no religious organization or association is an official co-organizer, although the local parish community does of course approve of the organization of this event and welcomes it in the church building.

The feast is organized according to a programme whose details change every year, although the same basic structure is maintained. When I took part in the Polish-German Christmas Eve on the Oder in 2016, huge torches were burning in front of the church entrance and one had to pass between them to get inside. The masters of the ceremony were Marta Szuster, a bilingual Mescherin resident and member of the local council, and Marek Brzeziński, an artist, social activist and politician from Gryfino. Every speech was translated into Polish or German. The main thread of each feast is memory and oral history. Usually, the programme is organized around the memories of specific people who have been connected with the region for many years. These are usually older people who remember the war or post-war times or their direct descendants who still live in the region. In 2016, the programme also included a presentation of the life of Hans Paasche, a German writer and pacifist who had probably been murdered by right-wing soldiers by 1920. The programme is accompanied by Christmas carols, classical music and Protestant hymns and songs. The event also incorporates the Polish tradition of sharing a wafer while exchanging Christmas greetings.

Despite the excessive use of elements that are rooted in the Christian religious tradition, the feast, according to organizers, has a secular character and can therefore be described as a nonreligious event. In an interview with one of the Polish organizers of this event, I asked about the potential participation of a pastor or priest or the possibility of a short common ecumenical prayer being spoken. In response, I was told that there would be neither a priest nor a pastor in attendance, no such prayer would be spoken and, furthermore, if someone tried to introduce one, then my interlocutor would give up his role as an organizer and would not participate. He emphasized that this is not a religious event but a meeting of neighbours that gives them a chance to get to know each other.

It seems that the church architecture, Christmas songs and music all serve a postreligious purpose. Although the feast could potentially have been held in the community meeting house, where everyone goes afterwards anyway for refreshments and conversations over a cup of tea, the church has been chosen as the preferred venue because it lends the event a certain ornate aura. Any elements that have their roots in religious worship (such as wafer sharing, carols or church architecture) are used to create an atmosphere of seriousness and sublimity. The beauty of the architecture, lights and music help to convince the participants, on an experiential, sensual level, that something special and important is taking place. One can say that the religious materiality helps to grant an aura of prominence and significance to the regional identity (shown through oral histories exemplified by selected biographies) and friendly Polish–German neighbourly relations.

Tourists, locals and believers

> State Churches (*Landeskirche*) offer many sights: There are not only old churches in the city and in the countryside, but also historical cemeteries with graves of famous people. Village churches open their gates every summer for numerous events and pilgrim routes, and conference houses invite you to go on hikes and to linger. Discover the ecclesiastical side of Berlin, Brandenburg and the Silesian Upper Lusatia![8]

My last short example concerning religious and nonreligious use concerns a group of visitors who come to a village church to admire its architecture and ornate interior. There, they meet a group of people involved in a religious ceremony. Which group are guests and which are hosts? The answer to this question is by no means a clear one. As the above quotation from the website of the Evangelical Church of Berlin and Upper Lusatia (EKBO) shows, church buildings can be considered important tourist sites (Isenberg and Steinecke 2013). If you take any standard guidebook to almost any European region, you would probably find a considerable number of church buildings described as sightseeing attractions. According to a classification proposed by Nolan and Nolan (1992), those buildings could be called 'religious tourist attractions', or sites where religiously motivated visitors encounter other visitors who are mostly interested in a given place because of its artistic or historical value. However, I think that the situation described below is even more complex.

In October 2017, I received an invitation to attend a guided tour of one of the churches in the Uckermark region. This church had been renovated in recent

320 *Agnieszka Halemba*

years, mostly thanks to the engagement of the people active in this church's Friends Association. The association had signed an agreement with the local religious community in 2009 to broaden the use of the building for 'cultural, ecologic and social use in the interests of the building's upkeep and the enrichment of life in the village'.[9] In this case, the official owner of the building is still a religious organization represented by a local parish. Still, as the situation that I observed showed, there was a strong feeling on the part of the nonreligious people involved in the renovation of the church that the building should primarily be treated as a place where the history of the village materializes, and only secondarily as a place of religious worship.

The tour was to be guided by the head of this village, who is also a museum worker in a nearby town. While showing us around the church and pointing out the ongoing renovations, our guide repeatedly stated that although the church building officially belongs to the EKBO, the actual collection of funds and organization of necessary work was carried out by local activists, who were not necessarily believers. In her narrative, the church authorities were presented as a distant controlling organization that does not understand local attitudes and feelings towards this place that are rooted in social memory. Instead, they treat the building as an object that has to be renovated according to professional rules established above the heads of the local community. She gave an example involving the commissioning of an architectural bureau to oversee the renovation of the outer walls. The association consulted an architect who lives and works in a nearby town and who could come to the site very often and see how the work was progressing. They reached a preliminary agreement, but the Church authorities insisted that the work had to be planned and overseen by an architectural bureau commissioned by the EKBO for the whole region. As their bureau is located more than 100 kilometres from the village, it was clear that the delegated architect would only be able to visit the site from time to time. This, according to our guide, led to several grave errors being made during the church's renovation. Most importantly, according to her, some parts of the church were renovated in ways that were not consulted carefully enough with village inhabitants. This, in her opinion, is problematic because the church is not only the key building in the spatial structure of the village but also a kind of materialization of the village's history. On its walls, one can read the local history, for example the level of flooding at various times, an inscription made by a particular person or a decision made by a particular pastor to paint a cornice. In many local churches in this region one can definitely find many objects related to local history, for example benches donated by particular families, boards containing the names of soldiers killed during the two world wars or sometimes paintings depicting local landscapes. Although our guide understood the need for professional supervision of the renovation, she also insisted on keeping the church building rooted in local history.

However, the most interesting situation occurred when our group gathered in the vestibule at the agreed time and was hoping to enter the church. We were informed by our guide that a couple of days earlier she had received a message that there would be a baptismal ceremony in the church at exactly the same time. As the tour had been advertised already for some time, she did not have the opportunity to inform all the affected people and change the starting hour; even more importantly, though, she thought that there was no reason to do so. She did not think that a religious ceremony should automatically take priority. After all, it was a local secular association that was gathering funds and organizing the church's restoration. Consequently, she considered the church building to be a place for the inhabitants of this village. She told us that she regarded this situation as a power game (*Machtspiel*) being played out between the church as an organization and the village to determine who was actually in charge of the place.

When we arrived, she first tried to lead us into the church despite the baptism taking place there. She wanted us just to sit in the benches at the back and wait for the ceremony to end, but one of the people attending the baptism asked us to leave and wait outside. The pastor was a guest from another parish, and he was so busy leading the important religious ritual that he had clearly not reacted quickly enough to the tour group's arrival. While he was leaving, he asked us what had happened and apologized for the situation.

While we were waiting in the vestibule, our guide made it very clear that she considered this to be a clear case of impudence (*Unverschämtheit*) on the part of a religious community who dared to think that religious use should have a priority in the church building. For her, it was much more important that the church is the historic heart of the local community and restored thanks to their efforts. The people organizing the baptism were informed that there was a tour planned in the church for exactly the same time that they had requested their ceremony for, and it was presumptuous of them to assume that the tour should have been moved. For our guide, a church was a nonreligious building and she was convinced of its importance for local identity. Although she was aware of its religious background, this should not, in her view, determine its present use.

It is worth asking what the main difference is between the case described above and religious tourist attractions as described by Nolan and Nolan (1992). Usually, tourist visits to religious sites are analyzed from the premise that the host is the church as an organization or believers as religious users. However, in the case described above, the guide and other nonreligious visitors see themselves as the primary users of the building and think that religious worship should be subjugated to the use of the church as a site of artistic and historical appeal to visitors and a local marker of identity.

Conclusions

Relations between religion, memory and heritage in the European context have been repeatedly noted. Daniele Hervieu-Leger's particular understanding of religion as a chain of memory directs our attention to the fact that religion in Europe is often treated as a depository and guardian of tradition, cultural memory and identity (2000). In many countries, religious organizations seem

322 *Agnieszka Halemba*

to agree to play this role as guardians of the past. This sometimes leads to the heritagization of religious places, which in turn implies a secular viewpoint being taken on things that are also experienced as religious (Paine 2013). This, in turn, may lead to a conflict or at least to the negotiation of meanings and practices (Salemink 2016). Birgit Meyer and Mattijs van de Port (2018) have suggested that anthropological research not only needs to show that a given identity, heritage site or social memory is socially constructed but also how, or through what means, its influence is actually brought into existence. How does this constructed reality become 'really real' for the people involved? These authors write about an 'aesthetics of persuasion' being required for people to view certain forms, things or practices as 'authentic'. The notion of authenticity in this case should be understood as an experiential one (Wang 1999). Within the European context, religious materiality tends to create a feeling among believers and non-believers alike that they are engaging in special activities outside of everyday life. In my opinion, religious architecture, music or rituals are used to create the 'realness of reality'; in other words, to arouse emotions and impressions that also operate on a pre-reflexive level. Religious materiality serves as a means to create moods and feelings that can also be experienced within the nonreligious field.

Religious communities worldwide produce impressive material objects ranging from masks, ritual clothing, painting and sculptures to buildings and other constructions. Within the context of religious use, those objects may be viewed as mediators between human and non-human actors. They are also sometimes seen as impressive and powerful even if they are not viewed as mediators of transcendence. The issue of how these objects should be dealt with in situations when they are removed from the religious sphere has become the subject of scholarly works focused on the reuse of churches (see e.g. Bauer 2011; Buttlar et al. 2012; Frings et al. 2007; Kiley 2004). However, none of the churches selected for investigation in this chapter has actually become a gym, restaurant or library. Instead, they are supposed to combine religious and secular uses, which can lead to a questioning of the borders between the former and latter.

Maybe we should not assume anymore that religious architecture in Europe makes the transcendent present, even for people who struggle to feel a religious sense of belonging (Davie 1994). On the one hand, religious architecture is used in negotiations over identities and in political struggles, yet on the other, it also enables researchers to examine the role played by religious organizations in public life. Still, the presence of such architecture also arouses affect and emotions that transcend questions of identity and politics, even (or more precisely, especially) in the case of people who do not see themselves as religious. Religious materiality is important for people who see themselves as being situated outside the religious field. One does not have to be a member of a religious group to argue for financial support for the building or rebuilding of a religious edifice. Religious buildings, with their particular visual appeal, evoke feelings and emotions within secularized contexts that lend even more significance to any issue – be it local identity, a feeling of community or Polish–German relations – that is tackled at such a place.

Religious architecture in Europe and beyond is perceived by many people, including those who declare themselves to be nonreligious, as an important and desirable element of public space (Davie 2006). Christopher Kiley drew attention, when writing about the adaptation of church buildings for non-religious purposes in the United States, to their place in the landscape, seeing them as 'anchors' whose powerful visual presence can, in his opinion, be considered a 'public good' (2004, 13). Still, who exactly should use these buildings and how exactly they should do this is an important and contested question. The boundaries created between the secular and religious are not so much variable as fluid, porous or gradually evolving. It is not a question of whether a given event, attitude or action belongs to a secular or religious order, but how much of it belongs to one of these orders and in what way at any particular moment.

Notes

1 https://europeanvaluesstudy.eu/methodology-data-documentation/survey-2017/ (accessed 27 April 2020).
2 The research on the Polish–German border was sponsored by a grant awarded by the Polish German Foundation for Science in 2015–16. Subsequent research on the church buildings in secular space was financed by grant 2019/33/B/HS3/02136 awarded by the National Science Centre in Poland.
3 https://de.wikipedia.org/wiki/Ged%C3%A4chtniskirche_Rosow (accessed 28 April 2020).
4 The greater part of this section and the two following sections are based on interviews and informal conversations conducted in the region. I do not give many details about my interlocutors because we agreed to preserve their anonymity. As they come from small communities in the case of Rosow and Mescherin, if I had provided the real names of villages, the combination of such personal details as gender, age and occupation could potentially have led to my interlocutors being identified, which I wanted to avoid. All the conversations took place between 2016 and 2019.
5 The Federation of Expellees is the German non-governmental head organization of various organized groups of German refugees and expellees, mainly committed to documenting the post–Second World War flight and expulsion of Germans. When the organization initiated the establishment of the Centre Against Expulsions, the Polish media, as well as Polish governmental agencies, were the most explicit critics. The main argument was that the concept of the Centre proposed by the Federation would make the suffering of the German expellees become equal or even stand out among the fate of other expelled groups throughout history, and especially during and after the Second World War.
6 https://kirche.rosow.de/Hintergrund.html (accessed 1 March 2021). Author's translation.
7 This attribution is for made the sake of brevity. The actual agreement was made between the association and the Pommersche Evangelische Kirche (PEK; Pomeranian Evangelical Church). The PEK was part of the EKD until 2012, when it was integrated into the Evangelisch-Lutherische Kirche in Norddeutschland (Nordkirche; Evangelical Lutheran Church in Northern Germany), which is also part of the EKD.
8 www.ekbo.de/themen/spiritualitaet-tourismus.html (accessed 1 March 2021). Author's translation.
9 This is a quotation from the website of this village. I cannot provide a reference as it would give away the name of the village. As the description of this situation could potentially lead to escalation of the local conflict, I decided to anonymize this particular place and therefore all the people involved.

References

Asad, Talal. 1993. *Genealogies of Religion: Discipline and Reasons of Power in Christianity and Islam*. Baltimore: Johns Hopkins University Press.

———. 2003. *Formations of the Secular: Christianity, Islam, Modernity*. Stanford, CA: Stanford University Press.

Balogh, Péter. 2013. "Sleeping Abroad but Working at Home: Cross-Border Residential Mobility Between Transnationalism and (Re)bordering." *Geografiska Annaler Series B: Human Geography* 95 (2): 189–204.

Bauer, Katrin. 2011. *Gotteshäuser zu verkaufen: Gemeindefusionen, Kirchenschließungen und Kirchenumnutzungen*. Münster: u.a.

Bloch, Maurice. 2008. "Why Religion Is Nothing Special but Is Central." *Philosophical Transactions of The Royal Society B: Biological Sciences* 363 (1499): 2055–61.

Buttlar, Adrian von, Gabi Dolff-Bonekämper, Michael S. Falser, Achim Hubel, Johannes Habisch, and Georg Mörsch. 2012. *Denkmalpflege statt Attrappenkult: Gegen die Rekonstruktion von Baudenkmälern – eine Anthologie*. Berlin: De Gruyter.

Cannell, Fenella. 2005. "The Christianity of Anthropology." *Journal of the Royal Anthropological Institute* 11 (2): 335–56.

———, ed. 2006. *The Anthropology of Christianity*. Durham, NC: Duke University Press.

Davie, Grace. 1994. *Religion in Britain Since 1945: Believing Without Belonging*. Oxford: Wiley-Blackwell.

———. 2006. Religion in Europe in the 21st Century: The Factors to Take into Account." *European Journal of Sociology/Archives Européennes de Sociologie* 47 (2): 271–96.

Engelke, Matthew. 2014. "Christianity and the Anthropology of Secular Humanism." *Current Anthropology* 55 (S10): S292–S301.

Frings, Thomas, Engelbert Honkomp, Alois Peitz, Andreas Lechtape, Michael Bönte, Christian Richters, and Gisbert Schmitz. 2007. *Gestaltete Umbrüche: Kirchen im Bistum Münster zwischen Neugestaltung und Umnutzung*. Münster: Dialogverlag.

Hafner, Johann, Helga Völkening, and Irene Becci. 2018. *Glaube in Potsdam Band I: Religiöse, spirituelle und weltanschauliche Gemeinschaften: Beschreibungen und Analysen*. Vol. 1. Baden-Baden: Ergon.

Halemba, Agnieszka. 2019. "Postreligijne I nierelijne wykorzystanie budynków kościelnych na przygraniczu polsko-niemieckim." *Etnografia Polska* 63 (1–2).

Hervieu-Léger, Daniele. 2000. *Religion as a Chain of Memory*. Translated by Simon Lee, 133. New Brunswick, NJ: Rutgers University Press.

Höhn, Hans-Joachim. 2006. "Renaissance of Religion. Clarifications on a Disputed Topic." *Herder Korrespondenz* 12: 605–8.

Houtman, Dick, and Birgit Meyer, eds. 2012. *Things: Religion and the Question of Materiality*. New York: Fordham University Press.

Isenberg, Wolfgang, and Albrecht Steinecke. 2013. "Kirchen und Klöster – touristische Dimensionen und Perspektiven." *Zeitschrift für Tourismuswissenschaft* 5 (2): 141–60.

Keane, Webb. 2003. "Semiotics and the Social Analysis of Material Things." *Language & Communication* 23 (3–4): 409–25.

Kiley, Christopher J. 2004. "Convert! The Adaptive Reuse of Churches." Thesis, MIT, Dept. of Urban Studies and Planning.

Lau, Burkhard, Karl Lau, Cezary Korzec, Karsten Scheller, and Dietrich Seeliger. 2018. *775 Jahre Rosow. Festschrift zum 775 Jubiläum*. Ortsbeirat Rosow: Gemeinde Mescherin.

Meyer, Birgit. 2010. "Aesthetics of Persuasion: Global Christianity and Pentecostalism's Sensational Forms." *South Atlantic Quarterly* 109 (4): 741–63.

Meyer, Birgit, and Mattijs van de Port. 2018. *Sense and Essence. Heritage and the Cultural Construction of the Real*. Oxford: Berghahn Books.

Nolan, Mary L., and Sidney Nolan. 1992. "Religious Sites as Tourism Attractions in Europe." *Annals of Tourism Research* 19 (1): 68–78.

Paine, Crispin. 2013. *Religious Objects in Museums: Private Lives and Public Duties*. London: Blooms.

Peperkamp, Esther, and Małgorzata Rajtar, eds. 2010. *Religion and the Secular in Eastern Germany, 1945 to the Present*. Leiden: Brill.

Pollack, Detlef. 2002. "The Change in Religion and Church in Eastern Germany After 1989: A Research Note." *Sociology of Religion* 63 (3): 373–87.

———. 2003. "Religiousness Inside and Outside the Church in Selected Post-Communist Countries of Central and Eastern Europe." *Social Compass* 50 (3): 321–34.

Pollack, Detlef, and Gert Pickel. 2000. *Religiöser und kirchlicher Wandel in Ostdeutschland 1989–1999*. Bd. 3. Opladen: Springer-Verlag.

Quack, Johannes. 2014. "Outline of a Relational Approach to 'Nonreligion'." *Method & Theory in the Study of Religion* 26 (4–5): 439–69.

Quack, Johannes, and Cora Schuh, eds. 2017. *Religious Indifference: New Perspectives from Studies on Secularization and Nonreligion*. Cham: Springer.

Robbins, Joel. 2007. "Continuity Thinking and the Problem of Christian Culture: Belief, Time, and the Anthropology of Christianity." *Current anthropology* 48 (1): 5–38.

Röger, Maren. 2016. *Ucieczka, wypędzenie I przesiedlenie. Medialne wspomnienia I debaty w Niemczech I w Polsce po 1989 roku*. Poznań: Wydawnictwo Nauka I Innowacje.

Rutkowska, Bogna. 2019. "Zamieszkując 'pogranicze'. Migracja przygraniczna z Polski do Niemiec w doświadczeniach dzieci I rodziców." *Etnografia Polska* 63: 23–41.

Salemink, Oskar. 2016. "Described, Inscribed, Written Off: Heritagization as (Dis)connection." In *Connected and Disconnected in Vietnam*, edited by Philip Taylor. Canberra: Australian National University Press.

Verkaaik, Oskar, ed. 2013. *Religious Architecture: Anthropological Perspectives*. Amsterdam: Amsterdam University Press.

Wang, Ning. 1999. "Rethinking Authenticity in Tourism Experience." *Annals of Tourism Research* 26 (2): 349–70.

Wohlrab-Sahr, Monika. 2011. "'Forced' Secularity? On the Appropriation of Repressive Secularization." *Religion and Society in Central and Eastern Europe* 4 (1): 63–77.

Wohlrab-Sahr, Monika, and Tom Kaden. 2014. "Exploring the Non-Religious. Societal Norms, Attitudes and Identities, Arenas of Conflict." *Archives de sciences sociales des religions* 167: 105–25.

Wohlrab-Sahr, Monika, Uta Karstein, and Thomas Schmidt-Lux. 2009. *Forcierte Säkularität: religiöser Wandel und Generationendynamik im Osten Deutschlands*. Frankfurt/New York: Campus Verlag.

Zaborski, Marcin. 2007. "Przeszłość w teraźniejszości. Niemieccy wypędzeni w polskich mediach." *Przegląd Zachodni* 319 (1): 199–215.

Part V

Transnational and vernacular memories

16 The political use of the cult of St Tryphon of Pechenga and its potential as a bridge-builder in the Arctic

Elina Kahla

Introduction

Until at least the fourteenth century, and in practice longer, the Barents Region,[1] with its vast Arctic Sea coastline, remained uncharted territory, where indigenous nomadic people, fishermen and hunters coexisted outside the jurisdiction of nation states. It is here where the civilizational border between Western and Eastern Christendom was settled in the second half of the sixteenth century. The rivalry between these two versions of Christianity led to confrontations, banditry and massacres. Meanwhile, Orthodox monk-missionaries sponsored by the Novgorod and Muscovite regimes also established their presence in the region (Kirkinen 1970, 1976; Korpela 2010). The region's most famous hero was originally a Russian military engineer named Tryphon (1495–1583). Later, he transformed himself into a missionary and founded the Pechenga Monastery.

As for the situation now, Tryphon's heritage in the Arctic has many faces. In Norway and Finland, it is alive in the local toponymy and shrines as well as among the indigenous people of the Kola (Skolt) Sámi,[2] a small ethnic group, and other (Orthodox) Christians in the region. Outside Russia, Tryphon's heritage is less politicized, with no nationalist connotations, and therefore also less popular. In Russia, the religious, political and nationalist interrelatedness is obvious. The institutional Russian Orthodox Church (ROC) controls Tryphon-related heritage, whereas the state border guard and defence administration restrict access to the sites of memory associated with the saint. There is no simple way to break out of this deadlock and move towards some form of rapprochement. This chapter elaborates on an under-researched aspect of the saint's heritage: the relationship between the institutional missionary and the Skolt Sámi, who inhabited territory crossing unmarked borders between nation states, moving with their reindeer herds and at times paying taxes simultaneously to three countries: Sweden, Denmark[3] and Russia (Kirkinen 1976, 374; Nielsen and Zaikov 2012). Their heritage is oral, and their prospects of sustaining their livelihood are being seriously jeopardized by conflicts and climate warming.

I am going to argue that by contrasting traditional Sámi stories representing the non-institutional, non-national aspects of Tryphon's heritage with

DOI: 10.4324/9781003264750-21

330 Elina Kahla

institutional Russian Orthodox authors' accounts of the saint, the scholar can discover several realms of the saint's cult as well as its contemporary potential, be it nationalist or non-nationalist, religious or secular, central or peripheral, or institutional as opposed to 'lived locally'. The saint's religious cult, which incorporates church feasts, intercessional prayers dedicated to him and geographical sites of cultural memory associated with him have separate meanings for different groups. These aspects of Tryphon's cult are especially precious to the small indigenous group of Skolt Sámi nomads who continue today to commemorate Tryphon as their baptizer into and enlightener of the Orthodox Christian faith.

The Skolts historically lived for many centuries in the Pechenga (or Petsamo, in Finnish) region, but in the aftermath of the First World War and the Peace Treaty of Tartu, signed in August 1920, the new state border led to some of their winter villages (or *siids*) being annexed to Finland from Russia, while the remaining *siids* stayed within Soviet Russia. In 1944, when the Soviet forces advanced into the region, the entire territory of Pechenga, which included the *siids* and the Orthodox monastery, was ceded by the Finns to the Soviets. The population were evacuated to the interior of Finland for good. For them, the lost Petsamo turned into a nostalgic site of memory cherished in memoir literature and memory societies (Paasilinna 1983; Kahla 2020). Losing Petsamo caused even deeper trauma for the evacuated Sámi due to the access they lost to lands and waters, as well as the loss of their reindeer herds, traditional livelihood and nomadic way of life.

In Finnish historiography on the Second World War, attention is often paid to national sentiments over the loss of Karelia (Fingerroos 2011). However, less attention has been paid to the loss of Petsamo, which had been part of Finland only for twenty-four years (1920–44) and was inhabited by Karelians and the Skolt Sámi who, unlike the other 90% of ethnic Finns, were not all Protestants but of Orthodox denomination. The Skolt Sámi were classed as a 'minority of a minority' until recently, when the growing cross-border and global movement of the Arctic indigenous peoples has increased their self-awareness and encouraged scholars to study them more (Valkeapää 2011; Nielsen et Zaikov 2012; Laptander 2020). For the non-Orthodox evacuees, Petsamo is more likely to represent a site of collective cultural and family, rather than religious, memory. Their memoirs only mention the Orthodox saint's cult in passing (Paasilinna 1983; Soini 1986). One evacuee from Petsamo, the important essayist and memoirist, Erno Paasilinna, draws a sharp contrast between Tryphon's veneration with that of his Finnish 'opponent', the sixteenth-century legendary war hero Pekka (Juho) Vesainen. The latter comes across as a kind of 'anti-Tryphon' and a marker of the antagonism between Western Christian and Orthodox civilizations.

Some Western memory studies scholars have suggested there should be *one* universal (unipolar) or cosmopolitan memory in Europe, and that should be ascribed to the Holocaust tragedy. Levy and Sznaider write 'the Holocaust is officially part of European memory and becomes a new founding moment for

The political use of the St Tryphon cult   331

the idea of European civilization' (Levy and Sznaider 2002, 102). As a scholar of memory and religion from a country located on the 1,300-kilometre northern civilizational border, I am inclined to call for a critical turn in the memory studies discipline towards an approach that is more multipolar, multivocal (even being informed by peripheral regions and their minorities) and translocal (crossing borders). The example of Petsamo/Pechenga deserves attention not only because it is contested territory with a violent, traumatic past, but also because it can offer some hope in virtue of its transcending national(ist) narratives and the history of mutual tolerance among groups living in harmony with the fragile Arctic environment.

The example of peaceful cohabitation is what the indigenous nomadic Sámi of Petsamo have to offer, and this is particularly worthy of the attention of majority ethnic groups. This chapter also illustrates the claim that religion is not only a category of faith but also a historical category describing relationships of power and is therefore dependent on a secular understanding and must be defined within a given historical context, and not as a separate, independent and unchangeable phenomenon (Asad 1993). I am going to question the value of building cults of national saints as if they were self-evident protectors of *one* nation state's interests. Clearly, Tryphon's veneration outside Russia testifies to the fact that such cults can transcend national agendas. As a consequence, the ROC has no pre-emptive right to claim Tryphon as a protector of the Russian faith and the territory of Holy Rus' alone. In fact, throughout the Communist regime, it was the faithful outside the jurisdiction of the ROC or the Russian Federation who preserved his heritage. For them, Tryphon is the special Arctic protector of the Sámi and all inhabitants of fragile landscapes with insecure livelihoods. When his legacy is conceived in this light, it becomes clear that he encompasses the potential of a uniting symbol or bridge-builder transcending national-political agendas.

Methodology

The method used in this chapter is based on a comparative reading of a number of oral and written accounts relating to Tryphon. I initially analyzed these narratives when undertaking research for a monograph I was writing on the history of the Pechenga Monastery in the Finnish period (1920–44) and its martyred hieromonk Paisi (Riabov, 1882–1940; Kahla 2020). These research materials included official documents, archives, travelogues and memoirs as well as Internet sites, discussion groups and audio-visual materials, including clerical sermons. I also participated in summer seminars organized by the Murmansk and Monchegorsk diocese in 2010–15 and visited sites associated with Tryphon as a pilgrim in September 2019.

The analyzed narratives can be divided into three parts depending on which of the following interest groups they best represent: the Sámi, Russian Orthodox institutional writers and non-Orthodox Westerners. The first category comprises Sámi oral tales dating back to Tryphon's lifetime that were later

332   *Elina Kahla*

collected by folklorists, ethnographers and philologists from the second half of the nineteenth century. The tales appeared in translation in several languages. These translations reflected tastes that were of their time and further influenced by the collectors and editors' background. The second category comprises a wide range of Russian-language historical, hagiographic and popular accounts in which Tryphon is represented as a national saint and protector of the Orthodox monarchy (Holy Rus') on the East-West border of civilizations. The first account I used in my research was drawn from a collection titled *The Canon to All Russian Saints* compiled by the monk Shelonin (Shelonin [1657] 2002), which appeared about a hundred years after Tryphon's death. Due to the devastation of the Pechenga Monastery, the next edition of Tryphon's vita had to wait until 1859 (Zhitie 1859). Throughout the atheist Soviet period, the commemoration of national saints and other material heritage testifying to Russia's imperial past was made all but taboo. The Pechenga Monastery valuables and part of the archives were evacuated to Finland in 1944.[4]

After the change of political system in the early 1990s, Russian researchers and clerical writers gained access to archives both within and outside Russia. As a result, scholarly knowledge of Tryphon's life was further enriched by new historiographical facts and the previously unexamined vantage points of clerical and secular authors. These have been compiled into new scholarly and popular editions (e.g. Kalugin 2003; Fedorov 1996, 2017; Koniushanets 2002; Mitrofan 2009, 2017). Interest in Tryphon's cult also increased in parallel with the resurgence of the ROC and cultural Orthodoxy. Zealous researchers aimed to rehabilitate the martyred clerical and monastic victims of Stalinist purges with a view to (some of) them being canonized. Simultaneously, in the Kola Arctic, attempts were being made to re-establish the Pechenga Monastery under the new ROC diocese of Murmansk and Monchegorsk, which had been established in 1995.

I start by introducing some accounts of the cult of the Venerable Tryphon of Pechenga and point to various aspects of the constantly negotiable and intertwined relationship between memory and religion, the political versus the nonpolitical, and the institutional realm versus the lived religion realm. The Russian institutional authors, be they chronicler-monks (*knizhniki*) like the seventeenth-century Sergei Shelonin from Solovetsky Monastery (year of birth and death unknown; see Sapozhnikova 2010) or secular writers like Prince Andrei Kurbski (1528–83), were following the patriotic-political guidelines created by Metropolitan Makarii (1482–1563) (Miller 1979). Makarii himself closely collaborated with the tsar and instructed venerable Orthodox monks that their activity must harmonize with the secular regime. Therefore, when reading accounts of Tryphon's miraculous assistance to Tsar Ivan (1530–84) and his son Feodor (1557–98) or his intercession over the protection of contested territories on the Arctic Sea coast, one should interpret these contributions as commissioned pieces of institutional writing operating within their own framework. The more institutionalized an author's position is, the more cautious they are about revealing any mismatches between the implicit agenda of the ascetic monk and that of

The political use of the St Tryphon cult 333

the secular authorities. This does not, however, mean that these authors would have been unaware of these mismatches.

Tryphon's dual agenda in the Kola Lapland was to maintain his personal ascetic penitence and to undertake missionary work among the Sámi. The main points on Tsar Ivan IV's agenda were to enlarge his empire to the North and to establish an international shipping route from Arkhangelsk to the Dutch seaports. The regime not only needed the monastery as a strategic forepost but also as a provider of intercessional prayers. The Sámi perspective differs from that of the institutional writers, in that the Sámi oral stories represent a non-national, non-political viewpoint and describe an irresolvable conflict of interest in a straightforward manner that does not involve any institutional framing or idealization of any of the actors. The second section of the chapter elaborates on the Russian-language accounts of Tryphon that paved the path to his recognition as an Arctic-style Russian national saint. In the third section, I will discuss the Sámi perspective before finally outlining the Tryphon's cult's potential as a non-partisan bridge-builder.

The composition of Tryphon's life and his development into a national Russian Orthodox saint

The well-known researcher of medieval North Russian Orthodox saints, historian Jukka Korpela, highlighted in a panel presentation (Korpela 2018) that Tryphon was an extraordinary figure among missionary-saints. Usually missionary-saints wrote literature for the people they baptized, as did Feodorit of Kola (1489–1571) or Stephan of Perm (1340–96; Korpela 2010). However, there is no record of Tryphon writing such texts for the Sámi. Moreover, Tryphon was not a hieromonk (a monk who is also a priest in the Orthodox Church), so he invited other priests to help him baptize the indigenous. According to Korpela, Tryphon was a bandit who formed an alliance with Tsar Ivan IV. The alliance was normative. The formation of the principality of Muscovy was a casual and heterogeneous process on the peripheries, in which monastery-led colonization and missionary work played an important part. The Pechenga Monastery was the first institutional manifestation of the ruler's power in the Arctic, and for that reason alone, important enough to originate a cult. Korpela doubts whether Tryphon was a traditional 'hermit in the desert' primarily focused on prayer. By contrast, post-Soviet researchers have claimed that his authentic motivation was religious penitence (Mitrofan 2009). I will now examine the steps that structured Tryphon's path to sainthood, taking into account reflections in recent critical research.

From his early life to his decision to move to Pechenga

According to the clerical-monastic canon, and in particular the edition of the canon published in 1859, the future Venerable Tryphon was born into a pious family in Torzhok (Zhitie 1859). His parents sent the boy, then named

334 Elina Kahla

Mitrophan, away from home at a young age. Tryphon's vita, as was customary in hagiography, provides no individual details about his early life and youth. Another accepted custom was that a saint's vita and cult must serve a *purpose*. As Kalugin writes, the origins of Tryphon's first vita can be traced to a command given by Afanasy, archbishop of Holmogory (Arkhangelsk), who needed the cult to help him keep discipline in his diocese (Kalugin 2003). This early account does not mention that the future saint would otherwise have become a bandit, nor that he accidentally took the life of his girlfriend and that it was this personal tragedy that motivated him to follow a life of penitence. Moreover, the compilation of texts had restrictions of a moral character imposed on it and was subject to state censorship (Kalugin 2003; Mitrofan 2009).

As further discoveries by such contemporary historians as Korpela and Kalugin have demonstrated, a number of rich sources exist that provide non-clerical information on Tryphon's later activities. In 1564, Tsar Ivan IV commissioned Tryphon to establish trade contacts with foreign merchants. According to a travelogue composed by the Dutchman Simon van Salingen, who met Tryphon in person in Kola, the monk said he had moved north to repent and that he had also stopped eating meat, drinking alcohol and using underwear (NNBW 2019). Tryphon's asceticism resembles the model set by previous saintly missionaries, such as Stephen of Perm, which generally involved heading north to save one's soul and evangelize pagans. The most detailed information relates to the years Tryphon spent by the Pechenga River amid the indigenous Sámi. He fought against many obstacles, including wild animals, bears and sea monsters. He also suffered much hardship, enduring hostility and even beatings by the pagan Sámi (Azbyka.ru 2019).

The latter stages of Tryphon's life, and his death

The community of ascetics developed; however, it was afflicted by crop failure, famine and internal riots. When things escalated, Tryphon left Pechenga for seven years. Information regarding those years is meagre. Only after seven years of absence did Tryphon receive the metropolitan's blessing to establish a fortress-like (autarchic) community of Orthodox monastic brethren. Only at that point was Tryphon tonsured as a monk, but he was not willing to accept the formal leadership of the monastery (Mitrofan 2009). When Tryphon grew old, he retreated to his solitary hut. According to the canon, Tryphon foresaw a tragedy and warned the brethren about it on his deathbed. He told the brethren to love each other and not to take up arms in the temple but rather to accept martyrdom, in the *imitatio Christi* sense.

Devastation of the Pechenga Monastery in 1589

The long Russo-Swedish war hit hardest the settlements that were in the north of Ostrobothnia, which was at the time officially beyond the Russian borders established by the Treaty of Nöteborg (1323). A guerrilla war without any possibility of outside assistance created a market for warlords to protect the

The political use of the St Tryphon cult   335

settlers (Kirkinen 1976). In his youth, Tryphon was a prominent figure in this warfare against the combined forces of the Swedes and Finns, who were commanded by the peasant leader Pekka Vesainen from Ostrobothnia. According to a legend, Vesainen led a raid on Pechenga during which many monks were killed (Virrankoski 1997). The monastery was indeed destroyed, and 116 of its inhabitants – including monks and workers, two of whom were women, and three of Tryphon's closest companions, the hieromonks Iona, Gury and Herman – died as martyrs in December 1589. After the raid, the surviving monks and workers moved southward to the fortress of Kola. Tryphon's veneration survived among the locals, but it took several centuries for his cult to reach the status of that of a national Russian Orthodox saint and a loyal ally of the Tsar, and for his posthumous miracles to form an organic part of its popularity.

Tryphon's locus fidelitatis – the miracles

In one famous posthumous miracle, Tryphon visited Tsar Ivan IV in a dream (Zhitie 1859). The dream preceded a real visit by Tryphon to the court, so this testifies to divine intercession. When Ivan recognizes Tryphon in the crowd of people wishing to get access to the tsar as the same man he had seen in his dream, he grants him a document (dated 11 November 1556) guaranteeing natural resources, land and water as well as a workforce of local Sámi who would be at the monastery's disposal (Koniushanets 2002, 13–14). In addition, Ivan's young son, the pious Tsarevich Fyodor, hands his precious mantle, embroidered with jewels and gold, to Tryphon, and says, 'as a foretaste of the Tsar's gifts' (Mitrofan 2017, 154–63).[5]

The canon mentions a second miracle that occurred when the young Tsar Fyodor Ioannovich was fighting against the Swedes in a battle that took place close to Narva in 1590. Tryphon appears to Fyodor in the latter's dream, warning him: 'Tsar, immediately step out from your tent, or death will catch you unawares!' (Azbyka.ru 2019). As a result, Fyodor saves his own life, and he wants to thank Tryphon, but he finds out that the venerable monk (starets) was already dead and the monastery had been devastated. These posthumous miracles represented from the Russian institutional viewpoint remind one of the historical context, which was dominated by the long tragedy of the Swedish-Russian war and the aforementioned need to create a harmonious locus fidelitatis (demonstration of a bond of trust and loyalty) between the ruler and the monk: each of them has both secular and sacral roles, and they are mutually dependent on each other.

The rebirth of the monastery and development of Tryphon's cult

The long and costly war completely drained the state's reserve funds, and in 1765 Catherine II commanded that the monasteries be closed down and their property confiscated. For almost two centuries, even though material heritage such as letters from the tsar, special coins and sacral items bore witness to the community's early period, Tryphon's cult only survived locally. The monastery

336   Elina Kahla

had buried Tryphon's relics and those of the 116 martyrs safely at the site of their deaths. In 1859, a new vita was published and eventually, in 1886, the Holy Synod undertook to rebuild the ancient monastery. The resurgence of interest in Tryphon's cult coincided with Russian national policy of the 1850s, which followed in the wake of the introduction, in 1833, of the so-called Official Nationality (or Orthodoxy, Autocracy and Nationality) theory, and a new wave of colonization to the North. As the case of Pechenga demonstrates, a strong paternalistic link formed between the tsar, the Church and the monastery institution (*Sluzhba prepodobnomu Trifonu* 1883).

Starting from the mid-1850s, new liturgical and popular publications on Tryphon appeared en masse, and subsequently his fame as a protector of Russian lands and its Orthodox faith against Westerners became explicit. The monastery developed into a cultural cradle with a rich library and a school for local children. Investments in the latest technology included the monastery's own hydropower plant. A railway to Romanov-na-Murmane (Murmansk) was completed and the monastery enjoyed wide privileges. In 1916, its status was upgraded to that of a *stauropigial* (administered by the patriarchate) monastery (Koniushanets 2002). Tryphon's cult reached the heights of its popularity, and the monastery attracted visitors and pilgrims. Small cheap booklets containing his vita sold well and this income was used for new investments. New monks and workers were recruited, the majority of whom arrived in Pechenga from the nearby Solovetsky Monastery (Robson 2004).

Tryphon's veneration after 1917

The Bolsheviks associated the national saints' veneration with the Russian monarchy. When the civil war and British intervention ended, the Pechenga monastery and the area around it were ceded to Finland under the terms of the Tartu Peace Treaty. During the Finnish period (1920–44), the monastery functioned under the authority of the autonomous Finnish Orthodox Church. Prayers of intercession that had previously been said on behalf of the Tsar and his family's health were invalidated. Daily prayers of intercession addressed to Tryphon as well as celebrations of his feasts continued: one on the day of his death (on 15/28 December) and another one devoted to his namesake, the Martyr Tryphon feast (on 2 February). Although pilgrims visited the monastery and its shrines, no new Tryphon-themed publications appeared. The Finns lost Petsamo to the Soviets first time in 1939, the second time in 1944 (Vuorio 1982). In autumn 1944, the fierce fighting between the retreating Wehrmacht and the advancing Red Army devastated the monastery, reducing it to ashes (Kiselev 1995).

After the systemic change of regime

After the Soviet regime had fallen and Communist heroes were not in demand anymore, demand reappeared for a new resurgence of the Tryphon cult. In sociological terms, the sacred and profane were turned upside down (Kivinen

The political use of the St Tryphon cult   337

and Humphreys 2020). As previously mentioned, the remote, militarized and sparsely populated Kola Region did not have its own diocese until December 1995. The new Murmansk and Monchegorsk diocese was officially established on the eve of 28 December, the official date when the memory of Venerable Tryphon is celebrated (*Murmanskaia i Monchegorskaia eparkhiia* 2019). The choice of opening date once again revitalized the memory of Tryphon and the 116 martyrs, presented as ideal heroes and protectors of the Russian faith.

By 2003, the ROC had prepared a significant number of candidates for canonization as new saints representing the region, and in the same year they were glorified and included in the Synaxis of the Saints of Kola. In addition to Tryphon, the list also includes such figures as Tryphon's mentor, Feodorit of Kola (1489–1571), the 116 martyrs of Pechenga who gave up their lives in 1589, Varlaam of Keretsk (ca. 1505–90) and other regional saints, as well as two Soviet-period New Martyrs: the priest Moisei Kozhin (d. 1930) and novice Feodor Abrosimov (d. 1941; *Sobor Kolskikh Sviatykh*). The combination of sixteenth and twentieth century names is a manifestation of the notion of the continuity of Russian Orthodoxy – with saints being seen as pearls in one endless chain – as well as an attempt by power-holders to draw attention to a spiritual resurgence by naming new heroes. The year 2003 marked the end of the intensive period of research when access had been granted to secret archives. At this point they were closed again, and the boom in the creation of new saints began to fade. Nevertheless, saints' cults continued to develop through cultural products. In 2006, the hierarchs conducted archaeological excavations at the site of the monastery ruins, hoping to uncover relics of saints' bones. But their efforts were not rewarded, and they only found pieces of Tryphon's melted silver cenotaph and the bones of fallen soldiers of both sides in the Second World War (Mitrofan 2017, 186). These excavations were part of the widespread activity known as *poisk* – literally, the 'search' for Second World War victims' remains (Zhurzhenko 2020).

The link between the saintly protector and the national idea has persisted. Andrei Koniushanets, a contemporary chronicler of the Pechenga Monastery, quotes an earlier patriotic Russian diplomat to Norway, Dmitrii Nikolaevich Ostrovsky, who in the presence of Tsar Alexander III praised the project in 1880 by saying: 'Pechenga monastery is a monument to the great Russian cause. Together with its reconstruction resurges the hope that the glorious past experienced by our North will come back to us with God's help!' (Koniushanets 2002, 4). The author follows the tradition of drawing an analogy between calls for Russian Orthodox people to display more cohesion and self-esteem and the monastery's resurgence, while also insinuating that the monastery institution per se embodies the magnificent Russian 'cause'. Koniushanets tends to repeat earlier writers' circular arguments about the contested territories – the *Norvezhskie zemli* (*Norwegian lands*) – which suggest that the territory is *iskonno russki* (primordially Russian) on the basis that Russia got to the region first because a Russian saint was active in the region before the Norwegians arrived.

338 *Elina Kahla*

The call for a resurgence in self-esteem also alludes to the chaotic situation in the 1990s, when the remote territory of the Kola Arctic faced the collapse of its institutional structures, including the army and navy (Moore 2002; Mitrofan 2010). Officers' families were living in poverty, criminals had the upper hand, and swindlers and soothsayers became more popular than ever. In sociological terms, society collapsed into anomie. In this situation, monastic-clerical, military and civil administrative power structures turned to each other for support. Previous taboos on religion or the commemoration of autocratic, Orthodox tsars were lifted. New popular research rehabilitated previously prohibited themes like the exploits of pre-1917 tsarist Army officers or royal philanthropy. Factions of royalists formed a notable group, which also had a strong presence in Kola. Metropolitan Mitrofan (Badanin), who was inaugurated in 2019, wrote a series of books, such as *Ikona Velikogo kniazia* (*The Icon of the Grand Duke*, 2012) and *Dukhovnye istoki russkoi revoliutsii* (*The Spiritual Origins of the Russian Revolution*, 2017), which elaborated on the consequences of the loss of the idea of Holy Rus' and shed light on the ideal of loyalty to the monarchy.

Other books by Mitrofan are devoted to the vitae of sixteenth-century saints and elaborate on the role that has been played by monastic institutions in the history of the region. According to Mitrofan, the Pechenga Monastery struggles even today to find a place for itself between two polar opposites: possession (*styazhanie*), or accepting sponsors' gifts and influence, versus non-possession (*nestyazhanie*), or committing to poverty and concentrating on prayer. Mitrofan concludes that the core reason for the monastery's devastation in 1589 was not the foreign invasion but rather the monks taking a 'possession stance' that made it difficult for them to resist the temptation to acquire riches (Mitrofan 2017, 148). The riches that the Pechenga Monastery accumulated from maritime trade only led to gluttony and debauchery (Mitrofan 2017, 190–94). In his view, Tryphon's vita depicts an ascetic prototype physically and mentally capable of fighting against inner and outer temptations (*iskushenie*) and maintaining control over the brethren through his personal example. After all, in the Arctic Hyperborea, only the toughest could make it (Mitrofan 2017, 150–53).

Contemporary promotion of the 'Russian cause' places great emphasis on Tryphon's divine intercession on behalf of the Russian rulers and his protection of the contested territories. In the next section, Tryphon's activity among the indigenous Sámi is presented from contrasting vantage points.

Tryphon and the indigenous Sámi: testimony to their mutual respect?

In ROC-produced institutional texts, many episodes in Tryphon's life describe his cohabitation with and work among the indigenous Sámi, who traditionally observed pre-Christian religious rituals and life practices and venerated their own Finno-Ugric gods. Tryphon is presented as fighting against the shamanic leaders, or *kebuns*, of the Sámi. It is they, rather than *all* the Sami, who are his major opponents, and it is they who insist on rebelling against the missionary.

The political use of the St Tryphon cult 339

The narratives describe the casting of spells and the worship of bats, snakes and rocks – all examples of practices that conflicted with Christian monotheism. The manner in which Tryphon deports himself in the thick of a perpetual state of conflict testifies to his possession of the virtue of Christian patience, his self-control and his self-abasement. Tryphon is described as having the physical and mental qualities of a strongman, yet he nevertheless refrains from using violence against the Sámi or against his rebellious brethren. He is described as carrying heavy logs and even a millstone on his shoulders.

Tryphon's iconography portrays him as an elderly bald man. According to the vernacular tradition, the Sámi tore his hair off to make him stop his missionary activity (Kharuzin 1890). Nevertheless, as the years went by, Tryphon learned their language and helped their fishermen by driving away scary 'sea monsters' (or whales) which were preventing them from fishing. His invaluable help formed part of his missionary activity and exemplified the value of his teaching that one should love one's neighbour. In Russian texts on Tryphon, when the missionary brings 'enlightenment through Christianity', this is presented as a valuable activity in itself. Importantly, the indigenous people do not deny the value of his good deeds either. I will now elaborate on the Sámi perspective. My reflections will be based on two Norwegian works, one by fiction writer Lars Staerk (*Adventures and Fairy Tales from South Varanger*) an ethnic Sámi, and another by a researcher of cross-cultural influences, Caroline Serck-Hanssen (Staerk 1984; Serck-Hanssen 2017, 255–65).

The perspective of the narrator of Staerk's Sámi tales is often that of a Sámi man, sometimes called Evvan (Ivan in Russian), who acts as an expert guide through the icy, windy, rocky, swampy, trackless, dark wilderness. The central focus of these tales is a conflict of interest between him and his non-Sámi clients, who are often armed and full of bad intentions. The most famous episode describes the fatal consequences that ensue when Evvan agrees, in late December 1589, to act as a guide for a gang of robbers who are determined to murder the monks of the Pechenga Monastery in late December. Evvan agrees to be their guide because he is desperate after years of famine and the depletion of his reindeer herd.

Other episodes describe Evvan's baptism, which he received in the greedy hope that he would be given gifts rather than because of his faith. When no gifts follow, he becomes disappointed. He fails to internalize the Christian teachings, and little by little, God's grace abandons him. Disappointed, Evvan guides the bandits to the monastery. However, when they are returning home after the bloodshed is over, Evvan has second thoughts. He cuts the straps yoking the line of reindeer together, and the reindeer and bandits fall into a ravine and meet their death. Evvan is the only survivor, which he acknowledges to himself in despair. He tries to quench his thirst by drinking water from a sacred chalice, his share of the loot. The water turns into blood; Evvan panics and tries to throw the chalice away, but it ascends to heaven on a pole of bright light. In these didactic tales, tragedy is the imminent result of instinctive human greed or grievances.

340   *Elina Kahla*

I shall now attempt to synthesize the perspective presented in the Sámi tales: Tryphon's person and legacy represent an ambiguous, yet venerable agency. There is a deep irresolvable conflict between Orthodox Christian teaching and the *kebuns'* orders as well as traditional religious practices. However, this conflict does not equate to the rejection of or indifference to Christian teaching. The tales vividly reveal the deep shock Evvan feels when he throws away the stolen chalice. This conflict, in my view, reveals the fundamental tragedy of Evvan, and not his alone. In fact, it reveals the tragedy of the entire Skolt Sámi community living on the civilizational border. Due to the community's strategic location and his own position as an unarmed indigenous dweller living in nature, Evvan has no choice but to accept all the work offers that come his way, even if they come from criminals. This conflict is irresolvable in the realm of faith and religion, where there is a need to do penance.

From Evvan's viewpoint, for a long time, the borders of nation states were unimportant (reindeer crossed these unmarked borders anyway), and statist-national sentiments even less so. The Sámi were nomads who continuously wandered with their herds between several locations around the year – the only ecologically sustainable method of ensuring critical access to the lichen needed by their reindeer. For centuries, landownership was an alien concept to them. They only had the right to *use* the natural resources, land and water. Their attitude to the surrounding land, water, flora and fauna is completely different from that of landowners: they cherish nature and wish to leave it as pristine as possible for future generations (Valkeapää 2011). The symbiosis they achieve between their life practices and nature is not only extremely worthy of the attention of today's memory scholars but also that of today's climate change theorists. Tryphon's relationship with the Sámi prompts the question of what the missionary could have learned from *them*, and indeed what non-indigenous scholars can learn from their ecologically sustainable way of life today. The urgency for dialogue is much more relevant now, when climate change is a global phenomenon, than during the colonization period, when the exploitation of natural resources was not on the agenda.

Although there is no written evidence of any dialogue between Tryphon and his monastic followers and the Sámi, it is safe to assume that their cohabitation had its mutual benefits. In addition to the evidence based on oral tradition, there is also an archive known as the *gramota* ('document'). It was hidden 'from ancient times' in the *siid* of Suonjel, which was located not far from the Pechenga Monastery. Evidence of the privileges Russian tsars granted to the community can be found in documents dating from between 1601 and 1775, which confirmed the Sámi's rights to the region 'for eternity'. The location of the archive was kept strictly secret. Only the head of the community knew its precise location. Its survival in a pine stump testifies to fact that the mutual respect between the interested parties must have lasted for centuries, or at least until the Second World War. It was eventually evacuated to Finland, along with the villagers, in 1944 and now forms part of the National Archives of Finland. As a unique testimony, the archive was entered in the UNESCO Memory of the World register in 2015 (UNESCO 2017).

The political use of the St Tryphon cult   341

For the Skolt Sámi, documents confirming the bond of trust between their community and the Russian monastery, and ultimately the Russian tsar, were invaluable. In extreme Arctic conditions, such trust was more valuable than gold. Every non-native wanderer hoping to find a safe path through the Sámi lands and cross the state border needed a competent and trusted guide, and the Sámi were ideally qualified to provide such guides. The *gramota* archive testifies to the mutual respect between the interested parties and offers a unique picture of conditions in the Arctic peripheries, where life looked very different to the centre (of state power). The *gramota* archive therefore exemplifies the benefits of secular agency and a commitment to legislative rights, whereas the Sámi oral tradition presents concrete irresolvable personal conflicts of interest revolving around sin, punishment and repentance within a local, very specific historical and climatic context.

From political saint to global bridge-builder

According to the oral tradition, Tryphon's veneration continued locally at the site of his burial. In 1708, an Uspenie (Dormition) church was erected there. Inside this church, a local sponsor built a silver cenotaph in his memory (Mitrofan 2017, 251). It was not until the mid-nineteenth century that the Tryphon cult assumed national forms of a larger scale, a development that was boosted by the modernization of the Russian North. Tsar Nicholas II was personally involved in the monastery's resurgence and he met Hegumen Ionafan (Baranov, 1849–1915) twice in person, in 1899 and 1907. Despite receiving strong institutional support, Tryphon's canonization as a national saint was not the smoothest of processes. Pechenga Monastery had barely survived from the period from the seventeenth to the nineteenth century. Written records of Tryphon's local veneration, let alone his canonization, had been lost. As previously mentioned, attempts to lift his remains and celebrate the transfer of his relics were not blessed with success. Ultimately, Tryphon was not included in the True List of Saints (*Vernyi mesiatseslov*) until 1903 (Mitrofan 2012, 252).

Another fact that attests to Tryphon's peculiar status within the institutional ROC is that he is commemorated in parallel in several synaxes (assemblies of saints), notably the Synaxes of Karelia (since 1957) and Novgorod (since 1981), and the Synaxis of the Saints of Kola (since 2003; Sobor Kol'skikh/Karel'skikh Sviatykh, 2020). The initiatives of these overlapping, territorial synaxes obviously serve secular, and sometimes (ecclesiastical) political, purposes, as was the case with the birth of the Synaxis of Karelian Enlighteners. In 1957, after the resolution of a schism between the FOC (see Finnish Orthodox Church 2020) and the ROC over a post-war (1945–57) canonical crisis caused by a dispute over the authority of the Orthodox monastery of New Valamo, the two parties celebrated their reconciliation by establishing, with the assistance of the Evangelical Lutheran Church of Finland, the Synaxis of All Karelian Enlighteners (or Saints). The list on this Synaxis includes a total of sixty-seven names of medieval saints; together, these saints form the imaginative space of the 'Karelian land', which does not correspond to the geographical reality presented by

342   *Elina Kahla*

any map. From the Finnish vantage point, the new Synaxis is associated with the historical-geographical cradle of Finnish Orthodoxy. In addition, the Synaxis is associated with ecumenical and ecclesiastical-political initiatives that are reminiscent of the normalization of inter-Orthodox relations and the regional protection provided through the saints' intercession.

In spite of the national saints' cults regularly being used, as discussed above, for political ends, such developments seldom disturb the practices of the observant faithful in their local communities. Although the institutional ROC has politicized Tryphon in its own interests, this has not prevented either the Skolt Sámi or the Arctic Norwegians, or even the entire FOC, from venerating him as *our* saint. The core Christian teachings – based on loving one's neighbour and not taking up arms, but accepting a martyr's death *in imitatio Christi* – are a uniting denominator for the faithful. Furthermore, as the Skolt Sámi tradition indicates, merging Christian teaching with the perspective taken by their own oral accounts is possible; the practice has survived to this day (*Pá̂ ss Treeffan Peäccmest: sää'mmaainâs* 2006, Paulaharju 1921).

Today, in the midst of heated debates on the issue of indigenous people's rights being seriously threatened by increasing concerns over the effects of climate warming, Tryphon's teachings based on Christian asceticism and peaceful cohabitation (transcending state borders) with wild fauna as well as different ethnic groups of various nationalities, identities and religious denominations should have even more resonance. Throughout the Barents Region, Sámi activists have built networks and combined their forces to accuse colonizers, including Christian missionaries, of all manner of evils, including the destruction of their livelihoods, soil and water, and ultimately, their identity. Their appeals have been met with some empathetic feedback (Kanninen – Ranta 2019).[6] In the Russian Federation, such protests are less welcome. Neither the regime nor the ROC has encouraged the Sámi, to say the least. It comes as no surprise that many contemporary ROC clerics may not even be aware of the ancient *siids* of the Sámi (they were destroyed during the Second World War). Forced assimilation appears to be the prevailing normative strategy, and the Sámi tragedy is nothing but a tiny chapter in a problem of 'warped mourning' in a 'land of the unburied' (Etkind 2013). This ignorance of Sámi rights can, at least partially, be explained by the ROC's dogmatic attitude to the Sámi's non-Christian practices, but it can also be accounted for by the tabooization of any discussion of the ethnic repressions (Stepanenko 2002). Stepanenko provides a thorough study on the repressions and deportations experienced by the Sámi throughout Stalinism. Even after this period, ethnic minorities (among them, the ethnic Finns of Kola) had no right of return to their traditional lands whatsoever. The ROC has so far not undertaken any serious dialogue with the Sámi giving sufficient attention to the indigenous people's experience and minority perspective. In the Murmansk Region, variations on neopaganism have arisen that seem to be attracting young people, including army and navy conscripts and those within the athletics community. These factions are presenting themselves as a counterweight to the rigorous nationalist ROC leadership, which

The political use of the St Tryphon cult   343

has been accused of corruption. Faced with such challenges to its authority, the ROC would benefit from integrating minority groups' experience of dialogue into their commemorative practices. Of course, knowledge about ethnic purges in the region would be a prerequisite for such a process of integration.

Outside Russia, Tryphon's veneration has been less 'warped'. Pilgrimages to holy sites or sites of memory associated with Tryphon have not only attracted Orthodox practitioners but also visits by secular travellers. The traditional visitors' route includes chapels and churches in three countries: St Georg's Chapel in Neiden in Norway; a church dedicated to the Saint Passion-Bearers Boris and Gleb on the Russian side of the border between Norway and Russia; and other churches in Sevettijärvi and Nellim in Finland. The two Finnish villages that hosted the Skolt Sámi who were evacuated after the Second World War built Orthodox churches and chapels for the new settlers' use.

The Tryphon-themed tours that are popular today represent an important part of Arctic cross-border cooperation and the peoples' diplomacy. Thanks to this institutionalized tradition, participants without Russian passports have also been granted an annual opportunity to visit the Church of Saints Boris and Gleb located in the border zone. Since 2014, however, the freezing of East-West political relations have restricted access to that church. However, very surprisingly, in this case too, there have been clear differences between the approach taken by the centre and the peripheries. By special local permission, Skolt Sámi pilgrims have been able to continue their traditional annual visits on 6 August to Borisoglebsk to celebrate the church's temple feast. In August 2019, a joint liturgical service took place. This testifies to the fact that the cherishing of local, cross-border collaboration is recognized as mutually beneficial and brings hope for a better future.

Another concrete example of the Tryphon cult is evident today on the Norwegian-Russian border. According to legend, Tryphon used to hide in caves from the Sámi (and various assailants). One of these caves is located on the seacoast near the newly constructed 'Trifon' E105 highway tunnel, which was opened in 2017 and links Norway and Russia. Not coincidentally, the Russians reconstructed a monument to Tryphon in the form of a cave and placed an icon inside it, whereas the Norwegian's main intention was to organize the financing of the expensive tunnel, which caters for both passenger and freight vehicles and leads to the town of Kirkenes (Nielsen 2017). The decision to name the tunnel after Tryphon demonstrates, in concrete terms, the extent to which both sides recognize the missionary saint's symbolical role as a bridge-builder. Although the tunnel is a secular (Norwegian) construction, and the reconstruction of the 'saint's cave' in the rocks (by the Russians) bears religious symbols, taken as a whole, both structures signify good neighbourly relations.

These sites of memory have the symbolic potential to assist with the working through of traumatic memories related to lost lands and bombed homes. Tunnels, like museums, are secular monuments, but they may still have religious undertones, as is clear from the decision to name the highway tunnel after Tryphon. The collections of the Grense (border) museum, which is dedicated

344 *Elina Kahla*

to regional history, incorporate the history of the Sámi, with whom Tryphon cohabited, as well as the Second World War events in the Norwegian town Kirkenes. Soothing traumatic memories requires knowledge of all interested parties' vantage points, and that is what the border museum seeks to achieve. The museum tells the story of the German occupation, which involved 100,000 soldiers, and the events surrounding the bombing of Kirkenes during its liberation by the Soviets. The texts accompanying the exhibits are in five languages, which is very welcome. The museum arose from a research collaboration and is open to anyone at no cost, unlike many other religious sites of memory, such as the Boris and Gleb church and the Tryphon cave in the border zone. Therefore, there is a need for professional researchers to verbalize how much religion and the religious imaginarium stand behind their field (see Bogumił and Yurchuk in this volume). Too often, memory scholars play by the rules set by the unipolar 'centre', whereas the peripheries' tragedies and heroes, and examples of peaceful cohabitation, lived religious practices and lessons learned, have had to wait their turn to be heard and shared.

Conclusion

The primary focus of this chapter was the construction of an Arctic saint's life story based on the person and activity of Venerable Tryphon of Pechenga and his relationship with the monastery he founded on contested territory at the civilizational border between Western and Eastern Christendom. I traced the rise and fall of the monastery through different epochs, arguing that each resurgence of the monastery involved a need to call upon its founder's protection. Today, the ROC is again developing the cults devoted to Tryphon and Feodorit as protectors of Russian interests in the region. Importantly, however, Tryphon's heritage has a wider potential, as is clear from Sámi tales and sites associated with Tryphon that are not only important for Russians but also for Norwegians, Finns and other groups of Arctic dwellers. Tryphon's bond of mutual benefit with the Skolt Sámi deserves more attention in future studies. Researchers should be asking what Tryphon learned from the Sámi, rather than exclusively focusing on the opposite scenario. Tryphon represents a paragon of the ascetic penitent, but his asceticism was paralleled by the asceticism practised by the Sámi, which was grounded in their traditional livelihood and life among nature as well as their rejection of traditional ownership and the ruthless exploitation of natural resources. Interdisciplinary, multipolar and multinational research should be undertaken that would enable the further investigation of religious heritage based on 'Tryphon's model' for practising tolerance, patience and the recognition of mutual interdependence when attempting to solve global challenges such as those presented by climate warming. Recognition of the ambiguous, but still venerated, heritage of sixteen-century saints should go hand in hand with reconciliation processes pertaining to twentieth-century civil traumas, in particular work on difficult memory and the rehabilitation of victims of mass purges. This process would require access being granted to

The political use of the St Tryphon cult   345

archive materials, the courage to publish research results, a bold attempt being made to separate institutional agencies from the living faithful, collaboration between religious and secular agencies and mutual respect.

Notes

1 The region is often referred to as the Barents Region or the Euro-Arctic Region. The area consists of the northernmost parts of Norway, Sweden, Finland and North-West Russia. The geographical area incorporates 1.75 million km² of land, of which about 75% is located in Russia. The Barents Region has over five million inhabitants, including several indigenous peoples: the Sami in all the four Barents countries, and the Nenets and Veps on the Russian side. www.barentscooperation.org/en/About/Learn-More/Barents-region, accessed 14 November 2019.
2 The Skolt Sámi (along with the Kildin, Ter and smaller Sámi communities of the Kola Peninsula) are, unlike all the other Sámi groups, Orthodox Christians.
3 Denmark and Norway were one country in this period.
4 The Petsamo Monastery collection is stored in the Orthodox Church Museum in Kuopio (Finland).
5 Later, Russian historians questioned this miracle's trustworthiness: Fyodor was not yet born in 1556. Mitrofan suggests that the miracle story merged two visits. Tryphon paid two visits to Kremlin, the first one in 1556, and the second one in 1576, when Tsarevich Fyodor was already nineteen years old.
6 Cf. Kanninen Jaana – Kukka Ranta, *Vastatuuleen. Saamen kansan pakkosuomalaistamisesta.* 2019. S&S. This volume is about the assimilation experiences of the Finnish Sámi Indigenous people and the ownership of the Arctic nature in the Sámi native region. In Finland, the government is preparing a reconciliation commission.

References

Asad, Talal. 1993. *Genealogies of Religion: Discipline and Reasons of Power in Christianity and Islam.* Baltimore: Johns Hopkins University Press. https://doi.org/10.2307/3712068.

Azbyka.ru. 2019. "Trifon Pechengskii." https://azbyka.ru/days/sv-trifon-pechengskij.

Etkind, Alexander. 2013. *Warped Mourning. Stories of the Undead in the Land of the Unburied.* Stanford, CA: Stanford University Press.

Fedorov, Pavel Viktorovich. 1996. *Istoriia Trifono-Pechengskogo monastyr'ia. 1886–1917 gg.* Murmansk: Murmanskii gosudarstvennyi pedagogicheskii universitet.

———. 2017. *Pravoslavnyi slovar' Kol'skogo severa.* 2-e dopolnennoe izdanie. Sankt-Petersburg. www.arcticandnorth.ru/Encyclopedia_Arctic/Prav-slovar-2-text.pdf.

Fingerroos, Outi. 2011. " 'Karelia Issue': The Politics and Memory of Karelia in Finland." In *Finland in World War II History, Memory, Interpretations. In History of Warfare Series*, Vol. 69, 483–517. Cham: Brill. https://doi.org/10.1163/9789004214330_013.

Finnish Orthodox Church. 2020. "Karjalan valistajat." https://ort.fi/karjalan-valistajat.

Kahla, Elina. 2020. *Petsamon marttyyri ja maailman pohjoisin luostari.* Helsinki: SKS.

Kalugin, V. V. 2003. "Zhitie Trifona Pechenskogo – pamiatnik severnorusskoi agiografii petrovskogo vremeni." In *Chelovek mezhdu tsarstvom I Imperiei. Sbornik materialov mezhdunarodnoi nauchnoi konferentsii*, 328–41. Moscow: RAN, In-t cheloveka.

Kanninen Jaana, and Ranta Kukka. 2019. *Vastatuuleen. Saamen kansan pakkosuomalaistamisesta.* Helsinki: S&S.

Kharuzin, Nikolai. 1890. *Russkie lopari.* Moscow: Imperatorskii Moskovskii universitet. Imperatorskoe Obshchestvo Liubitelei Estestvoznaniia, Antropologii I Ètnografii.

346 *Elina Kahla*

Kirkinen, Heikki. 1970. *Karjala idän ja lännen välissä I. Venäjän Karjala renessanssiajalla (1478–1617)*. Helsinki: Suomen historiallinen seura: Kirjayhtymä.

———. 1976. *Karjala idän ja lännen välissä II. Karjala taistelukenttänä*. Helsinki: Suomen historiallinen seura: Kirjayhtymä.

Kiselev, Aleksei Alekseevich. 1995. *Voina v Zapoliar'e: uchebnoe posobie dlia starshikh klassov gimnazii obshchcheobrazovatel'nykh shkol, litseev I gimnazii*. Murmansk. http://kolanord.ru/html_public/col_avtory/KiselevAA/KiselevAA_Voyna-v-Zapolyarje_1995/2/index.html.

Kivinen, Markku, and Brendan Humphreys, eds. 2020. *Russian Modernisation – A New Paradigm*. Abingdon: Routledge (Series on Russian and East European Studies).

Koniushanets, Andrei Ivanovich. 2002. *Sviataia obitel' na vershine Rossii*. Pechenga: Paraklit.

Korpela, Jukka. 2010. "Feodorit (Theodorit) Kol'skii: Missionary and Princely Agent." In *Religion und Integration im Moskauer Russland: Konzepte und Praktiken, Potentiale und Grenzen. 14–17 Jahrhundert*, 201–26. Berlin: Harassowitz Verlag.

———. 2018. "Bandit Trifon, the Muscovite Occupation of Arctic Shores and Its Religious Legitimization." Panel: St. Tryphon of Pechenga and Political Uses of History. Aleksanteri Conference, October 25.

Laptander, Roza. 2020. *When We Got Reindeer, We Moved to Live to in the Tundra: The Spoken and Silenced History of the Yamal Nenets*. Acta electronica Universitatis Lapponiensis 278. Rovaniemi: University of Lapland Printing Centre.

Levy, Daniel, and Natan Sznaider. 2002. "Memory Unbound: The Holocaust and the Formation of Cosmopolitan Memory." *European Journal of Social Theory*: 87–106. https://doi.org/10.1177/1368431002005001002.

Miller, David B. 1979. "The Velikie Minei Chetii and the Stepennaia Kniga of Metropolitan Makarii and the Origins of Russian National Consciousness." In *Forschungen zur Osteuropäischen Geschichte* 26 (1979): 263–382.

Mitrofan, Episkop (Badanin). 2009. *Prepodobnyi Trifon Pechengskii. Istoricheskie materialy k napisaniiu zhitiia*. Pravoslavnye podvizhniki Kol'skogo Severa: Kniga IV. Sankt-Peterburg and Murmansk: Ladan.

———. 2010. *Neugasimaia lampada "Kurska"*. Sankt-Peterburg and Murmansk: Ladan.

———. 2012. *Ikona Velikogo kniazia*. Sankt-Peterburg: Ladan.

———. 2017. *Kol'skii Sever v Srednie veka* [third volume]. Sankt-Peterburg: Ladan.

Moore, Robert. 2002. *A Time to Die. The Kursk Disaster*. London: Bantam Books.

Murmanskaia I Monchegorskaia eparkhiia. 2019. http://mmeparh.cerkov.ru/o-eparxii/.

Nielsen, Jens Petter, and Konstantin Zaikov. 2012. "Norway's Hard and Soft Borders Towards Russia." In *Imagined, Negotiated, Remembered: Constructing European Borders and Borderlands*, edited by Kimmo Katajala and Maria Lähteenmäki, 67–84. Zurich: LIT Verlag.

Nielsen, Thomas. 2017. "Member of Parliament Wants Russian Road Sign for Borderland Bridge." *Barents Observer*, October 1.

Nieuw Nederlandsch Biografisch Woordenboek (NNBW). 2019. Salingen, Simon van. http://ke.culture.gov-murman.ru/slovnik/?ELEMENT_ID=99713.

Paasilinna, Erno. 1983. *Maailman kourissa*. Helsinki: Otava.

På´ss Treeffan Peäccmest: sää'mmaainâs. 2006. Edited by Miia Moshnikoff and Satu Moshnikoff. Inari: Saamelaiskäräjät.

Paulaharju, Samuli. 1921. *Kolttain mailla. Kansatieteellisiä kuvauksia Kuollan-Lapista*. Helsinki: Kustannusosakeyhtiö Kirja.

Pechengskii monastyr', nyne ischeznuvshii s lica zemli. Predanie, dobavlennoe arkhivnymi dannymi. 1893. St. Petersburg: Izd. T. F. Kuz'mina.

Robson, Roy. 2004. *Solovki: The Story of Russia Told Through Its Most Remarkable Islands*. New Haven, CT: Yale University Press.

The political use of the St Tryphon cult 347

Sapozhnikova, Ol'ga Sergeevna. 2010. *Russki knizhnik XVII veka Sergii Shelonin*, 81–102. St Petersburg: Arkheo-Aletheia.

Serck-Hanssen, Caroline. 2017. *Helgen I grenseland. Arven fra Tryphon av Petsjenga*, 255–67. Stamsund: Orkana.

Shelonin, Sergii. 2002. *Kanon vsem russkim svyatym*. Moscow: Alfa I omega.

Sluzhba prepodobnomu Trifonu. 1883. Moscow: Sinodal'naia tipografiia.

Sobor = Sobor (Kol'skikh/Karel'skikh) Sviatykh. 2020. https://mospat.ru/calendar/sobor1.

Soini, Tuulikki. 1986. *Petsamo – Suomen siirtomaa*. Jyväskylä, Helsinki: Gummerus.

Staerk, Lars. 1984. *Eventyr og sagn fra Sør-Varanger, Muitalusat ja máidnasa Mátta-Várjjagis. Staerk, Lars*. Tana: Jår'galaed'dji.

Stepanenko, Aleksandr. 2002. *Rasstreliannaia sem'ia. Ocherki Kol'skikh saamov*. Murmansk: © Aleksandr Stepanenko.

Unesco Memory of the World. 2017. "Archive of the Skolt Sámi village of Suonjel." www. unesco.org/new/en/communication-and-information/memory-of-the-world/register/full-list-of-registered-heritage/registered-heritage-page-1/archive-of-the-skolt-sami-village-of-suonjel-suenjel/.

Valkeapää, Leena. 2011. *Luonnossa: vuoropuhelua Nils-Aslak Valkeapään tuotannon kanssa*. [Doctoral dissertation]. Helsinki: Maahenki.

Virrankoski, Pentti. 1997. "Vesainen, Pekka. Kansallisbiografia-verkkojulkaisu." In *Studia Biographica 4*. Helsinki: Suomalaisen Kirjallisuuden Seura. https://kansallisbiografia.fi/kansallisbiografia/henkilo/435.

Vuorio, Antero. 1982. *Petsamo talvisodan kourissa*. Helsinki: Kirjayhtymä.

Zhitie prepodobnago Trifona Pechengskago, prosvetitelja loparei. 1859. In *Pravoslavnyi sobesednik*, Ch. 2. Kazan': Sinodal'naia tipografiia.

Zhurzhenko, Tatiana. 2020. "Toisen maailmansodan muisto venäläisessä provinssimediassa (Novgorod ja Murmansk) [World War II Memories and Local Media in the Russian Province (Velikiy Novgorod and Murmansk)]." In *Sandarmohista Skolkovoon. Toim*, edited by Kaarina Aitamurto, Elina Kahla and Jussi Lassila, 181–95. Helsinki: Into Publishing House.

17 'Vernacular' and 'official' memories

Looking beyond the annual Hasidic pilgrimages to Uman

Alla Marchenko

Introduction: Hasidism and vernacular memory

Hasidism ('piety' in Hebrew) appeared on the territories of contemporary Poland and Ukraine (at that time, part of the Kingdom of Poland) in the middle of the eighteenth century. It arose as a movement in Judaism that sought to gain closer proximity to God through personal prayer and experience, and by gathering around a Hasidic leader called a *tsaddik* ('righteous man' in Hebrew) or *rebbe*. The important role played by the physical aspects of Hasidism (dancing, singing, public prayers, etc.) attracted wider audiences to the movement, ultimately transforming it into a response to existing social inequalities in society and an integral part of the modernization processes in Jewish history (Biale et al. 2018, 2).

Despite the fact that the Hasidim[1] only represent about 5% of world Jewry (Wodziński 2018b, 192), they shape the profile of pilgrimages to Eastern Europe and embody the 'typical religious Jew' for the non-Jewish locals there. As contemporary scholarship suggests, Hasidism has changed its role from being a protest movement to one of the defining movements in contemporary Judaism (Biale et al. 2018).

From its inception, Hasidism was a dynastic movement, which meant that the leadership in the Hasidic court (a group of believers) could be passed to the son of a rebbe or his favourite student. With the passage of time, different disciples or several of the tsaddik's children started to form their own courts. For instance, Rebbe Nachman, the founder of Breslov Hasidism, was the great grandson of the founder of Hasidism, Israel ben Eliezer, known as Ba'al Shem Tov ('Master of the Good Name' in Hebrew). The fact that Rebbe Nachman died in the town of Uman in 1810 and made his final testament there is the main reason accounting for the emergence of the Hasidic pilgrimage to the tsaddik's tomb. Most importantly, the founder of Breslov Hasidism[2] also became its last leader, because both of Rebbe Nachman's sons, Shlomo Efraim and Yakov, died prematurely and his most dedicated disciple, Nathan Sternharz (also known as Reb Noson), chose to spend his life disseminating Rebbe Nachman's teaching instead of promoting his own ambitions. The popularity of Breslov Hasidism (sometimes ironically referred to as 'dead Hasidism') is

DOI: 10.4324/9781003264750-22

partially explained by the absence of a living leader and partially by the fact that opportunities are more open for Jews to attach themselves to the movement. Rebbe Nachman is known to have promised:

> When my days are over and I leave this world, I will still intercede for anyone who comes to my grave, says Ten [particular – author's note] Psalms and gives a penny to charity. No matter how great his sins, I will do everything in my power, spanning the length and breadth of creation, to save him and cleanse him.
>
> (*The Essential Rabbi Nachman* 2006, 487)

This promise is often interpreted as an open invitation that is even extended to people with complicated biographies and life circumstances.

In this chapter, I analyze how vernacular and official local memory of Hasidic pilgrims are manifested in the public space of Uman and how these memories interact. This chapter starts with the main definitions and genealogy of collective memory connected to the Hasidic pilgrimages. Later, I show different perspectives for interpreting the Koliivshchyna rebellion within a contemporary context that are important both for the Hasidic pilgrims and the Ukrainian population of Uman. The last section discusses patterns of interaction between vernacular and official memory in the local space, and their structure and development.

My interpretations are based on materials I collected from web pages representing official Ukrainian institutions and available archival materials that refer to the development of Hasidic pilgrimage, as well as visual data from my personal observations in Uman in 2017–18. I also rely on the results of a survey conducted among Uman inhabitants in December 2018.[3]

Vernacular and official memories

In this chapter, I use the term 'collective memory' when referring to narratives about the past held by distinctive groups and embodied in commemorative practices, legends and oral histories. According to this interpretation, vernacular memory is a specific form of collective memory that is shared among members of a given community (Bodnar 1992; Marschall 2013), in contrast to official memory, which is always institutionalized and connected to local or national authorities. I have initially placed the most important concepts I discuss in parentheses to indicate that they reflect a variety of memories belonging to different subgroups within a given community or different institutions. Official memory is formed, supported and modified by dominant political elites, while vernacular memory mostly depends on the means by which it is communicated within the community.

It is important to note that vernacular memory of the Hasidic pilgrimages is deeply religious in character, and as such, it is a good example of how religion can help to form and retain the potential to remember, even under harsh

350   *Alla Marchenko*

restrictions. Historically, a significant proportion of the population of the town of Uman, which is known from written sources dating from the beginning of seventeenth century, were Jewish, although these Jews did not belong to the ruling political elite. For instance, a census conducted a hundred years ago (1920) showed that 57.1% of Uman's population were Jews, 29.7% were Ukrainians, 8.1% Russians and 3.1% Poles (Kuzniets 2005, 135).

After a period when it functioned as a privately owned Polish town (with Stanisław Szczęsny Potocki being the last owner), Uman became part of the Russian Empire in 1793. The dominant position occupied in the town by Christians meant that cultural memory of Uman's Jewish population was very much a matter for the Jewish community. One of the most heavily inhabited Jewish districts of pre-war Uman was located relatively far from the town's central square, and most of the town's Jewish inhabitants perished during the Holocaust. Memory of the Hasidic pilgrimages was erased from the local space several times due to general Soviet repressions against religion, which included a ban being placed in 1930 on any religious activities and a period of reconstruction following the Second World War that neglected any ethnic matters in favour of the promotion of a large framework incorporating the 'Soviet people' as a whole. The use of this framework was continued until the 1980s. At the same time, memory of the pilgrimages was kept in a vernacular form within Hasidic communities living outside Ukraine, and once the pilgrimages were allowed back into the town again, they came as an unexpected culture shock to many of Uman's inhabitants.

Depending on its means of transmission, collective memory can be divided into communicative memory and cultural memory (Assmann 1995, 126). Communicative memory includes patterns of memory based on personal communications, while cultural memory embraces repeated practices and knowledge from books, educational programmes and so on. It is possible to say that the communicative form was a characteristic feature of local collective memory of the Hasidim, though this obviously faded with time in the physical absence of the latter. It also played an important role in Hasidic communities, where it was combined with existing religious texts. The area around the current place of pilgrimage has been redeveloped a few times since the Second World War, which significantly changed the communicative memory of the locals connected to the space (Tchoukaleyska 2016). This has led to data discrepancies and different interpretations of the places that are once again connected to Jewish history in Uman today.

One good example of such a discrepancy is the location and boundaries of the old Jewish cemetery where Nachman was buried. Representatives of the Hasidic Jewish community marked the area of the cemetery with a yellow line on the pavement a few decades ago, basing the line's exact location on maps available to their Jewish community. Marking the cemetery's location was important for the community for at least two reasons connected with religion: first, not all groups of Jewish believers are allowed to step on the territory of a cemetery (even a former one); second, it is completely forbidden under Jewish

'Vernacular' and 'official' memories   351

law to 'disturb bodies' through construction or digging work. However, there is no information about this cemetery in the Ukrainian sources. This could be caused by the systematic erasure of cultural memory of religious communities (and especially those belonging to ethnic minorities) during Soviet times. At the same time, a Polish map dated to the early nineteenth century does not provide any evidence for a cemetery existing near the place of Nachman's burial. This discrepancy in the facts led a local memory keeper and researcher of Uman, Vladyslav Davydiuk, to the conclusion that any talks about the cemetery's existence in that area can be regarded as manipulative (Davydiuk 2019, 193).

In my analysis of memory interactions, I employ the classic scheme of social interactions developed by Robert Nisbet, which applies the notions of cooperation, exchange, competition, conflict and coercion (Nisbet 1970) to memory interactions taking place between specific communities. In this scheme, cooperation applies when there are elements of vernacular memory embedded in official memory, whereas exchange implies the mutual inclusion of elements (e.g. official memory is included in vernacular memory and vice versa) and the inclusion of mutual additions from various vernacular memories. Competition signifies that there are mutually exclusive elements in different memories that are in competition with each other (at the same time, official memory often dominates space by default, so only certain symbols known to a specific community may hint as to the existence of a rival version of past events). Conflict, in this context, occurs when there is a symbolic battle between different narratives of the same subject, and this may be supported by physical acts being perpetrated towards different symbols connected to it. Finally, coercion takes place when two memories interact in such a way that they cannot be differentiated from each other. This process may be explained by the subjectivity of collective memory potentially influenced by memory keepers.

The Breslov Hasidim in Uman. The importance and context of pilgrimages

It is hard to evaluate the proportion of Hasidim in Uman's local Jewish population before the Second World War, but they were most likely a minority within the Jewish ethnic minority. This means that the memory of the Breslov Hasidim was a link inside a long 'chain of memory' (Hervieu-Léger 2000) interrupted by Soviet secularization, the Second World War and the Holocaust.

According to research undertaken by Steven Zipperstein, a well-known anthropologist called Mark Zborowski, who later made his career in the United States, and his Jewish friends used to harass the Breslov Hasidim in pre-war Uman: 'We boys were standing in the doors and windows of the [synagogue], pulling them by their clothes, spitting in their faces, and throwing stones and dirt, while they were dancing and singing their prayers' (Zipperstein 2010, 39). The explanation given for this harassment was that the Breslov Hasidim of that time (Zborowski left Uman with his family in 1922) attracted the poorest social groups in the town. Another pre-war story, this time from the Soviet period,

352   *Alla Marchenko*

was told by Efim Rubin, whose family belonged to the Bratslav Hasidim and lived in Uman before 1941:

> What did people use to say [about Nachman – A.M.]? People used to pray in a house a little further from the centre. Usually people came there one by one, not in groups – not four or five people. A minyan [the ten Jewish men necessary for conducting prayer – A.M.] gathered there.[4]
>
> (Rubin 2005, 33:30–34:10)

Such cautiousness could be explained by the Soviet restrictions placed upon any religious service, but this short story also informs us about the small size of the community, or at least the small number of those who were continuing their prayers.

It should be emphasized that the story of the Hasidic pilgrimages[5] continued to be silenced in all non-Jewish sources, including fiction. One of the reasons for this could have been a general fear of repressions, and another reason may have been the absence of knowledge of or interest in the topic among the local cultural elite. The only person known to have written about the pre-war pilgrimages to Uman was Nadiia Surovtsova, a cultural activist and journalist whose works and memoirs were published only after her death in 1985:

> At the beginning of the twentieth century, we moved to Uman with my parents. I heard stories about the tsaddik and I knew that his grave is still visited by old and young Jews, with long sidelocks, in hats . . ., and these visitors gather around the grave of the tsaddik, sing merry songs, dance around the grave and then they move off somewhere.[6]
>
> (Surovtsova 1992, 143)

As we see, such memoirs do not shed much light on the meanings of such Hasidic rituals beyond the fact that they appeared bizarre when seen through the eyes of a child from a dominant Christian culture.

The sustainability of Hasidic memory was mostly reinforced by religious sources, including the stories of Rebbe Nachman and the personal accounts of different rabbis. The appearance of the Iron Curtain, Uman's relatively small size (its population vacillated between 50,000 and 80,000 people across different Soviet periods) and the specific character of the Hasidic community meant that it was extremely risky to visit the place of pilgrimage and those who wished to do so had to disguise themselves to avoid getting arrested.[7] Stories of such risky escapades have not only reinforced the image of a pilgrimage to Uman being a dangerous yet worthy experience for the Hasidim, but they have also added new heroes to vernacular memory of the Hasidim who symbolize the struggle for the right to pray at the tsaddik's grave.

It should be emphasized that visits to the tsaddik are one of a number of essential defining activities in the Hasidic world (Wodziński 2018a, 57). The Breslov Hasidim tradition of gathering in Uman before Rosh Hashanah ('head 'of the year' in Hebrew, the New Year according to the Jewish calendar) was launched in 1811, or the year after the Rebbe passed away, and lasted for more than a century, or until these gatherings were curtailed by the Soviet persecution of all religious activities. The tradition was officially revived in 1987, during the Perestroika period, when several dozen pilgrims took a trip to Uman. In the 2010s, the number of pilgrims grew to 30,000 or 35,000 visitors during the Rosh Hashanah celebrations, and many more visitors came throughout the year (*Press Center of National Police of Ukraine* 2019). These visits have become a visible part of the local landscape in a town of only 80,000 inhabitants. The Breslov Hasidim make up the core of the pilgrims travelling to Rebbe Nachman's grave.

Calculations by Marcin Wodziński, which he completed based on information he found in Hasidic phonebooks (these are exclusively distributed among Hasidic communities to help them find the contact information for other members), showed that there are around 7,096 Breslov Hasidim households in the world. Out of the thirty-nine most substantial groups of Hasidim, Breslov Hasidim are the fifth largest, after the Satmar Hasidim (26,078 households), Chabad-Lubavitch (16,376 households), Ger (11,859 households) and Belz (7,535 households) (Wodziński 2018a, 198–99).

The main Breslov Hasidism centres are located in Israel, particularly in Jerusalem, Bet Shemesh and Bnei Brak (Wodziński 2018a, 204). Nowadays, pilgrimages to Uman number among the largest Hasidic pilgrimages in the world, second only to those to Meron in Israel (where the sage Shimon bar Yohai was buried in the second century) and two new centres of pilgrimages: New York City (where the Lubavich Rebbe Menachem Mendl Shneerson was buried in 1994) and Kiryas Joel in the United States (where the Satmar Rebbe Yoel Teitelbaum was buried in 1979). The majority of Hasidic pilgrims come to Uman from Israel and the United States, but there are also visitors from many other countries.

The majority of Uman's inhabitants are Ukrainians and Orthodox Christians. According to the last national census of 2001, the proportion of Ukrainians in Uman's total population was 92.7%, and the proportion of Jews was 0.23% (*Natsionalnyi sklad mist* 2001). Even an update I received during informal talks I conducted in November 2019 informed me that the local Jewish community in Uman had 248 members at the time, and about seventy Hasidic families (mostly from Israel) had moved to Uman. Substantial Jewish infrastructure has appeared in the town since 1987 to support the pilgrimage, including scores of hotels, specialist shops and restaurants serving kosher food, as well as places to pray; for instance, thirty functioning synagogues in Uman were mentioned in a documentary made during the Rosh Hashanah celebrations (Pastyko 2019). Most of these places have been logistically supported by international sponsors and Jewish organizations, with the help of local service sector workers and those Hasidim who live in the town on a more or less permanent basis. At the same time, Uman has other touristic sites attracting tourists to the town that have nothing to do with its Jewish past. For instance, the best-known place is the 'Sofiivka' landscape park, which was built in the late eighteenth century on the initiative of Stanisław Szczęsny Potocki, the Polish count who owned the town during that period. This park recently received funding for a new 'Japanese part', which was completed in 2019. Another example of a popular tourist attraction is the modern complex of fountains built near the local river that open during the summer season. Besides those two well-known sites, Uman has a great deal of lesser-known objects of cultural heritage, for instance, a number of buildings of historical importance (dating from the seventeenth to the early twentieth century) in its central part (Spadshchyna 2020). Given the cultural and religious specificity of the Hasidic pilgrimage, the presence of such tourist attractions has separated the town's heritage space into several parts, with the heritage connected to the Hasidic pilgrimage remaining at the margins of the dominant cultural heritage.

Uman as a place of remembrance for the Koliivshchyna

According to the hagiography of Breslov Hasidim, Rebbe Nachman chose Uman as the place to die because it was a site where Jews had been murdered in large numbers in the 1768 Koliivshchyna ('impaling' in Ukrainian), an uprising of the Haydamaki (insurgents) against Polish domination. The *Umans'ka riznya* ('Uman Massacre' in Ukrainian) was an important focus in a well-known Ukrainian poem by Taras Shevchenko called *Haidamaky* and in *Taras Bulba*, a historical novel by Nikolai Gogol/Mykola Hohol. Estimates of the number of victims of the uprising vary from 3,000 to 18,000 people depending on the source (Mytsyk 2002, 127).

The topic of Koliivshchyna has always been present in representations of local history, but its discourses have varied. For instance, a Soviet guidebook provides such information:

> In the summer of 1768 Uman became one of the most important arenas of the peasant war of liberation in Ukraine under the guidance of a Zaporizhzhia Cossack, Maxym Zalizniak, and an Uman Cossack Centurion, Ivan Honta. The rebels captured a fortress by assault and started to prepare a campaign against the Polish gentry ('shliakhta' in Ukrainian) in the name of reunifying all the Ukrainian lands with Russia. This campaign, like many other disorganized and spontaneous peasant rebellions, failed. However, historians have admitted its progressive role.[8]
>
> (Zagranichny and Hraban 1982, 3–4)

Clearly, the Koliivshchyna was being presented in this guidebook from a 'class struggle' perspective as an attempt to argue for reunification with Russia and demonstrate that the Ukrainians were always fighting against Poland (the Jewry are notable for their absence in such accounts). The class struggle was one of the typical mechanisms behind the development of a Soviet-era topos that reframed Ukraine's earlier history as a series of struggles to reunify with Russia (Yekelchyk 2004; Kohut 2011).

In contemporary times, established narratives emphasize this uprising as a milestone in the town's history without any further evaluation or supporting details. This can be seen from the materials produced by the local Town Council's web pages (Uman Town Council 2019; *The Official Tourist Page of Uman* 2020). For instance, a brief historical outline on one of Uman Town Council's web pages provides such information:

> It is impossible to ignore the uprising in 1768 called "Koliivshchyna". It was in Uman that it reached its peak. "Koliivshchyna" was the last explosion of the people's anger. The number of Uman's inhabitants was significantly reduced and consisted of 1354 people in 1797.[9]
>
> (Uman Town Council 2019)

This citation hints that a massacre took place, but it does not say anything specific about it. Indeed, such a loss of inhabitants could have been provoked by other factors, for example, general destruction caused by invaders or economic decline. It is worth noting that the same text later connects Nachman's burial place to Koliivshchyna: 'He was buried in accordance with his will at an old Jewish cemetery where victims of the 1768 tragedy had been buried. He commanded his followers to pray over his grave to acquire spiritual cleansing and perfection' (Uman Town Council 2019).

A different text sheds light upon the narrative being maintained by the Uman Department of Tourism, which is also connected to the local Town Council: 'Uman's fate is connected with Breslov Hasidism. Thousands of pilgrims from more than 20 countries in the world come here every year to pray over the grave of their spiritual guide tsaddik Nachman' (*The Official Tourist Page of Uman* 2020). In the same text, there is a reference to Koliivshchyna: 'In 1768 Uman was a centre of the people's bold uprising – Koliivshchyna, which was led by Maxym Zalizniak and Ivan Honta' (*The Official Tourist Page of Uman* 2020). Clearly, local non-Jewish narratives do not include issues such as the massacre, the number of victims and the role played by the Jews in it. Consequently, the uprising is viewed in terms of the aforementioned 'class struggle' because the authors of these narratives believe it is important to preserve the town's particularity and avoid controversial interpretations. By contrast, a text written by the head of the Regional Archive in Cherkasy totally neglects to mention the topic of the uprising or the Jewish presence in the town from the seventeenth to the nineteenth century, the period to which this text refers (Klymenko 2016). This omission may be interpreted as an attempt to preserve the continuity of the Soviet tradition and maintain the existing emphasis on ethnic suffering and victimhood in the politics of memory in Ukraine. In general, the politics of memory in Ukraine is not much different from that of its European neighbours (e.g. the Ukrainian Institute of National Remembrance was modelled on its Polish equivalent), and the theme of suffering is at its very core. This can be explained by the many tragic events in the history of Ukraine, for example, the Holodomor and several other famines, the mass Soviet repressions in the

356   *Alla Marchenko*

twentieth century and the trauma of being deprived of its own statehood and divided between more powerful empires or states for centuries. The annexation of Crimea in 2014 and the ongoing military tensions in Donbas fuelled by Ukraine's eastern neighbour have further endangered Ukraine's integrity. All these factors reduce opportunities for memory agents to speak about tragedies and suffering in Ukraine that are outside the mainstream ethnic Ukrainian discourse. The contemporary shift in memory politics from the old reliance on Soviet discourses to the creation of new discourses more suited to an independent Ukraine have showed that every approach has its limitations (Portnov 2013; Shevel 2016; Zhurzhenko 2014), and sometimes there appears to be little option but to confront one myth with another (Yurchuk 2017).

It is worth noting that the most recent publication on Koliivshchyna (Tairova-Iakovleva 2019) re-evaluates the role played by Uman, presenting it as less central to the uprising, and makes no attempt to cover the topic of the Jewish victims.[10]

At the same time, Koliivshchyna remains an important milestone in Uman for many local institutions working with cultural memory. I attended a series of academic events connected to the topic of the Koliivshchyna in Uman. The most noticeable of these events was one dedicated to the anniversary of the start of the Koliivshchyna, which was co-organized by several institutions, including the local university. Representatives of various religious denominations were also involved in discussions, which were followed by an ecumenic prayer meeting (Uman State Pedagogical University, Department of History 2018). A monument to the leaders of the Koliivshchyna uprising, Ivan Honta, and Maxym Zalizniak, was erected in Uman at the end of 2015. The monument appeared due to the efforts of an organization called Umans'ke Kozatstvo ('Uman's Cossacks' in Ukrainian) and a crowdfunding campaign they conducted among Uman's inhabitants.

Although such a monument had been planned since 1968, its erection only really become part of the public agenda after the commencement of military operations in Donbas and Russia's annexation of Crimea. By this point, its supporters had begun to conceive of the Koliivshchyna as a historical example of the struggle for national ideas. The choice of location for the monument was based on its closeness to the Uman fortress, where the battle actually started. The exact location had been marked by a stone since the initial plans for the monument were developed. The monument emphasized Honta and Zalizniak's heroic masculinity – an important aspect of heroism for national identity building (Bureychak and Petrenko 2015). However, both the monument's location and the subjects portrayed on it were soon interpreted in Jewish circles as a symbolic representation of the Ukrainian side of Uman's negative response to the numerous Hasidic pilgrims. Notably, the Cossack organization in Uman that ran the monument campaign has always emphasized how important Christian Orthodox religion is for its identity, as can be seen from the image of the Holy Mary on the cover photo of its official page (*Umans'ke kozatstvo* 2020). This case illustrates a more general trend for linking religion to the Cossackdom that is so important for collective memory in Ukraine (Yurchuk 2014, 90–92).

Vernacular and official memories intertwined

Official memory in Uman is embodied in documents, such as those granting approval for the creation of a place of memory or a monument. It is visible in the naming and renaming of streets, lanes, squares and other physical features of the town, but also in official commemorative events. However, vernacular memory is embodied in the town in unofficial activities, such as the creation of inscriptions and symbols in public space. I have differentiated five patterns of memory interaction that are particularly visible in Uman space: (1) cooperation between official memory and the vernacular memory of pilgrims; (2) the exchange of various vernacular memories belonging to several competing groups of pilgrims; (3) a symbolic conflict between two opposing vernacular memories, one held by pilgrims and another by some locals, of the space; (4) the competition (and domination) of official memory over the vernacular memory of pilgrims; and (5) a symbolic conflict between official memory and the vernacular memory belonging to the Hasidic pilgrims.

The grave of Rebbe Nachman in its current form of an *ohel* ('tent' in Hebrew; also used to refer to a Jewish monumental tomb) represents cooperation between official memory and the pilgrims' vernacular memory. By cooperation, in this case, I mean that official institutions of various levels (from national to local) replied to numerous requests from the Hasidic representatives, but in a 'subordinate way' (by which I mean that the interpretation of any official document on a local level was guided by instructions from above).

In 1994, the President of Ukraine issued a decree in which he stated the importance of the 'cultural and historical centre' in Uman and emphasized how the authorities had responded to numerous appeals made by the Breslov Hasidim who lived in Uman (*Ukaz Prezydenta Ukrainy*: 1994). In 1995, the City Council of the Cherkasy Oblast, which includes Uman, entered the grave of Rebbe Nachman in the register of objects of cultural and historical heritage of local importance (*Dokumenty . . .* 1995, 21–22). Before then, the site of the rebbe's grave had been part of a private yard. The planning for the whole district has changed several times since the Second World War and, as I mentioned earlier, the exact location of both the grave and the old Jewish cemetery are controversial issues among various memory keepers. However, this place is, in itself, a manifestation of vernacular Hasidic memory.

While Hasidic vernacular memory had already incorporated the pilgrimage to Rebbe Nachman's *ohel* as an act of obeisance whose importance was self-explanatory for followers of Rebbe Nachman, the official Ukrainian organizations in Uman made it clear that they were not prepared to designate any object of heritage for the exclusive use of any one ethnic community – be it Ukrainian, Jewish or Hasidic. The situation in Uman, where informal commemoration practices had long served as a 'glue' for the Hasidic community, reversed the sequence of events generally associated with other well-known commemorations of a secular nature involving official and formalized practices. For instance, in the case of the Vietnam Veterans Memorial (Marschall 2013), the informal practices associated with the monument developed after the establishment of the formally designed memorial. The exact opposite was the case with Rebbe Nachman's memorial, a material *ohel*, which appeared at the place occupied by a yard in the late 1990s and became a religious manifestation to the world of already existing memory. Figure 17.1 shows one of the first sanctioned prayers in the private yard. It is important to note that it is the Hasidic communities that are responsible for communicating with visitors about the *ohel* and the surrounding space, and the dominant language of the space is Hebrew (Marchenko 2019).

The exchange of the various vernacular memories of several groups of pilgrims can be understood within the wider framework of pilgrimages. Although I have mentioned that the pilgrimage is a core experience for the Breslov community, there are many other pilgrims who come to Uman in search of a new experience. One of the explanations for these pilgrimages undertaken by people from outside the Breslov community could be the 'postmemory' (Hirsch and Miller 2011) experienced by people who feel the trauma of the Holocaust through their contact with the second generation following those who were its personal witnesses, and a consequent ancestral connection to the Jewish world that existed between the wars. In the case of the Hasidim, however, the dominant motif of their pilgrimage lies within the domain of religion: their relationship with the town is equated with a spiritual connection to Rabbi Nachman.

A district close to Rebbe Nachman's *ohel* is closely associated with the infrastructure needed to accommodate the pilgrims. The infrastructure this district provides not only includes places for religious rituals – such as synagogues, prayer houses and *mikva'ot* ('ritual baths' in Hebrew) – but also various accommodation options, kosher food, transport and medical services, and book and souvenir shops. The public space of this district, despite its linguistic homogeneity (there is a marked prevalence of Hebrew) is far from being homogenous when it comes to the pilgrims' affiliation. It is by no means unusual to hear mention of famous rabbis who are not connected with Rebbe Nachman or Uman in any way, but are used instead as an instrument for establishing an intra-Hasidic arena of commemoration.

This is what I call an exchange of various vernacular memories in the same space. Is this a space intended for the commemoration of Rebbe Nachman? Is it a place for uniting all Hasidim? Is it a place for all people regardless of their religious affiliation or for all followers of Judaism or for certain specific groups? For instance, in 2018 I noticed some large billboards commemorating the Lubavitch Hasidic Rebbe Menachem Mendl Shneerson, the Satmar Hasidic Rabbi Yoel Teitelbaum (both mentioned earlier within the context of the largest pilgrimages in the world), the Karaster Hasidic dynasty founder Yeshua Steinerand and the Chief Sephardi Rabbi of Israel Ovadia Yoseph (see Figure 17.2). Given that all of these rabbis, who all passed away recently, were very important for their communities yet had no direct relationship with Uman, their appearance could signify that Uman's position as a place of memory exclusively connected to Rebbe Nachman is being redefined.

'Vernacular' and 'official' memories 359

Figure 17.1 Hasidim praying in the yard of a private house near the grave of Rebbe Nachman. The photo was taken in 1993, photographer unknown. The photo is registered as 12527/photo 2911 in the archive of the Uman local museum.

Figure 17.2 A wall commemorating Chief Sephardi Rabbi of Israel Ovadia Yosef.
Source: Photo by Alla Marchenko, August 2018.

The symbolic conflict between two opposing vernacular memories – the first one belonging to the pilgrims and the second to some locals – is associated with a specific locality by the River Kamianka. This river is used by the pilgrims for ritual purposes, as it is located ten minutes' walking distance from the grave of Rebbe Nachman. In June 2013, a group of local activists representing the Council of Civic Organizations of Uman (*Rada gromads'kykh organizatsiy mista Umani*) installed a crucifix on the bank of the river opposite to the district. I interpret this crucifix as a manifestation of the vernacular memory of a group of locals who wish to emphasize (to the pilgrims) that Uman is a Christian land. This seems even more likely because the crucifix was erected on the 1025th anniversary of the baptism of Kyivan Rus'. The crucifix itself is more reminiscent of a Catholic than an Orthodox Christian symbol due to the presence on it of a separate structure representing the body of Jesus Christ. However, this peculiarity makes it more distinctive and visible from a distance.[11] The conflict has arisen from numerous desecrations of the crucifix. In particular, inscriptions in Hebrew have been daubed on it, it has been set on fire and parts of the symbolic body of Christ have been damaged. Each of these incidents received media coverage when they occurred. For instance, one of the first desecrations to be noted involving Hebrew letters happened soon after the crucifix had been installed ("Cross defaced near Ukraine grave of Rabbi Nachman" 2013). Another desecration that attracted attention, an arson attack, occurred in September 2018 ("In Uman, Hasidim set fire to the cross" 2018). A more recent, extraordinarily well-publicized desecration happened on 19 January 2019 – an important holiday for Orthodox Christians – which fuelled negative feelings among the local population towards the Hasidim. This time, a video from a street camera recorded several men in Hasidic dress damaging the crucifix. They were quickly found among a group of American pilgrims in Uman ("American Jews detained" 2019). The shockwaves sent out by this seemingly small-scale vernacular initiative turned the crucifix into an even more important symbol than it had been at the beginning. From then on, a police brigade began securing the object during mass pilgrimages. The case of the crucifix on the riverbank has opened up a conflict between two vernacular memories, both connected to religious symbols. For the Hasidim, the existence of an image of Jesus Christ in a space set aside for their prayers is insulting, because they believe it encourages idolatry. For the local activists, the crucifix is not just a religious symbol. It also symbolizes that the local land is owned by Christians and serves as a reminder to the Hasidic pilgrims of their status as guests. To the local population and journalists from the outside reporting on the desecration of the Christian symbol, this case is symptomatic of a generalized religious conflict between the Hasidim and the Christians.

The fourth pattern of memory interaction, or the competition (and domination) of official memory over the vernacular memory of pilgrims, appears to be the simplest to comprehend. Jews have always been the traditional 'Other', as exemplified by Polish society's 'production of Jewish space' (Matyjaszek 2019). I would like to examine how this pattern works in practice by referring to the politics of street naming and historical property possession.

The process of decommunization started in 1991, when Ukraine gained its independence. The primary aim of this process was to demolish symbols connected to the Communist regime. However, the most active decommunization phase started in May 2015, when the Parliament of Ukraine passed new laws, which were signed by the incumbent president of Ukraine, Petro Poroshenko. According to an interview conducted with the former head of the Ukrainian Institute of National Remembrance, this phase reached its culmination in early 2018, with the destruction of 2,500 monuments to Lenin and the renaming of 52,000 streets (Viatrovych 2018).[12] Two streets named, respectively, after Ivan Honta and Maxym Zalizniak have existed in Uman since Soviet times. Both of them are located far from the district containing the monument to these two men. The last wave of the so-called politics of decommunization in Ukraine (2015–19) coincided with a surge in nationalist sentiments. For instance, Haidamats'ka Street, which commemorated the Koliivshchyna insurgents, replaced a street named after Rafail Chorny (a Jewish Communist activist).

In 2018, Uman Town Council conducted a public hearing to deliberate on whether the street where Rebbe Nachman's grave is located should be renamed Rebbe Nachman Street (for more, see Marchenko 2019). However, those hearings ended when a conflict broke out with representatives of the

362 *Alla Marchenko*

local civic organization that had installed the crucifix on the Kamianka river-bank ("U mis'kradi Umani . . ." 2018). This conflict showed that renaming the street after Rebbe Nachman was interpreted as a solution favouring the Hasidic pilgrims that, at the same time, disregarded the interests of ethnic Ukrainians. In the end, the decision was taken to preserve the status quo, and the street containing Rebbe Nachman's *ohel* is still named after Hryhorii Kosynka, a Ukrainian writer.

The monument to Honta and Zalizniak is not only located near the histori-cal entrance to the fortress but also close to the pre-war Jewish district of Uman that is currently a pilgrimage site. On the opposite side of the monument, there is a local factory called Megommetr, which manufactures measurement devices. According to Breslov Hasidim sources (The Kloiz 2019) and Jewish encyclopaedias (Freeze 2010), a synagogue that belonged to Breslov Hasidim until 1930s was converted into one of the buildings of the local Megommetr factory. Such conversions were typical of what could happen to religious build-ings in the Soviet Union as part of the struggle against religion, conceived as the 'opium of people'. It is important to note the presence of a number of let-ters addressed by representatives of the Breslov Hasidim to Uman City Coun-cil relating to the return of three former synagogue buildings to the Breslov Hasidic community (two of these belonged to the Jewish community rather than the Hasidim). The first of these letters dates from the early 1990s (*Doku-menty* . . . 1993, 75). The responses given by the factory executives to whom Uman City Council forwarded the letters were unambiguous – the buildings are an essential part of the factory (*Dokumenty.* . . 1994, 3). The factory, which is located on a hill on the outskirts of Uman facing the highly visible monu-ment to Honta and Zalizniak, remains closed for external visiting.

It should be stressed that despite its recent construction and location on the outskirts of Uman, this monument is well known to the town's inhabitants. In 2018, unlabelled pictures of this monument and Rabbi Nachman's *ohel* were recognized by more than 80% of respondents participating in a mass survey (ReHerit Cultural Heritage Portal 2019). In all probability, both sites were recognized due to the photographs accompanying mass media coverage. This is particularly likely to be the case because, as Astrid Erll has emphasized, the role of mass media in triggering collective remembrance is especially effective when combined with narrative and pictures (Erll 2011, 128). The monument to the Koliivshchyna heroes was erected after the demolition of a monument to Lenin that had stood in the very centre of Uman (near the Town Council building) and can therefore be treated as a symbolic substitution. However, most official ceremonies in Uman are conducted near the monument to Taras Shevchenko, a Ukrainian writer and a figure commonly adopted as a positive hero in Ukraine (Yekelchyk 2004; Shevel 2016).[13]

It is worth noting that Uman's inhabitants tend to regard Honta and Zal-izniak as the most famous personalities in their town's history. In fact, 56% of respondents named them in response to an open question (see Diagram 17.1). Their opinion has been formed by the official narratives about Koliivshchyna

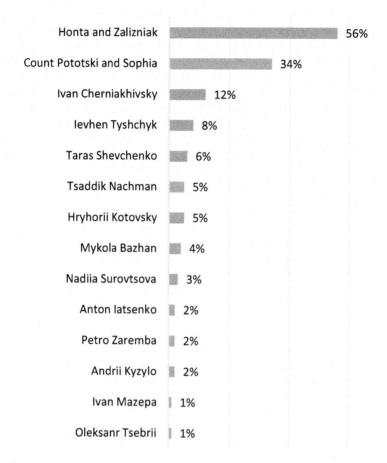

Diagram 17.1 Important personalities in the history of Uman.
Note: N = 800, survey of Uman inhabitants in November 2018.

discussed above as well as these distinctive personalities' contribution to Uman's history. At the same time, it is important to note that 5% of respondents named Rebbe Nachman as an important personality in Uman's history, which could be an early sign of the interiorization of this figure as common heritage (ReHerit Cultural Heritage Portal 2019).

Conclusions. Memory interactions between the past and the future

The Hasidic pilgrimage to Uman is a unique case of religious devotion in which memory of Rebbe Nachman was not only preserved through the hardest times of the Soviet ban on religion, but the once marginal status of the community of Breslov Hasidim who regard him as their founding father has been transformed to such an extent that it is now one of the most numerous Hasidic courts in the world. This 'chain of memory' was kept intact thanks to individual efforts and written accounts. The Hasidim's vernacular memory was shaped and supported as a form of resistance to the dominant politics of memory. The pilgrimage itself is a phenomenon full of paradoxes, the most notable being that the internal need of the Hasidim to separate themselves from the outside world is combined, in this case, with a great deal of international media attention being focused on Uman; a massive Hasidic pilgrimage is undertaken in the centre of a Christian Orthodox country with a long Jewish history yet few permanent Jewish residents today; and finally, there is a great deal of contradiction between the official narratives and the vernacular Hasidic narratives. The events of 1768, when the Koliivshchyna took place, are treated as formative and important for both memories, but from totally different perspectives. The absence of official documents able to support the claims made in many accounts connected to the pilgrimage and Jewish life in Uman before Second World War and the Holocaust leaves substantial space for speculation and for mutual distrust to develop between the representatives and keepers of both types of memory.

In this research, I have differentiated four patterns of memory interaction connected to the pilgrims' vernacular memory, local activists' vernacular memory and official memory in its institutionalized form. While the cooperation between official memory and the pilgrims' vernacular memory and the exchange of the various vernacular memories of several competing groups of pilgrims do not raise visible tensions, such tensions do become visible in two other patterns of memory, notably, the symbolic conflict between two opposing vernacular memories about the use of space, and competition between official memory and the vernacular memory belonging to the pilgrims.

The case of the Hasidic pilgrimage in Uman shows the close relationship between memory and religion, as it was born as a religious practice and set of rituals that have been maintained and adjusted to social circumstances. The different patterns of memory interaction discussed in this chapter show that the Hasidic pilgrimage has grown to be a politically significant phenomenon that touches on questions of various magnitude, ranging from the relations between various sources of symbolic power in the town to Ukraine's international image in mass media and official political discourses. It is worth noting that representatives of local churches in Uman do not make any public statements about the pilgrims or pilgrimage. This lack of engagement in the issue is due to the totally different mechanisms of memory and patterns of memorialization operating in Orthodox Christianity as opposed to Hasidic Judaism. The differences in interpretations of the Koliivshchyna incorporate ethnic, religious, political and economic contexts. Such complexity makes it difficult for the various sides to arrive at any common narrative that they can all accept.

Notes

1 'Hasidim' is the plural form of 'Hasid'. This Hebrew form has passed into English and its use is considered normative practice in academic literature on the topic nowadays.
2 The name of this group of Hasidim is taken from the town where Rebbe Nachman lived. This town may be pronounced in different ways: Bratslav (based on how the Ukrainian way of writing it), Bracław (based on the Polish way of writing it), or Breslov (used by most Hasidim). In this chapter, I will make consistent use of the last variant to maintain coherence and provide the vernacular Hasidic perspective. However, I admit that this version is not the only one used by the Hasidim. Some of them prefer the first spelling.
3 A survey in Uman was a part of the project 'ReHerit: Shared Responsibility for Common Heritage' (2018–20) funded by the European Union and implemented by the Center for Urban History of East Central Europe in cooperation with the Socioinform Ukrainian Center for Public Opinion Research. The survey included 800 face-to-face interviews in the households of a representative Uman population sampled by age and gender.
4 The informant spoke Yiddish: 'Vos me flegt redn? Me flegt kimen dovenen in a shtib a bisl vayt funem tsenter. Flegt men eyntsikvays do geyn, eyntsikvayz – nisht 4–5 menshn. Me hot minyan dortn' (transcribed and translated by Alla Marchenko).
5 The pilgrimages took place from 1811 (the first year after Rebbe Nachman's death) until the 1930s, when the repressions followed. Although there were some individual acts of pilgrimages and small group appeals during the Soviet times, the first officially allowed pilgrimages after the Iron Curtain times took place in 1987.
6 Translated by the author.
7 There are several well-known accounts of similar episodes, for instance, the account by Rabbi Gedaliah Fleer, who claimed to be the first American to manage to sneak into Uman during Iron Curtain times. He paid a visit there in the early 1960s.
8 Translated by the author.
9 All the quotations from the Uman Local Council's web pages were translated by the author.
10 According to a book presentation given by the author in September 2019, the reason for this apparent oversight was a lack of reliable documents.
11 I should mention that the same group of activists installed a cross on the building of the former Catholic church in the centre of Uman, now a museum and the Department of Art of the Museum of Local History. On Sundays, this building caters for the needs of Uman's small Catholic community, most of whom are of Polish origin. This is how this vernacular activism has increased its visibility in the town.
12 However, the new head of this institution, Anton Drobovych, who was elected in 2019, declared that finishing decommunization in Ukraine was one of his most important goals, implying that decommunization has not been completed yet.
13 Both monuments (to Taras Shevchenko and Honta and Zalizniak, respectively) are located relatively far from the centre, while the space of the former monument to Lenin has been transformed into an open square. According to my unofficial source, the erection of the monument to Honta and Zalizniak was not initially supported by the local authorities, and they were very slow to provide all the necessary documentation. This case shows a complicated process of interaction between official memory and the vernacular memory of locals that goes beyond the scope of this text.

References

"American Jews Detained Over Crucifix Vandalism in Uman, Ukraine." 2019. *Haaretz*. www.haaretz.com/world-news/american-jews-detained-over-crucifix-vandalism-in-uman-ukraine-1.6867346.
Assmann, Jan. 1995. "Collective Memory and Cultural Identity." *New German Critique* 65: 125–33.

366 Alla Marchenko

Biale, David, David Assaf, Benjamin Brown, Uriel Gellman, Samuel C. Heilman, Moshe Rosman, Gadi Sagiv, and Marcin Wodziński. 2018. *Hasidism: A New History*. Princeton, NJ: Princeton University Press.

Bodnar, John. 1992. *Remaking America: Public Memory, Commemoration, and Patriotism in the Twentieth Century*. Princeton, NJ: Princeton University Press.

Bureychak, Tetyana and Olena Petrenko. 2015. "Heroic Masculinity in Post-Soviet Ukraine: Cossacks, UPA and 'Svoboda.'" *East/West: Journal of Ukrainian Studies* 2 (2): 3–27.

"Cross Defaced Near Ukraine Grave of Rabbi Nachman." 2013. *Jewish Telegraphic Agency*. www.jta.org/2013/08/16/global/hasidim-deface-cross-in-uman-stirring-up-local-controversy.

Davydiuk, Vladyslav. 2019. *Istoriia Umani: mify ta dijsnist' v dokumentakh*. Uman: Vizavi.

Dokumenty pro istoryko-kul'turnii tsentr Bratslavs'kyh khasydiv u m. Umani. 1993. Vykonavchyi komitet Uman'skoi mis'koi rady narodnykh depytativ m.Umani. Fund 1, Description 2, Case 428a.

Dokumenty pro istoryko-kul'turnii tsentr Bratslavs'kyh khasydiv u m.Umani. 1994. Vykonavchyi komitet Uman'skoi mis'koi rady narodnykh depytativ m.Umani. Fund 1, Description 2, Case 451.

Dokumenty pro istoryko-kul'turnii tsentr Bratslavs'kyh khasydiv u m.Umani. 1995. Vykonavchyi komitet Uman'skoi mis'koi rady narodnykh depytativ m.Umani. Fund 1, Description 2, Case 884.

Erll, Astrid. 2011. *Memory in Culture. Palgrave Macmillan Memory Studies*. London: Palgrave Macmillan.

The Essential Rabbi Nachman. 2006. Translated by Avraham Greenbaum. Jerusalem: Azamra Institute.

Freeze, ChaeRan. 2010. "Uman." *YIVO Encyclopedia of Jews in Eastern Europe*. www.yivoencyclopedia.org/article.aspx/Uman.

Hervieu-Léger, Danièle. 2000. *Religion as a Chain of Memory*. New Brunswick, NJ: Rutgers University Press.

Hirsch, Marianne, and Nancy K. Miller, ed. 2011. *Rites of Return: Diaspora, Poetics and the Politics of Memory*. New York: Columbia University Press.

"In Uman, Hasidim Set Fire to the Cross." 2018. *Union of Orthodox Journalists*. https://spzh.news/en/news/55983-v-umani-khasidy-podozhgli-krest.

"The Kloiz. From the Hamber to the Megametor." 2019. *Breslov on the Internet* – www.breslov.com/uman/kloyz.html.

Klymenko, Tetiana. 2016. "Uman u XVII–XIX st: rozkvit ta zanepad." *Arkhivy Ukrainy* 1: 90–96.

Kohut, Zenon E. 2011. *Making Ukraine: Studies on Political Culture, Historical Narrative, and Identity*. Toronto: CIUS Press.

Kuzniets, Tetiana. 2005. *Naselennia Umanshczyny v XIX – na pochatku XX stolittia*. Kyiv: Kyiv University Poligraphic center.

Marchenko, Alla. 2019. "Mizh publichnym I prvatnym u mis'komu prostori: naratyvy, poviazani z palomnytstvom hasydiv do Umani." In *Anthropologia Religii: Porivnial'ni studii vid Prykarpattia do Kavkazu*, edited by Catherine Wanner and Iuliia Buiskikh, 190–218. Kyiv: Dukh I Litera.

Marschall, Sabine. 2013. "Collective Memory and Cultural Difference: Official vs. Vernacular Forms of Commemorating the Past." *Journal of South African and American Studies* 14 (1): 77–92.

Matyjaszek, Konrad. 2019. *Produkcja przestrzeni Żydowskiej w dawnej I współczesnej Polsce*. Kraków: Universitas.

Mytsyk, Iurii. 2002. *Uman kozats'ka I haidamats'ka*. Kyiv: KM Academia.

'Vernacular' and 'official' memories   367

Natsionalnyi sklad mist za perepysom 2001 roku. 2001. https://datatowel.in.ua/pop-composition/ethnic-cities.

Nisbet, Robert. 1970. *The Social Bond. An introduction to the Study of Society*. New York: Knopf.Pastyko, Kolian. 2019. "Shliakh Koena. A Documentary." https://hromadske.ua/posts/shlyah-koena-hromadskedoc.

The Official Tourist Page of Uman. 2020. "Istoriia Umani." http://umantravel.com.ua/istoriia/.

Portnov, Andriy. 2013. "Memory Wars in Post-Soviet Ukraine (1991–2010)." In *Memory and Theory in Eastern Europe*, edited by Uilleam Blacker, Alexander Etkind and Julie Fedor, 233–54. New York: Palgrave Macmillan.

Press Center of the National Police of Ukraine. 2019. "Blyz'ko 25 tysiach palomnykiv-khasydiv uzhe v Ukraini." *Press Center of National Police of Ukraine*. https://mvs.gov.ua/ua/news/24815_Blizko_25_tisyach_palomnikiv_hasidiv_vzhe_v_Ukraini.htm.

ReHerit Cultural Heritage Portal. 2019. "Rezul'taty sotsiologichnych doslidzen' kulturnoii spadshchyny w Umani ta L'vovi." https://reherit.org.ua/material/prezentatsiya-rezultativ-sotsiologichnyh-doslidzhen-kulturnoyi-spadshhyny-v-umani-ta-lvovi-2018/.

Rubin, Efim Isaakovich. 2005. "Interviewed by Dov-Ber Kerler, Jeffrey Veidlinger, and Dovid Katz on 26 June 2005." *AHEYM Project*. http://eviada.webhost.iu.edu/atm-playback.cfm?w=94&sn=MDV%20739&t=1804&sID=69&pID=162&sc=1.

Shevel, Oxana. 2016. "No Way Out? Post-Soviet Ukraine's Memory Wars in Comparative Perspective." In *Beyond the Euromaidan: Comparative Perspectives on Advancing Reform in Ukraine*, edited by Henry E. Hale and Robert W. Orttung, 21–40. Stanford, CA: Stanford University Press.

Spadshchyna. 2020. "Uman." *ReHerit Cultural Heritage Portal*. https://reherit.org.ua/spadshhyna/.

Surovtsova, Nadiia. 1992. "Bratslavs'kii tsadyk." *Ukraine-Israel* 1: 143–48.

Tairova-Iakovleva, Tetiana. 2019. *Koliivshchyna: velyki iliuzii*. Kyiv: Klio.

Tchoukaleyska, Roza. 2016. "Public Space and Memories of Migration: Erasing Diversity Through Urban Redevelopment in France." *Social and Cultural Geography* 17 (8): 1101–19.

Ukaz Prezydenta Ukrainy. 1994. "Pro stvorennia istoryko-kul'turnogo tsentru v misti Umani Cherkas'koii oblasti." *Zakonodavstvo Ukrainy*. http://zakon.rada.gov.ua/laws/show/283/94.

Uman State Pedagogical University. Department of History. 2018. "Ztsiliuiuchyranymynulogo." https://history.udpu.edu.ua/dopomoga-studentu/39-novyny/1351-ztsilyuyuchy-rany-mynuloho.

Uman Town Council. 2019. "Korotka istorychna dovidka. Nashe misto." http://uman-rada.gov.ua/index.php/nashe-misto.

Umans'ke kozatstvo. 2020. *Umans'kii kosh imeni Ivana Honty*. www.facebook.com/umankozak/.

"U mis'kradi Umani stalasia biika cherez pereimenuvannia vulytsi." 2018. *Correspondent*. https://ua.korrespondent.net/ukraine/4007592-u-miskradi-umani-stalasia-biika-cherez-pereimenuvannia-vulytsi.

Viatrovych, Volodymyr. 2018. "Dekomunizatsiia v Ukraini faktychno zavershena." *Ukrains'ka Pravda*. www.pravda.com.ua/news/2018/02/10/7171212/.

Wodziński, Marcin. 2018a. *Hasidism: Key Questions*. New York: Oxford University Press.

———. 2018b. *Historical Atlas of Hasidism*. Cartography by Waldemar Spallek. Princeton, NJ: Oxford University Press.

Yekelchyk, Sergei. 2004. "Ukrainskaia istoricheskaia pamiat I sovetskii kanon: kak opredelalos natsyonalnoe nasledie Ukrainy v stalinskuiu epohu." *Ab Imperio* 2: 77–124.

Yurchuk, Yuliya. 2014. *Reordering of Meaningful Worlds: Memory of the Organization of Ukrainian Nationalists and the Ukrainian Insurgent Army in post-Soviet Ukraine*. Stockholm: Acta.

———. 2017. "Reclaiming the Past, Confronting the Past: OUN – UPA Memory Politics and Nation Building in Ukraine (1991–2016)." In *War and Memory in Russia, Ukraine, and Belarus*, edited by Julie Fedor, Markku Kangaspuro, Jussi Lassila and Tatiana Zhurzhenko, 107–37. Basingstoke, Hampshire: Palgrave Macmillan.

Zagranichny, Petro, and Grygorii Hraban. 1982. *Uman*. Moscow: Tourist.

Zhurzhenko, Tatiana. 2014. "A Divided Nation? Reconsidering the Role of Identity Politics in the Ukraine Crisis." *Die Friedens-Warte* 89 (1/2): 249–67.

Zipperstein, Steven J. 2010. "Underground Man: The Curious Case of Mark Zborowski and a Writing of a Modern Jewish Classic." *Jewish Review of Books* (Summer): 38–42.

18 Memory as a religious mission?

Religion and nation in local commemoration practices in contemporary Poland

Małgorzata Głowacka-Grajper

Glory and martyrdom – national history through a religious lens

Two local communities and two kinds of victim

Since the times of Maurice Halbwachs, sociologists have thought of collective memory as the selective reconstruction of the past in response to the needs of the present (Halbwachs 1992). These needs are diverse in character, but in practice, they are often channelled through group identity projects that require suitable ancestors. Such projects attempt to justify claims to power, places and territory and seek to confirm current policies or social attitudes to contemporary problems. Consequently, two basic functions can be attributed to collective memory: the establishment of legitimacy (by adopting a given vision of the past that makes it possible to determine who should exercise power in a given group and why they should be allowed to do so) and the building of a collective identity (cf. Szacka 2006). Memory allows groups and individuals to determine who they are by referring to events and characters from the past and the values they represent. Memory impacts on group identity in three basic ways. First, it creates an awareness of being together in time; second, it enables the transmission of values and behavioural patterns, and third, it co-creates the symbolic language of the group, which becomes one of its distinguishing features and at the same time enables memory transmission (cf. Assmann 2011; Szacka 2006).

In this chapter, I will analyze the mnemonic situation of local communities in which transmitted values and the symbolic language of memory transmission are derived from the Roman Catholic religion and a vision in which the Polish nation is indisputably Catholic. I will present two empirical examples of the relationship between the religious and national narratives in local contexts. The first example is connected to the notion of sacrifice and glory, and the second to the notion of victimhood and martyrdom. This distinction between two radically different types of victim was introduced by the Korean historian Jie-Hyun Lim (2010). On the one hand, we are dealing with a passive victim par excellence suffering a senseless and anonymous death; for example, people

DOI: 10.4324/9781003264750-23

370   *Małgorzata Głowacka-Grajper*

slaughtered during the pacification of towns and villages or dying in civil wars instigated on religious and ethnic grounds. On the other hand, there are active victims who purposefully lay down their lives in the name of superior (often national) values. The former case type is best described as 'victimhood' and the second as 'sacrifice'. These two kinds of deaths are accompanied by two kinds of narrative: in the first case, death leads to suffering and martyrdom, and in the second, to victory and glory. Both narratives can be presented using the religious language of Catholicism. Both of the cases I analyze in this chapter are strongly associated with the cult of the Virgin Mary in Poland,[1] who is worshipped in two different ways: as a mother comforting the suffering nation and as a queen supporting Poland's victories.

The idea to investigate the two local cases presented in this chapter, notably, the communities of Radzymin and Kałków-Godów, arose from a research project devoted to local memory milieu in central Poland.[2] The first of these is a small town near the Polish capital of Warsaw, where the Polish army's victory over the Soviets in the Polish–Bolshevik War (perceived not only as a military act but also as a miracle performed by the Virgin Mary) is commemorated. The second is a small village near the Holy Cross Mountains whose population fell victim to German pacifications during the Second World War. After commemorating the local victims, the residents, led by a priest from a local parish, built a Sanctuary of Our Lady of Sorrows in their village in which the tragic events of Polish history of the last century are commemorated.

Both Radzymin and Kałków-Godów have become well known throughout the country – the first as a venue for annual state celebrations and the second as a nationwide place of pilgrimage visited by about 800,000 pilgrims a year. Although religious and national elements closely intertwine in the memory narratives of both places, vernacular memory is located differently in each one. In the first case, vernacular memory is a central component of the national narrative, and the local memory community present themselves as the guardians of both the nation's memory and the Catholic faith. Local memory activists from Radzymin are more focused on presenting the town as an exceptional place (not only the location of a national and religious miracle but also a site of strong, invincible memory). In the second case, vernacular memory has been absorbed by a narrative relating the suffering of the entire nation and is therefore only recognized by the local community. The local history is little known outside the community, but the place is famous for commemorating Poles as the suffering nation and presenting this suffering within the framework of Christian martyrdom. My analysis of these two examples will be used to show relations between religion and memory and the ways in which a social obligation to remember the past is reinforced by religious values and rituals.

The empirical material analyzed in this chapter comes from three kinds of sources: an ethnography of place (a detailed description of the different kinds of commemoration present in the public sphere), writings produced by local memory activists (e.g. books, leaflets, brochures and websites) and interviews with people engaged in the creation and maintenance of commemorative projects in both locations. My conclusions are based on the analysis of data from field research conducted in two stages. The first stage consisted of preparing a description for the ethnographic observation of both memorial sites. The objects in these sites were photographed and described. After this, a sociological description of the memory narratives in the two case studies was prepared, which consisted of an ethnographic description of the site and the analysis of websites and other written materials. During this second stage, study interviews were conducted.

During the research conducted in Radzymin, eleven interviews were conducted with memory activists. Any sites of memory and references to the past functioning in Radzymin's public space (e.g. murals, monuments and graves in the local cemetery) were described and documented photographically. Websites devoted to Radzymin's past and local commemorative activities were also analyzed, as were official materials on the town's history. In Kałków-Godów, eight interviews were conducted, which were then analyzed in conjunction with previously developed analytical narrative descriptions of the Sanctuary and its website.

Commemorative patterns and the Roman Catholic religion in Poland

Jay Winter (2015, 217) underlines that the concept of 'martyrdom' is still alive in Eastern Europe, and this term can accommodate local content and universal meaning, which facilitates the merging of individual and local suffering with the narrative of national identity and a collective past (cf. Zubrzycki in this volume). In Poland, however, the concept of national martyrdom assumes a particularly expressive form. From the period when Poland was wiped off the map of Europe (the late eighteenth century to the early twentieth century), the role the Roman Catholic Church played in shaping national identity and memory among Poles considerably increased in importance: 'The Catholic Church turned out to be the only institution which was able to penetrate the areas of the three Partitions. In the nineteenth century, Roman Catholicism, romantic nationalism and Slavic Messianism contributed to the new Polish civil religion' (Casanova 1994, 160). Over the course of over a hundred years, the Church acted as a substitute for the occupied state, becoming the greatest repository of history, culture, tradition and collective memory (Casanova 1994, 165), with the result that religious and nationalist elements became closely entwined.[3]

Later, in the communist era, the Catholic Church, which was perceived as a strong community and a moral authority supporting anti-communist activities, became one of the major oppositional forces (Grabowska 2004, 291). During that time, 'Polish Catholicism served as a public civic religion rather than a private religion for individual salvation' (Casanova 1994, 194). After 1989, the Church turned from an opponent of the communist state into a partner to the democratic state at a time when secularization processes were advancing (Grabowska 2004), leading to the Church being evaluated critically (e.g. as an institution excessively involved in politics). Nevertheless, its influence remained very strong, especially in the sphere of remembrance and commemoration of the past. Moreover, it seems that the 'memory boom' that Poland has witnessed in recent years has reinforced the position of religious language within the public domain and in commemorative practices and ceremonies. This shows that religion continues to be one of the major tools shaping Poles' collective identity (see Marody and Mandes 2006) and therefore, at least within this domain, religion continues to be inextricably interrelated with the public sphere.

Tragic events are built into a universal Christian pattern that uses religious language and symbols to reinforce the notion that a martyr's sacrifice enables subsequent generations to exist (cf. Lim 2010). According to this interpretation, memory becomes a social duty grounded in the beliefs that the dead should always be buried and remembered in prayers and religious rites and their burial places should be cared for. However, at the national level of commemoration, the dead cease to be ancestors and family members to whom certain psychological and religious obligations are due. Instead, they become representatives of a certain social category, for example, peasants, intelligentsia or Poles as a whole. Their physical presence (as victims) is not only a starting point in the space of the Polish state for political actions, but also, in the sphere of social memory, it is a point of departure for the creation of national memorial sites commemorating national martyrdom (see Verdery 1999).

Avishai Margalit (2004) notes that individual memory may be a question of knowing something or being aware of something, but the collective, intersubjective level of memory is always a question of values. The values prevalent in a given society not only determine what will be collectively remembered but also how events will be incorporated into the body of such communal memories. Dariusz Karłowicz (2005) refers to this process as the creation of 'axiological memory', by which he means memory as a collection of events and persons from the past bound together by a common pattern, value or set of values central to a given community: 'Axiological memory contains memories of specific actions taken by specific persons, which are treated as a kind of testimony or evidence of the existence of values; this is testimony given for a specific community' (2005, 37–38). Individual events are construed as being significant and worth remembering and passing on to subsequent generations because they actualize the values society considers to be important. The domain of axiological memory encompasses 'common ideals, not assessment of the status quo. It does not describe what we are, but what we would like to be' (2005, 36). It also allows division to be made into 'allies' and 'enemies', 'heroes' and 'traitors', and 'believers' and 'heretics'. One of the most important values in national narratives is the willingness to sacrifice one's life.

Researchers of nationalism note that the phenomenon of 'sacrificing one's life for the nation' is one of the most important elements that strengthen a sense of national community by helping to establish that community's ideals. Benedict Anderson (1986) called this kind of sacrifice 'secular salvation', by which he meant that a death for faith could be replaced by a death for nation in times of secularization. However, in a situation where belonging to a religious community and national identity are closely intertwined, both types of martyrdom (for nation and for faith) merge with each other. Both are types of death that connect the individual to the national community.

Radzymin – the commemoration of the 'miracle'

National politics and local memory

The local community in Radzymin protects the memory of what is known as the Warsaw Battle of 1920. This battle on the outskirts of Warsaw was the culmination of the Polish–Bolshevik War of 1919–21 (see Böhler 2018). This ended in success for the Polish troops after three days of bloody fighting. Radzymin was initially lost to the enemy on 13 August at approximately 7:00 p.m., when the Bolshevik army seized the town and captured 300 Polish soldiers. The town was regained on 15 August, the day on which the feast of the Ascension of the Virgin Mary is celebrated. The next day, a ceremonial service was held at a church in Radzymin in the presence of the archbishop of Warsaw, who handed the commander of the Polish army, General Józef Haller, the Medal of St Joan of Arc, with the blessing of Pope Benedict XV. The religious dimension of the victory was further reinforced by the fact that during one of the battle skirmishes, at the village of Ossów, a young priest called Ignacy Skorupka was killed, then buried with the highest honours in Warsaw and posthumously awarded the highest Polish military decoration: the Virtuti Militari Cross.

As a result of political changes that took place in Poland in the twentieth century, memory of Radzymin as 'the town of the Miracle on the Vistula' changed in character three times. In the interwar period, memory of the town was a very important component of Polish memory at both local and state levels. The building of the legend of the battle of Radzymin began the day after its completion (Drozdowski 1993). The aversion of various rightist political parties (supported by the Catholic Church) towards Józef Piłsudski (the commander of the Polish army) and their desire to undermine his contribution to the victory (by promoting an alternative narrative of the Mother of God as a supernatural force that had miraculously repelled the Bolsheviks) was of great importance in this process (Drozdowski 1993; Dwornicki 2011).

During the period from 1920 to 1923, collective and individual graves for those killed in the Battle of Warsaw were created at the parish cemetery, which also became a venue of choice for commemorative state ceremonies. Local and state memory were closely related to each other and mutually reinforced each other. During the period of the People's Republic of Poland (PRL), when Poland was subordinated to the Soviet Union, the situation at the state level changed radically. Memory of the Battle of August 1920 became uncomfortable, and attempts were made to oust it from Polish social memory (Ochman 2017). Efforts were made to eliminate all traces of commemoration of this event in public space and ensure that the name 'Radzymin' did not appear in public discourse at all (an objective partially served by the revocation of Radzymin's rights as a county capital in 1952). Thus, local and state memory were in opposition. Nevertheless, for the duration of the communist period, local

374 *Małgorzata Głowacka-Grajper*

identity did not change. In fact, the authorities' repression of local memory not only failed to weaken the community but even strengthened their identity as the inhabitants of 'the town of the miracle' (Wnuk 2015). And as soon as the political situation changed again in the late 1980s, the local community was ready to present its memory narrative on the national arena and regain its position as an important venue for state ceremonies. Memory of the Battle of Warsaw was restored after the beginning of the political transformation in 1989 (Ochman 2017, 2019), but the pre-war disputes over memory have not returned to the arena of nationwide discourse, as most modern Poles now regard most of them as impenetrable and invalidated (Nowik 2011).

The communist period was a time of social and economic stagnation for Radzymin. The town's anti-Bolshevik traditions and image led to it being passed over for all major investments, so it was not expanded and its railway connection with Warsaw was terminated. It became a small, provincial town, which gradually began to depopulate (Wnuk 2015). On the one hand, this inhibited its development, but on the other, it preserved the local community and its memory narratives and rituals.[4] A radical change came after 2000, when the town was discovered by developers building large housing estates for people working in and around Warsaw but unable to find affordable housing in the capital city. In just a few years, the town's population has almost doubled. This has led to the emergence of two almost numerically equal communities: rooted residents with a strong local identity, and a new population, neither integrated with each other nor with the people who have lived there for generations and consequently, not feeling any strong emotional ties to the town.

The first community is multigenerational, and their sense of rootedness comes from being 'the owners' of the place where they live as well as a common awareness of a shared past (both victorious and martyrological). The community's identity is based on the local religious, national and anti-communist traditions. The new residents are mostly young and middle-aged people working outside Radzymin who original come from different places in Poland with different identities. From the point of view of local memory activists, old and new residents can be distinguished from each other by their differing attitudes to the town's past, which is defined in terms of local patriotism. New inhabitants are presented by memory activists as not having integrated with the old ones:

> The situation in Radzymin is interesting. The number of inhabitants in Radzymin has increased because large new estates have been built and there is nothing really connecting . . . the activities of Radzymin's old residents with these newcomers. . . . the priest is trying to organize, we also joined in, such festivities for these residents. And the response from these inhabitants is meagre. The old residents of Radzymin tend to attend, while the new ones do not get involved. . . . Also this symbiosis, this cooperation between old residents and newcomers, has not been observed enough yet.
>
> (M., ca. 60 years old)

The perceived cultivation of memory of the battle as an 'admission ticket' to the local community prevails among our interlocutors from the middle and oldest generations. The integration of old and new residents is assessed through the prism of their involvement in commemorative activities. Even if they are socially active, interested in local government policy and want to have a say in it, they will not be regarded as fully integrated members of the community until they join the local 'memory community' and its rituals:

> I think, yes, that the residents of Radzymin identify themselves very strongly with this ceremony [the state ceremonies at the cemetery – author's note], although in recent years I have noticed a slightly different phenomenon that I often point out in conversations with friends and they notice it as well. Namely, attitudes are beginning to change when it comes to these ceremonies, but among the residents who came here recently, because Radzymin is one of the most dynamically developing towns, in population terms, in the Warsaw region. After all, ten years ago, there were 7,500 people living here. Now, there are almost 14,000. But what I have noticed is that even children who attend school here, as they often do, maybe it'll take a little time, but sometimes I'm irritated by such attitudes coming from pupils, they say such things to me as 'You're always harping on about this or that battle'. So I explain to them: 'If you lived here, you were born here, you must feel some emotional connection, [but] you just don't feel it'. [In the case of] those who have lived here for generations, that tradition was somehow cultivated.
>
> (M., ca. 50 years old)

This statement reflects the assumption among older residents that even knowledge and participation in commemorative rituals is not enough to achieve integration into their community. Emotions are still needed. To belong to the community, one should feel emotionally connected to its past. It can be concluded that the existence of such a 'community of emotions' was once taken for granted. The awareness that this is no longer the case causes irritation and the feeling that local traditions may be at risk. Memory activists are therefore facing another challenge that is perhaps more difficult to deal with than preserving the community's testimony to the struggles of 1920 during communist times. They must involve persons in their 'memory community' who have not undergone the same processes of socialization into local life (with its distinctive relationship to the past) as people from families rooted for generations in Radzymin.

The soldiers, the pope and the obligation to remember

Radzymin builds both its image and local identity upon two interrelated events: the Battle of Warsaw in 1920 and a much later visit paid to the town by Pope John Paul II, who came specifically because it is known as the place of 'the Miracle on the Vistula'. The close connection between these two elements is not coincidental. According to local memory activists, this connection results from the persistence of national-religious (Polish-Catholic) values in their community. The adoption of such an axiological framework determines what is commemorated and what interpretations are used to link together various events from the town's past into a single narrative sequence.

According to our interviewees, for generations, memory of the Battle of Warsaw was the most important element of a collection of memories of the Polish–Bolshevik War that were averse to communism and therefore could only be kept at some risk to the local community. However, after the beginning of the political transformation, the position of this memory changed, and it became one of the identity pillars of post-communist Poland (see Nowik 2011; Tarczyński 1990). At this point, new opportunities for using narratives about Radzymin's past opened up for the local government and community. The Battle of Warsaw eventually obscured all other elements of the town's past, especially when the national-religious narrative of the event was symbolically reinforced by the papal visit. The commemoration of both events is not only treated as a way of creating a local community with a specific identity but also as nationwide promotion for Radzymin. Memory has begun to be perceived as a key element in the building of local social capital, which is then used to promote the town and aid its development. At the same time, it is becoming the basis for the formation and maintenance of local social ties, so new residents appearing in Radzymin are expected to accept and internalize the dominant narratives of the city's past.

Narratives that outline attempts made in the communist period to destroy local memory of the events of 1920 and explain how these were resisted appeared in all the interviews we conducted. They are a living element of local memory and identity. It was not only the events of the 1920s that were incorporated into Radzymin's collective memory resource but also the activities undertaken by the local community to preserve the commemoration of these events in public space. In such a narrative, collective memory is much more than the habitual repetition of stories about the past. In fact, it would be more accurate to describe it as consciously undertaken action that involves sacrifices, hardships and consequences. Memory becomes the basis for social activities. In practice, this involves people taking specific actions to preserve places of remembrance and convey a narrative of the past, even when their actions contravene the official policy of the state. In this way, the local message of memory creates factual, narrative and axiological resources that can always be accessed, if necessary. As soon as the political condition begins to change, they can be launched and immediately presented in the public sphere.

According to the local discourse of remembrance, the inhabitants of Radzymin consistently, for successive generations, fulfil their obligation of remembrance and are eventually suitably rewarded for this, when the head of the Catholic Church, who happens to be one of the most famous Poles in the world, comes to their small, forgotten town. Thanks to his visit, life in the town changes radically. This narrative structure is visible, for example, in the following statement made by a priest who tends to the cemetery as well as building a John Paul II sanctuary in Radzymin:

> So what does John Paul II do? He arrives and recalls this event – on June 13; he says he wants to give thanks for this victory because he was born in 1920 and was later able to grow up in a free country, right? And from that moment, as it were, it acquires national importance, from the visit of John Paul II, to such an extent that we have a little laugh about it [and say] that it is the second Miracle on the Vistula. Well, because the pope was the first to come to Radzymin, [or indeed he came] at all, that is a miracle and that is how people perceive it, because everything changed from that moment, the town began to develop, because this town had 5,000 people, not even that. . . . And that's why there is no other place in Poland like Radzymin when it comes to such patriotic events, because here the history of 1920 intersects and the history of John Paul II intersects. And he comes and it's so symbolic, it really is a big thing and we, by building this church, we want to thank John Paul II who recalled [the battle], right? We are thanking him for giving thanks for the victory.
>
> (M., ca. 50 years old)

For the inhabitants of the town, who are a community with strong links to the Church, the pope's visit was an extremely important event. He was also a special pope – not only the head of the Church but also a Pole, for whom national issues were very important. He is perceived as a person who understood the way of thinking of the inhabitants of Radzymin and shared their emotions, not only because he professed the same national values but also because of his own biography. The fact that the pope was born in the year of the Battle of Warsaw makes him, in the eyes of many of our interlocutors, particularly strongly associated with that event. The homage he gave during his visit to the fallen soldiers as well as veterans of the Polish–Bolshevik War who were still alive is seen by the local community as the crowning achievement of all the activities they had undertaken over many years in an attempt to preserve memory of 1920. One can even say that the sequence of mutual symbolic thanks bestowed in Radzymin (residents thank those who died in battle by cultivating their memory; the pope thanks the residents for remembering the heroes; the residents thank the pope for giving thanks by building a sanctuary named after him) are a way of emphasizing the perseverance shown by the town's residents, who have cultivated and continue to cultivate memory of the events of 1920, as well as a kind of homage that the community pays to itself.

Moreover, the pope's visit is incorporated into the narrative of the history of Radzymin, where it is presented as an impetus for the town's development. Thus, the official restoration of hidden memory and the restoration of the town's opportunities for development are presented as being closely correlated. Consequently, by presenting Radzymin (to the whole of Poland and the rest of the world) as a model for the maintenance of patriotic collective memory,

378 *Małgorzata Głowacka-Grajper*

the local community are not only winning moral and symbolic recognition for their town but also 'economic' recognition. And this is treated as another 'miracle', and therefore a metaphysical reward. The 'capital of memory' eventually becomes monetized as 'financial capital', or investments in the town's development.

The papal visit was narrated in detail by our interlocutors, almost all of whom speak about it in the same way. It has also become an element of local memory, and every year there are celebrations commemorating that visit. Its significance to Radzymin can be demonstrated by the fact that many ordinary people, and not just priests, describe it in such great detail that they even include the exact landing time of the papal helicopter. The landing itself has also inspired the creation of another site of memory in public space. Near the parish cemetery that contains the mass graves of those killed in the Battle of Warsaw there is an empty square. It was in the middle of this square that the helicopter carrying John Paul II landed, and the place it touched down is clearly marked by the Radzymin coat of arms, which depicts the Eye of God's Providence. On a wall to the left, there is a large inscription referring to the Battle of Warsaw. All the military units that participated in it have also been listed.

Next to the landing site of the papal helicopter, another 'site of memory' begins: the Golgotha Road of the Polish Nation, which was built after John Paul II's visit in 1999. This commemorates those who took part in the battles at Radzymin. This road assumes the form of a path paved in grey and graphite – the colours of the Virtuti Militari Cross – which connects the parish cemetery to the Collegiate Church. Along the path, replicas of Virtuti Militari Crosses have been erected that commemorate regiments of the Polish Army, individual commanders and the residents of Radzymin. The commemorative narrative is at once heroic, victorious and martyrological. The events of August 1920 in Radzymin are presented as unique not only because of the battle's importance to the history of Poland and the world but also because of the great suffering of people belonging to one national community. The engagements in Radzymin were particularly bloody, with 300 Polish soldiers killed and 3,000 wounded. And although the battle narrative is victorious, it contains many martyrological elements that inscribe it in a more general narrative with a strong presence in Polish culture, that of the 'suffering of the Polish nation' (Casanova 1994; Porter-Szücs 2014). The notion of martyrdom or sacrifice is a key element connecting religious concepts and the history of a nation within collective memory. According to this notion, both religious and national memory are of a martyrological nature, and the sacrificing of life and the consequences of this sacrifice are defined as enabling factors that grant new life to individuals and the community (see Lim 2010). The primary purpose of both religious and national memory is to preserve the narrative of sacrifice in the name of one's neighbour and community for subsequent generations. The image of the victim presented in these narratives is similar. Such individuals are first and foremost innocent victims who constantly maintain their moral strength while defending what is right. They die because of who they are, namely, because of their identity, nationality or religion, but at the same time, through their deaths, they save the community to which they belong.

The main place where all the events of Radzymin's history, including this town's role in the fight for Poland's independence, are incorporated into a single narrative sequence contains a series of eighteen tablets placed alongside the mass grave of soldiers killed in the Battle of Warsaw. Each tablet contains a reference to a particular event or a specific person along with a photo from the period in question. The narrative presented on these stone tablets begins when Poland regained its independence after the First World War in November 1918 and presents the disarmament of the German troops stationed in Radzymin. The second tablet commemorates the visit of the Apostolic Nuncio, later Pius XI, to Radzymin in June 1920, and ten others are devoted to the events of the Battle of Warsaw of 1920 and to individual army units and people or the inhabitants of Radzymin. The thirteenth tablet commemorates the 'Consecration of the Chapel-Monument with the participation of the President of the Second Polish Republic Ignacy Mościcki' in October 1927. Three more tablets relate to the Second World War. The penultimate plaque commemorates a visit paid to Radzymin by the Polish Primate Stefan Wyszyński in June 1973 and his naming of the road to Warsaw as 'The Golgotha Road of the Polish Nation'. The tragic and heroic history of the town in the twentieth century culminates with a tablet dated 'June 13, 1999', which contains the inscription: 'Visit of the Holy Father John Paul II to the Cemetery of the Fallen in Radzymin, meeting with the soldiers of 1920'. These entanglements of religion and national history make the community of Radzymin guardians of both memory and faith.

Thus, activities commemorating the past become part of local history. This story not only consists of war events but also of various undertakings by the community to commemorate their war heroes. On the stone tablets in the cemetery, the local community presents itself in two ways: as a fighting community and as a remembering community. Fighting and remembering are analogous activities. In the event of an armed threat, they fight with weapons, but when memory and identity are threatened, they fight with acts of commemoration. In the first case, they are rewarded with their independence and freedom, and in the second, with recognition. In both cases, they are rewarded with glory and a reason to feel pride.

Kałków-Godów – from local tragedy to the sanctification of the martyrdom of the Polish nation

Local commemoration of the German pacifications

During the Second World War, some villages situated in the vicinity of present-day Kałków-Godów fell victim to the German policy of ensuring villagers bore collective responsibility for the actions of local partisans (Domański and Jankowski 2011). On 24 May and 11 November of 1943, divisions of the German military police carried out the pacification of the villages of Gębice and Żuchowiec.

380 *Małgorzata Głowacka-Grajper*

These two operations led to the deaths of a probable combined total of 136 people, of whom most came from these two villages, though there were other victims as well from the villages of Doły Biskupie, Godów and Krynki (*Główna Komisja* . . . 1980, 657). Those who survived the pacification had nothing to return to because whole villages had been burnt to the ground. The resultant depopulation of these two settlements led to them being incorporated into the village of Godów after the war. Today, this village is known as Kałków-Godów.

The residents of Kałków-Godów remember the pacifications of the neighbouring villages that the Germans carried out in 1943. There are still people alive today who directly witnessed these events or were raised in an atmosphere in which they were continuously reminded of murdered family members and neighbours. The victims of the pacifications of 24 May 1943 from Żuchowiec, Gębice and Doły Biskupie were initially buried by their relatives and neighbours in collective graves close to the burned villages. Later, their remains were exhumated and buried in the parish cemetery in Krynki, which is about nine kilometres from Kałków-Godów. However, at the site of the villagers' execution in the wood, one can also find another collective grave. The victims of the pacification of 11 November 1943 who were executed in the forest are buried there at 'the lodge', a site near to the place where they lost their lives.[5]

Memory of the murdered victims was transmitted orally within families until 1967, when Father Czesław Wala, the founder of the Sanctuary and its custos for many years (1982–2012), was dispatched to the parish of Krynki. During our visit to the Sanctuary, a local guide stressed that when Father Wala visited the villages lost between the forests, he noticed that

> the lives of many more local inhabitants are dominated by memories of the war; those settlements of Gębice and Żuchowiec were burned to the ground, destroyed, their inhabitants were murdered.
>
> (F., ca. 35 years old)

In the 1970s, the Council for the Protection of Struggle and Martyrdom Sites erected national memorials at two sites associated with the pacification that took place in May 1943. The central component of the national monument erected in 1970 that commemorates those residents of Żuchowiec who died in the May 1943 pacification was a granite stele. Today, this space is occupied by a statue of Our Lady, Queen of Poland, who has a crowned eagle emblazoned on her chest. The second monument bears the following inscription: 'A place sanctified by the martyrs' blood of 52 residents of the village of Gębice murdered by Nazis 24th May 1943. Honour to their Memory'. Every year in May, a Holy Mass and remembrance ceremony for those who were murdered are held on the anniversary of the May pacification. The monument by the statue of Our Lady, Queen of Poland serves as focal point for this ceremony, which is organized by management and teachers from the nearby elementary school in Godów in cooperation with local government representatives and clergymen from the local Sanctuary. By contrast, the events of November 1943 are

Memory as a religious mission? 381

mentioned during church services organized to mark National Independence Day (11 November) that are held during the Holy Mass for the Motherland celebrated at the church at the Sanctuary in Kałków-Godów.

The Sanctuary and the Golgotha of the Polish nation

The parish established in Kałków-Godów in 1981 was the first religious community in Poland to be dedicated to St Maximilian Maria Kolbe, a Polish Second World War martyr murdered at Auschwitz, beatified in 1971 and canonized in 1982. The introduction of martial law on 13 December 1981 provided the impetus for the creation of the Our Lady of Sorrows Sanctuary (Ryszka 2002). The construction of the shrine commenced in April 1982, though the local authorities were very inimical to the initiative. The following month, an image of the Blessed Virgin Mary with a crowned eagle on her breast was transferred to the shrine from a sanctuary in Licheń, a very important place linking the Marian cult to national ideology. Father Wala's parishioners and the inhabitants of neighbouring villages built the church with their own hands, completing the building in November 1983, after 153 days of labour.

Over time, Kałków increasingly began to assume the form of a site of memory commemorating the Polish nation's twentieth-century martyrology. The key year in this process was 1986, when the Golgotha of the Polish Nation was built in the Sanctuary's grounds. The building is thirty-three metres high and surmounted by a fifteen-metre-high oak Cross of Salvation, which is visible from far away and illuminated by night. This cross testifies to the 'cross's presence in the life of every person, in the life of the nation and the state' (Ryszka 2007). The five-storey stone building houses thirty chapels and oratories commemorating historical figures and events regarded as crucial for comprehending the Polish nation's fate in the twentieth century. Their dedicatees include important figures in the Polish church and tragic events from twentieth-century Polish history as well as orally and aurally challenged people from all over Poland. Space is also provided for national and regional activists affiliated to the Solidarity Independent Governing Trade Union, bus drivers, miners, railway workers and miners from all over Poland and Polish underground partisans active during the Second World War. There are chapels dedicated to Poles murdered and incarcerated in the East, including the Polish officers murdered at Katyn. By the entrance to the Golgotha, there is an expansive exhibition devoted to Poles honoured with the title of 'Righteous Among the Nations' for rescuing Jews during the Second World War. According to the official interpretation presented on the Sanctuary's website:

> The Golgotha was meant to commemorate the sacrifice of martyred Poles from ancient and modern times and to bear testimony to the fact that Poland has kept its faith in the Cross and the Gospel. Inside the Golgotha the latest Polish history has been recorded. . . . In this, Christ's Passion and the torments of the Polish nation merge into one.[6]

382 *Małgorzata Głowacka-Grajper*

The history of twentieth-century Poland and the tragic events that accompanied it have therefore been granted an unequivocal interpretation. The victims of the Second World War and the communist era are being presented as contemporary martyrs. Furthermore, their example is shaping models of morality and their sacrifice demands to be commemorated and venerated. The Golgotha of the Polish Nation is surmounted by a cross which, as the earlier mentioned guide explains during our visit,

> is supposed to remind us that the history of our nation, our lives are interwoven with pain, suffering, with the Catholic faith, that death, death as painful, as cruel as the death of Jesus Christ on the cross is an indelible part of our lives.
> (F., ca. 35 years old)

Although there are many oratories and remembrances of individuals on Golgotha, its general meaning relates to the whole Polish nation. The key element linking the history of salvation and that of the nation is the concept of sacrifice. The fundamental objective of both forms of memory is to preserve for future generations a narrative promoting sacrifice in the name of one's fellow man and the community. The term 'martyrdom' has therefore acquired a national dimension yet still retains its universal application. The religious language applied to the remembrance of victims of war and the communist era provokes and nurtures strong emotions. Moreover, it facilitates the transmission of memory of these victims because tragic historical events are becoming part of the universal schema of the martyred victim who makes it possible for future generations to live. If such an interpretation is applied, memory becomes a social and religious obligation.

Finally, it is worth noting that the Sanctuary's message is reinforced by the fact that it is located near the first sanctuary in Poland devoted to Relics of the True Cross. This was built on Święty Krzyż (Holy Cross Mountain), which is twenty kilometres from Kałków. According to the custos,

> our Sanctuary is at the foot of Święty Krzyż, it's as if these places were meant to harmonize with each other on national, religious and patriotic grounds.
> (M., ca. 50 years old)

In this way, the Sanctuary narrative, even though it focuses on twentieth-century events, is being incorporated into the much longer histories of both the Polish state and Polish Catholic Church.

After the Golgotha was constructed, the stone containing the plaque commemorating the victims of the pacification of Gębice and Żuchowiec was not brought into its space. The local tragedy is not commemorated within the bounds of the Golgotha in any manner whatsoever. A local woman working at the Sanctuary explained:

> but why duplicate these places? There's a monument here already, this is something even grander, everything concerning this site here is already

special and distinct, this is near the church and this is something very important; there [on the Golgotha] there is the martyrology of the Polish nation, and [the stone] here is [dedicated] to those people, those two villages and those who were murdered from those two villages.

(F., ca. 70 years old)

The Golgotha narrative is primarily of national purport, and the prevalence of this particular context means that the local community's primary concern is not to get their history incorporated into the Golgotha narrative. However, all the commemorations of the Second World War pacification do in fact allude to the same religious context of a history of salvation. These sites are therefore not in competition with each other either spatially, socially (i.e. in relation to the communities they serve) or in terms of their manner of interpretation (all of them show innocent victims and the enemy's bestiality). Instead, they function alongside each other. The ceremonies at local sites of memory only attract people united by family ties to the pacified villages, whereas the pilgrims and tourists visiting the Sanctuary primarily focus on its national-religious dimensions.

The residents of the village and the surrounding area have a somewhat different perspective on the Sanctuary. What comes to the fore in conversations with the oldest residents is the memory of how they joined forces to build the Sanctuary and the pride they feel in the fact that the local community have managed to create a unique place and a destination for numerous pilgrimages. The personal memories of individual locals who experienced the war and pacification are backgrounded. Residents seem satisfied that their story forms part of the story of a wider group and is being presented within the context of a nation's suffering. Such a presentation is treated as sufficient and fully adequate.

Conclusion: vernacular communities and the religious reinforcement of memory narratives

In Radzymin, the heroic martyrdom narrative of the past built over successive generations is of great importance for the local community. In fact, the preservation of memory and commemoration rituals define the community so strongly that anyone wishing to be accepted into it needs, above all, to accept the narrative and become actively involved in its transmission. The phenomenon that has existed in the town from the interwar period up to the present day is a manifestation of what Pierre Nora (1989) would describe as a *milieu de mémoire*, or a community living in the past. Memory of the local past is a visible element of social life. Not only does it permeate family and local life and the activities of institutions and individuals, but it is also present in public space. It is not seen as being limited to the private sphere. On the contrary, the past becomes an important basis for building socio-cultural capital and bolstering the position of the local community.

In the narrative of Radzymin's past, mutually reinforcing national and religious elements form an inseparable relationship. The interpretation of the Polish victory at the Battle of Warsaw as a miraculous event (on the basis that

384 *Małgorzata Głowacka-Grajper*

it was won on the day of the feast of the Assumption of the Blessed Virgin Mary, who is recognized in the national and religious tradition as the Queen of Poland) was strengthened by the visit of a Polish pope who happened to be born in the same year as that great victory. This interpretation of the victory as a miracle is nationwide in scope, but the confirmation, through a papal visit, of the importance of Radzymin as a site of memory has a local dimension. Memory activists have built among Radzymin's residents a sense of the town's uniqueness that has two foundations. First, the bloodiest engagements in one of the most important battles in the history of the world took place there. This is an element of 'grand history' that the inhabitants of the town had no influence on, although they passed an examination of their loyalty to the nation by taking part in the battle. Second, this is a town that also suffered because of its steadfast approach to preserving memory of the battle. The collective decision to preserve this memory can be seen as a conscious axiological choice made by the local community that soon become the most important component of its identity. According to local memory activists, Radzymin's image as a town determined to preserve memory at any cost has contributed to the accumulation of local social capital, which has helped promote the town as an attractive investment opportunity and thereby contributed to its development. Local memory activists define their contemporary challenge as saving this image in the face of rapid social changes.

At the Sanctuary in Kałków-Godów, the religious narrative dominates the narrative commemorating local history. From a grand historical perspective, the Gębice and Żuchowiec pacifications of 1943 were two instances of the small-scale local exterminations that occurred in their thousands during the war. However, from the local community's point of view, these were events that transformed their lives forever. The few survivors and the murder victims' relatives had to live on amid sites indelibly branded by the apocalypse they had suffered. For the communist authorities, the pacification sites provided even more historical evidence of the invaders' bestiality and were therefore exploited as such in the PRL's historical policy. This explains why, in the 1970s, a secular national memorial was erected at the main murder site of the May 1943 pacification, thereby incorporating these sites into a national network of Sites of Memory of the Struggle and Martyrdom of the Polish Nation. Over time, the local community erected religious memory markers in an attempt to sacralize secular monuments dating from the PRL.

The Golgotha of the Polish Nation was a very concrete contemporary response to both PRL-era historical policy, which excluded many social groups from national memory, and the memory environment of the nineties, when these excluded groups found their voice and began fighting for their story to be incorporated into the history of the nation. The portrayal of the past at the Sanctuary is mainly focused on these social groups' incorporation into a national history concentrated around motifs of suffering and martyrdom. This narrative reactivated a conceptual structure rooted in Polish culture that draws from Catholic models.

The memory communities in Radzymin and Kałków-Godów not only differ from each other because of the events that took place in each place, but also because of the actions of local memory actors. In Radzymin, a group of 'professional memory makers' developed (comprising activists associated with the local administration, teachers and priest), who set themselves the task of reproducing memory of the battle as a national event but also as an event from their family histories. Almost as soon as the battle was over, memorial rituals developed, which were supported by the actions of the army, Church and state. The local community became as attached to state and religious rituals as they did to memory of the battle itself. In Kałków-Godów, there were no local elites capable of creating rituals commemorating the local tragedy, so the local people commemorated the dead in the only way available to them: through religious rites devoted to the deceased. Although monuments were erected in the village by the state during communist times, only the local priest, in his role as a representative of the Catholic Church, created a narrative of suffering and martyrdom, which then became widely known outside the local community. In Radzymin, memory activists were looking for religious and national narratives that would enable them to confirm the extraordinary nature of their 'local homeland'. Indeed, their mission to remember local history also became a religious mission, and they believed that their religious beliefs and the institution of the Church confirmed the rightness of the path they had chosen. In Kałków-Godów, the inhabitants laid their local history on the altar of the national martyrdom narrative. The narrative of the suffering of the Polish nation modelled on Christ's life story and the masses celebrated on the anniversaries of the pacification of the villages do not make the local community's situation unique, but they do make it important when it is considered within the context of the history of the Polish nation and the universal history of salvation through martyrdom.

Researching the presence of religious language and symbols in the commemoration of the past leads to a more general question. What does the relationship between religion and memory look like today, and how do socio-cultural conditions affect how this relationship is understood? Religion, like collective memory, is a provider of rituals, but also of language and symbols that can connect the past, present and future. Ritual creates experience, as anthropologists have pointed out in classic works (see Douglas 2015). Experience is not only created by religious rituals but also secular ones, but even so, paying attention to religion while researching memory will allow scholars to discover a different type of memory experience, one in which a particular past (or particular events) is inscribed in the narrative of the nature of the world. Religion can make a historical event more meaningful by placing it within a universal context. It acts as a frame that allows individuals to remember and interpret various events by associating them with categories that they are familiar with from religious narratives. Memory that is immersed in religious rituals is axiological, not only because it is a carrier of values (such as sacrificing oneself for others or the collective), but also because it places the highest possible value on the act of remembering itself. This is hardly surprising when it is considered that remembering forms the basis of religion (Hervieu-Léger 2000). Remembering is a commitment. Indeed, religion owes its existence to continuous recollection

386 *Małgorzata Głowacka-Grajper*

and commemoration, which goes a long way to explaining why it is so well suited to the strengthening of memory narratives. Consequently, religion can be used by various institutions (such as the Church or the state) to build memory narratives, but understanding religious language and the religious vision of the world also enables us to understand how remembering functions at the local and individual level (in communities where religion is still an important element of social life). Thinking about relationships between the past, present and future in religious terms is not the only way to remember, but if this form of memory is ignored in memory research, it becomes extremely difficult to understand all the reasons why people remember and commemorate the past or consider remembering to be their duty.

Notes

1 Magdalena Zowczak (1987) emphasizes the importance in Polish folk culture of the relationship between the figure of the cultural hero and the Blessed Virgin: 'in heroic events she often appears as the hero's ally and guardian' (p. 150). Her image is also strongly grounded as a cultural hero who looks after Poles in a special way (p. 153).
2 Project 'Milieux de memoire in East-Central Europe – The Case of Poland', number 2013/09/D/H/S6/02630, supported by the National Science Centre in Poland, and headed by Zuzanna Bogumił.
3 For the place occupied by the Catholic religion in Polish historical narratives, see Porter-Szücs (2001) and Zubrzycki (2006).
4 For a more detailed analysis, see Głowacka-Grajper (2018).
5 For a more detailed analysis, see Bogumił and Głowacka-Grajper (2019).
6 Quotation from the official website of the Sanctuary, accessed 9 January 2018, www. kalkow.com.pl/view1.php?MMcat=g&MMarg=0.

References

Anderson, Benedict. 1986. *Imagined Communities: Reflections on the Origin and Spread of Nationalism*. London: Verso.
Assmann, Jan. 2011. *Cultural Memory and Early Civilization: Writing, Remembrance, and Political Imagination*. Cambridge: Cambridge University Press.
Bogumił, Zuzanna, and Małgorzata Głowacka-Grajper. 2019. *Milieux de mémoire in Late Modernity. Local Communities, Religion and Historical Politics*. Berlin: Peter Lang.
Böhler, Jochen. 2018. *Civil War in Central Europe, 1918–1921: The Reconstruction of Poland*. Oxford: Oxford University Press.
Casanova, José. 1994. *Public Religions in the Modern World*. Chicago: University of Chicago Press.
Domański, Tomasz, and Andrzej Jankowski. 2011. *Represje niemieckie na wsi kieleckiej 1939–1945*. Kielce: IPN.
Douglas, Mary. 2015. *Purity and Danger. An Analysis of Concept of Pollution and Taboo*. London: Routledge.
Drozdowski, Marian M. 1993. *Warszawa w obronie Rzeczypospolitej. Czerwiec – sierpień 1920*. Warszawa: Warszawska Oficyna Wydawnicza "Gryf", Instytut Historii PAN.
Dwornicki, Piotr. 2011. "Echa bitwy warszawskiej 1920 r. na łamach prasy prawicowej w Wielkopolsce." In *Wielkie rocznice w dyskursie publicznym I pamięci społecznej*, edited by Marceli Kosman. Poznań: Wydawnictwo Naukowe WNPiD UAM.

Memory as a religious mission? 387

Głowacka-Grajper, Małgorzata. 2018. "Pamięć jako kapitał społeczności lokalnej. Narracje o Bitwie Warszawskiej 1920 roku w Radzyminie." In *Stare I nowe tendencje w obszarze pamięci społecznej*, edited by Zuzanna Bogumił and Andrzej Szpociński. Warszawa: Wydawnictwo Scholar.

Główna Komisja Badania Zbrodni Hitlerowskich w Polsce. 1980. *Rejestr miejsc I faktów zbrodni popełnionych przez okupanta hitlerowskiego na ziemiach polskich w latach 1939–1945. Województwo kieleckie.* Warsaw: Ministerstwo Sprawiedliwości.

Grabowska, Mirosława. 2004. *Podział postkomunistyczny. Społeczne podstawy polityki w Polsce po 1989 roku.* Warszawa: Wydawnictwo Scholar.

Halbwachs, Maurice. 1992. *On Collective Memory.* Chicago: University of Chicago Press.

Hervieu-Léger, Daniele. 2000. *Religion as a Chain of Memory.* Translated by Simon Lee. New Brunswick, NJ: Rutgers University Press.

Karłowicz, Dariusz. 2005. "Pamięć aksjologiczna a historia." In *Pamięć I odpowiedzialność*, edited by Robert Kostro and Tomasz Merta. Kraków and Wrocław: Ośrodek Myśli Politycznej, Centrum Konserwatywne.

Lim, Jie-Hyun. 2010. "Victimhood Nationalism in Contested Memories: National Mourning and Global Accountability." In *Memory in a Global Age. Discourses, Practices and Trajectories*, edited by Aleida Assmann and Secastian Conrad. Basingstoke: Palgrave Macmillan.

Margalit, Avishai. 2004. *The Ethics of Memory.* Cambridge, MA: Harvard University Press.

Marody, Mirosława, and Sławomir Mandes. 2006. "On Functions of Religion in Molding the National Identity of Poles." *International Journal of Sociology* 35 (4): 49–68.

Nowik, Grzegorz. 2011. *Wojna światów. 1920 – Bitwa Warszawska.* Poznań: G&P Oficyna Wydawnicza, Muzeum Józefa Piłsudskiego w Sulejówku.

Nora, Pierre. 1989. "Between Memory and History: Les Lieux de Mémoire." *Representations* (26) (Spring 1989): 7–25.

Ochman, Ewa. 2017. "When and Why Is the Forgotten Past Recovered? The Battle of Warsaw, 1920 and the Role of Local Actors in the Production of Memory." *Memory Studies.* https://doi.org/10.1177/1750698017709874.

———. 2019. "Why Is Poland Unable to Celebrate Victories? 'The Miracle on the Vistula' a Century Later." *The Polish Review* 64 (2): 104–20.

Porter-Szücs, Brian. 2001. "The Catholic Nation: Religion, Identity, and the Narratives of Polish History." *The Slavic and East European Journal* 45 (2): 289–99.

———. 2014. *Poland in the Modern World. Beyond Martyrdom.* Chichester: Wiley Blackwell.

Ryszka, Czesław. 2002. *Kałków-Godów: Sanktuarium pod Świętym Krzyżem.* Warsaw: Wydawnictwo Sióstr Loretanek.

———. 2007. *Sanktuarium pod Świętym Krzyżem: Kałków-Godów.* Kraków and Radom: Wydawnictwo Sióstr Loretanek.

Szacka, Barbara. 2006. *Czas przeszły, pamięć, mit.* Warszawa: Wydawnictwo Naukowe Scholar.

Tarczyński, Marek. 1990. *Cud nad Wisłą. Bitwa Warszawska 1920.* Warszawa: Instytut Wydawniczy Związków Zawodowych.

Verdery, Katherine. 1999. *The Political Lives of Dead Bodies.* New York: Columbia University Press.

Winter, Jay. 2015. "War and Martyrdom in the Twentieth Century and After." *Journal of Soviet and Post-Soviet Politics and Society* 2: 217–56.

Wnuk, Jan. 2015. *Dzieje Radzymina.* Radzymin: Towarzystwo Przyjaciół Radzymina.

Zowczak, Magdalena. 1987. "Bohater jako święty." *Etnografia Polska* 31 (2): 139–59.

Zubrzycki, Geneviève. 2006. *The Crosses of Auschwitz: Nationalism and Religion in Post-Communist Poland.* Chicago: University of Chicago Press.

19 Critical juxtaposition in the post-war Japanese mnemoscape

Saint Maksymilian Kolbe of Auschwitz and the atomic bomb victims of Nagasaki

Jie-Hyun Lim

This chapter traces the trajectory of how memory of Saint Maksymilian Kolbe at Auschwitz and memory of the Catholic atomic bomb victims of Nagasaki have been juxtaposed in post-war Japan. The atomic bomb exploded in the sky over Nagasaki on 9 August 1945. Father Maksymilian Kolbe had returned to Poland in 1936 after six years' service as a missionary in Nagasaki and sacrificed himself to save another Auschwitz inmate on 14 August 1941. Despite the different time-framing, Kolbe's martyrdom at Auschwitz and the Catholic atomic bomb victimhood in Nagasaki have been connected mnemonically in post-war Japan. However, the two memories have coexisted separately in global memory space. The controversy over 'Kolbe's anti-Semitism' in Poland and the United States was disregarded among Japanese Catholics, whereas the *hansai* (燔祭, 'burnt offering') – a Japanese translation of 'holocaust' – in Takashi Nagai's eulogy for the Catholic victims in the ruins of Urakami Cathedral (delivered on 23 November 1945) did not receive much attention from the West. A simple juxtaposition of Auschwitz and Nagasaki through the figure of Maksymilian Kolbe may even unexpectedly expose a hidden mnemonic nexus capable of bridging East and West in the global memory space.

More often than not, transnational memory is used to justify and intensify mnemonic nationalism. As the rhetorical force of such terms as 'the Pacific Holocaust', 'the Japanese Holocaust', 'the Forgotten Asian Holocaust' or 'Poland's Holocaust' indicates, the cosmopolitanization of the Holocaust has often been subject to a nationalist desire to stress national victimhood. Juxtaposing non-Jewish national trauma with the Holocaust has been one way in which cosmopolitan memory has been re-territorialized to highlight individual cases of 'victimhood nationalism' in global memory space (Lim 2010, 138–62). The juxtaposition of Auschwitz and Nagasaki led to Saint Maksymilian Kolbe becoming a mnemonic code for victimhood nationalism in post-war Japan. This chapter aims to understand the religious sublimination of victimhood nationalism into the transnational memory formation by investigating the role

DOI: 10.4324/9781003264750-24

of the Saint Kolbe cult in the promotion of the Catholic sanctification of the Nagasaki atomic bomb victims in post-war Japan.

Methodologically, this chapter is located at the intersection of memory studies, global intellectual history and public history. It attempts to create a global intellectual history of the entangled memories of the Holocaust at Auschwitz and the atomic bombing in Nagasaki by way of textual criticism. This textual criticism focuses on vernacular memory more than official memory. I will also explore how memory of Auschwitz and memory of Nagasaki have been entangled by way of 'juxtaposition' in the post-war Japanese mnemoscape. Rather than drawing from sociological data, this chapter relies on such sources as novels, essays, travelogues, eulogies, films and visitor's books in museums, all of which belong to the realm of public history and vernacular memory in its interaction with the official memory. By examining one particular case – the strange juxtaposition of Saint Maksymilian Kolbe of Auschwitz and the Catholic *hibakusha* (atomic bomb victims) in Nagasaki – this chapter will show how public history, vernacular memory and official memory interact transnationally. The scope of the memory studies dimension of this chapter is transdisciplinary as much as transnational.

The 'Saint of Auschwitz' and the 'Saint of Nagasaki'

In Nagasaki's memory space, despite the resentment provoked by the deaths caused by the atomic bombing, these deaths have been wrapped in the religious halo of Catholicism. A link between these secular deaths and religious sanctity is formed by two Catholic martyrs who share a deep connection to Nagasaki: Maksymilian Kolbe, the Polish priest known as the 'Saint of Auschwitz', and Takashi Nagai, a Catholic layman reverently called the 'Saint of Nagasaki'. Kolbe, who worked as a missionary in Nagasaki between 1930 and 1936, sacrificed his life on 14 August 1941 to save a fellow prisoner, Franciszek Gajowniczek, in a punishment cell of Block 11 in the Auschwitz concentration camp. A Catholic physician and Nagasaki atomic bomb survivor, it was Takashi Nagai who originated the 'Urakami *hansai*/holocaust' theory. At the memorial Mass held at Urakami Cathedral for the atomic bomb victims on 23 November 1945, Nagai gave a eulogy quoting the word '*hansai*', a Japanese translation of the word 'holocaust' (burnt offering). The word occurs in chapter 22 of the book of Genesis, when God said to Abraham, 'Sacrifice him (Isaac) there as a burnt offering on a mountain I will show you'.

Thus, Nagai sublimated the tragedy of the atomic bomb victims of Nagasaki into a sacrificial offering made to God by turning them metonymically into a clean and unblemished lamb to be burnt alive. The Holocaust and the atomic bombing of Nagasaki became juxtaposed and entangled in the memory culture of post-war Japan through these two venerated figures. When the atomic bomb was dropped on 9 August 1945, Nagai was heavily wounded. By mid-August, his condition had deteriorated so much that he was in the throes of death.

390 *Jie-Hyun Lim*

Realizing that his time had come, Nagai made a general confession to a priest and received the Sacrament of the Anointing of the Sick (Nagai 2015, 126–28). While he was slowly drifting into unconsciousness, Nagai suddenly felt a cold sensation in his mouth and heard the sound of his mother whispering, 'This is Lourdes water'. He saw 'clearly the Lourdes Grotto with roses in full bloom and the pure image of the Holy Mother'. And Nagai heard a voice telling him to pray to Father Maksymilian Kolbe for intercession (Nagai 2015, 129–30).

Nagai was woken from his coma by the surprised voices of a doctor and nurse, who were saying that the bleeding had stopped. A miracle had occurred. Drinking the Lourdes water had allowed the wound to heal by itself. But the water that Nagai had drunk had not been brought from Lourdes of France, where the miracle of 1858 took place. Instead, it had come from a Nagasaki version of the Spring of Lourdes that Kolbe had built as an imitation of the original on a hill behind the Hongouchi Seminary in the Seibo no Kishi ('Knight of the Immaculate') Monastery. What makes this miracle on Nagai's deathbed remarkable is the presence of Father Kolbe. Not only was the fact that the water had come from the Lourdes Spring of the Hongouchi Seminary in the Seibo no Kishi Monastery a peculiar detail, but the part of this story where Nagai prays to Father Kolbe for intercession is particularly striking.

The acquaintanceship between Takashi Nagai and Maksymilian Kolbe dates back to before the outbreak of the war. Nagai paid a visit, in his capacity as a physician, to Kolbe at the Hongouchi Seminary in 1935. After the medical examination, Nagai found that Kolbe had a tuberculosis infection in both lungs. From a medical standpoint, it was incomprehensible that a priest who had lost about 80% of the functioning in both of his lungs due to persistent tuberculosis was passionately immersed in the publication of the Catholic journal, *Seibo no Kishi*, as well as missionary work. Kolbe was well aware of his advanced tuberculosis. That he continued to work hard at his mission despite his condition without ever losing his ability to smile was a mystery. When Nagai confessed that he could not figure out how Kolbe did this, the Polish priest held up his rosaries and said, 'This. This is how'. After the war, Nagai wrote a series of articles titled 'Records of the Atomic Wastelands' for *Seibo no Kishi*, beginning in 1947 and continuing right up until he died in 1951, all the time keeping up his memory of Kolbe.

In Nagasaki, which was considered the Holy Land of the East and called 'Little Rome', Catholicism has been the matrix of cultural memory. Incidentally, the date of the Japanese attack on Pearl Harbor in 1941 was 8 December, the Feast of the Immaculate Conception. Nagai recalled that upon hearing about the attack on Pearl Harbor, a premonition that Urakami might be completely turned into ashes sent a shiver down his spine. At the exact moment when the atomic bomb exploded in Nagasaki on 9 August 1945, confessions were being held for the local faithful at Urakami Cathedral. All the priests, sub-priests and lay followers who were gathered for the Mass marking the occasion of the approaching Feast of the Assumption of Mary on 15 August died on the spot (Nagai 2010, 262–63, 307). The name of the place where Nagai would later give his eulogy speech for the atomic bomb victims was also out of the ordinary. The official name of Urakami Cathedral, namely the Immaculate Conception Cathedral, had its origins in the Militia Immaculatae (Rycerstwo Niepokalanej), which was founded by Saint Maksymilian Kolbe.

Aside from the personal connection between Father Kolbe and Dr Nagai, memory of the atomic bombing in Nagasaki was intricately woven together with that of Christian persecution. Not only was Urakami Cathedral, already a symbol of Christian persecution, at the hypocentre of the blast, but the apocalyptic image of the atomic bombing served as an ideal motif that could be combined with cultural memory of Christian persecution. The persecution of Christians in Nagasaki had been widely known outside Japan even before the war. Raphael Lemkin, who formulated the term and concept of 'genocide', included the Christian persecution in Nagasaki in his world history of genocide, along with the colonial genocides in Namibia and the Congo of Africa, and the massacre of Roma, American Indians, Aztecs, Incas, Armenians and European Jews (Moses 2012, 276).

Once the image of the apocalypse was added to the existing history of Christian persecution in Nagasaki, the tragedy of the atomic bombing increasingly provoked associations with genocide. This explains the strong emphasis placed on the figure of Saint Maksymilian Kolbe within the memory culture of Nagasaki. Through the historical connection with Kolbe, who sacrificed himself for another at Auschwitz, the apocalyptic memory of the atomic bombing in Nagasaki was juxtaposed, though not entangled, with that of the Holocaust. This unique juxtaposition made it possible for atomic bomb survivors of Nagasaki to ensure that their own tragedy acquired a sense of universality by communicating with transnational memory of the Holocaust and reflecting on the pain of war and genocide. While mnemonic solidarity with Holocaust victims was emphasized in Nagasaki's memory culture, the historical context of the Asia-Pacific War, which led to the tragedy of the atomic bombing, was relatively overlooked. By de-contextualizing the Asia-Pacific War, Nagasaki's memory of the atomic bombing contributed to the formation of 'victimhood nationalism' in post-war Japan.

The Urakami 'Holocaust' and survivor's guilt

Soon after the atomic bombing, a rumour spread among the non-Christians in central Nagasaki that the victims of Urakami Cathedral had been punished for not worshipping the Japanese gods and worshipping a Western one instead (Treat 1995). Deeply rooted prejudice against the Christian *burakumin*/subalterns of Urakami was evident at the time. By contrast, the Christians of Nagasaki referred to the horrors of the atomic bombing, which had annihilated around 8,000 Christians living in the Urakami area, as the fifth persecution. They viewed the atomic bombing as an extension of the previous series of Christian persecutions, which started with Toyotomi Hideyoshi's repressions, then continued through the Tokugawa Shōgunate to the fourth persecution from the 1860s until 1873 after the opening of Japan. Urakami Cathedral was the largest cathedral in East Asia, which was built on a site where persecuted Japanese Catholics had previously had to step on *fumi-e*, or sacred images, and demonstrate to the state their apostasy (Maclelland 2015, 239). The construction of the Urakami Cathedral symbolized the revival and ultimate victory of Japanese Catholicism. Whether by nemesis or persecution, the believers of Urakami Cathedral had become victims of inevitable fate who were deprived of agency. Takashi Nagai's eulogy is significant in that it attempted to recover the lost agency among those victims.

The title of the manuscript was the 'Eulogy for the Joint Funeral for the Atomic-Bomb Deceased'.[1] In front of the Catholic attendants at the Mass, who held 8,000 candles, Nagai opened his speech by emphasizing that the fact that the Urakami Cathedral was at the hypocentre of the nuclear bomb blast was divine providence. Nagai asserted that it was no mere coincidence that the date of 15 August, when the whole world greeted the morning of peace following the Imperial Decision to end the war was pronounced, also happened to be the Feast of the Assumption of Mary. Instead of a chance event, this was the arcane providence of God. Nagai stated, 'The church of Urakami was placed on the altar of sacrifice as atonement for the sin of humankind that was the world war. It was chosen as a pure lamb, slaughtered, and burned' (Konishi 2014, 58). If Nagai's logic is to be taken to the extreme, the sacrifice of the Catholics of Urakami had brought a swift end to the war, saving billions of human lives that otherwise would have been ravaged. Furthermore, if the Catholics of Urakami, who had overcome persecution for 400 years and maintained their orthodox faith, had been chosen as a sacred offering on the altar of the Lord, that meant that they had been graced and blessed by God.

Nagai continued:

> Alas, the great Holocaust that was made in the presence of this cathedral on August ninth and duly ended the darkness of the great world war and shined the light of peace! Even in the nadir of sadness, we reverently viewed this as something beautiful, something pure, and something sacred.
> (Konishi 2014, 58–59)

Nagai's eulogy gave a resolute humanitarian meaning to the innocent deaths of the Catholics of Urakami Cathedral. As pure and unsullied lambs, they became the holy sacrifice of the great Holocaust, chosen to be offered on the altar of God and burned by the atomic bomb. They were also martyrs of peace, who died not only so that others would be absolved from their sins committed during the Second World War, but also so that the war could be brought an end, preventing any more sacrifice of innocents. Nagai's eulogy, which described Nagasaki's atomic bomb victims as offering their bodies to be burned on the altar of peace, just as a 'burnt offering' would be made to God, was a persuasive speech that sublimated their deaths into a sacrifice for peace. The 'Urakami

Juxtaposition in the Japanese mnemoscape 393

Holocaust' theory therefore implied that the atomic bomb victims of Nagasaki were to be remembered on equal terms to the Jewish victims of the Holocaust.[2]

Nagai's theory of the 'Urakami Holocaust' was not without its critics. Shinji Takahashi, a sociologist from Nagasaki, labelled the 'Urakami holocaust theory' as a discourse of 'double exemption' that erased the responsibility of the Japanese emperor for the war and that of the United States for the atomic bombing (Takahashi 1994). The poet and Nagasaki survivor Kan Yamada and the writer Inoue Hisashi joined the criticism. They argued that 'divine providence' obfuscates the question of who should be held accountable for the atomic bombing (Cheon 2013; Kwon 2014). It should also be noted that Dr Akizuki Tachiichiro, a student of Nagai, raised a similar criticism much earlier (Southhead 2016, 172–76). These critiques make a valid point about the political effect created by the eulogy: when the innocent deaths from the atomic bombing are sublimated into a holy sacrifice for world peace through 'divine providence', political responsibility is erased. By de-contextualizing and de-historicizing the Nagasaki victims, Japan's post-war memory culture and anti-nuclear pacifism also tend to neglect the atrocities of the Japanese empire. Nevertheless, the innocent atomic bomb victims could be assured of the existential value of their lives and the meaningful sacrifice inherent in their deaths through the notion of Catholic sublimation.

Among the Catholic mourners in Nagasaki, survivor's guilt was also quite common. In Nagai's words, 'In large-scale destructions such as an atomic bomb explosion, humans . . . die if they follow their conscience. In order not to die, one must turn away from one's conscience'. The extreme circumstances caused by an atomic bombing demanded a choice to be made between morality or rationality, between 'saving a friend who is groaning in pain in front of your eyes, sure to be engulfed in flames, or fleeing the scene and leaving your friend there to die'. Furthermore:

> If an atomic war is waged, any country would say, 'Do not be concerned about others, just save yourself. Don't even think about your duty. Your own life must be saved'. In situations like this, it is challenging to follow the teaching that 'you must love others; negate yourself and give love; fulfill your duty'.
>
> (Nagai 2015, 74–75)

Could Nagai's decision to name the house he lived in for the rest of his life *Nyokodo*, meaning 'love your neighbour as yourself', be seen as a sign that he was experiencing survivor's guilt that even the message of the Bible was unable to assuage?

As Primo Levi has argued, survivor's guilt is connected with 'the self-accusation of having failed in terms of human solidarity' (Levi 1989, 78). It is not surprising that a guilty conscience similar to that of the Holocaust survivors who emerged from concentration camps alive can be identified in Takashi

394 *Jie-Hyun Lim*

Nagai and other atomic bomb survivors. Survivor's guilt is readily apparent in Nagai, who asks himself:

> Haven't the survivors merely held up the hundreds of thousands of victims burned by the atomic bomb as examples, using them as the driving force to keep the peace movement going? Although the citizens affected by the atomic bombing (hibakusha) of Hiroshima and Nagasaki have been praying for peace, what sacrifices have they made for their prayers?
>
> (Nagai 2015, 189)

This guilt is distinctly different, by virtue of its self-reflexive existentialist tone, from Hiroshima's political victimhood. Memory in Hiroshima is more politicized due to the atomic bombing of Hiroshima being defined as a product of American racism and a symbol of absolute evil that ranks alongside the horrors of Auschwitz.

Surely there is some truth in the assertion that, in the case of Nagasaki, survivor's guilt at leaving dying friends behind gave rise to feelings of atonement or even a newfound respect for cases of martyrdom or self-sacrifice that contradicted the egoistic instinct to save oneself. Survivor's guilt is also apparent in the affectionate esteem Japanese Catholics felt towards the 'Saint of Auschwitz', Maksymilian Kolbe, who gave his life to save a fellow prisoner. Similarly, Brother Tōmei Ozaki wrote about his own survivor's guilt in a book titled *Kolbe Father of Nagasaki*. At the 'vigorous age of 17 years', Ozaki was exposed to radiation from the atomic bomb while he was working at an arms factory in Urakami. He would later recall: 'Seeing the chaos of the wounded lying around, I fled the scene in shock. Two months later, I entered the monastery' (Ozaki 2006, 226). Here, it is tacitly implied that his guilt at having 'fled the scene' and abandoning those who were dying from effects of the atomic bomb was the reason behind his decision to knock on the door of the Seibo no Kishi Monastery. That Brother Ozaki was drawn to the 'martyr of charity, Father Kolbe, who gave his life in place of another during the war' would have owed much to this guilt he was experiencing.

The author Shusaku Endō, who introduced Kolbe to many Japanese readers through the novel, *A Woman's Life, Part Two: The Case of Sachiko*, which was first serialized in *Asahi Shimbun*, also talks in the epilogue about the subtle consciousness one has as a survivor of one's own guilt:

> Rather than these difficult words, it may just be the honest feeling that 'we really all contrived to survive'. We all, contrived, to survive. But hidden behind this feeling are more complex emotions. They are the sadness and pain of knowing that even though I may have survived, the ones that I long for, loved, and was close friends with were lost during or after the war.
>
> (Endō 2017, 569)

As a devout Catholic, Endō portrays Kolbe in his novel as frequently quoting the Bible verse, 'There is no greater love than to lay down one's life for one's friends', thereby constantly evoking the guilt of those who had survived. Kolbe, who sacrificed his life by taking the place of a fellow prisoner, was thus a martyr who had made substitutionary atonement for the guilt of survivors.

The common theme running through *A Woman's Life, Part One* and *A Woman's Life, Part Two* is the self-sacrifice of devoting a pure and earnest love to another, to the extent of giving up one's life. Kiku, who appears in *Part One*, gives up her life for her beloved, Seikichi. Vomiting blood, she dies in front of the statue of the Mother Mary of Oura Cathedral. Kiku had given up everything, even defiling her own body, for her beloved Mother Mary, who comforts Kiku by saying, 'You have lived this world for love, just as my son (Jesus Christ) has', thereby creating an overlap between Kiku's love for Seikichi and her love of Christ (Endō 1986, 323–24).[3] The statue of the Mother Mary of Oura Cathedral is the one in front of which the 'Saint of Auschwitz', Father Kolbe, used to kneel down in prayer every day while he was teaching at Oura Seminary. In *Part Two*, Sachiko, who is Kiku's grandniece, is seen praying in front of the same statue of Mother Mary. Interestingly, the three protagonists in *A Woman's Life, Part Two* are Sachiko, Kiku's grandniece; Shuhei, the object of Sachiko's pure and ardent love, who dies in war as a kamikaze special forces soldier; and Father Kolbe. Part Two was written using a 'parallel plot' structure, in which the tragic love story between Sachiko and Shuhei intersects with the story of the priest, Maksymilian Kolbe. In the novel, Father Kolbe gives Sachiko a sacred printed image of Maria containing the Bible verse from John 15:13: 'There is no greater love than to lay down one's life for one's friends' (Endō 2017, 27–28).

Endō cites John 15:13 recurrently throughout the novel. For Endō, the minds of the lovers sacrificing themselves for their beloved are 'very similar to the mentality of a saint giving his life over to God, forsaking everything else' (Endō 1996, 64). The sacrificial love of Kiku, who gave her own life for her beloved, and the martyr's love of Father Kolbe, who gave his life in place of a fellow prisoner, allow survivors to realize their guilt and achieve a religious catharsis through substitutionary atonement. If Kolbe had left the crying Gajowniczek to die, he would have suffered from that sin for the rest of his life. In that case, he would have survived physically, but as a priest, he would have been as good as dead in spirit. Kolbe's sacrifice of his own life for a fellow prisoner is somewhat free from Primo Levi's self-criticism for failing through lack of human solidarity. The martyrdom at Auschwitz of Father Kolbe, with his secure connection to Nagasaki, was an excellent motif for the process of introspection provoked by the guilt experienced by the Catholic survivors of the Urakami holocaust.

Maksymilian Kolbe and the anti-Westernism of Japanese Catholics

Photographs of Kolbe taken during his stay in Nagasaki show the long, dark beard that was clearly his trademark, while later photos taken after he returned to Poland show him cleanly shaven. According to Tōmei Ozaki's interpretation, Kolbe had grown a long beard to soften his interactions with the Japanese

396 *Jie-Hyun Lim*

people by emulating the traditional image of a wise man of the East (Ozaki 2006, 219). Upon arriving at Nagasaki, Kolbe and his party were not only poorly received by Bishop Hayasaka of Oura Cathedral, who was sceptical about their missionary work based on the publication of the *Seibo no Kishi* journal. They were also, to their annoyance, suspected by the Japanese police of being Russian spies. As the landing of the American forces drew near, the pressure exerted on the Catholic Church by the Japanese military and the Special Higher Police intensified (Ozaki 2006, 169–71). Catholicism was not favourably perceived among Japanese society, and the image of the Catholic Church was identified with Western colonialism.

Even Shusaku Endō, who was a devout Catholic, could not but be conscious of the disapproving eyes being levelled at Catholicism for its involvement with colonialism. In *A Woman's Life, Part One*, Endō takes up the Church's complicity with Western colonialism, through the words of Shuntaro Hondo of the Nagasaki Magistrate's Office. Hondo asks pointedly, 'Why has the so-called Pope of the Christians kept mum about the rampant stealing, invading, and killing in the Eastern lands being committed by the Christian countries?' In the novel, Endō describes the embarrassment of a French priest, Father Petitjean, who has to admit the validity of Hondo's criticism of Christian hypocrisy, because there is no way of justifying the invasion and colonialization of Asia and Africa by Western Christian countries. Upon hearing Hondo's personal attack, which culminates in the words, 'Father Petitjean, while you have stirred up trouble in Japan and the village of Urakami and the Christians of Urakami are locked in prison, you are comfortably rested in this room', the blue-eyed French priest is at a loss for words (Endō 1986, 172–79).

It is here that the contrast between Father Kolbe from the East and Father Petitjean from the West is at its most pronounced. Indeed, Poland, as a (semi-) peripheral state of Europe, could in fact be regarded as 'the East within the West' and free from the guilt of colonialism, having been a nation oppressed by the three partitioning states of Russia, Prussia, and Austria for 120 years. Furthermore, Poland had maintained a close relationship with Japan because they had shared a common enemy, in Russia, since the Russo-Japanese War (Bandō 1995). Poland's underprivileged position gave Kolbe an advantage in the Japanese mind. For the Japanese, Kolbe was not from the West but the East (Wolff 1994; Kopp 2012; Kieniewicz 2013). According to the recollections of his fellow friars, Kolbe was treated poorly by Bishop Hayasaka and Father Urakawa of Oura Cathedral (Ozaki 2006, 109, 135). Missionaries from the West have rarely experienced such inferior treatment. Kolbe's childlike habit of calling the Holy Mother 'Mamusia' ('Mummy' in Polish), his insistence on living an impoverished but honest life and his simple way of doing missionary work that solely relied on *Seibo no Kishi* all made him distinctly different from other missionaries from Western colonial states (Ozaki 2006, 155–56).

Endō's portrayal of the arrival of Kolbe and his party at Nagasaki is also intriguing. Unlike typical Westerners, who tended to travel by first class, Kolbe and five other Polish friars took third-class seats in a ship named *Nagasakimaru*.

Juxtaposition in the Japanese mnemoscape 397

Tamaki, a Nagasaki police commissioner, was puzzled at the sight of them in the third-class cabin, carrying no more than a few pieces of clothing and a couple of books. Tamaki felt a sort of pity towards those poor 'Westerners' who hardly spoke a word of Japanese and very few words of English. Having disembarked, the group of Polish men stood around in the middle of the street rather than taking a rickshaw, carrying their suitcases and not knowing where to go, until they received some assistance from a certain Detective Kaneda, who escorted them to the road leading to Oura Cathedral (Endō 2017, 7–13). The mixture of curiosity, pity, and irritation the Polish clergy aroused in Detective Kaneda differed from the fear of Western colonialism felt by Hondo of the Nagasaki Magistrate's Office in his relations with Father Petitjean. Poland's (semi-)peripheral place in world history protected Kolbe from the accusation of being a Catholic colluding with Western colonialism. Being a missionary from the Global East, Kolbe was able to undermine the Japanese suspicion of Western colonialism. Endō's supposed encounter with Franz Fanon in Lyon may explain his sensitivity towards postcolonial problematics (Hill 2014).

The particular love for Maksymilian Kolbe felt by Ayako Sono, who documented the priest's life in the form of a biographical novel titled *Kiseki (Miracles)*, which spread knowledge about him throughout Japan, is remarkable too. Before attending Kolbe's beatification at the Vatican on 17 October 1971, Sono arrived in Poland on 21 September. With the guidance of Tadeusz K. Oblak, a Polish Jesuit, she searched for traces of Kolbe in Poland for more than three weeks. It was a long journey, starting at Zduńska Wola, which was Kolbe's hometown, then moving on to Niepokalanów Monastery, and Zakopane, where Kolbe stayed at a sanatorium to recover from his illness, and ending at the Auschwitz concentration camp in Oświęcim. Sono also visited Franciszek Gajowniczek, whose life was saved by Kolbe's sacrifice, and talked with him about Kolbe. While in Poland, Sono was astonished at how little was known about the story of Gajowniczek and Kolbe. By claiming that if this had been Japan, the media attention would have taken over Gajowniczek's everyday life, she tacitly accused the Polish media of indifference (Sono 2016, 15, 101–2). Sono published her travel notes as a series of articles, which ran for a year in the Catholic journal, *Catholic Club*, beginning in January 1972. Having gathered together her travelogue, which was based on the French version of Maria Winowska's biography of Kolbe, the materials she had collected during Sono's travels in Poland and her own sensibilities, she wrote *Kiseki*.

In Sono's understanding, Kolbe was a Catholic patriot. According to her, Kolbe had wanted to punish the foreign enemies that had occupied Poland, but he realized that real revenge lay in winning over people all around the world by spreading God's word rather than resorting to violence. She was also told an anecdote by Father Anselmo, whom she met in Kraków, according to which Kolbe's father had fought in the Brigade of the Polish Legions under Józef Piłsudski during the First World War. During a battle, Kolbe's father was captured by Soviet troops and executed (Sono 2016, 63, 68). The patriotism of Kolbe, whose father had devoted himself to the national movement, resonated

398 *Jie-Hyun Lim*

with the historical cliché of Polish Catholicism acting as the representative of the crucified nation. This may explain Ayako Sono's lenient attitude towards the Kolbe family's devotion to the nationalist cause.[4] Perhaps mindful of the controversy surrounding Kolbe's recognition as a Christian martyr at the time of his beatification, Sono wrote that the golden rule of Christianity is love, and to lay down one's life for one's friends, as Father Kolbe of Auschwitz did for Gajowniczek, is the greatest love. In other words, when devotion to Jesus is taken to its furthest point, it is accompanied by death. Had he ignored Gajowniczek's cries for mercy and his entreaties to be allowed to see his family again, Kolbe may have been alive physically, but as a priest and spiritually, he would have been as good as dead (Sono 2016, 112–15).

Sono reconfirms Kolbe's martyrdom, and Endō elaborated on this in his novel, *A Woman's Life, Part Two: The Case of Sachiko*, by ensuring that Sachiko of Nagasaki and Kolbe of Auschwitz cross paths. In his popular essay 'Father Kolbe', which has been included in a certified high school Japanese textbook, Endō defines the meaning of a miracle as follows:

> I do not think that a miracle is curing an incurable disease or turning a stone into gold. A miracle is doing what we cannot do. In the appalling purgatory of a Nazi concentration camp, Father Kolbe gave a love that we cannot give. This is what I call a miracle.
>
> (Endō 2018, 186)

The essay, short as it was, communicated Father Kolbe's love to the Japanese students who graduated from one of the high schools using the Japanese textbook in which it was printed. Once it had been published in a high school textbook, it contributed to making Father Kolbe's existence known to everyday Japanese people who were neither Catholics nor literary enthusiasts.

Meanwhile, on 21 September 1971, when Ayako Sono was at a Paris airport waiting to board a plane headed to Warsaw, a serious debate was going on in Poland over Father Kolbe's eligibility for his forthcoming beatification. *Tygodnik Powszechny*, a liberal Catholic weekly magazine published in Kraków that attracted widespread support from critical intellectuals, published a reader's letter questioning Kolbe's anti-Semitism. The writer of the letter was the critical left-wing intellectual and renowned Marxist economist, Jan Józef Lipski. In his letter, Lipski adopted the premise that Kolbe's beatification was an issue that by and large belonged to the Catholic Church, yet he still expressed concern from the perspective of the nation of Poland as a whole. He claimed that *Mały Dziennik*, of which Kolbe was the founder and editor-in-chief, was sycophantic towards extreme anti-Semitism and a breeding ground for hatred and contempt. That *Mały Dziennik* had close connections with members of the National Radical Camp (Obóz Narodowo-Radykalny [ONR]) was impossible for anyone to deny.[5] In Lipski's estimation, the assumption that Kolbe had admitted his wrongdoing and sought forgiveness solely because he had sacrificed his life for another was simply wishful thinking that had no basis in fact (Lipski, *Tygodnik Powszechny*, 19 September 1971).

The editors of *Tygodnik Powszechny* sent an inquiry about this matter to Dr Joachim Bar of the Catholic Theology Academy of Warsaw, who was due to host Kolbe's beatification. *Tygodnik Powszechny* posted an editor's note based on Dr Bar's response beneath Lipski's letter of critique. The refutation in the editor's note stated that in May 1935, when the first issue of *Mały Dziennik* had come out, Father Kolbe was not directly involved in the editing. Kolbe was still in Nagasaki at the time. The editor's note included a letter sent by Kolbe in Nagasaki to the acting editor-in-chief of the Polish devotional magazine *Rycerz Niepokalanej* on 12 July 1935. In the letter, Kolbe advises the editor 'to refrain from unnecessary hostility toward other people, parties, or nations. . . . speaking of the Jews, I would devote great attention not to stir up accidentally nor to intensify to a greater degree the hatred of our readers against them'. The editor's note added that after returning to Poland in 1936, Kolbe immersed himself in his work at the Niepokalanów monastery, and the editors in Warsaw published the content included in *Mały Dziennik* autonomously, without Kolbe's intervention (*Tygodnik Powszechny*, 19 September 1971). This controversy quickly sank into obscurity once *Tygodnik Powszechny* had run an article, on page 1, on the day of Kolbe's beatification (17 October), about Cardinal Karol Wojtyła raising Father Kolbe to the honours of the altar (Wojtyła, *Tygodnik Powszechny*, 17 October 1971).[6]

Although the controversy surrounding Kolbe's anti-Semitism made headlines just before Ayako Sono arrived at Warsaw, there is not a single word about it from her. There is no knowing for sure if Sono either intentionally kept silent about this matter or had no knowledge of it in the first place. Nevertheless, she did leave a clue that invites conjecture. Sono talks about the fact that Kolbe employed many belligerent expressions when he was setting up the Militia Immaculatae (Rycerstwo Niepokalanej). Kolbe was actually prompted to found the Militia Immaculatae by demonstrations taking place in Rome in 1917 to celebrate Freemasonry's 200th anniversary. Citing Maria Winowska's biography of Kolbe, Sono explains that when Father Kolbe saw 'a black flag showing the Archangel St. Michael beneath the feet of Lucifer . . . beneath the windows of the Vatican. . . . Right then, [Father Kolbe] conceived the idea of organizing an active society to counteract Freemasonry and other slaves of Lucifer' (Sono 2016, 63, 65). Kolbe was, in fact, steadfastly opposed to the Freemasons, and in his writings, they were often portrayed as part of an axis of evil that also recruited socialists and Jews (Kolbe 2010, 7). *The Protocols of the Elders of Zion*, an anti-Semitic text fabricated to spread the Jewish conspiracy theory, was sometimes quoted as supporting evidence for this claim (Kolbe 2010, 42).

Kolbe's recollection of the Freemason demonstrations at Rome is something that comes up often whenever controversy about his anti-Semitism arises. Significantly, Sono devoted attention to this passage at the critical time of his imminent beatification. Looking at Sono's actions afterwards, it makes sense that she would have turned a deaf ear to Kolbe's anti-Semitism even if she had heard about it. In 2015, Sono became the talk of the press worldwide for a column she contributed to *Sankei Shimbun* that praised South African apartheid and racial segregation as a potential model for migration policy in Japan. She

400 *Jie-Hyun Lim*

came under fire again in 2016 for unreservedly making discriminatory comments about people with disabilities (Lies and Umekawa 2015; McNeill 2015). Sono has mostly played the role of ideologue for the Abe regime, and it makes sense that from her ideological point of view, Kolbe's alleged anti-Semitism was never a particular problem.

Sono's indifference to the suspicions surrounding Kolbe's anti-Semitism goes hand in hand with her enthusiastic support for Catholic nationalism. Her positive views of nationalism and patriotism are consistent with her criticism of Kenzaburo Oe's book-length essay *Okinawa Notes*. In 'The Story Behind the Myth: Group Suicides on Okinawa and Tokashiki Islands', Sono took issue with Oe's critique of the former commander of the Kerama Islands who ordered about 430 residents to commit mass suicide. She accused Oe of standing in the 'viewpoint of God' and judging the commander who ordered the suicides of the island residents as sinful. How Sono felt about this matter is apparent in the following passage:

> Why should those who made the beautiful sacrifice of giving up their lives for their country be made into something less clean, their deaths defiled by someone saying after the war that they were forced to kill themselves by military order?
>
> (Ōe 2018, 107–11)

In Sono's memory, the residents of the Kerama Islands who died in an act of forced mass suicide are aligned with Father Kolbe, who died a martyr's death at Auschwitz, because all of them 'made the beautiful sacrifice of giving up their lives'.

Around the time of Kolbe's canonization in 1982, the controversy about his anti-Semitism re-emerged in major media outlets, including the *New York Times* and the *Washington Post* (Cohen 1982; Kamm 1982). Any international Catholic intellectual would have struggled to feign ignorance. The issue came up again in an obituary for Gajowniczek published in the 15 March 1995 issue of the *New York Times* (Binder 1995). The question of Kolbe's anti-Semitism was brought up again in John Gross's review of Patricia Treece's biography of Kolbe, 'A Man for Others: Maximilian Kolbe, Saint of Auschwitz, in the Words of Those Who Knew Him', which was published in the 17 February 1983 issue of the *New York Review of Books*. In this case, Gross's claim was refuted by some readers in the letters to the editor section, and a reply from Gross followed (Gross 1983a, 1983b). There is no denying that Kolbe believed in the authenticity of *The Protocols of the Elders of Zion* and that he claimed that the Masonic Mafia was instigating atheistic Communism and international Zionism was the driving force behind this.

However, Father Kolbe was not an extreme racist, because although he advocated the conversion of Jews, he did not reject those who had converted. He also sheltered about 1,500 Jews who were fleeing Nazi persecution and sought refuge in the monastery of Niepokalanów, which paints him in a different light. Clearly, these were not the actions of a radical anti-Semite. According to a testimony by Rosalia Kobla, who lived near the monastery, Father Kolbe advised that she should also give Jews bread to eat 'because all men are our brothers'. As Kolbe's advocates have argued, of the more than 10,000 letters and 369 editorials and columns he wrote, only thirty-one mentioned the Jewish question, and in these, his main concern was the conversion of Jews to Catholicism (Modras 1989, 373). Kolbe's perspective was different from that of the extreme anti-Semites who even shunned the Jews who had converted to Christianity. Father Kolbe was, after all, a product of his time. And even though he will never be free of the charge of anti-Semitism, it would also have been unrealistic to expect him to adopt the kind of ecumenical viewpoint that accepts Judaism as another tradition of Christianity.

Whether or not Kolbe was an anti-Semite is not my primary concern in this chapter. I am more interested in interpreting Japanese Catholic intellectuals' silence over the controversy regarding Father Kolbe's anti-Semitism. Their persistent silence is even more puzzling when contrasted with the enthusiasm with which Kolbe has been revered among Japanese Catholics. It is not surprising that Ayako Sono, who commended the apartheid system of South Africa as a model for migration policy in Japan, would not be concerned about Father Kolbe's anti-Semitism. However, it is perplexing to see Shusaku Endō, deemed a comparatively liberal Catholic intellectual, also keeping silent on this matter. Reconciling his silence on Kolbe's anti-Semitism with his postcolonial engagement with Franz Fanon in Lyon in the 1950s is still a challenge. Could it be that the silence maintained by Japanese Catholic intellectuals has more to do with the memory culture of post-war Nagasaki, or Japanese society in general, rather than their personal ideological dispositions?

Grassroots memory in re-citing and re-timing

It was not until after Father Kolbe's canonization on 10 October 1982 that he began to be known as a martyr of Auschwitz throughout the world. But earlier, on 7 June 1979, Pope John Paul II had delivered a sermon during his first visit to his mother country of Poland since his election, in which he said that Father Kolbe and Sister Edith Stein of the Carmelite Convent signified the triumph of the Catholic faith (John Paul II 1979). In February 1981, when the pope visited Nagasaki, he paid his respects before Kolbe's statue in the Seibo no Kishi Monastery in Hongouchi. In April of 1982, Mother Teresa paid a visit to Nagasaki. In Japan around the same time, between November 1980 and February 1982, Shusaku Endō wrote *A Woman's Life* in serialized form for *Asahi Shimbun*, and in 1981 started to gather data on Father Kolbe in Nagasaki and launched a campaign to raise the funds to build a memorial centre dedicated to him. Also, in 1981, the Modern Film Association and the Women's Society of Saint Paul of Japan produced a film titled *The Life of Father Kolbe: The Miracle of Love in Auschwitz*, which won the best movie prize at the 3rd Japanese Red Cross Film Festival. Japan's interest in Kolbe was no less enthusiastic than in

402 Jie-Hyun Lim

Poland. Considering that the first Polish biographical film of Kolbe, *Life for Life* (*Życie za życie*), was not made until 1991 and a documentary about him was not aired on Polish television until 2007, the scope of the Kolbe memory cult in Nagasaki and Japan has been quite impressive.

After Father Kolbe was beatified, he could have come to be regarded in Poland as a symbol of martyrdom against atheist communism. However, the visibility of Father Kolbe's martyrdom quickly faded due to an incident on 19 October 1984, in which another priest, Father Jerzy Popiełuszko, was brutally murdered after being kidnapped by the Communist secret police (Kaufman 1984). The anti-communist vernacular memory culture in Poland bestowed the status of representative martyr upon Popiełuszko (who had been killed by an atheist communist) rather than Kolbe. The political significance of the murder of Father Popiełuszko, who had fallen victim to a communist crime, outweighed that of the death of Father Kolbe, who had been killed by the Nazis. While persecution by Nazis had become a faint memory, memory of persecution by Communists was fresh and vivid. Even into the 1990s, the iconic twentieth-century martyr of the Polish Catholic Church was considered to be Father Popiełuszko rather than Father Kolbe.[7] By and large, memory of Father Kolbe in Poland remained within the religious milieu until the 'War of the Crosses at Auschwitz' broke out in the mid-1990s (Zubrzycki 2006; Bogumił and Głowacka-Grajper 2019). Eventually, the Polish Senate declared 2011 – the seventieth anniversary of Father Kolbe's martyrdom – as the Year of Saint Maximilian Kolbe.

Father Kolbe's popularity in Japan comes from his status as a moral referent for the sanctification and remembrance of the Nagasaki Catholic victims. A comparison could easily be drawn between the Catholic atomic bomb victims in Nagasaki, who had given up their lives on the altar of world peace as a 'burnt offering', and Father Kolbe, who sacrificed his own life to save another in Auschwitz. This idea was not only shared by Catholic intellectuals like Takashi Nagai or Shusaku Endō but also by quite a few ordinary Japanese people. Visitor books from the Oura Saint Kolbe Memorial Museum and the Kolbe Museum of Seibo no Kishi, despite their fragmentary nature, offer a glimpse into the way in which the Japanese think about Father Kolbe. Based on the number of visitor book entries, Japanese visitors are the most numerous, followed by Koreans. The number of Polish visitors is also continually increasing. The visitor books show that Japanese visitors are from various backgrounds, while Koreans and Poles are mostly Catholic pilgrims. Polish visitors mainly express their joy at finding a trace of another Pole, Father Kolbe, in Nagasaki. Korean Catholic pilgrims' entries tend to focus more on their wish for national unification and peace as well as for the happiness and well-being of their families and local church. It is interesting to note that no Polish visitor mentions Auschwitz.

Compared with the entries by Koreans and Poles, those by the Japanese predominantly mention their memory of visiting Auschwitz and a prayer for peace. The entries by the Japanese also mostly acknowledge that it was through one of Endō's essays or novels that they found out about Father Kolbe. Another commonality among the remarks made by the Japanese that stands out is the mention of the Great East Japan Earthquake. There is a particularly interesting long message, left on 17 March 2014, by a second-generation atomic bomb survivor who said he was the same age as when Father Kolbe died as a martyr. He wrote about his mother's sudden death and the radiation leak from the Fukushima nuclear power plant, before reminding everyone who must carry on under a capitalist system relying on atomic energy of the legacy of Father Kolbe's noble life. An entry made on 24 June 2018 says that a book written by Brother Zeno, who worked as a missionary in Japan alongside Father Kolbe, brought immense consolation to the victims of the Great East Japan Earthquake in 2011.

Father Kolbe has become a symbol that not only binds together three memories, namely, memory of the Christian persecution in Tokugawa in Japan, the Holocaust at Auschwitz, and the atomic bombing of Nagasaki, but is also binding these memories to memory of a more recent event, the Great East Japan Earthquake of 11 March 2011. The combining of these four memories signifies a restructuring and reorganization of time that is modifying the historical meaning of the Kolbe memorials. This process is evidenced by the manner in which Japanese grassroots memories are summoning memory of Father Kolbe at Auschwitz as a point of reference enabling better comprehension of today's tragedies, and then 're-citing' and 're-timing' that memory of Kolbe so it can be integrated into discourse of the Great East Japan Earthquake of 2011. The visitor book entries written by Japanese visitors show how they are drawing associations between grassroots memories of Auschwitz, Nagasaki and Fukushima by crossing global memory space in different time frames.

Japanese visitors to the Kolbe memorials in Oura and Hongouchi have prompted a re-citing and re-timing of the memory of the atomic bombing in Nagasaki and of Kolbe at Auschwitz in order to embed the Great East Japan Earthquake in their remembrance of Japanese victimhood. As a museum visitor study undertaken by the Ammunition Hill Museum in East Jerusalem shows, such a strategy of 're-citing' and 're-timing' the past and distant memory tends to fortify collective ethnonational memory (Noy 2018). Also, memory culture in Nagasaki is not free from the critique that it is de-historicizing and de-contextualizing Kolbe's martyrdom. According to this critique, that memory culture is allowing people to forget about the controversy surrounding Kolbe's anti-Semitism and be content to place Kolbe in the sacred realm as a saint who achieved a miracle of love in Auschwitz. The de-historicized memory of Father Kolbe shares the same logical structure as post-war Japan's victimhood memory, in which Japanese colonial and war atrocities against its Asian neighbours are overlooked. Instead, all the emphasis has been placed on Japan's status as the first and only victim of an atomic bombing. The first step towards genuinely honouring the sacrifices made in Auschwitz and Nagasaki would be to shift the focus away from justification, rationalization and any sort of fossilization of the memory in order to bring the meaning of sacrifice to life. As Slavoj Žižek formulated paradoxically, the only way this can be accomplished is to sacrifice the sacrifice (Žižek 2009, 175–77).

404 *Jie-Hyun Lim*

Notes

1 This chapter cites Nagai's handwritten version of the eulogy because the version of the eulogy republished in *The Bell of Nagasaki* has been criticized for being quite different from the original. The original version of the handwritten eulogy was published recently in the form of a facsimile (Konishi 2014, 55–68). I don't think that difference is so fundamental. The issue of the disparity between a republished version and the original also appears, more seriously, between the version republished in 1949 in Japanese and another one translated into Korean in 2011. Whereas the 1949 version has, 'When Urakami has burnt into ashes, God finally accepts this, hears the wrongdoing of humanity and reveals this to our emperor and has him make the holy decision to end of the war', the Korean version completely omits the part about the emperor making a holy decision.
2 According to the late Prof. Feliks Tych, a former director of the Jewish History Institute in Warsaw, Yad Vashem in Israel and ŻIH in Warsaw had argued among themselves over which side had first used the term 'Holocaust'. Whoever was right in this debate dating back to the 1950s, Nagai Takashi had already used the term 'Holocaust' (*hansai*) in 1945.
3 That the character of Seikichi, whom Kiku loves with her life, has the same name as Takashi Nagai's real son is another interesting detail.
4 Ayako Sono intentionally uses the term 'patriotism' when referring to the nationalist sympathies of Kolbe's family. The Polish dichotomy between 'good nationalism' and 'bad nationalism' seems be to relevant here.
5 Obóz Narodowych Radykalnych (ONR) displayed historical continuity with the anti-Semitism prevalent during the interwar period by organizing a large anti-immigrant and anti-Muslim protest in large Polish cities in Poland, including Warsaw. The protest included far rightists and was organized on 11 November 2018 to mark the centenary of Poland's liberation.
6 Cardinal Wojtyła, who later became Pope John Paul II, was a big admirer of Kolbe's; he hosted the canonization of Kolbe and paid a visit to sites associated with Kolbe in Nagasaki. This explains why criticism against Kolbe's anti-Semitism was received as wider criticism directed against John Paul II and the entire Catholic Church (Karjski 2010, 3).
7 Father Popiełuszko was already regarded within the Catholic Church as a martyr who had been beatified on 6 June 2010 and was waiting to be canonized. In 2014, he became the official patron of NSZZ Solidarność.

References

Bandō, Hiroshi. 1995. *Pōrando jin to Nichiro sensō*. Tokyo: Aoki Shoten.
Binder, David. 1995. "Franciszek Gajowniczek Dead; Priest Died for Him at Auschwitz." *The New York Times*, March 15. Accessed May 31, 2020. www.nytimes.com/1995/03/15/obituaries/franciszek-gajowniczek-dead-priest-died-for-him-at-auschwitz.html.
Bogumił, Zuzanna, and Małgorzata Głowacka-Grajper. 2019. *Milieux de mémoire in Late Modernity: Local Communities, Religion and Historical Politics*. Berlin: Peter Lang.
Cheon, Eunok. 2013. "Nagasak'ip'yŏnghwagihaeng I." *Ohmynews*, April 13. Accessed May 31, 2020. www.ohmynews.com/NWS_Web/View/at_pg.aspx?CNTN_CD=A0001857267.
Cohen, Richard. 1982. "Sainthood." *The Washington Post*, December 14. Accessed May 31, 2020. www.washingtonpost.com/archive/local/1982/12/14/sainthood/899d8e06-3209-4fd6-90de-d6798f76ee57/?noredirect=on.
"Editor's Note." 1971. *Tygodnik Powszechny* 38 (1182) (19 September).
Endō, Shusaku. 1986. *Onnano Isshō, Ippu • Kiku no baai, Yŏjaŭi ilsaeng, Part 1, Kik'uŭi kyŏngu*. Translated by Mun-hye Kong. Seoul: Hongseongsa.
———. 1996. *Kokoro no Yasoukyoku, Маŭmŭi yasanggok*. Seoul: Hongseongsa.
———. 2017. *Onnano Isshō, Nibu • Sachu no baai*. Tokyo: Shinchōsha.

Juxtaposition in the Japanese mnemoscape 405

———. 2018. *Korube Sinpu, Shinpen Kokugo Sōgō, Kaitēban.* Tokyo: Daishūkan Shoten.

Gross John. 1983a. "Life Saving." *The New York Review of Books*, February 17. Accessed May 31, 2020. www.nybooks.com/articles/1983/02/17/life-saving/.

———. 1983b. "Kolbe and Anti-Semitism." *The New York Review of Books*, April 14. Accessed May 31, 2020. www.nybooks.com/articles/1983/04/14/kolbe-anti-semitism-2/.

Hill, Christopher. 2014. "Crosse Geographies: Endō and Fanon in Lyon." *Representations* 128: 1.

Immaculate Conception Province Conventual Franciscans of Japan. 2005. *Sei Korube Rainichi Shichijugo Shūnen Kineneshi.* Nagasaki: Seibo no Kishisha.

Kamm, Henry. 1982. "The Saint of Auschwitz Is Canonized by Pope." *The New York Times*, October 11. Accessed May 31, 2020. www.nytimes.com/1982/10/11/world/the-saint-of-auschwitz-is-canonized-by-pope.html.

Karjski, Stanisław. 2010. "Przedmowa." In *Św. Maksymilian Maria Kolbe o masonerii i Żydach: pisma wybrane.* Krzeszowice: Dom Wydawniczy Ostoja.

Kaufman, Michale. 1984. "Poles Vow to Continue Slain Priest's Masses." *The New York Times*, 26 November. Accessed May 31, 2020. www.nytimes.com/1984/11/26/world/poles-vow-to-continue-slain-priest-s-masses.html.

Kieniewicz, Jan. 2013. "The Eastern Frontiers and the Civilisational Dimension of Europe." *Acta Poloniae Historica* 107.

Kolbe, Maksymilian. 2010. *Św. Maksymilian Maria Kolbe o masonerii i Żydach: pisma wybrane.* Krzeszowice: Dom Wydawniczy Ostoja

Konishi, Tetsuro. 2014. "The Original Manuscript of Takashi Nagai's Funeral Address at a Mass for the Victims of the Nagasaki Atomic Bomb." *Journal of Nagasaki University of Foreign Studies* 18.

Kopp, Kristin. 2012. *Germany's Wild East: Constructing Poland as Colonial Space.* Ann Arbor: University of Michigan Press.

Kwon, Hyuktae. 2014. "Nagasak' iŭi chongŭn ŏttŏk' eullyŏnna?" Accessed May 29, 2020. http://h21.hani.co.kr/arti/culture/culture_general/38589.html.

Levi, Primo. 1989. *The Drowned and the Saved.* Translated by Raymond Rosenthal. New York: Vintage Books.

Lies, Elaine, and Umekawa Takashi. 2015. "Japan PM Ex-adviser Praises Apartheid in Embarrassment for Abe." *Reuters*, February 13. Accessed May 31, 2020. www.reuters.com/article/us-japan-apartheid/japan-pm-ex-adviser-praises-apartheid-in-embarrassment-for-abe-idUSKBN0LH0M420150213.

Lim, Jie-Hyun. 2010. "Victimhood Nationalism in Contested Memories- National Mourning and Global Accountability." In *Memory in a Global Age: Discourses, Practices and Trajectories*, edited by Aleida Assmann and Sebastian Conrad. Basingstoke: Palgrave Macmillan.

Lipski, Jan Józef. 1971. "Ojciec Kolbe i *Mały Dziennik.*" *Tygodnik Powszechny* 38 (1182) (19 September).

Maclelland, Gwyn. 2015. "Guilt, Persecution, and Resurrection in Nagasaki: Atomic Memories and the Urakami Catholic Community." *Social Science Japan Journal* 18 (2).

McNeill, David. 2015. "Japanese Prime Minister Urged to Embrace Apartheid for Foreign Workers." *Independent*, February 13. Accessed May 31, 2020. www.independent.co.uk/news/world/asia/japanese-prime-minister-urged-to-embrace-apartheid-for-foreign-workers-10045647.html.

Modras, Ronald. 1989. "John Paul, St. Maximilian and anti-Semitism." In *Martyrs of Charity Part 2.* Washington, DC: St. Maximilian Kolbe Foundation.

Moses, A. Dirk. 2012. "The Holocaust and World History." In *The Holocaust and Historical Methodology*, edited by Dan Stone. New York: Berghahn Books.

406 *Jie-Hyun Lim*

Nagai, Takashi. 2010. *Horobinu mono wo. Yŏngwŏnhan kŏsŭl*. Translated by Sŭngu Lee. Seoul: Paorottal.

———. 2015. *Rosario no Kusari. Mukchual*. Translated by Sŭngu Lee. Seoul: Paorottal.

Noy, Chaim. 2018. "Memory, Media, and Museum Audience's Discourse of Remembering." *Critical Discourse Studies* 15 (1).

Ōe, Kenzaburō. 2018. *Teigishū. Marŭi chŏngŭi*. Revised Korean Translation by Tae-uk Song. Seoul: Myujint' ŭri.

Ozaki, Tōmei. 2006. *Nagasak'iŭi k'olbe*. Translated by Hee-il Kim. Geyeonggido: sŏngmogisahoe.

Paul II, John. 1979. "Apostolic Pilgrimage to Poland, Holy Mass at the Concentration Camp, Homily of His Holiness John Paul II." *Auschwitz-Bierkenau*, June 7. Accessed May 31, 2020. https://w2.vatican.va/content/john-paul-ii/en/homilies/1979/documents/hf_jp-ii_hom_19790607_polonia-brzezinka.html.

Sono, Ayako. 2016. *Miracles: A Novel*. Translated by Kevin Doak. Portland: Merwin Asia.

Southhead, Susan. 2016. *Nagasaki: Life After Nuclear War*. New York: Penguin Books.

Takahashi, Shinji. 1994. *Nagasaki ni atte Tetsugaku suru*. Tokyo: Hokuju.

Treat, John W. 1995. *Writing Ground Zero: Japanese Literature and the Atomic Bomb*. Chicago: University of Chicago Press.

Wojtyła, Kardynał Karol. 1971. "Znak Naszej Epoki." *Tygodnik Powszechny* 42 (1186) (September 17).

Wolff, Larry. 1994. *Inventing Eastern Europe*. Stanford, CA: Stanford University Press.

Žižek, Slavoj. 2009. *Shich'ajŏng kwanjŏm*. Translated by Seoyoung Kim. Seoul: Mat'i.

Zubrzycki, Geneviève. 2006. *The Crosses of Auschwitz: Nationalism and Religion in Post-Communist Poland*. Chicago: University of Chicago Press.

Afterword

From *Religion as a Chain of Memory* to memory from a postsecular perspective

Kathy Rousselet

While reflecting on the place of religion in the early 1990s, both in the French context and across highly secularized Western societies more broadly, French sociologist Danièle Hervieu-Léger (2000) defined religion as a 'chain of memory'. In the context of late modernity, she argues, the traditional forms of religious activity are losing their significance due to the increasing individualization of belief. Religion is not only developing outside institutions but also changing its form, so that it has become difficult to distinguish what is religious and what is not. Hervieu-Léger deals with the difficulties inherent in defining religion by proposing memory as a pivotal element. Religion, she says, is 'the particular form of believing which draws its legitimacy from reference to a tradition' (2000, 101). Thus, being religious in modernity increasingly means 'not so much knowing oneself begotten[1] as willing oneself so to be' (2000, 167). Moreover, choosing to belong to a small community is a more general element of high religious modernity.

This definition of religion, with its central reference to a tradition and lineage of beliefs, was initially elaborated with respect to the dissemination of belief in the West. It could, however, be deployed to analyze other contexts, not least post-communist societies. In Western Europe, Hervieu-Léger (1999) identified two seminal forms of new believer: the pilgrim and the convert. The pilgrim is characterized by the fluidity of his or her spiritual journey. Similarly, the anthropologist Zhanna Kormina (2019) identifies what she calls 'Orthodox nomads' in Russia, by which she means religious seekers who are in search of authenticity yet distance themselves from any institution.

It is clear that several contributions in this book are inspired by the work of Hervieu-Léger. In a comparative perspective, however, the definition of religion that she uses prompts us to look more closely at the relationship between tradition and religion(s), as well as at the vehicles of authority and the attitude of social actors towards institutions, be they religious or secular. Religious institutions occupy a different place in public space in Eastern as opposed to Western Europe. Even though Russian society is plural, it is pertinent to ask whether being religious in Russia (within the context of desecularization from above) means *knowing* oneself begotten rather than *willing* oneself to be. Furthermore, in the context studied by Hervieu-Léger, the central question

DOI: 10.4324/9781003264750-25

concerns the characterization of belief: we believe as our ancestors believed. But in societies such as Russia or Ukraine, it seems that religion is more a matter of practice. Religion therefore becomes the particular form of practice that draws its legitimacy from reference to a tradition.

Considering religion as a 'chain of memory' linked to a tradition is part of a wider reflection on the quest for continuity, especially in a post-communist context where, in the past, both researchers and politicians have emphasized discontinuity, notably in attitudes towards belief and practice. Secularization, however, has permeated both Western and post-communist societies, even if the sources are different in each case. And once lineages of belief have been largely disrupted, or even interrupted, religious and national institutions have, it seems, rediscovered and reinvented religious continuity. Moreover, the process has at times produced conflict between the new authorities and those who tried to maintain tradition at all costs during communist times. It follows that the religious practices that were maintained during the period of state atheism have been questioned by the current ecclesiastical authorities. The consequent rediscovery of theological ideas has provoked new debates – questions that are being revisited today, making use of the Internet and the appearance of 'fake icons' or 'fake-liturgical texts'.

Belief is increasingly unlikely to be transmitted in twenty-first-century Europe. But the legacies of the past remain. Religious traditions are being conveyed by both secular and religious actors who are particularly keen to affirm the cultural and moral aspects of the lineage. In most East European countries, traditions are being reinvented within a context of post-atheism, secularized societies and desecularization from above. In all these respects, they constitute a rich laboratory for studying the complex entanglements between religious, humanist and secularist positions that are not only present in post-communist contexts[2] but also in late modern societies more generally. They also make it possible to highlight the roles of actors characterized by researchers as nonreligious or postreligious.

This fascinating book, which adopts a postsecular approach, contributes to renewed reflection on the role of religion and memory, not only in the sociology of religion, but more especially, in memory studies. Up to now, scant attention has been paid to how religious factors influence the formation and evolution of memory in a field where secular approaches have largely dominated. In what follows, I have selected some of the threads that seem to me to link the different contributions set out in these chapters, connecting them where possible to the wider literature.

The sacralization of memory by legitimate secular and religious institutions

It is through re-reading the past that religious institutions legitimize themselves. While the religious landscape is becoming more pluralized, historical Churches, in cooperation with the political authorities, are competing to present themselves as authentic and to defend their status as 'traditional religions'. A process of 'patrimonialization' is most evident in the Ukrainian context, where Church-building is occurring at the same time as nation- and state-building, and where several institutions represent the same religious tradition. But the same phenomenon can be found elsewhere.

In postcolonial or post-conflict contexts, both secular and religious institutions value the nation and the homeland: they re-read the past by sacralizing events and places. In post-traumatic situations, the religious narrative becomes a narrative of salvation called upon when the past seems impossible to contemplate. For example, in the absence of international recognition, victims of the Armenian genocide were canonized by the Armenian Apostolic Church in 2015. And as the secular authorities deny and forget the Great Terror in Russia, the Russian Orthodox Church has taken up the memory of the many victims, canonizing some as New Martyrs. In so doing, the memory of the victims is not only sacralized but consolidated, rendering the traumatic events undeniable. At the same time, historical and political debate is largely avoided.

The mutual enhancement of secular memory and religious experience

Secular memory and religious experience can compete, as shown by the conflicts that have arisen over the use of religious buildings, such as Saint Isaac's Cathedral in Saint Petersburg. But they can also feed into each other. In the outskirts of Moscow, for example, at the Butovo Museum, where the bullets found in the mass grave or the everyday objects of a new saint are exhibited, the visitor is invited to share very immediately the experience of the prisoner: he or she enters an obscure, reconstructed barrack, accompanied by a background soundtrack. The aim is to trigger in the visitor an experience of memory that provokes affect and emotions, which can in turn nourish a specifically religious reaction.

Such a process makes up for the absence of the body of a saint, the traditional accompaniment to veneration in the history of the Church. In other words, this museum, like others, solves the 'problem of presence' and highlights the importance of supporting objects, smells and sounds. As for the religious dimension, this nourishes the experience of remembrance. Thus, hymns to the New Martyrs are an example of memory translated into religious language: they invite us to remember as well as to pray. Indeed, in some cases, the act of remembrance and religious experience are brought together in the very space in which the icon of the saint and the documentation of their life coexist. All that said, another question still arises: how does social memory, and in particular family memory, cohabit with the desire for 'impersonality' that exists in ritual memory?

The religious reading of the past and the political order

Both religious traditions and religious commemorations follow a specific political grammar. Reinvented religious traditions are woven according to a narrative of suffering or heroic memory in affinity with the political order. For example, in post-Maidan Ukraine, the Greek-Catholic Church emphasizes the Christian understanding of the heroic death. At the same time, the context of nationalism and its framework of 'us and them' are provoking a collision between religious traditions, the rise of fundamentalism, the increasing labelling of extremist threat and the presence in public life of certain religious traditions to the detriment of others, which is being supported by political institutions at national or local level.

Clearly, religious institutions are not only giving a new lease of life to more or less forgotten saints but filling the past with new saints who take on the role of heroes. Social networks contribute to their reputation and eventually ensure their pluralization. These processes, which can be observed in the Catholic, Orthodox and Armenian worlds, respond to the impulse of religious institutions to evangelize when faced with the loss of influence of the religious and the accelerated diversification of the religious offer (Michel 2011). The multiplication of saints ensures a strengthening of the legitimacy of religious institutions. However, behind their performative discourses, which present the saints as religious and moral examples, the true role of these saints in the universe of believers has yet to be demonstrated. This undoubtedly varies according to the religious culture in question and the specific saint being considered. In fact, the recent history of the veneration of New Martyrs in Russia shows that many of them have already been forgotten. But their role goes far beyond the world of believers; it is equally secular and political. In an increasingly patriotic and militarized Russia, for example, Alexander Nevsky occupies a prominent place and is presented as a warrior saint even though his image has become more pluralist; he also represents opposition to the West. Secular actors, and in particular historians and politicians, are contributing to the reputation of the canonized figures and the writing of their vitae. In contexts where politics is avoided in public space, saints become transmitters of political messages. The Russian imperial family offer another good example of this (Rousselet 2011).

Religious commemorations are shaped politically. At the end of the 1980s, in an international moment that linked political liberalism and religious freedom, the official commemoration of the baptism of Rus', which was followed by numerous individual baptisms, became a signal to the international community that the Soviet Union was emerging from state atheism and undergoing transformation. In post-traumatic contexts, the place of the individual in society, as well as more generally the relations between the individual and the collective, are thought out in various ways by social actors. Political logic cannot ignore the logic of ritual memory that selects elements of collective memory and, as already indicated, impersonalizes the saint. But the modalities of religious commemorations, which often take place in the absence of the remains of the victims, also have a political dimension. According to the varied grammars of politics, some emphasize the importance of naming and praying for each individual, while others, conversely, think about the history and future of a country rather than individual destinies. Some focus on a single social or national category, while others address all victims at the same time or create an opposition between the victims and the perpetrators.

Religious concepts as a tool for political language

Political language is increasingly using notions of belonging to the religious order, sometimes without the mediation of religious actors. Thus, religious notions are taking on secular connotations. In the later years of the Soviet Union, repentance was regarded by intellectuals and political actors as a tool for moral change that was crucial for the transformation of society and entry into a new political order. This notion of repentance was introduced in the Soviet Union at the end of the 1980s, largely through the Georgian film *Pokaianie* (*Repentance* [1987]), directed by Tengiz Abuladze, which was in essence an appeal for a trial of the past and for justice. In 1998, the call for repentance on the occasion of the commemoration of the assassination of the imperial family was taken up by both religious and political authorities.

In reconciliation policies, as shown by the example of South Africa, religious actors can themselves be the initiators of the process. But the religious notions that are used are often transformed by political actors. In post-dictatorial Chile, for example, the notions of God, forgiveness, soul and reconciliation used by Cardinal Henriquez were taken up by the political actors in the transition to democracy; the meaning of the 'soul of Chile' evolved in the discourses of the three presidents of the republic (Diaz 2014). Sometimes religious language is used by political groups who distance themselves from any kind of religion. When used to frame public debates, the rhetoric of forgiveness may convey less a Christian grammar than a grammar supportive of a demand for justice (Ben Hounet, Lefranc, and Puccio-Den 2014). In the Chinese context, the candle-light vigil commemorating the Tiananmen Square massacre urges solidarity with the survivors, truth, justice and the democratization of China.

I have listed a few examples of the subtle entanglements between memory and religion analyzed from a postsecular perspective. They display the religious and political grammars of contemporary societies as well as the relations between religious and political institutions, on the one hand, and political orders, on the other. As Hervieu-Léger (2015, 2017) explains in a more recent text written in homage to Grace Davie, political grammars have an effect on religious memory, just as religious grammars influence political memory and, more broadly, social and political practices in highly secularized societies. These entanglements allow us to attest that religious or secular institutions, through their interpretation of events, places and objects from the past, constantly provoke affects and emotions that create links in a wide variety of ways. They allow us to conclude that as the religious and the secular become progressively more hybridized, the boundaries being built between them by entrepreneurs of memory and a wide variety of social actors are becoming increasingly porous.

412 *Kathy Rousselet*

Notes

1 Here, 'begotten' was used within the context of looking to connect with a community in order to construct one's self-identity in a world in which one feels adrift.
2 This approach is close to that of Tobias Köllner (2018).

References

Ben, Hounet Yazid, Sandrine Lefranc, and Deborah Puccio-Den, eds. 2014. *Justice, Religion, réconciliation*. Paris: L'Harmattan, Collection de l'AFSR.

Diaz, Paola. 2014. "Thérapeutique politique de l'âme nationale. Une analyse du discours réconciliateur dans le Chili post dictatorial (1990–2004)." In *Justice, religion, réconciliation*, directed by Y. Ben Hounet, S. Lefranc and D. Puccio, 27–40. Paris: L'Harmattan, Collection de l'AFSR.

Hervieu-Léger Danièle. 1999. *Le pélerin et le converti. La religion en mouvement*. Paris: Flammarion.

———. 2000. *Religion as a Chain of Memory*. Translated by Simon Lee. New Brunswick, NJ: Rutgers University Press.

———. 2015. "Religion as a Grammar of Memory: Reflections on a Comparison Between Britain and France." In *Modernities, Memory and Mutations. Grace Davie and the Study of Religion*, edited by A. Day and M. Lovheim, 13–30. London: Ashgate.

———. 2017. "Grammaires politiques de la mémoire religieuse, grammaires religieuses de la mémoire politique: les cas britannique et français en perspective comparative." *Archives de sciences sociales des religions* 178: 197–220.

Köllner, Tobias, ed. 2018. *Orthodox Religion and Politics in Contemporary Eastern Europe: On Multiple Secularisms and Entanglements*. New York: Routledge.

Kormina, Zhanna. 2019. *Palomniki. Etnograficheskie ocherki pravoslavnogo nomadizma*. Moscow: High School of Economics.

Michel, Patrick. 2011. "Sanguinis effusione aut heroico virtutum exercitio – Éléments pour une anthropologie politique de la production et des usages contemporains de la sainteté canonisée." *Critique Internationale* 3 (52): 111–27.

Rousselet, Kathy. 2011. "Constructing Moralities Around the Tsarist Family." In *Multiple Moralities and Religions in Post-Soviet Russia*, edited by Jarrett Zigon, 146–67. New York: Berghahn Books.

Index

1913 Bucharest Treaty 229
1917 Revolution *see* revolution
Abe regime 400
Abraham 389
abrahamic 29, 31, 35
Abuladze, Tengiz 411
Afanasy: archbishop of Holmogory 334; bishop of Kovrov 287
Aleksy II 98, 100, 103
Alexander, Jeffrey 270
Aliti, Abdurahman 226
Allah 279
Alraid Association 268, 278, 281n13
Ammunition Hill Museum in East Jerusalem 403
Anatolian: ancestors 73, 77
Anderson, Benedict 372
Anselmo Fr 397
anti-Bolshevik 374
anti-Catholic 117; *see also* anti-Church; anti-religious
anti-Church 157, 159–62, 166, 169, 174; *see also* anti-Catholic; anti-religious
anti-clericalism 146, 169
anti-communism 134, 141–2, 146, 158, 162, 167, 168, 174, 228, 232, 371, 374, 401
anti-democratic 162, 163
anti-fascist 143, 225, 228
Anti-Fascist Assembly of the National Liberation of Macedonia (AANLM) 225–30
anti-Nazis 36, 139, 158, 164
anti-popular 162, 163, 166, 174
anti-religious 33, 39, 41, 157, 166, 174, 267; *see also* anti-Catholic; anti-Church
anti-Semitism 60, 139, 162, 164, 255–6, 257, 260, 388, 398, 399, 400–1, 403, 404n5, 404n6
anti-Soviet 36, 280
anti-Stalinist 36

anti-terrorist operation (ATO)
anti-Western 112, 117, 120, 395
Apartheid 399, 401
Aquinas, Thomas 136
Aram I 82, 83
Archangel St. Michael 399
Archbishop Jovan (Vraniškovski) 227
Archbishop Stefan 227
Arctic 329, 330, 331, 332, 333, 338, 341, 342, 343, 344, 345n1, 345n6
Arctic Sea 329, 332
Arkhangelsk 333, 334
Armenia 36, 69, 70, 72, 75; soviet 73, 74, 76–81, 82, 83, 84
Armenian Apostolic Church 69, 77–82, 409
Armenian Communist Party 73
Armenian Genocide Memorial Complex 74
Armenian Socialist Republic *see* Armenia, soviet
Arrow Cross regime 159, 164, 175n6
Asad, Talal 10, 11, 13, 18, 309
Asia-Pacific War 391
Assmann, Aleida 4
Assmann, Jan 3–4, 5, 6, 15, 30, 31, 32, 205, 269, 284
Association of Jewish Organizations and Communities (VAAD) 201, 206, 208, 210, 211, 213, 215
Assyrian Orthodox Church 82
Astrakhan 298
Atatürk 72
atheist 332, 402
atomic bomb 388–403; *see also* bombing; Hiroshima; Nagasaki
Auschwitz 20, 35, 36, 54, 55, 56, 58, 60, 63n6, 63n8, 134, 135, 381, 388, 389, 391, 394, 395, 397, 398, 400–3
Auschwitz-Birkenau *see* Auschwitz
Austria 50, 71, 139, 202, 396

414 *Index*

Austria-Hungary 138
Azerbaijan 74, 75, 77

Ba'al Shem Tov *see* ben Eliezer, Israel
Badiou, Alain 271
Balkan 224
Bar, Joachim 399
Baranek family 254, 257, 260
Barents Region 329, 342, 345n1
Bartholomew I 102, 103
Belz 353
Benedict XIV 135
Benedict XV 373
ben Eliezer, Israel 348
Benjamin, Walter 302
Berlin Wall 314
Betts, Peter 168
Bezbozhnik 298, *299*
Bieler, Andrea 269, 270, 273, 274
Black Sea xx, 299
Bolsheviks 72, 138, 140, 289, 298, 336, 373
Bolshevism 140
bombing 17, 20, 344, 389, 391, 393, 394, 403; *see also* atomic bomb
Borisoglebsk 234
Borzęcin 259, 260
Brak, Bnei 353
Brandenburg 310, 311, 319
Breslov Hasidism 348, 351–65; *see also* Hasidic; Jews
Brest Agreement 89
Brigade of the Polish Legions 397
Brzezinski, Marek 318
Buddhism 186, 187, 189, 194
Buddhist 188, 195
Bulgaria xxiii, 79, 230, 231
Bulgarian Orthodox Church 223
Buneva, Mara 19, 237n17; commemoration 223, 224, 230–5
Butcher, Brian A. 285, 304
Butovo Museum 409
Byzantine Church 78
Byzantine Empire *see* Byzantium
Byzantium 78, 115, 120, 298

canonization 127n2, 133, 135–7, 158, 173, 257, 286, 291, 337, 341, 400, 401, 404n6; commission 296
Cardinal Angelo Amato 81
Cardinal Henriquez 411
Čarnogurský, Ján 144, 145
Catherine II 335

Catholic Church 36, 81, 100, 202, 203, 227, 236n12, 312, 365n11; Hungarian 19, 157, 159–61, 166, 171–3; Japanese 396, 398, 404n6; Polish 243, 371, 373, 376, 382, 385, 402; Slovak 134, 135, 136, 141, 143–4, 151; *see also* Catholicism; Christianity
Catholic Club 397
Catholicism 5, 50, 52, 55, 56, 60, 61, 79, 91, 100, 137, 138, 147, 160, 207, 243, 247, 251, 260, 370, 371, 389, 390, 392, 396, 398, 401; *see also* Catholic Church; Christianity
Cemetery of the Fallen 379
Chabad-Lubavitch 353, 358
chain of memory xxii, 1, 29, 32, 91, 204, 321, 351, 364, 407, 408; *see also* Hervieu-Léger, Daniele; memory
Chaodu 188, 194, 195, 197
Chile 75, 411
China 181–97, 411
Chinese Communist Party 183
Chodówki forest 257, *258*, 260
Chorny, Rafail 361
Christensen, Hyldal 306n1
Christian Democratic Movement (KDH) 144, 145
christianitas 114
Christianity 117, 122, 140, 173, 191, 194, 195, 197, 248, 284, 329, 339, 398, 401; orthodox 127n4, 202, 217, 364; *see also* Catholic Church; Catholicism
Christianization 90–6, 98, 99, 101, 102, 104–6, 114; *see also* Kyivan Rus'
Christ Saviour Church 291
Chryzostom Korec, Ján 143, 144
civil 31, 38, 40, 42, 211, 212, 217, 334; duty 207; religion 16, 37, 50, 63n4, 371; rights 63n3, 181, 271; society 40, 203, 204, 206; war 85n1, 206, 207, 210, 211, 213, 215, 288, 336, 370
civilization 119, 146, 331
Cold War 18, 134, 141, 156, 167, 168, 151
colonialism 396, 397
Committee for Nationalities and Deported Citizens 277
communism 7, 36, 52, 56–8, 60, 61, 74, 80, 81, 142, 144, 150, 158, 160, 173, 174, 290, 376, 400, 402; anti 134, 141, 146, 162, 167
communitas 193
community 29, 50, 84, 91, 103, 171, 200, 201, 204, 205, 206, 211, 212, 244,

260, 268, 319, 334, 357, 358, 364, 371, 372, 379, 407; Armenian 69, 72, 81; Buddhist 195; Catholic 166, 256, 365n11; Christian 80, 193; Hungarian 167, 170, 172; international 145, 410; Islamic 227, 236n12; Jewish 15, 213, 227, 236n12, 246, 258, 350–3, 358, 362; local 245, 246, 247, 250, 252, 254, 258, 318, 320–2, 370, 373–9, 383–5; Muslim 268–70, 277, 280; national 6, 84, 147, 257, 373, 378; religious 14, 101, 119, 205, 227, 308, 312, 318, 320–2, 372, 381; Romani 259; Sámi 340–2, 349
Conference of Slovak Bishops 150
confessors *see* New Martyrs
Confucianism 189–91, 194, 195, 197
Constantinople 44n4, 78, 79, 81, 93, 94, 98, 102, 103, 203, 236n4
Coptic Orthodox Church 82
Cossack 354, 356
Council for the Protection of Struggle and Martyrdom Sites 380
Crimea 104, 204, 211, 214, 217, 218n16, 267–80, 280n5, 280n7, 281n12, 281n14; annexation 214, 356
Crimean Khanate 267, 268
cross 11, 18; 41, 49, 50, 62, 82, 122, 169, 247, 258, 259, 261n2, 261n4, 341, 361, 365n11, 381, 382; Auschwitz 54–8, 398; defenders 57, 59, 60, *61*; Katyń 58–61; Millennium 229; Red 261n3, 401; sacred religio-secular symbol 50–4; Virtuti Militari 373, 378
Csordas, Thomas 245
Czechoslovakia 138, 144

Daoism 186, 187, 189, 194, 195, 197
David, Magen 247
Davie, Grace 5, 18, 20, 411
Davydiuk, Vladyslav 351
Day of the Deportation of the Crimean Tatars 273, 274
Deleuze, Gilles 271
Democratic Federal Macedonia 225
Democratic Movement and Association of Catholic Organizations in Support of Patriotic Democratic Movements in China 191
Denmark 329, 345n3
Deportation Armenian 72; Crimean Tatars 212, 267–81; Jews 143
diaspora Armenian 69–83, 85n3; Hungarian 172; Macedonian 223, 226,

228, 229, 232; Russian 117, 127n4; Slovak 19; Ukrainian 89
Dink, Hrant 14
Doły Biskupie 380
Domańska, Ewa 244
Donbas 19, 104, 200–17, 218n16, 219n19, 356
Donskoy Monastery 298
Douglas, Mary 245
Drugie Doły 247, 250
Durkheim, Emil 49, 54, 62, 63n4

Eisenstein, Sergey 290
émigrés 63n3, 140, 141–5, 236n9
Endō, Shusaku 394–8, 401, 402
Erll, Astrid 362
Ethiopian Orthodox Church 82
Eucharist 285, 192
Euromaidan 207, 209, 212, 216, 217
European Union 12, 312, 314, 365n3
European Values Study 311
Euroregion Pomerania 314
Evangelical: Church in Germany (EKD) 311, 316, 323n7; Church of Berlin and Upper Lusatia (EKBO) 319, 320; Lutheran Church 323n7, 341; *see also* Lutheran; Protestant
Evvan 339, 340

Fanon, Franz 397, 401
Fascism 56, 74, 162
Feklyunina Valentina 119
Filaret (Denysenko) 97, 98, 101, 105, 107n6, 206, 210, 211, 213
Finland 20, 329, 330, 332, 333, 340, 341, 343, 345n1, 345n4, 345n6
First Armenian Republic 72, 81
First World War 70, 71, 72, 85n1, 139, 231, 318, 330, 379, 397
Florensky, Pavel 285, 287
France 70, 75, 79, 83, 91, 93, 190
Francis (Pope) 81
Fukushima 403

Gajowniczek, Franciszek 389, 395, 397, 398, 400
Gartz 318
Geghard Holy Lance 82
generation 6, 84, 105, 123, 141, 144, 150, 151, 184, 185, 193, 225, 234, 254, 272, 276, 280, 285, 288, 358, 403
Genesis 389
George V 81

416 *Index*

Georgia 36, 83
Ger 353
German Democratic Republic (GDR) 311, 314, 318
German–Polish Memorial for Flight, Expulsion and a New Beginning 312
Gębice 379, 380, 382, 384
Glazunov, Ilia 293, 293n14.2
Gligorov, Kiro 226
glory 37, 38, 41, 116, 124, 125, 369, 370, 379
Gogol, Nikolai 354
Golgotha 41, 82; Road of the Polish Nation 378, 379, 381–4
Gorbachev, Mikhail 74, 95, 96, 97
Gosheva, Ekaterina 233
Gospel 50, 81, 166, 255, 381
Grand Prince Vladimir 293
Great Cilician House 82
Great East Japan Earthquake 403
Great Terror 40, 286, 409
Greece 231
Greek-Catholic Church 410
Grense museum 343
Grenzsituation 33, 35, 44n2
Gryfino 318
Guerrilla 258, 273, 334
Gul, Abdullah 77
Gulag 37, 43, 286, 287, 290

Halakha 247, 258, 261n3
Halbwachs, Maurice 2–5, 16, 32, 33, 38, 44n1, 44n7, 136, 269, 369
Haller, Józef 373
Hasidic 17, 20, 348–50, 352–65, 365n2; *see also* Breslov Hasidism
Hayasaka Bishop 396
Haytarma 273, 274, 275, 280
Hegumen Ionafan 341
hermeneutics 181, 182
Hervieu-Léger, Daniele xxii, 5, 16, 29, 91–3, 106, 321, 407, 411; *see also* chain of memory
Hideyoshi, Toyotomi 391
Hiroshima 392; *see also* atomic bomb; Nagasaki
Hisashi, Inoue 393
Hizb ut-Tahrir 268, 281n14
Hlinka, Andrej 138, 139, 147
Holocaust 12, 17, 19, 20, 33–6, 55–6, 73, 243, 246–50, 256–8, 330, 350, 351, 358, 364, 388, 389, 391, 393, 403, 404n2; Armenian 70, 71; Japanese 388, 389; Urakami 391–5; *see also* Auschwitz

Holodomor 37, 355
Holy Cross Mountain 370, 382
Holy Mother 390, 396; *see also* Virgin Mary
Holy Rus' 42, 94, 288, 290, 331, 332, 338
Holy See 63n5
Hondo, Shuntaro 396, 397
Hong Kong 182–97, 197n2
Hongouchi Seminary 390, 401, 403
Honig, Raźla 246
Honta, Ivan 354–6, 361–5, 365n13, 365n13; *see also* Zalizniak, Maxym
Höhn, Hans Joachim 310, 311, 317
Hrushevskyi, Mykhailo 94
Hungary vi, 37, 138, 139, 156–75, 175n6
hymnography 20, 40, 284–306

icon 54, 123, 158, 161, 167, 174, 286, 338, 343, 409; *Assembly of New Martyrs* 286–306; Eternal Russia 293
iconography 15, 40, 52, 115, 117, 125, 284–306, 339
Ilinden 19, 223–35, 236n8, 236n10, 237n13
imaginarium 246, 257, 344
Indian Assyrian Orthodox Church 82
International Romani Caravan of Memory 259
Internal Macedonian Revolutionary Organization (IMRO) 231–2, 234
Iron Curtain 156, 158, 161, 167, 169, 172, 174, 352, 365n5, 365n7
Islam 71, 72, 78, 93, 209, 211, 217, 267–80
Israel 192, 208, 288, 348, 353, 358, *360*, 404n2
Ivan the Terrible 290, 303
Izborsk Club 120–1

January Uprising 52
Japan 20; post-war 388–403
Jarno, Józef 257
Jerusalem 16, 78, 80, 255, 353, 403
Jesus Christ 42, *51*, 52, 192–5, 255, 256, 257, 360, 361, 382, 395, 398
Jews 12, 13, 36, 56, 63n3, 69, 134, 138, 139, 143, 150, 200, 289; Uman 249–364; *see also* Breslov Hasidism
Joel, Kiryas 353
John Paul II *53*, 55, 81, 135, 136, 148, 375, 377–9, 399, 401, 404n6
Judaism 93, 243, 247, 248, 251, 255–7, 348, 358, 364, 401
Judas Iscariot 254

Kaczyński, Lech 58–60, 63n10
Kádár, János 161, 165, 169–74
Kaddish 246, 247, 248
Kalugin 332, 334
Kałków-Godów 370, 371, 379–85
Karekin II 77, 82, 83
Karelia 330, 341
Karłowicz, Dariusz 372
Katyn (also Katyń) 37, 58–60, 63n9, 381
Kerama Islands 400
Khrushchev's Thaw 73
Kiley, Christopher 323
Kiku 395, 404n2
Kirill, Patriarch of the ROC 111, 118, 119, 122, 207; Metropolitan of Kyiv 112, 118, 125
Kirkenes 343, 344
Kola *see* Skolt Sámi
Kolbe, Maximilian 17, 20, 135, 381, 388–403, 404n6
Koliivshchyna 349, 354–6, 361, 362, 364
Koreans 402
Kormina, Zhanna 125, 407
Korpela, Jukka 333, 334
Kosovo 222, 224
Kováč, Jozef 141
Kozhin, Moisei 337
Kraków 56, 58, 59, 60, 397, 398
Kruševo 225–6, 230, 237n14
Krynki 380
Kuchma, Leonid 99, 103
Kurakin, Sergei 299, 301, 302
Kurbski, Andrei 332
Kyivan Rus' 90–6, 101, 102, 105, 106, 112, 216, 217, 360; *see also* Christianization

Lacan, Jacques 286
Lapland 333
Latin America 192
Latosiński, Stanisław 255–7
Lebanon 75, 79, 81
Lemkin, Raphael 70, 391
Lenin 73, 288, 290, 361, 362, 365n13
Levi, Primo 393
Levy, Daniel 12, 330
lieux de memoire see sites of memory
Lim, Jie-Hyun 369
liminal 196, 244; experience 193, 194
liminality 193, 194
Lipski, Jan Józef 398
Lithuania 36
Löcknitz 318

Lourdes Grotto 390
Lublin 53, 246
Lutheran 16, 323n7, 341; *see also* Evangelical; Protestant
Luzhkov, Yury 302
Lyon 397, 401

Macedonian Orthodox Church 222, 223, 236–7n14
Macedonian Orthodox Church – Ohrid Archbishopric (MOC-OA) 222, 226–36
Maidan 203, 204, 218n4, 410
Makedonium memorial complex 226
Malke, Flavianus Michael 81
Maloyan, Ignatius 81
Mały Dziennik 398, 399
Mara Buneva 19, 223, 224; commemoration 230–35
Margalit, Avishai 372
martyrdom 35, 40, 45n10, 45n11, 52, 55–9, 70, 79, 80, 83, 395, 161, 164, 209, 217, 228, 261n4, 291, 293, 294, 334, 369–72, 378–86; Kolbe 388, 394, 398–402; Tiso 133–51
materiality 52, 54, 308, 311, 317, 319, 322
Mečiar, Vladimír 146
Mec Jeghern 77, 80, 84
Mecklenburg-Vorpommern 311
Medynsky, Vladimir 121
Mejlis 274–5, 277
Memorial for Flight, Expulsion and a New Beginning 312, 314
Memorial Society 40–2
memory: axiological 372, 376; communicative 185, 196, 201, 225, 269, 280, 350; cosmopolitan 12, 20, 330, 388; cultural 1–4, 7, 8, 15, 18, 30, 111, 112, 115–18, 123, 126, 160, 167, 173, 204, 206, 216, 269, 272, 276, 280, 321, 330, 350–1, 356, 390, 391; global 20, 29, 388, 403; liturgical 284–7, 304–5; local 251–60; postsecular 12; religious 3–8, 29, 31, 36, 122, 136, 157, 171, 201, 202, 204–6, 217, 218, 284–5, 305, 330, 386, 411; vernacular 348–9, 351–2, 357, 360–1, 364, 365n13, 370, 389, 402; *see also* chain of memory; non-sites of memory; sites of memory
Menorka 248, 249
Mescherin 318, 323n4
Messianism 50, 52, 63n5, 371
Metropolitan Makarii 107n5, 332
Metropolitan Petar 229

418 *Index*

Metropolitan Tikhon Shevkunov 39
Metropolitan Yuvenaly 296
Meyer, Birgit 322
Michlic Joanna 256
Middle East 72, 73, 115
Miechów 251, 254–7
Mihajlov, Ivan (Vančo) 323
milieux de memoire 3–4; *see also lieux de memoire*
milites Christi 115
Militia Immaculatae 391, 399
Mindszenty, József 19, 156–62, 164–75,
175n8
Miracle on the Vistula 373, 375, 377
Mirga-Tas, Małgorzata 259
Mitrofan (Badanin) 338, 345n5
mnemoscape 385
Monchegorsk 331, 332, 337
Moses 255
Mościcki, Ignacy 379
Mother Mary of Oura Cathedral 395–7
Mother Teresa 401
Mufti Said Ismagilov 209, 212, 214
Murmansk 331, 332, 336, 337, 342
Muscovite 113, 115
Museum of the Macedonian struggle for
Sovereignty and Independence 228
Muslim 36, 37, 92, 200, 201, 207, 209,
211, 215–17, 268, 404n5
Movement for Democratic Slovakia 146
Mytropolitan Onufrii 104

Nagai, Takashi 389–94, 402
Nagasaki 20, 388–403
Nagorno-Karabakh 75, 77, 81
nationalism 14, 50, 60, 72, 137, 138,
140–2, 146–7, 184, 256, 260, 371, 372,
400, 404n4, 410; victimhood 388, 391
nationhood 75, 225
Nazi 19, 34, 36, 56, 134, 138, 237n16,
246, 250, 252, 256, 257, 271, 398, 400;
anti- 139, 158, 164; pro- 144
necros 244, 245, 257
New Martyrs 133, 284–306, 337, 409, 410
New York Times 63n10, 167, 400
Nicholas II *see* Romanov family
Niepokalanów Monastery 397, 399, 400
Nikolko, Milana 270–1
Nisbet, Robert 351
NKVD 36, 58, 271
Nolan, Mary 319, 321
nonreligiosity 310
nonreligious 18, 19, 20, 43, 133, 151,
308–23, 408

non-sites of memory 243–60; *see also* sites
of memory
Nora, Pierre 3–5, 383
Norway 20, 329, 337, 343, 345n1, 345n3
Novgorod 112, 329, 341
Nuremberg trials 70

Oblak, Tadeusz K. 397
Obóz Narodowo-Radykalny (ONR) 398,
404n5
October Revolution *see* 1917 Revolution
Oe, Kenzaburo 400
Okinawa 400
Olick, Jeffrey 269
Orange Revolution 102
Orthodoxy 36, 38, 39, 43, 91, 93–4,
96–106, 119, 120, 332, 336, 337, 343
Ossów 373
Ostrovsky, Dmitrii Nikolaevich 337
Oświęcim *see* Auschwitz
Ottoman Empire 69, 71–3, 75, 77, 79,
81–3, 85n4, 85n2, 267
Ottoman Turkey *see* Ottoman Empire
Oura Seminary 395–7, 402, 403
Our Lady, Queen of Poland 380, 384
Our Lady of Sorrows Sanctuary *see*
Golgotha, Road of the Polish Nation
Ozaki, Tōmei 394, 396

Paasche, Hans 318
Paasilinna, Erno 330
pacification 370, 379, 380, 382–5
Paisi hieromonk 331
Pankov, Vladimir 237n19
Pasha, Djemal 71
Pasha, Enver 71
Pasieka, Agnieszka 245
Patriarch Pimen 96, 97, 98
Patriarch Tikhon 294, *295*, 298, *299*, 302
patrimonial Church 91–106
patrimonialization 16, 17, 93, 409
patrimony 16, 17, 90, 93
Pavelić, Ante 232
Pearl Harbor 390
Pechenga 329–44
Pekka, Vesainen (Juho) 330, 335
People's Republic of Poland (PRL)
373, 384
perestroika 74, 94–7, 106, 353
Perun 249
Petrich/ Pirin Macedonia 231
Petsamo *see* Pechenga
Petitjean Fr 396, 397

pilgrimage 50, 76, 142, 150, 370; Hasidic 348–64
Piłsudski, Józef 373, 397
Pius XI 379
Pius XII 141, 159, 167
Pogodin, Mikhail 94
Poland 4, 14, 18, 20, 35, 36, 49–62, 75, 139, 202, 243–61, 348, 354, 369–86, 388, 395–9, 401–2, 404n5
Polish–Bolshevik War 370, 373, 376–7
Popiełuszko, Jerzy Fr 402, 404n7
Poroshenko, Petro 104, 105, 361
postcolonial 6, 397, 401, 409
postreligious 16, 309–11, 319, 408
postsecular 1–18, 175n1, 251, 261, 305, 407–11; turn 2, 8–13, 15
postsecularism 8–13, 15
Prelić, Velmir 230, 231
profane 18, 49, 54, 97, 244, 366; *see also* secular
Prokhanov, Alexander 120, 121
Protestant 37, 160, 203, 243, 308–10, 312, 317, 318; *see also* Evangelical; Lutheran
Prussia 50, 396
pudu 187, 188
Putin, Vladimir 38, 83, 119, 121, 210, 302, *304*

Rabbinical Commission for Jewish Cemeteries 247
Radecznica 246–60
Radko *see* Mihajlov, Ivan (Vančo)
Rasputin 296
Rebbe Nachman 348–52, 354, 357–63, 365n1
Red Army 56, 139, 273, 294, 298, *300*, 314, 336
Republic Day *see* Ilinden
Republic of North Macedonia *see* Macedonia
revolution 44n7, 71; Cultural 188, 190; of Dignity 203, 212, 218n4; Hungarian 158, 160, 169, 170, 174; Orange 102; Russian 38, 39, 41, 93, 94, 117, 225, 284, 286–9, 291, 293–4, 298, 306, 338
Ricoeur, Paul 285
Righteous Among the Nations 255, 381
Roma Holocaust *see* Romani, genocide
Romani 259; genocide 259
Romanian Orthodoxy 36
Romanov family 284, 288, 295, 336; *see also* Tsar Nicholas II
Rosati, Massimo 11, 14

Rosh Hashanah 352, 353
Rosow 311–17, 323n4
Rothberg, Michael 17
Rubin, Efim 352
Russia – My History 39, 122
Russian Empire 72, 117, 202, 210, 271, 278, 350
Russian Orthodox Army 104
Russian Orthodox Church (ROC) 19, 89, 94–105, 202–7, 215, 217, 329, 331–2, 337–44
Russian Revolution *see* revolution
Russo-Japanese war 396
Russo-Swedish war 334
Ruthenian Orthodox Church 89
Rycerz Niepokalanej 399

Sachiko of Nagasaki 394–5, 398
Sacralization 7, 10, 19, 21n1, 32, 62, 69, 77–8, 82, 83, 117, 126, 201, 215, 217, 245, 259, 408
sacred 4, 5, 7–8, 16, 18, 20, 30, 40, 49–62, 82, 97, 133, 137, 151, 193, 204–5, 216–17, 225, 243–59, 269, 270, 273, 288, 289, 308, 310, 336, 339, 392, 395, 403
sacrum 245, 246, 251, 257, 260
Saint Petersburg 111, 115, 125, 126, 127n6, 409
Sanctuary of St Anthony of Padua 346
Sanjiao Heyi 189
Sargsyan, Serzh 76, 77, 83
Schenk, Frithjof Benjamin 111
Second Vatican Council *see* Vatican
Second World War 13, 14, 19, 37, 42, 72, 97, 134, 142, 207, 217n11, 225, 228, 232, 235, 237n16, 243, 251, 256, 267, 273, 276, 298, 302, 312, 314, 315, 323n5, 330, 337, 340, 342–4, 350–1, 357, 364, 370, 379, 381–3, 392
secular 2–20, 29–42, 45n10, 49–62, 97, 113, 122–6, 133–51, 175n1, 204, 223, 243–60, 268, 273, 274–5, 277–80, 281n10, 281n17, 286, 298, 305, 308–23, 330–45, 357, 372, 384–5, 389, 408–11; *see also* profane
secularization 3, 5, 9–11, 31, 35, 80, 92, 156, 166, 170, 351, 371, 372, 408
Seibo no Kishi Monastery 390, 394, 396, 401, 402
Seikichi 395, 404n3
Sendyka, Roma 244
Serbian Orthodox Church 223, 227

420 *Index*

Serck-Hanssen, Caroline 339
Seytablaev, Akhtem 275
Shelonin, Sergei 332
Shemesh, Bet 353
Shevchenko, Taras 97, 354, 362, 363, 365n13
Shevchuk, Sviatoslav 206, 218n11
Shirvanian, Aris 80
Shoah *see* Holocaust
Shōgunate, Tokugawa 391
Shuhei 395
Siedliska 251, 254, 257, 260
Simferopol 274, 276
sites of memory 3–4, 7, 14, 97, 112, 117, 145, 156, 157, 168, 226, 329, 343, 244, 371, 383, 384; *see also* non-sites of memory
Skolt Sámi 329–45
Skorupka, Ignacy 373
Skucha, Piotr 255
Slovakia 19, 37, 133–51
Slovak National Assembly (SNR) 146
Slovak National Uprising 139, 143, 146
Slovak People's Party 134, 138, 147
Social Democratic Union of Macedonia (SDSM) 222, 227, 228, 230
Solovetsky Monastery 332, 336
Sono, Ayako 377–401, 404n4
Soviet Bloc 156
Soviet Union 18, 36, 37, 43, 72–4, 82, 82, 89, 94–5, 98, 101, 117, 126, 168, 170, 210, 271, 281n3, 284, 288, 290, 294, 305, 362, 373, 410, 411
Spiritual Administration of Muslims of Crimea (SAMC) 268, 274–5, 277–8, 280, 281n12, 281n17
Spiritual Administrations of the Muslims of Ukraine DUMU 201–17; Umma 201–17
Staerk, Lars 339
St Alexander Nevsky xii, 19, 111–27, 410
Stalin 43, 117, 289, 290, 302, 303
St Boris 293, 343, 344; *see also* St Gleb
Steinerand, Yeshua 358
Stephen of Perm 334
Sternharz, Nathan 348
St Georg's Chapel in Neiden 343
St Gleb 293, 343, 344; *see also* St Boris
St Gregory the Illuminator 78, 82
St Isaac's Cathedral 409
St Maksymilian Kolbe 17, 20, 135, 381, 388–403, 404n6
St Prohor Pcinjski Monastery 226, 227, 228

St Tryphon of Pechenga 329–45, 345n5
St Volodymyr Hill 97, 103, 105
Sultan, Abdul Hamid II 71
Sultan, Amet-Han 275
Sultan Mustapha III 263n4
Suonjel 340
Surovtsova, Nadiia 352, 363
Sweden 115, 329, 345n1
Święty Krzyż *see* Holy Cross Mountain
symbol 18, 19, 49, 50–62, 63n8, 94, 116, 145, 150, 158, 159, 161, 167, 168, 173, 174, 196, 247, 249, 250, *252, 253,* 257, 302, 331, 360, 361, 391, 394, 402, 403; Nevsky 118, 121, 122, 125–6
Synodal Commission 40, 45n12
Syrian desert 72, 82, 83
Szczecin 316, 317, 318
Szczęsny Potocki, Stanisław 350, 354
Sznaider, Natan 12, 330
Szuster, Marta 318

Tachiichiro, Akizuki 393
Tamim, Sheikh Ahmed 211, 214
Tatars 20, 211, 212, 217, 267–80, 281n3, 280n6, 280n7, 280n10, 281n14
Tiananmen 195; commemoration 182; Mothers 181, 185, 186, 188, 191, 196; Square Massacre 181, 411, 195
Tiso, Jozef 19, 133–51, 151n2
Tito 225
Tokashiki Islands 400
Tokugawa 391, 403
Torzhok 333
Tower of Babel 302, *303*
tradition 3, 5, 6, 8, 12, 29, 30, 33, 45n10, 61, 79, 82, 91, 92, 143, 169, 203, 204, 247, 251, 269, 285, 318, 321, 337, 353, 354, 371, 375, 407; Armenian 81; Chinese 187; Confucian 189; Hasidim 352; Judaeo-Christian 3, 11, 12; oral 340, 341, 342; patriotic 57; revolutionary 38; religious 38, 90, 115, 192, 202, 217, 285–7, 305, 306n2, 308, 384, 401, 409; vernacular 339
traitor 71, 139, 170, 216, 254, 257, 272, 281n6, 372
trauma 5, 6, 7, 13, 33, 34, 35, 37, 41, 76, 171, 244, 305, 330; collective 70, 73, 84, 268, 269–80; Holocaust 356–8; intergenerational 69; national 388
Treaty of Nöteborg 334
Tsar Alexander III 337
Tsar Fyodor Ioannovich 335

Index   421

Tsar Nicholas II 341; *see also* Romanov family
Turkish Republic 72
Tygodnik Powszechny 60, 398–9

Uehling, Greta Lynn 271, 272, 273
Ukraine 17, 19, 20, 37, 63n9, 75, 89–106, 200–35, 268, 270, 273, 280n1, 281n13, 299, 348–64, 365n12, 408, 410
Ukrainian Autocephalous Orthodox Church (UAOC) 89, 90, 91, 98, 105, 107n5
Ukrainian Council of Churches and Religious Organizations (UCCRO) 203
Ukrainian Greek Catholic Church (UGCC) 89
Ukrainian Institute of National Remembrance 355, 361
Ukrainian Orthodox Church of the Kyiv Patriarchate (UOC-KP) 89–107, 201–17
Ukrainian Orthodox Church of the Moscow Patriarchate (UOC-MP) 89–106, 201–17
Ulma family 354, 257
Uman 348–65
UNESCO 340
United States 75, 76, 79, 85n4, 89, 140, 167, 169, 172, 213, 223, 323, 351, 353, 388, 393
Urakami Cathedral 388, 389, 390–2
Urakawa Fr 396
Uspensky Cathedral 290
USSR *see* Soviet Union
van de Port, Mattijs 322
van Salingen, Simon 334
Vatican 81, 135, 142, 143, 148–9, 151, 172, 173, 255, 256, 397, 399; Second Council 255, 260
Verdery, Katherine 233
Vergangenheitsbewältigung 34, 38
Verkaaik, Oskar 308
victimhood 19, 33, 34, 36, 44n3, 133, 159, 161, 209, 213, 255, 270, 370, 388, 394, 403; nationalism 388, 391
Victory Day 124
Vietnam Veterans Memorial 357
violence 115, 145, 168, 187, 191, 193, 244, 249, 250, 259, 260, 270, 273, 281n8, 339, 397

Virgin Mary 50, 370, 373, 381, 384; *see also* Holy Mother
Virtuti Militari Cross 373, 378
Vladimir city 112, 114, 115; Prince 38, 93, 102, 103, 112, 216, 293; *see also* St Volodymyr Hill
Volodymyr Prince *see* Vladimir city, Prince
Volodymyr (Romaniuk) 98
Volodymyr (Sabodan) 98
Vrtanes Mesrop Papazian 81

Wala, Czesław 380
Warsaw xix, xxii, 13, *51*, 52, 58, 59, 69, 370, 373–5, 398, 399, 404n2, 404n5
Warsaw Battle of 1920 373–9, 383; *see also* Polish–Bolshevik War
Washington Post 400
White, Stephen 119
Wierzbica 251, 251, 257, 260
Winowska, Maria 397, 399
Winter, Jay 10, 371
Wodziński, Marcin 353
Wojtyła, Karol *see* John Paul II
World War II *see* Second World War
Wyszynski, Stefan 379

Yakunin, Vladimir 122
Yamada, Kan 393
Yeltsin, Boris 302
Yerevan 73–7, 81
Young Turks 71
Yue Lan festival 187–8
Yugoslavia 222, 223, 226, 231, 232

Zakopane 397
Zalizniak, Maxym 354–6, 361–2, 365n13; *see also* Honta, Ivan
Zborowski, Mark 351
Zduńska Wola 397
zhenqing tong youming 186, 189, 190, 194
Zipperstein, Steven 351
Žižek, Slavoj 403
Zowczak, Magdalena 386n1
Zubrzycki, Geneviève 4, 11, 18
Żuchowiec 380, 382, 384
Zybała, Marianna 246–53
Zybała, Stanisław 246–53, *249, 250, 251, 252, 253*, 261n2

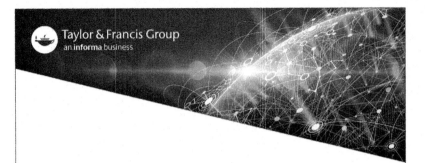